Staying Off the Beaten Track was fo
in 1982 and is now established as
bed-and-breakfast accommodation
in 1998, Elizabeth worked tirelessl
ensure that it remained unrivalled in its field; in more recent years she was supported in this task by her brother, Walter Gundrey.

In order to safeguard both the distinctive character and the principles underlying *Staying Off the Beaten Track*, Elizabeth passed ownership of the guide to the Staying Off the Beaten Track Trust. Day-to-day running of the guide is now in the hands of Jan Bowmer, who was appointed managing editor for the guide in 1998. Jan worked with Elizabeth for 10 years on *Staying Off the Beaten Track*, and so Arrow Books are confident that the guide will maintain its place in its field and its reputation as the only truly independent bed-and-breakfast accommodation guide.

VOUCHERS WORTH £18

(by courtesy of the houses concerned)

This voucher is worth **£6** at any establishment marked with a **V** sign in the pages of this book, provided it is presented **ON ARRIVAL** and not later. It is valid throughout **2002**, and may be used if a room is booked for **3** or more consecutive nights. Only one voucher usable per room.

This voucher is worth **£6** at any establishment marked with a **V** sign in the pages of this book, provided it is presented **ON ARRIVAL** and not later. It is valid throughout **2002**, and may be used if a room is booked for **3** or more consecutive nights. Only one voucher usable per room.

This voucher is worth **£6** at any establishment marked with a **V** sign in the pages of this book, provided it is presented **ON ARRIVAL** and not later. It is valid throughout **2002**, and may be used if a room is booked for **3** or more consecutive nights. Only one voucher usable per room.

OFFER OF NEXT EDITION

Using an out-of-date edition can lead to costly disappointments. A new edition appears every November, updated, with fresh entries added, some deleted and all revised, and with vouchers worth £18 valid for the next year. Make sure you are not using an out-of-date edition by sending a stamped self-addressed envelope to Explore Britain, Alston, Cumbria, CA9 3SL, for an order form on which you can apply for the 2003 edition even before it reaches the shops. No need for a letter: just put SOTBT 2003 on the top left corner of the envelope you send.

Complaints about matters which could not have been settled on the spot will be forwarded to proprietors. Please enclose a stamped addressed envelope if you want your complaint acknowledged. Letters should be addressed to Jan Bowmer (SOTBT), c/o Arrow Books, 20 Vauxhall Bridge Road, London SW1V 2SA.

STAYING OFF THE BEATEN TRACK

IN ENGLAND & WALES 2002

MANAGING EDITOR:
JAN BOWMER

A selection of moderately priced guest-houses, small hotels, farms and country houses

21st EDITION
2002

Edited by
Jacqueline Krendel

ARROW

Published by Arrow Books in 2001

1 3 5 7 9 10 8 6 4 2

First published in Great Britain 1982
by Hamlyn Paperbacks
Arrow edition (Sixth edition) first published 1986
Twenty-first edition 2001

Arrow Books
The Random House Group Limited
20 Vauxhall Bridge Road, London, SW1V 2SA

Random House Australia (Pty) Limited
20 Alfred Street, Milsons Point, Sydney,
New South Wales 2061, Australia

Random House New Zealand Limited
18 Poland Road, Glenfield,
Auckland 10, New Zealand

Random House (Pty) Limited
Endulini, 5a Jubilee Road,
Parktown 2193, South Africa

The Random House Group Limited Reg. No. 954009

www.randomhouse.co.uk

Designed and typeset by Bob Vickers
Maps copyright © 2001 Perrott CartoGraphics

Printed and bound in Great Britain by
Mackays of Chatham plc, Chatham, Kent

A CIP catalogue record for this book is available from the British Library

ISBN 0-09-941548-8

The publishers would like to thank all those owners who allowed us to use their drawings.
Additional line drawings by Rhona Garvin, Leslie Dean and others.

Acknowledgments

The publishers and the managing editor acknowledge with much appreciation the assistance of the rest of the SOTBT team (Jennifer Christie, Trevor Craddock, Elizabeth Griffin, Walter Gundrey, Jacqueline Krendel, Jonathan May, Kate McCarney, Frances Nicholson, Sarah Pring, May Smith, Bob Vickers and Nancy Webber) as well as of all the proprietors of houses.

CONTENTS

INTRODUCTION

THE COUNTRYSIDE REVISITED

'The sylvan slopes with corn-clad fields
Are hung, as if with golden shields,
Bright trophies of the sun!
Like a fair sister of the sky,
Unruffled doth the blue lake lie,
The mountains looking on.'

September, 1819 William Wordsworth

The pastoral idyll might not be quite as sublime as it was in Wordsworth's day, but the extraordinary diversity and scenic splendour of the British countryside still has an abiding appeal for millions of people – from the dedicated walker to the weekend escapee from city life. Preferences vary: some opt for spectacular coastlines or the exhilaration of windswept moorland and dramatic limestone gorges; others head for the quiet beauty of ancient forests and secluded river valleys; while the vista of gently rolling green hills studded with picturesque villages is a magnet for many, whatever the weather or season. There is something in the British landscape to suit every taste. And it is all the more remarkable that variety such as this can exist on so relatively small and densely populated an island. Even on the edge of sprawling conurbations, there remain pockets of unspoilt beauty – Burnham Beeches in Buckinghamshire and Cannock Chase in Staffordshire, to name but two.

Given the title of this book, it is hardly surprising that so many *Staying Off the Beaten Track* houses are ideally placed for visitors to experience the best that the British countryside can offer – from our great National Parks to designated Areas of Outstanding Natural Beauty and Heritage Coasts. Indeed, scenic surroundings – along with attractive furnishings, good food and genuine hospitality – are among the most important criteria for inclusion in the guide. Many proprietors themselves are enthusiasts for their particular areas and are only too happy to share their knowledge and give hints and tips on local beauty-spots, as well as provide detailed maps. A significant number of houses are located very close to national trails and from even more there is easy access to the countless footpaths and bridlepaths which crisscross the country. Some houses have special facilities for walkers, at others bicycles can be hired. Horseback riders, too, are catered for, as stabling is available on some properties. (A few of our houses also have fishing rights within their own grounds.) And for visitors without their own means of transport, there are certain hosts who are willing to drive guests to the starting-point of a day's exploration on foot and pick them up at journey's end.

Despite the vagaries of the British weather, the best time to visit the most beautiful parts of the countryside and coast is outside peak seasons and bank holiday periods. Many of our regular readers favour short breaks in spring, autumn and early summer, but even in mid-winter the scenery in such popular holiday areas as South Devon, the Cotswolds and the Lake District can be superb yet with far fewer people about.

So whether you are planning to walk, tour by car, cycle or ride, the choice of accommodation recommended in this guide – covering the length and breadth of England and Wales – will enable you to revisit perennially favourite countryside haunts, discover lesser-known byways or strike out in completely new directions.

SCENIC AREAS OF ENGLAND & WALES

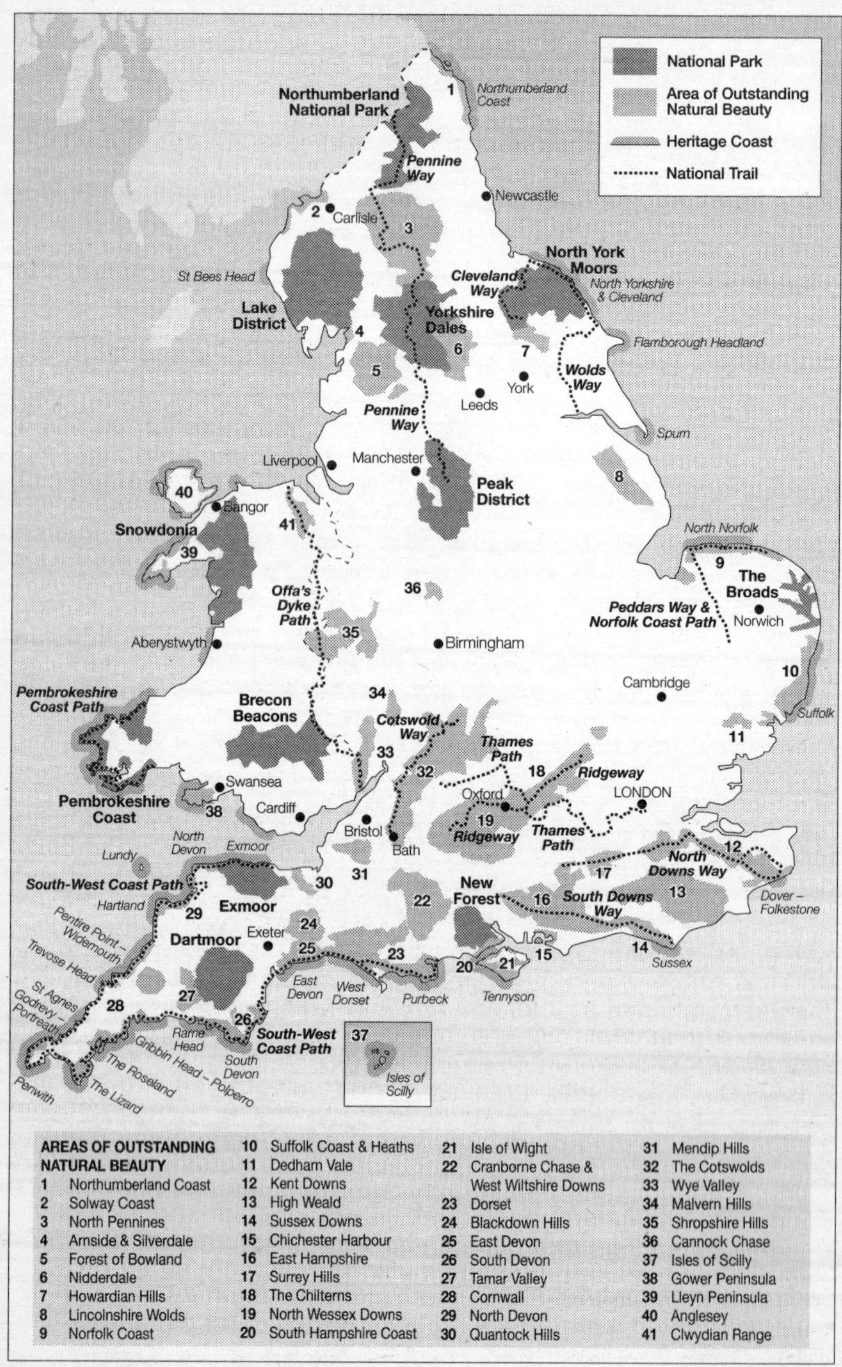

SOTBT HOUSES IN OR NEAR NATIONAL PARKS, THE BROADS & THE NEW FOREST

Below, we have identified those houses in this book which are geographically closest to the National Parks (including both The Broads and the New Forest Heritage Area), depicted on our map on p.viii. Inevitably, the list here is not exhaustive, as all of these protected landscapes can be quite easily reached from houses in neighbouring areas if you are prepared to travel just a little bit further from base.

Northumberland National Park

Lake District National Park

Yorkshire Dales National Park

North York Moors National Park

Peak District National Park

The Broads

New Forest

SOTBT HOUSES IN OR NEAR SELECTED AREAS OF OUTSTANDING NATURAL BEAUTY & HERITAGE COASTS

As you will see from our map on p.viii, there are over forty designated Areas of Outstanding Natural Beauty in England and Wales, as well as many individual stretches of Heritage Coastline. Below, we give just a sample selection of these specially protected scenic areas which have SOTBT houses in the vicinity. Again, the listings here are by no means comprehensive. For example, since all the Isles of Scilly are a designated Area of Outstanding Natural Beauty, we suggest you turn to the chapter on p.207 for our house recommendations there. It is also worth pointing out that some counties – e.g. Dorset, Gloucestershire and Cornwall – have such extensive Areas of Outstanding Natural Beauty that virtually every house in those chapters is within easy reach of particularly lovely countryside or coast.

For further information on the protected landscapes of England and Wales, contact:

The Countryside Agency, John Dower House, Crescent Place, Cheltenham, Gloucestershire, GL50 3RA. Tel: 01242 521381 (Fax: 01242 584270). Website: www.countryside.gov.uk

Countryside Council for Wales, Plas Penrhos, Ffordd Penrhos, Bangor, Gwynedd, LL57 2LQ. Tel: 01248 385500 (Fax: 01248 355782). Website: www.ccw.gov.uk

Association of National Park Authorities, 126 Bute Street, Cardiff, CF10 5LE. Tel: 029 20499966 (Fax: 029 20499980). Website: www.ANPA.gov.uk

Association for Areas of Outstanding Natural Beauty, The Old Police Station, Cotswold Heritage Centre, Northleach, Gloucestershire, GL54 3JH. Tel: 01451 862007 (Fax: 01451 862001). Website: www.aonb.org.uk

HOW TO HAVE A GOOD TIME

In the pages of this book you will find places to stay drawn from a wide spectrum of possibilities, some remote and truly 'off the beaten track', others more accessible and within striking distance of popular tourist attractions. There are working farms and converted barns, former mills and grand country mansions, old inns and small hotels, thatched country cottages and tucked-away coastal homes with spectacular sea views – each with its own character. The detailed descriptions are intended to bring out each house's individuality and to help the reader pick out the places that suit him or her best.

Some people have very particular requirements; and it is up to them to discuss these when telephoning to book. Many hosts in this book are more flexible than big hotels, and all are eager to help if they can. The sort of things to bear in mind are: a bad back, needing a very *firm mattress*; special *dietary* requirements, and *allergies* to feather pillows or animals; a strong preference for *separate tables* rather than a shared dining-table – or vice versa; *fewer courses* than on the fixed menu; *twin beds* rather than double beds – or vice versa; freedom to *smoke* – or freedom from it; a particular wish for *electric blanket*, *hot-water bottle*, etc. or a dislike of *duvets*; the need to arrive, depart or eat at *extra-early* or *extra-late* hours; an intention to pay by *credit card* (this should not be taken for granted, particularly at small guest-houses). Light sleepers should avoid rooms overlooking, for instance, a market square: not all houses in this book are rural.

The code letters that appear after the name of each house will help you identify houses suitable for children, dogs, people with mobility problems, users of public transport, etc.: for full explanation, see inside front cover. Please also use the 'how to book' checklist on page xiv when telephoning.

It's best to stay at least 2–3 days: you cannot possibly appreciate an area if you only stay overnight (prices per night are often less, too, if you stay on). The vouchers on page ii are usable for 3-night stays. At some houses, 1-night bookings may be refused.

When to go? Seaside resorts or other places suitable for children will be at their busiest (and dearest) in July–August and during half-term holidays (especially, in late May, which is also a bank holiday period). Houses which do *not* take children tend to have vacancies in July and August – even in the popular Cotswolds, for instance. Other peak periods are, of course, Easter, Christmas, New Year and the bank holiday in late August. There are local peaks, too (the Gold Cup races at Cheltenham or the regatta at Henley, for instance, are apt to fill hotels for miles around), and local troughs (Brighton, a conference centre, is least busy in high summer). In holiday areas, travel on any day other than a summer Saturday if you can. Make travel reservations well in advance.

One final tip on ensuring that you get all that you hope for: at the end of each season, throw away your current copy of the book and get next year's edition before it sells out in the bookshops later in the year (you can soon recoup its cost by using the fresh set of accommodation vouchers it contains). Here's why this is so important. Each edition contains scores of new entries, and existing houses are re-inspected on a regular cycle to ensure that standards have been maintained. Furthermore, every year entries are updated: prices change, so do telephone numbers, dinner menus and much else. Houses also change hands and using an out-of-date edition can therefore be extremely misleading, since it is the personal touch which so often recommends a particular house to our readers. Change of owner or inflated prices are the two most common reasons why houses are dropped; a third is that somewhere better – or of better value – is found nearby.

TELEPHONING TO BOOK: A CHECKLIST

Book well ahead: many of these houses have few rooms. Further, at some houses, rooms (even if similarly priced) vary in size or amenities: early applicants get the cheapest and/or best ones. Telephoning is preferable to writing to enquire about vacancies, and, in many cases, the best time is early evening.

1. Ask for the owner by the *name* given in this edition. (If there has been a change, standards and prices may differ.)
2. Mention that you are a reader of this book: sometimes there are discounts on offer exclusively for readers.
3. Specify *your precise needs* (such as en suite bathroom, if available), see previous page. (Do not turn up with children, dogs or disabilities if you have not checked that these are accepted or provided for.) Elderly people may wish to ensure that their room is not above the first floor.
4. Check *prices* – these, too, can change (particularly after spring). Ask whether there are any bargain breaks. Are credit cards accepted?
5. Ask what *deposit* to send (or quote a credit card number). Overseas visitors may be asked to pay up to 50 per cent.
6. State your intended *time of arrival*, what meals are wanted and at what times. (If you should then be late, telephone a warning – otherwise your room may be let to someone else. It is inconsiderate to arrive late for home-cooked meals prepared especially for you.) Most proprietors expect visitors to arrive about 5pm. In country lanes, finding your way after dark can be difficult.
7. Ask for precise instructions for *locating the house*: many are remote. Better still, ask for a brochure with map to be posted to you. Check where to park.
8. Few proprietors expect visitors to stay out of the house in the daytime; but if you want to stay in, check this when booking.

At houses where dinner is not served, a light supper can often be obtained (if ordered in advance), ranging from sandwiches to family 'pot luck'. (Packed lunches too.)

PRICES

This book came into being to provide a guide to good accommodation at prices suited to people of moderate means. That remains its policy.

In the current edition are houses at which it is possible to stay, at the time of publication, for as little as £16–£25 (London excepted) for b & b – that is, per person sharing a double room. However, for the best rooms in the house, or later in the year, you may well be asked for more. **Check when booking.** High-season prices start at different times. For instance, in the Isle of Wight few proprietors raise prices until summer (if then), while in the Lake District and Yorkshire Dales many put them up in spring.

The prices are as quoted when the book was in preparation during 2001. But sometimes unexpected costs force proprietors to increase their prices subsequently: becoming liable for VAT or business rates, for instance.

Inclusive terms for dinner, bed-and-breakfast can be much lower than those quoted here for these items taken separately. Many houses in this book have reduced rates for longer bookings or other discounts on offer, some exclusive to readers.

COUNTY DIRECTORY OF HOUSES AND HOTELS IN

ENGLAND

Prices are per person sharing a double room, at the beginning of the year. You may be quoted more later or for single occupancy.

Prices and other facts quoted at the head of each entry are as supplied by the proprietors.

County and Unitary Authority Map of England
SCOTLAND
NORTHUMBERLAND
Newcastle-upon-Tyne
COUNTY DURHAM
Middlesbrough
CUMBRIA
NORTH YORKSHIRE
EAST RIDING OF YORKSHIRE
LANCASHIRE
WEST YORKSHIRE
1
Manchester
Sheffield
Liverpool
CHESHIRE
DERBYSHIRE
NOTTINGHAMSHIRE
LINCOLNSHIRE
STAFFORDSHIRE
SHROPSHIRE
LEICESTERSHIRE
2
NORFOLK
Birmingham
WALES
(see page 314)
NORTHAMPTONSHIRE
CAMBRIDGESHIRE
HEREFORDSHIRE
WORCESTERSHIRE
WARWICKSHIRE
BEDFORDSHIRE
SUFFOLK
GLOUCESTERSHIRE
OXFORDSHIRE
BUCKINGHAMSHIRE
HERTFORDSHIRE
ESSEX
3
Bristol
4
LONDON
BERKSHIRE
WILTSHIRE
SURREY
KENT
SOMERSET
HAMPSHIRE
WEST SUSSEX
EAST SUSSEX
DEVON
DORSET
ISLE OF WIGHT
CORNWALL
ISLES OF SCILLY
CORNWALL
1 – NORTH LINCOLNSHIRE
2 – RUTLAND
3 – SOUTH GLOUCESTERSHIRE
4 – BATH & NORTH-EAST SOMERSET
0 Miles 50
0 Kilometres 80

BEDFORDSHIRE

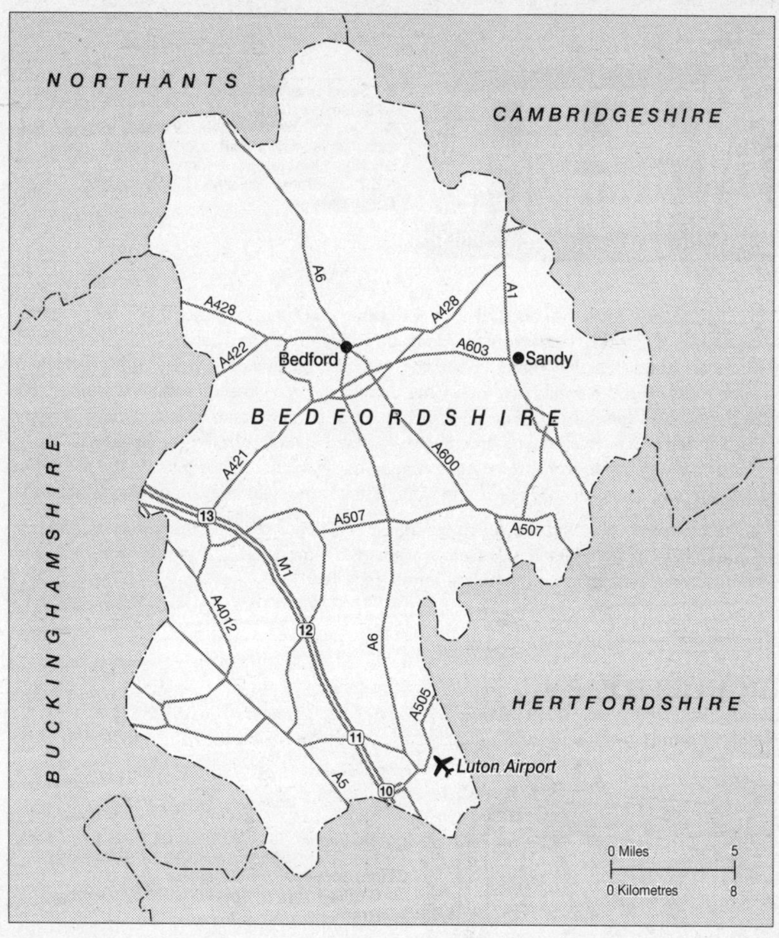

Addresses shown are to enable you to locate a house on a map. They are not necessarily complete postal addresses (though the essential post-code is included), and detailed directions for finding a house should be obtained from the owner.

1 THE GRANGE

C(5) D X

Sunderland Hill, Ravensden, Bedfordshire, MK44 2SH Tel: 01234 771771
North of Bedford. Nearest main road: A428 from Bedford towards St Neots (and M1, junction 14).

rear view

3 Bedrooms. £18 (less for 4 nights or more). Available: own bath/shower/toilet; TV. No smoking.
Dinner. £15 for 3 courses, sherry and coffee, from 6pm. Vegetarian or other special diets if ordered. No smoking. **Light suppers** if ordered.
1 Sitting-room. With stove, TV. No smoking.
Large garden

This large manor house has been divided into three dwellings, of which No. 1 is the handsome home of Patricia Roberts, with views downhill of terraced lawns and great cedars. Patricia has furnished the rooms in keeping with the architectural style, with chandeliers in each room. Good paintings (some by her daughter) hang on silky coral walls; silver, big velvet armchairs and Chippendale furniture are in one room; another has damask curtains and a Victorian sofa. Even the bathrooms are carpeted and have flowery wallpaper.

Dinner is very attractively presented. Salmon and pheasant often appear on the menu but guests can have whatever they like if it is ordered in advance. (Sunday lunch also available.)

Readers' comments: Nothing too much trouble. Food delicious. Charming hostess. Wished we could have stayed longer. Dinners imaginatively prepared. Elegantly furnished, and every comfort. Kind welcome, we felt at home. Excellent.

V

HIGHFIELD FARM

C D M X

Sandy, Bedfordshire, SG19 2AQ Tel: 01767 682332 (Fax: 01767 692503)
North of Sandy. Off the A1 from Biggleswade to Peterborough.

6 Bedrooms. £25–£30 (less for 7 nights or more). Available: own bath/shower/toilet; TV. No smoking.
Light suppers (by arrangement).
1 Sitting-room. With open fire, TV. No smoking.
Garden

Set well back from the A1, Highfield Farm is surrounded by fields of peas or wheat. Two single cottages a century ago, the house is now enlarged and painted sparkling white outside, with a trim lawn and colourful flowerbeds. The interior is equally immaculate, the six spotless bedrooms (two on the ground floor in former stables) having such features as bedheads matching the yew furniture hand-made locally. The L-shaped sitting-room has soft colours, a pretty Chinese carpet and comfortable armchairs. Every room is thoughtfully furnished by Margaret Codd; bathrooms, too, are good.

This is an area with many NT properties: Cardinal Wolsey's imposing dovecote and stables at Willington, the palatial mansions (and gardens) of Ascott and Waddesdon, Bernard Shaw's house at Ayot St Lawrence. There are Bunyan sights in and around Bedford (and in the town is a notable art gallery, the delightful Cecil Higgins Museum by the swan-frequented river). You can wander in Maulden Wood, look at Shuttleworth's historic aircraft collection or observe the 140 kinds of bird in the RSPB's headquarters reserve. Cambridge is less than 30 minutes away by car.

V

NARLY OAK LODGE

C(5) **M S X**

The Baulk, Green Lane, Clapham, Bedfordshire, MK41 6AA
Tel/Fax: 01234 350353
North of Bedford. Nearest main road: A6 from Bedford to Kettering.

3 Bedrooms. £20. All have own shower/toilet; TV. No smoking.
1 Sitting-room. No smoking.
Large garden

E-mail: FosterT@csdBedfordshire.gov.uk

Up a bumpy private road, past derelict World War II barracks, one comes to this modern red brick bungalow with far views across the Ouse Valley. The house was in fact built in 1939 as an RAF officers' mess, but was completely redeveloped, to a very high standard, in 1997 by Bedfordshire councillor Tom Foster and his wife Mollie. Tux, the Welsh border collie, gives guests a friendly welcome.

Inside, all is immaculate. There is a conservatory-style sitting-area with an abundance of green plants. Each bedroom is individually named (the Churchill or the Victoria suite, for example) and comfortably furnished with pretty colour schemes and good carpets. The breakfast-room is made interesting with military memorabilia, including an antique Parachute Regiment kettledrum, and has fine views over the garden and valley below.

Guests dine in nearby Clapham. For keen anglers, there is fishing on the Great Ouse; golf and horse-riding facilities are also close. Twinwood airfield, from where Glenn Miller took off on his last fateful flight, is only quarter of a mile away. London itself is easily accessible by road or rail from here.

NORTH END BARNS

C M S X

Riseley Road, Bletsoe, Bedfordshire, MK44 1QT Tel/Fax: 01234 781320
North of Bedford. Nearest main road: A6 from Bedford to Kettering.

8 Bedrooms. £22.50. Available: own bath/shower/toilet; TV. No smoking.
Large garden

Deep in rural Bedfordshire and surrounded by arable fields is this 16th-century, creeper-covered, thatched farmhouse where farmer Paul Forster and his wife Chris provide high-quality, bed-and-breakfast accommodation. A duck-pond, weeping willow and grazing sheep all add to the tranquillity of the scene.

Guests' bedrooms are in the sympathetically converted outbuilding. There are colourful quilted bedspreads, sturdy old barn beams, good pine furnishings, bright and imaginative colour schemes, and pristine bathrooms throughout. A ground-floor room has been specially adapted for wheelchair access. Laundry facilities also available.

Breakfast (comprising a wide choice, cooked to order by Chris) is taken round a large communal table in the farmhouse itself, where there is also a snug bedroom with its own beamed bathroom. Guests can dine at the Fox and Hounds (good steaks, lively atmosphere) in Riseley, or at the Falcon Inn (sophisticated, French-style cuisine) in Bletsoe, which is even closer.

In the vicinity are quiet villages, pleasant country walks, a clay-pigeon-shooting complex, fishing on Grafham Water, and Thurleigh Autodrome, where high-speed cars can be hired by the day.

ORCHARD COTTAGE

C M P T S

1 High Street, Wrestlingworth, Bedfordshire, SG19 2EW Tel: 01767 631355

East of Bedford. Nearest main road: A1 from Baldock to Biggleswade.

4 Bedrooms. £21–£24. No smoking.
1 Sitting-room. With open fire, TV. No smoking.
Large garden

A talented lady lives at thatched Orchard Cottage, once the village bakery and now a tea-room. Joan Strong makes delicate bobbin-lace – an old craft for which the area was once famous – while some of the furniture in the house was made by her husband, Owen. The pleasant rooms have views of fields, or of the garden enclosed by high Cupressus hedges. From the large sitting-room (with log fire) glass doors open on to a paved terrace. For dinner, sample food at the many inns in this area.

Much Bedfordshire scenery is lovely (some of it in the care of the National Trust). Wide open spaces alternate with wooded hills, there are thatched cottages, old mills and winding streams – many of them tributaries of the beautiful Great Ouse. Woburn Abbey (with deer and safari park) is one of England's grandest stately homes and contains a superb collection of paintings. Gardens worth seeking out include Wrest Park and Old Warden's Swiss Garden.

Readers' comments: Very good value. Spotless and comfortable.

For explanation of code letters and V symbol, see inside front cover.

Book well ahead: many of these houses have few rooms. Do not expect dinner if you have not booked it or if you arrive late.

At houses where dinner is not served, a light supper can often be obtained (if ordered in advance), ranging from sandwiches to family 'pot luck'. (Packed lunches too.)

Prices for single occupancy may be higher than those quoted here. Houses that charge singles no more, or only 10% more, than half the price of a double room (except possibly at peak periods) are indicated by the 'S' symbol.

BERKSHIRE

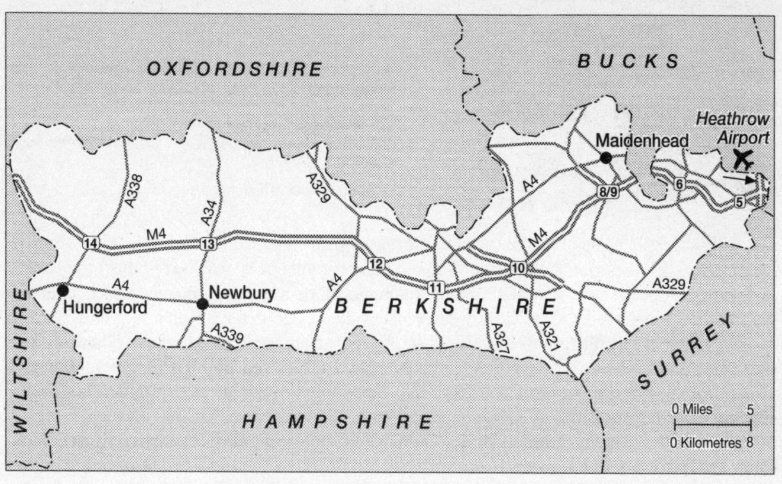

YOU AND THE LAW

Once your booking has been confirmed – orally or in writing – a contract exists between you and the proprietor. He/she is legally bound to provide accommodation as booked; and you are legally bound to pay for this accommodation. If unable to take up the booking – even because of sickness – you still remain liable for a very substantial proportion of the charges (in addition to losing your deposit).

If you have to cancel, let the proprietor know as soon as possible; then he/she may be able to re-let the accommodation (in which case you would be liable to pay only a re-letting cost or forfeit your deposit). Phone if you are going to arrive late.

(A note to overseas readers. It may be an acceptable practice elsewhere to make bookings at several houses for the same date, choosing only later which one to patronize; but this way of doing things is not the British practice and you are legally liable to compensate any proprietors whom you let down in this way.)

Berkshire

DUMBLEDORE

C(9) **D X**

Warren Row, Berkshire, RG10 8QS Tel/Fax: 01628 822723
West of Maidenhead. Nearest main road: A4 from Maidenhead to Reading (also M4, junction 8/9; and M40, junction 4).

3 Bedrooms. £25 **(one room for readers of this book only)**–£35. Available: own bath/toilet; TV. No smoking.
Light suppers if ordered.
2 Sitting-rooms. With stove, TV (in one). No smoking.
Garden

E-mail: laviniarashleigh@faxvia.net

Tubs of flowering plants line the cobbled entrance to this handsome timber and brick house (originally four workmen's cottages). The oldest part dates back to Tudor times, the extension being added some 150 years later. Its unusual name is a Berkshire word meaning 'bumblebee'.

The pretty bedrooms, with board-and-latch doors and lead-paned windows, are decorated in cottage style. One bright blue room overlooks the garden and tennis court. (There is also a heated swimming-pool in the grounds.) Bathrooms, although not en suite, are private and have a charming mix of modern fittings and old timbering. Lavinia Rashleigh serves breakfast in the heavily beamed dining-hall, where her two Norfolk terriers, Casper and Cato, are likely to greet guests.

For evening meals, there is a pub in Warren Row itself and a good restaurant in the nearby village of Crazies Hill. Lavinia can also direct visitors to other local food pubs in easy driving distance. The house is well placed for quick access to Heathrow Airport, as well as the multiple attractions of Henley, Oxford and Windsor. Some of the most picturesque stretches of the River Thames (best explored by boat) are close by.

Berkshire

HOLT LODGE

C D S X

Kintbury, Berkshire, RG17 9SX Tel/Fax: 01488 668244
West of Newbury. Nearest main road: A4 from Newbury to Hungerford (and M4, junctions 13/14).

rear view

4 Bedrooms. £25 (less for 14 nights or more). Available: own bath/shower/toilet; TV. No smoking.
1 Sitting-room. With open fire.
Large garden

E-mail: johnfreeland@holtlodge.freeserve.co.uk

This dignified early Georgian house, the family home of John and Beroë Freeland, stands on a working farm surrounded by 350 acres of pasture for beef-cattle and sheep. Inside, the well-proportioned rooms are beautifully furnished with antiques, oriental rugs and kelims, interesting paintings and etchings. In the big sitting/dining-room, capacious armchairs face out on to the garden through the French windows.

Up an elegant oak stairway, each bedroom has its own character: the pretty pink and blue single overlooks a pond; the purple and green double has handsome walnut furniture; and a third room, with good country views, has family photos and Renoir prints on the walls. A poppy-themed bathroom is particularly attractive.

There is ample choice of places for evening meals (two in walking distance). Stabling for horses can be provided.

Holt Lodge is a handy base for cyclists and walkers, and for those wishing to venture further afield – Marlborough, Oxford and Winchester are all easily reached. From nearby Kintbury, there are horse-drawn barge trips (summer only) along the Kennet & Avon Canal.

Reader's comments: Warm and comfortable; a very charming couple; delightful.

LODGE DOWN

C X

Berkshire

Lambourn, Berkshire, RG17 7BJ Tel/Fax: 01672 540304
North of Hungerford. Nearest main road: A338 from Hungerford to Wantage (and M4, junction 14).

rear view

3 Bedrooms. £22.50. Available: own bath/shower/toilet. No smoking.
Light suppers if ordered.
1 Sitting-room. With open fire, TV, piano.
Large garden

Down a long drive, one eventually comes to an open vista of rolling downs stretching towards the Uffington White Horse. Built in the 1950s, Lodge Down is ideally positioned to take advantage of this panoramic view.

In the enormous parquet-floored sitting-room, with wing chairs, white corner alcoves, Bukhara rugs and old family photos, guests can relax round a big open fire. Upstairs, bedrooms are conventionally furnished, but two have the benefit of those far country views, while the third overlooks a bluebell wood which forms part of the extensive grounds surrounding the house. Breakfast is served by Sally Cook in the dining-room which faces a walled garden, where roses, catmint and lavender grow.

Lambourn is one of the most famous racehorse centres in the country. From the house, guests can watch horses being exercised on the gallops opposite; visits to stables can sometimes be arranged; and the local Hare & Hounds pub (good for evening meals) has strong racing connections. Newbury itself is close by. For those with more esoteric interests, Avebury stone circle and the Wiltshire crop circles are within easy driving distance. **V**

MARSHGATE COTTAGE HOTEL

C D M PT

Berkshire

Marsh Lane, Hungerford, Berkshire, RG17 0QN Tel: 01488 682307
(Fax: 01488 685475)
Nearest main road: A338 from Hungerford to Salisbury (and M4, junction 14).

10 Bedrooms. £25 **to SOTBT readers only** (in November, January and February)–£29. All have own shower/toilet; TV; views of canal (most). No smoking.
Light suppers by arrangement. Vegetarian or special diets if ordered. No smoking.
2 Sitting-areas. With open fire (in one). No smoking. Honesty bar.
Large garden
E-mail: reservations@marshgate.co.uk

The marshes which give this thatched cottage its name stretch down to the 18th-century Kennet & Avon Canal, a haven for birds and wildflowers. But it is a traditionally designed extension, with much exposed brickwork and polished floorboards, which provides the cosy and cottagey guest accommodation.

The small hotel is now owned by Carole and Chris Ticehurst (a former teacher-cum-cordon-bleu-cook and business executive) who have upgraded the rooms to a high standard. Bedrooms (most of which are on the ground floor) are well equipped and have new pine furniture, pretty colour schemes and immaculate shower-rooms. The bright breakfast-room, decorated in colourful pastel shades to match the crockery, has separate pine tables and an adjoining, conservatory-style sitting-area. A patio with garden benches allows views of canal life, including passing narrow-boats and the marsh ducks which roam freely about.

In addition to many eating-places, there is a plethora of antique shops in Hungerford. This is a good walking and cycling area. Barge trips also available. (Heathrow is an hour away.)

Reader's comments: Chris and Carole doing a wonderful job; the place is spotless; breakfast excellent; location superb; warm hospitality.

Berkshire

WILTON HOUSE

C(8) **PT**

33 High Street, Hungerford, Berkshire, RG17 0NF Tel: 01488 684228
(Fax: 01488 685037)
On A338 from Wantage to Hungerford (also near A4 from Newbury to Hungerford; and M4, junction 14).

2 Bedrooms. £25 **(one room to readers of this book only)**–£27. Both have own bath/shower/toilet; TV. No smoking.
1 Sitting-room. With open fire.
Small garden

E-mail: welfares@hotmail.com

Readers of this book who stayed at Deborah Welfare's previous home in Oxfordshire will realize that she has furnished this one with equal flair and elegance. Described by Pevsner as the 'most ambitious house in Hungerford', the classic Queen Anne brick façade conceals its origins as a much older mediaeval hall-house. Off the flagstoned entrance hall is a formal Regency dining-room, where guests' breakfast options may include home-grown fruit compote and such treats as scrambled eggs with smoked salmon (Deborah uses organic ingredients whenever possible).

In the cream-panelled Georgian drawing-room, green sofas are drawn round an open fire and surrounded by fine antiques and period pieces. A grandfather clock ticks away in the background. Guest bedrooms (and bathrooms) are stylish, spacious and immaculate. In one there is an outsize double bed; in the other, a truly splendid Victorian copper and brass bedstead. Throughout the house panelled walls are painted in delicate shades and complemented by lovely prints and paintings.

Hungerford – a mecca for antique-hunters – is well endowed with pubs and other places to dine, all just a short walk away.

Berkshire

WOODPECKER COTTAGE

C(8) **M**

Star Lane, Warren Row, Berkshire, RG10 8QS Tel: 01628 822772
(Fax: 01628 822125)
West of Maidenhead. Nearest main road: A4 from Maidenhead to Reading (also M4, junction 8/9; and M40, junction 4).

rear view

3 Bedrooms. £22.50 **to readers of this book only**–£27.50. All have own bath/shower/toilet; TV. No smoking.
1 Sitting-room. With wood-burning stove. No smoking.
Large garden

E-mail: power@woodpecker.co.uk

There really are woodpeckers here – three kinds – for the cottage is deep in bluebell woods, their many old tracks frequented by birdwatchers. A pretty garden and croquet lawn add to the attractions, and all this within a half-hour's drive of Heathrow Airport, Windsor and Henley. The house is also a good base for day trips into London.

Flint-walled cowsheds were converted and extensions added to create this attractive home. One ground-floor bedroom overlooks a fish pond, sundial and rock garden; all have woodland views. There's an en suite single room, a small 'snug', and a dining-room where Chippendale-style chairs surround the large breakfast-table. Although Joanna Power does not provide evening meals, there is a village pub in easy walking distance, as well as a wide choice of eating-places within a two-mile radius.

V

Readers' comments: Excellent. Attentive and very welcoming. Fantastic breakfast. Will stay again. Totally uncontrived atmosphere.

BUCKINGHAMSHIRE

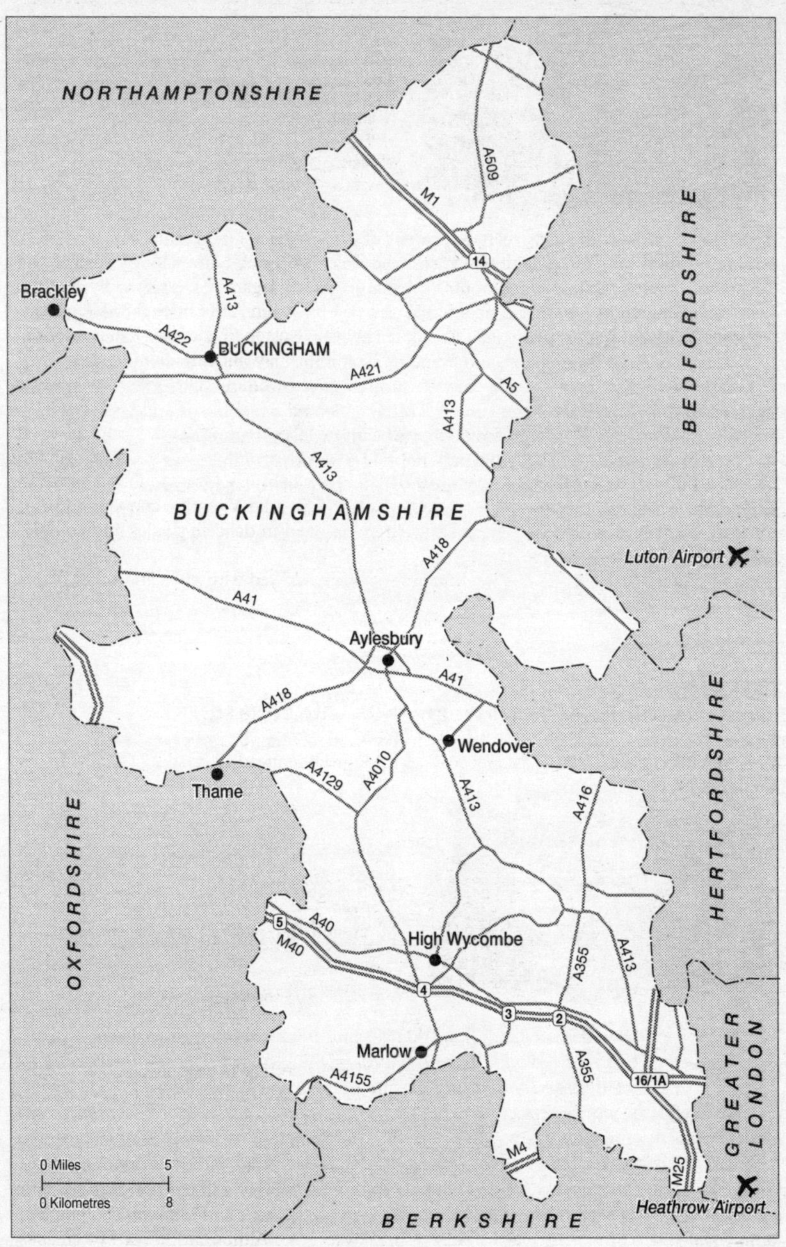

Months when houses are shown as closed are inclusive.

Buckinghamshire

FIELD COTTAGE

C(12)

St Leonards, Buckinghamshire, HP23 6NS Tel: 01494 837602 (Mobile: 07803 295337)
South-east of Wendover. Nearest main road: A413 from Amersham to Aylesbury.

3 Bedrooms. £25 **(one room for readers of this book only)**–£35. Less for 3 nights or more. Available: own bath/shower/toilet; TV. No smoking.
1 Sitting-room. With stove. No smoking.
Garden

E-mail: michael.jepson@lineone.net

Tucked away in a surprisingly secluded corner of Buckinghamshire, Field Cottage – true to its name – abuts arable farmland which stretches towards the Ridgeway long-distance footpath. It is a pretty, white-painted house (originally two workmen's cottages) with roses and clematis trailing up its façade and panoramic views on three sides. In the bright conservatory, brimming with geranium, hydrangea and bougainvillea, Sue Jepson serves generous breakfasts – assorted fresh fruit, yogurt and home-made muffins, as well as the regular fare.

Guests have their own elegant, antique-furnished, cream and coral sitting-room which leads on to the attractive cottage-garden. Upstairs, behind white board-and-latch doors are tasteful and immaculately decorated bedrooms with excellent bathrooms.

For evening meals, Sue recommends the Old Swan (half a mile away) which, in summer, can be reached on foot across country. The proximity of the Ridgeway is an obvious attraction for walkers, but there are also National Trust properties nearby. In autumn the surrounding beech woods are ablaze with colour, while in spring bluebells cut a painted swathe through the greenery.

V *Reader's comments:* Lovely home and garden; a real find.

Buckinghamshire

FOXHILL

C(5) **S**

Kingsey, Buckinghamshire, HP17 8LZ Tel/Fax: 01844 291650
East of Thame. On A4129 from Princes Risborough to Thame (and near M40, junctions 7/8).

3 Bedrooms. £24–£25. Available: own shower; TV. No smoking.
Light suppers if ordered.
1 Sitting-room. With TV. No smoking.
Large garden
Closed from December to February.

The instant impression is delightful: sparkling white house beyond green lawns where a pool, frequented by mallard ducks, is crossed by an arching stone bridge. At the back of the house is a well-tended garden with heated swimming-pool and Wendy house.

The interior is just as attractive. The house having been the home of architect Nick Hooper and his family for many years, it is not surprising that its modernization was done with care to respect its 16th-century origins. In the hall, floored with polished red quarry-tiles, a wrought-iron staircase leads up to bedrooms with beamed ceilings and restful colour schemes. The breakfast-room (which also serves as a sitting-room) has brown gingham tablecloths and rush-seated chairs. Here Mary-Joyce – a warm, gentle hostess – usually serves only breakfast, recommending pubs and restaurants in surrounding villages for evening meals. The ancient market town of Thame is only a few minutes away.

Readers' comments: Wonderfully kind hosts, lovely home, top of our list! Beautiful house.
V The Hoopers and their home are charming. Hospitality excellent.

LITTLE PARMOOR

C S X

Parmoor Lane, Frieth, Buckinghamshire, RG9 6NL Tel: 01494 881447 (Fax: 01494 883012)

North-west of Marlow. Nearest main road: A40 from Oxford to High Wycombe (also M40, junctions 4/5; and M4, junction 8/9).

3 Bedrooms. £24–£30 (less for 2 nights or more). Available: own bath/shower/toilet; TV. No smoking.
1 Sitting-room. With open fire. No smoking.
Large garden

Within a mere half-hour of Heathrow (and only a little longer to London) is a peaceful spot among the lovely Chiltern Hills, and in it this attractive house built in 1724.

Inside are green and white panelling, antiques, a log fire and watercolours painted by Wynyard Wallace's grandfather. An elegant pine staircase leads to two large, well-appointed, panelled bedrooms and another, smaller double often let for single occupancy. Julia Wallace provides breakfast which can sometimes be taken under the vine outside. The house stands in a designated Area of Outstanding Natural Beauty and is surrounded by footpaths for glorious country walks. There are plenty of excellent pubs and other eating-places in which to dine.

Readers' comments: Made us feel part of the family. Lovely. Most impressed by the warmth of welcome. Excellent. Charming people. Thoughtful, caring hospitality. Kindness itself. Brilliant hospitality.

MILL FARMHOUSE

C D S X

Westbury, Buckinghamshire, NN13 5JS Tel/Fax: 01280 704843

East of Brackley. Nearest main road: A422 from Brackley to Buckingham.

3 Bedrooms. £25 (less for 3 nights or more). Available: own bath/shower/toilet; TV.
Light suppers if ordered. Vegetarian or other special diets if ordered.
1 Sitting-room. With open fire, TV.
Large garden

The mill itself is now used as workshops, and the miller's stone house (built in the 18th century) is the heart of a 1000-acre farm with sheep, cattle and horses. The building has been immaculately restored and furnished by the Owens. Although the old, deep-set casements and shutters remain, as do panelled oak doors and other traditional features, Jacqueline has used pretty fabrics and colours to give a light and attractive look to the bedrooms – a wisteria frieze, figured cotton spreads and velvet bedheads in one, for instance; while another has a smart apricot and eau-de-nil colour scheme. These rooms are reached by a stair rising from the sitting/dining-room, which has a big refectory table, hunting-prints on cream walls and leather armchairs and a sofa. Handsome carved oak furniture recalls the past while sliding glass doors to the garden are wholly of today (as is the covered, heated swimming-pool).

The garden has stone-walled terraces and shrubs with foliage and berries selected to be colourful even in winter. There is stabling for horses – this is good riding country. Guests dine at local pubs or in Buckingham (six miles away) where there is a choice of restaurants.

Reader's comments: Everything was superb; Mr and Mrs Owen the most delightful people; light suppers absolutely tip-top.

Buckinghamshire

POLETREES FARM

C M S X

Ludgershall Road, Brill, Buckinghamshire, HP18 9TZ Tel/Fax: 01844 238276
West of Aylesbury. Nearest main road: A41 from Aylesbury to Bicester (and M40, junction 9).

3 Bedrooms. £25–£30. One has own shower/toilet; TV. No smoking.
Dinner (by arrangement). £15 for 4 courses and coffee, at 6.30pm. Vegetarian or other special diets if ordered. **Light suppers** if ordered.
1 Sitting-room. With TV. No smoking.
Large garden

There is clematis round the porch, baskets brimming with begonias and lobelias hang on the walls, and all around are roses, apple-trees and views of fields. Inside, stone walls, oak beams and an inglenook with a rare window beside it have survived five centuries. The water for the house still comes from a spring. Anita Cooper has furnished her ancient home well and has collections of old railway keys and of earthenware boots.

Bedrooms are pleasantly decorated too, with handsome walnut furniture. One room, in a quite superbly converted pigsty, is particularly comfortable and well equipped.

Dinner may comprise such dishes as home-made soup, roast pork, chocolate mousse, and cheese with fruit (cold suppers in high summer). The nearby village of Ludgershall is where Wycliffe started his great work of translating the Bible into English.

V

Readers' comments: Fantastic weekend! Very friendly; felt totally at home. Comfortable, and lovely breakfasts. Would recommend Poletrees time and time again.

Buckinghamshire

WHITEWEBBS

C(7) **PT X**

Grange Road, off Lower Road, Chalfont St Peter, Buckinghamshire, SL9 9AQ
Tel: 01753 884105
South-east of High Wycombe. Nearest main road: A413 from Amersham to Denham (also M40, junction 1a; and M25, junction 16).

2 Bedrooms. £25. Available: own bath/shower/toilet; TV. No smoking.
Light suppers if ordered. No smoking.
Small garden

This house, secluded by tall oaks and pines, was built in 1928 on ground belonging to the nearby Grange, once the home of William Penn's father-in-law (who sailed with him on the *Mayflower*). Now it is the home of artist Maureen Marsh, who specializes in portraits of houses and country views: visitors are welcome to see her studio and little printing-press.

Often tea (with home-produced raspberry jam and cakes) is served in the pretty garden – or visitors can use the kitchen to make their own at any hour. Upstairs are trim, cottagey, well-equipped bedrooms, and everywhere Maureen's delightful watercolours.

The fascinating Chiltern Open-air Museum of Historic Buildings is just a short drive away.

V

Readers' comments: Warm hospitality. Large, airy and comfortable rooms. One feels like a family guest. Delicious breakfasts. Extremely pretty. Food and ambience perfect. Comfortable and charming. Welcoming, caring; lovely room, excellent breakfast.

CAMBRIDGESHIRE

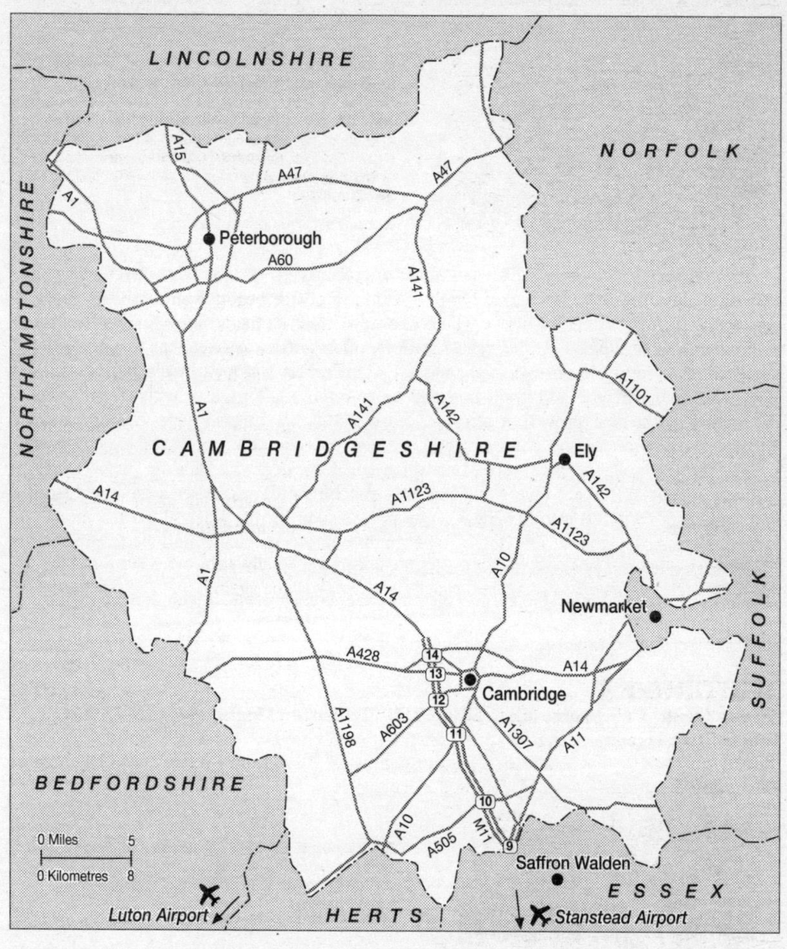

Facts (prices, etc.) at the top of entries are supplied by the proprietors themselves. While every effort is made to ensure that these are correct at the time of going to press, they may alter thereafter: please check when you book.

Cambridgeshire

FINCH FARMHOUSE C(5)

28 Fen Road, Bassingbourn, Cambridgeshire, SG8 5PQ Tel: 01763 242019 (Fax: 01763 241907)

South-west of Cambridge. Nearest main road: A1198 from Godmanchester to Royston (and M11, junction 10).

2 Bedrooms. £22 (less for 7 nights or more). Both have own bath/shower/toilet; TV. No smoking.
Dinner (by arrangement). £9.50–£11.50 for 2–3 courses and coffee (or £16.50 for 3-course cordon bleu menu), at 6–8pm (not weekends). Vegetarian or other special diets if ordered. No smoking. **Light suppers** if ordered.
1 Sitting-room. With open fire, TV. No smoking.
Small garden

E-mail: btmurray@dial.pipex.com

Charlotte Murray's culinary skills were much appreciated by readers who stayed at her former home in Longstowe, and good food remains one of the principal reasons for coming to this attractive mid-Victorian house where she now lives. In the striking, deep red dining-room with bold bird prints on the walls, Charlotte offers guests meals cooked to a professional standard. A cordon bleu menu might include Camembert wrapped in filo pastry, chicken fillet with crème fraîche and grain mustard sauce, then apple mousse with caramel sauce. Alternatively, she will provide a simpler, more traditional English supper – home-made watercress soup, a roast and plum tart, for example. (Lunches, too, are available on request.)

The light, pleasingly uncluttered bedrooms are decorated with delicate pink-and-white or powder-blue-and-white toile wallpaper and matching curtains. After a day's sightseeing in Cambridge (only 20 minutes away), guests can relax in the peaceful garden or by the hearth in the sitting-room. The house itself – with white bargeboards and a canopied porch – was originally built as an ale house for Irish agricultural labourers.

V *Reader's comments:* Memorable cordon bleu cooking. Nice hostess. Lovely supper.

Cambridgeshire

THE GROVE C

Sutton Gault, Cambridgeshire, CB6 2BD Tel/Fax: 01353 777196

West of Ely. Nearest main road: A142 from Ely to Chatteris.

2 Bedrooms. £23. Both have own bath/shower/ toilet; views of river. No smoking.
1 Sitting-room. With open fire, TV, piano.
Large garden

The Grove, surrounded by lime trees (unusual in the Fens), was built for a Dutch drainage engineer around 1750, and later 'Victorianized'. It stands almost alone before a bridge which crosses the New Bedford River. This is an idyllic place for birdwatchers, especially to view waders.

Stella Anderson, an amiable hostess, serves breakfast in the highly polished oak dining-room, or in the kitchen, with large baskets and bunches of dried flowers seemingly growing out from the beams, blue-and-white gingham curtains, plates on the wall and a royal blue Aga. French doors lead on to a terrace and garden with snowdrops, aconites and daffodils under tall trees bedecked with bird-boxes. Beyond is a field with sheep and an all-weather tennis court.

The twin room is spacious; the light and airy double room enjoys the garden views. Three heavy oak beams in the ceiling date from the original construction; dark green and white tiles make its bathroom sparkle.

V There is an excellent inn next door.

HILL HOUSE FARM

C(12)

9 Main Street, Coveney, Cambridgeshire, CB6 2DJ Tel: 01353 778369
West of Ely. Nearest main road: A142 from Ely to Chatteris.

3 Bedrooms. £22–£24 (less for 5 nights or more). All have own shower/toilet; TV. No smoking.
1 Sitting-room. No smoking.
Small garden

The Nix family have been farmers in Coveney since 1640, when they arrived from Holland to work on the Fens drainage scheme. At that time Coveney was an 'island in the bay' from which one travelled by boat to Ely, three miles away. From the guests' lounge is a panoramic view of the Fens, with Ely Cathedral a focal point in the distance.

Mrs Nix is a very attentive and welcoming hostess. Her breakfasts include kippers and croissants as well as a full farmhouse option.

There are three en suite bedrooms, one on the ground floor (with its own entrance). Double and twin rooms are approached via an outdoor staircase. Everything is immaculate. Outside there are a terrace and small garden where guests may sit.

The house is very well placed to visit not only Ely, Cambridge, Peterborough (another fine cathedral) and Newmarket but also the scenic parts of Norfolk and Suffolk. For those who love wildlife, Welney's bird reserve and Wicken Fen are near.

Readers' comments: Very comfortable and attractive. Delicious breakfast. Made most welcome.

OLD EGREMONT HOUSE

C(12) **PT**

31 Egremont Street, Ely, Cambridgeshire, CB6 1AE Tel: 01353 663118
(Fax: 01353 614516)
Nearest main road: A10 from Cambridge to King's Lynn.

Cambridgeshire

rear view

2 Bedrooms. £24–£25 (less for 3 nights or more). Both have own bath/toilet; TV. No smoking.
Large garden
Closed in late December.

The 300-year-old house has been filled by Sheila Friend-Smith with attractive furnishings, the garden is exceptional and there is a cathedral view.

One bedsitting-room has a cream carpet and beribboned duvet, sprigged wallpaper and stripped pine furniture. There are armchairs from which to enjoy a view of the winding flower garden and its herbaceous bed; from the other bedroom one sees the neat vegetable garden where Victorian hedges of box flank the symmetrical paths, and the tennis lawn. The house is full of interesting things to look at: Jeremy's collection of clocks (one is silent, being gravity-operated), pretty Portuguese tiles in bathrooms (and some depicting old military costumes), embroideries from Jordan and stone-rubbings from Thailand. Breakfast is served at a big, gleaming, mahogany table surrounded by Chippendale-style chairs, with antique china, numerous books and prints around.

Guests dine at the Old Fire Engine (restaurant) or at the Stage Coach (carvery), both of which are in walking distance.

Cambridgeshire

OLD WELL COTTAGE

C

Main Street, Shudy Camps, Cambridgeshire, CB1 6RA Tel: 01799 584387 (Fax: 01799 584486)

North-east of Saffron Walden. Nearest main road: A1307 from Cambridge to Haverhill (and M11, junction 9).

2 Bedrooms. £22–£23 (less for 3 nights or more). Both have own TV. No smoking.
Dinner (by arrangement). £10–£15 for 2–4 courses and coffee, at times to suit guests. Vegetarian or other special diets if ordered. No smoking. **Light suppers** if ordered.
Garden

E-mail: robsamvet@aol.com

Shudy Camps was originally part of a Roman settlement and at its edge stands this long, low, cream-painted cottage whose walls are covered in distinctive pargeting.

Guests' accommodation is at one end of the cottage and comprises two homely and pleasantly decorated bedrooms and a compact dining-room. Here, Jackie Edmonds, an experienced caterer, serves such evening meals as broccoli and Stilton soup, pork roulade, mini-meringue nests with raspberries in a coulis, and cheese.

One of the bedrooms is a pretty single with a pink rosebud Laura Ashley wallpaper and a quilted cream and rose-patterned bedspread. The larger, double room is comfortably equipped with a two-seater sofa. As the quarry-tiled shower-room and toilet are shared, Jackie only lets both bedrooms when a group of friends or family are travelling together. Scones and tea are offered on arrival, and in summer guests can sit by the little pond in the front garden. All around are arable fields, numerous footpaths and country quiet.

Popular sightseeing options from here include: Jacobean Audley End House, Duxford aircraft museum, Chilford Hall vineyard, and the attractive market town of Saffron Walden.

Cambridgeshire

QUEENSBERRY

C D PT

196 Carter Street, Fordham, Cambridgeshire, CB7 5JU Tel: 01638 720916 (Fax: 01638 720233)

North of Newmarket. Nearest main road: A142 from Newmarket to Ely.

3 Bedrooms. £25–£30 (less for 3 nights or more). One has own shower/toilet; TV (in all). No smoking.
1 Sitting-room. With open fire, piano. No smoking.
Small garden

A little gem of a place, especially for those interested in horseracing. Jan Roper, ebullient and welcoming, and Malcolm, a former amateur jockey, are keen to show you maps and information about training yards, race meetings and horse sales in the area.

Their house is full of interesting furniture, prints (15 by Spy in the dining-room) and china – including a Japanese tea service. Silver-framed family portraits adorn the piano and there is an abundance of silk flowers. Bedrooms are delightfully furnished.

Malcolm makes fresh orange juice to serve with breakfast at the mahogany dining-table. A traditional Coles wallpaper gives warmth to this room, where there are also fruit pot-pourris and displays of china in cabinets. Guests may order haddock, kippers, traditional farmhouse food and croissants. Jams are home-made.

Jan loves making sponges for tea when guests arrive and she will provide full set teas if given notice. Although evening meals are no longer served, there are four eating-places within a 10-minute walk from the house.

Reader's comments: Made to feel at home immediately; specially good breakfast; sorry not to be there longer.

ROSENDALE LODGE

C(7) M PT X

223 Main Street, Witchford, Cambridgeshire, CB6 2HT Tel: 01353 667700 (Fax: 01353 667799)

West of Ely. Nearest main road: A142 from Ely to Chatteris.

4 Bedrooms. £25–£30 (less for 4 nights or more). Available: own bath/shower/toilet; TV. No smoking.
Dinner (by arrangement). £8–£10 for 2–3 courses and coffee, at 7–8pm. Vegetarian diets if ordered. No smoking. **Light suppers** if ordered.
1 Sitting-room. No smoking.
Garden

This partly brick-clad, timber-framed house with overhanging gables was only built a few years ago and its interior combines the best of modern comfort with stylish period furnishings. Val Pickford has a collector's eye for antiques and many of the interesting pieces with which she has filled the rooms of her home were acquired at auction. Bedrooms here are particularly attractive – individually furnished in Victorian or Edwardian style, with huge beds, comfortable sofas and thoughtful hospitality trays. Shower-rooms, too, are impressive and spacious enough to accommodate antique, marble-topped washstands. A ground-floor suite, fully adapted for disabled guests, is no less characterful.

The splendid, galleried dining-cum-sitting-room has a vast brick inglenook at one end, crystal chandeliers and a handsome mahogany sideboard. Val will prepare homely evening meals – celery soup, roast beef and plum pie, for instance – and she offers an extensive choice at breakfast.

Ely is close by and the rest of East Anglia is also easily accessible from here.

Readers' comments: Hospitable and welcoming hosts. Extremely comfortable rooms, furnished and decorated with real taste. Marvellous breakfast. We loved staying there.

V

SPINNEY ABBEY

C(5)

Wicken, Cambridgeshire, CB7 5XQ Tel: 01353 720971

South of Ely. Nearest main road: A10 from Cambridge to Ely (and M11, junction 9).

3 Bedrooms. £23. Available: own bath/shower/toilet; TV. No smoking.
1 Sitting-room. With TV. Piano.
Large garden

E-mail: spinney.abbey@tesco.net

The original Spinney Abbey was closed by Henry VIII, became a private house and was later pulled down. Its stones were used to build a new house in 1775. This is now the home of Valerie Fuller who has three serene and spacious bedrooms, decorated in pastel shades, with comfortable armchairs and good private bathrooms. From the adjoining farm lands are views into ancient Wicken Fen, a National Trust nature reserve. There is a tennis court, too. The nearby village pub serves evening meals.

Ely has one of Europe's most glorious cathedrals, a multiplicity of pinnacles and spires outside, lofty vista within. The city still has an 18th-century air, and there is a particularly attractive riverside walk linking its quays. Cambridge and Newmarket are also at hand.

Readers' comments: Excellent hostess, capable and friendly. Very comfortable. Accommodation, service and food exceptionally good. Lovely hostess. Very welcoming.

SPRINGFIELD

C PT S X

16 Horn Lane, Linton, Cambridgeshire, CB1 6HT Tel: 01223 891383

South-east of Cambridge. Nearest main road: A1307 from Haverhill towards Cambridge (and M11, junctions 9/10).

2 Bedrooms. £25–£27 (less for 2 nights or more). Available: own bath/toilet; TV; views of river. No smoking.

1 Sitting-room. With open fire, TV, piano. No smoking.

Large garden

The spring which gives this 19th-century house its name rises in a carp pond at the far end of the garden – or, rather, gardens; for there is a succession of hedge-enclosed areas. One of these (almost islanded by a twist of the River Granta) is equipped for children.

The house is of gracious design, its gables decorated with fretted bargeboards and at its side a spacious conservatory (where breakfast is often served) which Judith Rossiter has filled with white flowering plants. Adjoining it is a comfortable sitting-room. Bedrooms are on the second floor, furnished with antiques including old maps of America and other Americana (Fred is descended from George Washington's aide-de-camp). At dusk you might hear the distant roar of lions from nearby Linton Zoo.

V *Readers' comments:* Very comfortable, and a really splendid breakfast. Charming and very comfortable. Warm welcome. Strongly recommended. Excellent.

Houses which accept the discount vouchers on page ii are marked with a V symbol next to the relevant entries.

Where wine is not available (meaning it is on sale or can be fetched for you), you are nearly always welcome to bring in your own drinks.

Prices are per person sharing a room at the beginning of the year. However, for the best rooms in the house or later in the year, you may well be asked for more.

If you find places in England and Wales that you feel should be visited for possible inclusion in a future edition of SOTBT, please write and let us know. Send your descriptions (including full name of establishment, address and current b & b price per person) to Jan Bowmer, c/o Arrow Books, Random House, 20 Vauxhall Bridge Road, London, SW1V 2SA.

CHESHIRE

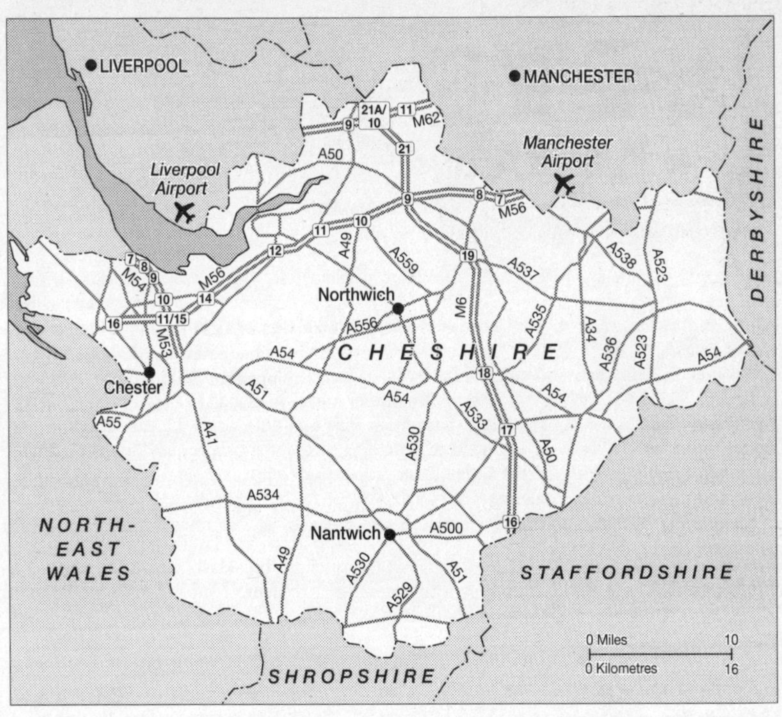

You stand a better chance of finding the right accommodation at the right price in the right area if you are using an up-to-date edition of this book, which is revised every year. Obtain an order form for the next edition (published in November) by sending a stamped addressed envelope, with 'SOTBT 2003' in the top left-hand corner, to Explore Britain, Alston, Cumbria, CA9 3SL.

Cheshire

BARRATWICH

PT S X

Cuddington Lane, Cuddington, Cheshire, CW8 2SZ Tel: 01606 882412
South-west of Northwich. Nearest main road: A49 from Whitchurch to Warrington.

3 Bedrooms. £20–£22 (less for 2 nights or more). All have TV. No smoking.
Light suppers if ordered.
Large garden

Just beyond the Delamere Forest is Cuddington village and this Victorian cottage with a large garden from which to enjoy the fine views of open countryside. These include a valley trout lake that, like many other Cheshire meres (old marl diggings), attracts unusual birds – and birdwatchers.

Visitors enter a white-and-celadon hall with galleried staircase leading to fresh, cottagey bedrooms – one with white boarded wall, another with stencilled decoration. Mary Riley prides herself on her good breakfasts, with fresh fruit and farm eggs. This is served in the dining-room, which has been extended to provide a pleasant sitting-area at one end. While Mary will usually provide a light supper, the nearest pub which serves food is only a mile away, and there are more restaurants in Northwich.

Sightseeing options include the unusual salt museum at Northwich and Arley Hall mansion.

Readers' comments: A warm welcome. Warmth and hospitality; setting peaceful. Delightful. Charming; hosts most helpful and friendly. How welcome I was made.

Cheshire

CASTLE HOUSE

C D PT S X

23 Castle Street, Chester, Cheshire, CH1 2DS Tel/Fax: 01244 350354
Nearest main road: A483 from Wrexham to Chester (and M56, junction 16).

5 Bedrooms. £24 **to readers of this book only.** Sunday half-price if part of 3-night booking, November to March. Available: own bath/shower/toilet; TV.
1 Sitting-room. With open fire. No smoking.
Small garden

Right in the middle of the city but in a quiet by-road, this interesting house has a breakfast-room which dates from 1540 behind an 18th-century frontage and staircase. The arms of Elizabeth I (with English lion and Welsh dragon) are over the fireplace. It is both the Marls' own home and a guest-house with modern bedrooms that are exceptionally well furnished and equipped. Bed-and-breakfast only, for Chester has so many good restaurants; but visitors are welcome to use the kitchen. Newspapers and local phone calls are free. Coyle Marl, a local businessman, is an enthusiast for Chester and loves to tell visitors about its lesser-known charms.

Chester's cathedral of red stone dates back to the 14th century and the city's zoo is outstanding.

V

Readers' comments: Breakfasts absolutely first class. Excellent room and hospitality. Delightful hosts. So welcoming and friendly. Breakfast a delight. Liked it immensely. Very atmospheric. Superb position, comfortable, excellent food. A week well spent.

LEA FARM

C D

Wrinehill Road, Wybunbury, Cheshire, CW5 7NS Tel/Fax: 01270 841429
East of Nantwich. Nearest main road: A500 from Stoke-on-Trent to Nantwich (and M6, junction 16).

3 Bedrooms. £19–£21 (less for 3 nights or more). Available: own bath/shower/toilet; TV. No smoking.
Dinner (by arrangement). £12 for 3 courses and coffee, at 6.45pm. No smoking. **Light suppers** if ordered.
1 Sitting-room. With open fire, TV. No smoking.
Garden

Jean and Alan Callwood's peacocks may grace you with their company at breakfast-time, for they often appear at the French windows, right on cue, nonchalantly peering in and then suddenly startling themselves with their own reflections.

This solid, pre-World War II farmhouse was built by Alan's parents. It is part of a 150-acre dairy-farm where Alan and his son Jonathan keep a herd of pedigree Holstein-Friesians, producing milk for local cheese-makers. Accommodation is homely and comfortable. Good-sized bedrooms have patterned carpets and frilled bedspreads; while in the sitting-room, green velours sofas and armchairs are drawn round the hearth. Jean provides generous, traditional farmhouse breakfasts and dinners (soup, roast beef and apple pie, for instance). Alternatively, two pubs in the village offer reasonably priced food.

Guests who enjoy visiting gardens will appreciate that there are four in the vicinity: Stapeley Water Gardens, Biddulph Grange, the Dorothy Clive Gardens and Bridgemere Garden World. Jodrell Bank combines scientific interest with an arboretum. Stately homes nearby include the Halls at Dorfold, Gawsworth and Little Moreton.

Reader's comments: Courteous host and hostess, quiet rural location and very reasonable prices. V

Cheshire

MITCHELL'S

C D PT

28 Hough Green, Chester, Cheshire, CH4 8JQ Tel: 01244 679004 (Fax: 01244 659567)
On A5104 from Chester to Saltney.

6 Bedrooms. £24–£26 (less for 3 nights or more in low season only). All have own shower/toilet; TV. No smoking.
1 Sitting-room. With open fire, TV, piano.
Small garden

E-mail: mitoches@dialstart.net

On the south side of the city, this handsome house, built in 1856, has large windows and fine, high-ceilinged rooms with moulded cornices which Helen and Colin Mitchell have furnished in period: buttoned velvet chairs, old clocks, even a Victorian baby-chair and sewing-machine. Some rooms have a leafy outlook and there is a lily-pool cascade that is lit up at night. There is parking space (an asset in Chester), with buses to the centre passing outside.

The city is, of course, of outstanding interest – second only to Bath and York in what there is to see. It is surrounded by ancient walls of red sandstone, just outside which is a large Roman amphitheatre. The most unusual feature, however, is the Rows: here, steps from street level lead up to balustraded galleries overhanging the pavements, serving a second level of small shops above the ones below.

Reader's comments: Welcome friendly, help and advice forthcoming.

Cheshire

NEWTON HALL

D

Newton Lane, Tattenhall, Cheshire, CH3 9NE Tel: 01829 770153 (Fax: 01829 770655)

South-east of Chester. Nearest main road: A41 from Whitchurch to Chester.

3 Bedrooms. £22.50–£27.50. One has own bath/shower/toilet; TV. No smoking.
1 Sitting-room. With TV. No smoking.
Large garden

E-mail: newton.hall@farming.co.uk

The centre of a big dairy-farm, Newton Hall is a 300-year-old house surrounded by gardens and with fine views of both Beeston and Peckforton castles. Anne Arden's rooms have an air of solid comfort (the blue bedroom is particularly beautiful, with handsome Victorian mahogany furniture and an en suite bathroom). In the breakfast-room are wheelback chairs, oak table and dresser, the original quarry-tiles, a brick fireplace, huge beams and oak doors with great iron hinges. Like those in the sitting-room, its casements open on to sweeping lawns.

The walled city of Chester is famous for its cathedral, castle and Rows, an outstanding zoo as well, and the River Dee for salmon. At nearby Bunbury, alabaster monuments are a feature of the church; and from Brown Knowl you can go up Bickerton Hill to get stunning views across Wales. Except for the hills in this part of the county, Cheshire consists mostly of level pastureland which supports the cows whose milk has made Cheshire cheese into a classic variety.

Readers' comments: Exceptionally charming. Hostess of great care. Most warmly received. Outstanding. Very pleasant. Exceeded our expectations. Lovely room and gracious hostess.

Cheshire

ROUGHLOW FARMHOUSE

C(6) X

Chapel Lane, Willington, Cheshire, CW6 0PG Tel/Fax: 01829 751199

East of Chester. Nearest main road: A54 from Congleton towards Chester (and M6, junction 18).

3 Bedrooms. £25–£35. All have own bath/shower/toilet. No smoking.
3 Sitting-rooms. With open fire/stove, TV, piano. No smoking.
Large garden

E-mail: sutcliffe@roughlow.freeserve.co.uk

Warm sandstone was used to build this 200-year-old farmhouse, well sited 450 feet up for superb views towards Shropshire in one direction and Wales in another.

From a graceful sitting-room in shades of pink and grey, stairs wind up to the bedrooms. There is an enormous suite above the barn with beamed sitting-room and pretty quilts contrasting with bedheads of white bamboo; beyond it is a luxurious, outsize shower. Sally Sutcliffe used to be an interior decorator and this shows in her choice of colours, antiques, and pictures by a local artist. The Sutcliffes are both collectors of art and have amassed an interesting collection of contemporary watercolours.

There is a tennis court for guests' use. One can dine well at the village pub (a mile away). Motor-racing enthusiasts head for nearby Oulton Park; while a little further afield are such varied National Trust properties (with gardens) as Tatton Park, Erdigg Hall and 700-year-old Chirk Castle.

Readers' comments: Superb bedrooms. Quite enchanting. Beautifully appointed, peaceful, elegant. Absolutely delighted with the reception we received. Delightfully secluded. Breath-taking views.

TILSTON LODGE

C S X

Cheshire

Tilston, Cheshire, SY14 7DR Tel/Fax: 01829 250223
South of Chester. Nearest main road: A41 from Chester to Whitchurch.

3 Bedrooms. £25–£35 (less for 3 nights or more). Bargain breaks. All have own bath/shower/toilet; TV. No smoking.
Dinner (by arrangement). From £15 for 3 courses and coffee, at times to suit guests. Vegetarian or other special diets if ordered. No smoking.
1 Sitting-room. With open fire, TV, piano. No smoking.
Large garden

Handy for North Wales as well as historic Chester, the pretty village of Tilston is surrounded by the Peckforton and Bickerton hills. Tilston Lodge, set in 16 acres of grounds which include award-winning gardens and two big ponds to attract wildfowl, is now home to Kathie Ritchie and her collection of rare breeds. The original Victorian features include a handsomely tiled hall with pretty marble fireplace and galleried mahogany staircase. Kathie has made patchwork bedspreads; stencilled woodbines on walls; draped a four-poster with lace; and collected an array of Victorian jugs. In the raspberry-walled dining-room – with William-and-Mary-style chairs, good linen and silver – she serves imaginative meals using home-grown produce, local lamb, Cheshire and other local cheeses. Alternatively, guests may dine at the excellent village pub. You might be offered duck eggs for breakfast; jams and marmalade are home-made.

Readers' comments: Excellent in every way. Fine bedroom and bathroom. Very good, quiet setting.

V

For a list of SOTBT houses that are in or close to the great National Parks of England and Wales, see p.ix.

Readers' comments quoted in the book are from letters sent directly to us: they are not supplied via the proprietors.

Some proprietors stipulate a minimum stay of two nights at weekends or peak seasons; or they will accept one-nighters only at short notice (that is, only if no lengthier booking has yet been made).

Complaints about matters which could not have been settled on the spot will be forwarded to proprietors. Please enclose a stamped addressed envelope if you want your complaint acknowledged.

CORNWALL

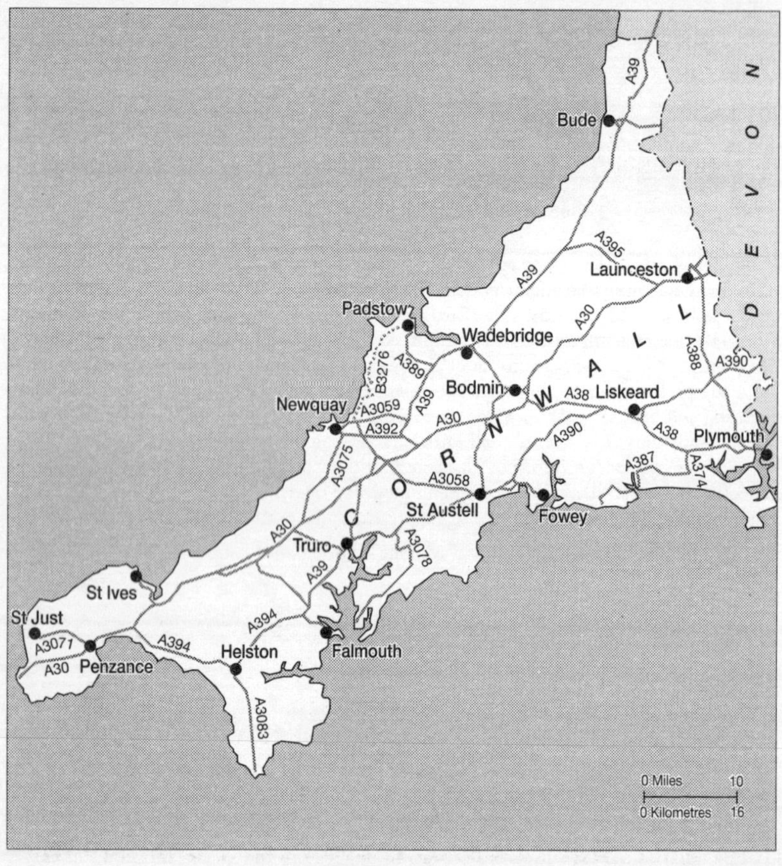

Some houses offer special discounts to readers using the current edition of this book. Always state you are an SOTBT reader when ringing to book or when using E-mail.

BOSCEAN COUNTRY HOTEL

C(5) **X**

Boswedden Road, St Just, Cornwall, TR19 7QP Tel/Fax: 01736 788748
Nearest main road: A3071 from Penzance to St Just.

10 Bedrooms. £23 (less for 7 nights or more). Available: own bath/shower/toilet; views of sea. No smoking.
Dinner (by arrangement). £13 for 4 courses and coffee, at 7pm. Vegetarian or other special diets if ordered. Wine available. No smoking. **Light suppers** if ordered.
1 Sitting-room. With open fire, TV. No smoking. **Bar.**
Large garden

E-mail: boscean@aol.com

This dignified house was originally built as a gentleman's residence, and Dennis and Linda Wilson, during their sympathetic modernization, have taken care not to disturb its many old features. Especially impressive are the oak staircase and oak panelling, the timber for which came mostly from a 19th-century Royal Navy ship. See if you can find the hidden panel. A tip – it is in the spacious hall, where guests sit with pre-dinner drinks around a log fire. Hanging throughout the house are pictures and maps depicting Cornish mining history which, along with Cornish antiquarian books, are Dennis's great interests.

Bedrooms are a delightful mix of furnishings and colours, some flowery, others more modern. In the bar, the walls are a stunning combination of mulberry-red and deep green, while plum is the predominant hue of the dining-room. For evening meals (home-made), Linda uses locally produced meat and vegetables; fresh fish is delivered daily. A typical menu (with some choices): turnip and dill soup, followed by beef, ale and mushroom pie, then rum and banana trifle, and cheese. Guests may have an unlimited number of desserts.

BOSILLION

C(10) **PT**

Grampound, Cornwall, TR2 4QY Tel: 01726 883327
East of Truro. Nearest main road: A390 from St Austell to Truro.

Cornwall

1 Bedroom. £23–£30 (with continental breakfast). Has own bath/shower/toilet; TV. No smoking.
Large garden

Only before and after photographs could show the Herculean effort put in by Jonathon and Annabel Croggon to transform an old barn into an adjunct of their home, with private accommodation for guests. The site was mentioned in Domesday Book and there has been a Croggon here since 1630.

In the huge bedsitting-room, a soft grey velvet sofa contrasts with the blue-printed beige curtains which, in turn, match the shaped, padded headboards with tufted buttons. The fabrics (honeysuckle-patterned cotton with turquoise and pink butterflies in the white bathroom) are especially pretty, and were chosen and made up with imagination by Annabel, who used to work for Colefax & Fowler.

From the bedroom, stable doors open on to a terrace where a bulldozer was used to create tiered banks which are festooned with ceanothus, camelias, azaleas and hydrangeas. Annabel, a delightful young hostess, brings continental breakfast to the bedroom, and for dinner, guests can eat at the excellent Chinese restaurant or village pub just a few minutes away.

Cornwall

BOSWEDDEN HOUSE HOTEL

C D P T S

Cape Cornwall, St Just-in-Penwith, Cornwall, TR19 7NJ Tel/Fax: 01736 788733
West of St Just. Nearest main road: A3071 from Penzance to St Just.

8 Bedrooms. £21–£25 (less for 2 nights or more). Available: own bath/shower/toilet; views of sea. No smoking.
Dinner (by arrangement). £8–£12 for 2–3 courses and coffee, at 7.30pm. Vegetarian or other special diets if ordered. Wine available. No smoking. **Light suppers** if ordered.
1 Sitting-room. With open fire, TV. No smoking. **Bar.**
Large garden

E-mail: relax@boswedden.free-online.co.uk

Built at the beginning of the 19th century as a mine captain's mansion, this large white house is just a short distance from Cape Cornwall – the only cape in England – where great rolling breakers rise up from the Atlantic and batter the spectacular coastline.

However, all is calm inside the rooms of Thelma Griffiths' house, where relaxation therapies are available and also a heated, indoor swimming-pool on a seasonal basis. On chilly evenings a fire is lit in the sitting-room, where cream embossed wallpaper is offset by the heather colours in the curtains and cushions.

Thelma, formerly catering manager at Reading University, might offer such dinners as prawn cocktail, chicken breasts in white wine and asparagus sauce, and passion cake. These are served in the large, bright dining-room with a grey-green and rose-pink colour scheme. The immaculate bedrooms and bathrooms are all different.

V This wild and beautiful part of Cornwall is steeped in Celtic history. Land's End is nearby as are the cliffside Minack Theatre and coastal beauty-spots.

Cornwall

CARNEGGAN HOUSE

C D S

Lanteglos-by-Fowey, Cornwall, PL23 1NW Tel/Fax: 01726 870327
East of St Austell. Nearest main road: A390 from Liskeard to St Austell.

3 Bedrooms. £22–£28 (less for 7 nights or more). Available: own bath/shower/toilet; TV; views of sea.
Dinner (by arrangement). £10–£15 for 3 courses and coffee, at 7.30pm. Vegetarian or other special diets if ordered. Wine available. **Light suppers** if ordered.
1 Sitting-room. With open fire, piano.
Large garden
Closed from December to January.

Folklore has it that 'the angels dance at Carneggan'. Sue and Alan Shakerley can vouch for this rare but wondrous sight which occurs when the moon shines on the sea and the wind blows through the leaves of the sycamore trees in a certain way. The result is shooting, dancing, silvery lights.

This 18th-century house was built to withstand the storms which sweep in from the English Channel; and, inside, the antique furniture, heavily draped curtains in rich colours and collections of books and china combine to create a home of warmth and interest. In the sitting-room is a series of paintings of Alan's father astride his horses. The bedrooms are pretty and the largest of all has comfortable chairs in a bay window for guests to enjoy the spectacular sea views.

Sue's dinners comprise organic meat (some of it reared by them) and organic vegetables when in season. A typical menu: smoked Scottish salmon, beef stew with vegetables, and lemon cream pie.

Reader's comments: A wonderful place; a charming house; an 'at home' every evening.

CLARE HOUSE

C(12) PT

20 Broad Street, Penryn, Cornwall, TR10 8JH Tel: 01326 373294

North-west of Falmouth. Nearest main road: A39 from Truro to Falmouth.

Cornwall

2 Bedrooms. £25 (less for 3 nights or more). Available: own bath/shower/toilet; TV; views of river. No smoking.

1 Sitting-room. With open fire, TV. No smoking.

Garden

For the long-distance traveller, this 17th-century town house is a haven of warmth and comfort. Hosts Jack and Jean Hewitt have lovingly restored a much-neglected house, built originally for a sea merchant, and have furnished it in keeping with the period. Guests are greeted with tea and cake in the elegant sitting-room, where an off-white, satin striped wall-paper provides a foil for the terracotta curtains and apple-green sofas and chairs. Tea can also be taken in the conservatory beneath the century-old grapevine, or in the secluded garden where plants flourish until late in the year. Throughout the house are paintings done by Jean, a gifted amateur artist.

The bedrooms, which lead off a wide landing, are spacious and pretty (hyacinth-blue and yellow in one, yellows and almond-white in the other). Separate from the bedrooms is a cubby-hole stocked with beverages and biscuits.

For dinner, there is a choice of places within walking distance or, further afield, the noted Pandora restaurant, overlooking Restronguet Creek.

Reader's comments: Impressed by the hospitality; high standard of accommodation and excellent breakfasts.

CLIFF HOUSE

PT S X

Devonport Hill, Kingsand, Cornwall, PL10 1NJ Tel: 01752 823110 (Fax: 01752 822595)

South-west of Plymouth. Nearest main road: A374 from Plymouth towards Looe.

Cornwall

3 Bedrooms. £20–£30 (less for 3 nights or more). Available: own bath/shower/toilet; views of sea. No smoking.

Dinner (by arrangement). £20 for aperitif, 4 courses and coffee, at times to suit guests. Less for fewer courses and without aperitif. Vegetarian or other special diets if ordered. Wine available. No smoking.

Light suppers if ordered.

2 Sitting-rooms. With stove, TV, balcony, piano. No smoking.

Small garden

E-mail: chkingsand@aol.com

In a fishing village on the Rame peninsula, an Area of Outstanding Natural Beauty, is 17th-century Cliff House – perched high above the sea and within a few yards of the south Cornwall coastal path.

From its hexagonal bay windows or the verandah, one can watch naval ships passing in and out of Plymouth Sound or children playing on the sands of Cawsand Bay. To make the most of these views, the sitting-room is on the first floor. On the walls of the house are paintings by local artists that are for sale. Some bedrooms, too, enjoy the fine views – the largest having armchairs in the bay window. Some visitors have found parking awkward.

Ann Heasman is an enthusiastic wholefood cook of such meals as lentil pâté with spiced fruit salad, carbonnade of beef, and chocolate roulade. She bakes her own bread.

Readers' comments: Lovely, friendly welcome, dinners delicious, beautiful landscape, would go again time after time. Made us feel instantly at home; house so friendly, comfortable and stylish; cooking absolutely superb. Front rooms superb, breakfast very good.

V

COBBLERS COTTAGE

PT

Nantithet, Cury, Cornwall, TR12 7RB Tel/Fax: 01326 241342
South-east of Helston. Nearest main road: A3083 from Helston to the Lizard.

3 Bedrooms. £22–£24 (less for 7 nights or more). All have own bath/shower/toilet; TV. No smoking.
Dinner. £12 for 3 courses and coffee, at 6.30pm. Vegetarian or other special diets if ordered. No smoking. **Light suppers** if ordered.
1 Sitting-room. With open fire, TV. No smoking.
Large garden

The history of David and Hilary Lugg's attractive pink-painted stone cottage is waiting to be explored; the house certainly dates from the 17th century and has been, in turn, a school and a cobbler's shop: the local shoemaker used to keep the tools of his trade in one of the upstairs rooms. Today no traces of chalk-dust or leather linger in the pretty bedrooms (one pink, another palest celadon) with their sloping ceilings, deep-set windows and good bathrooms, nor downstairs in the cosy beamed sitting-room where brass and copper gleam round the stove in the big stone fireplace. Lace tablecloths add an elegant touch to the dining-room, where Hilary might serve, for example, pork in apple and onion sauce (accompanied by generous quantities of vegetables), a delectable trifle, and cheeses.

The family has farmed the same land in Cury (now run by David and Hilary's son and daughter-in-law – see **Tregaddra Farm** entry) for five generations.

Reader's comments: The friendliness and kindness of our hosts, the nicely appointed house and the good meals made our stay an extremely enjoyable experience.

CREED HOUSE

C(8)

Grampound, Cornwall, TR2 4SL Tel: 01872 530372
South-west of St Austell. Nearest main road: A390 from St Austell to Truro.

rear view

3 Bedrooms. £23–£30. All have own bath/shower/toilet. No smoking preferred.
Light suppers if ordered. No smoking preferred.
1 Sitting-room. With log stove, TV. No smoking preferred.
Large garden

Virtually in the centre of Cornwall, and within easy reach of many of its most famous gardens, lie five less well-known but no less beautiful acres of spectacular landscaping: the grounds of Creed House, a Georgian rectory dating from about 1730, whose sweeping lawns, walled herbaceous garden and stream-fed ponds provide an entrancing outlook for Lally Croggon's guests. These gardens are occasionally open to the public. Lally serves lavish breakfasts round the Georgian mahogany table in the elegant dining-room, often with an open fire in the grate. The russet-and-cream sitting-room is furnished with comfortable, squashy sofas and Persian rugs on the floor. Bedrooms are light and airy, with pastel walls and Colefax & Fowler fabrics.

Despite – or perhaps because of – the fact that she grew up in India and lived in Malaya, Lally's forte is the creation of an English country house-party atmosphere, in some of the most gracious surroundings in this book. The Eden Project can be easily visited from here.

Readers' comments: Excellent; the best of 'old world' b & b. Marvellous hostess, outstanding value. A highlight. Delightful; delicious breakfast, magnificent garden.

THE CROFT
D PT

Coverack, Cornwall, TR12 6TF Tel/Fax: 01326 280387
South-east of Helston. Nearest main road: A3083 from Helston to the Lizard.

3 Bedrooms. £18–£20 (less for 4 nights or more). Available: own bath/shower/toilet; views of sea; balcony (one). No smoking.
Dinner. £11.50 for 3 courses and coffee, at 7–7.30pm. Vegetarian or other special diets only. No smoking.
1 Sitting-room. With TV. No smoking.
Garden. No smoking.

The charm of the Croft lies not in any elegance of exterior or entrance, though it is a handsome house (with ample parking space), but rather in the empathetic character of its host, a photographer who came here from London in 1993, and in its quite outstanding position within a stone's throw of the sea. Views from two of the bedrooms are truly spectacular. One has an enclosed balcony from which to relish these to the full, and the lie of the land is such that the prospect from both the dining-room and the sitting-room downstairs is just as mesmerizing. Peter Chéze-Brown's terraced gardens end at the drop to the beach and are probably the only no-smoking grounds in this book, because plants have been chosen for their scent. Indoors, walls are hung with memorable paintings and prints.

Meals are strictly vegetarian, so guests are surprised by the 'bacon' and 'sausages' supplied for meat-eating breakfasters; at dinner, Peter's soups are gaining an international reputation. Bread is home-made.

Readers' comments: Extremely friendly, you feel totally relaxed, and the best breakfast I've ever had; superb view. Wonderful host, food delicious and plenty of it. **V**

DEGEMBRIS FARM
C S

St Newlyn East, Cornwall, TR8 5HY Tel: 01872 510555 (Fax: 01872 510230)
South-east of Newquay. Nearest main road: A3058 from St Austell to Newquay.

5 Bedrooms. £22–£25. Bargain breaks. Available: own bath/shower/toilet; TV.
Dinner. £12.50 for 4 courses and coffee, at 6.30pm. Vegetarian or other special diets if ordered. **Light suppers** if ordered.
1 Sitting-room. With open fire, TV, piano.
Garden

E-mail: kathy@degembris.co.uk

A survey published in the 1830s recorded the name as the much more Cornish-sounding Tregembris. From the parking area a few steep steps lead up to the pretty sloping front garden (wonderful views over the wooded valley) and the unusual slate-clad house, over 200 years old. It is now the hub of a busy working farm which has been in Roger Woodley's family since his great-uncle bought it from the Trerice estate in 1915. Kathy is happy to let guests wander into the traditional farmhouse kitchen but meals are served in the low-beamed dining-room, originally the farm's dairy. A typical dinner: soup, a roast or casserole, blackberry-and-apple pie, and cheese. The attractive, individually furnished bedrooms vary in size from a small, flowery single to a spacious family room.

In spring the surrounding woodland walks are carpeted with bluebells. Newquay is close, Truro not far in the other direction, and the magnificent beaches of Cornwall's west coast are within easy reach.

Readers' comments: Delightful farmhouse; charming hostess; quiet and comfortable. Highly recommended. Portions generous. Cooking of highest standard. **V**

Cornwall

EDNOVEAN FARM

PT

Perranuthnoe, Cornwall, TR20 9LZ Tel: 01736 711883 (Fax: 01736 710480)
East of Penzance. Nearest main road: A394 from Helston towards Penzance.

3 Bedrooms. £25–£35. Available: own bath/toilet; TV; views of sea. No smoking.
Light suppers if ordered.
1 Sitting-room. No smoking.
Small garden

E-mail: info@ednoveanfarm.co.uk

Everything is upside-down at Ednovean: bedrooms on the ground floor, open-plan living area upstairs; breakfast by candlelight in this immaculate conversion of a 17th-century barn set in 22 acres of farmland where Christine and Charles Taylor train horses for shows and eventing. The dividing slabs from old pigpens form the hall floor; and the other materials used in the rebuilding were all recycled too – one wooden window-sill bears the unmistakable signs of ship's beetle.

The bedrooms and outstanding bathrooms vary to suit every taste: one has a hand-carved four-poster bed with a white cotton sofa; another lovely room (with private patio and wonderful views) has a French bed and chandelier (here the colours are deep blue with pale grey-washed walls); and in contrast is a gold room with Christine's stencils. Two of the bedrooms open into a sitting-room which has slate floors and oriental carpeting, and from the green and yellow garden room, with terrace, are views of St Michael's Mount and four harbours.

Reader's comments: Superb rooms, excellent food.

Cornwall

THE HAVEN

S

Rezare, Cornwall, PL15 9NX Tel: 01579 370247 (Fax: 01579 370664)
South of Launceston. Nearest main road: A388 from Launceston to Saltash.

2 Bedrooms. £20–£25 (less for 3 nights or more). Both have own bath/shower/toilet; TV. No smoking.
Dinner (by arrangement). £12 for 2 courses and coffee, at times to suit guests. Vegetarian or other special diets if ordered. No smoking.
2 Sitting-rooms. With log-burner (in one), TV. No smoking.
Small garden
Closed from December to February.

E-mail: Frontline.west@btinternet.com

The Haven is exactly that: mid-way between Bodmin Moor and Dartmoor, the only sounds likely to disturb guests here are the noises of a passing tractor or of cows going to the milking sheds further down the lane. Derelict some years ago, Malcolm and Ann George have now completed the restoration of this 16th-century, white-painted farmhouse. They have retained inglenook fireplaces, slate flooring and beamed ceilings, while former stables are now a pretty annexe providing accommodation which can be let on a b & b or self-catering basis. In the downstairs bedroom, there is a wrought-iron and brass bed complemented by Laura Ashley fabrics and antique pine furniture. From the galleried sitting-room above are views across the moors.

The front door of the main house opens into a long room, which has the breakfast-table at one end and squashy sofas at the other. Upstairs is another attractive bedroom, with embroidered bedlinen and a blue and white colour scheme.

V

For dinner, Ann might serve chicken breasts with sage, and blackberry and apple pie with Cornish clotted cream. Alternatively, there are good dining-pubs nearby.

HURDON FARM

C M S

Cornwall

Hurdon, Cornwall, PL15 9LS Tel: 01566 772955
South of Launceston. Nearest main road: A30 from Launceston to Bodmin.

6 Bedrooms. £21–£24. Available: own bath/toilet; TV. No smoking.
Dinner. £12.50 for 4 courses and coffee, at 6.30pm (not Sundays). Vegetarian or other special diets if ordered. No smoking. **Light suppers** if ordered.
1 Sitting-room. With woodstove, TV. No smoking.
Large garden
Closed from November to mid-April.

The 18th-century stone house is in a picturesque area, not far from Dartmoor and Bodmin Moor (both the north and south coasts are within reach, too). It has large sash windows with the original panelled shutters and built-in dressers in the dining-room. The sitting-room has large and comfortable chairs and a great log stove.

Upstairs, all is spick-and-span with fresh paintwork and light, bright colour schemes in the bedrooms. There is also a family suite on the ground floor.

Meals, often prepared by Margaret Smith's daughter Nicola, are above average 'farm-house fare'. Soups are accompanied by home-made rolls; lamb by such vegetables as courgettes au gratin; puddings include pavlovas and home-made ice creams. She uses the farm's own produce and clotted cream.

Readers' comments: Superb atmosphere. Idyllic – we were spoilt! Excellent meals, very comfortable, very reasonable. Enjoyable and relaxing. We return year after year. Well above average farm cooking. Food of the highest standard. Everything immaculate.

LAMPEN MILL

C PT S X

Cornwall

St Neot, Cornwall, PL14 6PB Tel/Fax: 01579 321119
North-west of Liskeard. Nearest main road: A38 from Liskeard to Bodmin.

3 Bedrooms. £25–£30. Available: own bath/shower/toilet; TV; views of river. No smoking.
Light suppers if ordered.
1 Sitting-room. With stove. No smoking.
Large garden

A drive winds between woodland trees, then over a humpback bridge and a clapper bridge, and finally before you is the millpond reflecting the Pearces' lovingly restored mill house. Nestling in the Glynn Valley, designated an Area of Outstanding Natural Beauty, the mill is mentioned in Domesday Book.

Chris, a builder (working in stone is his hobby), and Heather, an energetic and thoughtful hostess, took the mill over when it was derelict. Now, the accommodation set aside for guests features much Columbian pine and a unique spiral staircase crafted by Chris's father. Bedrooms, with their flowery fabrics and wallpapers, are especially pretty. The breakfast-room, which has pot-plants, gold velvet high-backed chairs and a wood-burner in the granite and stone inglenook, opens into the conservatory. From there, visitors can observe the abundant bird life which inhabits the millpond and garden. Old wrought-iron lights salvaged from a railway station illuminate the grounds at night.

In the immediate vicinity are Dobwalls Adventure Park for families and Carnglaze Slate Caverns – abandoned mining chambers.

Cornwall

LILAC COTTAGE

C D PT

5 Church Road, Lanivet, Cornwall, PL30 5EZ Tel/Fax: 01208 832083 (Mobile: 07747 832914)

South-west of Bodmin. Nearest main road: A30 from Bodmin to Redruth.

3 Bedrooms. £20 (less for 5 nights or more). No smoking.
1 Sitting-room. With TV. Restricted smoking.
Garden
Closed from December to January.

E-mail: janaustin@talk21.com

Conveniently situated between Cornwall's north and south coasts, and halfway along the Saints' Way, which links Padstow to Fowey, Lilac Cottage is likely to appeal to both walkers and families.

Overlooking the village green, this 19th-century terraced cottage opens to reveal spacious accommodation. The sitting-cum-breakfast-room is massed with paintings (John Austin is an avid collector). Discreetly placed is John's guitar which he enjoys playing for musically minded guests.

The bedrooms, with their flowery bedlinen, stencilling and hand-made patchwork quilts, are pretty and restful. Off one is a stairway to a hidden eyrie, created especially for children. It houses table and chairs for small people (although the single beds are full-sized), pencils, paints, jigsaws and games. Jan and John have been known to light candles in the large bathroom, draw a hot scented bath and place beside it a gratis glass of wine for the really travel-weary.

Guests dine at the local pub, a two-minute walk away.

Readers' comments: A very welcome rest; hearty breakfast; beautifully furnished. More than delighted with the standard of accommodation; our stay really special; wonderful garden.

Cornwall

LITTLE BRYATON

C D PT S X

Morwenstow, Cornwall, EX23 9SU Tel: 01288 331755

North of Bude. Nearest main road: A39 from Bude to Bideford.

3–4 Bedrooms. £21.50–£24 (less for 7 nights or more). All have own bath/shower/toilet; TV. No smoking.
Dinner (by arrangement). £11 for 3 courses and coffee, at times to suit guests. Vegetarian or other special diets if ordered. **Light suppers** if ordered.
2 Sitting-rooms. With stove (in one), TV (in one), piano (in one).
Garden

E-mail: little.bryaton@dial.pipex.com

For 300 years or more this farmhouse has stood not far from some of the most spectacular coastal scenery in Britain. Towering cliffs and granite boulders are lashed by enormous seas rolling in from the Atlantic, while at other times it is serenely beautiful.

Paul and Jan Hudson are a hospitable couple and Jan has won admiration for her candlelit suppers, which are served in the beamed library/dining-room. An evening meal might comprise carrot-and-coriander soup, pork and apricots served on rice with toasted almonds, and orange and rhubarb pie. Afterwards, one can relax in the comfortable conservatory overlooking the lawned gardens, or in a sitting-room with wood-burner and grand piano.

The low-ceilinged bedrooms have white walls and pretty fabrics. One has its own entrance and sitting-room. Paul, a retired police officer, is an indefatigable walker and he has prepared notated maps of circular walks for guests.

V

Readers' comments: Food excellent; lovely bedroom. Made us feel so welcome; accommodation and food of excellent quality; could not have been more helpful. Superb meals, friendly, welcoming. Jan a superb cook; oasis of calm.

LUNEY BARTON HOUSE

C(15) S

Cornwall

Lower Sticker, Cornwall, PL26 7JH Tel/Fax: 01726 882219
South-west of St Austell. Nearest main road: A390 from St Austell to Truro.

3 Bedrooms. £22–£25. Available: own bath/shower/toilet; TV. No smoking.
Dinner (by arrangement). £16 for 4 courses and coffee, at times to suit guests. Vegetarian or other special diets if ordered. No smoking. **Light suppers** if ordered.
1 Sitting-room. With open fire. No smoking.
Large garden

E-mail: info@luneybarton.com

Cornish stone and granite give this old Georgian house a mellowness which is echoed inside by its welcoming hosts, Michael (Rick) and Mary Rickaby. Access to this rural retreat is via a narrow, private lane off a country road and yet it is within easy driving distance of National Trust houses and gardens, as well as the Eden Project.

Rick, who was in the merchant navy, and Mary, a Canadian and former nurse, have combined their various interests to the benefit of their guests. The maritime influence is reflected in the many pictures; and native art and sculpture from Canada are clustered in niches and on shelves.

Old plates and platters decorate the breakfast-cum-dining-room. The Rickabys are imaginative cooks and dinner could comprise carrot-and-ginger soup, roast beef with all the trimmings, and orange slices marinated in Grand Marnier with a crisp caramel topping.

One spacious bedroom, in almond-white and ink-blue, has a quilted bedspread made and embroidered for Mary, by her sister.

Reader's comments: The welcome was second to none; nothing is too much trouble; beautiful rooms. Exceptionally delightful; the food was five-star.

MARINA HOTEL

D PT X

Cornwall

The Esplanade, Fowey, Cornwall, PL23 1HY Tel: 01726 833315
(Fax: 01726 832779)
East of St Austell. Nearest main road: A390 from Lostwithiel to St Austell.

rear view

13 Bedrooms. £58–£74 **including dinner** (less for 3 nights or more). Available: own bath/shower/toilet; TV; views of sea; balcony.
Dinner. 3 courses and coffee, at 7–8.30pm. Vegetarian or other special diets if ordered. Wine available. No smoking. **Light suppers.**
3 Sitting-rooms. With TV. **Bar.**
Small garden

E-mail: marina.hotel@dial.pipex.com

Built in 1830 as a seaside retreat for the Bishop of Truro, this fine house has been furnished with the elegance it deserves. The handsome mouldings, arches and panelling of the hall and octagonal landing are now decorated in green and burgundy; and each bedroom is different – a pale colour scheme in one; sprigged covers and pine in another; four with covered verandahs of lacy ironwork facing the tiny walled garden and waterfront beyond it. The dining-room has spectacular views, but meals can also be taken alfresco on the decking overlooking the river. A self-contained suite has its own kitchenette and a private garden.

The manager, James Coggan, gives equal attention to the standard of the food. At dinner, you might choose your main dish from a selection that includes (for instance) boned chicken in a sauce of mushrooms and cider, beef Wellington, rack of lamb and local fish in a variety of ways.

Cornwall

MEAVER FARMHOUSE

D P T X

Mullion, Cornwall, TR12 7DN Tel: 01326 240128 (Fax: 01326 240011)
South-west of Helston. Nearest main road: A3083 from Helston to the Lizard.

3 Bedrooms. £23.50 (less for 3 nights or more). All have own bath/toilet; TV. No smoking.
1 Sitting-room. With open fire. No smoking.
Large garden

E-mail: meaverfarm@eclipse.co.uk

It is hard to believe that this cosy cottage was once classed as unfit for human habitation. Thankfully, Russell and Janet Stanland ignored the warning, and they have turned their 18th-century farmhouse into a warm and restful haven from buffeting Cornish winds. One enters a beamed, low-ceilinged room, where guests are served breakfast at a pine table made by Russell, who is a wood-turner. Another feature is the Royal Crown Devonware collected by Janet and her ancestors.

The sitting-room has logs piled on the hearth and softly draped voile at the window gives it a light and airy feel. Two bedrooms have four-poster beds (one is king-size), while a third room has dramatic headboards from the Inter-Continental Hotel in Vienna. Large candles are a soothing extra in the lovely bathrooms.

Russell and Janet are willing to chauffeur walkers to and from their various starting-points and destinations. Nearby Mullion has several restaurants and pubs for dinner.

Reader's comments: High quality accommodation for a very reasonable price; will definitely stay again.

Cornwall

MOTHER IVEY COTTAGE

C D S X

Trevose Head, Cornwall, PL28 8SL Tel/Fax: 01841 520329
West of Padstow. Nearest main road: B3276 from Padstow to Newquay.

2 Bedrooms. £22.50–£25 (less for 7 nights or more). Both have own bath/toilet; views of sea. No smoking.
Dinner (by arrangement). £12 for 3 courses and coffee, at times to suit guests. Vegetarian diets if ordered. Limited smoking. **Light suppers** if ordered.
Large garden

E-mail: woosnammills@compuserve.com

This sturdy, slate cottage, occupying a marvellous clifftop position, is in an ideal holiday spot. The coastal footpath runs behind the property, nearby is Trevose golf course and immediately below the garden wall are the golden sands of Mother Ivey Bay. (The name may be a corruption of 'Martha' Ivey, the last in a line of Iveys who lived in the area.)

Prior to 1920, the cottage was used for processing the catches landed by fishing boats on the beach below. It is now the home of Antony and Phyllida Woosnam Mills whose family have been here for 60 years. The sitting/dining-room is warmed by a wood-burner and meals are served round an oak table. The two bedrooms (one has deep cream velvet curtains and crewel bedspreads) are simply but comfortably furnished. Electric blankets and heaters are provided as there is no central heating. Guests fall asleep to the sound of waves lapping below and awake to wonderful views of the rocky coastline.

For dinner, Phyllida may serve fresh fish in a delicate sauce, then strawberry mousse and Cornish cheeses. Packed lunches are also available.

NANCHERROW

C(10) **PT**

61 Trevean Way, Pentire, Cornwall, TR7 1TW Tel: 01637 878080
South-west of Newquay. Nearest main road: A392 from Indian Queens towards Newquay.

3 Bedrooms. £20–£22 (less for 3 nights or more). Bargain breaks. Available: own bath/shower/toilet; views of river. No smoking.
Dinner (by arrangement). £12–£14 for 2–3 courses and coffee, at 7pm. Vegetarian or other special diets if ordered. Wine available. No smoking. **Light suppers** if ordered.
1 Sitting-room. With TV. No smoking.
Small garden
Closed from Christmas to early January.

Modern houses line the Gannel estuary and none is more contemporary than the Californian/Spanish-style house of John and Christina Rayner. Set one tier back from the estuary and on a hill, the house has been designed to take maximum advantage of its position. Sunlight floods through the large windows which overlook the tidal sands, as do the wide, tiled terraces.

Inside, small fronded plants adorn the apricot sitting-room, which has an arch through to the breakfast-room. John and Christina have a small antique shop where their special interests are porcelain, coloured glass and early Victoriana. Lovely examples of these are spread throughout the house, as are an interesting mix of pictures, particularly Russell Flint prints – favourites of Christina. Downstairs is the guests' sitting-room/library, with striking, claret-red velvet-upholstered furniture. Two of the stylish bedrooms are suitable for a family or group of friends travelling together. A typical dinner menu: home-made mushroom soup, coq au vin, and crème brûlée.

A little footpath leads to the water where, at low tide, it is possible to walk to Crantock beach. Trerice House and gardens (NT) are a 10-minute drive away. V

OLD MILL HOUSE

C(14) **PT S**

Little Petherick, Cornwall, PL27 7QT Tel: 01841 540388 (Fax: 08700 569360)
South of Padstow. On A389 from Padstow towards Wadebridge.

4 Bedrooms. £25–£29 **includes a 10% discount to readers of this book only.** Available: own shower/toilet; views of river. No smoking.
1 Sitting-room. With TV, piano. Restricted smoking.
Small garden
Closed from November to March.

E-mail: dwalker@oldmillbandb.demon.co.uk

This picturesque 16th-century converted corn mill was the first house David and Debbie Walker looked at when they returned from Barbados (where they had been working for an English educational publisher). And it immediately captivated them. The old waterwheel is still in the leat, Little Petherick creek meanders through the garden and the village is in an Area of Outstanding Natural Beauty.

Breakfast is served at separate tables in a spacious, low-ceilinged room, where comfortable seating is grouped at one end, below a large mural of man and horse ploughing. The bedrooms – all looking into the garden – are very individual. One is furnished with rich brocaded chairs, another has an old pine chest of drawers and wardrobe, while in a third are floor-sweeping, ruby-red velvet curtains.

Although Debbie does not provide dinner, she is able to offer guests an aperitif, which can be enjoyed beside the garden stream in the fading light of a summer's day. For evening meals, there are good pubs and restaurants within a 10-minute drive.

The nearby coastline is celebrated for its many beautiful beaches and coves.

Cornwall

OLD RECTORY

D

St John, Torpoint, Cornwall, PL11 3AW Tel: 01752 822275 (Fax: 01752 823322)
West of Plymouth. Nearest main road: A374 from Torpoint towards Looe.

3 Bedrooms. £25–£47.50 (less for 3 nights or more). Available: own bath/shower/toilet. No smoking.
1 Sitting-room. With open fire, TV. No smoking.
Large garden
Closed in January and February.

E-mail: clive@oldrectory-stjohn.co.uk

At the head of a tidal creek – designated a special habitat for wildlife – is this exceptional house surrounded by gardens with a variety of subtropical and lush waterside plantation. There is also a leat, millpond and bluebell wood.

When Clive Poole and his wife Button bought their home, they set out to create a luxurious but essentially relaxed retreat. Button, who is noted for her interior design and flower arrangements, has transformed the rooms. The sitting-room is made exotic with silk fabrics embroidered in rich golds and yellows. Large sofas and chairs are drawn up round a log fire; and board-games, books and a CD player are to hand. Bedrooms (and bathrooms) are superb. One is furnished with a Regency four-poster which was discovered in a hay loft.

Breakfast, served at a billiard table (with a special top), includes poached fruits, herby mushrooms on toast, scrambled eggs with smoked salmon, and various breads. Guests can walk to the local pub for dinner.

V *Readers' comments:* Delightful house in a wonderful, peaceful setting; breakfasts memorable; welcoming and most helpful hosts; rooms ample and comfortable.

Cornwall

OLDE TREDORE HOUSE

C PT X

St Issey, Cornwall, PL27 7QS Tel: 01841 540291
West of Wadebridge. Nearest main road: A389 from Padstow towards Wadebridge.

3 Bedrooms. £23–£26. All have own bath/shower/toilet; TV. No smoking.
1 Sitting-room. With open fire. Restricted smoking.
Garden

Late Georgian and early Victorian additions to the original farmhouse have combined to create a house of considerable harmony and generous proportions. More recently, the interior has been greatly enhanced by the efforts of Bob and Gill Claridge. They stripped the painted staircase to reveal carved mahogany, built spacious bathrooms where there were none, and have filled the rooms with fine furniture and pictures.

Guests breakfast round a polished table of boardroom-size proportions. An equally impressive dresser holds Bob's collection of old whisky jugs and decanters. In the sitting-room, the pinky hue of the marble fire-surround is picked up by the softest pinks and blues in the swagged velvet curtains. These, in turn, blend well with the pink and grey armchairs and sofas.

The lovely bedrooms have embossed wallpapers and frilled and embroidered bedlinen. One is exceptional: it has a mahogany four-poster bed with fully draped canopy, and a handsome wardrobe. There is a separate suite of two bedrooms and a bathroom. All have views of surrounding farmland.

Guest dine at nearby pubs and restaurants.

V *Reader's comments:* It was beautiful yet homely; food excellent and hosts so helpful.

OLD VICARAGE

C S

Morwenstow, Cornwall, EX23 9SR Tel: 01288 331369 (Fax: 01288 356077)
North of Bude. Nearest main road: A39 from Bude to Bideford.

Cornwall

3 Bedrooms. £25–£28. Available: own bath/shower/toilet; views of sea. No smoking.
Dinner. £20 for aperitif, 4 courses, wine and coffee, at 7.30pm (not Mondays and Tuesdays). Vegetarian or other special diets if ordered. No smoking. **Light suppers** if ordered.
2 Sitting-rooms. With open fire/stove, TV. No smoking (in one). **Bar.**
Large garden
Closed in December and January.

Find Morwenstow church and you are within calling distance of the Old Vicarage, although you might think you are never coming to it as you descend the winding, wooded drive. Then you will see the extraordinary chimneys of this splendid Victorian pile, each reputedly modelled on the tower of a church with which its first incumbent had been associated.

Jill and Richard Wellby have created an elegant and comfortable ambience for their visitors, while retaining such original features as the handsome slate-and-tile hall floor and the marble fireplace in the dining-room. The sitting-room is pink and grey, with claret velvet curtains and a carved stone fireplace. Up the shallow staircase, all the bedrooms have arched windows and an individual style. There is a billiard-room up here, too, with a bar.

A typical dinner might comprise crab bisque, chicken in herbs, and summer pudding with Cornish cream, followed by cheese and biscuits.

Readers' comments: Delightful, a mouthwatering place, a gastronomic feast. We especially loved it. Fantastic. Really superb meal, everything charmingly presented.

OLD VICARAGE

C(5)

Treneglos, Cornwall, PL15 8UQ Tel/Fax: 01566 781351
North-west of Launceston. Nearest main road: A395 from Launceston towards Camelford.

Cornwall

2 Bedrooms. £25. Available: own bath/shower/toilet. No smoking.
1 Sitting-room. With TV, piano. No smoking.
Large garden
Closed from November to February.

E-mail: maggie@fancourt.freeserve.co.uk

At the idyllically situated, 18th-century Old Vicarage, Maggie Fancourt grows old-fashioned, fragrant sweetpeas and shrub roses for her guests, as well as organically produced fruit. There is ample choice for breakfast, which is served in the elegant blue-and-cream dining-room with its lovely Chinese-style curtains. Cream teas with scones and home-made jam are irresistible. In the bedrooms, Maggie's attention to detail extends even to the coathangers, which are covered in fabric to match the pretty flowered wallpaper. (Home-baked biscuits are also provided.)

For evening meals, guests venture to the local pub, the Eliot Arms (with 73 antique clocks!).

From Launceston you can visit the majestic and romantic north Cornish coast, or head inland to wild Bodmin Moor to discover hidden, unspoilt villages. The area is full of Arthurian legends; Daphne du Maurier's Jamaica Inn is on the moor.

Readers' comments: Well furnished; good base for visiting coast and countryside.

Cornwall

OLD VICARAGE HOTEL

C D PT

Parc-an-Creet, St Ives, Cornwall, TR26 2ES Tel: 01736 796124 (Fax: 01736 796343)
Nearest main road: A30 from Redruth to Penzance.

8 Bedrooms. £23 (less for 7 nights or more). All have own bath/shower/toilet; TV.
Light suppers by arrangement.
1 Sitting-room. With open fire, TV. **Bar.** Piano.
Large garden
Closed from November to Easter.

E-mail: holidays@oldvicarage.com

Built of silvery granite in the 1850s, this hotel (among houses on the outskirts of St Ives) is entered via a small conservatory and a great iron-hinged door of ecclesiastical shape, which opens into a hall with red-and-black tiled floor. Jack Sykes, who runs the hotel with his daughter Dianne, has done his best to preserve this period ambience. The bar is furnished with crimson-and-gold flock wallpaper and all kinds of Victoriana. Big windows and handsome fireplaces feature throughout; and the Sykeses have put in excellent carpets, along with good, solid furniture – a 'thirties walnut suite in one bedroom, and velvet-upholstered bedheads. The Anna French fabrics and wallpapers were designed by Dianne and many of the paintings in the house are hers too. One room has a refurbished Victorian loo, preserved in all its glory of blue lilies and rushes. In addition, there's a sitting-room and a blue-and-gold dining-room.

Readers' comments: Excellent in every way. Attention to detail outstanding. Cannot praise highly enough. So good, beautifully kept, warm welcome. Thoroughly recommended. Atmosphere most civilized, attention to detail impeccable. Lovely house.

V

Cornwall

PORTEATH BARN

C(12) D

St Minver, Cornwall, PL27 6RA Tel: 01208 863605 (Fax: 01208 863954)
North-west of Wadebridge. Nearest main road: A39 from Camelford to Wadebridge.

3 Bedrooms. £22.50–£30 (less for 2 nights or more).
Light suppers if ordered.
1 Sitting-room. With stove.
Large garden

E-mail: mbloor@ukonline.co.uk

Sheep and cows were the last occupants of Michael and Jo Bloor's massive old barn, which was a wreck when they found it. To oversee the restoration work they lived in a caravan on site for many months. They now have a rag-slate roofed home modernized to the highest standard. Every room has French windows, so the house is flooded with natural light, and throughout Jo has used National Trust colours such as old gold and terracotta to offset the wonderful fabrics. There is a clever mix of antique and modern pieces and Jo's flair is so evident that two guests asked her to design and furnish the interior of their recently acquired home.

Visitors eat round an old refectory table and on sunny days the terraces catch the last rays of the evening sun. Another sun-trap is the round house where, formerly, an animal walked in circles to drive the barn shaft.

Porteath is in a secluded valley yet it is only a short walk from the South-West Coast Path and Epphaven Cove, a small inlet. Also nearby is the Bee Centre, a haven for honey-lovers.

V

RESTORMEL MANOR

C D P T S

Lostwithiel, Cornwall, PL22 0HN Tel: 01208 873444 (Fax: 01208 873455)
South of Bodmin. Nearest main road: A390 from St Austell towards Liskeard.

4 Bedrooms. £25–£29 (less for 4 nights or more). One has own shower. No smoking.
Light suppers if ordered. Wine available.
1 Sitting-room. With open woodstove, TV, piano.
Large garden

Sitting beneath the 13th-century castle of the same name is this house of grand proportions in which Robert and Rosamund Woodard have created a warm and congenial atmosphere. Sir Robert, the last Rear-Admiral of HM Yacht *Britannia*, and Lady Woodard, whose interests include fine arts and gardening, enjoy sharing with their guests the history related to this marvellous site. The manor is built on the foundations of a 13th-century chapel and Crusaders sailed down the Fowey River from here on their way to France. Lady Woodard's family, the Edgcumbes, have been associated with the castle for several centuries. The sitting-room, dominated by a huge granite inglenook, is filled with family portraits including one of Fanny Lucy Shelley, a cousin of the poet. One wing (which can be used for self-catering) has its own entrance. Bedrooms are spacious and simply furnished.

The Woodards' garden slopes down to a bridge across the Fowey and a short uphill walk leads to the Duchy of Cornwall Nurseries, visited by people from all over the country in search of rare plants. The Eden Project is also easily reached from here.

ST GENNYS HOUSE

C(5)

St Gennys, Cornwall, EX23 0NW Tel: 01840 230384 (Fax: 01840 230537)
South of Bude. Nearest main road: A39 from Bude to Wadebridge.

Cornwall

3 Bedrooms. £22–£30 (less for 4 nights or more). One has own bath/shower/toilet. No smoking.
Dinner (by arrangement). £15 for 3 courses and coffee, at times to suit guests. Vegetarian or other special diets if ordered. **Light suppers** if ordered.
1 Sitting-room. With open fire, TV.
Large garden

This old vicarage is in a secluded part of Cornwall where the trees bend to the prevailing winds and bay windows in the sitting-room afford spectacular views of the seas beyond. Part 16th-century with Georgian and Edwardian additions, the house has been furnished in appropriate style by its present owners, Anthony and Jane Farquhar. Among their many paintings is a portrait of John Wesley, the founder of Methodism; it was given to this former Anglican rectory by the local Methodist church in recognition of the hospitality John Wesley received there.

In the handsome dining-room, with its large oval oak table and terracotta-and-blue watersilk curtains, Jane serves such meals as mushroom soup with garlic bread, baked ham accompanied by ratatouille, French beans and new potatoes, and fruit salad with clotted cream, or chocolate mousse. Two of the pretty bedrooms overlook a walled garden.

From the house it is a 10-minute walk to the cliffs and South-West Coast Path. All along this rugged coastline are picturesque fishing villages such as Boscastle, Tintagel (with Arthurian associations) and Port Isaac, but the inland scenery deserves to be explored too.

V

Cornwall

TREGADDRA FARM

C

Cury, Cornwall, TR12 7BB Tel/Fax: 01326 240235
South of Helston. Nearest main road: A3083 from Helston to the Lizard.

5 Bedrooms. £21–£25. Bargain breaks. Available: own bath/shower/toilet; views of sea; balcony. No smoking.
2 Sitting-rooms. With open fire (in one), TV. No smoking.
Large garden

E-mail: holidays@tregaddra.freeserve.co.uk

A beautifully kept garden of winding flowerbeds, tennis court and spacious swimming-pool (heated) is the setting for this immaculate house, built in the 18th century but much modernized since. Two upstairs bedrooms have balconies. All around are distant views, especially fine when the sun is setting over the sea. Goonhilly's satellite station and a wind farm on the moors are quite spectacular too.

Rooms are well furnished in conventional style, and comfortable. When evenings are chilly, logs blaze in a granite inglenook, and there is a glass sun-room to make the most of the mild climate in this very southerly part of England. There is a warm drying room in a barn for the use of cyclists and walkers.

For dinner, June Lugg recommends the Hazelphron Inn at Gunwalloe, six miles away. There is also a wide variety of other eating-places just a bit further afield.

Reader's comments: Very fine location and views, accommodation best we had, very willing and helpful owner.

Cornwall

TREGLOWN HOUSE

C D

Haywood Farm, St Mabyn, Cornwall, PL30 3BU Tel/Fax: 01208 841896
North-east of Wadebridge. Nearest main road: A39 from Wadebridge to Camelford.

3 Bedrooms. £23–£25 (less for 3 nights or more). Available: own bath/shower/toilet; TV. No smoking.
1 Sitting-room. With open fire, TV, piano.
Large garden

E-mail: treglownhouse@stmabyn.fsnet.co.uk

Lord Falmouth built this sturdy house with its granite lintels and Delabole slate roof at the end of the 19th century. Its owner now is Carol Fielding-Brown who, with her warmth and humour, has created a home-away-from-home atmosphere. She renamed the house using her mother's maiden name to remind her of her distant Cornish connections.

Pecking around beneath a large oak tree is a variety of rare fowl which provide breakfast-time eggs, and in the five-acre meadow goats and small steers graze. On arrival, guests are treated to a tea-tray with home-baked scones served on the sunny terrace or, on chilly days, in the sitting-room with its welcoming open fire. The house has an eclectic mix of furniture: two eye-catching gilt-framed pictures of waterfalls were painted by Carol's great-aunt. Bedrooms are simple but attractive. Breakfast options include such specialities as home-made Staffordshire oat cakes, and 'thunder and lightning' – which is clotted cream and honey. (High teas for children, if requested.)

For dinner, guests can eat at the excellent St Mabyn pub which is a walk away.

V

Reader's comments: Lovely farmhouse; welcoming, warm; great breakfast.

TREGOLLS FARM

C S

St Wenn, Cornwall, PL30 5PG Tel/Fax: 01208 812154

West of Bodmin. Nearest main road: A30 from Exeter to Penzance and A39 from Wadebridge to Truro.

4 Bedrooms. £16–£17.50 (less for 3 nights or more). One has own shower. No smoking.
Dinner. £9.25 for 3 courses and coffee, at 7pm. Vegetarian or other special diets if ordered. No smoking. **Light suppers** if ordered.
1 Sitting-room. With stove, TV. No smoking.
Garden

Tregolls is more or less bang in the middle of Cornwall, making it an ideal centre from which to explore the whole beautiful and endlessly varying county. The old stone-built farmhouse is the hub of a 107-acre mixed farm, rearing cattle and sheep (with some arable crops); it has been in the Hawkey family for over 50 years, and Marilyn's husband was born here. Bedrooms – with handsome stripped pine doors – are prettily furnished and comfortable; one double room has its own shower and coronet drapes over the bedhead, and there's a single room too. Those at the front share the lovely view to be had from both the sitting- and the dining-rooms downstairs: across the sloping garden to the rolling countryside beyond, as far as the eye can see.

The farm's own beef and lamb may appear in the dining-room (whose walls are hung with Marilyn's collection of attractive china plates), followed by, perhaps, blackberry and apple pie (with custard *and* Cornish cream), or queen of puddings.

Readers' comments: Beautiful views, beautifully decorated bedrooms, excellent home-cooked food. Cheerful welcome, we were looked after well.

TREGONGON HOUSE

C(10)

Ruan High Lanes, Cornwall, TR2 5LD Tel: 01872 501708

South-east of Truro. Nearest main road: A3078 from Tregony to St Mawes.

2 Bedrooms. £25 (less for 3 nights or more). Both have own bath/shower/toilet; TV. No smoking.
Dinner. £14 for 4 courses and coffee, at 7pm. Vegetarian or other special diets if ordered. No smoking.
1 Sitting-room. With woodstove, piano. No smoking.
9 acres including gardens
Closed from October to April.

The present house, built on classic Georgian lines, replaced a much older farmhouse; today, Tregongon, with its remaining nine acres of land (including lovely gardens and paddocks for two horses), is the home of Joan and Terry Scullion, who moved down here from Cheshire in 1987.

Bedrooms are charming, bright with chintz and pine; both command magnificent country views, and one has its own small sitting-room from which to enjoy them, as well as a pretty pink-and-green bathroom. A baby grand piano takes pride of place in the downstairs sitting-room, where the exposed stone of the original timber-frame walls is white-painted. Through an alcove, the book-filled dining-room is the setting for such meals as seafood Mornay pancakes; roast duckling with orange, caramel and brandy sauce; and brown bread ice cream.

Reader's comments: Peace and quiet in a tastefully furnished house; delicious home cooking and a truly *en famille* atmosphere; highly recommended.

Cornwall

Cornwall

TRENESTRAL FARM

C D M S

Ruan High Lanes, Cornwall, TR2 5LX Tel: 01872 501259
South-east of Truro. Nearest main road: A3078 from Tregony to St Mawes.

3 Bedrooms. £20. No smoking.
Dinner (by arrangement). £11 for 3 courses and coffee, at times to suit guests. Vegetarian or other special diets if ordered. No smoking. **Light suppers** if ordered.
1 Sitting-room. With TV. No smoking.
Garden
Closed from November to February.

A farm holiday for walkers, a beach holiday, or just a country holiday for townies: Trenestral offers all of these, situated as it is within easy reach of the South-West Coast Path, a choice of fine beaches (south-facing Pendower is the closest) and the cathedral city of Truro. Accommodation is homely and comfortable: there are books and games in the sitting-room (with far views over the surrounding farmland and countryside; guests take breakfast here, too, in high-backed, rush-seated chairs round the communal table). The family room looks out over a 200-year-old stone barn on one side and has a circular window set into the roughcast stone wall on another. It's a mixed farm – beef, sheep and cereals – and the Palmers rear pedigree Charolais cattle which they sometimes show. Ann's farmhouse meals might feature Trenestral's own produce; alternatively, visitors dine at the pleasant Roseland Inn a mile away in Philleigh, which welcomes children and provides good-value food.

V *Reader's comments:* Very warm, relaxed welcome; lovely space and peace; delightful hostess; will certainly return.

Cornwall

TREROSEWILL FARM

C PT S

Paradise, Boscastle, Cornwall, PL35 0BL Tel/Fax: 01840 250545
South-west of Bude. Nearest main road: A39 from Wadebridge to Bude.

6 Bedrooms. £21–£25 (less for 2 nights or more). Bargain breaks. Available: own bath/shower/toilet; TV; views of sea. No smoking.
1 Sitting-room. With log stove, TV. No smoking. **Bar.**
Large garden
Closed from mid-November to mid-February.

Perched high above the picturesque fishing village of Boscastle is this modern farmhouse built by Steve and Cheryl Nicholls, whose families have farmed and fished in this area for generations. In each bedroom is a copy of an old newspaper photograph of Steve's great-grandfather, who was rescued and brought home by a Welsh fishing vessel after his own boat had foundered and he had been given up for lost. In the photograph, he is wearing a Guernsey sweater knitted in the traditional Boscastle style: each fishing village had its own distinctive pattern so that bodies salvaged after accidents at sea could be brought home to their own communities for identification and burial.

Bedrooms are delightful, varying considerably in size but all prettily decorated in pastel shades and flowered fabrics; several have sea views. One has a brass bed, another a four-poster. Downstairs in the cheerful peppermint-green breakfast-room is a piano for occasional evening sing-songs. There are two restaurants and a dining-pub just 500 yards' walk down the lane.

V *Reader's comments:* Extremely welcoming and comfortable, fantastic breakfast, beautiful views.

TREWERRY MILL

C(7) PT S

St Newlyn East, Cornwall, TR8 5GS Tel/Fax: 01872 510345
South-east of Newquay. Nearest main road: A3058 from Newquay to St Austell.

6 Bedrooms. £20–£26 (less for 7 nights or more). Available: own shower/toilet; views of river. No smoking.
Light suppers if ordered. Vegetarian or other special diets if ordered. Wine available. No smoking.
1 Sitting-room. With open fire, TV, bar. No smoking.
Large garden
Closed from December to January.

E-mail: trewerry.mill@which.net

Trewerry Mill was built in 1639 to provide flour for the household of the nearby Elizabethan manor, Trerice (now a National Trust property), and corn continued to be milled here until after the Second World War.

One passes through a stone-flagged hall to a sitting-room with log fire and a window through which there is a view inside the old waterwheel. Bedrooms are not large, but neat and comfortable. Extensive, tranquil gardens lead down to a pond and the River Gannel, and include a length of the old Newquay to Perranporth railway line, with its arched bridge over the river.

Light suppers only, but morning coffee, lunches and cream teas are served in the garden on warm summer days (your table may be made from an old millstone). David and Terri Clark can recommend local walks and a variety of nearby eating-places to guests.

Readers' comments: Nothing too much trouble. Gloriously quiet and peaceful, wonderful care and attention. Marvellous garden. Warm welcome, good food.

V

WHEATLEY FARM

C

Maxworthy, Cornwall, PL15 8LY Tel/Fax: 01566 781232
North-west of Launceston. Nearest main road: A39 from Wadebridge to Bude.

4 Bedrooms. £19–£24 (less for 2 nights or more). Bargain breaks. Available: own bath/shower/toilet; TV. No smoking.
Dinner (by arrangement). From £13 for 4 courses and coffee, at about 7pm. Vegetarian or other special diets if ordered. No smoking. **Light suppers** if ordered.
1 Sitting-room. With woodstove, TV. No smoking.
Large garden
Closed from November to February.

E-mail: wheatleyfrm@compuserve.com

Wheatley has been in the same family for generations; Raymond and Valerie Griffin's son will be the fifth in succession to work this substantial dairy and sheep farm deep in the rolling Cornish countryside. The handsome farmhouse was built in 1871 by the Duke of Bedford; when the Griffins repaired an ageing window, they discovered the ducal seal stamped in the original oak lintel.

One enters the house through the imposing hall. It is beautifully decorated in shades of green, with floral curtains and frieze. The sitting-room, too, is sumptuous and welcoming, and there is a granite inglenook with cloam (bread) oven in the dining-room, which also has a magnificent antique mahogany table and matching sideboard.

Upstairs, the bedrooms are attractively furnished with country-style pine; one has a four-poster and en suite corner bath.

A typical dinner might be home-made soup or pâté, home-produced or local beef or lamb, rhubarb-and-blackcurrant crumble topped with Cornish clotted cream, and local cheeses.

V

WOODLANDS

C S

Trewollock, Gorran Haven, Cornwall, PL26 6NS Tel: 01726 843821

South of St Austell. Nearest main road: A390 from St Austell to Truro.

5 Bedrooms. £20–£25. Available: own shower/toilet; TV; views of sea. No smoking.
Light suppers if ordered (in low season only).
Large garden

E-mail: woodlands@gorranhaven.fsbusiness.co.uk

When Paul and Dianne Harrison were seeking a new lifestyle following Paul's retirement from the police, they alighted upon Woodlands, a 1930s house standing on a prominent site with panoramic sea views and a path leading to the sands and rocks below. In the garden is a pair of spring-fed ponds – the top one has fish and waterlilies, and by the other are seats from which to enjoy the scenery.

Inside, all is immaculate. The breakfast/sitting-room, with its deep green curtains and sponge-painted green and white walls, has cheerful little posies on the tables; in one sunny corner are two sofas. The bedrooms are compact, but light and airy with flower-sprigged wallpapers and pretty fabrics, and the bathrooms are tip-top.

Dianne is happy to provide packed lunches for walkers and will serve cream teas in the garden by prior arrangement. There are numerous pubs and restaurants in the surrounding villages providing a variety of good meals. On summer evenings, the Harrisons sometimes hold impromptu barbecues for their guests. The Cornish coastal path is close by and the Lost Gardens of Heligan and the Eden Project are just a few miles away.

Private bathrooms are not necessarily en suite.

Many houses in this book are situated in or very near to Areas of Outstanding Natural Beauty and protected Heritage Coasts. For a selection of these houses, see p.xi.

COMPLAINTS: If anything was not of reasonable standard (e.g. chilly bedroom or badly cooked food) you are entitled to claim a reduction on your bill, but *only if* you had previously told the proprietor and given him or her a chance to put matters right. In a court case involving a restaurant meal, it was ruled that, because a customer had not made a specific complaint at the time, he had no right subsequently to withhold payment (he had cancelled his cheque). The moral is obvious: if dissatisfied, you are expected to say so at once and not later. Houses are regularly inspected; and complaints will be forwarded to proprietors for their comments. Write to: Jan Bowmer (SOTBT), c/o Arrow Books, 20 Vauxhall Bridge Road, London SW1V 2SA. Please enclose a stamped addressed envelope if you want her to acknowledge receipt of your complaint.

CUMBRIA

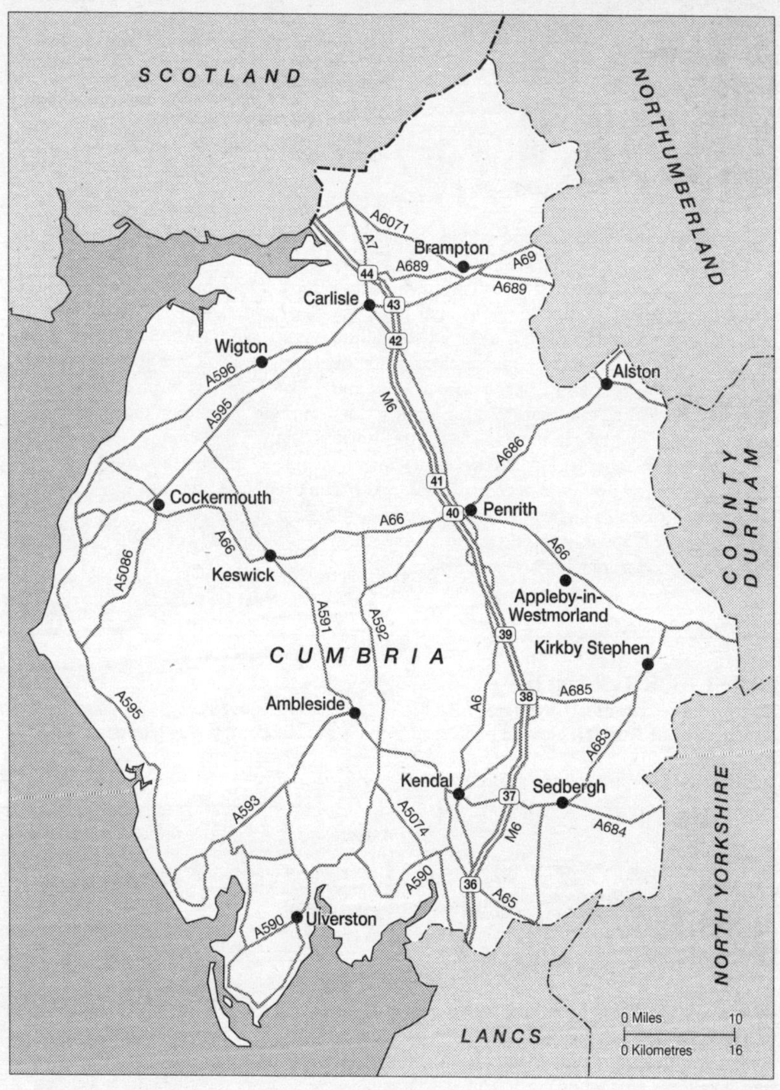

Prices are per person sharing a room at the beginning of the year. However, for the best rooms in the house or later in the year, you may well be asked for more.

Cumbria

ALDERSHAW

CDS

Grisedale, Cumbria, LA10 5PS Tel/Fax: 01539 621211
East of Sedbergh. Nearest main road: A684 from Hawes to Sedbergh.

3 Bedrooms. £20–£25. One has own shower/toilet; TV. No smoking.
Dinner (by arrangement). £14.50 for 4 courses and coffee, at 7–8pm. Vegetarian or other special diets if ordered. **Light suppers** if ordered.
1 Sitting-room. With stove, TV, piano.
Small garden

Only just outside Yorkshire and within the Dales National Park, this house – among the remotest in this book – stands high above Garsdale (at the top of Wensleydale). It is reached by its own gated track off a quiet, narrow road. Fundamentally from the 17th century, it was largely rebuilt a decade and a half ago by a builder and woodcarver, who did most of his work in oak: there is a carved owl on the staircase and worked branches among the rafters and in the striking mantelpiece in the big sitting-room. Once part of the barn, this is – like the bedrooms – at first-floor level, and – like them – is furnished with some character. According to season, you can sit by a wood-burning stove or on the imaginatively laid out terrace and take in the fine view of this isolated dale.

Dinner with Peter and Mary Robinson might include Cumbrian air-dried ham with melon; pheasant with German red cabbage; and banana soufflé. Otherwise, the Moorcock Inn (one of England's highest) offers conventional pub food not far away.

The house is roughly equidistant from the magnificent waterfalls of Cautley Spout (in Cumbria) and Hardraw Force (in Yorkshire).

Cumbria

BIRSLACK GRANGE

CDM

Hutton Lane, Levens, Cumbria, LA8 8PA Tel: 015395 60989
South-west of Kendal. Nearest main road: A590 from Kendal towards Ulverston (and M6, junction 36).

4 Bedrooms. £22. Bargain breaks. All have own bath/shower/toilet. No smoking.
Light suppers if ordered. No smoking.
1 Sitting-room. With open fire, TV. No smoking.
Large garden

In a converted barn, John and Jean Carrington-Birch offer comfortable accommodation overlooking the Lyth Valley, famous for damsons. As well as an easily accessible ground-floor room, there is a family suite. In the dining-room, where Jean provides much-appreciated breakfasts (including fresh fruit salad) and simple suppers to order, her collection of china is displayed on an Irish dresser – like a Welsh dresser but bigger. Also around are souvenirs of John's many stays in Africa, where he advises on printing.

The house is close to two mansions. Levens Hall, still in family hands, is Elizabethan, with Jacobean plasterwork and woodwork and contemporary furniture. In an outhouse is a collection of model steam engines. The gardens have been maintained to their original late 17th-century design, including the famous topiary. Nearby Sizergh Castle (NT) has a 14th-century peel tower at its heart. The gardens were among the favourites of the late Dr Alan Gemmell of 'Gardeners' Question Time' fame.

V *Readers' comments:* Good fortune to stay. Delicious breakfast.

CRACROP FARM

D S

Cumbria

Kirkcambeck, Cumbria, CA8 2BW Tel: 016977 48245 (Fax: 016977 48333)
North of Brampton. Nearest main road: A6071 from Brampton to Longtown.

3 Bedrooms. £25 **to readers of this book only** –£27.50. Available: own shower/toilet; TV. No smoking.
Dinner (by arrangement). £15 for 3 courses and coffee, at 7pm. Vegetarian or other special diets if ordered. No smoking. **Light suppers** if ordered.
1 Sitting-room. With open fire, TV. No smoking.
Large garden

Agriculture and forestry still predominate in the Border hills, truly unspoiled countryside. Typically for the area, Cracrop is principally a stock farm, where the friendly Stobarts are pleased if visitors take an interest in the work. Semi-finalists in a local conservation competition, they have produced an excellent farm trail leaflet which gives an insight into the holding and its interesting past, and also leaflets for walks of a few miles from the house. Sturdier walkers have plenty of routes to follow, too.

If walking is not exertion enough, in the Victorian house are an exercise bike, a rowing-machine and other such equipment; and to recuperate in, a sauna (for an extra charge) and a spa bath. Then you can relax in the garden to the sound of the ornamental stream.

Bedrooms are sizeable, two giving views of the northern Pennines and the Lake District hills, the other of the farmyard. Each has its own character, with colour-coordinated furnishings. The downstairs rooms are comfortably furnished in conventional style.

A typical meal: salmon mousse, a traditional roast, rhubarb crumble and cream. Alternatively, there is a choice of pubs for dinner.

Readers' comments: Superior accommodation. Truly excellent, could not be faulted.

CROSBY HOUSE

C S

Cumbria

Crosby-on-Eden, Cumbria, CA6 4QZ Tel: 01228 573239 (Fax: 01228 573338)
North-east of Carlisle. Nearest main road: A689 from Carlisle to Brampton (and M6, junction 44).

2 Bedrooms. £20–£24 (less for 3 nights or more). Both have own bath/shower/toilet; TV. No smoking.
Light suppers if ordered.
1 Sitting-room. With open fire, TV. No smoking.
Large garden

E-mail: deirdre@norbyways.demon.co.uk

With its symmetrical Georgian front and park-like grounds (with tennis court) approached by a tree-lined drive, Crosby House is almost a mansion. The sitting- and dining-rooms are large and high-ceilinged, and Deirdre and Michael Dickson have furnished them appropriately. On the walls (mostly in shades and tones of yellow) are paintings and etchings, and old legal documents related to the house and the area. Bedrooms have full-sized and well-equipped bathrooms (one with a sauna).

For evening meals, there is a choice within easy walking distance: good pub meals at the village inn, or a lavish table d'hôte at the hotel which adjoins the grounds of Crosby House.

Though convenient for those en route between England and Scotland, this deserves to be more than a stopover, for the area has much to offer: Hadrian's Wall is close, as is Carlisle, with cathedral, castle and museum (creatively laid out by the designers responsible for Jorvik at York). The Lake District and southern Scotland are accessible, but the immediate Border countryside is rewarding for its peacefulness and open views.

V

Cumbria

FELL EDGE

C(10) S

High Ireby, Cumbria, CA7 1HF Tel: 016973 71397
North-west of Keswick. Nearest main road: A591 from Keswick towards Carlisle.

2 Bedrooms. £20 (less for 7 nights or more). Available: own bath/shower/toilet; TV. No smoking.
Dinner. £10 for 4 courses and coffee, at 6.30pm. Vegetarian or other special diets if ordered. No smoking.
1 Sitting-room. With open fire, piano. No smoking.
Small garden

In the tiny, remote hamlet of High Ireby, Fell Edge, which was built in the 18th century as a chapel, is the home of the highly musical Allison family. This is a place for people who appreciate quietness and views – of the northern fells in one direction and, across the garden which Arthur Allison has laid out, as far as Dumfries in the other. The garden contributes to such dinner menus as tomato and basil soup, pork in raisin sauce, and meringue glacé. (Some people may find the stairs rather steep.)

Apart from the northern Lake District, the area is worth exploring for its own sake. People who resist the lure of the Lakes can visit Holm Cultram Abbey, the saltmarshes of the Solway Firth (where salmon are still netted in the old way) and the site of the end of Hadrian's Wall. The Allisons have produced a leaflet of local walks of various standards.

V *Readers' comments:* Stayed there twice and been very satisfied. Wonderful hospitality. Each meal well cooked and well presented. Charming hosts for whom nothing was too much.

Cumbria

FOLDGATE FARM

S

Corney, near Bootle village, Cumbria, LA19 5TN Tel: 01229 718660
North-west of Ulverston. Nearest main road: A595 from Whitehaven towards Millom.

3 Bedrooms. £18–£20 (less for 3 nights or more). No smoking.
Dinner (by arrangement). £10 for 4 courses and coffee, at 6pm. Vegetarian or other special diets if ordered. No smoking. **Light suppers** if ordered.
1 Sitting-room. With open fire, TV. No smoking.
Small garden
Closed in December.

A real Cumbrian farm near Millom, and well outside the main tourist areas, it covers 170 acres on which are kept sheep as well as some cattle. The approach to the farm is through a cobbled yard, with a great stone byre and stables at one side, Muscovy ducks perching on a dry-stone wall, and pots filled with stonecrop, London pride or primroses.

Guests sometimes eat with the family, by a dresser where mugs hang, the clothes airer suspended overhead and a grandfather clock ticking in one corner. There are bacon-hooks in the ceiling, shepherds' crooks stacked in the hall, and a bright coal fire in the evenings.

Mary Hogg serves real country fare here: Cumberland sausage, 'tatie pot', plum pudding with rum sauce, farm duckling, Herdwick lamb or mutton, rum butter on bread, currant cake with tea on arrival and at bedtime, and jams made from local produce.

V *Readers' comments:* Excellent food, good company. A great success. Never a dull moment! Food, atmosphere and welcome couldn't be faulted. Delighted with our welcome, the food and all the local attractions. Delightful experience, we can't wait to return.

THE HERMITAGE

Shap, Cumbria, CA10 3LX Tel: 01931 716671
South of Penrith. On A6 from Kendal to Penrith (and near M6, junction 39).

3 Bedrooms. £19–£24 (less for 3 nights or more). Bargain breaks. Available: own bath/shower/toilet; TV. No smoking.
Dinner. £10.50 for 3 courses and coffee, from 7pm. Vegetarian or other special diets if ordered. No smoking. **Light suppers** if ordered.
2 Sitting-rooms. With open fire, TV. Piano. No smoking.
Garden

This house is perhaps so called because it was built, at least three centuries ago, of stone from Shap Abbey (whose ruins can still be visited). It is a rambling house of beams and low ceilings. A previous owner added a stained-glass window and carved panelling from Lowther Castle a few miles away, now only a shell (of which Jean Jackson has collected a number of old pictures), and in a recent extension, Jean has used window-frames from a demolished cottage at the back of the house. A bedroom in the old part, with lavishly flowery decoration, has a particularly spacious bathroom.

Though the house stands on a main road, there is now little through traffic.

For evening meals, there is a choice of half a dozen dishes at each course, including local ingredients and garden produce – robust fare much appreciated by the Coast-to-Coast walkers and cyclists with whom the house is popular.

Readers' comments: Beautifully decorated and furnished; a most welcoming hostess. An exceptionally good find. Good food; clean and comfortable; will go again.

HIGH WINDY HALL C

Middleton Road, Garrigill, Cumbria, CA9 3EZ Tel: 01434 381547 (Fax: 01434 382477)
South-east of Alston. Nearest main road: A686 from Penrith to Alston.

rear view

5 Bedrooms. £25 **(to SOTBT readers who must mention this book when making a reservation)** –£35. Less for 2 nights or more. Bargain breaks. Available: own bath/shower/toilet; TV; balcony. No smoking.
Dinner (by arrangement). £18–£22 for 2–3 courses and coffee, at 8pm or at times to suit guests. Vegetarian or other special diets if ordered. Wine available. No smoking. **Light suppers** if ordered.
1 Sitting-room. With open fire, TV.
Small garden
Closed from December to mid-March.

E-mail: sales@hwh.u-net.com

Pauline and Bob Platts built this small hotel next to their then holiday cottage. Of local stone and in local style, it was planned by them to overlook the wide valley of the South Tyne, with Cross Fell – the highest point of the Pennines – in the distance. All the sizeable bedrooms take advantage of this pastoral panorama of open fields and dry-stone walls, with only sheep and a few old houses to be seen.

The rooms are decoratively furnished in a 19th-century manner. There are lots of pictures of local landscapes on the walls and a specially commissioned stained-glass window at the head of the stairs. In the restaurant are a grand Victorian sideboard of carved oak and a set of large mirrors in art nouveau frames. Here guests have a choice of three dishes at each course, cooked by the Platts' son Cameron, a professional chef: one might have coriander-and-crab cake, leg of lamb with saffron couscous, and lemon curd tart.

At 1500 feet, almost at the top of England's hilly spine, the hotel is on a little-used minor road, with the isolated town of Alston four miles away.

Cumbria

HULLERBANK

C(12)

Talkin, Cumbria, CA8 1LB Tel/Fax: 016977 46668
South of Brampton. Nearest main road: A69 from Carlisle to Brampton (and M6, junction 43).

3 Bedrooms. £23–£23.50 (less for 7 nights or more). Bargain breaks. Available: own bath/shower/toilet; TV. No smoking.
1 Sitting-room. With open fire, TV. No smoking.
Small garden
Closed from mid-December to mid-January.

Little Talkin village is in an interesting part of the country, surrounded by fells that are popular with walkers and near a country park and tarn with various watersports. Talkin used to be a stopping-place for monks making their way to Lanercost Priory: part of this is in ruins, but the lovely nave is still used as a church and what was the guests' solar is a village hall.

In a secluded spot, just half a mile from the village, Hullerbank offers farmhouse accommodation at its most comfortable. Though this is only a 14-acre smallholding, Brian and Sheila Stobbart are local farming people. B & b only, but guests can dine at two nearby pubs.

Readers' comments: Very friendly. I can definitely recommend Hullerbank. Very comfortable and spotlessly clean. Delightful house. Breakfasts exceptionally good. Hosts extremely considerate, excellent accommodation. Good value.

Cumbria

ING HILL LODGE

D

Mallerstang Dale, Cumbria, CA17 4JT Tel: 017683 71153
South of Kirkby Stephen. Nearest main road: A685 from Tebay to Brough.

3 Bedrooms. £20–£25 (less for 7 nights or more). Bargain breaks. Available: own shower/toilet; TV; views of river. No smoking.
Light suppers if ordered. Wine available. No smoking.
1 Sitting-room. With open fire.
Large garden

Mallerstang must be the Cumbrian valley least known to tourists. Yet it is rich in associations, real or legendary: King Arthur, Dick Turpin, the Romans and the Vikings, Thomas à Becket, Michael Faraday. Ing Hill – built probably as a hunting-lodge in 1820 – stands above the valley floor, and the views are splendid, especially from the bedrooms. The latter have neatly coordinated fabrics and ingenious bedheads-cum-backrests designed by Tony Sawyer. A retired surveyor, he has done all the design and conversion.

Light suppers only, but for more substantial dinners there are several pubs nearby and a bistro in Kirkby Stephen.

V

Readers' comments: Standard of a top hotel. Thrilled by standard of accommodation. Marvellous hospitality. Delightful furnishings and location. Accommodation outstanding. Made us so very welcome. Standard exceptional. Sheer paradise.

MILL BECK COTTAGE

C(5) S

Cumbria

Water Street, Morland, Cumbria, CA10 3AY Tel: 01931 714567
(Mobile: 0780 8562738)
North-west of Appleby-in-Westmorland. Nearest main road: A6 from Kendal to Penrith (and M6, junction 39).

2 Bedrooms. £22–£25 (less for 3 nights or more). Bargain breaks. Both have TV; views of river. No smoking.
Dinner (by arrangement). £12.50 for 3 courses and coffee, at times to suit guests. Vegetarian or other special diets if ordered. Wine available. No smoking.
Light suppers if ordered.
1 Sitting-room. With stove, TV. No smoking.
Small garden

The Eden Valley is scattered with peaceful villages, their houses built of red sandstone. Morland, like its Saxon church, is the oldest of them. Alongside Water Street runs Morland Beck, and the bedrooms of this old cottage overlook the stream, with its little sluice, foot-bridge and grassy banks, where you may see a heron dining on minnows.

Inside, you can hardly see the walls for an intriguing collection of paintings, prints, photographs and watercolours (some of the latter by Hardre Jackson herself). Many are mementoes of distant countries, for the Jacksons are well travelled and Derek Jackson was an expedition leader after leaving the Parachute Regiment. The sunny bedrooms, pleasantly furnished in cottage style, share one guests' bathroom.

If you dine here, you may get, for example, cream of vegetable soup, navarin of local lamb, and chocolate gâteau with raspberries. Otherwise, the Jacksons will direct (or even drive) you to good inns. Morland is on the Cumbrian Way long-distance footpath and not far from Appleby, with its Norman castle and old church (with fine organ).

Readers' comments: Unspoilt, unpretentious and excellently furnished; excellent cook.

V

THE MILL HOTEL

C D S

Cumbria

Mungrisdale, Cumbria, CA11 0XR Tel: 017687 79659
West of Penrith. Nearest main road: A66 from Keswick to Penrith (and M6, junction 40).

9 Bedrooms. £49–£59 **including dinner, to readers of this book.** Less for 3 nights or more. Available: own bath/shower/toilet; TV; views of river.
Dinner. 5 courses and coffee, at 7pm. Vegetarian or other special diets if ordered. Wine available. No smoking. **Light suppers** if ordered.
2 Sitting-rooms. With open fire, TV.
Large garden
Closed from November to February.

In a peaceful spot, with little more than the sound of the River Glenderamackin rushing down its rocky bed, the Mill Hotel (adjoining, but not connected with, the Mill Inn) is a simple white house with moss on the slate roof. A small conservatory faces a stone terrace and a lawn with seats by the water's edge.

Eleanor and Richard Quinlan believe that dinner is the high point of a stay. A typical menu might include a tartlet of wild mushrooms; green bean and apple soup with freshly baked soda bread; quail with orange, brandy and thyme; and steamed marmalade pudding. There is always a vegetarian option.

The main sitting-room is pretty and there is a small TV room with well-filled bookshelves. In the dining-room each oak table has willow-pattern china, candles and a nosegay. Around are pictures from Richard's collections of Victorian paintings and of wooden bygones.

Readers' comments: Beautiful, quiet, excellent food. Service attentive and friendly. Food is superb. Outstanding. Interesting dinner with Mozart background. Charming. Hospitality exceptional, food absolutely delicious. Ambience, food and accommodation wonderful.

V

Cumbria

OWL BROOK

CDMSX

High Lorton, Cumbria, CA13 9TX Tel: 01900 85333
South-east of Cockermouth. Nearest main road: A66 from Keswick to Cockermouth.

3 Bedrooms. £16.50–£17.50 (less for 6 nights or more). Bargain breaks. TV. No smoking.
Dinner (by arrangement). £12.50 for 4 courses and coffee, at 7pm. Vegetarian or other special diets if ordered. No smoking. **Light suppers** if ordered.
Small garden

At the western end of spectacular Whinlatter Pass is Ann Roberts's architect-designed and attractive bungalow of green lakeland slate with pine ceilings. It was built some years ago, and all the airy bedrooms have fine views. Dinner might comprise soup, risotto, and fresh fruit salad, using wholefood ingredients. Guests are welcome to share the Roberts' sitting-room.

Whinlatter Pass, running from the direction of Keswick and beautiful Derwent Water, rises through woodland to give magnificent views, but it is not too alarming for cautious motorists. The Vale of Lorton is less popular than the central Lake District but no less beautiful. Loweswater, Buttermere and Crummock Water are quiet lakes nearby. Much of the woodland in this area is owned by the National Trust, which was founded in the Lake District. The Whinlatter Forest Park is run by the Forestry Commission, which has provided picnic sites and a new visitor centre containing a restaurant.

'A yew tree stands in Lorton vale', wrote Wordsworth. It stands today, though storm-damaged, and was once featured in a TV series on notable trees.

Readers' comments: Beautiful views and utter tranquillity. Breakfasts were superb. Very friendly family atmosphere.

Cumbria

SPOONEY GREEN

D PT S X

Spooney Green Lane, Keswick, Cumbria, CA12 4PS Tel: 017687 72601
Nearest main road: A66 from Penrith to Keswick.

2 Bedrooms. £20–£25 (less for 3 nights or more). Both have own bath/shower/toilet; TV. No smoking.
Dinner (by arrangement). £10 for 3 courses and coffee, at times to suit guests. Vegetarian or other special diets if ordered. No smoking. **Light suppers** if ordered.
Large garden

E-mail: spooneygreen@beeb.net

In a secluded rural setting yet within walking distance of an attractive town, Spooney Green has it all. An early 18th-century house, it has been particularly pleasantly decorated by the Wallaces. The double room, for example, is predominantly blue, with fleur-de-lys wallpaper, and the furniture is of wrought iron and cane (it includes an easy chair and a desk to make up for the absence of a sitting-room). Like the equally smart twin-bedded room, it gives excellent views, across an outstanding garden with a pool and lots of wildlife, of the Lake District hills, into which easy or more strenuous walks start from the house. (Ian Wallace, a retired dentist, leads walking parties and is a member of the mountain rescue team.)

In the dining-room, Sandra might serve salmon mousse, venison casserole, and sticky-toffee pudding. Otherwise, there is a big choice of eating-places in Keswick itself. Derwent Water, one of the most beautiful of the lakes, is close by.

V

Readers' comments: Beautiful and very comfortable accommodation; lovely views; made to feel welcome and at home; breakfast very good indeed; view spectacular.

SUMMERLANDS TOWER

Endmoor, Cumbria, LA8 0ED Tel/Fax: 015395 61081

South of Kendal. Nearest main road: A65 from Kirkby Lonsdale to Kendal (and M6, junction 36).

Cumbria

2 Bedrooms. £24–£29.50. Available: own bath/shower/toilet; TV. No smoking.
Light suppers if ordered. Vegetarian or other special diets if ordered. No smoking.
1 Sitting-room. With piano. No smoking.
Large garden
Closed from December to February.

A mansion built for a mill-owner in 1846 is now three dwellings, of which this is one. A fraction of the Jacobethan house it may be, but its scale is still huge, with large, high-ceilinged rooms and vast windows looking out on to three acres of lawns and shrubberies. From the hall which is the guests' sitting-room – with a carved stone fireplace inscribed 'Where friends meet hearts warm' – a massive oak staircase leads to bedrooms with lavish bathrooms. In the larger room is an unusual pair of symmetrically matching brass bedsteads. As well as antiques, the house contains some interesting souvenirs of Michael and Hazel Green's trips abroad, such as a small carpet loom from Pakistan. Hazel (who used to be craft teacher to the blind) makes her own muesli and uses free-range eggs and local sausages for breakfasts. The house is close not only to the Lake District but to the westernmost of the Yorkshire Dales as well.

Reader's comments: We stayed three nights, would love to stay again, nor would we hesitate to recommend it to our friends.

V

SWALEDALE WATCH C M S

Whelpo, Caldbeck, Cumbria, CA7 8HQ Tel/Fax: 016974 78409

South-east of Wigton. Nearest main road: A595 from Carlisle to Cockermouth (and M6, junction 41).

Cumbria

4 Bedrooms. £18–£21. Available: own bath/shower/toilet; TV; views of river. No smoking.
Dinner (Tuesday to Thursday and Saturdays). From £12 for 3 courses and coffee, at 7pm. Vegetarian or other special diets if ordered. No smoking. **Light suppers** if ordered.
2 Sitting-rooms. With open fire/stove, TV. No smoking.
Large garden

E-mail: nan.savage@talk21.com

At Whelpo ('Wolf's lair'), Swaledale Watch is a sheep farm, named after the breed kept here. There are bedrooms in the modern farmhouse, where there is a comfortable L-shaped sitting-room, and also two in a converted byre which share a sitting-room and a kitchenette. Guests eat in a big dining-room in the house, which is set in fine scenery and good walking country just inside the Lake District National Park. Cookery enthusiast Nan Savage serves, for instance, Highland prawns, chicken baked with honey, and chocolate roll; bread rolls are home-baked.

Caldbeck is one of the Lake District's prettiest villages, with an old inn (handy for lunch), a churchyard where lie John Peel and the real-life heroine of Melvyn Bragg's *Maid of Buttermere*, and a restored watermill for craft shops and a good vegetarian restaurant. Near Caldbeck is Carrock Fell, known for the variety of minerals that can be found there.

Reader's comments: Delightful place, food of remarkably high quality and value.

V

Cumbria

TOWN END

D

Satterthwaite, Cumbria, LA12 8LN Tel: 01229 860936
South of Ambleside. Nearest main road: A590 from Kendal to Ulverston.

1 Bedroom. £20 (less for 4 nights or more). Has own bath/shower/toilet. No smoking.
Light suppers if ordered.
1 Sitting-room. With fire. No smoking.
Small garden
Closed in December and January.

This Georgian house was once the police station of the village on whose edge it stands. It has been neatly restored by Helen and Jeff Bright, and they keep it spotless in spite of their two young children! Those who stay in the one bedroom, with its pine bedstead and views, across farmland, of Grizedale Forest, have the exclusive use of both sitting-room and breakfast-room, and of a bathroom prettily decorated in blue. Helen makes a point of using local and free-range ingredients for her generous breakfasts. The Eagle's Head, almost next door, serves evening meals.

Both keen walkers in the area before they moved here a few years ago, the Brights are well informed about the best routes for hikers and cyclists. There are tens of miles of paths and cycle tracks in Grizedale Forest itself, some starting close to the house. Within the great forest you will come across an assortment of specially commissioned sculptures here and there. The forest's visitor centre contains the expected souvenir shop and café, and an informative tree nursery.

V

Cumbria

VIOLET BANK

PT

Hawkshead, Cumbria, LA22 0PL Tel: 015394 36222
South-west of Ambleside. Nearest main road: A591 from Windermere to Keswick.

2 Bedrooms. £20. No smoking.
1 Sitting-room. With open fire/stove, TV. No smoking.
Large garden

E-mail: CHP@violetbank.freeserve.co.uk

Tucked up a lane half a mile from Hawkshead, Violet Bank is an 18th-century farmhouse with Victorian improvements, including a striking fireplace of coloured marble in the dining-room, which Nancy Penrice has furnished with mostly 19th-century antiques. Around the house are pictures and relics of shooting and fishing – prints and paintings, old gunsmiths' equipment, an aggressive-looking stuffed pike. Chris has a collection of country bygones which he keeps in the slate-shelved dairy and will show to fellow enthusiasts.

The Penrices keep ducks, geese (the latter of the Toulouse breed, which are friendlier than most) and two pointers (plus a collection of pictures of the breed).

Hawkshead, picturesque and pedestrianized, is handy for a choice of good evening meals. The village is mostly owned (and strictly conserved) by the National Trust, which was founded in this part of the world. It is one of the Lake District's most popular tourist destinations, not least because of the school that Wordsworth attended (now a museum). The Beatrix Potter Gallery, with its exhibition of original illustrations, is also a major attraction.

WILLOW COTTAGE **PT**

Bassenthwaite, Cumbria, CA12 4QP Tel: 017687 76440

North-west of Keswick. Nearest main road: A591 from Keswick towards Carlisle.

2 Bedrooms. £22.50–£25 (less for 7 nights or more). Both have own bath/toilet. No smoking.
1 Sitting-room. With stove. No smoking.
Small garden

You will sleep under gnarled rafters at Willow Cottage, which Chris Beaty and her husband have carefully converted from an ancient barn (together with self-catering accommodation next door). One bedroom has views of Skiddaw, the other the use of a big cast-iron bath. At the foot of the staircase (on which hangs Chris's collection of antique baby-linen) is a beamed sitting-cum-breakfast-room, with comfortable seats facing an iron stove in a nook. A smaller room has French windows opening on to a paved area by the vegetable and herb garden, where guests often sit to gaze at the mountains. The cottage is attractively decorated, with unobtrusive stencilling and furniture-painting by Chris. She offers some choice at breakfast; many guests dine at the Sun Inn a few hundred yards away.

Bassenthwaite Lake, to which the village has given its name, is popular with small-boat sailors, but this, the most northerly part of the Lake District National Park, is never as crowded as the more popular centre, and Cockermouth is one of the least spoiled of the towns. For good pub lunches, Ireby and Caldbeck are not far.

Reader's comments: Breakfast generous in scope and size; comfortable and cosy; we'd stay again.

V

YEW TREE COTTAGE C(12) **D PT S**

35 Loftus Hill, Sedbergh, Cumbria, LA10 5SQ Tel: 01539 621600

East of Kendal. On A684 from Kendal to Hawes (and M6, junction 37).

2 Bedrooms. £20 (less for 3 nights or more). No smoking.
Light suppers if ordered. Vegetarian or other special diets if ordered. Wine available.
1 Sitting-room. With TV.
Small garden

Anne Jones has lovingly restored this tiny cottage, keeping intact such details as pine panelling and cast-iron grates, using plain colours for the walls and carpets, and furnishing it in simple country style. On the walls are flower pictures, Anne's own samplers, and drawings by her daughter (including the animal portraits in which she specializes).

One of a row on the edge of Sedbergh – a small and characterful town where one can dine – the cottage is at the start of a rewarding drive for the motorist who can cope with steep, winding and narrow roads: past a good craft gallery, through cobbled Dent, by a spectacular Victorian railway viaduct and alongside a little river running over limestone pavements. Outside the town, at Brigflatts, is one of the oldest Quaker meeting houses in the country – a tranquil and historic place. On the other side is England's highest single-drop waterfall, Cautley Spout.

Readers' comments: Lovely, elegant, warm, welcoming and comfortable. Delightful welcome, charming hospitality. Our favourite; a real find; good breakfasts and such good value.

V

DERBYSHIRE

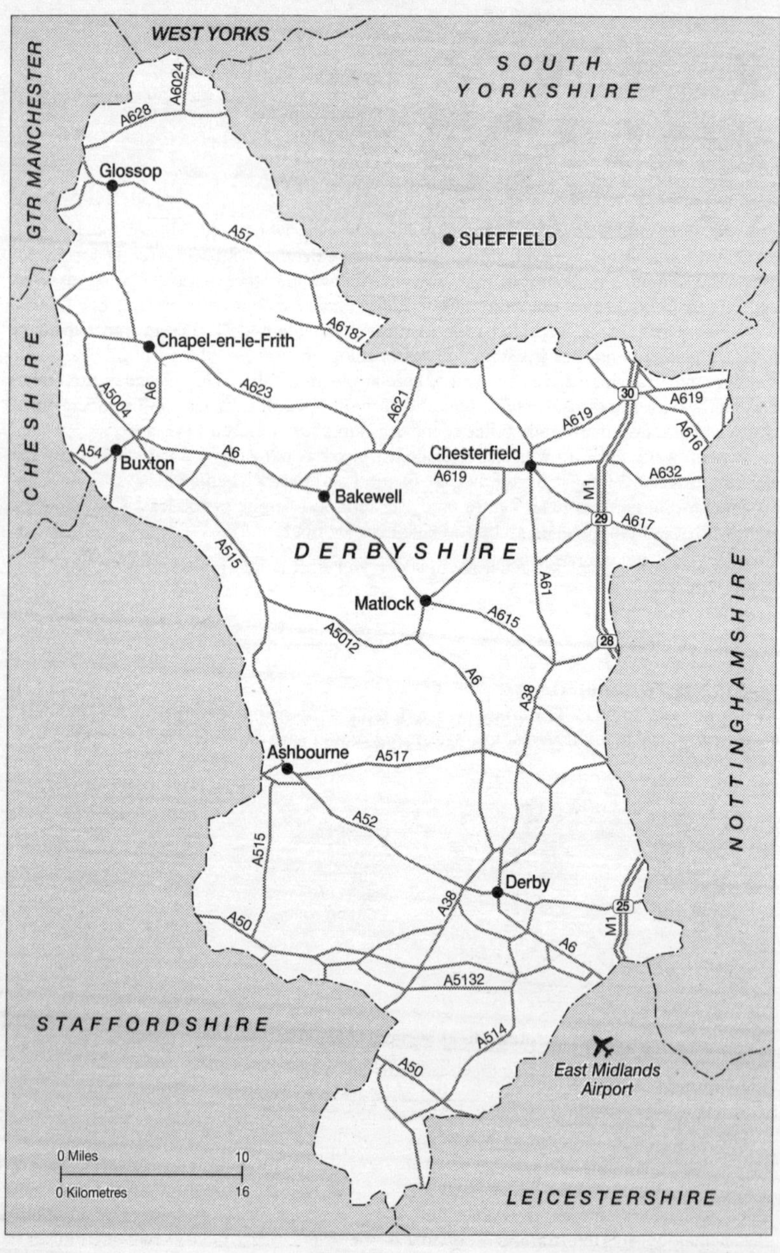

For explanation of code letters and **V** symbol, see inside front cover.

BARMS FARMHOUSE

Fairfield, Derbyshire, SK17 7HW Tel: 01298 77723 (Fax: 01298 78692)
North of Buxton. On A6 from Buxton to Stockport.

rear view

3 Bedrooms. £23–£25 (less for 7 nights or more). Bargain breaks. Available: own bath/shower/toilet; TV. No smoking.
1 Sitting-room. With TV. No smoking.
Small garden

E-mail: info@peakpracticegolf.co.uk

Derbyshire

One mile out of the Georgian spa town of Buxton and overlooking the High Peak golf course is this former dairy-farm. When John Naden's grandfather bought the farm in the 1930s, it had three separate dwellings. Now, Lorraine and John have refurbished the farmhouse to provide comfortable accommodation of a high standard.

You can be as independent as you choose here, since guests have a separate entrance and their own key. Upstairs, the three well-equipped double bedrooms (located at one end of the farmhouse, away from the family) have king-size beds with brass bedsteads. The bathrooms are excellent (two of the rooms also have separate power-shower cubicles), with sparkling gold-plated taps.

Off the dining-room is an oak-beamed sitting-room containing plenty of literature on what to see and do in the area. As Lorraine has two young children, she does not provide evening meals, but a short drive away are several pubs with good food, or you could eat in nearby Buxton. V

BOWER LODGE D

Well Lane, Repton, Derbyshire, DE65 6EY Tel: 01283 702245 (Fax: 01283 704361)
South-west of Derby. Nearest main road: A38 from Derby to Burton-upon-Trent (and M1, junction 23a).

6 Bedrooms. £25–£32 (less for 4 nights or more). Available: own bath/shower/toilet; TV.
Dinner. £17 for 4 courses and coffee, at 7.45pm. Vegetarian or other special diets if ordered. Wine available. **Light suppers** if ordered.
2 Sitting-rooms. With open fires, TV. No smoking in one.
Large garden

Derbyshire

Mercian kings made Repton their capital over a thousand years ago. All down the High Street are scores of historic stone buildings, many now used by Repton's public school; and at the end is this lane of large houses in wooded grounds (one by Lutyens).

Rooms here are spacious and handsome, elegantly furnished by Elizabeth Plant. In one pretty sitting-room with Corinthian pillars, she has used chinoiserie fabrics and festoon blinds, with old china and good paintings around; in another, leafy fabrics contrast with apricot-coloured walls, French doors opening on to a terrace. The dining-room has pretty china and placemats (the separate breakfast-room can be used by any visitors who prefer to eat on their own). Here Elizabeth – who does outside catering too – serves such meals as melon, coq-au-vin, brandy ice cream, and cheese (vegetables come from the garden).

Bedrooms are well furnished and, in some cases, have views of fine trees and the lily-pond. For overseas visitors, two airports are conveniently near.

Reader's comments: Cooking superb, very friendly host.

Derbyshire

CRESSBROOK HALL

C D M

Cressbrook, Derbyshire, SK17 8SY Tel: 0800 3583003 (free) (Fax: 01298 871845)
East of Buxton. Nearest main road: A6 from Buxton to Bakewell.

3 Bedrooms (plus 5 in cottages). £25–£47.50. Bargain breaks. Available: own bath/shower/toilet; TV; views of river. No smoking.
Dinner (by arrangement). From £18.50 for 3 courses and coffee, at 7pm. Vegetarian or other special diets if ordered. Wine available. No smoking. **Light suppers** if ordered.
1 Sitting-room. With open fire, TV, piano. No smoking preferred.
Large garden

A spectacular mansion in a spectacular setting, looking over a deep limestone gorge. The gorge is almost alpine; the extensive gardens were laid out by an assistant to Paxton (of Chatsworth and Crystal Palace fame), and the rooms are of exceptional splendour.

Some bedrooms are on two floors of the main house: one has a remarkable domed ceiling and a bay window from which to enjoy the superb view. Others are in lodges mostly for self-catering (with optional meals in the Hall).

Bobby Hull-Bailey and her husband added a conservatory, where meals are sometimes served instead of in the big dining-room. A typical dinner: melon, stuffed lamb parcels, and oranges in Cointreau (breakfasts are equally ample).

The Hull-Baileys have provided a sunbed, sauna and games room (fee for the first two) as well as a children's play area.

V

Readers' comments: Idyllic.Welcomed with warmth and sincerity. Strongly recommended.

Derbyshire

DELF VIEW HOUSE

Church Street, Eyam, Derbyshire, S32 5QH Tel: 01433 631533 (Fax: 01433 631972)
North of Bakewell. Nearest main road: A623 from Chapel-en-le-Frith towards Chesterfield.

3 Bedrooms. £25–£32 (less for 3 nights or more). All have own bath/shower/toilet; TV. No smoking.
Light suppers if ordered.
1 Sitting-room. With open fire, piano. No smoking.
Large garden

E-mail: lewis@delfview.demon.co.uk

In 1665, infection from the Great Plague travelled from London to Eyam in a roll of cloth. Heroically, the villagers cut themselves off lest they should infect others in the county. They held their church services outdoors in a hollow called the Cucklet Delf, above which was this gritstone house (much enlarged in 1830).

Today, Delf View is one of the most elegant houses in this book, lovingly restored by architect David Lewis and his wife. They have furnished it with such outstanding antiques as silver-legged beds from France painted with romantic pastoral scenes, a Sheraton four-poster, an inlaid fortepiano of 1820 and a ship made by Napoleonic prisoners-of-war. Sometimes candles are lit in the crystal chandelier of the blue sitting-room. There are a sunken bath in a brown-and-gold bathroom, embroidered towels, Augustus John drawings . . . and to complement all this you may be offered at breakfast a soufflé omelette or apples poached in Calvados, as well as local bacon and so forth. Outside is a garden with croquet lawn which overlooks the Delf.

V

Readers' comments: Very pleasing room and excellent breakfast. A truly memorable stay. Absolutely superb.

THE HOLLOW **C S**

Little Longstone, Derbyshire, DE45 1NN Tel: 01629 640746
North-west of Bakewell. Nearest main road: A6 from Bakewell to Buxton.

2 Bedrooms. £22.50–£25. Available: own bath/shower/toilet; TV. No smoking.
Light suppers if ordered. Vegetarian breakfasts if ordered. No smoking.
Small garden

As you enter this handsome stone house, part of which dates back 300 years, the overwhelming impression is one of sheer elegance. For Elizabeth Chadwick has filled it with stylish antiques and imaginative furnishings. You step straight on to the beech-panelled floor of the dining-room. Cherrywood chairs with gold-coloured damask seats surround an imposing mahogany table, and deep red velvet drapes hang at the windows. Up a gracious wooden staircase are impressive, south-facing bedrooms with stone fireplaces, Victorian-style dressing-tables and such touches as frosted green candles in one, Somerset patchwork cushions in another.

Outside is a glorious landscaped garden, beyond which lies the Monsal Trail. The majestic scenery of Monsal Dale is a short stroll away. There are several good pubs and restaurants in the area, the nearest being the Packhorse pub across the road.

Readers' comments: What a find! The situation is idyllic, the accommodation exquisite, the breakfast a sheer extravagance. Delightful hosts. We couldn't have found a more perfect place. Wonderful home and glorious garden; nothing was too much trouble.

HOLLY COTTAGE **C D S**

Rowland, Derbyshire, DE45 1NR Tel: 01629 640624
North of Bakewell. Nearest main road: A6 from Bakewell to Buxton.

2 Bedrooms. £23–£24 (less for 4 nights or more). No smoking.
Dinner. £10–£13.50 for 2–3 courses and coffee, at 7pm. Vegetarian or other special diets if ordered. No smoking. **Light suppers** if ordered.
2 Sitting-rooms. With open fire/stove, TV, piano. No smoking.
Small garden
Closed from November to February.

As one of England's golf champions (1972), Mary Everard used to travel the world but eventually chose the quiet hamlet of Rowland in which to settle down. Here, at 18th-century Holly Cottage, she welcomes guests to her elegant sitting-room, a pale blue and green dining-room furnished with old maple chairs from America, and pretty bedrooms with white board doors. A typical dinner menu: home-made mushroom soup; sweet-and-sour pork or fish pie, with vegetables from the garden; Bakewell tart and crème fraîche. For breakfast, bread, rolls and muffins are home-baked; jams and marmalade home-made.

If you want more than just the hill scenery, there are stately homes to visit, spectacular show caverns at Castleton, Matlock Bath and Buxton, the market town of Bakewell, and Sheffield for its many and varied attractions: excellent art gallery, cathedral and industrial heritage museum with steel craftsmen ('the little mesters') at work.

Readers' comments: Excellent in every way. Lovely house, warm welcome, good food and wonderful setting. Excellent and friendly hostess; we hope to return.

Derbyshire

HORSLEYGATE HALL C(5)

Horsleygate Lane, Holmesfield, Derbyshire, S18 7WD Tel: 0114 2890333
North-west of Chesterfield. Nearest main road: A621 from Baslow to Sheffield.

3 Bedrooms. £23–£25. One has own bath/shower/toilet. No smoking.
1 Sitting-room. With open fire, TV. No smoking.
Large garden

Garden enthusiasts, in particular, will enjoy staying here because Margaret Ford has created a fascinating terraced garden of hidden patios, woodland paths, rock garden, herbaceous beds and brimming stone troughs. The house (part early Victorian, part Georgian) had hardly been touched for generations, but its original features were intact and have now been carefully restored.

The Fords painted the panelling in the sitting-room apricot and grey, with fabrics to match. What was once the children's schoolroom is now a breakfast-room. Here and elsewhere are Margaret's 'flea market' finds which add to the character of the house.

There are spacious bedrooms, some with armchairs from which to enjoy the superb Peak District scenery. Stripped pine doors and baths set in alcoves are features of the house.

For evening meals, Margaret points guests in the direction of local pubs.

Readers' comments: Very impressed. Picturesque and quiet location, with good views. Friendly and helpful. Enjoyed our stay tremendously.

Derbyshire

JASMINE COTTAGE S

Thorpe, Derbyshire, DE6 2AW Tel: 01335 350465
North of Ashbourne. Nearest main road: A515 from Ashbourne to Buxton.

2 Bedrooms. £20–£25 (less for 2 nights or more). Available: own bath/shower/toilet. No smoking.
Dinner (by arrangement). £12 for 3 courses and coffee, at 7pm. Vegetarian or other special diets if ordered. No smoking. **Light suppers** if ordered.
1 Sitting-room. With wood-burner, TV. No smoking.
Garden

Virginia creeper tangles with jasmine and clings to the limestone walls of this particularly pretty, old Dales cottage. In the front garden, stone troughs and planters are full of colour and a herbaceous border slopes down to a rushing stream.

Elizabeth and Roger Round moved here from their former home at Broadlow Ash Farm, which appeared in earlier editions of this guide. Roger still farms but says he is taking things a little easier – he has evenings off! There is a peaceful atmosphere in the large and comfortable sitting-room where you can relax in a rocking-chair, disturbed only by the slow tick-tock of a grandfather clock. Here and elsewhere are nice old pieces of family furniture, all polished to a high sheen.

For an evening meal, Elizabeth might prepare asparagus soup, local smoked trout, and raspberry tart. Good farmhouse breakfasts include freshly squeezed orange juice.

For cyclists and walkers, Ashbourne is the starting-point of the Tissington Trail, which runs along the bed of a disused railway track to Parsley Hey. The Halls at nearby Sudbury and Kedleston (both NT) are worth visiting.

V

MOUNT TABOR HOUSE

C PT S

Crich, Derbyshire, DE4 5DG Tel: 01773 857008 (Mobile: 07977 078266)
South-east of Matlock. Nearest main road: A6 from Matlock to Derby (and M1, junctions 26/28).

Derbyshire

2 Bedrooms. £25–£27 (less for 3 nights or more). Bargain breaks. Available: own bath/shower/toilet; TV. No smoking.
Dinner (by arrangement). £17.50 for 3 courses and coffee, from 7pm. Vegetarian or other special diets if ordered. No smoking. **Light suppers** if ordered.
1 Sitting-room. With TV. No smoking.
Small garden

E-mail: mountabor@email.msn.com

High in the Derbyshire Peaks lies the village of Crich. The name derives from an old English word meaning mound or hill; and Crich Stand, a memorial dedicated to the men of the Sherwood Foresters Regiment who died in the Great War, can be seen for miles around. In the centre of the village is Mount Tabor House, a former Methodist chapel which served the community for more than a hundred years. Converted several years ago, this fine Victorian building, with its exposed stone walls and Gothic-style windows, most retaining their original stained glass, is now owned by Fay and Steve Whitehead.

Bedrooms are on the lower ground floor in what was once the schoolroom. One in restful blues contains a king-size antique pine bed.

Candlelit dinners are served in the large living/dining-area upstairs, or on the balcony in warm weather. The atmosphere is peaceful and the views of the Amber Valley are stunning. Fay uses local and organic produce for meals such as goat's cheese en croûte, roast monkfish niçoise, and lemon and chocolate mousse.

Trout fishing and hot-air ballooning are amongst the many things you can do in this lovely area. The National Tramway Museum in Crich itself is well worth visiting.

OLD ORCHARD

C S

Stoney Lane, Thorpe, Derbyshire, DE6 2AW Tel/Fax: 01335 350410
North-west of Ashbourne. Nearest main road: A515 from Ashbourne to Buxton.

Derbyshire

4 Bedrooms. £21–£25 (less for 3 nights or more). Available: own shower/toilet.
1 Sitting-room. With open fire, TV. No smoking.
Small garden
Closed from December to February.

Dovedale is one of the loveliest parts of the Peak District; and in this area there are particularly fine views of it where the Manifold Valley runs down into the dale (at the foot of Thorpe Cloud – one of several 1000-foot hills here).

On the edge of Thorpe village is a very prettily sited stone house in traditional style, which stands where once an orchard of damson trees grew. This is the comfortable home of Barbara Challinor and her husband; keen gardeners, as is obvious from the herbaceous beds, stone terraces, rock garden and stream with waterfalls in their sloping, landscaped grounds.

This part of the National Park is known as 'the White Peak' because the underlying rock is limestone (further north, in 'the Dark Peak', the geology changes). There is a network of paths around here by which to explore Milldale, Wolfscote Dale and Beresford Dale.

But scenery is not the only attraction of the area. There are the stately homes of Chatsworth and Haddon Hall to visit, the old towns of Matlock and Bakewell, and busy Ashbourne with a splendid church and antique salerooms.

Readers' comments: Ideal hostess. Excellent: went out of her way to make us welcome. Excellent accommodation, homely and friendly people. Most satisfying accommodation with friendly atmosphere.

Derbyshire

POTTING SHED

C PT

Bank Hall, Chapel-en-le-Frith, Derbyshire, SK23 9UB Tel: 01298 812656 or 0161 3388134

West of Chapel-en-le-Frith. Nearest main road: A6 from Buxton to Chapel-en-le-Frith.

2 Bedrooms. £25. Both have own shower/toilet; TV. No smoking.
Light suppers if ordered.
1 Sitting-room. No smoking.
Large garden

This gritstone cottage occupies the site of an old kitchen garden for the erstwhile Bank Hall estate. Remnants such as an old glasshouse remain, but Sandra and Mike Ashton's garden is ornamental. Pretty herbaceous borders contrast with tree peonies and old-fashioned varieties of rose and geranium; a pond and bog garden lie where there was once a banana-house.

There is a Mediterranean air to the cottage itself, for Sandra has used warm terracottas and reds, counterbalanced by cooler shades of blue and green. Breakfast is served in the conservatory, which looks out over the dramatic scenery of the Dark Peak. The ground-floor bedrooms – decorated with flair, using old stripped-pine furniture – have their own entrances and open out on to the walled garden. All about are colourful examples of Sandra's ever-expanding collection of ceramics. For evening meals, try the Veccia Italia in Chapel.

Walking routes planned by the Ashtons (themselves keen walkers) are available for guests. Nearby Castleton is where the unique Blue John mineral stone is found.

V *Reader's comments:* The garden is a delight, the welcome the warmest I have come across; a very special place.

Derbyshire

WAYSIDE COTTAGE

C(7) D PT X

106 Padfield Main Road, Padfield, Derbyshire, SK13 1ET Tel: 01457 866495

North-east of Glossop. Nearest main road: A57 from Glossop to Manchester (and M67, junction 3).

2 Bedrooms. £20–£22.50 (less for 3 nights or more). Bargain breaks. Available: own bath/shower/toilet; TV. No smoking.
Light suppers if ordered.
1 Sitting-room. With stove, TV.
Small garden

E-mail: wayside106@tesco.net

For Marcia and Graeme Dodd, moving into Wayside Cottage was both the fulfilment of a long-held wish and a very civilized, amicable arrangement. Having lived opposite the house for many years, they and its then owners quite simply swapped homes.

To this already beautifully renovated 17th-century cottage the Dodds added a pretty garden room of slate and stone, with colourful windows of reclaimed stained glass. Here, while breakfasting, guests can look out past the cherry-trees to a little stream with miniature bridge.

Bedrooms are stylish and attractive. One has a golfing theme (one of Graeme's enthusiasms), the other a more period feel, enhanced by a 17th-century canopied oak bed and other antique finds. Afternoon tea is offered on arrival, including home-baked treats (Marcia is in catering). In winter, this is served in the low-beamed sitting-room in front of a glowing stove. Good and reasonably priced evening meals can be had at the quiet village pub, a half-minute walk away.

V *Reader's comments:* Very nice people – we were made members of the family immediately; as good a b & b as we are ever likely to find.

WELLHEAD FARM

CDS

Wormhill, Derbyshire, SK17 8SL Tel: 01298 871023
East of Buxton. Nearest main road: A6 from Buxton to Bakewell.

4 Bedrooms. £22–£28 (less for 4 nights or more). Available: own bath/shower/toilet. No smoking.
Dinner. £14.50 for 4 courses and coffee, at 6–8pm. Vegetarian or other special diets if ordered. **Light suppers** if ordered.
2 Sitting-rooms. With woodstove, TV. No smoking in one.

When Yvonne and Barry Peirson moved to this 400-year-old limestone farmhouse with stone-slabbed roof, there was no running water – it had to be pumped up from the well in the cellar. Here the original slabs of stone on which animals were cut up (to be sold on the black market during the war) are still to be found.

Today, this characterful, oak-beamed house (and adjoining tea-room) is filled with a homely mixture of antiques and personal memorabilia. Stairs lead up from the main sitting-room to pretty, cottage-style bedrooms (some have four-posters, and one is a family room).

Yvonne serves such dinners as devilled mushrooms; chicken breasts with white sauce, nuts and grapes; pavlova; and cheese. In summer, you can take the footpath along the river to the Angler's Rest pub in Miller's Dale (the Peirsons will collect you), just one of several excellent walks in the area.

Readers' comments: Very friendly and informal atmosphere, quiet and comfortable, good food, a highlight of the trip. Outgoing, friendly people, willing to put themselves to any amount of trouble.

V

WOLFSCOTE GRANGE

CS

Hartington, Derbyshire, SK17 0AX Tel: 01298 84342
North-west of Ashbourne. Nearest main road: A515 from Ashbourne to Buxton.

3 Bedrooms. £20–£25. Bargain breaks. One has own shower/toilet. No smoking.
Light suppers if ordered. Vegetarian or other special diets if ordered.
1 Sitting-room. With open fire/stove, TV.
Large garden
Closed in December and January.

Truly remote, Wolfscote Grange is an isolated beef and sheep farm, parts of the ancient building dating back to the 13th century. Just outside, the land drops down 200 feet to the River Dove. Jane Gibbs keeps her rooms as traditional as is compatible with modern comfort: in keeping with the narrow, mullioned windows and low rafters, her armchairs are cretonne-covered and antique sporting-guns hang on the walls. Frequently, television companies seek out this authentic setting for costume dramas. Twists and steps lead you to bed: for the best view, ask for the pink room.

Hartington is a pretty village, its busy past as market and lead-mining town now long gone. Arbor Low, nearby, is a place of mystery – a circle of white stones erected on a windswept site 4000 years ago and with burial mounds nearby. Beyond it lies possibly the most perfect mediaeval stately home in this country: turreted Haddon Hall, with terraced gardens descending to a sparkling river. Across high heather moors lies Matlock – there is a mining museum worth visiting here.

V

DEVON

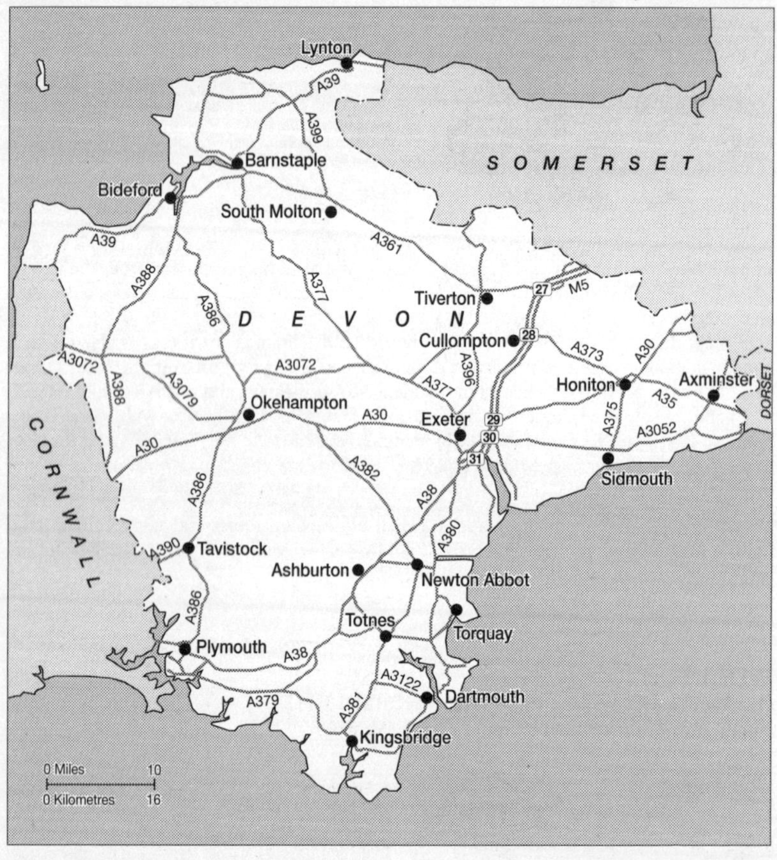

THANK YOU . . . to those who send details of their own finds, for possible future inclusion in the book. Do not be disappointed if your candidate does not appear in the very next edition. Recommendations from unknown members of the public are never published without verification, and it takes time to get round each part of England and Wales in turn. Please, however, do not send details of houses already featured in many other guides, nor any that are more expensive than those in this book (see page xiv).

AYRMER HOUSE

S

Devon

Ringmore, Devon, TQ7 4HL Tel: 01548 810391
West of Kingsbridge. Nearest main road: A379 from Kingsbridge to Plymouth.

4 Bedrooms. £22–£26 (less for 3 nights or more). Available: own bath/shower/toilet; TV; views of sea; balcony. No smoking.
1 Sitting-room. With open fire, TV. No smoking.
Garden

The superb view down a broad valley to the sea (where the Eddystone lighthouse flashes at night) is what brings many visitors here: big picture-windows, a terrace and a wide verandah outside three of the bedrooms make the most of it. This is National Trust land, threaded by a stream and path to the secluded beach and to the long coastal walk which can take you to Salcombe or to Plymouth.

Jim and Ella Dodds, who keep sheep on this land, have a most unusual farmhouse – completely modern and with such natural features as walls of timber or stone, polished slate for floors or hearth, and an open-tread staircase to one bedroom suite with its own sitting-room. William Morris fabrics contrast with white walls in most rooms.

Home-made bread and preserves are served at breakfast. For dinner, there is a very good pub just 300 yards away.

Around the attractive resort of Salcombe there is outstanding coastal scenery (especially at the National Trust's Bolt Head), mild enough for orange and lemon trees.

Readers' comments: Delightful house and view. Charmingly decorated. Warmly welcomed, home-from-home atmosphere, excellent service, most restful.

V

BARK HOUSE HOTEL

Devon

Oakford Bridge, Devon, EX16 9HZ Tel: 01398 351236
North of Tiverton. On A396 from Exeter to Minehead.

5 Bedrooms. £25–£51.75 (less for 2 nights or more full board). All have own bath/shower/toilet; TV; views of river.
Dinner. £25 for 3 courses and coffee, at 7.15–8.45pm. Vegetarian diets if ordered. Wine available.
Light suppers if ordered.
1 Sitting-room. With open fire.
Large garden
Restricted opening from November to end of March.

In the sylvan setting of the River Exe and its valley meadows, lies a stone building of unusual origin. A former tannery (the oak bark was brought from Exmoor Forest), it now serves walkers who want to explore Exmoor and the lovely Exe Valley, or visitors to the nearby National Trust houses and gardens. Bark House's owner, Alastair Kameen, is an enthusiastic self-taught cook, and his partner, Justine Hill, makes guests welcome with such touches as fresh flowers in every bedroom.

In the low-ceilinged dining-room, one may sit down to a dinner of, for example, courgette and rosemary soup, fillet of brill with tarragon and vermouth sauce, and steamed sponge pudding with butterscotch sauce and fresh egg custard.

The bedrooms overlook the road (busy during the day; quiet in the evenings) and beyond that to a tranquil rural setting. One huge bedroom has its own ancient arched door to a rock garden and rock pool.

Readers' comments: So impressed with the reception that we returned. They look after guests' every need. Outstanding culinary skills.

Devon

THE BEEHIVE

C(13)

Steep Hill, Maidencombe, Devon, TQ1 4TS Tel: 01803 314647
North of Torquay. Nearest main road: A380 from Exeter towards Paignton.

3 Bedrooms. £20–£21. Available: own bath/shower/toilet; TV; views of sea; balcony (one).
Large garden

The stunning views across Lyme Bay are one of the many rewarding features of this handsome and immaculate house, set in a country lane which winds down to a sandy cove. Norman and Dorothy Sibthorp fell in love with the site and Norman designed a home to enhance its vantage point. Around the house, with its beautifully tended garden, are high granite terraces where guests can sun themselves.

Light flows through large windows and sliding glass doors into rooms where soft pastels are offset by dusky pink carpeting. Bedrooms, with flowery fabrics, have lovely coastal views, and a telescope is available to keep abreast with activity at sea. One particularly spacious bedroom, with its own wrought-iron balcony, is occasionally available. A short walk down the lane brings guests to the Thatched Tavern which is noted for its meals.

All the coast along here has a Mediterranean air. It is one of the most popular parts of Devon, though Maidencombe is well tucked away from the crowds.

V *Readers' comments:* Beautifully decorated. Never met hosts who were kinder and more anxious to please. Thoroughly enjoyed our stay. Superb quality, exceptional hospitality.

Devon

BEERA FARM

C X

Milton Abbot, Devon, PL19 8PL Tel/Fax: 01822 870216 (Mobile: 07974 957966)
North-west of Tavistock. Nearest main road: A30 from Okehampton to Launceston.

3 Bedrooms. £25 (less for 2 and 7 nights or more). All have own shower/toilet; TV. No smoking.
Dinner (by arrangement). £13–£15 for 2–3 courses and coffee, at times to suit guests. Vegetarian or other special diets if ordered. No smoking. **Light suppers** if ordered.
1 Sitting-room. With open fire, TV, piano. No smoking.
Large garden

E-mail: robert.tucker@farming.co.uk

The kitchen and outbuildings of this large, traditional, stone-built Victorian farmhouse gained fame when they were used in the popular BBC TV series 'The Vet'. The house, set in the heart of the Tamar Valley, is owned by Robert and Hilary Tucker (the surrounding 180 acres are farmed by Robert). This young couple have decorated their home with great panache, and have sought out such old pieces of furniture as the oak tables and antique velvet-covered chairs in the dining-room. Here Hilary, a former chef, serves evening meals which might comprise smoked bacon and cheese soufflé, poached chicken in white wine sauce, and warm sticky-toffee and banana pudding.

The bedrooms, two with marbled-slate, Victorian fireplaces, are quite delightful. One has a canopied four-poster bed, tea-rose-patterned wallpaper and rug-covered, polished floorboards. Another, with an old pine wardrobe (made for the house when it was built), has Jacobean-style soft furnishings.

Hilary, a seemingly unhurried young mother, welcomes her guests with a cream tea.

V *Reader's comments:* Hospitality at its best; excellent food; warm welcome and high standards.

Devon

BICKLEIGH COTTAGE HOTEL

PT S

Bickleigh, Devon, EX16 8RJ Tel: 01884 855230

South of Tiverton. On A396 from Exeter to Tiverton (and near M5, junction 27).

4 Bedrooms. £22.50–£25 (less for 7 nights or more). All have own shower/toilet; views of river. No smoking.
1 Sitting-room. With TV.
Large garden
Closed from November to March.

Built about 1640 and later extended, this very picturesque thatched cottage has been run as a small hotel by the same family for over 60 years. It stands on a busy road by the River Exe, with a foaming weir a few yards downstream: a typically Devonian beauty-spot.

The rooms downstairs are full of antiques such as old chests and carved oak chairs, as well as a collection of blue glass and other interesting trifles including articles of Honiton lace made by Mrs Cochrane, which are for sale. The bedrooms are more simply furnished, though one has a four-poster bed. All are quiet and river-facing. Outside is a pretty riverside garden and a glasshouse containing a collection of cacti and succulents.

Bed-and-breakfast only, but there are three places within 150 yards that offer good and varied evening meals. Nearby sightseeing attractions include opulent Knightshayes Court (NT) with beautiful gardens and moated Bickleigh Castle.

Readers' comments: Delightful. A favourite place. Beautiful position. Delightful cottage and scenery. Lovely setting, lots of history and charm. Very friendly. Excellent.

Devon

BROOKSIDE

C D S X

Lustleigh, Devon, TQ13 9TJ Tel/Fax: 01647 277310

North-west of Newton Abbot. Nearest main road: A382 from Bovey Tracey to Moretonhampstead.

rear view

3 Bedrooms. £22 (less for 4 nights or more). All have views of river. No smoking.
Light suppers if ordered.
1 Sitting-room. With woodstove, TV. No smoking.
Small garden

A show village of the Dartmoor National Park, Lustleigh is sometimes crowded with sightseers – but even then Brookside, well tucked away, is peaceful. The landscaped garden is raised up on what was once a railway embankment. Round it winds the River Wrey, and one can sit above its waters on the little bridge across which trains once puffed their way.

One enters Judy Claxton's old house through a combined sitting/breakfast-room, which has a great granite hearth (with woodstove) at one end. A twisting stair rises to bedrooms furnished in simple cottage style. The house was originally a thatched cottage belonging to a 15th-century farm, now the Cleave Inn, which serves good dinners.

An excellent area for birdwatching; mountain bikes and guided walks available.

Readers' comments: Excellent hospitality, tranquil surroundings. Beautiful views. Superb breakfasts; efficient and charming hosts; a haven of peace.

V

Devon

CIDER HOUSE

C D PT

Buckland Abbey, Yelverton, Devon, PL20 6EZ Tel: 01822 853285 (Fax: 01822 853626)
South of Tavistock. Nearest main road: A386 from Tavistock to Plymouth.

2 Bedrooms. £25–£30 (less for 2 nights or more). Both have own bath/shower/toilet; TV (in one). No smoking.
Dinner (by arrangement for 4 people). £20 for 4 courses and coffee, at times to suit guests. Vegetarian or other special diets if ordered. No smoking. **Light suppers** if ordered.
1 Sitting-room. With open fire, TV. Piano. No smoking.
Large garden

E-mail: michael.stone@cider-house.co.uk

For history-buffs and garden-lovers, Michael and Sarah Stone's beautiful old house is a must. Nestling beneath 13th-century Buckland Abbey, later the residence of Sir Francis Drake, the Cider House has served as both the abbey's refectory and Drake's cider barn. Inside the great granite walls, all is warm and welcoming, while outside, in a valley above the River Tavy, flourish gardens of great beauty and wildness.

Breakfast is eaten in a sunny corner of the big kitchen where Sarah has stencilled white-painted floorboards. Here and elsewhere are pictures done by the Stones' artist daughter and Sarah's father. The sitting-room is a particularly pretty room and French doors open to allow in the fragrance of a white wisteria. Spacious bedrooms are light and bright, with their soft yellows, pinks and whites and delicate, flower-printed friezes.

Guests dine by candlelight in a room with pale cinnamon walls. Here Sarah might serve local smoked trout with horseradish and gooseberry sauce, casseroled venison with home-grown organic vegetables, fruit tarts and local cheeses.

V

Reader's comments: Warm and attentive hostess; high standard of accommodation; a pearl.

Devon

CORBYNS BRIMLEY

C(12) M

Higher Brimley, Bovey Tracey, Devon, TQ13 9JT Tel: 01626 833332
North-west of Newton Abbot. Nearest main road: A38 from Exeter to Plymouth.

2 Bedrooms. £25–£27 (less for 3 nights or more). One has own shower/toilet. No smoking.
Light suppers if ordered. Vegetarian or other special diets if ordered. No smoking.
1 Sitting-room. With open fire/stove, TV. No smoking.
Large garden
Closed from mid-December to mid-January.

Dartmoor National Park is one of the jewels of Devon and here in this lovely setting stands a white stone-walled and thatched cottage. Now the home of Christopher and Hazel White, its origins as a Devon long-house can be traced back 450 years. In the breakfast-room, guests are seated round a large mahogany table; and while Hazel cooks breakfast in the adjoining open-plan kitchen she enjoys chatting to her visitors.

Over the years, the Whites have assembled a variety of interesting collections, which include Cicely Mary Barker's 'Flower Fairies' plates, glass paperweights, and Christopher's model vintage cars and carriages at the top of the stairs. The sitting-room, with comfortable sofa and chairs, is warmed by a large wood-burner; and the bedrooms have splendid country views and such thoughtful touches as fresh flowers, hair-dryers and electric blankets. Snack suppers, or guests can dine at one of the local inns or restaurants.

Worth seeking out is Grimspound ('Grim' is Saxon for the god Woden) where the remains of over 20 Bronze Age huts can be seen.

V

Readers' comments: Superb views, splendid accommodation, caring proprietors; shall return again and again.

EAST WOODLANDS FARMHOUSE

C(10) S

Newton Tracey, Devon, EX31 3PP Tel: 01271 858776 (Fax: 01271 858784)
South-west of Barnstaple. Nearest main road: A39 from Barnstaple to Bideford.

2 Bedrooms. £20–£24 (less for 3 nights or more). Both have own shower/toilet. No smoking.
Dinner (by arrangement). £14 for 3–4 courses and coffee, at 7.30pm. Vegetarian or other special diets if ordered. No smoking.
1 Sitting-room. With wood-burner, TV. No smoking.
Large garden

E-mail: HardingFarmhouse@aol.com

Meeting people and cooking are two of Ann Harding's pleasures and she decided that doing bed-and-breakfast would be an ideal way to combine them. She and her husband Richard, a retired police officer, live in a 450-year-old stone and cob farmhouse. It is surrounded by a one-acre garden which they are developing, with a pond as its focal point. The house retains many original features such as inglenook fireplaces, a bread oven, creamer and a panelled stairway.

Throughout the house are examples of Ann and Richard's handicrafts, as well as delicate watercolours painted by Richard's mother. The embroidered wall-hangings are the work of Ann, while Richard's wire sculptures, drawings and ceramics add a thoroughly modern touch. One pink-toned bedroom has floral curtains and a flowery border on the wallpaper, while the other is in vibrant greens and yellows.

Ann's dinner menu might include carrot-and-orange soup, honey-baked pork steaks with plums, and chocolate and coffee torte.

Garden-lovers will head for Tapeley Park and RHS Rosemoor, both of which are close by.

Reader's comments: Lovely house, excellent b & b; good bedrooms, nice meals. **V**

EAST WORTH FARMHOUSE

C M(limited) **S**

Northlew, Devon, EX20 3PN Tel/Fax: 01409 221757
North-west of Okehampton. Nearest main road: A386 from Tavistock to Great Torrington.

3 Bedrooms. £25 (less for 4 nights or more). Available: own bath/shower/toilet; TV. No smoking.
Dinner (by arrangement). £15 for 4 courses and coffee, at 7–8.30pm. Vegetarian or other special diets if ordered. Wine available. No smoking. **Light suppers** if ordered.
Large garden
Closed from November to February.

The 17th-century construction of this Devon long-house was authenticated by an original Bible safe. A cobbled cross passage links the main house to what was a barn, which now provides immaculate accommodation for guests. They are greeted here by Rosalind Haddon, who serves tea either in the sitting/dining-room or the garden. A feature of the garden is the 'lookout' from where deer can be observed.

A downstairs bedroom is suitable for someone of limited mobility: although the bedroom is accessible by wheelchair, the bathroom (which has a grab bar beside the bath) is not. Upstairs there are two rooms, and Rosalind will arrange them to suit visitors' needs. A pretty bedroom and shower-room adjoin another little room; and this can be equipped as a nursery, as a private sitting-room, or as an additional bedroom when friends or family are travelling together.

A typical dinner: pumpkin soup, poached salmon, fruit crumble, and Devonshire cheeses.

Readers' comments: Accommodation and food first class; Rosalind delightful. Extremely kind and helpful; food delicious; one of the nicest places I have visited.

Devon

FUCHSIA COTTAGE

C M P T S

Burscott Lane, Higher Clovelly, Devon, EX39 5RR Tel: 01237 431398
West of Bideford. Nearest main road: A39 from Bideford to Bude.

3 Bedrooms. £19 (less for 6 nights or more). Available: own bath/shower/toilet; TV; views of sea. No smoking.
Small garden

E-mail: tomsuecurtis.fuchsiacot@currantbun.com

This is not a 'ye olde' cottage but a 1970s house lying towards the end of a lane, with rural views to the sea beyond. Run by Tom and Sue Curtis, a welcoming and friendly couple, the house is set back from Clovelly, one of Britain's most picturesque villages. Steep cobbled streets lead down to a 14th-century harbour where donkeys are still used to convey luggage and empty beer barrels. For those who cannot face the upward climb, transport is available.

Breakfast is served in the Curtises' sitting-room, sunlit in the mornings and filled with pictures – one of which shows Clovelly school where Tom taught for many years. The pretty bedrooms, supplied with hot-water bottles and electric blankets, have their own armchairs, and a downstairs room is suitable for a wheelchair.

Coastal walks in this area are renowned and the Curtises will take walkers to the start of their ramble or pick them up at day's end. They will also transport guests' luggage to their next destination. Local hotels, restaurants and pubs are available for evening meals.

V

Devon

GOLDCOMBE FARMHOUSE

C D X

Gittisham, Devon, EX14 3AB Tel: 01404 42559
South-west of Honiton. Nearest main road: A30 from Honiton to Exeter.

3 Bedrooms. £18.50–£22.50 (less for 4 nights or more). Available: own bath/shower/toilet. No smoking.
Dinner (by arrangement). £12.50 for 3 courses and coffee, at 7.30pm. Vegetarian or other special diets if ordered. No smoking. **Light suppers** if ordered.
1 Sitting-room. With open fire, TV. Piano.
Large garden

At old and picturesque Goldcombe Farmhouse (near pretty Gittisham), renovations have revealed a rare feature – a screen wall of oak planks dividing rooms downstairs. The house has beautiful views across the Otter Valley and towards far Dartmoor. A sun-room and one ground-floor bedroom open on to the garden with its lavender bushes and old apple-trees. Further accommodation is in a barn conversion. There are a grass tennis court and a games barn. One breakfasts in the hall, with a view into the kitchen where Ann Stansell, a trained cook, also produces cordon bleu meals (only by arrangement), such as grilled avocado with bacon and Brie, casseroled pheasant, and apple galette made with her own apples.

Northward, the Blackdown Hills are an Area of Outstanding Natural Beauty, and in the opposite direction is a lovely coastline dotted with such old-fashioned resorts as Sidmouth, Branscombe and Beer. Visitors also enjoy the nearby donkey sanctuary, Bicton Park and the old Seaton–Colyton tramway.

Readers' comments: Comfortable, breakfast generous, hosts discreet and friendly. Very good. An unalloyed pleasure.

V

GOODMANS HOUSE

CDSX

Devon

Furley, Devon, EX13 7TU Tel: 01404 881690
North-west of Axminster. Nearest main road: A30 from Honiton to Chard (and M5, junction 25).

7 Bedrooms. £25–£28 (less for 3 nights or more). Bargain breaks. All have own bath/toilet; TV. Private lounges (some). No smoking.
Dinner (by arrangement). £20 for aperitif, 3 courses and coffee, at 7pm. Vegetarian or other special diets if ordered. Wine available. No smoking.
1 Sitting-room. No smoking.
Large garden
Closed from November to early February, except Christmas and New Year.

This mostly 18th-century house is elegant without being formal. Complimentary aperitifs are served in the Georgian garden room, before a candlelit dinner in an arched dining-room with inglenooks at each end. The bedrooms are some of the most attractive in this book, with handsome bathrooms. The gardens and over nine acres of grounds are exceptional.

Alternatively, some families prefer to have accommodation in the well-equipped garden cottages. Robert and Patricia Spencer, who were hoteliers, use much organic produce for such meals as creamy scallop and monkfish soup, roast lamb with imaginatively prepared vegetables, and exotic fresh fruits in Malibu with clotted cream.

Readers' comments: Breathtaking scenery, very caring hosts, delicious food. A super place. I can't think of anywhere nicer to spend a few days. A unique and very special place. Cannot speak too highly of it. Food superb. Made most welcome; nothing too much trouble.

GREENCOTT

CS

Devon

Landscove, Devon, TQ13 7LZ Tel: 01803 762649
South-east of Ashburton. Nearest main road: A38 from Plymouth to Exeter.

2 Bedrooms. £18–£19 (less for 7 nights or more). Bargain breaks. Both have own bath/shower/toilet.
Dinner. £9 for 4 courses and coffee, at 7pm. Vegetarian or other special diets if ordered. **Light suppers** if ordered.
1 Sitting-room. With TV.
Small garden

From Sue Townsend's immaculate tile-hung 1970s house you can see Haytor Rocks. There are two attractive en suite bedrooms; and from the quarry-tiled kitchen (with Aga) one steps through glass patio doors straight into the colourful garden. The light and airy rooms have panoramic views and are restfully furnished. After a starter such as melon or pâté, dinner will probably include a roast, or steak pie, perhaps followed by fruit pie with Devonshire cream, then cheese and coffee. The nationally renowned Hillhouse garden centre is close, and for steam enthusiasts the South Devon Railway in the Dart Valley.

Also in the vicinity are plenty of inns, theatres and concerts including those at Dartington's celebrated arts and crafts centres. Totnes, a centre for complementary medicine, has its castle and streets of ancient buildings.

Readers' comments: Sue is one of the best cooks; food beautifully presented. Warm welcome, good food. Sensational cook. Caring hostess. Superb food.

V

Devon

HINES HILL

C(12) **S**

East Prawle, Devon, TQ7 2BZ Tel/Fax: 01548 511263

South-east of Kingsbridge. Nearest main road: A379 from Kingsbridge to Dartmouth.

3 Bedrooms. £25–£29 (less for 3 nights or more). Available: own bath/shower/toilet; TV; views of sea. No smoking.
1 Sitting-room. With open fire. No smoking.
Large garden
Closed from October to Easter.

This luxuriously furnished modern house has big windows to make the most of spectacular sea views from the 400-foot promontory, and a terrace overlooking the tiny sandy beach below. Many oriental pieces are among the antiques, and the elegant soft furnishings were made by Sylvia Morris herself.

Guests can dine at one of the two village pubs, both of which are within walking distance.

Nearby is Salcombe, Devon's southernmost resort, and arguably its most beautiful one. Even orange and lemon trees grow here which, together with palms, remind one of parts of the Mediterranean. The estuary is very popular for sailing, garden-lovers come to see Sharpitor (NT), walkers make for the viewpoints of Bolberry Down and Bolt Head. All along the coast from here to Plymouth are picturesque waterfront villages.

Readers' comments: Wonderful views, peaceful, furnished to a high standard, attentive and helpful.

Devon

HOLE MILL

D X

Branscombe, Devon, EX12 3BX Tel: 01297 680314

East of Sidmouth. Nearest main road: A3052 from Lyme Regis to Sidmouth.

3 Bedrooms. £18–£21 (less for 3 nights or more). All have views of stream. No smoking.
Light suppers if ordered, or guests can use kitchen.
1 Sitting-room. With open fire, TV. Piano. No smoking.
Large garden

A scenic lane winds up then very sharply down – one hears rushing water and clucking hens before the former cornmill comes into sight below. Within the thick and crooked stone walls are beamy rooms reached by steps up or down, which Rod and Amanda Hart have furnished in antique style, with a collection of clocks (they aren't allowed to chime upstairs!), Victorian bric-a-brac, and a cage with son Adrian's family of enchanting, bushy-tailed chinchillas. In one bedroom is a particularly high iron bedstead from which you can watch the bubbling stream and the comings and goings of deer.

If you want more than a snack supper, the village has a choice of pubs and restaurants; a lift can usually be arranged. The Harts are infinitely flexible, even willing to serve breakfast at any hour: 2.20pm is the record!

Readers' comments: House done up beautifully, peaceful. Goose eggs for breakfast! Charming couple. Best breakfast ever. Idyllic setting with heavenly garden. Hosts couldn't have been more thoughtful. Wished we could have stayed longer. Friendly and flexible hosts.

JUBILEE COTTAGE

C(10) **PT S**

Devon

75 Chapel Street, Sidbury, Devon, EX10 0RQ Tel: 01395 597295
North of Sidmouth. Nearest main road: A375 from Sidmouth to Honiton.

3 Bedrooms. £18–£20 (less for 7 nights or more). Available: own TV. No smoking.
1 Sitting-room. With stove, TV. No smoking.
Garden

E-mail: rd.coles@talk21.com

16th-century, thatched Jubilee Cottage overlooks the lovely Sid Valley. All bedrooms are neat and pleasant with friezes of flowers and pretty bedlinen – two spacious back rooms have a good view of Buckley Hill. Front rooms, facing Chapel Street, are double-glazed. There is a snug sitting-room, and all walls are of very thick, white-painted cob (solid clay, built up lump by lump). Major Coles and his German-born wife Marianne do not provide evening meals, but Marianne can make reservations at local pubs (the Blue Ball in the next village is recommended). Breakfast is sometimes served on the sunny patio which overlooks a pond and waterfall in the secluded garden.

This, the more accessible part of Devon, is exceptionally fertile and most of the cream for which Devon is famous comes from here. Birdwatchers and others who appreciate quiet prefer this part to the so-called 'riviera' coast further along. The area is full of historical associations (ancestral homes of Raleigh and Drake, Marlborough and Coleridge, for instance). Sidmouth is a particularly charming old resort.

Reader's comments: Enjoyable time, good accommodation.

V

KERSCOTT FARM

PT

Devon

Ashmill, Devon, EX36 4QG Tel: 01769 550262 (Fax: 01769 550910)
East of South Molton. Nearest main road: A361 from Tiverton to Barnstaple.

3 Bedrooms. £21–£23. Available: own bath/shower/ toilet. No smoking.
Dinner (by arrangement). £10 for 3 courses and coffee, at 6.30pm. Vegetarian diets if ordered. No smoking. **Light suppers** if ordered.
1 Sitting-room. With stove, TV. No smoking.
Small garden

Stepping into 16th-century Kerscott Farm is like travelling back in time. John and Theresa Sampson, who farm the 120 acres surrounding their home, have preserved old farming implements, family prints and photographs, oil lamps and much more. And they have cleverly grouped and displayed these pieces of rural history throughout the spacious rooms, creating a harmonious home. In the guests' sitting-room, brasses and horse tackle hang above the massive inglenook fireplace. The focal point of the dining-room is the centuries-old oven for making clotted cream, built into the wall. The bedrooms have a mix of pretty fabrics and antique furniture.

Theresa, who has been awarded the accolade of 'top farmhouse landlady', enjoys cooking: a typical dinner could be tomato, noodle and pepper soup with home-baked herb rolls, roast beef with four vegetables, and orange and rhubarb crumble with home-made custard. Mentioned in Domesday Book, the farm has its own springs and wells which are constantly monitored for purity.

Kerscott has Exmoor horn sheep, a pedigree herd of Devon Red Ruby beef-cattle that have won prizes, pigs, geese, white doves, and friendly dogs and cats.

V

LOWER MARSH FARM

C D M P T S

Marsh Green, Devon, EX5 2EX Tel: 01404 822432
East of Exeter. Nearest main road: A30 from Exeter to Honiton (and M5, junctions 29/30).

3 Bedrooms. £23–£26 (less for 5 nights or more). Available: own bath/shower/toilet; TV. No smoking.
Light suppers if ordered.
1 Sitting-room. With open fire, TV.
Large garden

Old-fashioned roses frame the windows and festoon the walls of this 17th-century farmhouse; and in the grounds, with its orchard, ponds, streams and meadows (the latter home to sheep and horses), there are weeping willows, oaks and beeches.

James and Sian Wroe have modernized the interior sympathetically to retain such interesting period features as H-hinged cupboards and chamfered crossbeams. In the low-ceilinged, beamed breakfast-room, terracotta-pink walls are offset by an old pine refectory table and dresser. An ancient and gnarled ship's timber is part of the upstairs hallway and one bedroom is entered through a small chapel-like doorway (remember to duck your head). The bedrooms, with their green, cream and pink colour schemes, are warm and restful.

Marsh Green is an unspoilt little hamlet frequented by horse-riders – Sian could well be among them. Guests dine at the Jack in the Green pub, just a short drive away.

V

Reader's comments: Nothing was too much trouble; delightful host; most delicious breakfasts; accommodation comfortable and room spacious.

YOU AND THE LAW

Once your booking has been confirmed – orally or in writing – a contract exists between you and the proprietor. He/she is legally bound to provide accommodation as booked; and you are legally bound to pay for this accommodation. If unable to take up the booking – even because of sickness – you still remain liable for a very substantial proportion of the charges (in addition to losing your deposit).

If you have to cancel, let the proprietor know as soon as possible; then he/she may be able to re-let the accommodation (in which case you would be liable to pay only a re-letting cost or forfeit your deposit). Phone if you are going to arrive late.

(A note to overseas readers. It may be an acceptable practice elsewhere to make bookings at several houses for the same date, choosing only later which one to patronize; but this way of doing things is not the British practice and you are legally liable to compensate any proprietors whom you let down in this way.)

MARSH MILLS

C D P T S

Devon

Aveton Gifford, Devon, TQ7 4JW Tel/Fax: 01548 550549
West of Kingsbridge. Nearest main road: A379 from Kingsbridge to Plymouth.

4 Bedrooms. £20–£22. Available: own bath/shower/toilet; TV; views of river.
Large garden

E-mail: newsham@marshmills.co.uk

The river and creeks surrounding this Georgian mill house are ideal for exploration by canoe or dinghy, which can be launched from John and Margaret Newsham's own jetty. Alternatively, guests can just wander along the leat path which winds through orchard and garden, where one is likely to come upon chickens and ducks. There are also goats, sheep and donkeys on this smallholding. (Outbuildings provide ample shelter for mountain bikes and walkers' gear, as well as boats.)

The bedrooms, from where the rushing water of the mill-leat is audible, are simple but comfortable. One, with fawn and pink colourings, looks towards a shrub-filled garden that rises steeply behind the house. Another has grey, blue and soft pink wallpaper which matches the colour of the two-seater sofa. Electric heaters are provided as the rooms are not centrally heated.

Breakfast is served in a sunny room which doubles as a sitting-room. Guests can dine at the local pub – a two-minute walk away – where the speciality is Thai food, cooked by the landlord's Thai wife.

Reader's comments: Made most welcome, breakfast excellent; the setting is beautiful.

V

THE MILL

C P T S X

Devon

Lower Washfield, Devon, EX16 9PD Tel/Fax: 01884 255297
North of Tiverton. Nearest main road: A361 from Tiverton to Barnstaple (and M5, junction 27).

4 Bedrooms. £19–£21 (less for 7 nights or more). Available: own bath/shower/toilet; TV; views of river. Limited smoking.
Dinner (by arrangement). £10 for 3 courses and coffee, at times to suit guests. Vegetarian or other special diets if ordered. No smoking. **Light suppers** if ordered.
1 Sitting-room. With stove, TV. No smoking.
Large garden

E-mail: arnold@washfield.freeserve.co.uk

An old mill, with its leat feeding into the River Exe, has been converted by Roger and Liz Arnold into a centre ideally suited to families and country-lovers. Their home is surrounded by Roger's 120-acre dairy-farm where picnics, paddling, swimming and riverside walks can be enjoyed in privacy.

Beamed ceilings, whitewashed walls and exposed stone are reminders of the mill's origins. Breakfast is served in the large dining-hall or the adjacent sun-room, where guests are often visited by ducks and their offspring looking for titbits. For wet days, there is a spacious sitting-room warmed by a wood-burner, and which has a selection of games and videos.

At one end of the house is a mini-suite of two bedrooms with bathroom. Another bedroom, with a deep blue colour scheme, is appropriately named the kingfisher room. And from here that elusive bird can sometimes be seen.

For dinner, Liz might offer seafood ramekins, lamb or pork chops with seasonal vegetables, and a selection of such home-made desserts as steamed treacle pudding.

V

Devon

MOLE COTTAGE

C P T S

Chittlehamholt, Devon, EX37 9HF Tel/Fax: 01769 540471
South-west of South Molton. Nearest main road: A377 from Exeter to Barnstaple.

3 Bedrooms. £23 **to readers of this book only** –£30 (less for 3 nights or more). Available: own bath/shower/toilet; TV; views of river. No smoking.
Large garden
Closed from late December to early January.

E-mail: arch.ceramics@sosi.net

The excellent fishing – salmon, trout and sea-trout – in the River Mole inspired a local lord to build his fishing-lodge by the 'garden' pool in the 17th century. The lodge is now the wisteria-clad home of Mark and Pauline Donaldson. A road divides the cottage from its river garden, where those not intent on fishing can sit in the octagonal summer-house; or, when the weather is fine, guests can use the barbecue. Mark and Pauline, an imaginative couple, have utilized the steep, wooded hill behind their cottage for a 10-hole crazy golf course. Mark, an architectural ceramics designer (his exotic designs are evident throughout the cottage), exports his pottery worldwide and he offers residential courses (when evening meals are provided).

If requested, Pauline will serve breakfast in guests' bedrooms, where the Donaldsons have thoughtfully provided small cane tables and chairs; and for walkers there is a drying-room. Most b & b guests dine at the local village pub and the Donaldsons can arrange a chauffeur service there and back – it's not that far, but up a very steep hill.

Devon

OVERCOMBE HOTEL

C D M P T S X

Old Station Road, Horrabridge, Devon, PL20 7RA Tel/Fax: 01822 853501
South-east of Tavistock. On A386 from Plymouth to Tavistock.

8 Bedrooms. £23–£25 (less for 7 nights or more). Bargain breaks. All have own bath/shower/toilet; TV. No smoking.
Dinner (by arrangement). £14 for 4 courses and coffee, at 7.30pm. Vegetarian or other special diets if ordered in advance. Wine available. No smoking.
1 Sitting-room. With TV, piano, bar. No smoking.
Small garden

Conveniently placed for exploring Dartmoor and the coast, this comfortable small hotel is run on friendly and relaxed terms by its owners, John and Gillian Wright. The rooms reflect the interests of these two avid collectors: over the years Gillian has amassed paintings, while John's passion is yesteryear's Matchbox cars – a collection nearing the 2000 mark. Gillian is now acquiring Cornish paintings and will display, for sale, work by local artists.

The sitting-room, with green and pink glazed cotton curtains and forest-green walls, opens on to a patio which has access for a wheelchair. A downstairs bedroom has also been fully equipped for the disabled traveller. The four-poster bedroom, with white embroidered canopy and bedcovers and wallpaper embossed with posies of roses, is popular with honeymooners. Several of the rooms have views of Dartmoor.

In the sunny dining-room, Gillian might serve crispy mushrooms, followed by peppered sirloin steak with brandy sauce, and Bakewell tart.

Within easy reach are the shire horse, glass-blowing and paperweight centres, Buckland Abbey, Tavistock's pannier market and the city of Plymouth.

PARFORD WELL

C(8) S

Devon

Sandy Park, Devon, TQ13 8JW Tel: 01647 433353
East of Okehampton. Nearest main road: A30 from Okehampton to Exeter (and M5, junction 31).

3 Bedrooms. £25–£30. Available: own bath/shower/toilet. No smoking.
1 Sitting-room. With stove, TV. No smoking.
Garden

When Tim Daniel, a former hotelier, decided to return to his ancestral roots, he chose a house which stands below the extravagantly styled Castle Drogo. And the well, from which the house took its name, is still to be found in the garden. It was bequeathed to the parishioners of Sandy Park in 1876 for domestic use.

Tim, who is a discerning collector of paintings and *objets d'art*, also has a good eye for colour. In the attractive sitting-room, with its off-white silk curtains and honey-yellow sofas, there is a prominent, Turneresque-style oil painting of Venice, and an inherited virginal that can be played by guests. There are two breakfast-rooms – one with a large oak table and a spectacular piece of artwork by modernist Lydia Baumann. The other, perfect for a twosome, also has something special: the rich cream cotton curtains once belonged to the Queen Mother. The bedrooms, which have almond-white walls, are given colour with glazed chintz and exotically patterned headboards. For dinners, Tim recommends the Sandy Park Inn, just a short walk away.

Reader's comment: Run most professionally.

PENPARK

C S

Devon

Bickington, Devon, TQ12 6LH Tel: 01626 821314 (Fax: 01626 821101)
West of Newton Abbot. Nearest main road: A38 from Exeter to Plymouth.

3 Bedrooms. £23–£28 (less for 2 nights or more). Available: own bath/shower/toilet; TV; balcony. No smoking.
Light suppers if ordered.
1 Sitting-room. With open fire, TV. No smoking.
Large garden

E-mail: gregson.penpark@ukgateway.net

This lovely country house, situated within Dartmoor National Park, was designed by Sir Clough Williams-Ellis (of Portmeirion fame) and has been much enhanced by Michael Gregson, a former Royal Marine, and his wife Madeleine. The light and spacious rooms exude elegance and charm, with their wealth of antique furniture, family portraits and *objets d'art*.

Breakfast is served in the sunny dining-room, which is furnished with mahogany and oak and has rag-rolled fern-green walls, or on the south-facing terrace.

One bedroom, with a two-seater settee and armchair, has pale peach walls complemented by fabrics in pastel shades. The windows and balcony overlook the gardens and beech woodland. Another bedroom, hung mostly with French prints, has the use of a pretty sitting-room.

Buzzards can be spotted nesting in the extensive grounds, an all-weather tennis court is available and there are wonderful views in all directions. Guests dine at the local pub, a three-minute walk away, or there is a good choice of eating-places slightly further afield.

Reader's comments: The welcome, the standard and hospitality among the best we have encountered.

V

Devon

PRESTON FARMHOUSE

C S

Harberton, Devon, TQ9 7SW Tel: 01803 862235
South of Totnes. Nearest main road: A381 from Totnes to Kingsbridge.

3 Bedrooms. £22.50 (less for 2 nights or more). Available: own bath/shower/toilet; TV. No smoking.
Dinner (by arrangement). £14 for 4 courses and coffee, at 7pm. Vegetarian or other special diets if ordered. No smoking.
2 Sitting-rooms. With woodstove, TV. No smoking.
Small garden

The Steers' house, built in 1680, has been in the same farming family for generations: Isabelle was born in it. All the bedrooms are spacious and light and have pretty coordinated fabrics. Next to the farmhouse kitchen is the dining-room, with beams and inglenook. At the back is a sunny courtyard, and an ancient iron-studded door.

There is good home cooking at dinner, with dishes as varied as fresh salmon from the River Dart, chicken Marengo, roasts, pies, baked Alaska, treacle pudding. The ingredients are mostly home-grown or local. (Alternatively, the local 13th-century pub has an imaginative dinner menu.) Breakfast comes on 'help-yourself' platters – conventional bacon and eggs or more unusual things like hog's pudding or smoked haddock.

Harberton is a picturesque cluster of old cottages with colourful gardens, set in a valley.

Readers' comments: Quite simply the best b & b. Most comfortable and delightful four days. Truly a gem. Unusual combination of efficiency, courtesy and kindness; food excellent. Delightful place to stay. Cannot praise too highly. Food and accommodation first class.

V

Devon

RIVERSDALE

C PT

Weare Giffard, Devon, EX39 4QR Tel: 01237 423676
South of Bideford. Nearest main road: A386 from Bideford to Great Torrington.

4 Bedrooms. £22–£25 (less for 7 nights or more). Available: own bath/shower/toilet; TV; views of river. No smoking.
2 Sitting-rooms. With stove (in one). No smoking.
Large garden
Closed from November to February.

For readers who thrilled to Henry Williamson's adventures of Tarka the Otter or those who yearn for quiet, the village of Weare Giffard is an ideal choice. When Eddie and Maggie Ellison lighted upon Riversdale, it was virtually derelict. Paintwork has laboriously been removed to reveal many fine pine features. Two bedrooms, which have views over stream and ponds, are small and pretty with pale walls highlighted with Maggie's stencilling. (A further two, with their own lounge, adjoin the main house.) A beamed sitting-room leads to the elegant dining-room where breakfast is served. Typically, this might include porridge, smoked haddock, cold meats and home-made jams. For evening meals, the village pub is just 50 yards away.

The Ellisons' home is immensely appealing, with its weeping willows in the garden and private fishing beat on the River Torridge. RHS Rosemoor, the Civil War town of Great Torrington, and the beaches of Westward Ho! and Instow are close by.

Readers' comments: Will return; the owners are friendly and helpful; it has all the facilities a holiday-maker could want.

SAMPSONS THATCH HOTEL & RESTAURANT **D M PT X**

Devon

Preston, Devon, TQ12 3PP Tel/Fax: 01626 354913
North of Newton Abbot. Nearest main road: A380 from Newton Abbot towards Exeter (and M5, junction 31).

10 Bedrooms. £20–£40 (less for 3 nights or more). Bargain breaks. Available: own bath/shower/toilet; TV. No smoking.
Dinner. £14.50 for 3 courses and coffee, or à la carte, from 7pm. Vegetarian or other special diets if ordered. Wine available. No smoking.
1 Sitting-room. With open fire. **Bar.**
Large garden

E-mail: nigel@sampsonsfarm.com

To this traditional Devon house, all whitewash and thatch, came a Cornish farming family who gave it a new way of life – as a renowned restaurant and small hotel. Nigel Bell runs both the restaurant and bed-and-breakfast with the help of his mother, Hazel.

Gourmet-class meals could include scallops with garlic, after which one might have the house speciality – a half-duckling in orange sauce with vegetables cooked to perfection – and then a lemon ice cream with biscuity topping. (There is a good wine list too.) Dinner is served in a low, cosy dining-room, with candle-lamps. Beyond the small bar is a snug, timbered sitting-room with log fire in an inglenook.

The way to the bedrooms (two with four-poster) is all steps and twists, for the house has grown in a higgledy-piggledy way since its probable beginnings in the 15th century. There are more bedrooms in two immacutely converted barns across the courtyard.

Readers' comments: Most welcoming, food excellent. Restaurant fabulous; very helpful. Hospitality outstanding, food exceptional. V

SLOOP INN **C D**

Devon

Bantham, Devon, TQ7 3AJ Tel: 01548 560489 (Fax: 01548 561940)
West of Kingsbridge. Nearest main road: A379 from Kingsbridge to Plymouth.

5 Bedrooms. £22–£35 **to readers of this book only until Easter.** Less for 4 nights or more. Bargain breaks. Available: own bath/shower/toilet; TV; views of sea/river.
Dinner. From £12 for 3 courses à la carte, at 7–10pm. Vegetarian or special diets if ordered. Wine available. Cigarette smoking only. **Light suppers.**
Bars. Cigarette smoking only.

It goes without saying that this 400-year-old inn by the sea has a history of smuggling. Owned by Neil Girling, the inn is unspoilt: everything one hopes that a village inn will be but rarely is, low-beamed, stone-flagged and snug. One of its several bars is made from old boat-timbers. Here you can take on the locals at a game of darts or table-skittles after enjoying an excellent bar meal; or stroll down to the sandy dunes to watch the sun set over the sea. Bathing, building sandcastles and exploring rock pools delight children; and there is surfing. Many of the plainly furnished bedrooms have a view of the sea or River Avon. (Sometimes the traffic noise is noticeable.) Early arrival outside pub hours can be arranged.

Soups are home-made and ham home-cooked; smoked salmon, crabs and steaks are all local produce. Fish is, of course, particularly good and fresh. All portions are generous.

Readers' comments: Food very good. A most enjoyable stay. Quiet, peaceful, idyllic scenery. Excellently furnished. Food the best I've eaten lately. Really comfortable. V

SOUTH HOOE CAPTAIN'S HOUSE

C D PT S X

Hole's Hole, Bere Alston, Yelverton, Devon, PL20 7BW Tel: 01822 840329 (Mobile: 07971 525558)

South-west of Tavistock. Nearest main road: A386 from Plymouth to Tavistock.

3 Bedrooms. £23–£25. Available: own bath/shower/toilet; views of river. No smoking.
Dinner (by arrangement). £15 for 4 courses and coffee, at times to suit guests. Vegetarian or other special diets if ordered. No smoking. **Light suppers** if ordered.
1 Sitting-room. With open fire, TV. No smoking.
Large garden

E-mail: southhooe@aol.com

Seen from the distance, Trish Dugmore's house appears to cling to a cliff of hanging oaks, but once you arrive all is rock-solid, with wondrous views over the Tamar River. From this old mine captain's house, a path leads steeply down to a landing stage for small boats; deep-water moorings can also be arranged. Trish is a flexible hostess and so breakfast might be served in the kitchen, the dining-room or outside on the lawn, and dinner likewise – alfresco dinners are candlelit.

The dining-room reflects Trish's Scottish heritage, with curtains and chair coverings in the Drummond tartan of her clan. Throughout the house are her mother's watercolours; and in one bathroom, there are blown-up photographs of Trish's three children in a donkey-drawn cart. (Martha, the donkey, lives close to the house and enjoys bowls of tea and carrots at any hour!) The simply furnished bedrooms have estuary views.

Dinner might comprise gazpacho, Tamar sea trout (caught by a neighbour) with home-grown vegetables, lemon roulade, and cheese and oatcakes to finish.

Readers' comments: Exceptionally comfortable, made most welcome. Perfect relaxation and tranquillity; idyllic setting.

STOWFORD HOUSE

Stowford, Devon, EX20 4BZ Tel: 01566 783415 (Fax: 01566 783109)

South-west of Okehampton. Nearest main road: A30 from Okehampton to Launceston.

4 Bedrooms. £23–£29 (less for 7 nights or more). Available: own bath/shower/toilet; TV. No smoking.
Dinner (by arrangement). £14 for 3 courses and coffee, at 7.30pm. Vegetarian or other special diets if ordered. Wine available. No smoking.
1 Sitting-room. With open fire, TV. No smoking.
Large garden

E-mail: alison@stowfordhouse.com

A chance sighting in an estate agent's window gave John Bennett and his partner Alison Pardoe the opportunity to fulfil their wish to own a former Georgian rectory and provide high-quality bed-and-breakfast accommodation. This pleasant young couple have acquired a fine house where the handsome front door, graceful interior archway and impressive staircase are reminders of its 18th-century origins.

The drawing-room is especially attractive. Here, gold wallpaper complements brocades and deep vermilion settees and chairs. In the candlelit dining-room, which has dusky pink walls, dark blue tablecloths and carpet, Alison serves such evening meals as fennel, Gruyère and onion tartlet, chicken with caramelized onions, and Ricotta, ginger and chocolate mousse.

Bedrooms are bright, airy and individually furnished. Some overlook the large garden which is at its best in May. One particularly sunny and spacious room, decorated in pretty pinks and yellow, has a three-seater sofa.

At nearby Lydford Gorge, one can walk by foaming waters with oak woods hanging overhead to the roaring 200-foot waterfall known as the White Lady.

V

Reader's comments: Excellent stay; wonderful food; delightful atmosphere; very welcoming.

TOWER INN

C(4) **D PT X**

Church Road, Slapton, Devon, TQ7 2PN Tel: 01548 580216
South-west of Dartmouth. Nearest main road: A379 from Dartmouth to Torcross.

3 Bedrooms. £25–£27.50. All have own shower/toilet; TV. No smoking.
Dinner. A la carte, from £15 for 3 courses and coffee, at 6–9.30pm (7pm in winter). Vegetarian or other special diets if ordered. Wine available.
Bar
Walled garden

E-mail: towerinn@slapton.org

Central to this picturesque, old village is Josh and Nicola Acfield's historic inn, which was originally part of the 14th-century Collegiate Chantry of St Mary, founded by Sir Guy de Brian, standard-bearer to King Edward III.

A narrow entrance leads to a small courtyard carpark fronting the whitewashed pub. Inside, it is just as we want inns to be – beamed, low ceilings, flagstone floors, wine-coloured walls and the glow of log fires (no vending machines). But it is the food (an award-winning chef is in the kitchen) which draws people here time and again. Tables and sconces are candlelit for dinner, when the varied menu might include smoked prawns with dill mayonnaise, braised lamb shank on celeriac and mint mash, and treacle tart.

The accommodation here, with its own entrance, is simple: bedrooms have pale green walls and chintzy curtains. Southwards are the superb beaches of Slapton Sands, the Slapton Ley freshwater lake and nature reserve, and various memorials testifying to the presence of American servicemen, who in 1943-44 took over this whole area to practise the D-Day landings.

Reader's comments: Exceptional; near to lovely coastline.

TWITCHEN FARM

C D M S X

Challacombe, Devon, EX31 4TT Tel: 01598 763568 (Fax: 01598 763310)
North-east of Barnstaple. Nearest main road: A399 from Ilfracombe to South Molton.

Devon

8 Bedrooms. £20–£27. All have own bath/shower/toilet; TV. No smoking.
Dinner (by arrangement). £16 for 3 courses and coffee, at 7pm. Vegetarian or other special diets if ordered.
1 Sitting-room. With TV.
Large garden

E-mail: holidays@twitchen.co.uk

The rugged beauty of Exmoor stretches as far as the eye can see and for this reason Twitchen Farm (from the Old English 'twicen', meaning the fork of a road) appeals to walkers, horse-riders and families. An ideal way of seeing the Exmoor ponies and red deer is to hire a waggon pulled by shire horses (available at a neighbouring farm).

Sisters Helen Asher and Jaye Jones originally took over a shell surrounded by derelict barns. The house is now filled with finds from auction rooms. Bedrooms in both the house and the converted barns have carpets, curtains and bed coverings in complementary shades. A Persian rug inherited from their great-grandfather hangs on the sitting-room wall; and to while away the evenings, board-games are supplied.

A fine Ham stone fireplace surrounding a wood-burning stove is a feature of the dining-room. Jaye, a professional cook, might offer leak and potato soup, coq au vin with fresh vegetables (organic), and sherry trifle. Bread comes from a nearby organic bakery. Gourmet weekends and celebrations can also be catered for, and stabling provided for guests' horses.

Devon

UPTON

C(12) **PT S**

Cullompton, Devon, EX15 1RA Tel/Fax: 01884 33097
South-east of Tiverton. Nearest main road: A373 from Cullompton to Honiton (and M5, junction 28).

3 Bedrooms. £22–£27 (less for 7 nights or more). All have own bath/shower/toilet; TV. No smoking.
1 Sitting-room. With stove, TV. No smoking.
Large garden

A driveway, flanked on one side by lawns and rosebeds and on the other by fields where racehorses graze, leads to a large, pink-washed, 17th-century farmhouse. Home to farmer Chris Down (a renowned amateur jockey), his wife Fay and son Richard, it has a simply spectacular interior. Fay has revealed a wealth of history by stripping away lath and plaster, lime wash and centuries of 'modernization' by successive generations. One unique discovery is a quotation written by a workman in the 1760s, which reads: 'When this you see remember me; speak by me as you find; I'm not like the weather cock which changeth with the wind.' Ceilings are now beamed, oak panelling lines the walls, huge stone fireplaces have been uncovered, and fine furniture left behind by previous owners and retrieved from outbuildings adorns these beautiful rooms. The bedrooms have richly coloured fabrics and newly installed bathrooms.

In addition to coarse fishing in their lake, croquet and stabling are offered by Upton's thoughtful hosts. Country pubs and restaurants are a short drive away.

Readers' comments: Were made very welcome; delicious breakfasts; peace and beautiful countryside. Supremely comfortable with a charming hostess.

Devon

WELLPRITTON FARM

C(5) **D X**

Holne, Devon, TQ13 7RX Tel: 01364 631273
West of Ashburton. Nearest main road: A38 from Exeter to Plymouth.

5 Bedrooms. £20–£22.50. Bargain breaks. Available: own bath/shower/toilet; TV. No smoking.
Dinner (by arrangement). £10–£12.50 for 2–3 courses and coffee, at 7pm. Vegetarian or other special diets if ordered. No smoking.
1 Sitting-room. With TV. No smoking.
Small garden

Tucked away in a fold of the gentle hills south of Dartmoor is this small farm where sheep and hens are kept; horses and goats too. (Children's riding by arrangement.) From the farm there are views of the moors.

The bedrooms are prettily furnished and supplied with fruit-squash and biscuits as well as tea. There are two family units of two rooms and a shower, and a ground-floor suite. A comfortable sitting-room is available to guests.

After a starter such as pâté, the main course at dinner might be roast lamb or poached salmon fillet with lemon butter sauce, followed by bread-and-butter pudding or treacle tart.

V *As this edition went to press, we learned that Wellpritton Farm had changed hands. The new owners are Susan and David Grey.*

WHITSTONE FARM

C(15) **PT**

Bovey Tracey, Devon, TQ13 9NA Tel: 01626 832258 (Fax: 01626 836494)
North of Newton Abbot. Nearest main road: A382 from Newton Abbot to Moretonhampstead.

3 Bedrooms. £25–£32.50 (less for 3 nights or more). Available: own bath/shower/toilet; TV. No smoking.
Dinner (by arrangement). £16–£18.50 for 2–3 courses and coffee, at times to suit guests. Vegetarian or other special diets if ordered. No smoking. **Light suppers** if ordered.
1 Sitting-room. With open fire. No smoking.
Large garden

E-mail: katie@reynolds2000.co.uk

A semi-derelict house and overgrown grounds have been turned into near-perfection within a year by Alan and Katie Bunn. On the three acres of land, planted with more than 250 specimen trees, there are drifts of daffodils and bluebells; while indoors, bedrooms are equally attractive. One has a kingsize bed, another a queensize. In the most spacious – all rose-pinks and white – an archway between two banks of cupboards leads to a large shower-room with its own separate lavatory.

Meals are served round a turn-of-the-century oak table which once did service in the boardroom of Alan's company. Katie, a past president of Ladies' Circle International (Round Table), is an imaginative cook. Dinner might include cheese-stuffed peaches with brandy topping, poached salmon with saffron sauce, and home-made trifle. Waxed pine gives warmth to the pretty sitting-room where guests are offered pre-dinner sherry.

Readers' comments: Delightful house, marvellous views, beautiful garden. Food excellent; nothing too much trouble. A pleasure to have such old-fashioned hospitality; food mouth-watering. Rooms of superior quality and superbly equipped; a treat to stay at this home. V

WOODLANDS

C(12) **PT S**

Lynbridge Road, Lynton, Devon, EX35 6AX Tel: 01598 752324 (Fax: 01598 753828)
Nearest main road: A39 from Minehead to Lynton.

6 Bedrooms. £20–£22 (less for 3 nights or more). All have own bath/shower/toilet; TV; views of river; balcony. No smoking.
Dinner (by arrangement). £13.95 for 3 courses and coffee, at 7pm. Vegetarian or other special diets if ordered. Wine available. No smoking. **Light suppers** if ordered.
1 Sitting-room. With open fire, TV. No smoking.
Large garden
Closed from November to February.

E-mail: info@woodlandsguesthouse.co.uk

The wonderful scenery and the quiet charm of the countryside prompted the Victorians to name Lynton and its sister village Lynmouth the 'Little Switzerland of England'. Today, it is still the tranquillity and the ruggedness which draws visitors to the area: you can go to the Valley of Rocks, an extraordinary site of weathered rock formations where wild goats roam the valley, or perhaps walk to Lynmouth, whose praises have been sung by Wordsworth, Coleridge and Southey. Another spectacular feature is the unique water-operated cliff railway, dating from 1890, which links Lynmouth with Lynton.

Woodlands, seemingly suspended from the hillside, has pretty, airy bedrooms and a sun lounge with views of a cascade weaving its way down to the West Lyn River. One bedroom opens on to a balcony from which to enjoy the same scene. For walkers, there is a drying-room with a washing machine.

A typical evening meal might comprise carrot-and-coriander soup, pan-fried breast of chicken with new potatoes and fresh vegetables, and apple crumble with custard.

As this edition went to press, we learned that Woodlands had changed hands. The new owners are Peter and Carole Hood.

WOODY BAY HOTEL

CDS

Woody Bay, Parracombe, Devon, EX31 4QX Tel: 01598 763264
West of Lynton. Nearest main road: A39 from Lynton to Barnstaple.

10 Bedrooms. £25 **to readers of this book only** –£32 (less for 2 nights or more). Bargain breaks. Available: own bath/shower/toilet; TV; views of sea; balcony.
Dinner. £20.50 for 3 courses and coffee, at 7.15–8.30pm. Vegetarian or other special diets if ordered. Wine available. No smoking. **Light suppers** if ordered.
1 Sitting-room. With open fire. Piano. No smoking.
Bar.
Large garden
Closed in January.

E-mail: reception@woodybayhotel.fsnet.co.uk

The views and the food draw guests back time and again to this small Victorian hotel, which is set on the coastal edge of Exmoor National Park. Every room, including the bedrooms, has a panoramic outlook on woods and ocean. The bay itself, a 15-minute walk away, is reached via a path which winds through beech and oak. Parents and children can spend the day here swimming and sandcastle-building. Alternatively, there is marvellous walking: a track, for instance, passes through a tunnel of trees which hugs the very edge of the cliffs.

The hotel sitting-room has been furnished with a high degree of comfort by Martin and Collette Petch, who want their less energetic guests simply to enjoy their surroundings. Accommodation in the pleasant bedrooms is varied. One has a small balcony and a gold-draped four-poster bed.

Martin, an enthusiastic cook, prepares dishes to order. Fresh, locally caught fish is a house speciality. Dinner choices might include sea bass or Devon beef fillet, then bread-and-butter pudding or plums in Marsala.

Reader's comments: Wonderful, spent the best New Year of my life there; a star.

For a list of SOTBT houses that are in or close to the great National Parks of England and Wales, see p.ix.

Houses which accept the discount vouchers on page ii are marked with a V symbol next to the relevant entries.

Book well ahead: many of these houses have few rooms. Do not expect dinner if you have not booked it or if you arrive late.

Addresses shown are to enable you to locate a house on a map. They are not necessarily complete postal addresses (though the essential post-code is included), and detailed directions for finding a house should be obtained from the owner.

DORSET

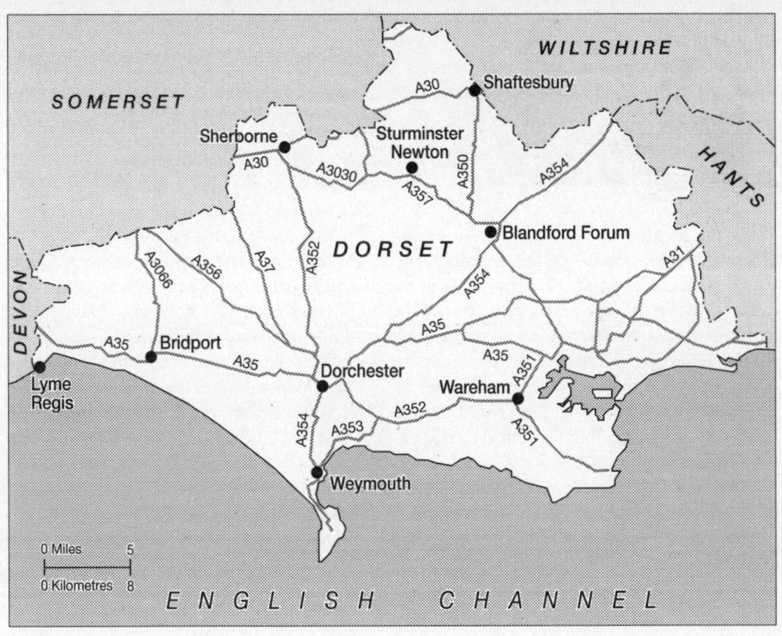

APPLYING FOR INCLUSION IN SOTBT **Many proprietors ask for their houses to be included in this book, and – although few can be accepted – such applications are welcomed, particularly from areas not already well covered; *provided that* the b & b price is within the book's limits (see page xiv). Ideally, either dinner or light snacks should be available in the evening. There is no charge for an entry but, compiling the book being expensive, nearly all proprietors make a contribution at the end of each year (no bills are issued). Every house has to be visited first and it may be some time before this takes place. Brochures, prices, menus, etc. should be posted to: Jan Bowmer (SOTBT), c/o Arrow Books, 20 Vauxhall Bridge Road, London SW1V 2SA. No phone calls please.**

Dorset

BRADLE FARM

C(8) S

Church Knowle, Dorset, BH20 5NU Tel: 01929 480712 (Fax: 01929 481144)
South of Wareham. Nearest main road: A351 from Wareham to Swanage.

3 Bedrooms. £23–£25 (less for 3 nights or more). Bargain breaks. All have own bath/shower/toilet; TV.
Light suppers if ordered.
1 Sitting-room. With stove.
Large garden

E-mail: hole.bradle@farmersweekly.net

From this handsome Victorian house of local Purbeck stone there are beautiful views – across the duck-pond – of the so-called Isle of Purbeck and of the gaunt ruins of Corfe Castle looming over all. Window-seats at the shuttered casements help you to make the most of these, with unlimited help-yourself tea and home-made cake in hand. Upstairs, low corridors lead to bedrooms (one is particularly spacious) with similar views.

The Hole family, represented these days by John and Gillian, have lived here for generations, with what is now 1400 acres of their mixed farm (cows, sheep, corn) stretching right down to the sea and up to high Swyre Head. The long coastal footpath goes through their land: you can watch milking and lambing or help feed the chickens . . . or just laze by the log stove.

Although Gillian sometimes provides guests with snack suppers, she will make bookings at the thatched New Inn which serves good Dorset meals – it has a skittle alley too.

The coast is only one and a half miles from the house, with beautiful walks there and inland as well.

V *Readers' comments:* Superb. Welcoming hospitality.

Dorset

BROADSTONE BARN

C(12) S

Walditch, Dorset, DT6 4LA Tel: 01308 427430
East of Bridport. Nearest main road: A35 from Bridport to Dorchester.

3 Bedrooms. £22.50–£25 (minimum 2 nights). Less for 4 nights or more. Available: own bath/shower/toilet. No smoking.
1 Sitting-room. With log stove, TV. No smoking.
Closed from November to March.

E-mail: broadstone@dial.pipex.com

A fine old barn of golden stone was most handsomely converted, with its original character carefully retained, to make this beautiful house. Rugged stone walls and slate floors contrast with a splendid open-tread spiral staircase with a rope handrail. Val and Guy Barnes have grouped sofas round the stove in the sitting-room, with glass doors on both sides. In the dining-room, a particularly impressive pine table and fiddleback chairs stand under old rafters still exposed to view and a new gallery where there are wicker armchairs. Adjoining this gallery are attractive bedrooms (one has windows on three sides); one of the bathrooms is particularly elegant, its tiles patterned with cornstalks. Outdoors is an area chequered with cobbles and paving around a raised, circular lily-pond; a small lawn with seats; and a vegetable garden frequented by badgers.

At breakfast, not only marmalade and bread are home-made but yogurt and fruit compote too; the bacon and eggs come from a local farm. There is unlimited tea and coffee available in the sitting-room at all times.

Dorset is a wonderful county for walkers, particularly along the nearby coast, while those who want to explore it on wheels can borrow mountain bicycles at the house.

CERNE RIVER COTTAGE

C PT

8 The Folly, Cerne Abbas, Dorset, DT2 7JR Tel: 01300 341355
North of Dorchester. Nearest main road: A352 from Dorchester to Sherborne.

Dorset

2 Bedrooms. £24–£28. Available: own bath/shower/toilet. No smoking.
1 Sitting-room. With open fire, TV. No smoking.
Small garden

A good view of the Cerne Abbas giant, an enormous pagan chalk-cut figure, is afforded from the twin room of this pretty, 18th-century thatched cottage. At one time a master tanner's house, it is now the home of Ginny Williams-Ellis, her husband Nick, a landscape gardener, and their children. Not surprisingly, their garden (where guests can have breakfast in summer) is particularly pleasant, with the River Cerne meandering through it.

They have worked hard to restore their home. In the dining-room guests can enjoy local organic milk and eggs for their breakfast, as well as a range of home-made marmalade and jams. Bedrooms are simply furnished in pastel shades; the double has a brass bedstead and view of the garden. Good evening meals can be had at any of Cerne's inns. The village has a fine church, abbey ruins and a working pottery to visit.

Readers' comments: Thoroughly recommended. Made very comfortable.

V

CHURCH COTTAGE

C PT S

West Knighton, Dorset, DT2 8PF Tel: 01305 852243
South-east of Dorchester. Nearest main road: A352 from Wareham to Dorchester.

Dorset

2 Bedrooms. £23–£25 (less for 3 nights or more). Both have own bath/shower/toilet; TV. No smoking.
Garden
Closed from mid-December to mid-January.
E-mail: info@church-cottage.com

Tucked up next to the wall surrounding the village's 12th-century church is this 300-year-old cottage, which was once a cheese-house and creamery. In more recent times it has become the home of Peter and Renée East, who took on the task of restoring a house which had not been touched for 30 years.

The Easts have been sympathetic modernizers and they are relaxed and accommodating hosts. Guests are offered a leisurely breakfast, where the menu includes the freshest of free-range eggs, home-made jams, marmalade, yogurt and fruit salad. It is served in a cosy room which has a sitting-area too. Renée can also provide reflexology treatment, an extension of her interest in remedial yoga.

The cottagey bedrooms (hyacinth-blue for one, soft apple-green for the other) have antique iron and brass bedsteads fitted with king-size mattresses.

The village pub is recommended for dinner. Thomas Hardy fans will appreciate the fact that the church was renovated by his brother and by Hardy himself, wearing his 'architect's' hat. At the time, he was also writing his last major novel, *Jude the Obscure*.

V

Dorset

FROGMORE FARM

C D M X

Chideock, Dorset, DT6 6HT Tel: 01308 456159
West of Bridport. On A35 from Bridport to Honiton.

3 Bedrooms. £20 (less for 2 nights or more). Bargain breaks. Available: own bath/shower/toilet; TV; views of sea. No smoking.
Dinner (by arrangement). £10 for 2 courses and coffee, at 7pm. Vegetarian or other special diets if ordered. No smoking. **Light suppers** if ordered.
1 Sitting-room. With stove, TV. No smoking.
Large garden

Nestling in a valley with distant sea views is a sturdy farmhouse with a wide, colonnaded verandah leading to lawns and a rambling garden. From there, two paths – both quite rugged walking – finish at the shore's edge. Tony and Susan Norman's home is ideally placed to explore some of Dorset's finest coastline, while within their own 90 acres, deer, fox, badger and bat can be observed.

Throughout the house are reminders of its name – frogs (of the inanimate kind) pop up everywhere, even on tiles in one of the bathrooms. Susan, an inveterate collector, has put an American church organ in the comfortable sitting-room; in another spot is an old cash register; and in a window alcove, a series of Toby jugs.

The sunny bedrooms are full of colour, with patterned curtains and carpets. One spacious room has its own entrance, and a converted stable in the garden is a mini-suite, with a kitchen and secluded courtyard.

Susan is a traditional cook and dinner might comprise a roast with meat from their own stock or steak and kidney pie, followed by rice pudding or apple pie.

Dorset

GOLD COURT

C(10) PT

St John's Hill, Wareham, Dorset, BH20 4LZ Tel/Fax: 01929 553320
Nearest main road: A351 from Poole to Swanage.

3 Bedrooms. £25. All have own bath/shower/toilet; TV; views of river.
Dinner (by arrangement in winter only). £10 for 3 courses and coffee, at 7.30–8pm. Vegetarian or other special diets if ordered.
Walled garden

Long before the Great Fire of Wareham in 1762 the local goldsmith lived and worked on this spot; hence the name of the present Georgian house, rebuilt on the 13th-century foundations of that former dwelling. Anthea and Michael Hipwell came here from the Old Vicarage, Affpuddle, in 1998, and offer the same unbeatable level of care enjoyed by readers in their former home: their attention to detail extends through elegance and comfort to the provision of an old-fashioned Roberts radio in every bedroom. Dinner – offered in winter only – might comprise chicken and tarragon in lemon sauce, tarte tatin, cheese and coffee; at other times Wareham's wealth of restaurants provides ample choice.

Situated as it is on the very edge of Dorset's designated Area of Outstanding Natural Beauty, Wareham in general – and Gold Court House in particular – is ideally placed for walkers and cyclists who want to explore this lovely part of the south coast. The River Frome runs just minutes from the house; there are excellent walks here, or along the Purbeck Way to Corfe Castle (you can return by bus).

GRAY'S FARMHOUSE

C D S

Dorset

Clift Lane, Toller Porcorum, Dorset, DT2 0EJ Tel/Fax: 01308 485574
North-east of Bridport. Nearest main road: A356 from Crewkerne towards Dorchester.

2 Bedrooms. £25–£30 (less for 3 nights or more). Bargain breaks. Both have own bath/shower/toilet; TV. No smoking.
Large garden

E-mail: rosie@farmhousebnb.co.uk

Rosie and Roger Britton's house is set in one of west Dorset's hidden beauty-spots. Not far away are Kingcombe nature reserve and Eggardon Hill, one of the finest hill forts in this area. From the grounds of the farmhouse, guests have direct access to a network of footpaths and bridleways through ancient wildflower meadows and woodland teeming with wildlife.

So that she would have more time to paint, Rosie, like her husband, took early retirement from the teaching profession. Examples of her work, which hang throughout the house, show her to be a gifted artist.

The 1840s farmhouse retains many of its original features and Rosie's eye for colour has enhanced this interesting home. From the spacious double bedroom, there are views of the garden sloping down to a stream and the countryside beyond.

Breakfast is served in the kitchen, warmed by a large range, or in the dining-room where French doors open on to the garden. The menu includes newly laid free-range eggs, and such options as black pudding and kippers. Guests can dine at pubs which are a 10-minute drive away.

V

HOLYLEAS HOUSE

C D P T S

Dorset

Buckland Newton, Dorset, DT2 7DP Tel: 01300 345214 (Fax: 01305 264488)
North of Dorchester. Nearest main road: A352 from Dorchester to Sherborne.

3 Bedrooms. £22.50–£25. Available: own bath/shower/toilet; TV. No smoking.
Light suppers if ordered.
1 Sitting-room. With open fire. No smoking.
Small garden

E-mail: tiabunkall@holyleas.fsnet.co.uk

On arrival, you might find a wood-engraved notice hanging on the front door, saying: 'I'm pottering in the garden'. For the half-acre walled garden, with its herbaceous border, is owner Tia Bunkall's passion and provides a delightful backdrop to this gracious, mid-19th-century country house.

The guests' sitting-room, which overlooks the village cricket pitch (Tia's husband Julian is an enthusiastic player), is especially pretty. Pelmeted curtains of Colefax & Fowler fabric in green and cream, and splashed with pink tea-roses, complement the colours of the sofa and chairs. Antique furnishings, table lamps and the warm glow of a log fire all further contribute to making this a most restful room.

In the bedrooms, which have views across open countryside, Tia has used flowery fabrics in sunshine yellow, blues and peach. Bathrobes and hot-water bottles are provided. Forest-green walls, polished floorboards, mahogany furniture and another open hearth set the scene in the breakfast-room. There are several good pubs nearby for dinner.

The famous prehistoric giant is cut into the hillside at Cerne Abbas, close by. All around are Hardy sites and associations.

V

Dorset

KIMMERIDGE FARMHOUSE C(10)

Kimmeridge, Dorset, BH20 5PE Tel: 01929 480990
South of Wareham. Nearest main road: A351 from Wareham to Swanage.

3 Bedrooms. £22–£24 (less for 3 nights or more mid-week, in low season). Bargain breaks. All have own bath/shower/toilet; TV. No smoking.
Dinner (by arrangement). £12.50–£15 for 2–3 courses and coffee, at 7pm. Vegetarian or other special diets if ordered. No smoking. **Light suppers** if ordered.
1 Sitting-area. No smoking.
Large garden

With fields reaching right to the cliff edge and Kimmeridge Bay only a short walk away, Kimmeridge Farmhouse is set in a particularly attractive part of coastal Dorset.

The present 1830s farmhouse is next to the village church, and itself has 14th-century monastic origins. Accommodation is both stylish and comfortable. One bedroom, in blue and white, has smart chintz curtains edged with a blue fringe, while others have swags and tailed pelmets or green-and-cream check upholstered headboards, all made by Annette Hole. A cosy sitting-area on the first floor overlooks the garden, and has plenty of information on things to see and do in the area. Jeremy Hole is happy to show guests aspects of daily life on the farm, such as milking or lambing.

Annette serves traditional farmhouse breakfasts and such evening meals as tomato and basil soup, chicken casserole in cream and mushroom sauce, and raspberry pavlova or fruit salad to finish. (Cream teas and packed lunches now available too.) After dinner, you could stroll across the fields to the headland and see one of Britain's many forgotten follies: Clavell Tower. It was built in 1820 by a reclusive vicar, but is now sadly derelict.

V

Dorset

LINTON COTTAGE PT

Abbotsbury, Dorset, DT3 4JL Tel/Fax: 01305 871339
North-west of Weymouth. Nearest main road: A35 from Dorchester to Bridport.

3 Bedrooms. £22.50–£28 (less for 7 nights or more). Bargain breaks. All have own bath/shower/toilet; TV. No smoking.
1 Sitting-room. With open fire. No smoking.
Small garden
Closed from Christmas to mid-January.

E-mail: queenbee@abbotsbury.co.uk

Find the roadside beehive with the signs: 'Honey and Dorset Apple Cake for Sale' and you have found the home of John and Maralyn Harman. The honey from John's hives is on the breakfast-table and either the apple cake or Welsh cake, in honour of Maralyn's ancestry, is provided in the packed lunches if requested. The Harmans are an enterprising family: Maralyn and her three cello-playing children organize musical evenings and holidays in their music room.

The breakfast-cum-sitting-room, with gold and burgundy walls and a border frieze to match the fruits in the curtains, has views of 14th-century St Catherine's Chapel. Upstairs, the simply furnished bedrooms, which have bed canopies and pretty wallpapers, look across farming land. There is also a ground-floor bedroom.

Both the privately owned village, which has many picture-postcard cottages, and the surrounding area are steeped in history. Within walking distance are the remains of the 11th-century Benedictine abbey, its tithe barn and Britain's only nesting colony of mute swans, founded by the monks. For evening meals, there are several nearby pubs.

LOWER FIFEHEAD FARM

C D S

Fifehead St Quintin, Sturminster Newton, Dorset, DT10 2AP Tel/Fax: 01258 817335
West of Blandford Forum. Nearest main road: A357 from Blandford Forum towards Sherborne.

3 Bedrooms. £22.50–£27.50 (less for 7 nights or more). Available: own bath/shower/toilet. No smoking.
Light suppers if ordered.
1 Sitting-room. With open fire, TV. No smoking.
Large garden

This farmhouse, which has the date 1739 carved on one wall but is believed to have 15th-century origins, merited mention by the architectural historian Nikolaus Pevsner, who wrote after his visit: 'It is worth a pilgrimage to look at the roped mullion windows'.

The 400-acre dairy-farm, owned by Brian and Jill Miller, is in the Develish Valley and on the edge of Blackmore Vale, beloved by Thomas Hardy fans. Jill, who rides and keeps horses, was thrilled when one of them won a hunter-chase race at Cheltenham.

Bedrooms are comfortable and the colour blue – Jill's favourite – is to be seen in studded velvet headboards, carpets and a patchwork quilt with a wedding-rings pattern. A mahogany banqueting table is the centrepiece of the breakfast-room. In here, shelves hold a turn-of-the-century dinner service, designed by Jill's grandmother at the time of her wedding.

For dinner, guests can walk to Plumber Manor, situated on a weir, or drive to nearby pubs.

Reader's comments: Spotlessly clean and comfortable; the silence of the night broken only by foxes and owls.

V

MELBURY MILL

Melbury Abbas, Dorset, SP7 0DB Tel: 01747 852163
South of Shaftesbury. Nearest main road: A350 from Shaftesbury to Blandford Forum.

3 Bedrooms. £25–£27.50. All have own bath/shower/toilet. No smoking.
1 Sitting-room. With woodstove, TV. No smoking.
Large garden

By lovely Cranborne Chase, a watermill at Melbury Abbas was mentioned in Domesday Book. On its Saxon foundations the present Melbury Mill was built in the 18th century (its historic wheel still turns). Trained as an architect, Richard Bradley-Watson has done a beautiful conversion of beamed outbuildings to provide two exceptionally good bedrooms with en suite facilities overlooking the millpond. In the house itself there is a third, large bedroom, sitting-room with woodstove, and a stone-flagged dining-room. For dinners, there are pubs within a two-mile radius. Lovely walks along lanes and footpaths lead to Melbury Beacon and Fontmell Down, both owned by the National Trust.

There are plenty of good drives around here. For instance, one might go via Mere to visit the world-famous landscaped gardens and lake of Stourhead and the 18th-century mansion itself (full of art treasures). Alternatively, one could drive to Tollard Royal on a road of hairpin bends that is an outstanding scenic route.

Readers' comments: Unsurpassed for peace. Very hospitable and comfortable. Delightful; room lovely, breakfast excellent; we can recommend it wholeheartedly. Rooms extremely comfortable, hosts charming and setting delightful.

Dorset

MUSTON MANOR

C(10) **D PT**

Piddlehinton, Dorset, DT2 7SY Tel/Fax: 01305 848242
North-east of Dorchester. Nearest main road: A35 from Poole to Dorchester.

2 Bedrooms. £22–£30 (less for 4 nights or more). Both have own bath/shower/toilet; TV. No smoking.
Light suppers if ordered.
2 Sitting-rooms. With open fire (in one). No smoking.
Large garden

For over three centuries the ancestral home of a branch of the Churchill family, Muston Manor is a beautifully proportioned, 17th-century, ochre-coloured brick mansion, with mullioned windows, dormers and a handsome two-storeyed porch. Paddy and Barry Paine have lived here for some 25 years and now offer b & b in their elegant and spacious home.

One suite of three rooms comprises a bedroom in blues and cream, which looks out over the five acres of grounds, a sitting-room with comfortable yellow wing-chairs and, leading off this, an attractive bathroom with pink ribbon-patterned walls. The other bedroom is equally attractive, as is the light and airy main sitting-room downstairs. The breakfast-room, overlooking the heated swimming-pool, houses Barry's collection of Wisdens and a group of commemorative plates marking an Arctic expedition led by one of his ancestors.

For evening meals, the village has three pubs offering varied and imaginative menus. Athelhampton, one of England's finest 15th-century houses, is nearby, while on a less grand
V scale the church at Piddletrenthide is also worth a visit.

Dorset

OLD FORGE

C PT S

Fanners Yard, Compton Abbas, Dorset, SP7 0NQ Tel/Fax: 01747 811881
South of Shaftesbury. On A350 from Shaftesbury to Blandford Forum.

3 Bedrooms. £22.50 **(one room for readers of this book only)**–£25. Available: own bath/shower/toilet; TV. No smoking.
1 Sitting-room. With stove. No smoking.
Large garden

Tim and Lucy Kerridge are a young couple who take pride and joy in preserving the past. And they are to be admired for their perseverance in taking over a series of derelict buildings and transforming what was the village wheelwright's workshop into a home of considerable charm and character. Tim, who is passionate about maintaining Dorset's heritage, also restores post-war classic cars. Rescued beams, stone and templates have been incorporated into the house; while for the warm and pretty bedrooms with sloping ceilings, Lucy has found such treasures as a wrought-iron bedstead with little 19th-century oil paintings set in the frame, stencilled Edwardian furniture and a Dutch pine bed.

Outside, the garden leads to walks through a network of lanes and bridleways across the surrounding downs. No evening meals, but pub food is available within one mile.

The ancient nearby town of Shaftesbury is perched high on a hilltop overlooking the lovely Blackmore Vale, and from its centre the famous, cobbled street of Gold Hill makes a steep descent.

Readers' comments: Charming couple; wonderful breakfast. Nothing to criticize, only praise.

POWERSTOCK MILL FARM

CDS

Dorset

Powerstock, Dorset, DT6 3SL Tel: 01308 485213 (Fax: 01308 485123)
North-east of Bridport. Nearest main road: A3066 from Bridport to Beaminster.

3 Bedrooms. £22 (less for 3 nights or more).
Dinner (by arrangement). £10–£15 for 2–4 courses and coffee, at times to suit guests. Vegetarian or other special diets if ordered. **Light suppers** if ordered.
1 Sitting-room. With open fire, TV.
Large garden

The great iron waterwheel at this farm ceased to turn long ago but the wandering stream still goes by the old farmhouse in its secluded valley, so sheltered that palms grow there. It can be reached by a dramatic drive over Eggardon Hill (the 'Egdon Heath' of Hardy and Holst) and along lanes where celandines and bluebells throng the banks. The sea is only five miles away.

This is a truly traditional farm: board ceilings, tiled floors, dresser with blue-and-white china, coal fire and the slow tick of a grandfather clock – with the landowner's ducal coat-of-arms on one wall. There are cows, chickens and ducks around; and for dinner, using organic produce, Elaine Marsh serves a proper farm meal – soup, a roast, apple crumble, and cheeses.

There are Iron Age hill forts, and many literary associations in this lovely area.

Readers' comments: A lovely farm. Pretty and spotless bedrooms. Warm welcome, delicious breakfast, hope to go back.

V

RASHWOOD LODGE

C(5) PT

Dorset

Clappentail Lane, Lyme Regis, Dorset, DT7 3LZ Tel: 01297 445700
Nearest main road: A35 from Dorchester to Honiton.

3 Bedrooms. £22–£26. Available: own bath/shower/toilet; TV; views of sea. No smoking.
Garden
Closed from December to January.

Lyme is one of those delightful small coastal towns which has not sold its soul to tourism. It has many claims to fame: Jane Austen associations; fossils found along its beaches; the landing of the Duke of Monmouth in 1685 to start his abortive rebellion; and the historic Cobb where *The French Lieutenant's Woman* was filmed (the author John Fowles lives locally). It is here that Mike (a builder) and Diana Lake have created a home of considerable charm. Set in gardens of immaculately kept lawns and shrubs, this octagonal-shaped house was built to take advantage of Dorset sunshine and views of the sea – a 15-minute stroll away.

The light and airy bedrooms have flower-sprigged wallpapers and white embroidered bedlinen. One double has a king-size bed, and a pretty, little twin-bedded room has the sole use of a spacious blue and white bathroom, where cherubs romp on the tiles and the window is draped with a scroll of voile. The breakfast-room and entrance hall hold Diana's collections of decorative china. For dinner, there are numerous pubs within walking distance.

V

Dorset

RED HOUSE

C(8) PT

Sidmouth Road, Lyme Regis, Dorset, DT7 3ES Tel/Fax: 01297 442055
Nearest main road: A3052 from Lyme Regis to Exeter.

3 Bedrooms. £20–£27 (less for 4 nights or more). Available: own bath/toilet; TV; views of sea. No smoking.
Light suppers (on first night of stay only) if ordered.
Garden
Closed from December to February.

E-mail: red.house@virgin.net

This dignified 'twenties house was built for Aldis (inventor of the famous signal-lamps which bear his name) on a superb site with a 40-mile sea view south-east as far as Portland Bill. It is a house with handsome features – iron-studded oak doors, leaded casements and window-seats, for example. On sunny mornings, you can take breakfast on the wide verandah and enjoy sea breezes while you eat; at your feet, sloping lawns with colourful rhododendrons, camellias, fuchsias and wisteria. On chilly mornings, breakfast is served in an attractive room with a fire. (For dinner, Lyme Regis has a plethora of eating-places.)

Each bedroom is equipped with armchairs, TV, a refrigerator, and fresh flowers – the aim being to provide individual bedsitters for guests, as there is no full-size sitting-room.

The house is full of pictures and objects from the Normans' overseas postings (Anthony was in the Navy) and in the garden is a timber cabin where Vicky makes exceptionally pretty cloth dolls: she also teaches this skill.

Readers' comments: Splendid views and pleasant gardens. Rooms perfectly equipped. Top rate.

Dorset

REW COTTAGE

C D PT

Buckland Newton, Dorset, DT2 7DN Tel/Fax: 01300 345467
South of Sherborne. Nearest main road: A352 from Sherborne to Dorchester.

3 Bedrooms. £22.50–£25 (less for 5 nights or more). Available: own bath/shower/toilet; TV. No smoking.
Light suppers if ordered.
1 Sitting-room. With open fire, TV, piano.
Large garden

Approaching Buckland Newton from Dorchester by the cross-country route, look out for a signpost, just south of the village, with a collection of perhaps the most intriguing village names in the whole county: Mappowder, Folly and Plush. The first was home to T.F. Powys whose literary writings, along with those of his brothers, plunge one into the Dorset–Somerset scene.

At Rew Cottage the emphasis is on informality. Visitors share Annette and Rupert McCarthy's large sitting-room, and breakfast is taken in the cosy kitchen. Bedrooms, all with rural views, are prettily furnished, with mementoes of the McCarthys' years spent abroad dotted about. As a retired cavalry officer, Rupert is a keen horseman and knows every inch of the surrounding countryside, so he can advise guests on interesting walks. One takes you to the Iron Age ramparts at Dungeon Hill, carpeted with violets and primroses in springtime.

For evening meals, try the Brace of Pheasants at Plush or the Smith's Arms at Godmanstone, England's tiniest pub. Mediaeval Sherborne's superb 15th-century abbey of golden stone deserves a lingering visit as do its two castles, one with gardens and parkland designed by Capability Brown.

V

SEAHILL HOUSE

C(8) **PT S**

Dorset

Seahill Lane, Seatown, Dorset, DT6 6JT Tel: 01297 489801 (Fax: 01297 489526)
West of Bridport. Nearest main road: A35 from Bridport to Axminster.

3 Bedrooms. £25–£27 (less for 2 nights or more). Available: own shower/toilet; TV; views of sea. No smoking.
Light suppers if ordered.
1 Sitting-room. With TV. No smoking.
Large garden

E-mail: jane@seahill.co.uk

High up on Dorset's Heritage Coast and in a designated Area of Outstanding Natural Beauty, this handsome house occupies a spectacular position. From its many windows are sweeping views of sea, countryside and rolling hills, as well as Golden Cap, the highest point on the south coast.

Seatown, a small hamlet of thatched and stone cottages grouped round the mouth of the River Winniford, attracts both walkers (the South-West Coast Path passes through here) and fossil-seekers. But for guests who want a less strenuous holiday, Adrian and Jane Tamone have thoughtfully provided wind-sheltered seats in their extensive grounds, from which sea views can be enjoyed.

Two of the pretty bedrooms, one yellow, one blue, with complementary bedlinen and wicker chairs, share a large bathroom. A third twin room, decorated in peach, has an en suite shower.

The Aga-cooked breakfast is served round a William IVth table in the blue and terracotta dining-room, or in fine weather it may be served outside on the patio. For dinner, guests stroll down a rural lane to the unspoilt Seatown pub. V

STICKLAND FARMHOUSE

C(9) **M PT S X**

Dorset

Winterborne Stickland, Dorset, DT11 0NT Tel/Fax: 01258 880119
West of Blandford Forum. Nearest main road: A354 from Blandford to Dorchester.

3 Bedrooms. £22.50–£25 (less for 5 nights or more). All have own shower/toilet; TV. No smoking.
1 Sitting-room. With stove, TV. No smoking.
Garden

Within a few miles of Bulbarrow Hill, one of the highest vantage points in the county, Winterborne Stickland is another secluded Dorset village. Here, this cob, brick and flint former farmhouse is full of unusual family pieces accumulated over the years by Sandy and Paul Crofton-Atkins. Tapestries made by Paul's mother and decorative colonial mirrors sit comfortably beside intricately tooled leather-bound volumes and antique pieces from South America and Sandy's family home in Ireland.

Bedrooms are all individual. One, downstairs, has exposed brick walls hung with family portraits, and Florida fishing scenes in vibrant colours displayed in its shower-room. The breakfast-room is cosy and stylish. For evening meals, the Shire Horse pub in the village has a good menu.

At Turnworth, the next village northwards, is the only Dorset church whose restoration was supervised, and in part designed, by Thomas Hardy during his time as an architect. Eastwards lies Chettle House, a fine example of the English baroque style; the handsome market town of Blandford Forum; and Wimborne Minster where Kingston Lacy has outstanding paintings and wooded parkland for relaxing walks. V

Dorset

STOURCASTLE LODGE

X

Gough's Close, Sturminster Newton, Dorset, DT10 1BU Tel: 01258 472320 (Fax: 01258 473381)

South-west of Shaftesbury. Nearest main road: A357 from Blandford Forum to Wincanton.

5 Bedrooms. £25–£38 **(less 10% for 2 nights or more half board to readers showing the current edition of this book on arrival).** Available: own bath/shower/toilet; TV. No smoking.
Dinner. £19.50 for 4 courses and coffee, at 7.30pm. Vegetarian or other special diets if ordered. No smoking.
1 Sitting-room. With open fire.
Large garden

Gourmets seek out this secluded town house, for peace as well as good food. Although just off the market place, Gough's Close is traffic-free and quiet: a narrow lane opening out into a green and pleasant place, with the River Stour beyond. The 17th-century Lodge has been agreeably furnished by Jill Hookham-Bassett, with soft greens and pinks predominating. Everything is spick-and-span, the bedrooms cottagey in style, and all have garden views.

Ken and Jill, who achieved a gold star for cooking when she trained at Ealing Technical College, provide food well above average. A typical dinner might be kedgeree, chicken cooked in tarragon and mushroom sauce, and charlotte Malakoff (made with cream and almonds). An unassuming house with a lot to offer in the way of hospitality.

Readers' comments: Jill's cooking was superb. Delightful. Made to feel welcome and at home. Room charming. Enjoyed our visit so much. Delicious food. Evening meal was highlight of my stay; breakfast faultless with vast array of choice.

Dorset

SYCAMORES

C(9) PT

Littlehurst Close, Charmouth, Dorset, DT6 6RZ Tel: 01297 560926

West of Bridport. Nearest main road: A35 from Bridport to Axminster.

2 Bedrooms. £20–£22.50 (less for 3 nights or more). Available: own bath/shower/toilet; TV. No smoking.
Small garden
Closed from early December to January.

Secreted away in this small, unspoilt seaside village is a large old garden, surrounded by equally old stone walls. Three white Georgian-style houses have been built here and one is the home of Jenny Betteridge and her husband Mike, an estate agent.

Jenny, the most welcoming of hostesses, has chosen warm peach and autumnal shades for both the breakfast-room and one of the bedrooms. In contrast, the twin-bedded room, with a view of the church tower and within the sound of its bells, has Oxford-blue bedcovers and curved headboards with blue-and-white pleated trims to match the curtains. Because the bedrooms share a spacious, interconnecting bathroom, Jenny will only make the second bedroom available if a family or group of friends are travelling together. Guests can dine at local pubs which are within walking distance.

Views from the house include Stonebarrow Hill, where there are scenic and undemanding walks across National Trust land. The beach is only five minutes away.

Reader's comments: A lovely house; made to feel very welcome; Mrs Betteridge is charming; fantastic breakfast.

V

VARTREES HOUSE

C(10) **D PT S**

Moreton, Dorset, DT2 8BE Tel: 01305 852704
East of Dorchester. Nearest main road: A35 from Dorchester to Poole.

Dorset

3 Bedrooms. £20–£25. One has own shower. No smoking.
1 Sitting-room. With TV, piano.
Large garden

When Thomas Hardy's most trusted friend, the inspired eccentric Hermann Lea, built himself this handsome house, Hardy helped to name it Vartrees, after the nearby River Frome – once Var. It is in Arts and Crafts style, with much use of Japanese oak, maple, exposed brickwork, iron-latched doors, and big windows overlooking three acres of woodland garden, brilliant with colour at azalea time.

It is now the home of Doris Haggett, an entertaining and much-travelled hostess. Pen and ink sketches of Samoan faces, Indian silk paintings and Moroccan artefacts decorate the spacious and comfortable rooms. Breakfast is served around a D-end Georgian table. Afterwards, guests gravitate to the terrace from where the birds, squirrels and deer which inhabit the garden can be seen. For dinner, there is an excellent pub within a 10-minute walk.

Moreton's parish church is notable for its Laurence Whistler engraved glass windows and as the burial place of T.E. Lawrence. This is the valley ('green trough of sappiness') where Tess of the D'Urbervilles was a dairymaid. The sea is only a short drive away.

Reader's comments: Stunning, unique, peaceful.

V

WHITFIELD FARM COTTAGE

C(6) **M PT S**

Poundbury Road, near Bradford Peverell, Dorset, DT2 9SL Tel/Fax: 01305 260233
West of Dorchester. Nearest main road: A37 from Yeovil to Dorchester.

Dorset

3 Bedrooms. £25 (less for 5 nights or more). Available: own bath/shower/toilet; TV. No smoking.
Light suppers (by arrangement on night of arrival only). Vegetarian or other special diets if ordered. No smoking.
1 Sitting-room. With open fire, TV. No smoking.
Large garden
Closed at Easter.

E-mail: dc.whitfield@clara.net

After 30 years of army postings – and 17 house moves – Jackie and David Charles (he, a retired Parachute Regiment officer) have finally settled into this attractive 200-year-old thatched cottage on the outskirts of Dorchester. One bedroom on the ground floor has accomplished watercolours of rural scenes by a local artist on the walls and a smart shower-room. It is almost self-contained – having its own garden entrance and a comfortable sofa to relax upon. Alternatively, you may sit in the oak-beamed sitting-room, pink damasked sofas drawn up by the inglenook fireplace and family photos dotted around.

Breakfast (with morning papers provided) is taken in the quarry-tiled and stripped-pine kitchen where hand-painted ceramic tiles and plates complement the shiny blue Aga. Home-made jams and local honey are usually available. Historic Dorchester, which has plenty of restaurants, is minutes away (a bypass is just within earshot of the house, but bedrooms are quiet). Even nearer are the Keep military museum and New Barn Field Centre which has a re-creation of an Iron Age homestead, pottery demonstrations and a nature trail.

V

Dorset

WYNARDS FARM

C(5) **D PT S**

Chaldon Road, Winfrith Newburgh, Dorset, DT2 8DQ Tel: 01305 852660
(Fax: 01395 854094)

West of Wareham. Nearest main road: A352 from Wareham towards Dorchester.

3 Bedrooms. £20–£25 (less for 7 nights or more). All have own shower/toilet; TV.
Large garden

E-mail: canaven@hotmail.com

Framed Ordnance Survey maps on bedroom walls point to one of the main pursuits available from this comfortable house. For it is surrounded by good walking country and one of the most popular routes starts from the doorstep. A newly instated path takes walkers along an ancient watermeadow and around the perimeter of an organic farm where Jersey cows can be seen grazing. Some of this farm's produce is used for the breakfasts, which are served in a delightful room. Antiques, collected over the years by Ray and Judy Canaven, have found a home in here. On the mantelpiece are rosettes awarded to their horse-riding daughters, while framed photos and a mounted porthole testify to the Canavens' interest in sailing and scuba diving.

Each bedroom has its own entrance and shower-room. Two have been skilfully built into the high sloping eaves above a garage, where large skylights allow in flooding sunlight and afford tranquil countryside views. A third bedroom opens into the garden. All have restful colour schemes and, as there is no sitting-room, are equipped with chairs, books and sightseeing information. Guests dine at recommended local pubs.

V

Dorset

YELLOWHAM FARMHOUSE

C(6) **PT S X**

Yellowham Wood, Dorchester, Dorset, DT2 8RW Tel: 01305 262892
(Fax: 01305 257707)

East of Dorchester. Nearest main road: A35 from Dorchester to Bere Regis.

4 Bedrooms. £25 (less for 3 nights or more). All have own bath/shower/toilet; TV. No smoking.
Dinner (by arrangement). £14.95 for 3 courses and coffee, at 7.30–8pm. Vegetarian or other special diets if ordered. Wine available. No smoking.
1 Sitting-room. With stove. No smoking.
Large garden

E-mail: b&b@yellowham.freeserve.co.uk

National Hunt racehorses bred by Kay Birchenhough are the first sight to greet you on the approach to Yellowham. Twenty years ago, Kay and her husband Tony, whose hobby is racing classic cars, built this two-storey, red brick house where they now offer stylish and streamlined accommodation. Ground-floor bedrooms have pine ceilings, pale lemon walls, and lemon and grey bathrooms. The large breakfast-room is linked to a wonderful sitting-room by a wall of sliding glass doors. Furnishings in the sitting-room are ultra-modern, and the Chinese bamboo settee and chairs made for comfort.

Nestling in the lee of a 130-acre wood (with a variety of walks) is a woodland garden where afternoon teas and pre-dinner drinks are served in summer. Also in the grounds are a hard tennis court and a croquet lawn.

Kay is helped for six months of the year by her daughter Ellie, who is a Prue Leith-trained cook. Dinner might comprise spinach and blue cheese filo tartlets; pan-fried fillets of lemon sole with cucumber and sautéed potatoes; and brandy-snap baskets filled with coconut ice cream and fresh raspberries.

V

YOAH COTTAGE

C(7) **D S**

West Knighton, Dorset, DT2 8PE Tel: 01305 852087

South-east of Dorchester. Nearest main road: A352 from Dorchester to Wareham.

2 Bedrooms. £18.50–£25 (less for 7 nights or more). Available: own bath/toilet. No smoking.
Dinner (by arrangement). £14 for 3 courses and coffee, at 7.30pm. Vegetarian or other special diets if ordered. No smoking. **Light suppers** if ordered.
1 Sitting-room. With open fire, TV. No smoking.
Large garden
Closed at Easter.

In every room of this picturesque cottage, all whitewash and thatch, are ceramic sheep, pigs, poultry, Noah's Arks or Gardens of Eden – which both Furse and Rosemary Swann make in their studio at the back. The great beam over one of the inglenook fireplaces carries the date 1622. Rooms are low and white-walled, the staircases narrow and steep, floors stone-flagged, windows small and deep-set.

The Swanns have filled the house with an immensely varied collection of treasures. Bedrooms are attractive (the pretty bathrooms are on the ground floor).

Rosemary, who lived in Sweden for many years, specializes in cooking such classic Scandinavian dishes as gravlax, Swedish Royal pot roast, and poached apricots with vanilla cream, as well as her own recipes. Furse prepares breakfasts; and he makes all the jams.

Readers' comments: Most beautiful and characterful. Delightful atmosphere. Idyllic. A memorable place to stay. Truly outstanding. Cottage and food wonderful, hosts extremely welcoming.

Private bathrooms are not necessarily en suite.

Months when houses are shown as closed are inclusive.

Facts (prices, etc.) at the top of entries are supplied by the proprietors themselves. While every effort is made to ensure that these are correct at the time of going to press, they may alter thereafter: please check when you book.

To find the right accommodation in the right area at the right price, use an up-to-date edition of this book – revised every year. For an order form for the next edition (published in November), send a stamped addressed envelope, with 'SOTBT 2003 in the top left-hand corner, to Explore Britain, Alston, Cumbria, CA9 3SL.

County DURHAM

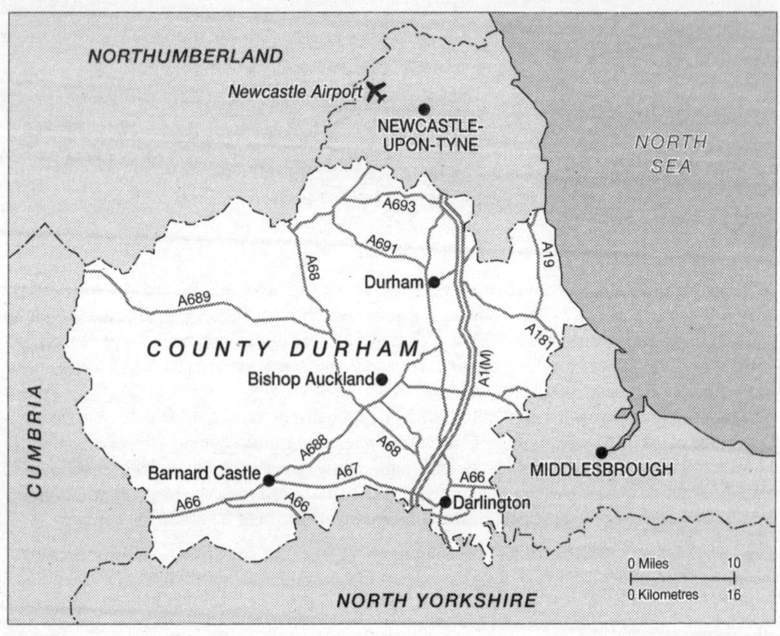

COMPLAINTS: If anything was not of reasonable standard (e.g. chilly bedroom or badly cooked food) you are entitled to claim a reduction on your bill, but *only if* you had previously told the proprietor and given him or her a chance to put matters right. In a court case involving a restaurant meal, it was ruled that, because a customer had not made a specific complaint at the time, he had no right subsequently to withhold payment (he had cancelled his cheque). The moral is obvious: if dissatisfied, you are expected to say so at once and not later. Houses are regularly inspected; and complaints will be forwarded to proprietors for their comments. Write to: Jan Bowmer (SOTBT), c/o Arrow Books, 20 Vauxhall Bridge Road, London SW1V 2SA. Please enclose a stamped addressed envelope if you want her to acknowledge receipt of your complaint.

CLOUD HIGH

C(10)

Eggleston, County Durham, DL12 0AU Tel/Fax: 01833 650644
North-west of Barnard Castle. Nearest main road: A688 from Barnard Castle to Staindrop.

3 Bedrooms. £22.50–£25. Available: own bath/shower/toilet; TV; balcony. No smoking.
Dinner (by arrangement). £17.50 for 3 courses and coffee, at 7.30pm. Vegetarian diets if ordered. Wine available. No smoking. **Light suppers** if ordered.
1 Sitting-room. With TV. No smoking.
Garden

With views almost to the coast from the garden and from the balcony of one of the bedrooms, Cloud High is a pre-war house with character (and a 'folly' the Bells have built in the garden). A post-war addition is the conservatory, where Frank and Eileen sometimes serve meals – usually prepared by Frank, who enjoys making such dishes as smoked salmon with prawns, peppered steak, and a choice of desserts. Breakfasts are well out of the ordinary, usually with an assortment of garnished fresh fruit on offer.

The balcony room is particularly spacious, with an extra-large bed and two settees. It is off a first-floor sitting-room with comfortable armchairs and plenty of books about this little-known area. The nearest sights are Eggleston Hall Gardens – beautiful, and with an excellent nursery – and spectacular High Force (England's highest waterfall).

Readers' comments: Made very welcome, excellent dinners, extremely comfortable, delightful place. Really outstanding; friendly hosts; cordon bleu breakfasts.

V

DEMESNES MILL

C(7) **PT**

Barnard Castle, County Durham, DL12 8PE Tel: 01833 637929 (Fax: 01833 637974)
Nearest main road: A66 from Scotch Corner towards Brough.

3 Bedrooms. £25–£37.50. Available: own bath/shower/toilet; TV; views of river; balcony. No smoking.
1 Sitting-room. With open fire, TV. No smoking.
Small garden
Closed from November to March.

E-mail: millbb2@ic24.net

After 25 years in Canada, Joan and Bob Young returned to their native county and fell for a near-derelict mill on the River Tees. Years of hard and patient work have transformed it.

Where two pairs of millstones once ground flour is now a long sitting-room furnished in antique style. Windows overlook the rushing river immediately below and a new conservatory at one end gives a splendid downriver view of a natural weir, where herons, dippers and kingfishers are often seen. Under the beamed ceiling supported by cast-iron columns, some of the mill mechanism survives. Off the sitting-room is the breakfast-area where Joan's visitors help themselves from an extensive buffet with fresh-baked bread. The big bedrooms upstairs, which overlook the weir, are decorated elaborately and have bathrooms equipped to high standards. A new barn conversion provides luxury self-contained accommodation.

The mill is approached across the Demesnes, a big public open space almost in the centre of Barnard Castle, where numerous eating-places are within walking distance for dinner.

Readers' comments: Wonderful house, everything about it marvellous, dramatic surroundings; made so welcome. Wonderful setting, made to feel so at home.

V

County Durham

GREENWELL FARM

C D M P T S

Tow Law, County Durham, DL13 4PH Tel: 01388 527248 (Fax: 01388 526785)
West of Durham. Nearest main road: A68 from Darlington towards Corbridge.

6 Bedrooms. £22.50–£27.50 (less for 3 nights or more). Bargain breaks. All have own bath/shower/toilet. No smoking.
Dinner (by arrangement). £15 for 4 courses and coffee, at 7pm. Vegetarian or other special diets if ordered. **Light suppers** if ordered.
2 Sitting-rooms. With TV. No smoking.
Small garden
Closed in late December.

There has been a farm here at least since early mediaeval times, as attests the Boldon Book (the Northumbrian equivalent of Domesday Book, which did not include the north of England). Now one of the barns has been converted and extended to provide accommodation, with bedrooms on two floors. On the upper storey is a spacious dining-cum-sitting-room, and there are more seats below. Another lounge, converted from a gin-gang, where a tethered horse was used to turn a millstone, is suitable for small conferences.

The farm is big, largely self-sufficient agriculturally, and run with a care to conservation: wildlife is nurtured, there is a large nature reserve, and the Vickers family have produced a farm-trail booklet to help visitors to enjoy it.

Beef and lamb from the farm, as well as home-produced vegetables, fruit and eggs, are used in the meals which Linda comes across from the farmhouse to prepare: fish pâté, lamb cutlets, and a big choice of puddings might be on offer.

V The historic city of Durham – with its magnificent Romanesque cathedral, Norman castle, museums, university and botanic garden – is within easy driving distance.

County Durham

GROVE HOUSE

C(8) S

Hamsterley Forest, County Durham, DL13 3NL Tel: 01388 488203
(Fax: 01388 488174)
West of Bishop Auckland. Nearest main road: A68 from Darlington to Corbridge.

3 Bedrooms. £23–£28.50. Available: own bath/shower/toilet. No smoking.
Dinner. £22.50 for 4 courses and coffee, at 7.30pm. Vegetarian or other special diets if ordered. No smoking. **Light suppers** if ordered.
2 Sitting-rooms. With open fire, TV. No smoking.
Large garden
Closed from mid-December to mid-January.

E-mail: xov47@dial.pipex.com

Amid a 5000-acre Forestry Commission holding, a few houses are buried in the original forest. Among them is Grove House, once an aristocrat's shooting-box, surrounded by its own big gardens. The windows of the prettily furnished guest-rooms look across the garden or into the forest. Birdsong is the loudest sound you will hear.

The downstairs rooms have a touch of aristocratic grandeur and some unusual fittings from Germany (notice the art deco doorhandles). Helene Close prepares all the food from fresh ingredients. A typical dinner: warm smoked-haddock creams, pork tenderloin stuffed with celery and onion fondue, Normandy apple tart, and cheese. She discusses guests' preferences beforehand. Bicycle hire and pony trekking are available.

Readers' comments: Fairytale house in beautiful setting. A wonderful 'find'; it was perfect. Idyllic. Exceptionally varied menus, beautifully cooked. Marvellous situation, food and welcome. A trip to paradise! Of a very high standard in every way.

LANDS FARM

C PT

Westgate-in-Weardale, County Durham, DL13 1SN Tel: 01388 517210
West of Bishop Auckland. Nearest main road: A689 from Crook to Alston.

2 Bedrooms. £23 (less for 5 nights or more). Both have own bath/shower/toilet; TV; views of river.
1 Sitting-room
Large garden

The very friendly John and Barbara Reed run this stock-farm in little-known Weardale. The house stands on a narrow lane which runs along the valley side, with the Reeds' sheep and cattle grazing in fields bounded by dry-stone walls and trees. Inside, there is an oak-furnished breakfast-room with armchairs, and a conservatory gives pleasant views of countryside beyond the garden with its barn. One bedroom is pleasantly furnished in pine. At the end of the lane, the village pub offers bar snacks; fuller meals are obtainable at plenty of places a drive away, including a new and well thought of one within two miles.

The area is of much interest both botanically and geologically. Frosterley 'marble' was quarried nearby and can be seen in such places as York Minster and Durham Cathedral. By one of the waterfalls on Rookhope Burn, not far from the farm, a Roman altar was found in the last century; the village of Rookhope is where W.H. Auden 'became aware of self and not-self' – the area, which he visited in his youth, made a great impression on him. Up the valley is Killhope Wheel, a huge waterwheel which has been restored to demonstrate the lead-mining industry which was once the mainstay of the north Pennines.

Readers' comments: An excellent weekend. Beautifully decorated, hostess charming and very knowledgeable about the beauty-spots. Delightful couple, lovely situation. V

LANE HEAD FARM

D X

Hutton Magna, County Durham, DL11 7HF Tel: 01833 627378
South-east of Barnard Castle. Nearest main road: A66 from Scotch Corner to Brough.

3 Bedrooms. £20. Available: own bath/shower/toilet; TV (in two). No smoking.
Light suppers if ordered.
1 Sitting-room. With open fire, TV.
Large garden

You could bring your horse on holiday here (or your dogs), to stay in the range of loose-boxes which were built when this farm was used to train racehorses. Its current total of 500 acres is now mostly arable, with wide views across the Vale of York. There are Roman remains in the area and ever since their time there has been a highway in the gap in the Pennines through which the busy A66 now runs.

Sue Ormston's bedrooms are tucked under the sloping roof of this wide, creeper-clad house, which was built two or three centuries ago. There is a cosy sitting-room for guests, who have their own entrance, and also a kitchen for them to use if they want hot drinks and so on. Sue offers no evening meal because numerous pubs offering outstandingly good meals are a feature of North Yorkshire – the farm is just on the county boundary.

As well as being close to the Yorkshire Dales, the house is near beautiful Teesdale, which is much less well known. (The Teesdale Way for walkers is also close.) Nearby are Palladian Rokeby House and, by the Tees, the ruins of Eggleston Abbey.

Reader's comments: Excellent for accommodation, value, homeliness and location.

SPRING LODGE

C D PT

Newgate, Barnard Castle, County Durham, DL12 8NW Tel: 01833 638110
Nearest main road: A67 from Darlington to Barnard Castle.

3 Bedrooms. £22.50–£27.50 (less for 3 nights or more). All have own bath/shower/toilet; TV.
Light suppers if ordered. Vegetarian or special diets if ordered.
1 Sitting-room. With open fire.
Large garden

This imposing Regency house was nearly derelict when Sarah-Jane Ormston and her husband acquired it a few years ago, and the garden had almost reverted to a state of nature. The house is now back to its former impressive self, with the formal gardens restored (two bedrooms overlook them). A flamboyant red-rose wallpaper adorns the high-ceilinged entrance hall, and in the guests' sitting-room, a panorama of the kings and queens of Scotland has been utilized as a frieze. (The Winnie-the-Pooh murals in here are Sarah-Jane's handiwork.)

The house is just opposite the entrance to the Bowes Museum. Built in the 19th century, in the style of a château, by an ancestor of the Queen Mother, this houses a remarkable collection that includes – as well as French furniture and many old master paintings – ship models, toys, antiquities, natural history and geological specimens, and a life-size silver automaton of a swan. The whole is like an enormous cabinet of curiosities.

V For full-scale evening meals, there is a good choice within walking distance in picturesque Barnard Castle, with the old market cross at its centre.

Book well ahead: many of these houses have few rooms. Do not expect dinner if you have not booked it or if you arrive late.

Where wine is not available (meaning it is on sale or can be fetched for you), you are nearly always welcome to bring in your own drinks.

Some proprietors stipulate a minimum stay of two nights at weekends or peak seasons; or they will accept one-nighters only at short notice (that is, only if no lengthier booking has yet been made).

Prices for single occupancy may be higher than those quoted here. Houses that charge singles no more, or only 10% more, than half the price of a double room (except possibly at peak periods) are indicated by the 'S' symbol.

ESSEX

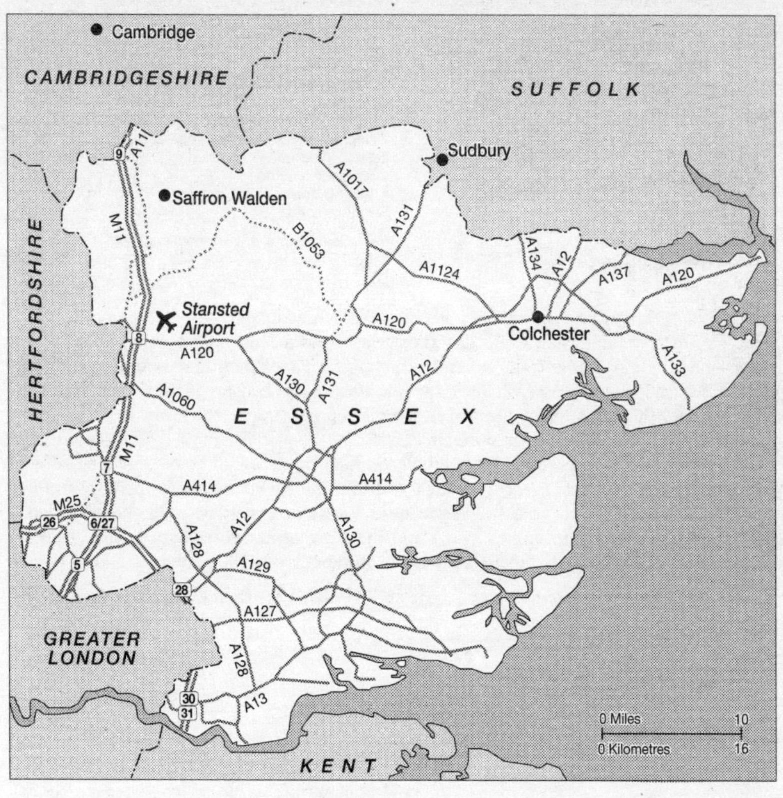

Prices are per person sharing a room at the beginning of the year. However, for the best rooms in the house or later in the year, you may well be asked for more.

Essex

BEECH VILLA

C D P T S X

1 Borough Lane, Saffron Walden, Essex, CB11 4AF Tel: 01799 516891
(Fax: 01799 521390)
Nearest main road: B1053 from Saffron Walden to Braintree (and M11, junction 9).

3 Bedrooms. £20–£22.50 (less for 5 nights or more). One has own shower/toilet. No smoking.
Dinner (by arrangement). £12 for 3 courses and coffee, at 6.30–7.30pm. Vegetarian or other special diets if ordered. Wine available. No smoking. **Light suppers** if ordered.
1 Sitting-room. With open fire, TV. No smoking.
Small garden

E-mail: jamesbutler3@compuserve.com

This pretty villa was built in 1820: its glass-roofed verandah with cast-iron columns is very typical of the period. Inside is a little sitting-room, and a pink-walled dining-room with a piano and Victorian-style chairs around a mahogany table. Bedrooms are pleasantly furnished: e.g. stripped pine, ice-blue walls, white Portuguese bedspreads and blue-and-white china in one. Breakfast may be served in the airy conservatory, which looks out on to the garden where Jiffy, the long-haired rabbit, resides.

Marilyn Butler will produce such simple evening meals as home-made soup, salmon, and trifle (she has a wide range of homely dishes). She trained in aromatherapy, and you can book a session during your stay if you want a relaxing experience. The house is handy for Stansted Airport (20 minutes away) and there are attractive villages in the vicinity – Thaxted, Finchingfield and Great Bardfield, for instance.

V *Readers' comments:* Made to feel so welcome and relaxed. Very friendly and knowledgeable.

Essex

BULMER TYE HOUSE

C D S X

Bulmer Tye, Essex, CO10 7ED Tel/Fax: 01787 269315
South-west of Sudbury. Nearest main road: A131 from Halstead to Sudbury.

4 Bedrooms. £20. Two singles have own bath/toilet. No smoking.
Dinner (by arrangement). £10 for 2 or 3 courses and coffee, at times to suit guests. Vegetarian or other special diets if ordered. No smoking. **Light suppers** if ordered.
3 Sitting-rooms. With open fires, TV, piano. No smoking.
Large garden

E-mail: noelriley@hotmail.com

One of Gainsborough's most famous paintings is of the Andrews family and it was one of their sons, a parson, who in the 18th century 'modernized' this house, most of which dates back to the reign of Elizabeth I. Today its old timbers resonate to the sound of music (played by family or guests), for Peter Owen is a maker of very fine clavichords – and of much of the interesting furniture seen in the rooms. His wife Noël is an authority on antiques, so not surprisingly there are some unusual period pieces in the house. The Owens have contrasted the antiques with strong modern patterns.

Guests eat with the family in the quarry-tiled kitchen. Garden produce goes into soups and puddings; wine is home-made and Peter bakes the bread. Popular dishes include beef-and-lentil flan, fish pie, a cheesy bread-and-butter pudding with stir-fried vegetables. For breakfast, you will be offered home-made muesli and marmalade, as well as free-range eggs (no fry-ups). Some of Suffolk's showpiece villages are easily reached from here.

Readers' comments: Characterful house, beautiful garden, very informal and friendly. Very interesting house, superb garden.

1 GUNTER'S COTTAGES

Thaxted Road, Saffron Walden, Essex, CB10 2UT Tel: 01799 522091
South-east of Saffron Walden. Nearest main road: A1301 from Cambridge to Saffron Walden (and M11, junction 9).

Essex

1 Bedroom. £19.50 (less for 3 nights or more). Has own bath/toilet; TV. No smoking.
Light suppers if ordered. Vegetarian diets if ordered. No smoking.
Small garden

Originally built in 1840 as homes for farmworkers' families, these cottages have now been combined and modernized. The special attraction of staying at No. 1 is a heated, indoor swimming-pool built on to the back. This is directly accessible from the guests' self-contained suite of bedroom and bathroom.

In the spacious dining-room, with its blue Wedgwood collection, Pat Goddard serves sandwiches if you do not want to go into the town for a meal. An interesting feature of Gunter's is the pargeting: decorative exterior plasterwork, usually found only on the historic houses of Essex and Suffolk, but here a modern artist-craftsman has created some outstanding work – particularly the owl and the huntsman on, of all things, garage walls. To the rear of the house are cornfields, and the Goddards can recommend several pleasant walks locally.

Reader's comment: Welcoming and helpful.

V

OLLIVER'S FARMHOUSE

C(10)

Toppesfield, Essex, CO9 4LS Tel: 01787 237642 (Fax: 01787 237602)
North-west of Colchester. Nearest main road: A1017 from Braintree towards Haverhill.

Essex

2 Bedrooms. £23–£30 (less for 3 nights or more). One has own shower/toilet; TV (in both). No smoking.
Light suppers if ordered. No smoking.
1 Sitting-room. With open fire, piano. No smoking.
Large garden

E-mail: sueblackie@fsmail.net

To the attraction of a historic (16th-century) house is added that of a particularly interesting garden created by Sue Blackie, a qualified landscape gardener. Her award-winning architect husband James makes wine from the small vineyard adjoining the garden: Domesday Book records a vineyard in the Toppesfield area.

In the huge sitting-room, with a correspondingly huge brick fireplace and chamfered ceiling beams, hang some of the modern paintings which James collects. Further paintings fill the terracotta walls of the landing, where latched board doors open into bedrooms with old china, garden flowers, and pleasant colour schemes. Breakfast is served in the antique-furnished dining-room or outside on the sun-trapping terrace.

As to the garden (at its best in spring), this consists of a whole series of experiences as one area opens into another, with something for each season, and each with its own colour scheme. Up a mossy-roofed barn Sue has trained jasmine, clematis and a grapevine. A deep iron vat is now a lily-pool, inhabited by goldfish.The White Hart in nearby Great Yeldham has built up a popular following for its fine cuisine.

YARDLEYS

C S

Orchard Pightle, Hadstock, Essex, CB1 6PQ Tel/Fax: 01223 891822
South-east of Cambridge. Nearest main road: A1307 from Cambridge to Haverhill (and M11, junctions 9/10).

3 Bedrooms. £23–£25 (less for 3 nights or more). Bargain breaks. Available: own bath/shower/toilet. No smoking.
Dinner (by arrangement). £10.50–£12 for 3 courses and coffee, at times to suit guests. Vegetarian or other special diets if ordered. No smoking. **Light suppers** if ordered.
1 Sitting-room. With TV. No smoking.
Garden

E-mail: yardleys@waitrose.com

In picturesque Hadstock, almost in Cambridgeshire, is a flowery close called Orchard Pightle ('pightle' is an old word for an enclosure) within which is Gillian Ludgate's modern home. Upstairs are well-equipped bedrooms in pale colours, neat and airy, with private or en suite bathrooms; and at the back there is a conservatory brimming with flowers, where meals are sometimes served. Gillian is a keen cook, serving suppers or such meals as salmon mousse, chicken breasts with tarragon and orange, and pavlova. Breakfast may include garden fruit, local sausages, her own jam, and organic free-range eggs.

Cambridge and the attractive town of Saffron Walden are within easy reach. The Imperial War Museum's collection of historic aircraft (at Duxford) is also close by.

Readers' comments: All sorts of generous little extras, excellent evening meals. Lovely place; the most pleasant of hosts; food second to none. Made to feel like family friends. Every need was met; meals were varied and delightfully cooked and served.

V

For explanation of code letters and V symbol, see inside front cover.

Major tourist attractions, such as Stratford-upon-Avon, Bath and Cambridge, can often be easily reached from houses in adjacent counties.

Some houses offer special discounts to readers using the current edition of this book. Always state you are an SOTBT reader when ringing to book or when using E-mail.

At houses where dinner is not served, a light supper can often be obtained (if ordered in advance), ranging from sandwiches to family 'pot luck'. (Packed lunches too.)

GLOUCESTERSHIRE
(including South Gloucestershire)

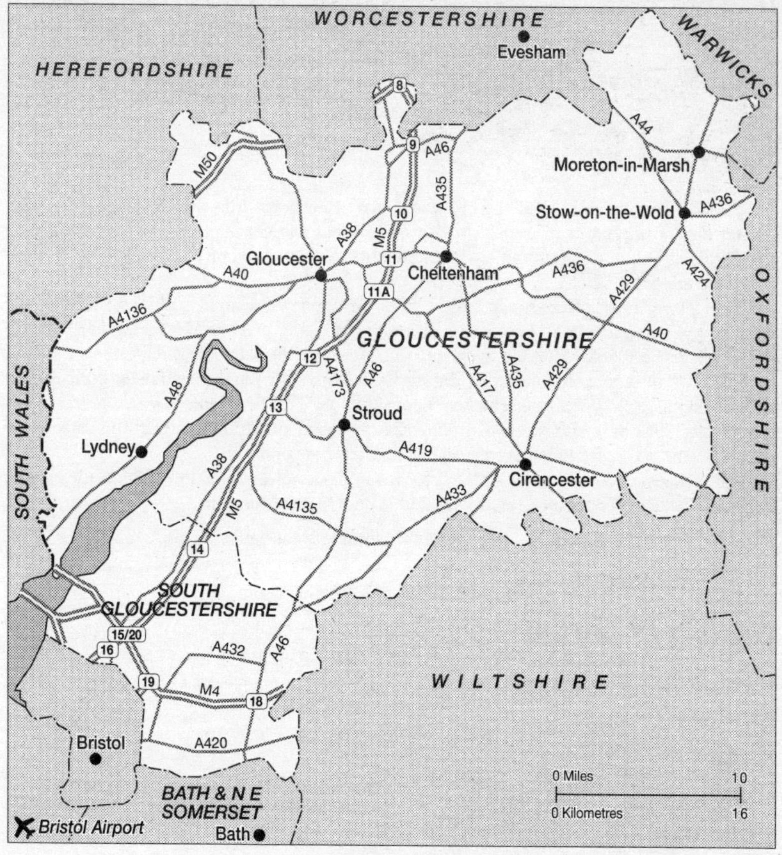

Houses which accept the discount vouchers on page ii are marked with a V symbol next to the relevant entries.

Gloucestershire

AARON FARM

C D PT X

Nympsfield Road, Nailsworth, Gloucestershire, GL6 0ET Tel: 01453 833598 (Fax: 01453 833626)
South of Stroud. Nearest main road: A46 from Stroud to Bath (and M5, junction 13).

3 Bedrooms. £21–£22 (less for 3 nights or more). All have own bath/shower/toilet; TV. No smoking.
Dinner (by arrangement). £14 for 3 courses and coffee, from 6–8pm. Vegetarian or other special diets if ordered. No smoking. **Light suppers** if ordered.
1 Sitting-room. With open fire, piano. No smoking.
Small garden
E-mail: AaronFarm@aol.com

On a road rising steeply out of the old wool town of Nailsworth in the Cotswold Hills, this former farmhouse has been transformed by its present owners, Patrick and June Mulligan, to provide stylish and comfortable accommodation. A separate entrance for guests ensures complete privacy.

There is a huge sitting-room which, save for a pile of scatter cushions under a tall window providing a splash of colour, is decorated in restful creams. With a log fire burning in the attractive Cotswold-stone fireplace, this is a tranquil place in which to relax after a long day's sightseeing. In the small dining-room with individual pine tables, June serves such meals as eggs florentine, chicken Véronique with fresh vegetables, and home-made profiteroles. The pink and green bedrooms are of a good size and the one at the back has a pleasant view across the small garden to playing-fields beyond.

Aaron Farm is conveniently situated for many places of interest, including Sudeley and Berkeley Castles, Westonbirt Arboretum and Woodchester Mansion.

V *Reader's comment*: Delightful couple for whom nothing is too much trouble.

Gloucestershire

DAMSELLS LODGE

C M PT S

The Park, Painswick, Gloucestershire, GL6 6SR Tel: 01452 813777
North of Stroud. Nearest main road: A46 from Stroud to Cheltenham (and M5, junction 11a).

3 Bedrooms. £24 **(one room for readers of this book only)**–£27. Less for 3 nights or more. Available: own bath/shower/toilet; TV. No smoking.
Light suppers if ordered.
1 Sitting-room. With log stove, TV, piano.
Small garden

This very comfortable house was originally the lodge to the nearby mansion. It is in a peaceful rural lane and has truly spectacular views from every window across a small garden of lawns, stone terrace and flowering shrubs.

Judy Cooke is a welcoming hostess who soon makes friends with her visitors. The huge sitting-room has windows on three sides, and a big log stove. Everywhere there are thick carpets and good furniture (even the bathroom is pretty luxurious). Perhaps the best bedroom is one separate from the house: a one-floor garden annexe, with huge sliding windows through which to step straight on to the lawn or to view the distant hills while still in bed, and ideal for anyone who finds stairs difficult.

Readers' comments: Immaculate; lovely setting, gorgeous view. Absolutely marvellous. Delightful hosts. Wonderful, homely place. Perfect setting. First-class accommodation. Warm welcome. Impeccably kept house, quiet. Great place to stay. Marvellous breakfast.

DORNDEN

C D

Church Lane, Old Sodbury, South Gloucestershire, BS37 6NB Tel: 01454 313325 (Fax: 01454 312263)

North-east of Bristol. Nearest main road: A432 from Bristol to Old Sodbury (and M4, junction 18).

South Gloucestershire

9 Bedrooms. £23–£29 (less for 2 nights at weekends or 4 mid-week). Available: own bath/shower/toilet; TV. No smoking.
Dinner (by arrangement). £11.50 for 3 courses and coffee, at 6.45pm. Vegetarian or other special diets if ordered. No smoking.
1 Sitting-room. With piano. No smoking.
Large garden
Closed from mid-September to mid-October.

E-mail: dorndenguesthouse@tinyworld.co.uk

An immaculate garden surrounds the big guest-house – flowerbeds and box-hedges in trim and neat array, with a large vegetable and fruit garden to supply the kitchen. From its lawns and grass tennis court, set high up, there are splendid views.

This is the place for a quiet stay, well placed for exploring the scenic counties around it. All the rooms are sedate and comfortable in a style appropriate to what it was in mid-Victorian days – a vicarage – and with features of the period still retained, from the beautifully polished tiles of the hall to the terrace on to which the sitting-room opens.

Daphne Paz serves traditional favourites at dinner – such as roasts, steak and kidney pie, sticky-toffee pudding, pies or crumbles: very moderately priced.

Readers' comments: Strongly recommended. Cooking of high standard. Excellent value. Very friendly. Always excellent, delightful hosts. Friendly attitude, always ready for a laugh.

V

FAIRVIEW FARMHOUSE

C(8)

Bledington Road, Stow-on-the-Wold, Gloucestershire, GL54 1JH
Tel/Fax: 01451 830279

East of Stow-on-the-Wold. Nearest main road: A436 from Stow-on-the-Wold towards Chipping Norton.

Gloucestershire

6 Bedrooms. £24–£27.50 (less for 5 nights or more). Bargain breaks. Available: own bath/shower/toilet; TV. No smoking.
Light suppers if ordered.
2 Sitting-rooms. With open fire (in one).
Large garden

In the more peaceful south of the Cotswolds, Fairview Farmhouse is the home of Susan, a fitness instructor, and Andrew Davis. Guests can choose between accommodation in the main house or in a separate annexe. Bedrooms, all of a high standard, are smartly decorated in pinks, greens and chintzes, with four-posters in some rooms and draped canopies above beds in others. Fair views indeed – of rolling countryside to Icomb Hill. Light suppers only, but menus from local eateries are available and transport can sometimes be arranged.

A main attraction of the region is the Cotswold Farm Park, home to the Rare Breeds Survival Trust. For gardens, go to Sezincote, Hidcote or Batsford (the last has a Japanese-style arboretum). Stow-on-the-Wold merits unhurried exploration: it's a little town of antique and craft shops, restaurants and byways.

Reader's comment: Wonderful hosts.

Gloucestershire

FRESHFIELDS

C(5) PT

2 Hayden Lane, Staverton, Gloucestershire, GL51 0SR Tel: 01242 680830
West of Cheltenham. Nearest main road: A40 from Cheltenham to Gloucester (and M5, junction 11).

3 Bedrooms. £20 (less for 2 nights or more). With TV. No smoking.
1 Sitting-room. With open fire, TV. No smoking.
Small garden

When you arrive at Bill and Margaret Gooch's much-modernized 1920s house, you might be greeted by one of their friendly dogs who will accompany you up a path, past a pretty garden filled with shrubs, flowers and vegetables, with a dovecote to one side. Bill and Margaret's pride in their comfortably furnished house is evident, as is their genuine warmth and desire to make you feel completely at home.

The sitting-room is full of family photos, and throughout the winter an open fire burns in the Cotswold-stone fireplace, one of the many things which Bill has created since the couple's arrival here in the mid-1960s. This room is shared with them and usually one or two of their three cats. Breakfast is served in the bright conservatory which looks on to a rockery, complete with fish-pond and water feature, and fields beyond. The simply furnished bedrooms, including two snug singles, are spick-and-span, and guests share the use of a roomy bathroom upstairs or a good shower-room on the ground floor.

B & b only, but there are decent food pubs close by.

Gloucestershire

GUITING GUEST-HOUSE

C D PT S

Post Office Lane, Guiting Power, Gloucestershire, GL54 5TU Tel: 01451 850470 (Fax: 01451 850034)
West of Stow-on-the-Wold. Nearest main road: A436 from Andoversford towards Stow-on-the-Wold.

5 Bedrooms. £24–£29 (less for 5 nights or more). All have own bath/shower/toilet; TV. No smoking.
Dinner (by arrangement). £19 for 4 courses and coffee, at 7pm. Vegetarian or other special diets if ordered. No smoking. **Light suppers** if ordered.
2 Sitting-rooms. With open fire, TV (in one). No smoking.
Small garden

E-mail: Guiting.guest_house@virgin.net

This is a quintessential Cotswold village with stone cross on a green and wisteria clambering up mellow walls. Changes to the 450-year-old guest-house have been done with sensitivity. New pine doors have wood latches; the dining-room floor is made of solid elm; logs blaze in a stone fireplace; and in the snug sitting-room are flagstones covered with oriental rugs. Bedrooms are pleasantly decorated, with such touches as beribboned cushions or an old cane-backed rocking-chair, and four-posters.

Yvonne Sylvester will cook whatever you want, but a favourite menu is trout from a nearby fish farm, chicken in lime-and-ginger sauce, strawberry baskets with cream, and cheeses.

Readers' comments: Made us so welcome. Beautiful house. One of the happiest breaks I've had. Nothing too much trouble. Charming, faultless, relaxing, ideal. Very relaxed atmosphere. Our favourite, will definitely return. Marvellous cook, tasteful rooms. Superb food.

GUNN MILL HOUSE

C D X

Lower Spout Lane, Mitcheldean, Gloucestershire, GL17 0EA Tel/Fax: 01594 827577
West of Gloucester. Nearest main road: A48 from Gloucester to Chepstow (and M50, junction 4).

8 Bedrooms. £25–£40 (less for 5 nights or more). Bargain breaks. Available: own bath/shower/toilet; TV. No smoking.
Dinner (by arrangement). £24.50 for 4 courses and coffee, at 8pm. Vegetarian or other special diets if ordered. Wine available. No smoking. **Light suppers** if ordered.
3 Sitting-rooms. With open fire (in two), TV (in one). No smoking.
Large garden

E-mail: info@gunnmillhouse.co.uk

There are mill ruins in the grounds of this elegant Georgian house, which is set in five acres of gardens and paddock at the northernmost tip of the Forest of Dean. Originally built for the mill owner, it is now the home of David and Caroline Anderson and their daughter Holly. The Andersons have restored the house with great flair and imagination and, having been involved for many years in the film industry, they have filled it with fascinating mementoes from the various international locations they have visited.

One spacious and stylishly furnished room has a beamed dining-area at one end and sofas cosily grouped round a fireplace of local stone at the other. All around are photos of the family and of film stars with whom the couple have worked. The bedrooms are of a very high standard. Six are in converted outhouses across a courtyard. Some of these have their own sitting-rooms and one has a four-poster bed.

The Andersons enjoy cooking for their guests and serve such dinners as chestnut soup, trout in fragrant Thai spices, cheeseboard, and mascarpone torte.

Readers' comments: Strongly recommended. Genuine hospitality, food excellent.

HOLLY HOUSE

C M

Ebrington, Gloucestershire, GL55 6NL Tel: 01386 593213 (Fax: 01386 593181)
North of Moreton-in-Marsh. Nearest main road: A429 from Moreton-in-Marsh towards Warwick.

4 Bedrooms. £22–£25. Available: own bath/shower/toilet; TV. No smoking.
Light suppers if ordered. Vegetarian or other special diets if ordered. No smoking.
1 Sitting-room. No smoking.
Small garden

E-mail: Jeff.Hutsby@care4free.net

Holly House was built in the early 1900s by a local brewery to house the landlord of the nearby pub. Candida Hutsby's family arrived in the area at about the same time and half a century later, her grandfather bought the house. Candida and her husband Jeffrey eventually acquired it and set about converting it into the stylish home it is today.

You enter the house through an olive-green hallway where two paintings of the village, done by Candida's grandfather, hang. In the plum and gold dining-room, a cabinet displays a fine collection of dolls. One window overlooks the village green where Morris Men dance in summer. The neat bedrooms, with lemon and cream walls and pine beds, are reached across a courtyard. Two are in what was originally the village wheelwright shop and the others are in a converted barn. There is a garden room, too, from which you can enjoy views over fields towards Blockley Hill and Moreton-in-Marsh.

Evening meals can be had at the Ebrington Arms or at the highly praised Churchill Arms in Paxford. Picturesque Chipping Campden and Hidcote Manor Garden are near.

V

MANOR FARMHOUSE

S X

Wormington, Gloucestershire, WR12 7NL Tel: 01386 584302 (Fax: 01386 584649)
South-east of Evesham. Nearest main road: A46 from Evesham towards Tewkesbury (and M5, junction 9).

3 Bedrooms. £19–£22 (less for 3 nights or more). All have own shower/toilet. No smoking.
Light suppers if ordered.
1 Sitting-room. With open fire, TV.
Small garden

E-mail: pauline@smith-russell.softnet.co.uk

Once this house was known as Charity Farm because 'dole' was dispensed to wayfarers. There are leaded casements in the comfortable sitting-room, a stone inglenook in the hall, slabs of Welsh slate on the floor, steps and turns everywhere on one's way up to beamy all-white bedrooms well furnished with mahogany pieces. There's still a cheese-room dating from the time when this was a dairy-farm.

What was once a cattle-yard is now a very attractive court with lawn, fountain and stone sinks planted with flowers. To one side is an old granary of brick and timber which dates, like the house itself, from the 15th century. From the stable door five small ponies watch visitors' comings and goings. On the farm are shooting and trout fishing.

Pauline Russell usually serves only breakfast, recommending for other meals Olivers wine bar in Broadway – best known of all the picturesque villages hereabouts.

V *Readers' comments:* Lovely farmhouse; looked after us so well. Friendly, good value.

Gloucestershire

OLD RECTORY

C D

Rodmarton, Gloucestershire, GL7 6PE Tel: 01285 841246 (Fax: 01285 841488)
South-west of Cirencester. Nearest main road: A433 from Cirencester to Tetbury (and M4, junction 15).

2 Bedrooms. £23–£25 (less for 5 nights or more). Both have own bath/toilet. No smoking.
Dinner (by arrangement). £12.50–£15 for 2–3 courses and coffee, from 7–9pm. Vegetarian or other special diets if ordered. No smoking. **Light suppers** if ordered.
1 Sitting-room. With open fire, TV.
Small garden

E-mail: Jfitz@globalnet.co.uk

This substantial house, owned by the Church until the mid-1960s, has a datestone with the year 1632, although its present owners, John and Mary FitzGerald, believe that parts of it may be even older. What is certain is that the house was considerably enlarged in the latter half of the 19th century, the new part including a large entrance hall with broad staircase and a Cotswold-stone façade with a tall mullioned window at its centre.

The guests' sitting-room, with mustard-coloured walls and turquoise flower-patterned drapes, is in the older part of the house. During the 19th-century remodelling, its ceiling was raised, giving the room a spacious feel. In the cosy, beamed dining-room, Mary, who is cordon bleu trained, serves such dinners as garlic mushrooms, chicken cooked in herbs with Parma ham, and apple flan with apricot glaze. Bedrooms are beamed and ample in size, with good bathrooms.

Rodmarton is close to the source of the River Thames and there are lovely walks in the area.

Reader's comments: Extremely well looked after, food excellent; John and Mary were friendly and most helpful and made our stay memorable.

V

PARKVIEW

C(1) D PT S X

4 Pittville Crescent, Cheltenham, Gloucestershire, GL52 2QZ Tel: 01242 575567
Nearest main road: A435 from Evesham to Cheltenham.

3 Bedrooms. £20–£25 (less for 3 nights or more). Bargain breaks. One has own shower/toilet; TV (in all). No smoking.
1 Sitting-room. With TV, piano. No smoking.
Small garden

In springtime a cherry tree in bloom marks Parkview. Overlooking Pittville Park, this elegant Georgian house in a quiet residential area is a useful base for exploring the town, or for travelling further into the Cotswolds. The stairway of the house is lined with Sandra and John Sparrey's interesting finds from local auctions: old playbills, sepia-toned photographs and a land deed with George IV's royal seal. Bedrooms, all with washbasins, are pleasantly furnished; one has a lovely art nouveau-style dressing-suite.

Cheltenham's Regency houses date from its heyday as a fashionable spa: the Duke of Wellington regularly came here whenever rheumatism or affairs of state got him down. The town needs repeated visits to see everything: the birthplace of composer Gustav Holst, the Pump Room (where you can still 'take the waters'), the elegant Promenade and Montpellier area, distinguished art gallery, and lovely gardens. Racegoers throng here at Gold Cup time; others come for various arts festivals. There are innumerable restaurants, pubs and wine bars where visitors can dine well.

V

POSTLIP HALL FARM

C D

Winchcombe, Gloucestershire, GL54 5AQ Tel/Fax: 01242 603351
North-east of Cheltenham. Nearest main road: A435 from Cheltenham towards Evesham.

Gloucestershire

3 Bedrooms. £22.50 (less for 4 nights or more). Available: own bath/shower/toilet; TV. No smoking.
Light suppers if ordered. Vegetarian or other special diets if ordered.
1 Sitting-room. With stove, TV. No smoking.
Large garden

This livestock farm, situated at the end of a sweeping and tree-lined drive in the hamlet of Postlip, was at one time part of the local Broadway family estate. Fine views of 15th-century Postlip Hall, with its magnificent gabled frontage, are to be had from this modern farmhouse of Cotswold stone.

Valerie and Joe Albutt have created a comfortable atmosphere for their guests. The large sitting-room, with panoramic views, has brocade sofas and armchairs and two recliners gathered around a wood-burning stove. Bedrooms are of a good size. One in beige and peach has unusual antique headboards; another, with double aspect, has views of open farmland and the old Hall beyond.

The farm adjoins Cleeve Common, at 1800 acres the largest area of common land in the county, so there are attractive cross-country walks, one of which takes you to nearby Winchcombe, a picturesque village that was the capital of the ancient kingdom of Mercia. Sudeley Castle, too, is a short walk away.

Readers' comments: Immaculate. Breakfast the best ever.

Gloucestershire

ROOSTERS

C D S

Todenham, Gloucestershire, GL56 9PA Tel/Fax: 01608 650645
North-east of Moreton-in-Marsh. Nearest main road: A429 from Moreton-in-Marsh to Warwick.

3 Bedrooms. £23–£25 (less for 4 nights or more). Bargain breaks. Available: own bath/shower/toilet; TV. No smoking.
Dinner (by arrangement). £18 for 3 courses and coffee, at 7.30pm. Less for 2 courses. Vegetarian or other special diets if ordered. **Light suppers** if ordered.
1 Sitting-room. With open fire. No smoking.
Large garden

Situated near the old 'four shires' stone, this 17th-century cottage provides an ideal base for touring not only the Cotswold villages but also Stratford-upon-Avon (only 20 minutes away) and, further afield, Cheltenham to the west or Warwick and Leamington Spa to the north.

Returning after a busy day sightseeing, and having been greeted by Rosie the golden retriever, you can relax by the inglenook fireplace with its gleaming copper cowl and admire Chris Longmore's eclectic collection of china, before she serves dinner. Chris and her husband Paul, a former golf professional, lived for some time in Sweden, so after perhaps broccoli-and-cheese soup you might be served Scandinavian pork, followed by a more traditional summer pudding or strawberry cheesecake.

Bedrooms are all individual, comfortable and furnished with imagination. One in yellow and blue has unusual pale pine and leather scrolled headboards, and a striking golden pine and green bathroom. Another has pretty rose-stencilled walls and white lace bedspreads. Some of Paul's grandfather's watercolour landscapes adorn the walls in the low-beamed hallways.

Gloucestershire

STEPPING STONE

C(12) D M(limited) S

Rectory Lane, Great Rissington, Gloucestershire, GL54 2LL Tel: 01451 821385 (Fax: 01451 821008)
East of Cheltenham. Nearest main road: A40 from Cheltenham to Witney.

5 Bedrooms. £20–£27.50 (less for 3 nights or more). Bargain breaks. Available: own bath/shower/toilet; TV; balcony (one). No smoking.
Dinner (by arrangement). £15 for 3 courses and coffee, at 7pm. Vegetarian or other special diets if ordered. Wine available. No smoking. **Light suppers** if ordered.
Large garden

E-mail: ststbandb@aol.com

Well placed to explore the Cotswolds, Sandra and Roger Freeman's modern stone-built home blends in beautifully with its surroundings. Bedrooms are decorated in creams and chintzes, with comfortable pink velour armchairs. Two stylish and well-equipped self-contained suites, with their own sitting-areas, are in separate buildings, both looking out over the secluded garden which is lit at night. The studio flat at first-floor level has its own balcony, and the garden room a little patio beside the lawn. You may spot ducks and chickens waddling past, sometimes with one of the Freemans' cats in pursuit; or sheep in the paddock providing a lawn-mowing service. For dinner, Roger might prepare garlic mushrooms, followed by baked plaice or a roast, with ice cream to finish.

The house is midway between two famous Cotswold villages – Bourton-on-the-Water and Burford. Most people come here simply for the scenery, but also in the vicinity is Sudeley Castle, once the home of Catherine Parr. Only a little further away are Oxford, Warwick and Woodstock (with Blenheim Palace).

V

TILED HOUSE FARM

C(10) M S

Oxlynch Lane, Oxlynch, Gloucestershire, GL10 3DF Tel/Fax: 01453 822363

North-west of Stroud. Nearest main road: A419 from Stroud to Stonehouse (and M5, junction 13).

3 Bedrooms. £19–£22 (less for 4 nights or more). Available: own bath/shower/toilet. No smoking.
Light suppers if ordered. Vegetarian or other special diets if ordered. No smoking.
1 Sitting-room. With open fire, TV. No smoking.
Large garden
Closed in December.

E-mail: dmj@ukgateway.net

Four-hundred-year-old Tiled House Farm was the first house in the area to have the innovation of tiles to replace thatch on its roof, hence its name. In the big sitting-room, with huge stone fireplace, the original bacon-hooks in the beams and gun-racks above the hearth still remain. Steep stairs go up from the dining-room (which overlooks the farmyard) to some of the bedrooms, the largest of which has timber-framed walls; there is also a self-contained ground-floor suite with good bathroom; here a strange little 'gothick' window was uncovered in a thick stone wall when renovations were being done.

For visitors not wanting to go out, Diane Jeffery will make an inexpensive meal of, say, tuna mousse with salad, baked potato and garlic bread, or chicken casserole, followed by apricot gâteau with cream.

The Rococo Garden at nearby Painswick is a popular draw for visitors, as is the Slimbridge Wildfowl Trust.

Readers' comments: First-class accommodation, superb breakfast. Delightful. Charming and welcoming hosts, nothing too much trouble. Spotlessly clean, breakfasts first class.

TYERSALL

D S

St Briavels, Gloucestershire, GL15 6RT Tel: 01594 530215

West of Lydney. Nearest main road: A466 from Chepstow to Monmouth.

2 Bedrooms. £20. One has own bath/shower/toilet. No smoking.
Dinner (by arrangement). £12 for 3 courses and coffee, at times to suit guests. Vegetarian or other special diets if ordered. No smoking. **Light suppers** if ordered.
1 Sitting-room. With stove, TV. No smoking.
Large garden
Closed from December to February.

Woodland surrounds this 18th-century, wisteria-clad former farmhouse above the River Wye, and high up in Jane Morgan's two-acre garden there are seats from which to enjoy the lovely views across the valley and savour the peace and tranquillity of this secluded spot. Garden-lovers will appreciate the abundance of azaleas and rhododendrons.

Jane's interests are evident throughout the house. On the walls are photos recording her travels abroad; and the life studies in clay dotted around the place are her own work. There are good views from the simply furnished bedrooms and from the spacious sitting-room.

Jane makes her own bread, jam and pâté. For dinner, home-grown organic vegetables may be served as an accompaniment to a main course of chicken and ham pie, preceded by home-made tomato soup, with a refreshing raspberry mousse to finish.

Tyersall is on the edge of the ancient Forest of Dean, an area of great beauty and wildlife interest. There are the remains of Roman iron mines and many other attractions. Offa's Dyke is just a stone's throw away and Tintern Abbey is a short drive from the house. **V**

Gloucestershire

WICKSELM

C D PT S

Station Road, Berkeley, Gloucestershire, GL13 9RL Tel: 01453 810639
South-west of Gloucester. Nearest main road: A38 from Gloucester to Bristol (and M5, junction 14).

2 Bedrooms. £18–£20 (less for 3 nights or more). Available: own bath/shower/toilet.
Light suppers if ordered. Vegetarian or other special diets if ordered.
1 Sitting-room. With open fire, TV.
Large garden

E-mail: wickselm@binternet.com

This small Georgian town has a fascinating history. Within the walls of its Norman castle, home of the Berkeley family for more than 800 years, Edward II was brutally murdered in 1327. Two centuries later, the family played host to Sir Francis Drake, who would stay when en route to the Forest of Dean to select timbers for his ships. Dr Edward Jenner, who pioneered vaccination, lived here and there is a museum devoted to his life and work.

Set in 15 acres of parkland on the outskirts of the town, Wickselm is an imposing and spacious, grey stone Georgian house with high moulded ceilings and tall shuttered windows. Retired farmer Richard Lippiatt and his wife Chris, who now breed horses as a hobby, receive guests in a relaxed and informal atmosphere. The comfortable sitting-room is full of family photos and personal mementoes and the large, simply furnished bedrooms, reached via an impressive stone staircase, have good views.

Berkeley Castle is open to the public between Easter and September. The Slimbridge Wildfowl and Wetlands Trust is also nearby. There are pubs and restaurants within a few minutes' walk.

V

Gloucestershire

WINDRUSH HOUSE

S

Hazleton, Gloucestershire, GL54 4EB Tel: 01451 860364
South-west of Stow-on-the-Wold. Nearest main road: A40 from Cheltenham to Oxford.

4 Bedrooms. £20–£25. Bargain breaks. Available: own bath/shower/toilet; TV. No smoking.
Dinner. £19.50 for 3 courses and coffee, at 7.30pm. Vegetarian diets if ordered. Wine available. **Light suppers** if ordered.
2 Sitting-rooms. With open fire (in one), TV, piano (in one). No smoking.
Large garden
Closed from mid-December to mid-February.

The greatest attraction of this small guest-house built of Cotswold stone is Sydney Harrison's outstanding cooking. Not only is everything impeccably prepared – vegetables delicately sliced and lightly cooked, bread home-baked, breakfast orange juice freshly squeezed – but she has a repertoire of imaginative dishes that puts many an expensive restaurant in the shade.

Sydney's friendly welcome is manifest the moment you arrive, and a free glass of sherry awaits you in your room. As to the house itself, this is furnished with much attention to comfort, and in tranquil colours. All the rooms are immaculate, the furnishings traditional.

The house stands in a quiet spot some 800 feet up in the Cotswold Hills, where the air is bracing and the views are of far fields and grazing sheep. It is on the outskirts of a rambling village of old stone farmhouses and close to beautiful Northleach.

Readers' comments: First-rate; inventive menu. Excellent food. Food outstanding; what a find! Superb cooking. Excellent in every way, especially food and wine. The best cook we've found in England. Delightful, scenic and peaceful location.

WYCK HILL LODGE

M

Wyck Hill, Stow-on-the-Wold, Gloucestershire, GL54 1HT Tel: 01451 830141
On A424 from Stow-on-the-Wold to Burford.

3 Bedrooms. £24–£25 (less for 4 nights or more). Available: own bath/shower/toilet; TV. No smoking.
2 Sitting-rooms. With open fire (in one). No smoking.
Garden
Closed from November to February.

E-mail: gkhwyck@compuserve.com

This picturesque house, now the home of Eddie and Gloria Holbrook, was built around 1800 as the lodge to a nearby mansion. It is surrounded by very lovely gardens, where guests can have afternoon tea in summer and enjoy far views across Bourton Vale. There are good walks straight from the door.

In the L-shaped sitting-room are comfortable sofas, and, in winter, a crackling fire. A small reading-room is particularly attractive: like some other rooms, it has windows set in pointed arches with stained-glass panes at the top. There is a view of the terraced garden (with pond) and far hills. Two of the bedrooms (one opening on to the garden) are on the ground floor, and there is another upstairs – this is a big, two-level room with easy chairs.

At breakfast, Gloria offers plenty of choices – smoked haddock, for instance. For evening meals, there are two good restaurants close by and a wider choice in Stow itself.

Readers' comments: Breakfast very good. Beautiful house with magnificent views. Ideally sited for exploring the Cotswolds. Immaculate; every effort is made to make visitors feel at home. An absolute gem; perfect in every way; our very favourite b & b.

Prices are per person sharing a room at the beginning of the year.

Many houses in this book are situated in or very near to Areas of Outstanding Natural Beauty and protected Heritage Coasts. For a selection of these houses, see p.xi.

Complaints about matters which could not have been settled on the spot will be forwarded to proprietors. Please enclose a stamped addressed envelope if you want your complaint acknowledged.

Addresses shown are to enable you to locate a house on a map. They are not necessarily complete postal addresses (though the essential post-code is included), and detailed directions for finding a house should be obtained from the owner.

HAMPSHIRE

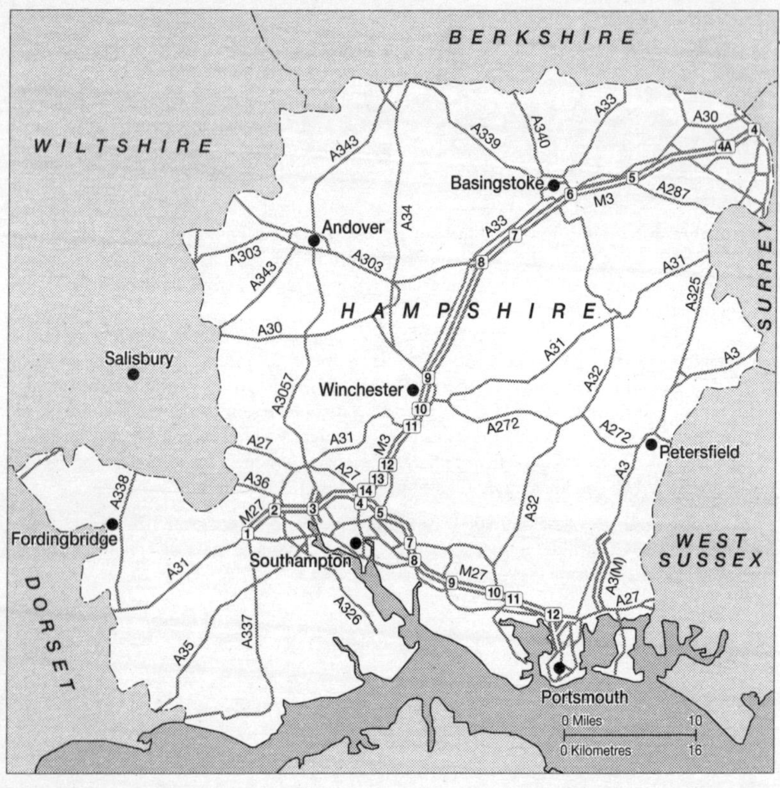

If you find places in England and Wales that you feel should be visited for possible inclusion in a future edition of SOTBT, please write and let us know. Send your descriptions (including full name of establishment, address and current b & b price per person) to Jan Bowmer, c/o Arrow Books, Random House, 20 Vauxhall Bridge Road, London, SW1V 2SA.

BROADWATER

CX

Amport, Hampshire, SP11 8AY Tel/Fax: 01264 772240
West of Andover. Nearest main road: A303 from Andover to Amesbury.

2 Bedrooms. £25–£30. Available: own bath/shower/toilet. No smoking.
Light suppers only. Vegetarian or other special diets if ordered.
1 Sitting-room. With open fire, TV.
Small garden

E-mail: carolyn@dmac.co.uk

Stonehenge, that great megalithic monument on Salisbury Plain, is only a few miles from the quiet and unspoilt village of Amport. Indeed, discoveries such as flint instruments and burial mounds have been made in the area, suggesting that man has lived here for 5000 years.

Broadwater was built near Pill Hill Brook, a clear chalk stream, in the 1600s. The cottage is attractively furnished by Carolyn Mallam and, with its pretty garden (full of roses, lavender, herbs and fruit trees), is a peaceful place. In the beamed sitting/dining-room are watercolours painted by a relative who served in Nelson's fleet. The simply furnished bedrooms are cosy, with views of the garden and surrounding countryside.

Books and board games are thoughtfully provided for children; and Carolyn is willing to serve light suppers (including home-made bread), recommending local inns, such as the Black Swan at Monxton, for more substantial meals.

In the immediate vicinity are the Hawk Conservancy, the Danebury Iron Age hill fort, and the Museum of Army Flying. The cathedral towns of Salisbury and Winchester are also near and the New Forest is only a 30-minute drive away.

V

CAMS

CDS

Hambledon, Hampshire, PO7 4SP Tel: 023 92632865 (Fax: 023 92632691)
North of Portsmouth. Nearest main road: A3 from Portsmouth to Petersfield.

3 Bedrooms. £22–£25 (less for 4 nights or more). Available: own bath/shower/toilet; TV. No smoking.
Light suppers if ordered.
1 Sitting-room. With open fire, TV. No smoking.
Large garden

Hampshire is rich in historic houses: this is one. With 16th-century origins, it derives its name from the de Camoys family, who owned land locally. Its 17th-century pine-panelled dining-room is impressive, with marble fireplace and shuttered glass doors opening on to the garden; beyond a haha sheep graze (beside a tennis court). Spindle-backed rush chairs surround a great circular table of polished yew, where breakfast is served. In the sitting-room, chinoiserie curtains and pink walls make a pleasing background to antique furniture. Up the impressive staircase are pretty bedrooms: the oldest, in pink and white, has beamy walls and leaded windows. For dinners Valerie Fawcett recommends the Vine, a five-minute walk away, or the Bat and Ball, a short drive from the house.

Portsmouth, from where ferries sail to the Isle of Wight and France, is 10 miles away. Also near are Winchester and Chichester. The Queen Elizabeth Country Park, with its many outdoor activities, is worth a visit. Within the park is Butser Hill, the highest point on the South Downs, where you can enjoy superb views.

V

Hampshire

COTTAGE CREST

C

Castle Hill, Woodgreen, Hampshire, SP6 2AX Tel: 01725 512009
South of Salisbury. Nearest main road: A338 from Ringwood to Salisbury.

3 Bedrooms. £24 (less for 3 nights or more). Available: own shower/toilet; TV; views of river. No smoking.
Light suppers if ordered.
1 Sitting/dining-room
Large garden

Bedrooms in the Cadmans' home are some of the most beautiful and well-equipped in this book. A great brass bed with pink-and-white lacy linen is in one: an L-shaped room with windows on two sides from which to enjoy superb views of sunsets over the River Avon in the valley below. A garden suite with private sitting-room faces this view. There are comfortable armchairs, attractive antiques and personal ornaments throughout.

One can sit on a paved terrace with a little pond, or take a zigzag path down to a lower garden frequented by deer, or walk straight into the New Forest.

Particularly picturesque villages nearby include Breamore (with 16th-century Breamore House open to the public, and a mediaeval maze), Rockbourne (Roman villa close to it), and the hamlets of Moyles Court and Burley.

Readers' comments: Delightful, made so welcome, very comfortable. Most charming and friendly. Very warm welcome. Made most comfortable. Garden suite beautifully furnished, and with fresh flowers. Charming hostess, friendly and interesting too.

Hampshire

GREEN PATCH

Furze Hill, Fordingbridge, Hampshire, SP6 2PS Tel: 01425 652387
(Fax: 01425 656594)
West of Southampton. Nearest main road: A31 from Southampton to Ringwood.

3 Bedrooms. £23.50–£27.50. Available: own bath/shower/toilet; TV. No smoking.
Light suppers only. Vegetarian or other special diets if ordered. No smoking.
1 Sitting-room. No smoking.
Large garden

Closed in December and January.

Nestling in a hillside with the New Forest as a backdrop, this 1920s house offers total peace and seclusion.

Eating breakfast in the oak-panelled dining-room is a treat, not least because of the wide and interesting choice of dishes which Meg Mulcahy is happy to prepare. Porridge with whisky and maple syrup might be on the menu, or eggs Benedict, sweetcorn pancakes, kippers, soft cod roes on toast, or scrambled eggs with smoked trout on a toasted muffin; and, of course, the more usual fare.

All year round, guests can relax in the plant-filled conservatory. There is a fridge here, and on summer days you are welcome to barbecue your own food on the adjoining patio, whilst enjoying lovely views of the forest.

Meg offers light suppers only, but there are several eating-places nearby.

Flower-painting is a hobby which she particularly enjoys, and examples of her work and that of the celebrated botanical artist Marianne North are displayed in the spotless bedrooms, some of which have very good views.

V

LAND OF NOD

C(12)

Headley, Bordon, Hampshire, GU35 8SJ Tel: 01428 713609 (Fax: 01428 717698)
North-east of Petersfield. Nearest main road: A3 from Guildford to Petersfield.

2 Bedrooms. £25 **to readers of this book only** –£40. Bargain breaks. Available: own bath/toilet; TV; balcony. No smoking.
Dinner (by arrangement). £20 for 3 courses and wine, at 7pm. Vegetarian or other special diets if ordered. No smoking.
Large garden

'And Cain went out from the presence of the Lord and dwelt in the land of Nod' (Genesis). They say that in the 16th century a man called Cain was excommunicated by the local vicar for some misdemeanour and came to live in a house on this site. The name has remained but this is the third house to be built here amid 100 acres of private estate. It was built in 1939 by Jeremy Whitaker's father: Whitakers have lived here since 1884.

The elegant red-brick house is surrounded by beautiful gardens with some formal areas and much informal woodland (tennis and croquet too). There are good views from the spacious bedrooms, which have comfortable armchairs (there is no guests' sitting-room).

The dining-room takes the Orient as its theme, having been inspired by a piece of antique Japanese needlework which hangs here. Hand-painted chinoiserie panels adorn the walls and the circular resin dining-table is surrounded by specially made Chinese-style chairs in rosewood. A typical dinner menu: cucumber mousse; hot ham in cranberry sauce with seasonal vegetables; rhubarb fool. Both fruit and vegetables are home-grown. Jeremy and Philippa Whitaker are interesting people, having travelled widely. V

MALT COTTAGE

C PT(limited)

Upper Clatford, Hampshire, SP11 7QL Tel: 01264 323469 (Fax: 01264 334100)
South of Andover. Nearest main road: A303 from Andover to Amesbury.

3 Bedrooms. £22.50–£35. Available: own bath/shower/ toilet; TV. No smoking.
Light suppers if ordered. No smoking.
1 Sitting-room. With log stove. No smoking.
Large garden

E-mail: rooms@maltcottage.co.uk

Such was his interest in gardens that Richard Mason gave up a career in industry in order to design them for a living. His wife Patsy has always been a keen gardener too, so it's hardly surprising that the six acres of land which they have gradually acquired is now an area of great beauty which guests can enjoy at their leisure. There is a formal garden containing a variety of shrubs and trees, including Liquidambar with its stunning autumnal colour. There are ponds and a rose arbour and, beyond all this, a chalk stream with trout and meadowland where wildlife flourishes. You might spot a kingfisher on one of its visits or the swans who come to nest every year.

The cottage itself, once a malting barn, is elegant and spacious. The entrance hall leads to a beamed dining-area where guests eat at an Edwardian refectory table. The sitting-room, in pastel shades, features a large inglenook fireplace and log-burning stove. Bedrooms are comfortable and some have garden views.

Light suppers only, but guests can eat at the Mayfly, a short drive away, with its attractive waterside setting.

MAYS FARMHOUSE

C(7) D

Longwood Dean, Hampshire, SO21 1JS Tel: 01962 777486 (Fax: 01962 777747)

South-east of Winchester. Nearest main road: A272 from Winchester to Petersfield (and M3, junction 9).

3 Bedrooms. £25 (less for 4 nights or more). Available: own bath/shower/toilet; TV. No smoking.
Dinner (by arrangement). £14.50 for 4 courses and coffee, at 7pm. Vegetarian or other special diets if ordered. No smoking. **Light suppers** if ordered.
1 Sitting-room. With open fire, TV, piano. No smoking.
Large garden

E-mail: maysfarm@fsnet.co.uk

Twelve-foot trees grew in the kitchen and the 16th-century house had no roof. Undeterred, James Ashby (expert in renovations) bought and transformed it to the highest standards – unvarnished oak beams in the dining-room are now complemented by a woodblock floor, and a handsome log stove stands in the old inglenook, for instance.

Rosalie has painted bedroom furniture decoratively – she runs classes on how to do this (on Mondays). All the rooms have views of the Ashbys' white goats, and of a pretty garden and the woods beyond. One has a Jacuzzi-style bath. A stair-lift is available for those who need it. Dinner (with fresh garden produce) might include pheasant pâté, pork in orange and cider sauce, and a raspberry flan.

Nearby Winchester was England's capital in the days of King Alfred (indeed, it had been a considerable town long before that, during the long Roman occupation). The Norman cathedral dominates all, its most famous bishop – William of Wykeham – being the founder of one of England's great public schools, Winchester College (which can be visited).

V

Hampshire

MORNINGTON HOUSE

C D S

Hambledon, Hampshire, PO7 4RU Tel/Fax: 023 92632704

North of Portsmouth. Nearest main road: A3 from Portsmouth to Petersfield.

2 Bedrooms. £19 (less for 3 nights or more). No smoking.
Light suppers if ordered.
1 Sitting-room. With open fire, TV, piano.
Large garden

In 1760, the year when Mornington House was built, Hambledon was the premier cricket club in England (still going strong) and laid down today's complicated rules.

Charles Lutyens, for many years chairman of the club, is a great-nephew of Sir Edwin Lutyens and may show the architect's Delhi plans to interested visitors as they relax in the bay-windowed sitting-room or the adjoining conservatory with grapevine overhead. There are splendid views over brimming herbaceous flowerbeds, beech hedges, rooftops and church. In the garden is a swimming-pool (unheated).

Everywhere are interesting antiques – an inlaid escritoire from Holland, Edwardian chairs painted with garlands. In the dining-room, 'spitting images' of Disraeli and Gladstone preside over the breakfast-table, and an unusual rocking horse is a magnet to little children.

One bedroom, with lace spread and bamboo bedheads, leads to a bathroom with another bedroom, in blue and white, adjoining it. The Vine pub, five minutes' walk away, is recommended for evening meals.

Readers' comments: Delightful. Lovely welcome and attention. Look forward to returning. Delightful house, charming hosts. Excellent supper. So comfortable. Shall return. My vote for the b & b of the year. Very pleasant, every kindness. A warm, inviting welcome.

V

SANDY CORNER

D S

Ogdens North, Fordingbridge, Hampshire, SP6 2QD Tel: 01425 657295
West of Southampton. Nearest main road: A338 from Fordingbridge to Ringwood (and M27, junction 1).

2 Bedrooms. £23–£25 (less for 4 nights or more). Both have own bath/toilet. No smoking.
Dinner (by arrangement). £15 for 3 courses and coffee, at 7pm. Vegetarian diets if ordered. No smoking. **Light suppers** if ordered.
1 Sitting-room. With TV. No smoking.
Garden

As you may guess by its name, Sandy Corner lies in that part of the New Forest where gravel soil predominates, forming splendid moorlike countryside of gorse, heath and birch. Archaeologist Sue Browne's quiet and attractive 1930s home, looking out over the heathland, is an ideal base for exploring the forest – either on foot, by bicycle (available for hire locally) or on horseback.

Inside, the décor is minimalist in style, with modern etchings and kilim rugs providing colourful embellishments to pale walls and wooden floors. Bedrooms, one of which is on the ground floor, are light and uncluttered. Sue uses only top-quality ingredients in the preparation of her meals. Dinner might comprise home-made tomato soup, followed by chicken casserole, and fruit salad. Packed lunches can also be provided. The house is usually closed to guests during the daytime.

The flora and fauna of the New Forest are a significant attraction for many visitors. You might spot a wild gladiolus, or see one of the many rare species of bats and predatory birds swooping overhead. Ponies and deer still roam; and you could attend one of the specially organized badger watches.

Hampshire

SOUTH FARM

East Meon, Hampshire, GU32 1EZ Tel: 01730 823261 (Fax: 01730 823614)
West of Petersfield. Nearest main road: A272 from Winchester to Petersfield.

3 Bedrooms. £23–£25. Available: own bath/toilet; views of river. No smoking.
Light suppers if ordered. Vegetarian or other special diets if ordered. Wine available.
1 Sitting-room. With open fire, TV. No smoking.
Large garden

The approach to the farm is delightful. There are specimen trees on a lawn (ash, chestnut), an old granary and a grapevine under glass. In the 500-year-old house is a brick-floored dining-room with huge inglenook, rush ladderback chairs and a big oak table. The very large sitting-room has antique furniture and chinoiserie curtains in gold and blue. Bedrooms have been very agreeably furnished by Jane Atkinson: one with poppy fabrics, for instance; in another are exposed beams and a lace bedspread. An oak-panelled room has a peony fabric. All are outstanding.

The house is full of flowers because Jane, an accomplished flower-arranger, regularly has large deliveries from Covent Garden market. You can dine at the George or Izaak Walton inns in East Meon if you want more than a light supper.

The Meon Valley, amid the South Downs, has churches that go back to Saxon times, flint-walled houses and prehistoric burial mounds.

Reader's comments: Wonderful b & b, superb hostess.

Hampshire

STREET FARMHOUSE

C PT S X

Alton Road, South Warnborough, Hampshire, RG29 1RS Tel/Fax: 01256 862225
South-east of Basingstoke. Nearest main road: A287 from Odiham to Farnham (and M3, junction 5).

3 Bedrooms. £18–£26 (less for 3 nights or more). Available: own bath/shower/toilet; TV. No smoking.
Dinner (by arrangement). £16 for 4 courses and coffee, at 7.30pm. Vegetarian or other special diets if ordered. No smoking. **Light suppers** if ordered.
1 Sitting-room. With log stove, TV.
Large garden

E-mail: streetfarmhouse@btinternet.com

Two 16th-century cottages were combined into one to make this attractive house, beamed and with inglenook fireplace, in an ancient village through which a stream runs. Wendy Turner's choice of furnishings admirably complements the old house. There are prettily carved chairs in the pale green dining-room; pine doors have been stripped and brick walls exposed; buttoned chairs in rust-colour covers are gathered around a log stove in the sitting-room. Bedrooms are very pleasant – for instance, furnished with chest-of-drawers of woven cane, with very good armchairs and colour schemes. One bathroom has an oval bath in peach and a bidet. Standards throughout are high and in the garden there is a heated swimming-pool. Dinner might include pork in cider with apricots, and raspberry pavlova.

Readers' comments: An outstanding experience. A place of great character; seldom have we met such friendly people. Excellent in all respects. Our third visit, excellent value.
V Beautifully kept. Made most welcome; warm and comfortable.

Hampshire

VINE FARMHOUSE

Bentley, Hampshire, GU34 4PW Tel/Fax: 01420 23262
South-east of Basingstoke. Nearest main road: A31 from Farnham to Alton (and M3, junction 5).

2 Bedrooms. £20–£25 (less for 4 nights or more). Bargain breaks. One has own bath/toilet; views of river. No smoking.
Large garden

E-mail: vinefarm@aol.com

The River Wey runs within a few yards of this turn-of-the-century farmhouse and, with an acre or so of informal garden and farmland beyond, this is indeed a secluded spot.

The circular entrance hall is just one of the many additions made by the present owners, Gail and David Sinclair. The red-and-cream striped fabric covering the walls in the dining-room gives it a cosy feel, and guests can enjoy fine views of the river and fields beyond while eating breakfast around a circular table. For other meals, you could try the Hen and Chicken or the Anchor in nearby Froyle.

Hunting prints and family photos line the staircase and landing. One small bedroom in blue and yellow has a shared bathroom; the other has windows with good views at each end.

Barn owls breed in a box at the side of the house and, about three miles away, in 20 acres of parkland, is Birdworld with its numerous species of birds. Jane Austen's house is at nearby Chawton. Ten minutes away you can board the Watercress Line, a steam railway which passes through beautiful countryside between Alton and Alresford.

WALNUT COTTAGE

C(14) **M PT**

Old Romsey Road, Cadnam, Hampshire, SO40 2NP Tel/Fax: 023 80812275

West of Southampton. Nearest main road: A31 from Ringwood towards Winchester (and M27, junction1).

3 Bedrooms. £23. Available: own bath/shower/toilet; TV. No smoking.
2 Sitting-rooms. With open fire (in one), TV. No smoking.
Small garden

Old Romsey Road no longer leads anywhere (its days ended when a nearby motorway replaced it). Little, white Walnut Cottage stands in a pretty garden (with an old well) which traps the sun. One bedroom opens on to this.

All the rooms have been attractively furnished by Charlotte and Eric Osgood, who did much of the work themselves. There are two sitting-rooms, one with windows on three sides. For meals other than breakfast, Charlotte recommends the White Hart Inn nearby.

The cottage is on the edge of the New Forest (it was originally occupied by foresters) and is a good choice for an October break, when the forest colours are superb.

Readers' comments: Beautifully located, most helpful people. Delightful couple, charming rooms, comfortable; superb breakfasts. Faultless accommodation and welcome. Made most welcome; situation ideal. Have returned 9 times. Bedrooms very attractive and comfortable.

WEIR COTTAGE

C (5)

Bickton, Hampshire, SP6 2HA Tel: 01425 655813

South of Salisbury. Nearest main road: A338 from Ringwood to Salisbury.

Hampshire

2 Bedrooms. £23–£25 (less for 5 nights or more). Available: own bath/shower/toilet; views of river. No smoking.
Dinner. £15 for 3 courses and coffee, at 8pm. Vegetarian or other special diets if ordered. Wine available. No smoking. **Light suppers** if ordered.
1 Sitting-room. With TV. No smoking.
Large garden

Near Fordingbridge, Weir Cottage was once the flour store for the nearby watermill (now converted). Seated on the sofa in a turquoise and white ground-floor bedroom, one has a view of the tranquil watermeadows of the River Avon. On the sunny upper floor is another bedroom, and a vast room with rafters above a long chestnut table where dinner is served. Breakfast-tables are placed to make the most of the mill-race view. From another window one can see the garden – winding herbaceous beds and a paved terrace with swing-seat.

Philippa Duckworth serves such meals as cucumber mousse, local pheasant with vegetables from the garden, and rhubarb fool.

There are two pianos in the house, played not only by Geoffrey but by guests too. A retired brigadier, he also catches the trout which often appear on the dinner-table. His father, and the Duckworths' daughter, painted the watercolours seen on the walls.

To the north lies Salisbury and its cathedral, but most people stay here to enjoy the New Forest – William the Conqueror's hunting reserve nearly a thousand years ago.

HEREFORDSHIRE

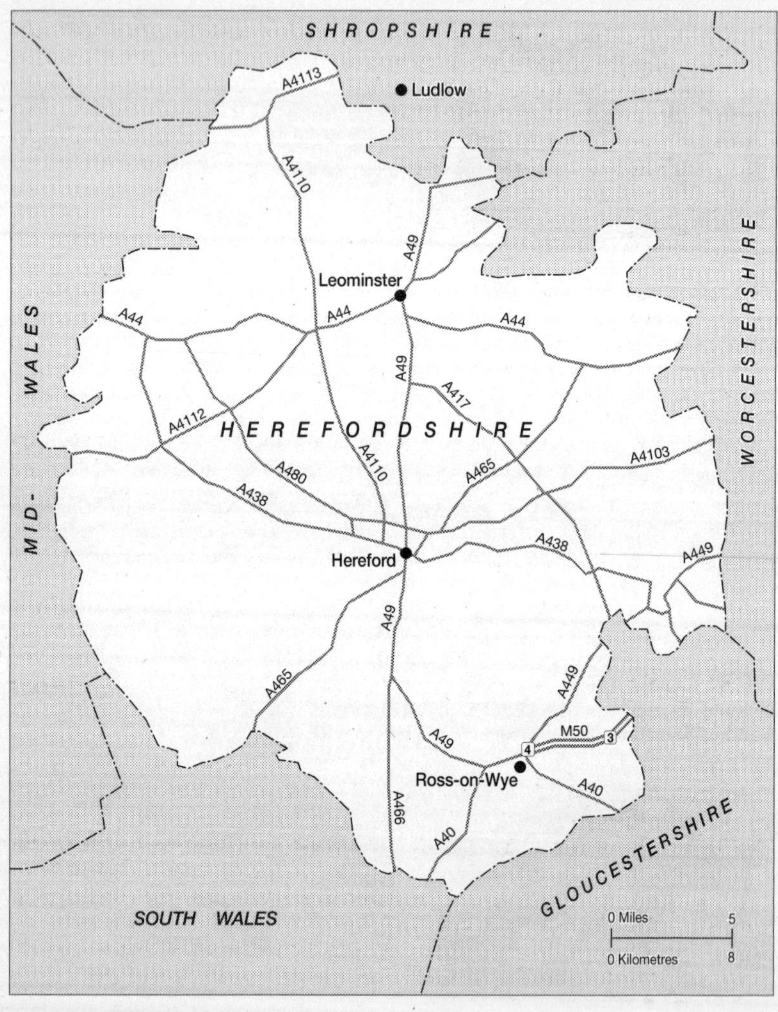

Facts (prices, etc.) at the top of entries are supplied by the proprietors themselves. While every effort is made to ensure that these are correct at the time of going to press, they may alter thereafter: please check when you book.

CWM CRAIG FARM

C S X

Bolston Road, Little Dewchurch, Herefordshire, HR2 6PS Tel/Fax: 01432 840250

North-west of Ross-on-Wye. Nearest main road: A49 from Ross-on-Wye to Hereford (and M50, junction 4).

Herefordshire

3 Bedrooms. £19 (less for 4 nights or more). Available: own bath/shower/toilet; TV. No smoking.
2 Sitting-rooms. With open fire, TV. No smoking (in one).
Large garden

This 18th-century farm in the Wye Valley would be a good choice for a family. Children can watch cattle being fed, and use the games room, which has a snooker table and dart-board. A good family room (with figured walnut suite and shapely bevelled mirrors) has books, television and games; also a particularly good shower-room. There is a second dining-room (with kitchen) reserved for those who want to bring in their own food, a utility room, and an attractive garden.

All rooms are high and light, kept in immaculate condition by Gladys Lee, with far views through their large sash windows. Fine architectural details, including marble fireplaces, are complemented by pink velvet wing chairs or others in William Morris covers.

Readers' comments: Lovely, friendly people. Amazing attention to detail – three kinds of marmalade. Quite entranced: I defy anyone to better it. Bright and cheerful (a lot like the hostess); extremely good value.

V

GRAFTON VILLA FARM

C(5) **PT S**

Grafton, Herefordshire, HR2 8ED Tel/Fax: 01432 268689

South of Hereford. On A49 from Hereford to Ross-on-Wye.

Herefordshire

3 Bedrooms. £22–£23 (less for 2 nights or more). Available: own bath/shower/toilet; TV. No smoking.
Light suppers if ordered.
1 Sitting-room. With open fire, TV. No smoking.
Large garden

E-mail: jennielayton@ereal.com

The 18th-century farmhouse, set well back from the road, is furnished with antiques and well-chosen fabrics. Each bedroom is named after the woodland of which it has a view (Aconbury, Dinedor, Haywood), for the panoramic scenery in every direction is one of the attractions of staying here. The pretty family room also overlooks the farmyard with its free-ranging chickens and ducks – sometimes foals too. Bath- and shower-rooms are good; the little sitting-room snug, its velvet chairs grouped around the fire. The terracotta dining-room, with hunting-prints and leather dining-chairs, looks on to an attractive courtyard garden with a cider-press stone fountain.

Jennie Layton's award-winning breakfasts include poached prunes and apricots flavoured with bramble tea, Herefordshire apple juice, pork sausages and preserves, and home-made bread. For evening meals, good pub food is available locally.

The house is close to the cathedral city of Hereford and within a few miles there are other historic towns such as Ledbury, Ross-on-Wye and Hay-on-Wye ('book city').

V

Herefordshire

HERMITAGE MANOR

C(12)

Canon Pyon, Herefordshire, HR4 8NR Tel/Fax: 01432 760317
North-west of Hereford. Off A4110 from Hereford towards Knighton.

3 Bedrooms. £25 **(one room to readers of this book only)**–£27.50. Minimum 2 nights. All have own bath/shower/toilet; TV. No smoking.
2 Sitting-rooms. With open fire, piano (in one). No smoking.
Large garden
Closed from mid-November to February.

An *escalier d'honneur* sweeps grandly up to the front door which opens into a room of baronial splendour, its ceiling decorated with Tudor roses and strapwork, motifs which are repeated on the oak-panelled walls. Through stone-mullioned bay windows are some of the finest views from any house in this book. There is also a very lovely music room (damask walls and velvet chairs are in soft blue; the limewood fireplace has carved garlands).

The bedrooms, and their bathrooms, are of the highest standard and very large. No. 4 has a view of a hillside spring flowing through stepped pools of pinkish limestone (from a quarry in the area) which Shirley Hickling created when she was converting this exceptional house. She and her partner Bert Morgan provide bed-and-breakfast only – but there are good inns nearby, and Hereford is only 10 minutes away. (Croquet and bowls in the garden.)

Readers' comments: Magnificent view, magnificent bedrooms. So outstanding that we stayed several times this year and last. So pleased by house and view we stayed longer. Fantastic, delightful host and hostess. The equal of 4-star hotels. Probably the best b & b.

Herefordshire

HIGHFIELD

PT S

Ivington Road, Leominster, Herefordshire, HR6 8QD Tel: 01568 613216
Nearest main road: A44 from Worcester to Leominster.

3 Bedrooms. £20–£24 (less for 2 nights or more). Available: own bath/shower/toilet. No smoking.
Dinner. £13.50 for 3 courses and coffee, at 7–7.30pm or when requested. Vegetarian or other special diets if ordered. Wine available. No smoking. **Light suppers** if ordered.
2 Sitting-rooms. With open fire, TV. No smoking (in one).
Large garden
E-mail: info@stay-at-highfield.co.uk

The big comfortable house, built in Edwardian times, stands among fields just outside the old market town of Leominster. Twin sisters Catherine and Marguerite Fothergill, who learnt cooking from Robert Carrier and Prue Leith, have furnished the house handsomely – Chippendale-style chairs in the dining-room, for instance.

Not only are dinners very special but breakfasts too can be memorable – with such options (given notice) as home-made brioches, fishcakes, kedgeree, or home-cooked ham.

For other meals, residents can take the house menu or (after their first night) can choose a special one which might include asparagus and cheese tartlets; cider-baked gammon with raisin sauce; profiteroles or pear pie with brandy cream, or local cheeses to finish.

Readers' comments: Cooking, service and friendliness made my stay seem like a house party. Excellent food and attention. Ideal. Everything perfect. Evening meal splendid.

V

LINDEN HOUSE

C(8) **PT X**

14 Church Street, Ross-on-Wye, Herefordshire, HR9 5HN
Tel: 01989 565373 (Fax: 01989 565575)
Nearest main road: A40 from Gloucester to Monmouth (and M50, junction 4).

Herefordshire

5 Bedrooms. £21–£25. Available: own shower/toilet; TV. No smoking.

Although close to the central market square of this historic town, the guest-house is in a quiet street opposite the church. It was built in 1680 but its façade was altered in the 18th century. At every sash window there is a window-box ablaze with flowers during summer.

Indoors, Clare and Patrick O'Reilly have stencilled the bedroom walls. Some of the rooms are small (and there is no sitting-room) but all are pretty, and there are four with an attractive view of the old churchyard. Most rooms have period beds.

Much is home-made, such as the marmalades and jams at breakfast. A vegetarian cooked breakfast is also available.

The old market town of Ross is ideally placed for touring some of the best parts of England and Wales, midway in a scenic corridor between Hereford and Chepstow.

V

OLD MILL

C D M PT S X

Hoarwithy, Herefordshire, HR2 6QH Tel/Fax: 01432 840602
North-west of Ross-on-Wye. Nearest main road: A49 from Hereford to Ross-on-Wye (and M50, junction 4).

Herefordshire

6 Bedrooms. £20–£22 (less for 5 nights or more). Available: own bath/shower/toilet. No smoking.
Dinner. £12–£13 for 3 courses and coffee, at 7pm. Vegetarian or other special diets if ordered. No smoking. **Light suppers** if ordered.
1 Sitting-room. With open fire, TV. No smoking.
Large garden

Picturesque Hoarwithy, on the River Wye, has not only an exceptional Italianate church, with much use of marble, porphyry and other exotic materials, but also a good guest-house in this 18th-century building The mill race flows through the garden, clematis and roses grow up the front of the cream-painted house. Beyond a tiled and stone-walled hall is a beamed sitting-room with woodstove and a dining-room of scarlet-clothed tables (a typical meal: melon-and-prawn cocktail, chicken casserole, chocolate roulade). Carol Probert has furnished the bedrooms (including one ground-floor double) in cottage style.

Visitors come to this area not only for the surrounding scenery (the Black Mountains, Malvern Hills and Forest of Dean) but to go antique-hunting in Ross-on-Wye. A trip to Symonds Yat is a 'must': around the foot of this rock, 500 feet high, the great River Wye makes a loop that almost turns it into an island and in every direction are superb views of river, wooded slopes and fields.

Readers' comments: Hospitable and helpful. Excellent accommodation. Made to feel very much at home, food excellent. Friendly welcome, picturesque building, pleasant outlook, dinners imaginative. A lovely room; friendly hospitality.

Herefordshire

OLD RECTORY

C PT

Byford, Herefordshire, HR4 7LD Tel: 01981 590218 (Fax: 01981 590499)
West of Hereford. Nearest main road: A438 from Hereford to Brecon.

3 Bedrooms. £24–£25 (less for 3 nights or more). Available: own bath/shower/toilet; TV. No smoking.
Dinner (by arrangement). £13 for 3 courses and coffee, at 7pm. Vegetarian or other special diets if ordered. No smoking. **Light suppers** if ordered.
1 Sitting-room. No smoking.
Large garden
Closed from December to February.

E-mail: jo@cm-ltd.com

An enormous cedar of Lebanon dominates the garden outside the Rectory, a handsome brick house which, though built in 1830, is Georgian in style – having big, well-proportioned rooms and great sash windows which make the most of the very fine views of hills and church. Audrey Mayson and husband Charles have put a great deal of loving care into not only the restoration of the big house (adding Victorian-style bathrooms) but also the landscaping of the formerly neglected garden. The house is run in an informal, caring way.

The sitting/dining-room has pale green walls, deep pine-shuttered windows, pine-panelled doors, and the Maysons' collection of unusual Escher pictures. For dinner Audrey serves such dishes as Piedmont roasted peppers, almond chicken with home-grown vegetables, and hazelnut meringue. At breakfast, home-made preserves are offered. Local crafts are on display.

Readers' comments: Very friendly, relaxed and roomy. Good food. Outstanding. Such spacious and elegant rooms. Cannot recommend too highly.

Herefordshire

OLD RECTORY

PT S

Ewyas Harold, Herefordshire, HR2 0EY Tel/Fax: 01981 240498
South-west of Hereford. Nearest main road: A465 from Hereford to Abergavenny.

3 Bedrooms. £22–£25 (less for 3 nights or more). Bargain breaks. Available: own bath/toilet; TV. No smoking.
Dinner (by arrangement). £13.50 for 3 courses and coffee, at 7pm. Vegetarian or other special diets if ordered. No smoking. **Light suppers** if ordered.
1 Sitting-room. With open fire, piano. No smoking.
Large garden

Close to the Welsh border, Ewyas Harold tells of its early history in its name. Once this whole region was part of the Welsh province of Ewyas. Before the Normans came, however, Harold – Earl of Hereford and Edward the Confessor's successor – made a foray into this area and seized much of its territory. The present inhabitants of the Georgian Old Rectory can trace their roots to that period, for there were Juckes who came over with William the Conqueror.

Jenny and Chrix, previously Cotswold farmers, have an elegantly furnished home, sporting prints hanging alongside portraits of Jenny's Royalist ancestors. Bedrooms are stylish and neat. The dining-room, with antique furniture, has French doors leading on to the secluded garden where there is a small summer-house on rotating runners to follow the sun's course, and common land beyond. Guests may relax in the shuttered sitting-room after an evening meal which might comprise leek and potato soup, gammon with ratatouille and potatoes dauphinoise, and apple and apricot tart.

Reader's comments: Friendly, easy hospitality; roomy, comfortable house and delightful garden; all like a foretaste of paradise.

ORCHARD FARMHOUSE

D PT S

Mordiford, Herefordshire, HR1 4EJ Tel: 01432 870253
South-east of Hereford. Nearest main road: A438 from Hereford to Ledbury.

3 Bedrooms. £19–£20 (less for 4 nights or more). Bargain breaks. One has own bath/toilet; views of river (two). No smoking.
Dinner (by arrangement). £12 for 3 courses and coffee, from 7pm. Vegetarian or other special diets if ordered. Wine available. No smoking. **Light suppers** if ordered.
2 Sitting-rooms. With open fire, TV (in one). No smoking. Bar.
Garden

Country antiques and Victorian china decorate this 17th-century house of reddish stone walls, inglenooks, flagged floors and beams. An old Norwegian stove (decorated with reindeer) warms one sitting-room. Pink and pine bedrooms with wicker armchairs have high ceilings and nice bathrooms; two front rooms have views of the Black Mountains. The dining-room has rush chairs and a dresser with more china dishes. You may spot deer, foxes and even badgers; also kestrels and buzzards, cowslips and violets – for the house is in an Area of Special Scientific Interest within the Wye Valley, itself an Area of Outstanding Natural Beauty.

Fishing can be arranged on the Wye, the Lugg or the Frome (all within a mile); guided walking holidays are available, and Ken James also runs driving courses.

Angela specializes in good farmhouse cooking. Dinner might comprise home-made leek and potato soup, lamb cooked in cider, honey and rosemary, and home-made apple pie, for example. Bread rolls are home-made; most produce is local.

V

STONE HOUSE FARM

C D PT S X

Tillington, Herefordshire, HR4 8LP Tel: 01432 760631
North-west of Hereford. Nearest main road: A4110 from Hereford towards Leominster.

3 Bedrooms. £17.50 (less for 3 nights or more). Bargain breaks. Available: own bath/shower/toilet. No smoking.
Dinner. £12 for 4 courses and coffee, at times to suit guests. Vegetarian or other special diets if ordered. Wine available. No smoking. **Light suppers** if ordered.
2 Sitting-rooms. With open fire/stove, TV, piano (in one). No smoking (in one).
Garden

Judy Seaborne's very good home cooking is the main attraction of Stone House Farm. The setting is very peaceful, with fine views, and children in particular enjoy spring visits when there are lambs, calves and foals to be seen. A typical meal: home-made soup, a roast, fruit pie – served from Royal Worcester dishes, in a dining-room with log stove. (Sunday lunch is also available by arrangement.) Made of solid stone from a local quarry, the house stands well back from the country lane. There is an old pump in the front garden which feeds a small pond.

Nearby are Hereford and its cathedral; Hay-on-Wye for secondhand bookshops; the lovely River Wye with footpaths alongside. Many visitors, with 'The Black-and-White Village Trail' in hand, motor from one picturesque village to the next.

Readers' comments: Well fed and received with great friendliness. Food of high quality and ample. Most welcoming; excellent cook. A real farmhouse experience.

V

UPPER BUCKTON

C X

Leintwardine, Herefordshire, SY7 0JU Tel: 01547 540634
West of Ludlow. Nearest main road: A4113 from Knighton towards Ludlow.

3 Bedrooms. £25–£30 (less for 5 nights or more). All have own bath/shower/toilet; views of river. No smoking.
Dinner. £20 for 4 courses and coffee, at 7pm. Vegetarian or other special diets if ordered. Wine available. No smoking. **Light suppers** if ordered (for late arrivals).
1 Sitting-room. With open fire, TV. No smoking.
Large garden

Yvonne Lloyd is an accomplished cook, serving such starters as pears with grilled goat's cheese or stuffed mushrooms; then roasts, salmon, or chicken with orange and almonds; vacherins or chocolate roulade. It is largely her reputation for good food which brings visitors here – that, and the peace and quiet of this 18th-century house (the heart of a 300-acre sheep and cereal farm) in which antiques furnish the comfortable rooms.

Yvonne has a decorative touch, with a taste for ribbon-and-posy fabrics in one room, poppies in another, for instance. All the frilled or pleated valances are made by her.

Outside is a verandah on which to sit with pre-dinner drink or after-dinner coffee to enjoy the view towards the high ridge of the Wigmore Rolls. There is a croquet lawn, and other outdoor games.

This is very good country for walking and birdwatching, or for leisurely drives.

Readers' comments: Outstanding location. Marvellous hosts, lovely house, food excellent. We felt completely at home. Could not have been more warmly and sensitively welcomed. Super retreat for jaded townies. Bedrooms delightful. House beautifully furnished.

UPPER NEWTON FARM

C S X

Kinnersley, Herefordshire, HR3 6QB Tel/Fax: 01544 327727
North-west of Hereford. Off A4112 from Kinnersley towards Leominster.

5 Bedrooms. £25. Bargain breaks. All have own bath/shower/toilet; TV. No smoking.
Light suppers if ordered. Vegetarian or other special diets if ordered. No smoking.
3 Sitting-rooms. With open fire (in one), TV. No smoking.
Large garden
E-mail: enquiries@bordertrails.u-net.com

Jon Taylor's family has lived at Upper Newton for a hundred years, but the handsome black-and-white house at the heart of this mixed beef and arable farm (cider orchards too) has been there a lot longer than that: the oldest part (now the tiled hall) dates back to 1640. Most of the bed-and-breakfast accommodation is in the converted stable block and comprises a couple of two-bedroomed cottages, each of which is let only as a single booking, whether for one person, a couple or a group. As well as bedrooms (one with four-poster), each cottage has a sitting-room (toy box and children's videos in one), a small but well-equipped kitchen area and access to an enclosed herb garden. There is an additional four-poster bedroom, with its own sitting-room, in the main house.

From time to time Pearl Taylor runs courses in crafts, interior design and cookery, so the additional decorative touches – the stencilling and the clever use of fabric hangings and trimmings – are hers. (She has won the accolade of AA Landlady of the Year.) There are always fresh flowers in the rooms, and home-made cakes or biscuits on arrival.

Breakfast is served in the farmhouse, in the spacious dining-room with an open fre. Light suppers only, but Pearl will advise on the best eating-places in the area.

VAULD FARMHOUSE

C(12) **PT X**

The Vauld, Herefordshire, HR1 3HA Tel: 01568 797898
North of Hereford. Nearest main road: A49 from Hereford to Leominster.

4 Bedrooms. £25–£30 (less for 3 nights or more). Available: own bath/shower/toilet; TV.
Dinner (by arrangement). From £18 for 4 courses and coffee, at 7.30pm (not Sundays). No smoking. **Light suppers** if ordered.
Sitting-rooms: see text.
Large garden

'Sleepy hollow', the locals call this area where the ancient farmhouse lies hidden, its creamy, black-timbered walls lopsided with age (it was built in 1510). One steps through the front door into a great room with stone-slabbed floor, half-timbered walls, log fire and colossal beams overhead.

Those who book the granary suite (which has its own stone staircase from outside) have a private sitting-room, with deep velvet armchairs, bathroom and a choice of bedrooms (one a gallery). Other visitors may prefer the ground-floor oak room with four-poster (this, too, has its own entrance and bathroom). The house is well endowed with private sitting-areas.

Jean Bengry will prepare dinners using much fresh local produce. A typical menu: stuffed mushrooms, duck breasts, apple and hazelnut tart, and a selection of cheeses.

Readers' comments: None of us wanted to leave. Nothing was too much trouble. Made us completely at home. A superb break. What a wonderful place! The food was a treat. Enchanting. Our fourth visit, always excellent. Wonderful hostess. Attractively decorated.

For a list of SOTBT houses that are in or close to the great National Parks of England and Wales, see p.ix.

Readers' comments quoted in the book are from letters sent directly to us: they are not supplied via the proprietors.

When writing to the managing editor, if you want an acknowledgment please enclose a stamped addressed envelope.

Some proprietors stipulate a minimum stay of two nights at weekends or peak seasons; or they will accept one-nighters only at short notice (that is, only if no lengthier booking has yet been made).

HERTFORDSHIRE

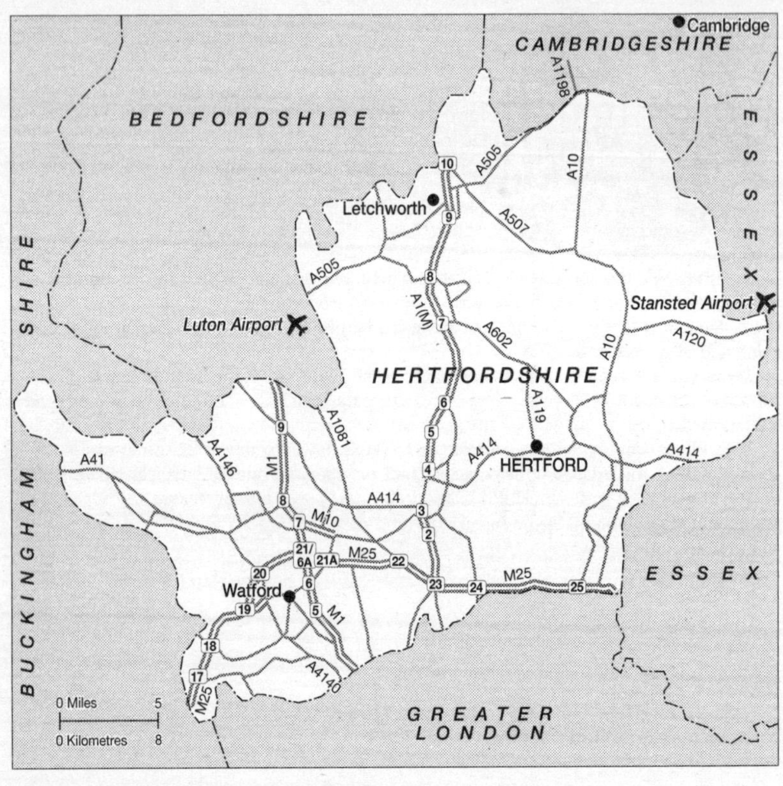

To find the right accommodation in the right area at the right price, use an up-to-date edition of this book – revised every year. For an order form for the next edition (published in November), send a stamped addressed envelope, with 'SOTBT 2003 in the top left-hand corner, to Explore Britain, Alston, Cumbria, CA9 3SL.

FAIRHAVEN

C PT

102 Old North Road, Kneesworth, Hertfordshire, SG8 5JR Tel/Fax: 01763 249471
South-west of Cambridge. On A1198 from Royston to Godmanchester (also near A1(M), junction 10 and M11, junction 10).

3 Bedrooms. £19 (less for 4 nights). Available: own TV. No smoking.
Light suppers if ordered. Vegetarian diets if ordered. No smoking.
1 Conservatory/sitting-room. No smoking.
Garden

Despite its somewhat bland exterior and position on a busy main road, Fairhaven is a welcoming base from which to explore four counties (Hertfordshire, Cambridgeshire, Bedfordshire and Essex). Guests' bedrooms in this much-converted 1930s bungalow are most attractively and comfortably furnished; windows are double-glazed. In the hall are Diana Watson's dried flower arrangements and a striking collection of commemorative china and glassware. Breakfast is taken in a pretty room with pale apricot walls and handsome old pine furniture. Fresh yogurt (made by husband Peter) is always available, and, in addition to home-made bread and preserves, Diana takes great care to serve locally supplied bacon and sausages.

After a hard day's sightseeing, guests can relax in the plant-filled conservatory or sip a glass of wine in the small summer-house. The peaceful garden is well tended, with pergola, trailing honeysuckle and colourful flowerbeds.

For full-scale dinners, Diana has produced a map pinpointing worthwhile eateries – all within 5–10 minutes' drive.

Apart from such tourist honeypots as Cambridge, families enjoy visiting Wimpole Hall with its grand house, home farm, fine walks, parkland and gardens.

V

SCHOOL HOUSE

C

Newnham, Hertfordshire, SG7 5LA Tel: 01462 742815
North-east of Letchworth. Nearest main road: A1 from Borehamwood to Biggleswade (and A1(M), junction 10).

2 Bedrooms. £23–£25. Available: own bath/shower/toilet; TV. No smoking.
Dinner (by arrangement). £10 for 2 courses, at 7–8.30pm. Vegetarian or other special diets if ordered. Wine available. No smoking. **Light suppers** if ordered.
1 Sitting-room. With open fire, TV. No smoking.
Large garden
Closed from early December to mid-January.

Farrs have farmed here for generations; but this house had different beginnings, being first a village school – hence the bell high up on the lemon-coloured façade – and then a shooting-lodge. All around are fields and deep peace. (In the grounds there is a tennis court.)

Trish Farr has an eye for striking colours, and every room seems to sing – with walls of brilliant viridian in the characterful sitting-room, coral in the quarry-tiled hall, raspberry or mint in the bedrooms. There are such distinctive touches as butterfly tiles in a fireplace, a budgerigar-patterned bedspread, and unusual antiques or junk-shop finds.

As she has four teenage children, she serves only simple meals (like chicken casserole and fresh fruit with cream) and breakfast, sometimes eaten on the terrace. But there are lots of inns offering good food, particularly in nearby Ashwell – famous for its high-towered church, music festivals and old houses. Newnham's own 12th-century church, with frescoes of St Christopher, is also worth a visit. Luton Airport is easily reached from here.

Reader's comments: Superb cook, price very modest.

Hertfordshire

Hertfordshire

WOODCOTE HOUSE C

7 The Grove, Whippendell, King's Langley, Hertfordshire, WD4 9JF
Tel: 01923 262077 (Fax: 01923 266198)
North-west of Watford. Nearest main road: A4251 from M25, junction 20, towards Tring (and M1, junction 6).

side and rear view

4 Bedrooms. £23–£26 (less for 2 nights or more). Available: own bath/shower/toilet; TV. No smoking.
Light suppers if ordered.
1 Sitting-area. With TV. No smoking.
Large garden
Closed at Easter.

E-mail: Leveridge@btinternet.com

Perched at the top of a cul-de-sac, this Scandinavian-style, timber-framed house overlooks a large sloping garden, with oak, ash and maple trees, towards open farmland. Although it is close to the motorway network and very conveniently placed for both Heathrow and Luton airports, as well as quick access to London, all is quiet hereabouts.

Throughout the house, the dark attractive timbering of its construction is much in evidence. Bedrooms (with good bath- or shower-rooms tucked away behind wooden doors) are comfortable but unfussy – two are singles. In the oak-furnished breakfast-room, where there is also a piano, 'breakfast chef' and retired printer Colin Leveridge provides guests with such options as kippers and smoked haddock in addition to the usual fare. Occasionally, breakfast may be taken on the sunny terrace.

For evening meals, there are two good food pubs in nearby Chipperfield, or Annette (an occupational therapist) will serve soup-and-sandwich suppers if requested.There are pleasant walks in the vicinity (along the Grand Union Canal, for example), riding stables next door and cricket on the green in King's Langley.

V

Prices are per person sharing a room at the beginning of the year.

Book well ahead: many of these houses have few rooms. Do not expect dinner if you have not booked it or if you arrive late.

Major tourist attractions, such as Stratford-upon-Avon, Bath and Cambridge, can often be easily reached from houses in adjacent counties.

THANK YOU . . . to those who send details of their own finds, for possible future inclusion in the book. Do not be disappointed if your candidate does not appear in the very next edition. Recommendations from unknown members of the public are never published without verification, and it takes time to get round each part of England and Wales in turn. Please, however, do not send details of houses already featured in many other guides, nor any that are more expensive than those in this book (see page xiv).

KENT

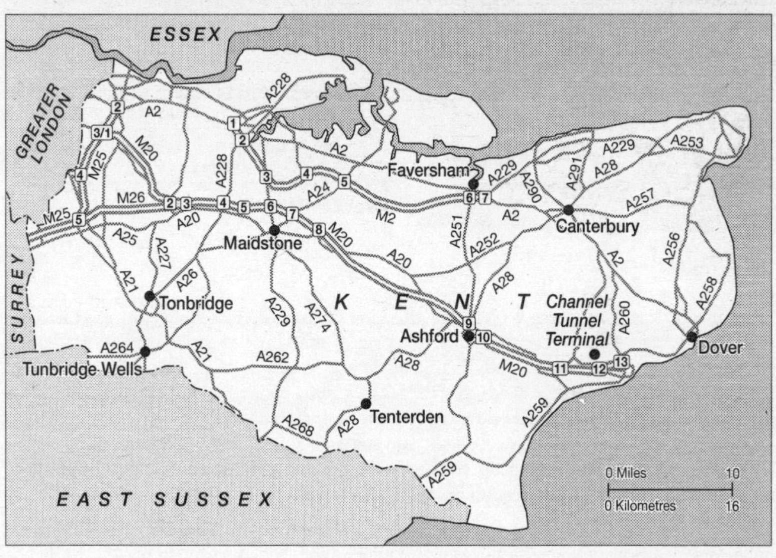

APPLYING FOR INCLUSION IN SOTBT Many proprietors ask for their houses to be included in this book, and – although few can be accepted – such applications are welcomed, particularly from areas not already well covered; *provided that* the b & b price is within the book's limits (see page xiv). Ideally, either dinner or light snacks should be available in the evening. There is no charge for an entry but, compiling the book being expensive, nearly all proprietors make a contribution at the end of each year (no bills are issued). Every house has to be visited first and it may be some time before this takes place. Brochures, prices, menus, etc. should be posted to: Jan Bowmer (SOTBT), c/o Arrow Books, 20 Vauxhall Bridge Road, London SW1V 2SA. No phone calls please.

Kent

BARNFIELD FARM

C S

near Charing, Kent, TN27 0BN Tel/Fax: 01233 712421

North-west of Ashford. Nearest main road: A20 from Maidstone to Ashford (and M20, junctions 8/9).

5 Bedrooms. £23–£24 (less for 7 nights or more). Some have views of river. No smoking.
Dinner. £12.50 for 3 courses and coffee, at 7pm. Vegetarian or special diets if ordered. Wine available. No smoking. **Light suppers** if ordered.
2 Sitting-rooms. With open fires, TV. No smoking.
Large garden with tennis court.

This historic farmhouse was built about the time of the Battle of Agincourt (1415). One steps into a large hall, where the oak framework of the house is exposed to view (draped with hop bines) and a cask holding shepherds' crooks stands in one corner – for outside are sheep pastures, with arable fields beyond. The dining-room has an exceptionally large inglenook, and an especially fine door made from a church chest.

Bedrooms are fresh and unpretentious, and some overlook the River Stour.

Phillada Pym serves such meals as egg mayonnaise, casseroled lamb cutlets, and chocolate mousse – loading a hot-tray on the sideboard for second helpings.

V

Readers' comments: Enjoyed our stay very much; a warm welcome. Unobtrusive but charming hostess. Delightful house and garden. Excellent meal. Nicely secluded position. A house full of treasures and perfectly beautiful. Delightful.

Kent

BOWER FARMHOUSE

C D PT S

Bossingham Road, Stelling Minnis, Kent, CT4 6BB Tel: 01227 709430

South of Canterbury. Nearest main road: A2 from Dover towards Canterbury (and M20, junction 11).

2 Bedrooms. £22–£24 (less for 5 nights or more). Both have own bath/shower/toilet.
1 Sitting-room. With open fire, TV, piano.
Garden

E-mail: book@bowerbb.freeserve.co.uk

This 300-year-old house with exposed oak beams and central staircase was in Victorian times a small school. It is now the home of Anne and Nick Hunt, he a secondary school head, their teenage daughters and their two cats and dogs. There is a cosy sitting-room with old and modern watercolours, wing chairs and two chesterfields in warm reds, and a piano. The double bedroom has pastel striped and sprigged wallpaper and pretty patchwork bedspreads; the other twin room (also with its own bathroom) has peach curtains, fine walnut veneered furniture and headboards, and a gently sloping floor encouraging one bedwards! Home-made bread and eggs from the Hunts' own chickens are served at breakfast.

The Minnis or common land of 125 acres lies opposite the house; two nature reserves and a rural heritage centre are close by. Canterbury, the Shuttle terminal, Dover and Folkestone are only short drives away.

V

Reader's comments: Delightful house, charming hosts.

BULLTOWN FARMHOUSE

C X

Kent

Bulltown, West Brabourne, Kent, TN25 5NB Tel: 01233 813505 (Fax: 01227 709544)
East of Ashford. Nearest main road: A20 from Ashford to Folkestone (and M20, junction 10).

3 Bedrooms. £22.50 (less for 3 nights or more). All have own bath/shower/toilet. No smoking.
Light suppers if ordered.
1 Sitting-room. With open fire, TV, piano. No smoking.
Large garden

The Wiltons' geese will probably announce your arrival at Bulltown Farmhouse, a beautifully restored, 15th-century, timber-framed house tucked away in a tiny North Downs hamlet. Rooms are spacious and high-ceilinged – you are more likely to weave in and out of exposed beams than to duck under them.

The whitewashed bedrooms are stylishly furnished, with individual touches. There is a prettily embroidered chintz and white bedspread in one; another has an Indian crewelwork rug and an old meat-safe used as a bedside cabinet. In the oak-furnished and quarry-tiled dining-room, Lilly Wilton serves breakfasts and light suppers. She and Julian are a friendly young couple: he runs an interior design business, but his passion is restoring and driving vintage cars. For evening meals, there are three good pubs nearby.

Country walks are an obvious attraction hereabouts. The Crundale Valley is particularly quiet and unspoilt. There is a nature reserve at Wye and a craft centre at Smeeth. And, of course, you are ideally placed for day trips to France.

Reader's comment: Superb in all respects.

V

CATHEDRAL GATE HOTEL

C D PT X

Kent

36 Burgate, Canterbury, Kent, CT1 2HA Tel: 01227 464381 (Fax: 01227 462800)
(M2, junction 7, is near.)

27 Bedrooms. £22.50–£40.50. Full English breakfast extra from February. Bargain breaks. Available: own bath/shower/toilet; TV; telephone; views of cathedral.
Dinner. £13 for 3 courses, at 7–9pm. Vegetarian or other special diets if ordered. Wine available. No smoking. **Light suppers.**
2 Sitting-rooms. Bar.
E-mail: cgate@cgate.demon.co.uk

The cathedral has a great, sculpted, mediaeval gateway. Tucked beside it is a row of shops and restaurants, above part of which is this upstairs guest-house (which has direct access to the cathedral precincts), not luxurious but characterful. Bedrooms are reached via a maze of narrow corridors and creaking stairways. Most are quiet; and some at the top have superlative views of the cathedral – floodlit at night (during summer).

When the small hotel was taken over by Caroline Jubber and her husband, they greatly improved the bedrooms while retaining ancient beams, leaded casements and bow windows. Breakfast (except in January, continental unless you pay extra) is brought to you in the small dining-room or in your bedroom. There are municipal carparks (for which there is a charge) several minutes' walk away.

Readers' comments: Incredible situation. Very nice people. Location superb. Delicious breakfasts. We can't wait to return.

V

Kent

CHARCOTT FARMHOUSE

C D PT

Charcott, Leigh, Kent, TN11 8LG Tel: 01892 870024 (Fax: 01892 870158)
West of Tonbridge. Nearest main road: A21 from Sevenoaks to Tonbridge.

3 Bedrooms. £22.50. All have own bath/shower/toilet. No smoking.
Light suppers if ordered.
1 Sitting-room. With TV, piano.
Large garden

E-mail: nicholasmorris@charcott.freeserve.co.uk

The breakfasts which Nick Morris serves in the elegant maroon and white dining-room of this 18th-century, tile-hung farmhouse are a major event. You may be offered wholemeal porridge oats with Jersey cream, home-made brioche, kippers or kedgeree, in addition to the more usual fare. One is very much *en famille* here, what with four cats, Polly the dog, and the Morrises' two children in residence.

There is a snug sitting-room; and one attractive, beamy, ground-floor bedroom overlooks the pond and chicken coop. Up a twisty staircase are two more neat bedrooms. You may notice Ginny's watercolours on the walls or Nick's photographs. After a varied career in the army and in industry, he is now a professional photographer and often works at nearby Penshurst Place, one of England's great mediaeval manor houses. For evening meals, the Greyhound pub is a short stroll from the farmhouse.

Within a few miles are half a dozen NT properties, Tudeley church with stained-glass windows by Chagall, and Chiddingstone, one of the Weald's prettiest villages.

V *Reader's comments:* The welcome was warm and hospitable, breakfast was extremely good.

Kent

CRABTREE FARMHOUSE

C D PT(limited) **S**

Tamley Lane, Hastingleigh, Kent, TN25 5HW Tel/Fax: 01233 750327
East of Ashford. Nearest main road: A28 from Ashford to Canterbury (and M20, junction 10).

2 Bedrooms. £22 (less for 3 nights or more). Both have own bath/shower/toilet. No smoking.
Dinner (by arrangement). £12.50 for 3 courses and coffee, at times to suit guests. **Light suppers** if ordered.
1 Sitting-room. With TV. Piano.
Large garden

Roz Bacon fell in love with Crabtree Farmhouse many years ago, and when the opportunity arose to acquire it, she and her husband Chris leapt at the chance. The reasons for their enthusiasm are plain to see. Set high up in the peaceful, rolling North Downs, this is a particularly charming, whitewashed and pantiled cottage. Built in 1746, it is surrounded by a pretty flint-walled garden where holyhocks grow beside traditional English roses.

The comfortable bedrooms are at either end of the house. One is in the original cottage, where beams are exposed and floors slope; the other is in the eaves of the extension, formerly an old weatherboarded barn. Breakfast is served in a snug little panelled room off the kitchen, and evening meals – perhaps vichyssoise, beef and orange casserole, and home-made ginger ice cream – in the grander, ochre-coloured dining-room.

Nearby Canterbury is best visited outside the summer months, and Roz can direct you to its quieter parts. The North Downs Way is half a mile from the house and the Channel Tunnel a 20-minute drive away.

V

DEAN COURT FARM **C D S X**

Kent

Challock Lane, Westwell, Kent, TN25 4NH Tel: 01233 712924
North-west of Ashford. Nearest main road: A20 from Maidstone to Ashford (and M20, junction 9).

3 Bedrooms. £22.50. One has own bath/shower.
Dinner (by arrangement). £10 for 3 courses and coffee, at times to suit guests. Vegetarian or other special diets if ordered. Wine available. **Light suppers** if ordered.
2 Sitting-rooms. With open fire (in one). TV.
Large garden

Among rolling hills with fine views is Dean Court Farm, a 200-acre sheep farm close to the Pilgrims' Way. The house's name is listed in Domesday Book, but the present building is only 200 years old, with some 20th-century additions – for example, the garden room, which has comfortable cane furniture and views over Eastwell Park, which the farm borders. Tony Lister, a chartered surveyor, and his wife Susan encourage an informal family atmosphere. They both have a good eye for pictures, which cover the walls. Accommodation is simple, with good-sized rooms. One has pink-striped walls, another exposed beams covered with rosettes from family successes in three-day eventing. There is a good walk around the farm perimeter, and interesting wildlife. An evening meal may comprise chicken casserole, a fruity pudding, cheese, and a glass of wine.

For a scenic drive, go across the North Downs to the valley of the River Stour, taking in the Tudor village of Chilham and then on to Hastingleigh.

FRITH FARM HOUSE **C**(10)

Kent

Otterden, Kent, ME13 0DD Tel: 01795 890701 (Fax: 01795 890009)
South-west of Faversham. Nearest main road: A20 from Maidstone to Charing (and M2, junction 6).

3 Bedrooms. £25–£32 (less for 3 nights or more). Available: own shower/toilet; TV. No smoking.
Dinner (by arrangement). £19.50 for 4 courses and coffee, from 7pm. Vegetarian or other special diets if ordered. No smoking. **Light suppers** if ordered.
1 Sitting-room. With open fire. No smoking.
Large garden

E-mail: markham@frith.force9.co.uk

Once, there were cherry orchards as far as the eye could see: now Frith has only six acres. (From their fruit Susan Chesterfield makes sorbets for her gourmet dinners.)

Those cherry trees also financed the building in 1820 of this very fine house. Maroon damask wallpapers and sofas are in keeping with its style. The bedrooms are beautifully decorated and very well equipped (one has a four-poster).

In a very lovely dining-room, fiddleback chairs and a collection of antique plates contrast with a bold geometrical Kazak print used for the curtains, and with the white dishes of German bone china on which Susan serves such meals as avocado with taramasalata, sorbet, lamb steaks with capers, and meringues glacés. Breakfast is served in the polygonal conservatory. An indoor heated swimming-pool is available for guests.

The house is so high up on the North Downs that its views extend – in the case of one of the pretty bedrooms – as far as the Isle of Sheppey. Canterbury is near.

Reader's comments: Extremely helpful, beautiful home, delicious dinner. V

Kent

THE GRANARY

C PT S X

Rock Farm, Gibbs Hill, Nettlestead, Kent, ME18 5HT Tel: 01622 814547 (Fax: 01622 813905)
South-west of Maidstone. Nearest main road: A26 from Maidstone to Tonbridge (and M20, junction 4).

4 Bedrooms. £25–£35. Available: Both have own bath/shower/toilet; TV. No smoking.
Light suppers if ordered.
1 Sitting-room. With stove, TV. No smoking.
Garden

E-mail: robcorfe@thegranary-bnb.co.uk

Gone are the days when Kent produced most of the hops for Britain's beers, and the Corfe family, who until recently were hop-farmers, have moved with the times. Their land is now turned over to arable- and fruit-farming, and they have converted an early 19th-century barn into a smart and comfortable family home.

The attractive main bedroom, once the threshing area, has a king-size bed framed by the old roof supports, while a smaller double has exposed brick walls and a bright turquoise colour scheme. Two additional bedrooms have recently been created on the ground floor. Gail's breakfasts, produced using local ingredients, are served in the state-of-the-art kitchen, from which a small gallery looks down on to the red and gold sitting-room.

Rock Farm House gardens are open to the public in summer under the National Gardens Scheme; and there is also a plant nursery on the land which you are welcome to visit. For meals other than light suppers, there is a restaurant in nearby Wateringbury, or at the Whitbread Hop Farm in Beltring, which also has a museum devoted to hop-farming and rural crafts.

Kent

HEAVERS

C D

Ryarsh, West Malling, Kent, ME19 5JU Tel: 01732 842074 (Fax: 01732 842043)
West of Maidstone. Nearest main road: A228 from Tonbridge to Rochester (and M20, junction 4).

2 Bedrooms. £19–£21. Bargain breaks. No smoking.
Dinner (by arrangement). £14 for 4 courses and coffee, at 7.30pm. Vegetarian or other special diets if ordered. Wine available. No smoking. **Light suppers** if ordered.
1 Sitting-room. With open fire, TV, piano. No smoking.
Large garden

E-mail: jamesed@compuserve.com

Perched on a hilltop, this 17th-century red brick farmhouse with dormer windows in the roof and clematis around the porch is at the heart of a smallholding.

The cosy sitting-room has very comfortable armchairs grouped around the brick hearth (stacked with logs), which still has the old bread oven alongside.

Jean Edwards enjoys cooking a wide selection of dishes. She bakes her own bread; honey, eggs and lamb are home-produced.

Beamed bedrooms are small but prettily furnished. Through the windows are views of the Downs or of the garden which, even in winter, is colourful.

Readers' comments: Very good indeed. As charming as could be; convivial hosts; mouth-watering and plentiful food. Charming house, food delicious. Well-informed, witty and helpful hosts. Gourmet dinners.

HOATH HOUSE

C

Kent

Penshurst Road, Chiddingstone Hoath, Kent, TN8 7DB Tel: 01342 850362
North-west of Tunbridge Wells. Nearest main road: A264 from Tunbridge Wells to East Grinstead.

3 Bedrooms. £25–£30 (less for 2 nights or more). One has own bath/toilet; TV (in all). No smoking.
Dinner (by arrangement). £15 for 3 courses and coffee, at 8pm. Vegetarian dishes if ordered. No smoking. **Light suppers** if ordered.
1 Sitting-room. With open fire, piano. No smoking.
Large garden
Closed from December to February.

Hoath House is a building of exceptional mediaeval interest which, starting as a simple hall house, has had wings and other additions built on through the centuries. The massive, chamfered beams of the sitting-room, its lattice-paned windows and the plastered walls where the hand-prints of builders can still be seen, are impressive.

To reach the upstairs bedrooms one passes through passages with 18th-century ancestral portraits and other family heirlooms. A vast family bedroom has a sofa in the bay window. There is an enormous bathroom in 'thirties style. (The en suite bedroom is in a ground-floor annexe.)

Jane Streatfeild provides straightforward dinners: home-made soup or pâté; devilled chicken; fruit fool or pie. Seasonal fruit and vegetables come from the garden.

Readers' comments: Fascinating house. Helpful and welcoming. Wonderful, interesting house. Like stepping back into the first Elizabethan age. Stunning views. Could not have been kinder. Charming, very interesting. Quite an experience to stay here.

JESSOPS

C(12) **M PT S X**

Kent

Tonbridge Road, Bough Beech, Kent, TN8 7AU Tel: 01892 870428
North-west of Tunbridge Wells. Nearest main road: A21 from Sevenoaks to Tonbridge (and M25, junction 5).

3 Bedrooms. £24–£25 (less for 3 nights or more). Available: own shower/toilet; TV. No smoking.
1 Sitting-room. With open fire, TV, piano. No smoking.
Large garden

In the scenic and fertile Kentish Weald is 15th-century Jessops, home of artist Frank Stark, whose landscapes line the walls. Every room has unusual antiques and other interesting finds from afar. There are beams and lattice windows, and, in some parts of the house, the original wattle-and-daub walls. Outside are a flowery garden and the Starks' hens, geese, ducks and dogs. Judith's excellent breakfasts include varied home-made breads, croissants and her own marmalade. For evening meals, Judith can recommend several good pubs in the area.

Lanes meander through the Wealden hills, among orchards and hop fields. This is one of the most fertile places in Europe, yet with no prairie-sized fields to spoil the scene: small is beautiful. Only the stately homes are of great size – and magnificence: Penshurst, Hever Castle, Knole and Ightham Mote, in particular.

Readers' comments: We were made very welcome. Breakfasts were excellent. Nothing was too much trouble. Very warm and interesting hosts. Will definitely return.

Kent

LAMBERDEN HOUSE

C D S

Rye Road, Sandhurst, Kent, TN18 5PH Tel: 01580 850968 (Fax: 01580 850121)
South-west of Tenterden. On A268 from Flimwell to Rye.

3 Bedrooms. £25–£27.50 (less for 3 nights or more). Available: own bath/shower/toilet; TV. No smoking.
Dinner (by arrangement). £17.50 for 4 courses and coffee, at 6–7pm. Vegetarian or other special diets if ordered. No smoking. **Light suppers** if ordered.
Large garden

E-mail: Croysdill@lamberden.freeserve.co.uk

Margie and Julian Croysdill's home occupies the barn of a converted oast house, one of a small group of former farm buildings which have far-reaching views across the Weald of Kent.

Homely and comfortable accommodation is provided, with fresh flowers in the rooms taken from Margie's traditional English garden (with heated swimming-pool). She is a good cook and serves evening meals by candlelight in the warm-toned dining-room, where family photos hang beside Graham Miles landscape prints of the surrounding countryside. You might start with a home-made vegetable soup, followed by pheasant casserole, apple and blackberry crumble, and then cheese.

Julian, a semi-retired solicitor, has great enthusiasm for, and knowledge of, the county and will happily point you towards its interesting but less-frequented corners. For garden-lovers, within a 10-minute drive are Sissinghurst, Pashley Manor and Great Dixter, where you will find Christopher Lloyd's marvellously varied and colourful gardens, as well as a Lutyens-restored mediaeval house. From here, continue across country to 14th-century Bodiam Castle (NT), perhaps the most romantic castle ruin in the whole of England.

V

Kent

NUMBER TEN

C D M P T S X

Modest Corner, Southborough, Kent, TN4 0LS Tel/Fax: 01892 522450
North of Tunbridge Wells. Nearest main road: A21 from Sevenoaks to Hastings.

3 Bedrooms. £20–£25. Bargain breaks. One has own shower/toilet; TV (in all). No smoking.
Dinner. £12.50 for 3 courses and coffee, at 8pm. Vegetarian or other special diets if ordered. Wine available. No smoking. **Light suppers** if ordered.
Small garden

E-mail: modestanneke@lineone.net

On a wooded hillside close to Tunbridge Wells is a hidden hamlet, well called Modest Corner. Here is the equally modest home of Dutch-born picture-framer Anneke Leemhuis. The bedrooms are simple, furnished with pine and Laura Ashley wallpapers and fabrics. The upstairs bedroom has fine views. Meals (such as lamb with ratatouille, followed by trifle) are eaten in Anneke's new kitchen. Visitors can explore the many footpaths in the surrounding countryside. The house is only five minutes from a station with fast trains to London.

Elegant Tunbridge Wells is all you expect of an 18th-century spa that once rivalled Bath. The famous 'Pantiles' is a colonnaded pedestrian precinct among attractive shops (you can taste the waters from the spring there) and close by is a fine 17th-century church dedicated to King Charles I.

Readers' comments: Homely atmosphere, wonderful walks. Unequalled hospitality and helpfulness. I have stayed four times and am continually impressed. Delightful and comfortable stay; thoughtful hostess.

V

SHIRKOAK FARM

C(10) **PT**

Woodchurch, Kent, TN26 3PZ Tel: 01233 860056 (Fax: 01233 861402)
East of Tenterden. Nearest main road: A28 from Tenterden to Ashford (and M20, junction 9).

3 Bedrooms. £25 **to SOTBT readers only**–£28. Available: own bath/shower/toilet; TV. No smoking.
Light suppers if ordered.
1 Sitting-room. With open fire, TV. No smoking.
Large garden
Closed in December and February.

E-mail: shirkoakfarm@aol.com

For a small village, Woodchurch has much to offer the visitor: a working windmill, the South of England Rare Breeds Centre and one of Kent's most beautiful churches. In addition, there is the fine accommodation offered by Tessa and Michael Leadbeater in their 18th-century tile-hung farmhouse. Bedrooms are smart and spotless, with very good bathrooms. The focal point of the salmon-pink and cream sitting-room is the old inglenook, with deep sofas and chairs drawn around it. Victorian landscape scenes hang on the walls.

Breakfast, which includes eggs from the Leadbeaters' chickens and much home-made produce, is served in the elegant dining-room overlooking a large pond – its banks full of daffodils in springtime. Guests are welcome to use the tennis court and games room which has a full-size billiard table.

The Leadbeaters are well travelled (Michael was a keen long-distance yacht racer) and they both enjoy bridge and walking their two friendly dogs. Smallhythe Place (NT) and Tenterden (good restaurants for evening meals) are close by.

Reader's comments: The best SOTBT [house] we have encountered; extremely well-appointed bedroom; we will be back.

SUNSHINE COTTAGE

C M PT X

The Green, Shepherdswell, Kent, CT15 7LQ Tel: 01304 831359 or 831218
North-west of Dover. Nearest main road: A2 from Dover towards Canterbury (also M2, junction 7; and M20, junction 13).

6 Bedrooms. £23–£27.50 (less for 7 nights or more). Available: own bath/shower/toilet. No smoking.
2 Sitting-rooms. With open fire, TV. No smoking.
Small garden

Neither shepherd nor well gave this pretty village its name: the Saxons knew it as Sibert's Wold. Sunshine Cottage, built in 1635, is now the home of Barry and Lyn Popple.

One steps into a cosy sitting-room with shaggy, cocoa-coloured carpet and low beams, a velvet sofa facing a brick inglenook that has logs piled high and hop bines draped across it. Breakfast is served in a dining-room where antique pine is complemented by coir matting, dressers display antique plates, old pews and stickback chairs surround tables laid with pretty china. Lyn is happy to provide home-made cakes with afternoon tea, and for dinners, she recommends the Crown in Eythorne or the Bell in Lydden, both a short drive away.

There is one ground-floor bedroom (with shower), decorated with pretty fabrics. Those upstairs vary in size and style; several have antique iron bedsteads and some have views of the village green. Barry is an artist and some of his pictures are on the walls.

Readers' comments: Full of treasures. A relaxed cottage atmosphere. Made us very welcome. Quite delightful.

V

Kent

WALNUT TREE FARMHOUSE C(3)

Lynsore Bottom, Upper Hardres, Kent, CT4 6EG Tel: 01227 709375
South of Canterbury. Nearest main road: A2 from Dover towards Canterbury.

2 Bedrooms. £24–£25 (less for 3 nights or more). Both have own shower/toilet. No smoking.
Light suppers by arrangement.
Large garden
Closed from December to March.

With its thatched roof, this house has one of the prettiest exteriors in Kent. Inside, too, it is full of charm. Gerald Wilton makes furniture, very decorative carved signboards, colourful decoy ducks and much else – including the long oak table which looks as if it, like the house itself, dates from the 14th century.

Guests' bedrooms in the house are reached by steep stairs. (Others may be available in a converted barn usually used as a self-catering cottage.) Every wall and floor slopes a little. Crisp white fabrics, flower-sprigged, and pine fitments combine to give rooms an airy, cottagey feel. An attic room with low windows has the ancient king-post that supports the whole structure. In the garden is a swimming-pool. (For evening meals, Sheila Wilton recommends the nearby Duck Inn.)

V *Readers' comments:* Have returned many times, most exceptional. A lot of thought and care; made most welcome. Beautifully furnished. Made to feel like guests of the family.

For explanation of code letters and V symbol, see inside front cover.

Where wine is not available (meaning it is on sale or can be fetched for you), you are nearly always welcome to bring in your own drinks.

Many houses in this book are situated in or very near to Areas of Outstanding Natural Beauty and protected Heritage Coasts. For a selection of these houses, see p.xi.

Complaints about matters which could not have been settled on the spot will be forwarded to proprietors. Please enclose a stamped addressed envelope if you want your complaint acknowledged.

LANCASHIRE

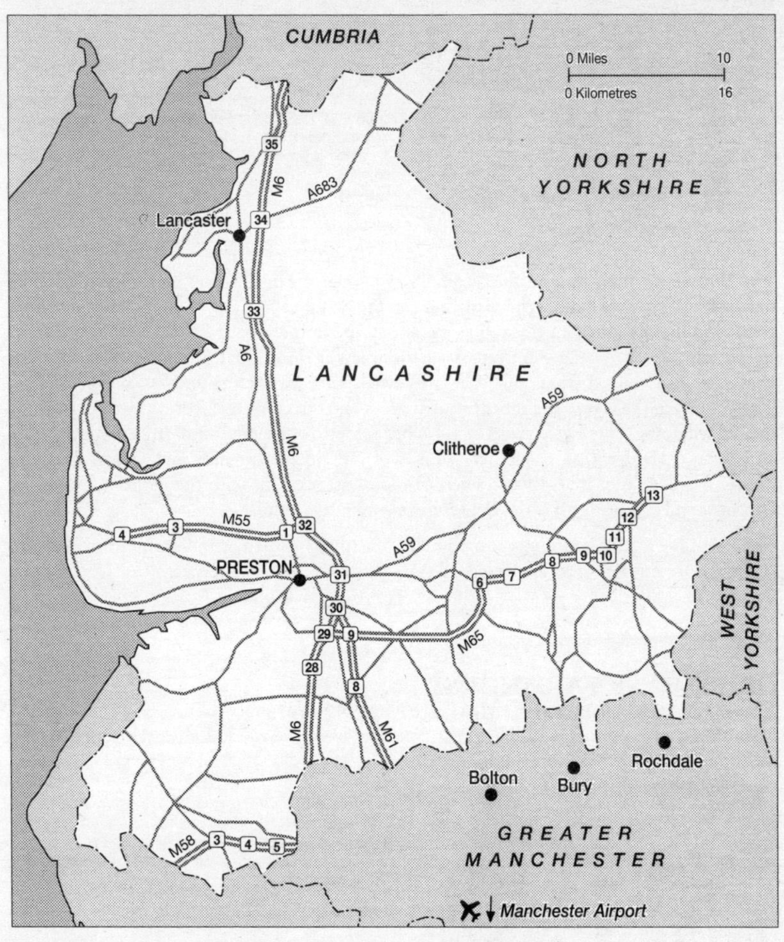

Prices are per person sharing a room at the beginning of the year. However, for the best rooms in the house or later in the year, you may well be asked for more.

Lancashire

THE BOWER

C(12) **D PT X**

Yealand Conyers, Lancashire, LA5 9SF Tel: 01524 734585
North of Lancaster. Nearest main road: A6 from Lancaster to Kendal (and M6, junction 35).

2 Bedrooms. £23–£33.50. Both have own bath/shower/toilet; TV. No smoking.
Dinner (by arrangement). £22 for 4 courses and coffee, at 7.30pm. Vegetarian or other special diets if ordered. No smoking. **Light suppers** if ordered.
1 Sitting-room. With open fire, TV, piano. No smoking.
Garden

The Bower was built as a farmhouse in 1745 and later gentrified. (The cast-iron porch is handsome.) There is a modern harpsichord in the entrance hall and hi-fi in both the sitting-room and the dining-room (as well as a piano in the former), for Michael Rothwell teaches music (also bridge). Sally-Ann serves such dinners as individual Stilton soufflés, chicken chasseur, pears in red wine, and cheese. A two-course 'kitchen supper' is often available. The colours in the rooms are mostly muted greys and pinks, with elaborate floral curtains at the tall windows. These give views across a big garden, to the summit of Ingleborough.

Leighton Hall, with a collection of birds of prey in the grounds and Gillow furniture inside, is a couple of miles away. There are local associations with the earliest days of the Quakers, and at Carnforth is the *Brief Encounter* railway station.

V *Readers' comments:* Charming young couple, charming garden, comfortable dining-room, superb bedroom with every convenience. Most enjoyable in every respect.

Lancashire

GREENBANK FARMHOUSE

Abbeystead, Lancashire, LA2 9BA Tel/Fax: 01524 792063
South-east of Lancaster. Nearest main road: A6 from Preston to Lancaster (and M6, junction 33).

3 Bedrooms. £20–£25 (less for 4 nights or more). Available: own bath/shower/toilet; TV. No smoking.
Large garden

E-mail: bowpicfram@madasafish.com

The Taits used to be dairy-farmers and now run a picture-framing business, so it is not surprising that there are lots of framed pictures of cattle on the walls of their home. It is a modernized farmhouse extending into the dairy where cheese was made, with a double-height window where the barn doors used to be. This lights the stairs to the bedrooms, where on each window-sill is an account identifying the specific features of countryside (fells and fields) that the rooms overlook – a thoughtful touch, typical of Sally's hospitality.

Breakfast is served in a small room which houses Sally's collection of honeypots and Simon's collection of model buses. For evening meals, you can be driven (if you wish) to the local pub. Guests are welcome to join the Taits in the family sitting-room, with its big stone fireplace and beams hung with horse-brasses.

The setting is an attractive part of rural Lancashire, near the (almost treeless) Forest of Bowland, with its wild landscape and picturesque villages.

V *Readers' comments:* Beautiful house, superb surroundings, lovely room, very comfortable, great view, delicious breakfast.

HERON LODGE

D PT S X

Lancashire

Edgworth, Lancashire, BL7 0DS Tel/Fax: 01204 852262
North of Bolton. Nearest main road: A676 from Bolton to Ramsbottom.

3 Bedrooms. £25 (less for 7 nights or more). Available: own bath/shower/toilet; TV; views of river. No smoking.
Light suppers if ordered. No smoking.
1 Sitting-room. With open fire, TV. No smoking.
Large garden

E-mail: heronlodge@hotmail.com

Moorside villages like Edgworth should serve as a reminder that in this part of England you are never far from beautiful countryside.

There had been a building on this site for as long as anyone could remember when the Miltons bought the single-storey property in the late 1980s and set about converting it into an immaculate, traditionally styled family house. The dining-room incorporates a massive old beam from a derelict barn, and local stone has been used in the construction.

Bedrooms have generous floral curtains, and lacy covers on Victorian brass bedsteads (one king-size) in two of them. Edwardian-style fittings in the excellent shower-rooms enhance the period atmosphere. Another bedroom at the back of the house is a very pretty L-shaped twin with patchwork quilts and has an attractive adjoining bathroom.

Guests tend to converge on the comfortable quarry-tiled kitchen, especially on baking days; for Roland Milton, who has lived in the village all his life, is renowned for his boiled fruit cake and rhubarb pies. There is a variety of good, reasonably priced eating-places within easy reach.

V

LEACHES FARM

C(8) D S

Lancashire

Ashworth, Rochdale, Lancashire, OL11 5UN Tel: 01706 641116/7 or 224307
North-east of Bury. Nearest main road: A680 from Rochdale to Edenfield (and M66, junctions 1/2).

3 Bedrooms. £20–£22 (less for 6 nights or more).
1 Sitting-room. With open fire, TV, piano.
Garden
Closed in late December.

Once part of a shooting estate belonging to an old Cheshire family (whose name survives on the inn-sign of the nearby pub, the Egerton Arms), 17th century Leaches Farm, along with the rest of the estate, was sold at the end of the war to pay death duties. Being one of the better farmhouses on the estate, Leaches was upgraded by the present tenant into the homely place it is today, with open fires, beamed ceilings, board-and-latch doors and a somewhat steep staircase leading to the shared bathroom and three very comfortable bedrooms, including an attractive single bursting with books.

Views are spectacular, whether of moorland or, at night, the lights of Manchester a few miles to the south. For, despite its remote Pennine feel, Leaches Farm – where Jane and Michael Neave and their family have reared beef and sheep for over 40 years – is close enough to the north-west's motorway complex to make both Liverpool and Leeds, as well as Manchester itself, easily reachable. Closer still, though, is the East Lancs Railway between Rawtenstall and Bury – a boon for steam enthusiasts. For dinner, guests are recommended to try two excellent pubs just a mile away in either direction.

V

Lancashire

MIDDLE FLASS LODGE

D S X

Settle Road, Bolton-by-Bowland, Lancashire, BB7 4NY Tel: 01200 447259 (Fax: 01200 447300)

North of Clitheroe. Nearest main road: A59 from Skipton to Clitheroe.

5 Bedrooms. £23–£30 (less for 3 nights or more). Bargain breaks. All have own bath/shower/toilet; TV. No smoking.
Dinner. From £19 for 3 courses and coffee, at 6–7pm. Vegetarian or other special diets if ordered. Wine available. No smoking. **Light suppers** if ordered.
1 Sitting-room. With stove, TV. No smoking.
Small garden

Nigel Quayle, a head chef, and Joan Simpson, also a catering professional, converted their guest-house and restaurant from a farmhouse and its outbuildings, putting neat bedrooms into the old cowbyre to take advantage of the outlook. In the restaurant below, they offer a varied choice. You might pick a mushroom dish to start with, and the roast of the day or fresh fish – the choice of the latter depending on the best available. There are puddings of every kind, and a suitable wine list. The small sitting-room is at one end of the dining-room.

Middle Flass Lodge is on the west of the Forest of Bowland, only parts of which are wooded in spite of its name. Enclosing the Trough of Bowland, it is an area of open fells and little valleys where streams gurgle over limestone beds. Within it are picturesque Slaidburn and Browsholme Hall, a family-owned house, occasionally open to the public.

Readers' comments: Food of excellent quality. A warm welcome; proprietors always interested and helpful; food uniformly excellent. Top-rate professionalism; first class.

V

Lancashire

PETER BARN

C(5)

Cross Lane, Waddington, Lancashire, BB7 3JH Tel: 01200 428585 (Messages: 01200 422381)

North-west of Clitheroe. Nearest main road: A59 from Preston to Clitheroe.

3 Bedrooms. £24–£26 (less for 3 nights or more). Bargain breaks. Available: own bath/shower/toilet; TV. No smoking.
Light suppers if ordered.
1 Sitting-room. With open fire, TV. No smoking.
Large garden

On a single-track road that runs through a tunnel of trees, Peter Barn was once a tithe barn. The upper floor is exclusively for guests. The large, airy sitting-room is reached by an open-tread staircase and has a roof made of old church rafters. By a stone fireplace are comfortable settees and armchairs, near the head of the staircase is the breakfast-area, and off the other end of this well-proportioned space are the bedrooms and bathroom. (The arrangement is such that a large family would have the use of a virtually self-contained flat.) Much of the furniture is antique, and the mantel clock was made by Gordon Smith's grandfather.

Jean Smith has the greenest of fingers, for the one-acre garden is a remarkable achievement, having been a field when the house was converted 25 years ago. Now it is beautifully landscaped and lovingly tended. There is no shortage of places for an evening meal, not least in Clitheroe, the lively market town a couple of miles away.

Readers' comments: Wonderful experience. Highlight of our holiday. Like being entertained by friends. A visit is pure pleasure; can't wait to return. 'Readers' comments' all exceeded. Delights of home and garden cannot be easy to match. We hit the bull's-eye; perfect.

V

LEICESTERSHIRE
(including Rutland)

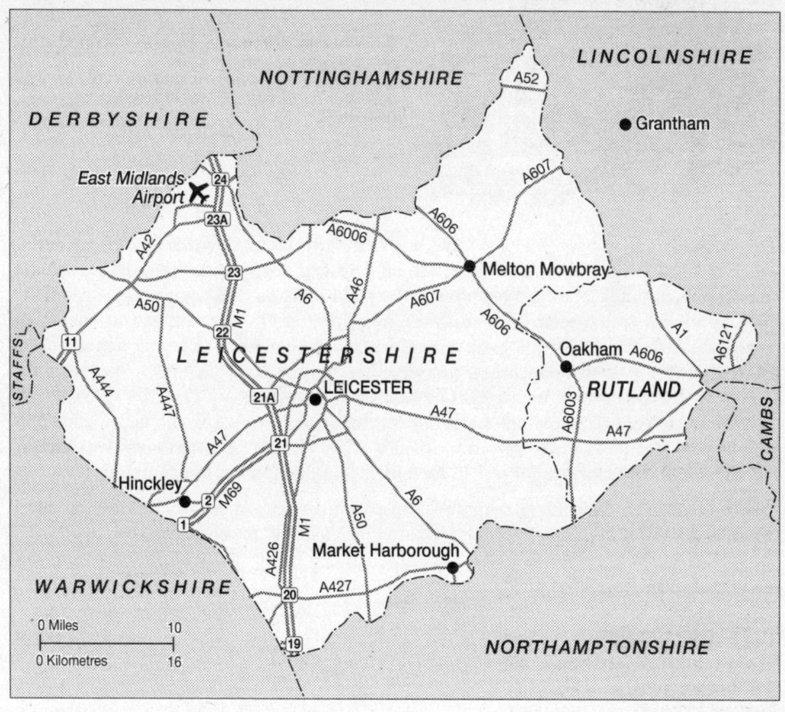

Addresses shown are to enable you to locate a house on a map. They are not necessarily complete postal addresses (though the essential post-code is included), and detailed directions for finding a house should be obtained from the owner.

Leicestershire

CHURCH COTTAGE

C(1) PT S X

The Green, Holwell, Leicestershire, LE14 4SZ Tel: 01664 444255
North-west of Melton Mowbray. Nearest main road: A606 from Melton Mowbray to Nottingham.

2 Bedrooms. £20 (less for 4 nights or more). One has own bath/shower/toilet. No smoking.
Light suppers if ordered. No smoking.
1 Sitting-room. With TV. No smoking.
Garden

The conservation village of Holwell has a particularly ancient church (1200) alongside which is 18th-century Church Cottage, full of steps and turns inside. Here Brenda Bailey gives visitors not only a beamed bedroom with brass bed and a well-equipped bathroom but their own small sitting-room too, and their own front door. There is also an extremely pretty pink twin room. Brenda hand-embroiders all the bedlinen; cakes, scones and fresh fruit are always available. Breakfasts are served in her dining-room, which overlooks the sloping, landscaped garden with a summer-house for guests' use.

Melton Mowbray is a pleasant market town (from which you can go home laden with its famous pork pies), and is well placed for visiting other historic Leicestershire towns such as Loughborough and Oakham (as well as Grantham and Stamford in Lincolnshire).

Readers' comments: Delightful, beautiful. Superb hospitality. Amazing breakfast on silver salver. A delightful weekend; impressed by attention to detail. Lovely host.

Leicestershire

THE GRANGE

C M PT X

New Road, Burton Lazars, Leicestershire, LE14 2UU Tel/Fax: 01664 560775
South-east of Melton Mowbray. Nearest main road: A606 from Melton Mowbray to Oakham.

4 Bedrooms. £22.25–£25 (less for 3 nights or more). Available: own bath/shower/toilet; TV; balcony. No smoking.
Light suppers if ordered. Wine available.
1 Sitting-room. With open fire.
Large garden

This was once the home of the McAlpine family – a creeper-covered country house in 18th-century style with such features as leaded window-panes, arches, prettily plastered ceiling and barley-sugar banisters on the oak staircase.

Pam Holden has decorated the rooms with imagination, and hung the walls with good paintings. In the elegant and spacious aquamarine sitting-room are shell-pink armchairs. The handsome dining-room has rosewood and mahogany tables which are complemented by Pam's tapestry-covered chairs. There are two ground-floor bedrooms, one with hand-made quilted bedspreads and a large bathroom, the other with a white-draped four-poster; a yellow bedroom upstairs has a superb country view and its own balcony.

Landscaped grounds include a sunken garden, orchard and paved terrace with chairs from which to enjoy the view across terraced lawns to the Vale of Stapleford.

Guests dine at local restaurants. There is plenty to do in the area – visiting Belvoir Castle or Burghley House, and the open-air attractions of Rutland Water, for example.

MEDBOURNE GRANGE

C X

Medbourne, Leicestershire, LE16 8EF Tel: 01858 565249 (Fax: 01858 565257)
North-east of Market Harborough. Nearest main road: A427 from Market Harborough to Corby.

Leicestershire

3 Bedrooms. £20–£23 (less for 3 nights or more). Available: own shower/toilet.
Light suppers if ordered.
1 Sitting-room. With TV. No smoking.
Large garden

At Nevill Holt's great 17th-century Hall (now a school) Emerald Cunard held her salons, attended by the leading political and literary lions of the Edwardian era. Medbourne Grange was a principal farm on its large estate, a dignified house standing at the heart of 500 acres of mainly arable fields.

Sally Beaty has furnished it attractively: the capacious, cut-velvet armchairs are of the same soft blue as the sitting-room carpet; one beige-and-green bedroom (with far view) has a carved walnut suite, another (also with panoramic country view) has a sofa-bed too and can be used as a family room.

Outside are stone troughs of flowers and, sheltered by old walls, a heated swimming-pool; while beyond lies the valley of the River Welland which flows all the way to The Wash.

Reader's comments: An excellent stay, fully recommended.

OLD MANSE

C PT

37 Swingbridge Street, Foxton, Leicestershire, LE16 7RH Tel: 01858 545456
North-west of Market Harborough. Nearest main road: A6 from Market Harborough to Leicester.

Leicestershire

3 Bedrooms. £23. Available: own bath/shower/toilet; TV. No smoking.
Light suppers if ordered.
3 Sitting-rooms. With open fire (in one), TV (in one), piano (in one). No smoking.
Large garden

Ancient and tiny Foxton, its 13th-century church restored by John of Gaunt and preached in by Wycliffe, is famous for its 'staircase' of 10 locks on the Grand Union Canal, which raises boats 75 feet uphill (there are a canal museum and horse-drawn barge trips). The village pub has an ambitious menu and an attractive conservatory dining-room.

The Old Manse was built in the 17th century, just beyond a swing-bridge over the canal; and in it the Baptist minister later ran a school. Now it is home to the Pickerings as well as their collection of classic cars and rare breeds of hen.

Rooms are elegant and immaculate, and there is a fine garden – open to the public at times – with an array of fuchsias. Some of the light and flowery bedrooms have a good view of this. Downstairs, a huge conservatory has bamboo armchairs and sofas with pale green upholstery; the formal sitting-room houses a grand piano; and in the study there is a big collection of Rita's saucy china fairings. Altogether, a characterful house in a little-known spot of considerable interest; and surrounded by such sights as Boughton House, Canons Ashby and Rockingham Castle.

V

Leicestershire

PEACOCK FARMHOUSE

C D M P T X

Redmile, Leicestershire, NG13 0GQ Tel: 01949 842475 (Fax: 01949 843127)
West of Grantham. Nearest main road: A52 from Nottingham to Grantham.

8 Bedrooms. £25 **to SOTBT readers only in low season**–£28. Less for 7 nights or more. Bargain breaks. Available: own bath/shower/toilet; TV.
Dinner. £15.50 for 3 courses and coffee, at 7.15pm. Vegetarian or other special diets if ordered. Wine available. No smoking. **Light suppers** if ordered.
1 Sitting-room. With open fire. No smoking. **Bar.**
Large garden

E-mail: peacockfarm@primeuk.net

This guest-house with restaurant (built as a farm in the 18th century) is ideal for a break when doing a long north–south journey on the nearby A1, particularly with children.

It is in the outstandingly beautiful Vale of Belvoir, with the Duke of Rutland's Belvoir Castle (full of art treasures) rearing its battlemented walls high above a nearby hilltop.

The Needs have created a happy family atmosphere here. Children can safely play in the garden which has a large lawn, hammock, swings, bicycles, barbecue, and farm pets. There is also a playroom with snooker and table tennis. All the bedrooms (several suitable for families) are on the ground floor. A mini 'coach house' and modern brick bungalow in the grounds provide additional accommodation.

Meals are prepared by Nicky Need, a vivacious hostess, and include home-made bread and soups, herbs from the garden and much local produce. Beef and venison carbonnade and 'tipsy' bread-and-butter pudding are dinner-menu favourites.

V *Readers' comments:* Good food, delightful hosts. Room attractively furnished, meal excellent.

Rutland

RUTLAND COTTAGES

C S X

5 Cedar Street, Braunston, Rutland, LE15 8QS Tel: 01572 722049
South-west of Oakham. Nearest main road: A6003 from Oakham to Kettering.

4 Bedrooms. £23–£25. All have own bath/shower/toilet; TV. No smoking.
2 Sitting-rooms. With open fire, TV. No smoking.
Small garden

E-mail: rbeadman@compuserve.com

A 17th-century bakehouse is the home of John and Connie Beadman (keen gardeners); and in addition they own two fully equipped and cosy cottages (one next door, the other down the garden path) which are let on a bed-and-breakfast basis. All guests take breakfast together in the beamed dining-room of the main house (on Sundays, cooked breakfasts are available only between 7.30 and 8.30am). Visitors can dine at two inns in this pretty conservation village of golden stone.

Guests may also use the Beadmans' huge and pleasantly furnished sitting-room (it has a see-through stone fireplace in the middle, and a 'curfew window' through which the village watchman could check that the baker's fires had been properly extinguished for the night). Connie often helps visitors trace their family history locally.

Readers' comments: Most friendly. Cottage excellent. Nothing is too much trouble. The accommodation is first class. Very pleasant welcome, excellent. Good breakfast. Warm V welcome. Most helpful and friendly. B & b at its very best in every way.

WATER MEADOWS FARMHOUSE

C D X

Billington Road East, Elmesthorpe, Leicestershire, LE9 7SB Tel: 01455 843417
North-east of Hinckley. Nearest main road: A47 from Hinckley to Leicester (also M69, junction 1; and M1, junction 21).

3 Bedrooms. £17.50 (less for 3 nights or more). Available: own toilet; TV. No smoking.
Light suppers if ordered.
1 Sitting-room. With open fire, TV.
Large garden

E-mail: june-peter@watermeadowsfarm.fsnet.co.uk

In the depression of the 1930s, smallholdings with houses were provided through the Land Settlement Association, a 'self-sufficiency' scheme eventually abandoned. Peter Robinson bought two of these plots (which are on the site of a lost mediaeval village and Roman remains) and has gradually turned them into his own private conservation area, creating tracts of woodland and wetland where over 80 species of birds have been spotted.

Bedrooms are good: for instance, a huge family room with sofa and large TV (concealed in a fitment) has fine inlaid Edwardian furniture and windows on three sides from which to enjoy the garden – floodlit at night.

June is an accomplished cook, and every day breakfast is different, with such unusual choices as kidneys or cheese-and-potato pancakes. Bread and preserves are home-made. Guests dine at the local inn, designed by Voysey, who lived nearby.

Houses which accept the discount vouchers on page ii are marked with a V symbol next to the relevant entries.

Some houses offer special discounts to readers using the current edition of this book. Always state you are an SOTBT reader when ringing to book or when using E-mail.

At houses where dinner is not served, a light supper can often be obtained (if ordered in advance), ranging from sandwiches to family 'pot luck'. (Packed lunches too.)

Prices for single occupancy may be higher than those quoted here. Houses that charge singles no more, or only 10% more, than half the price of a double room (except possibly at peak periods) are indicated by the 'S' symbol.

LINCOLNSHIRE

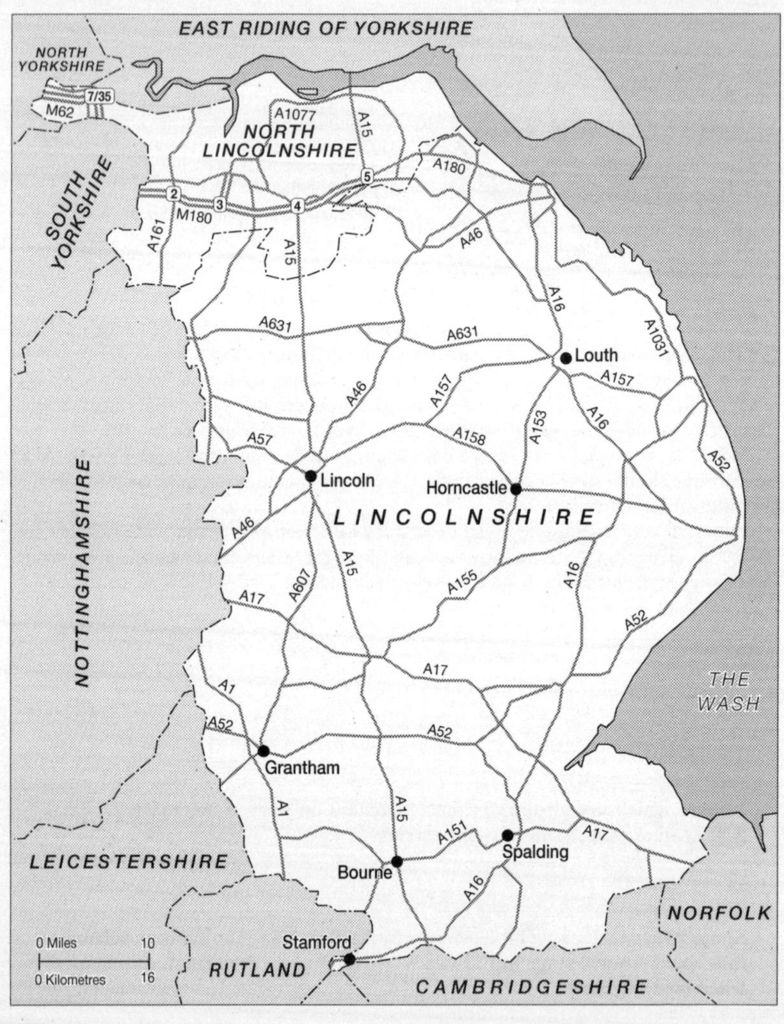

Readers' comments quoted in the book are from letters sent directly to us: they are not supplied via the proprietors.

BAUMBER PARK **C D PT S**

Baumber, Lincolnshire, LN9 5NE Tel: 01507 578235 (Fax: 01507 578417)
North-west of Horncastle. Nearest main road: A158 from Lincoln to Horncastle.

3 Bedrooms. £25 (less for 3 nights or more). Available: own shower/toilet; TV. No smoking.
Dinner (by arrangement). £10–£12 for 2–3 courses and coffee, from 7pm. Vegetarian or other special diets if ordered. **Light suppers** if ordered.
1 Sitting-room. With open fire, TV, piano.
Large garden

Unspoilt countryside, a niche in racing history and the quiet comfort of a sedate Victorian farmhouse provide ample reason for staying at Baumber Park. Once a stud farm (the 1875 Derby-winner was bred here), the house is now the hub of a mixed arable and beef-cattle farm, whose Lincoln Reds can be seen calving under cover during the winter months.

The spick-and-span bedrooms are decorated in soft colours which blend well with the traditional furnishings and the tranquil country views. Meals are taken in the blue and pale grey dining-room, around a mahogany table with balloon-back chairs. An antique linen-press and a fossil-embedded marble fireplace add character to this bay-windowed room. Both at breakfast and dinner, home-grown and farm-reared produce feature prominently in Clare Harrison's wholesome fare. A typical evening meal: steak-and-kidney pie, followed by chocolate pots or pavlova.

The Harrisons are enthusiasts for the countryside and happy to share their knowledge with guests. There is a pond wildlife-haven in the grounds, as well as a grass tennis court. Nearby Horncastle is a mini-mecca for antiques. V

BODKIN LODGE **C**(12) **M**

Torrington Lane, East Barkwith, Lincolnshire, LN8 5RY Tel: 01673 858249
North-east of Lincoln. Nearest main road: A157 from Wragby to Louth.

2 Bedrooms. £25–£27. Available: own bath/shower/toilet; TV. No smoking.
Dinner (by arrangement). £15 for 3–4 courses and coffee, at 7.30pm. Vegetarian or other special diets if ordered. No smoking. **Light suppers** if ordered.
1 Sitting-room. With open fire, TV, piano. No smoking.
Large garden
Closed from mid-December to January.

Anne and Richard Stamp have furnished Bodkin Lodge with great care, adding much character to this stylish home. From the entrance hall, doors open on to a light, airy sitting-room with floor-to-ceiling windows and far-reaching views (towards Lincoln Cathedral in one direction, the Wolds in another). Paintings and ornate mirrors hang on the walls, and French windows lead on to a terrace, where breakfast may be served in the summer.

Impressive, ground-floor bedrooms have direct access to the garden, and each has its own private terrace. In warm weather, guests can relax in the Victorian-style glass-house.

Anne (who occasionally writes short stories for women's magazines) serves meals such as smoked haddock and chive creams; lamb with apricot stuffing; and almond and pear flan.

Lincolnshire is the county to choose if you want to unwind in the peace of a remote and solitary countryside, where the skies are open wide and the pace is slow-changing.

Readers' comments: The standard of food, presentation, etc. could not have been bettered. Wonderful ambience, perfect hosts. Exceptionally comfortable. Never found such de luxe facilities, gracious hospitality and delicious meals. Wish we had stayed longer.

Lincolnshire

CAWTHORPE HALL

C D M

Bourne, Lincolnshire, PE10 0AB Tel: 01778 423830 (Fax: 01778 426620)
North-east of Stamford. Nearest main road: A15 from Bourne to Sleaford.

4 Bedrooms. £25 **(one room for readers of this book only)**–£30. Available: own bath/shower/toilet. No smoking.
1 Sitting-room. With stove, TV. No smoking. Piano and harmonium.
Large garden

E-mail: bandb@rosewater.com

On the edge of a bluebell wood, Georgian Cawthorpe Hall is surrounded by gardens and three acres of scented rose fields from which Ozric Armstrong produces English rose oil and water.

One enters the house into an impressive double-arched hallway, off of which is a huge studio extension built in the early 1900s by a Royal Academician (two of whose paintings hang in the hall). This grand and lofty space serves as the guests' sitting-cum-breakfast-room. It is filled with sofas, wicker armchairs and a big collection of bold, modern canvases by the Armstrongs' artist daughter, Dominique.

Bedrooms are pleasant and spacious; one on the ground floor has a woodstove and an en suite bathroom with free-standing tub and Portuguese wall tiles. Dotted around are attractive pieces of mahogany furniture from Madeira, where Chantal Armstrong was born.

In summer, afternoon teas are served on the lawn. The Wishing Well in nearby Dyke is a popular dining-pub, and Grimsthorpe Castle a local sightseeing attraction.

V *Reader's comments:* Well-travelled and delightful couple, treated us as house-guests; totally relaxed atmosphere, beautiful room.

Lincolnshire

COACH HOUSE

PT S

Belton-by-Grantham, Lincolnshire, NG32 2LW Tel: 01476 573636
North of Grantham. Nearest main road: A607 from Grantham to Lincoln.

4 Bedrooms. £21. Bargain breaks. All have own bath/shower/toilet; TV. No smoking.
1 Sitting-room. With TV. No smoking.
Large garden
Closed in January.

For an overnight stop on the long haul from Cambridge to York, the coaches once paused here at an inn, next door to which the buildings of Ancaster stone that are now the Nortons' home were stables surrounding a coach yard.

Bernard Norton has created such attractive features as a second, sun-trapping courtyard with a fountain in the centre of a circle of blue-brick paving: an attractive view to enjoy while breakfasting. The guests' sitting-room has French windows which open on to the garden. There are ground-floor bedrooms (one with courtyard view, one with none) and others upstairs – be prepared for rafters and steps – which have roof-lights. Sue has made ruffled pelmets and, on one bed, a prettily draped corona, using silky pink or rose-patterned fabrics.

For evening meals, there are several eating-places locally.

All around the conservation village is National Trust land with good walks.

Readers' comments: Delightfully situated, very attractively furnished. Very friendly and helpful. A lovely stay, food good.

THE GRANGE C(12)

Torrington Lane, East Barkwith, Lincolnshire, LN8 5RY Tel: 01673 858670
North-east of Lincoln. Nearest main road: A157 from Wragby to Louth.

2 Bedrooms. £23. Available: own bath/shower/toilet; TV. No smoking.
Dinner (by arrangement). £14 for 4 courses, sherry and coffee, at 7pm. Vegetarian or other special diets if ordered. No smoking. **Light suppers** if ordered.
1 Sitting-room. With open fire. No smoking.
Large garden
Closed in late December.

Set in acres of farmland (mainly arable) which adjoin a conservation area, this late-Georgian house is on a working farm. Jonathan Stamp runs the farm business with the help of his father, Richard (see **Bodkin Lodge**). Built in 1820, the house has sash windows deep-set in shuttered embrasures. The hall has a stained-glass door, black-and-white floor tiles, and a graceful staircase leading up to attractive bedrooms.

The elegant dining-room has fine views of the surrounding countryside. Here, Sarah Stamp (a trained home economist and accomplished cook) serves, for example, watercress and salmon roulade; chicken in white wine and tarragon sauce; chocolate brownie gâteau.

Outside is a lawn with topiary, swing-settee, croquet and tennis.

The Grange, which sits on a farm trail, has won three conservation awards, and has a private trout lake (where guests can fish or relax with a picnic).

Reader's comments: Very warm welcome, excellent accommodation and first-class dinner and breakfast; so peaceful; will certainly go again. Thoroughly enjoyed our stay; the beautiful house, warmth and friendliness make it a must to return.

MEWS HOUSE C M S X

Great Ponton, Lincolnshire, NG33 5AG Tel/Fax: 01476 530311
(Mobile: 07980 598328)
South of Grantham. Nearest main road: A1 from Stamford to Grantham.

Lincolnshire

rear view

1 Bedroom. £20–£25. Has own bath/shower/toilet. No smoking.
1 Sitting-room. With TV, piano. No smoking.
Large garden
E-mail: accommodation@themewshouse.freeserve.co.uk

Though just off the busy A1, all is quiet as you enter the cobbled courtyard of this handsome brick house. Built in 1810, it was once part of the neighbouring residence, and locally born Paul and Celia Carpenter have taken immense care to bring it and the surrounding land to their present appealing condition. Throughout the house, a love of horses is evident in the many equestrian pictures – especially in the Carpenters' sumptuous drawing-room.

Guests have sole use of a comfortable, self-contained suite, which can be let on a single, double or family basis. Disabled travellers, in particular, will appreciate the specially adapted bathroom and the fact that *all* the accommodation is on the ground floor.

Breakfast is served in a smart dining-room, with French doors leading on to the lovely walled garden from which there is direct access to the Gingerbread Way – a plus for walkers. In the grounds, the Carpenters have created private sitting-areas where guests can relax.

For dinner, visitors go to nearby village pubs or into Grantham. Belton House and Sir Isaac Newton's birthplace at Woolsthorpe Manor (both NT) are within easy driving distance. V

PIPWELL MANOR

C(12)

Saracen's Head, Lincolnshire, PE12 8AL Tel/Fax: 01406 423119
North-east of Spalding. Nearest main road: A17 from King's Lynn to Sleaford.

4 Bedrooms. £22–£24. Bargain breaks. Available: own bath/shower/toilet. No smoking.
1 Sitting-room. With open fire, TV. No smoking.
Large garden

To the attraction of an imaginatively decorated 18th-century house is added that of a five-inch-gauge steam railway (rides available) which runs through the flowery garden. Here, in fine weather, Lesley Honnor serves tea and home-made cakes on guests' arrival.

Indoors, every room bears the hallmark of Lesley's flair for colour and creative touch. Bedrooms are delightful, with eye-catching colour schemes complemented by well-chosen fabrics and furnishings. Nearly all the cushions, covers and lovely curtains were made by Lesley and the delicate stencilling in some of the equally attractive bathrooms is also hers. The cosy sitting-room has a log fire surrounded by chintz-covered sofas, and in the pretty pink-and-cream breakfast-room, with dried flowers festooned over the mantelpiece, guests are treated to eggs from the Honnors' own hens as well as stewed fruit from the garden.

Standing in a quiet Fenland village, Pipwell Manor is well placed for visiting the spring flower fields for which this area is renowned, Boston with its Pilgrim Fathers' connection, and the cathedral cities of Ely, Peterborough and Lincoln. There are local inns for evening meals. (Free bicycles on request.)

V

ROSE COTTAGE

C D X

7 High Street, South Witham, Lincolnshire, NG33 5QB Tel: 01572 767757
(Fax: 01572 767199)
North-west of Stamford. Nearest main road: A1 from Stamford to Grantham.

3 Bedrooms. £23. Available: own bath/shower/toilet; TV (on request). No smoking.
Dinner (by arrangement). £15 for 4 courses, wine and coffee, at times to suit guests. Vegetarian or other special diets if ordered. No smoking.
1 Sitting-room. With open fire, TV. No smoking. Piano.
Large garden

E-mail: bob@vankimmenade.freeserve.co.uk

A profusion of yellow and pink roses and a Montana clematis ramble up the façade of this Lincolnshire limestone cottage. In the original part, dating back to 1760, is a mellow, mahogany-furnished dining-room, with an exposed stone wall at one end and a limestone fireplace at the other. Here, Veronica Van Kimmenade (a former news journalist) sometimes serves such dinners as home-made carrot-and-orange soup, pork or chicken with Madeira and cream, and lemon meringue pie. She is an amenable hostess, offering guests sherry on arrival and a big choice for breakfast.

The neat, cottage-style bedrooms are comfortably furnished (one with a two-seater sofa) and decorated in pretty colours – turquoise and pink, white and poppy-red, for example.

Outside, there's a picturesque courtyard, a patio and two gardens – plenty of space to relax and roam. Alternatively, guests can unwind in the snug sitting-room.

Situated on the Lincolnshire/Rutland border, Rose Cottage is a convenient base for exploring the historic towns and great houses in this area, as well as enjoying traditional country pursuits. (Stabling and grazing for horses are available.)

V

SPROXTON LODGE FARM

C S

Skillington, Lincolnshire, NG33 5HJ Tel: 01476 860307
South of Grantham. Nearest main road: A1 from Grantham to Stamford.

3 Bedrooms. £18–£20. All have TV. No smoking.
Dinner (by arrangement). £7 for 2 courses and coffee, at 6pm. Vegetarian or other special diets if ordered. No smoking. **Light suppers** if ordered.
1 Sitting-room. With open fire, TV. No smoking.
Large garden

18th-century Sproxton Lodge is popular with walkers because the long Viking Way borders its fields. This is a homely, working farm – with silver ploughing-trophies won by Ted on display to prove it. He still has his very first tractor of 45 years ago, now almost a museum piece. Unpretentious comfort (and an enormous, carpeted bathroom) is what hospitable Eileen Whatton offers here, with dinners or snacks by arrangement. Bathrobes are provided for the guests in the bedrooms.

There are many popular sights in this region: Belvoir Castle, Belton House, Stapleford Park, Rutland Water and Wollaton Hall in its park; also Holme Pierrepont Hall, Doddington Hall, and Newstead Abbey (Byron's home). Eastwood has D.H. Lawrence's birthplace. Lincoln (cathedral), Southwell (minster), Sherwood Forest (Robin Hood display) and Nottingham are also near – the last a much underrated city. There is an arts museum in the castle and others at its foot (the lace museum is fascinating), river trips and walks through the Georgian quarter. The historic market towns of Stamford (in particular) and Newark are of great interest. One can shop for local Stilton, crafts and Nottingham lace.

WESTBROOK HOUSE

C PT(limited) **S X**

Gayton le Marsh, Lincolnshire, LN13 0NW Tel: 01507 450624
South-east of Louth. Nearest main road: A157 from Louth towards Mablethorpe.

3 Bedrooms. £22 (less for 2 nights or more). Available: own bath/shower/toilet; TV. No smoking.
Dinner (by arrangement). £10 for 3 courses and coffee, at 6.30–9pm. Vegetarian or other special diets if ordered. Wine available. No smoking. **Light suppers** if ordered.
1 Sitting-area. With TV. No smoking.
Small garden

In a tranquil, tiny hamlet, just a few miles from the sea in one direction and the Lincolnshire Wolds in the other, stands this immaculate guest-house which combines the best of modern comfort with traditional hospitality.

One steps straight into the sunny conservatory dining-room which, with its contemporary design and vibrant colours of yellow, terracotta and splashes of blue, sets the tone for the rest of the house. Most of the pale pine fitments and furniture, including the open-tread staircase which leads up to the galleried sitting-area, were made by owner Stewart Thompson, who also cooks all the meals. Bedrooms – decorated in those same glorious hues – are exceptionally smart and thoughtfully equipped.

Local Lincolnshire produce is served at breakfast, while an evening meal might comprise tuna salad, pork chops in cider sauce, and home-made banoffee pie. In warm weather, guests can unwind in the little patio-garden.

Visitors, who venture up the coast in late autumn, can witness the extraordinary sight of a colony of grey seals pupping on the beach, blissfully oblivious to the roar of RAF fighter jets in training overhead. Nearby Louth is an attractive market town and its 16th-century parish church has the tallest spire in England.

V

EXPLANATION OF CODE LETTERS

(These appear, where applicable, with each entry.)

C Suitable for families with children. Sometimes a minimum age is stipulated, in which case this is indicated by a numeral; thus **C**(5) means children over 5 years old are accepted. In most cases, houses that accept children offer reduced rates and special meals. They may provide cots and high chairs; or games and sports for older children. Please enquire when booking. And do not expect young children to be lodged free, as babies are. Families which pick establishments with plenty of games, swimming-pool, animals, etc., or that are near free museums, parks and walks, can save a lot on keeping youngsters entertained. (Readers wanting total quiet may wish to avoid houses coded **C**.)

D Dogs permitted. A charge is rarely made, but it is often a stipulation that you must ask before bringing one; the dog may have to sleep in your car, or be banned from certain rooms.

M Suitable for those with mobility problems. Needs vary: whenever we have used the code letter **M**, this indicates that not only is there a ground-floor bedroom and bathroom, but these, and doorways, have sufficient width for a wheelchair, and steps are few. For precise details, ask when booking.

PT Accessible by public transport. It is not essential to have a car in order to get off the beaten track because public transport is mostly available, albeit on a somewhat infrequent basis in many deep rural areas. Houses indicated by the code **PT** have a railway station or coach stop within a reasonable distance, from which you can walk or take a taxi (quite a number of hosts will even pick you up, free, in their own car). The symbol **PT** further indicates that there are also some buses for sightseeing, but these may be few. Ask when booking.

S Indicates those houses which charge single people no more, or only 10% more, than half the price of a double room (except, possibly, at peak periods).

X Visitors are accepted at Christmas, though Christmas meals are not necessarily provided. Some hotels and farms offer special Christmas holidays; but, unless otherwise indicated (by the code letter **X** at top of entry), those in this book will then be closed. Even if a house is not shown as being open at Christmas, it may open immediately thereafter – please enquire.

V Houses which accept the discount vouchers on page ii of this book.

LONDON

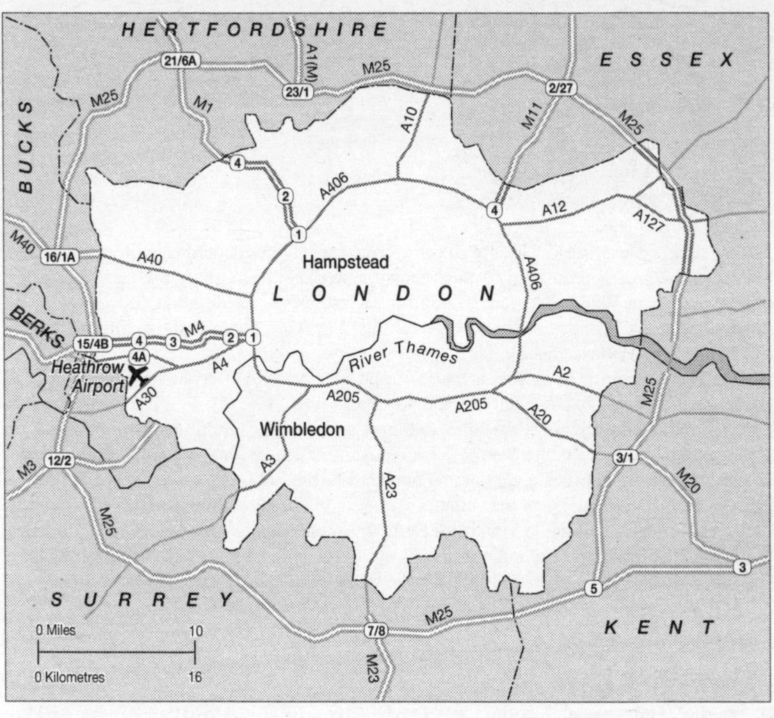

You stand a better chance of finding the right accommodation at the right price in the right area if you are using an up-to-date edition of this book, which is revised every year. Obtain an order form for the next edition (published in November) by sending a stamped addressed envelope, with 'SOTBT 2003' in the top left-hand corner, to Explore Britain, Alston, Cumbria, CA9 3SL.

London

THE COTTAGE PT S

1A Kemplay Road, Hampstead, London, NW3 1TA Tel: 020 7794 0365
Nearest main road: A502 (Rosslyn Hill) from Hampstead towards Camden Town.

4 Bedrooms. £33–£35 (less for 3 nights or more). Available: own shower/toilet; TV; balcony (three). No smoking.
Small garden

In the heart of Hampstead, close to the chic boutiques, cosmopolitan cafés and restaurants for which the area is renowned, is this yellow-painted, cottage-style house of 18th-century origin where Jean Wilde welcomes bed-and-breakfast guests. Inside, there is everything one might expect of a Hampstead house – interesting *objets d'art*, books and paintings, antiques, and the owner's evident creative flair.

The best bedroom, decorated in maroon and cream, has an old brass bed and a large terrace, which overlooks a quintessential London scene. Two of the other very pleasant bedrooms also have their own balconies (a bonus as there is no communal sitting-room).

Breakfast is served in the warm, country-style kitchen around an antique pine table. Guests can choose between a continental breakfast or the full English cooked version (at no extra cost). Occasionally, Jean may offer breakfast in the pretty walled garden.

Except at night, parking in Hampstead can be problematic, so visitors are recommended to use the Heath carpark, eight minutes' walk away. Hampstead Heath itself, the tube station and other places of literary, historic and artistic interest are quickly and easily accessible.

London

LANGORF HOTEL C PT X

20 Frognal, Hampstead, London, NW3 6AG Tel: 020 7794 4483 (Fax: 020 7435 9055)
Toll-free from USA on: 1-800-925-4731
Nearest main road: A41 (Finchley Road) from London to Aylesbury (M1, junction 1, is near).

31 Bedrooms. £34 (with continental breakfast) **to readers of this book sharing a double room.** All have own bath/shower/toilet; TV; same day laundry/cleaning service.
Light snacks etc. (24 hours). **Bar.**
Small garden

E-mail: langorf@aol.com

For readers visiting London, we have negotiated a very special price at a small but luxurious hotel in a quiet residential road (with good access into the centre); no single occupancy.

The bedrooms are elegant: modern furniture is complemented by excellent soft furnishings, and all bathroom fitments are of the highest quality. There are remote-control TV sets in each room, direct-dial telephones, hair-dryers, etc. Some bedrooms are on the ground floor, others are served by a lift. Twenty-four-hour room service for snacks and drinks.

Downstairs, an attractive coral reception/sitting-area leads into the airy breakfast-room, which overlooks a leafy garden. Here one helps oneself from a buffet of some two dozen items that include assorted fruits, ham, cheeses, croissants and much else. Individual dietary requirements can be catered for, if the hotel is forewarned. The manager is Caroline Haynes.

Readers' comments: Very nice and helpful staff. Wonderful gem, everything superb. Each guest very special. The best value we have found in London. Excellent value for the city.

ROTHESAY

C M P T X

198 Kingston Road, Wimbledon, London, SW19 3NU Tel: 020 8715 1335 (Fax: 020 8715 1336)

Nearest main road: A3 from Guildford towards Wimbledon.

3 Bedrooms. £28.50–£36 (with continental breakfast). All have own bath/shower/toilet; TV; balcony (one). No smoking.
1 Sitting-room. With TV. No smoking.
Small garden

In a conservation area that was developed by horticultural pioneer John Innes, this mid-Victorian house retains many of its original and distinctive architectural features. Despite its position on a busy road, off-street parking is available, and bedrooms to the side and rear are quiet. All are spacious and bright and can accommodate families of three or even four people. One on the ground floor has its own kitchenette, and a huge upstairs one overlooking the garden has a resplendent bathroom with Jacuzzi bath surrounded by pink marble. The pale blue room (with silky wallpaper and painted oak headboards) is also attractive. Throughout there are polished floorboards strewn with Persian and Chinese rugs and stripped red pine doors.

Breakfast is taken round a long oval dining-table and although it is billed as 'continental', German-born Traude Konig provides guests with platters of ham and salami, four different types of cheese, pancakes, and a selection of European breads and home-made jams.

From Wimbledon tube and railway station (a brisk 10-minute walk away), there are frequent fast trains into Waterloo in one direction and to Hampton Court in the other. V

Private bathrooms are not necessarily en suite.

Months when houses are shown as closed are inclusive.

Book well ahead: many of these houses have few rooms. Do not expect dinner if you have not booked it or if you arrive late.

Facts (prices, etc.) at the top of entries are supplied by the proprietors themselves. While every effort is made to ensure that these are correct at the time of going to press, they may alter thereafter: please check when you book.

NORFOLK

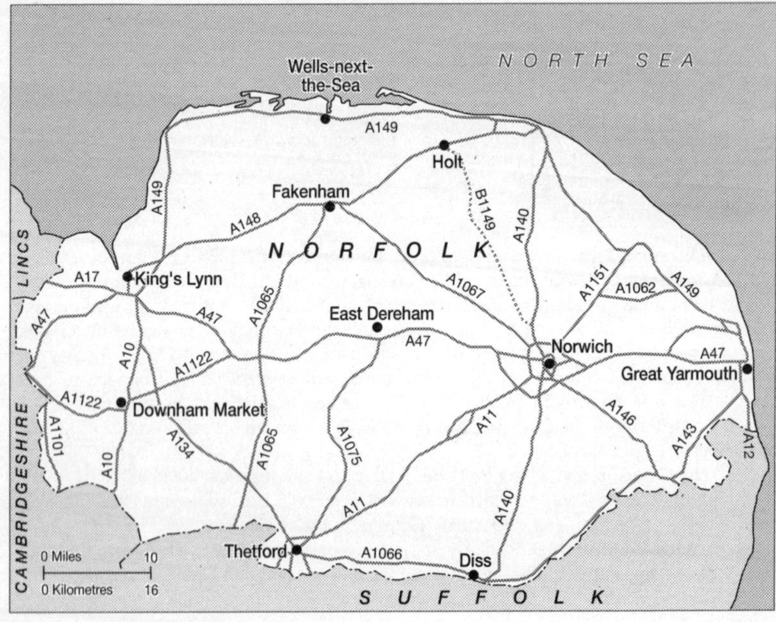

COMPLAINTS: If anything was not of reasonable standard (e.g. chilly bedroom or badly cooked food) you are entitled to claim a reduction on your bill, but *only if* you had previously told the proprietor and given him or her a chance to put matters right. In a court case involving a restaurant meal, it was ruled that, because a customer had not made a specific complaint at the time, he had no right subsequently to withhold payment (he had cancelled his cheque). The moral is obvious: if dissatisfied, you are expected to say so at once and not later. Houses are regularly inspected; and complaints will be forwarded to proprietors for their comments. Write to: Jan Bowmer (SOTBT), c/o Arrow Books, 20 Vauxhall Bridge Road, London SW1V 2SA. Please enclose a stamped addressed envelope if you want her to acknowledge receipt of your complaint.

BERRY HALL

C(10) S

Great Walsingham, Norfolk, NR22 6DZ Tel: 01328 820267
North of Fakenham. Nearest main road: A149 from Sheringham to Wells-next-the-Sea.

Norfolk

5 Bedrooms. £24. Available: own bath/toilet. No smoking.
Dinner. £12 for 3 courses and coffee, at 6.45pm. Vegetarian or other special diets if ordered. No smoking.
1 Sitting-room. With open fire, TV. No smoking.
Large garden

This is a fine Tudor house in big grounds named after the merchant who built it in 1532. Once, Rupert Brooke's family lived here. Now it is the home of Joan Sheaf. Many rooms, all very big, have fine panelling; in the hall are a flagstone floor and impressive oak ceiling; Delft tiles, depicting scenes of Goa, decorate the dining-room. There is a great balustraded staircase and unusual antiques. The sitting-room overlooks the large, pleasant garden with rosebeds and a magnificent copper beech tree, beyond which lies a moat with ducks. For dinner there are such dishes as watercress soup, then lamb noisettes in sherry sauce, and meringues with strawberries.

Less than an hour away are many stately homes and National Trust properties – Blickling, Felbrigg, Houghton, Holkham and Oxburgh Halls, and Sandringham House, the royal Christmas residence. Nearby Thursford has a steam museum and an organ collection.

Readers' comments: Most attractive, comfortable and spacious. Food cooked to perfection. Charming and characterful. Lovely home; spacious room.

BURGH PARVA HALL

C D S X

Melton Constable, Norfolk, NR24 2PU Tel/Fax: 01263 862569
South of Holt. Nearest main road: A148 from Fakenham to Cromer.

Norfolk

2 Bedrooms. £20–£22 (less for 7 nights or more).
Dinner (by arrangement). £15 for 3 courses and coffee, at 7.30pm. Vegetarian or other special diets if ordered. **Light suppers** if ordered.
Small garden

E-mail: judy.heal@btinternet.com

Burgh Parva Hall was a farm in the 16th century; in the 1840s an imposing wing was added. It is the only house left at Burgh (pronounced 'borough') Parva, for the village was destroyed after the Great Plague of 1665.

One enters through the dining-hall where logs crackle under the ogee arch of the fire-place. Furniture is old in style, rooms huge; your bedroom will have a sofa or armchairs from which to enjoy the view through sash windows – fine sunsets. Judy or William Heal will either give you a lift to and from a local inn for dinner, or by arrangement you may dine at the house.

Nearby Holt is a picturesque market town; and the very beautiful heritage coastline is only a few miles away. The bird sanctuary and seal colony at Blakeney are worth a visit.

Readers' comments: Impressive house, excellent breakfasts. Very helpful. Bedroom was enormous, breakfast great; wonderful to stay in such a lovely old house.

V

Norfolk

CEDAR LODGE

D S

West Tofts, Norfolk, IP26 5DB Tel/Fax: 01842 878281

North-west of Thetford. Nearest main road: A134 from Thetford towards Downham Market.

3 Bedrooms. £23. Bargain breaks. Available: own bath/shower/toilet; TV. No smoking.
Dinner (by arrangement). £15–£20 for 4–5 courses and coffee, at times to suit guests. Vegetarian or other special diets if ordered. **Light suppers** if ordered.
1 Sitting-room. With open fire, TV.
Garden

It is largely the exceptional food which brings visitors to Christine Collins's home – she is a member of The Master Chefs of Great Britain. Situated on the edge of Thetford Forest, her Colt cedar house has timber walls of treble thickness to keep it warm in winter and cool in summer. There are large picture-windows from which to appreciate the apple-blossom in the garden and the leafy scene beyond.

Indoors, soft blues and celadon green contrast with timber walls and a hearth of light stone; in the dining-room, buttoned leather chairs surround a lovely yew table, laid with silver at dinner; bedrooms are light and airy.

As to meals, a typical dinner might comprise: a warm provençale tartlet; Dover sole fillets with a pea purée sauce; fillet of lamb on a bed of rosti, Savoy cabbage and Puy lentils, served with a jus; tarte au citron; and cheeses. During the winter there are catering weekends for guests, and cookery demonstrations.

Readers' comments: Food excellent. Peaceful. Extremely hospitable and helpful.

Norfolk

COLLEGE FARMHOUSE

C(7) **S X**

Thompson, Norfolk, IP24 1QG Tel/Fax: 01953 483318

North of Thetford. Nearest main road: A1075 from Thetford to East Dereham.

3 Bedrooms. £23–£25. Available: own bath/shower/toilet; TV.
Large garden

E-mail: collegefarm@amstrad.net

Priests used to live in College Farmhouse until Henry VIII disbanded them. Later owners added oak panelling, a coat-of-arms and other features. There are Gothic windows; walls (some three feet thick) have odd curves. Lavender Garnier has collected interesting furniture, family portraits (it was an ancestor who selected dark blue as Oxford's boat-race colour), and attractive fabrics for bedrooms that have armchairs and TV (no sitting-room). A lovely old garden slopes down to eel-ponds. Bicycles for hire. Inn food one mile away.

Thompson is in an attractive, leafy part of Norfolk, where the landscape undulates and villages are pretty. Thetford was the birthplace of Thomas Paine and there is a statue of him in the town.

Readers' comments: Warm hospitality. Magical peace in a beautiful house. Very comfortable, warm and friendly. Breakfasts a joy. Excellent. As near perfect as makes no difference; excellent value. Quite wonderful. Perfection?

DIAL HOUSE

PT X

Railway Road, Downham Market, Norfolk, PE38 9EB Tel: 01366 388358
Nearest main road: A10 from King's Lynn to Ely.

3 Bedrooms. £17.50–£22.50. Bargain breaks. All have own bath/shower/toilet; TV. No smoking.
Dinner (by arrangement). £15 for 3 courses and coffee, at 7pm. Vegetarian or other special diets if ordered. No smoking. **Light suppers** if ordered.
1 Sitting-room. With TV. No smoking.
Small garden

E-mail: bookings@thedialhouse.co.uk

Former banker David Murray has restored the sundial which gives this house its name. He and his wife Ann have furnished their home with comfort very much in mind and filled it with family photos and paintings which reflect their eclectic taste. Built of local stone, much of the house dates from the 18th century, though it may have had its origins in Jacobean times.

The sitting- and dining-rooms, both spacious and light, are linked by a long, low corridor. Upstairs, bedrooms are cosy, one with pretty stained-glass windows.

Once restaurateurs, Ann and David are no strangers to cooking and can offer dinner for up to 16 people. A typical menu might include marinated mushrooms and red peppers in balsamic vinegar; tender pork chop with a mild mustard, onion and rosemary sauce; and pineapple and grapes in Muscat wine to finish.

On the edge of the Fens, Downham Market is well placed for visiting Ely, King's Lynn, several bird reserves, including Welney, and many National Trust properties. This is a good area for cycling and bikes can be hired from the Dial House.

GREENACRES FARM

D

Wood Green, Long Stratton, Norfolk, NR15 2RR Tel/Fax: 01508 530261
South of Norwich. Nearest main road: A140 from Norwich towards Diss.

3 Bedrooms. £25 (minimum 2 nights)–£27.50. Less for 7 nights or more. Available: own bath/shower/toilet; TV. No smoking.
1 Sitting-room. With wood-burner, TV, piano. No smoking.
Large garden

E-mail: greenacresfarm@tinyworld.co.uk

17th-century Greenacres Farm is right on the edge of a 30-acre common with ponds and ancient woods. Bedrooms are comfortable, with own shower or bath. In the huge snooker room you can peer into the floodlit depths of a 60-foot well as old as the house itself. There is also a tennis court. Joanna Douglas is trained in therapeutic massage, aromatherapy and reflexology, and guests can book a session during their stay. For evening meals, Joanna recommends the Crown at nearby Pulham Market.

This is an excellent spot from which to explore in all directions. Bressingham has fine gardens and steam engines. The Broads are near; and to the north lies Norwich, one of the most beautiful of mediaeval cities, complete with castle and cathedral, as well as craft and antique shops in cobbled byways. Just outside the city, the Sainsbury Centre for Visual Arts, in a building designed by Norman Foster, is exceptional.

Reader's comment: Very friendly and quiet.

Norfolk

HIDEAWAY

D S

Red Lion Yard, Wells-next-the-Sea, Norfolk, NR23 1AX Tel/Fax: 01328 710524
Nearest main road: A149 from Cromer to Hunstanton.

3 Bedrooms. £20.50–£22 (less for 7 nights or more). Bargain breaks. Available: own bath/shower/toilet; TV. No smoking.
1 Sitting-room. With TV. No smoking. Bar (smoking permitted).
Small garden
Closed from mid-December to mid-January.

Aptly named, these converted stables are – although only 200 yards from the harbour – so tucked away that they take some finding! Beyond a secluded courtyard garden (the nicest of the bedrooms is actually in this), a door opens into a small sitting-area. Beyond this lie further bedrooms, compact in size and neat rather than characterful in style – all on the ground floor. You can use the sauna or spa bath for a small charge. And, a considerable asset in the town centre, Hideaway has its own parking space.

Ex-teacher Madeline Higgs and her helpers run the guest-house on well-organized lines. Packed lunches are available and there is a microwave and toaster for visitors' use. Except on special winter weekend breaks, dinner is not provided, but guests can walk to one of the many eating-places nearby. This part of Norfolk is well endowed with things to do or see – from stately homes to nature reserves of differing kinds.

Readers' comments: We have returned many times. Most hospitable. Winter weekends are very, very good value. Pleasantly informal. Comfortable rooms.

Norfolk

HONEYHILLS

D S

Bircham Newton, Norfolk, PE31 6QR Tel: 01485 578266
North-east of King's Lynn. Nearest main road: A148 from King's Lynn to Fakenham.

2 Bedrooms. £17.50–£22.50. No smoking.
1 Sitting-room. With TV. No smoking.
Garden

Some hundred years ago, bees were kept in hives on nearby hills, thus giving this pretty flint cottage its name. All is spick-and-span within and former hotelier Lesley Piper has created a relaxing atmosphere. At one end of the beamed sitting-room are brick-red sofas and at the other, breakfast is served at a Victorian mahogany table. One wall is lined with books and there are paintings here and elsewhere by local artists. Beyond this room is an attractive cottage-garden crammed with herbaceous borders giving colour for much of the year. Bedrooms with bright patchwork quilts are small and neat. The bathroom is shared.

This is good walking country. There are many footpaths hereabouts and unspoilt sandy beaches too. Several stately homes, including Sandringham, are close, as are bird reserves and a golf course. The tiny 13th-century church in the village is also worth a visit.

For evening meals, try one of the many eating-places in Burnham Market or Brancaster.

Reader's comments: A true find; the welcome couldn't have been warmer. Garden was truly spectacular. I will definitely be returning.

KIMBERLEY HOME FARM

C S

Norfolk

Wymondham, Norfolk, NR18 0RW Tel: 01953 603137 (Fax: 01953 604836)
South-west of Norwich. Nearest main road: A11 from Norwich to Thetford.

4 Bedrooms. £20–£25. Available: own bath/shower/toilet.
Dinner. £15 for 3 courses and coffee, at times to suit guests. Wine available. **Light suppers** if ordered.
1 Sitting-room. With open fire, TV.
Large garden
Closed from December to March.

This is an attractively furnished farmhouse with stables at the front and a large garden at the back, on to which the glass doors of the large sitting-room open. There is a pond with ducks and a hard tennis court. Apart from the hundreds of acres of crops, the main activity at Kimberley is training and racing horses.

The bedrooms are particularly pretty, the bathroom excellent, and the dining-room has a long Regency table. Jenny Bloom is not only a superb cook but a generous one, leaving pheasants or joints of meat on a hot-tray from which guests may help themselves. Starters are imaginative (avocado mousse, for instance), and puddings delicious.

You can have the exclusive use of rooms if you wish, or get more involved with the family and the farm. There is a very good attic family-suite.

Readers' comments: Total peace, comfortable rooms, delicious food. Comfortable, and very good food. Excellent. Very warm welcome. Lovely people. Delicious supper. Nothing was too much trouble: very highly rated. Fun, very welcoming.

LODGE FARM

C(8) D S

Norfolk

Bressingham, Norfolk, IP22 2BQ Tel/Fax: 01379 687629
West of Diss. Nearest main road: A1066 from Thetford to Diss.

3 Bedrooms. £18–£20 (less for 3 nights or more).
Light suppers if ordered. Vegetarian or other special diets if ordered. Wine available.
1 Sitting-room. With open fire.
Large garden

Henry VIII had a 'palace' for hunting near here and at the boundaries of his great estate were lodges, of which this was one. Its windows and pink walls give little hint that the house goes back so far, but inside are chamfered beams, low ceilings, odd steps and angles.

David and Pat Bateson have furniture that is very much in keeping – for instance, a wedding-chest dated 1682; a big refectory table; and an iron fireback of 1582 which furnishes the great inglenook where logs blaze on chilly nights. The simple bedrooms are cottagey in style, one lime-and-white, one (with brass bed) pink-and-white. This is a lovely place for a family holiday, with plenty of sightseeing outings likely to appeal to older children. Outside is a garden and the Batesons' smallholding (they keep sheep, ducks and horses).

For a full dinner, most visitors drive to South Lopham or to the Red Lion at Kenninghall, which has a particularly good vegetarian section.

Readers' comments: Made so welcome. Delightful weekend. Reasonable bill.

V

Norfolk

OLD BAKEHOUSE

C

33–35 High Street, Little Walsingham, Norfolk, NR22 6BZ Tel/Fax: 01328 820454
North of Fakenham. Nearest main road: A148 from King's Lynn to Cromer.

3 Bedrooms. £24.50 (less for 7 nights or more). All have own bath/shower/toilet; TV.
Dinner. £13.75 for 3 courses and coffee, at 7pm. Vegetarian or other special diets if ordered. Wine available. No smoking.
1 Bar/lounge
Closed from mid-January to mid-February.

Over a restaurant, renowned for good food, are excellent bedrooms, double-glazed to reduce street noise and comfortably furnished with settees and armchairs.

From 1550 until recent times, part of this house was a bakery and the old brick ovens are still to be seen. Above an ancient cellar bar is a large, lofty dining-room – in the 18th century it was a corn exchange. There is a great brick fireplace at one end, and a huge iron-hinged door. Chris and Helen Padley serve such delectable table d'hôte meals as fresh peaches baked with cheese and herbs; banana-stuffed chicken with a mild curry-and-almond sauce; and ice-cream coffee-cake; there is a wider à la carte choice too.

A pilgrimage centre since the Middle Ages, the village has a museum charting the history of the pilgrims.

Readers' comments: Gourmet food; friendly and efficient. Loving attention to detail; food superb. Food wonderful. Comfortable rooms, friendly and accommodating hosts. Food first class. Took real pains to make us welcome.

Norfolk

OLD PUMPHOUSE

C(5) D PT S

Holman Road, Aylsham, Norfolk, NR11 6BY Tel/Fax: 01263 733789
North of Norwich. Nearest main road: A140 from Norwich to Cromer.

6 Bedrooms. £19–£24 (less for 7 nights or more). Available: own bath/shower/toilet; TV. No smoking.
Light suppers (from October to April) if ordered.
2 Sitting-areas. With open fire (in one), TV (in one). No smoking.
Small garden

This house, built in the 1750s, takes its name from the quaint, thatch-roofed town pump which faces it. The warm pale ochre of its façade has also been used indoors to create a gentle elegance, enlivened by Lynda's displays of equestrian equipment and Tony's accomplished photography of aircraft and Himalayan mountains.

The Richardsons have decorated the comfortable and well-equipped bedrooms with strong colour schemes. One, in pimento-red, has a four-poster bed with tented hangings made by Lynda; while another has an Indian theme – silk cushions and prints, and etchings of old Delhi. A corner annexe, with space for additional bedding, lends versatility to the family room. The spotless bathrooms have Laura Ashley wallpapers.

There is a cosy sitting-area at one end of the spacious dining-room, which has pillar-box red walls offset by stripped pine shutters and floorboards. Its deep sash windows overlook the pretty rear garden, with an ornamental pond and seating in secluded corners. Good breakfasts here are assured, as the Richardsons were previously restaurateurs.

Blickling Hall is close by, and the Bure Valley Railway terminates at Aylsham.

OLD RECTORY

C S

Rectory Lane, Framingham Pigot, Norfolk, NR14 7QQ Tel: 01508 493082
South-east of Norwich. Nearest main road: A146 from Norwich to Lowestoft.

3 Bedrooms. £22 (less for 7 nights or more). Bargain breaks. Two have own bath/toilet. No smoking.
1 Sitting-room. With open fire, TV. No smoking.
Large garden

A church has stood in this tiny hamlet since Saxon times. The present one dates from the 19th century and its Georgian-style rectory is now home to Susan and David Thurman.

An old pew in the hallway is the only reminder of its ecclesiastical connection. Furniture throughout the rest of the house has been attractively re-upholstered by Susan, who gives lessons in the subject during the winter months.

In the comfortable sitting-room, shared with the Thurmans, a turquoise-coloured sofa makes a pleasing contrast to the pale blue walls and floral curtains. Plants line the window-sill of the cream-and-green dining-room and beyond is a lovely view of the garden, beautifully transformed by Susan and David from the wilderness it once was.

Eggs for breakfast are supplied by the couple's own hens, and for evening meals, good inns such as the Gull are a few minutes away by car. Nearby Norwich also offers a variety of eating-places and much in the way of historic interest too. This is a good base for visiting the 100 or so 'round tower' churches for which this part of Norfolk is renowned.

V

PEACOCK HOUSE

C D S X

Peacock Lane, Old Beetley, Norfolk, NR20 4DG Tel: 01362 860371
North of East Dereham. Nearest main road: A47 from East Dereham to Norwich.

rear view

3 Bedrooms. £21–£22.50. Available: own bath/shower/toilet; TV. No smoking.
Dinner (by arrangement). £14.50 for 3 courses and coffee, at 7pm (not Wednesdays). Vegetarian or other special diets if ordered. Wine available. No smoking.
1 Sitting-room. With open fire, TV. No smoking.
Large garden

E-mail: PeackH@aol.com

Once a farm, the tranquil house hides its Elizabethan beams behind a façade added in Victorian times. On arrival, guests are taken by Jenny Bell into their own sitting-room and given home-made flapjacks or scones with tea. There is an open fire on cold days – or when it is sunny you may prefer to wander out to the large lawn, with old apple-trees and a pond, surrounded by fields with the Bells' sheep and chickens (lambs among the daffodils in spring). Croquet is also available.

Upstairs are rooms with antique bedsteads, co-ordinated duvets and curtains, exposed timbers, and a really huge bathroom in one. Breakfasts, served in the handsomely beamed dining-room, are both generous and varied (home-produced eggs and local sausages are very popular with guests); and as to dinner, Jenny serves such meals as carrot-and-coriander soup, salmon fillet with red pepper and tomato sauce, and raspberry pavlova.

Readers' comments: Truly rural. Wonderful welcome. Spared no efforts in caring for our comfort. Tastefully furnished; lovely room.

Norfolk

REGENCY HOUSE

C D P T S X

Neatishead, Norfolk, NR12 8AD Tel/Fax: 01692 630233

North-east of Norwich. Nearest main road: A1151 from Norwich to Stalham.

5 Bedrooms. £22–£24 **(less for 2 nights or more to readers of this book).** Available: own bath/shower/toilet; TV.

Light suppers if ordered.

2 Sitting-rooms. With open fire (in one).

Small garden

Closed in November.

E-mail: wrigleyregency@talk21.com

In the Norfolk Broads, former *Daily Express* reporter Sue Wrigley and her husband Alan (a keen gardener) run this 18th-century guest-house to an immaculate standard.

The breakfasts are outstanding: standard issue is 2 sausages, 4 rashers of bacon, 6 mushrooms, 2 whole tomatoes, 2 slices of fried bread and as many eggs as you request! But if you prefer it, Sue will produce a low-cholesterol option or vegetarian breakfast instead. This is served in an oak-panelled room with willow-pattern crockery on tables that were specially made by a local craftsman. Bedrooms have Laura Ashley fabrics (two have king-size beds) and fresh flowers. Bathrooms are excellent. The main sitting-room has a beamed ceiling and looks on to the colourful garden. For dinner, there is a choice of eating-places within yards of the guest-house.

V

Readers' comments: Lovely furnishings. Amazing breakfasts, generous hospitality. The best b & b we've stayed in. Very neat, well-appointed rooms. Excellent in every way. Highly recommended. Very warm welcome, lots of creature comforts.

Norfolk

TOWER COTTAGE

C(8)

Black Street, Winterton-on-Sea, Norfolk, NR29 4AP Tel: 01493 394053

North of Great Yarmouth. Nearest main road: A149 from Great Yarmouth to Cromer.

3 Bedrooms. £19–£21 (less for 7 nights or more). Available: own bath/shower/toilet; TV (in all). No smoking (in two).

Small garden

E-mail: towercott@aladdinscave.net

The ancient flint church in this peaceful, unspoilt village has the second highest tower in Norfolk and you can see it for miles around. Just across the road stands Alan and Muriel Webster's attractive 18th-century cottage, only a few minutes' walk from a sandy beach. Alan spent several years at sea, travelling the world as a master mariner, and photos of some of the ships on which he sailed are hung in the hallway of their charming home.

Bedrooms are neat and unpretentious. Two are on the ground floor and one of these, in a small converted barn, has its own sitting-area.

Breakfast includes home-made preserves and is served in the snug dining-room in winter and in the pretty conservatory hung with a grapevine in summer. For evening meals, the Fisherman's Return in the village comes highly recommended and there's a good range of other dining-places within a short drive.

The Broads are close, and sailing and windsurfing are popular pursuits in the area. Great Yarmouth has plenty of holiday entertainments that are aimed at families.

WHITE HALL

C

Carbrooke, Norfolk, IP25 6SG Tel: 01953 885950 (Fax: 01953 884420)

North-east of Thetford. Nearest main road: A1075 from Thetford to East Dereham.

3 Bedrooms. £21–£23 (less for 4 nights or more). One has own bath/toilet. No smoking.
Light suppers if ordered.
1 Sitting-room. With open fire, TV, piano.
Large garden

The hamlet was already an ancient settlement when the Romans came here. In the mediaeval church, the hammerbeam roof and rood-screen are particularly fine. White Hall is, by contrast, quite a recent addition to the scene – little more than two centuries old. An elegant Georgian house, it is surrounded by grounds where you may encounter guinea-fowl and bantams.

Inside, Shirley and David Carr have furnished the sitting-room with peony sofas facing the marble fireplace, and the light bedrooms with pink roses or green-sprigged fabrics complementing white or apple-green walls. The dining-room has a big log stove and, like other rooms, large, shuttered sash windows through which to enjoy tranquil views.

For active visitors, croquet, bicycles and badminton are available.

Readers' comments: I felt like a very privileged guest. Delightful couple, easy-going attitude. Staying there was a real pleasure. Nothing too much trouble. Beautifully decorated. Friendly and welcoming. Excellent decor. Best one yet, helpful and charming owners.

For a list of SOTBT houses that are in or close to the great National Parks of England and Wales, see p.ix.

When writing to the managing editor, if you want an acknowledgment please enclose a stamped addressed envelope.

Prices are per person sharing a room at the beginning of the year. However, for the best rooms in the house or later in the year, you may well be asked for more.

Addresses shown are to enable you to locate a house on a map. They are not necessarily complete postal addresses (though the essential post-code is included), and detailed directions for finding a house should be obtained from the owner.

NORTHAMPTONSHIRE

Some proprietors stipulate a minimum stay of two nights at weekends or peak seasons; or they will accept one-nighters only at short notice (that is, only if no lengthier booking has yet been made).

CASTLE FARM

C X

Fotheringhay, Northamptonshire, PE8 5HZ Tel/Fax: 01832 226200

South-west of Peterborough. Nearest main road: A605 from Peterborough to Oundle.

Northamptonshire

5 Bedrooms. £25–£28 (less for 5 nights or more). Available: own bath/shower/toilet; TV; views of river. No smoking.

1 Sitting-room. With open fire, TV.

Large garden

In the castle that was once here, Richard III was born. Later, Mary Queen of Scots' heart was secretly buried in the mound on which the keep stood: part of the land belonging to Castle Farm today. The thistles that grow here are called Queen Mary's Tears.

At the Victorian farm, one steps straight into Stephanie Gould's huge quarry-tiled kitchen where a pine staircase rises to spacious bedrooms that are spick-and-span, all with nice views. There are good bath- or shower-rooms, and much stripped pine. The big sitting-room, too, has a view to enjoy – of the swift River Nene beyond the lawn, and a picturesque bridge. In an outbuilding, there are two even more luxurious bedrooms.

One can eat well (albeit expensively) at the nearby Falcon Inn. To the south is Oundle (famous for its public school), a delightful little town within a loop of the River Nene, on which you can go boating.

Readers' comments: Very relaxed. Good breakfast. Lovely view. Beautifully furnished. Excellent room. Friendly young hostess. Could not have been more hospitable. Rooms excellent and very up-market. Excellent facilities.

DAIRY FARM

C D M S

St Andrews Lane, Cranford St Andrew, Northamptonshire, NN14 4AQ

Tel: 01536 330273

East of Kettering. Nearest main road: A14 from Kettering towards Cambridge.

Northamptonshire

3 Bedrooms. £22–£32 (less for 4 nights or more). Available: own bath/shower/toilet; TV. No smoking.

Dinner (by arrangement). £15 for 3 courses and coffee, at 7pm. Vegetarian or other special diets if ordered. No smoking. **Light suppers** if ordered.

1 Sitting-room. With open fire, TV. No smoking.

Garden

This is not in fact a dairy-farm but arable and sheep. Its name derives from the old dairy around which the manor house was built, in 1610. It is a fine building with mullioned lattice windows in limestone walls and a thatched roof. Its noble chimney-stacks, finials on the gables, dormer windows and dignified porch give it great character. In the grounds stands a circular stone dovecote (mediaeval) with unique rotating ladder inside.

Audrey and John Clarke have hung old family portraits in the sitting-room, and furnished the house with things like oak chests and ladderback chairs that are in keeping with it. Some bedrooms, one with four-poster, overlook church and mansion nearby.

Meals consist of straightforward home cooking – soups, roasts, fruit pies – using fruit and vegetables from the garden. Visitors enjoy croquet, good walks and cycling.

Readers' comments: Very special, will return. Delicious food; attentive hosts. Very kind; food plentiful; peaceful. Delightful house and setting. Good, friendly reception. Good food, relaxed atmosphere.

V

Northamptonshire

MURCOTT MILL

C D P T S X

Long Buckby, Northamptonshire, NN6 7QR Tel: 01327 842236 (Fax: 01327 844524)
North-west of Northampton. Nearest main road: A428 from Northampton to Rugby (and M1, junction 17).

3 Bedrooms. £20–£25. Available: own bath/shower/toilet; TV.
Dinner (by arrangement). £7.50 for 2 courses and coffee, at 7.30pm. Vegetarian or other special diets if ordered. No smoking. **Light suppers** if ordered.
1 Sitting-room. With open fire, TV.
Small garden

E-mail: bhart6@compuserve.com

This 18th-century house, approached via a long, private drive, is a mill no longer but a farm. Carrie, descendant of the original owner, married Australian Brian Hart who (reversing the usual order of things!) immigrated here to keep sheep and raise a young family. The house – no ordinary mill – has big bay windows, marble fireplaces, handsome doors, alcoves and pretty plasterwork, all of which Carrie has complemented with restful colour schemes. She serves snacks or such traditional meals as roast lamb and treacle pudding. The light and pleasant sitting-room, with eau-de-nil wallpaper, looks on to the garden where there are green and copper beeches.

The mill is well placed for seeking out not only the pretty and unspoilt villages hidden in Northamptonshire's unappreciated lanes but also such masterpieces as the stately homes of Canons Ashby and Castle Ashby, Cottesbrooke (inspiration for Jane Austen's *Mansfield Park*), mediaeval Deene Park, Kirby and Lamport Halls. Althorp is also close by.

V

Northamptonshire

OLD VICARAGE

C D

Laxton, Northamptonshire, NN17 3AT Tel: 01780 450248 (Fax: 01780 450398)
North-east of Corby. Nearest main road: A43 from Kettering to Stamford.

4 Bedrooms. £20.50 (less for 5 nights or more). All have TV.
1 Sitting-room. With open fire, TV. Piano.
Large garden

E-mail: susan@marthahill.co.uk

Humphrey Repton, famous as a landscape gardener, designed the whole village of Laxton in 1804; which is why this house is so attractive, in 'gothick' style. Susan Hill-Brookes and her husband have filled every room with Victorian landscapes and still-lifes, portraits of dogs, period pieces and other treasures. The guests' elegant sitting-room is bright and airy and overlooks the garden. A twisting stair at the back leads to old-fashioned, cottagey bedrooms. There is a small, unheated swimming-pool; also a croquet lawn, assorted farm animals (their own hens provide the breakfast eggs), dogs and horses. One can dine well at the Queen's Head in Bulwick (one and a half miles away).

This is a good area for walking or cycling (bikes for hire) and other country pursuits, and for sightseeing too: the historic schools at Uppingham and Oundle, the mediaeval town of Stamford, Rockingham Castle, and the stately home of Burghley where horse trials take place every September. On Rutland Water, fishing and sailing are available.

V

RECTORY FARM

C D

Sulgrave, Northamptonshire, OX17 2SG Tel: 01295 760261 (Fax: 01295 760089)
North-east of Banbury. Nearest main road: A43 from Northampton towards Oxford (and M40, junction 11).

3 Bedrooms. £20–£22 (less for 5 nights or more). All have own TV. No smoking.
Dinner (by arrangement). £15 for 3 courses and coffee, at 7.30–9pm. Vegetarian or other special diets if ordered. Wine available. No smoking.
1 Sitting-room. With open fire. Piano. No smoking.
Small garden

E-mail: rectoryfarm@talk21.com

George Washington's ancestors lived at Sulgrave Manor, which remained in the Washington family for 120 years and is now a museum. Overlooking the manor house is 17th-century Rectory Farm, thatched without and stone-flagged within. Generously proportioned rooms have wide, panelled doors and deep-set windows with white shutters behind cream curtains that contrast with rust-red rugs on the floor and the peonies on the capacious armchairs. Bedrooms are in pleasant country-house style (one has extra long, mahogany-framed beds); and from the window of the upstairs landing you can see both the Stars and Stripes and the Union Jack flying over Sulgrave Manor.

Joanna Smyth-Osbourne, despite bringing up a family, finds time to produce such beautifully cooked dinners as parsnip soup flavoured with ginger and orange, pork-and-apple ragoût, and a delicious kiwi fruit ice cream. Meals are served in the dining-room where there is also a piano and a sturdy rocking-horse for children to play on. Outside are sheep, ponies, feathery-legged bantams and pheasants strutting the autumn fields. Joanna can recommend several lovely walks nearby.

SHUCKBURGH ARMS

C M

Stoke Doyle, Northamptonshire, PE8 5TG Tel: 01832 272339 (Fax: 01832 275230)
South-west of Oundle. Nearest main road: A605 from Peterborough to Oundle.

Northamptonshire

5 Bedrooms. £20 **to readers mentioning SOTBT when booking**. All have own shower/toilet; TV.
Dinner. £10–£15 for 2 courses and coffee, from 7–9.30pm. Vegetarian or other special diets if ordered. Wine available. No smoking.
1 Bar. With open fire.
Small garden

E-mail: paulkirkby@shuckburgharms.co.uk

The quintessential English pub is something of a rarity these days, but the character of this 17th-century inn remains unspoiled. Paul Kirkby has added the comfort of burgundy velvet chesterfields and pine-panelled walls in the bar, where logs blaze in a stone inglenook. Food (in bar or restaurant) is excellent; portions are generous. Casseroles (from wild boar to venison and even kangaroo) are a speciality of the house and there are real ales to sample. The mulberry-and-white en suite bedrooms are not only of the highest standard but well segregated from the inn by a garden, which has an extensive children's play area. Just off the main bar, guests can join locals playing traditional Northamptonshire skittles.

Oundle is as attractive as many Cotswold towns, for the local stone is the same, but much less frequented by tourists. The buildings of its famous public school are like an Oxford college. One can take steam train trips on the Nene Valley Railway, and (at Kettering) Wicksteed Park is an ideal place to take children. Fotheringhay, where Mary Queen of Scots was executed, has a particularly fine church with interesting tombs.

UPTON MILL

C D S

Upton, Northamptonshire, NN5 4UY Tel/Fax: 01604 753277

West of Northampton. Nearest main road: A45 from Northampton to Daventry (and M1, junctions 15a/16).

3 Bedrooms. £25–£27 (less for 2 nights or more). One has own bath/toilet; TV (in all); views of river (two). No smoking.

Dinner (by arrangement). From £12 for 4 courses and coffee, at times to suit guests. Vegetarian or other special diets if ordered. **Light suppers** if ordered.

1 Sitting-room. With piano.

Large garden

Closed from Christmas to Easter.

It's hard to believe there is such a peaceful haven for wildlife just off the busy A45. Built right across the bubbling River Nene, Upton Mill (mentioned in Domesday Book), now a farmhouse, is the focal point of many lovely footpaths: they were first trodden by farmers carrying grain to the mill. From the dining-room (with a locally made yew table and a Jacobean-style carved wooden sideboard) and adjoining sun-room, one steps into a garden on the river bank, with pond for moorhens beyond and over 1000 acres for sheep and cows.

Jane Spokes prepares such dinners as watercress soup, cumin-spiced lamb, lemon soufflé or a selection of home-made ice creams, and cheese; in warm weather meals may be served in the garden.

The area is excellent for birdwatching (kingfishers and swans may be observed from bedroom windows); fishing is available in the millpond, and just a short walk away are two large lakes with ducks.

WOLD FARM

C D P T S X

Old, Northamptonshire, NN6 9RJ Tel/Fax: 01604 781258

North of Northampton. Nearest main road: A508 from Northampton to Market Harborough (also M1, junction 15; and M1–A1 link).

5 Bedrooms. £25–£30 (less for 3 nights or more). Available: own bath/shower/toilet; TV. No smoking.

2 Sitting-rooms. With open fire (in one), TV. No smoking. Billiards.

Garden

This 18th-century house has particularly attractive rooms (including a spacious suite), and two delightful gardens with rose pergola and a swing-seat. A former granary has been converted into a garden-cottage where there are more bedrooms (en suite). In the main sitting-room are alcoves of Italian porcelain and Hummel figures; the dining-room has a carved 17th-century sideboard; and in the breakfast-room there is an inglenook fireplace and a dresser with the exhortation: 'Nourish thyself with lively vivacity'. Oak beams, well-chosen fabrics and pretty window-seats add further character to the rooms.

Anne Engler (once a 'Tiller girl') only serves breakfast. For evening meals, guests stroll to the village pub. A feature of the landscape round here is the network of 18th- and 19th-century canals. At Stoke Bruerne, a waterways museum tells the whole story of the canals (boat trips too).

V

Readers' comments: Very thoughtful attention. Harmony and friendliness. Exactingly high standard. Kind and generous. It excels. Attractive garden. Pretty and very comfortable room.

NORTHUMBERLAND

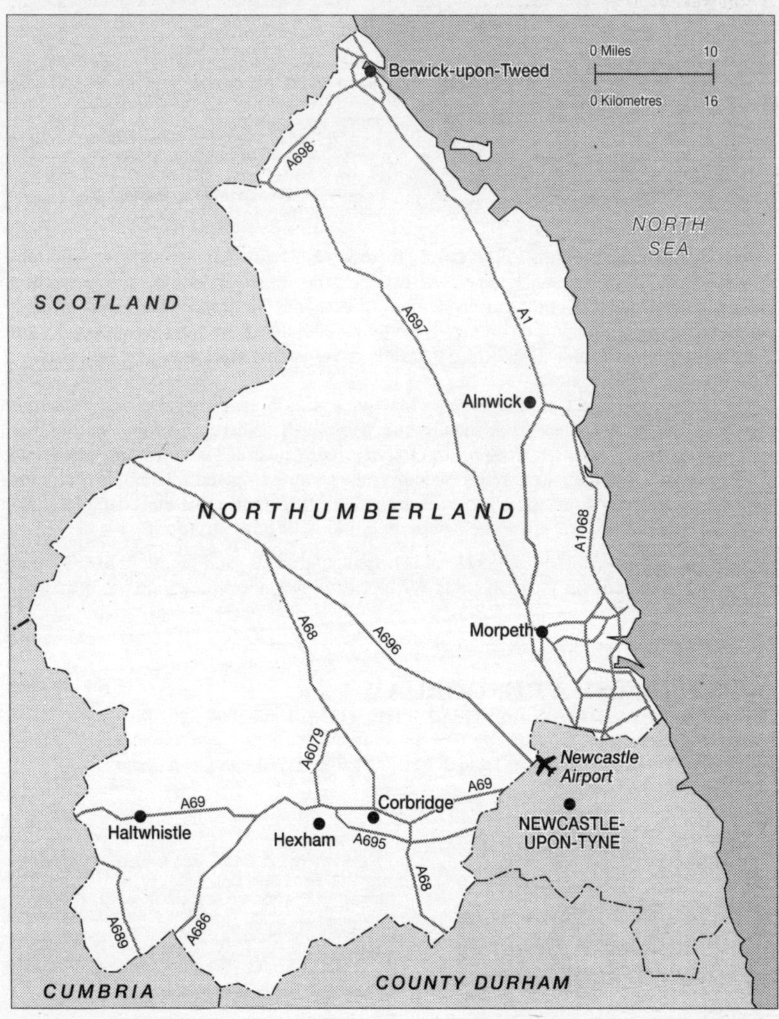

Houses which accept the discount vouchers on page ii are marked with a V symbol next to the relevant entries.

Northumberland

BILTON BARNS C

Bilton, Alnmouth, Northumberland, NE66 2TB Tel: 01665 830427
(Fax: 01665 830063)
South-east of Alnwick. Nearest main road: A1 from Newcastle to Berwick-upon-Tweed.

3 Bedrooms. £21–£26 (less for 7 nights or more). Bargain breaks. All have own shower/toilet; TV; views of sea. No smoking.
Dinner (by arrangement). £14 for 3 courses and coffee, at 6.30pm. Vegetarian diets if ordered.
2 Sitting-rooms. With open fire. Piano.
Garden
Closed from mid-October to Easter.

On a 400-acre mixed farm is Bilton Barns, an early 18th-century house with very spacious rooms, which – like the sun lounge – all overlook the sweep of Alnmouth Bay across a croquet lawn. One bedroom, furnished entirely in cane, has windows on two sides, giving it a particularly fine outlook. For dinner, Dorothy Jackson offers, for instance, smoked trout from Craster, a roast, and sticky-toffee pudding, or something more elaborate on occasion. A farm walk can be arranged.

From here, you could explore the grand coastline with its sandy beaches and numerous castles. The nearest of these is at picturesque Warkworth (galleries here for craft and art too), which was the home of Hotspur. In *Henry IV Part 1* he called it 'this worm eaten hold of ragged stone', but parts were refurbished over the centuries. Inland is Cragside (NT), the mansion designed for Lord Armstrong, the armaments king. One of the most complete late-Victorian houses there are, it was the first in the world to be lit by electricity.

Readers' comments: Most hospitable and helpful. Spacious and comfortable. Dinner delicious. I would heartily recommend it. We received a warm welcome from our hostess.

Northumberland

COACH HOUSE AT CROOKHAM C D M S

Cornhill-on-Tweed, Northumberland, TD12 4TD Tel: 01890 820293
(Fax: 01890 820284)
South-west of Berwick-upon-Tweed. On A697 from Wooler to Coldstream.

11 Bedrooms. £23–£39 (less for 7 nights or more). Available: own bath/shower/toilet; TV.
Dinner. £17.50 for 4 courses and coffee, at 7.30pm. Vegetarian or other special diets if ordered. Wine available. No smoking.
1 Sitting-room. With open fire.
Large garden
Closed from November to Easter.

E-mail: thecoachhouse@englandmail.com

Close to the site of Flodden Field, this is a group of several old farm buildings forming a square. What was the coach house itself is now the sitting-room, with lofty beamed ceiling and great arched windows and an enormous brick fireplace.

The highly individual bedrooms have interesting paintings, and fridges. Lynne Anderson used to travel a great deal and so has a lot of practical ideas about what travellers need.

Breakfasts are excellent; and for dinner there is a choice of 6 starters; a roast or casserole; puddings or one of 15 home-made ice creams. Organic produce is used increasingly.

Readers' comments: The very best breakfast, and Lynne is exceptionally good at making guests at ease. Outstanding. Charm, friendliness, service; cannot be too highly praised. Everything a guest might want. Cooking superb; we hope to return. A warm welcome; meals delicious.

V

GAIRSHIELD FARM

C(8)

Whitley Chapel, Northumberland, NE47 0HS Tel: 01434 673562
South-east of Hexham. Nearest main road: A69 from Haltwhistle to Hexham.

1 Bedroom. £20 (less for 3 nights or more). Has own bath/toilet. No smoking.
Dinner (by arrangement). £10–£12 for 2–3 courses and coffee, at times to suit guests. Vegetarian or other special diets if ordered. Wine available. No smoking.
Light suppers if ordered.
1 Sitting-room. With stove, TV. No smoking.
Small garden
Closed from November to Easter.

High and remote, this unpretentious hill farm is just the place for people who like breezy open space. It stands at over 1000 feet, with wide views over rolling pastoral countryside, and is reached by a long road which serves only other hill farms and leads nowhere. Empty though the area seems, it has a long history (on which Hilary Kristensen has written a book). What were ancient tracks and drove-roads are now the footpaths and bridleways which today's walkers, cyclists and riders enjoy.

The one bedroom, which has its own large bathroom, can sleep a family of three or even four. It is pleasantly decorated in mostly pastel shades, like the cosy private living-room. Hilary's meals are made from, as far as possible, British organic ingredients. One of her dinners, when required, might consist of soup or melon, chicken and mushroom casserole, and trifle, but most visitors dine in country pubs or else in Hexham for more exotic fare.

The farm's livestock includes not only commercial sheep, but the rare long-woolled Wensleydales, as well as a donkey and horse – there is stabling for your own horses. V

THE HERMITAGE

C(10) S

Swinburne, Northumberland, NE48 4DG Tel: 01434 681248 (Fax: 01434 681110)
North of Corbridge. On A6079 from Hexham towards Rothbury.

3 Bedrooms. £25–£30. All have own bath/shower/toilet. No smoking.
Light suppers if ordered.
1 Sitting-room. With open fire, TV.
Large garden
Closed from October to February.

E-mail: stewart@thehermitagenow.freeserve.co.uk

The Hermitage used to be the agent's house of Swinburne Castle, now demolished, the family seat of Catherine Stewart's family since the 1700s. At the end of a half-mile drive with a big lodge at the roadside, it is surrounded by trees where deer and foxes live.

The rooms are gracefully proportioned and all are furnished largely with family antiques, such as the circular mahogany breakfast-table, and oil paintings. The sitting-room is long enough for the television set at one end not to disturb people at the other; like two of the bedrooms, it overlooks the garden and park. The third bedroom faces the vegetable gardens and the stables of the Stewarts' horses. The cast-iron baths are capacious! There is a private chapel where Mass is celebrated every Sunday.

Two inns for good evening meals are a short drive away, and so are the Roman wall and any number of castles and mansions.

Readers' comments: Best b & b ever. Rooms beautiful and spacious, the gardens lovely. Bedrooms magnificent, very comfortable and luxurious. Friendly and relaxed hosts. Delicious breakfasts, beautiful views; an experience not to be missed. A memorable visit.

Northumberland

HIGH LETHAM FARMHOUSE

C(12) **D PT**

Low Cocklaw Road, Berwick-upon-Tweed, Northumberland, TD15 1UX
Tel: 01289 306585 (Fax: 01289 304194)
Nearest main road: A1 from Alnwick towards Edinburgh.

rear view

3 Bedrooms. £24–£34 (less for 3 nights or more). All have own bath/shower/toilet; TV; views of river (two). No smoking.
Dinner (by arrangement). £17.50–£22 for 3–4 courses and coffee, at times to suit guests. Vegetarian or other special diets if ordered. Wine available. No smoking.
2 Sitting-rooms. With open fire/stove, TV. No smoking.
Large garden

E-mail: HLFS@fantasyprints.co.uk

Situated in open countryside north of the River Tweed, the house has views extending for tens of miles over the river to the Cheviots in the south and the Eildon Hills in the west.

A Georgian house, once the property of the mayor of Berwick, it is furnished mostly with antiques, both in the large bedrooms and in the long downstairs sitting-room, where you also eat at one big table. This you should enjoy doing, for Susan Persse was a professional cook in the City of London and Richard was a wine-shipper. A possible dinner: Eyemouth seafood chowder, venison, and ice cream made with local honey. Vegetables come from the garden beyond the box-hedged croquet lawn.

Birdwatching, fly-fishing and sea-angling are popular pursuits round here (there is a rod-room in the house). There are numerous historic buildings to visit on either side of the nearby Scottish border, and the centre of Berwick itself is only two miles away.

Readers' comments: Gracefully proportioned house with spectacular views; our hosts made us feel that they enjoyed meeting us. House delightful and very comfortable, dinner delicious; made us extremely welcome.

Northumberland

HIGH STEADS

C(8) **D X**

Lowick, Northumberland, TD15 2QE Tel/Fax: 01289 388689
South of Berwick-upon-Tweed. Nearest main road: A1 from Alnwick to Berwick.

2 Bedrooms. £22.50–£25 (less for 7 nights or more). Both have own bath/shower/toilet. No smoking.
Light suppers if ordered.
1 Sitting-room. With TV. No smoking.
Large garden

E-mail: HighStead@aol.com

Under the wide skies of north Northumberland, the first-floor sitting-room of this 18th-century former farmhouse gives views, through unusual ogival windows, of the Cheviots and the Kyloe Hills, with even a glimpse of the sea. Containing much antique furniture (including a Georgian dolls' house), the room is partly panelled and has been painted by Margo Newington-Bridges in the muted Georgian colours she has used throughout.

The staircase is ornamented with a display of old golf clubs in an arrangement made by a local blacksmith and with prints of Edinburgh, Margo's home town. In the oak-furnished breakfast-room, you eat at a massive 400-year-old table (used by Simon's family to shelter from air raids during the Second World War!). Breakfast choices are made the night before from an unusual menu which includes such things as *pain perdu* and 'gentleman's omelette', cooked by Simon. Evening meals are available at two inns in the nearby village.

V To one side of Lowick is Holy Island (with Lindisfarne Castle and ruined priory) and to the other is the model village of Ford.

HOLMHEAD

C PT X

Greenhead, Northumberland, CA6 7HY Tel/Fax: 016977 47402
West of Haltwhistle. Nearest main road: A69 from Carlisle to Hexham.

4 Bedrooms. £25–£29 (less for 7 nights or more). Bargain breaks. All have own shower/toilet. No smoking.
Dinner. £19.95 for 4 courses and coffee, at 7.30pm. Vegetarian or other special diets if ordered. Wine available. No smoking. **Light snacks.**
1 Sitting-room. With TV, organ. No smoking.
Large garden
Closed from mid-December to mid-January.

E-mail: Holmhead@hadrianswall.freeserve.co.uk

Beside a salmon river, just where the walkers' Pennine Way crosses Hadrian's Wall, this remote house has the ruins of Thirlwall Castle looming overhead, within view through the windows of the guests' large and comfortable upstairs sitting-room.

Although some of the bedrooms are small, there are all kinds of unexpected 'extras': a foot-massager for weary walkers; pure spring water; table tennis; snacks at any hour. Pauline Staff makes all the preserves, chutneys, cakes, bread and scones. A typical dinner: melon with kiwi fruit; trout in hollandaise sauce; almond meringue with wild raspberries. Out of season, a ground-floor flat may be available for b & b, and groups can be accommodated over Christmas. Breakfast choices include haggis, black pudding, kedgeree, muffins and crumpets.

Pauline has a diploma in archaeology and local history and is a qualified guide.

Readers' comments: Excellent accommodation; highlight was the food. Delightful place. Situation beautiful, food excellent. Mealtime a joy. Kindness and hospitality terrific. Food memorably good. Comfortable; very knowledgeable hostess. Superb breakfast.

V

LOUGHBROW HOUSE

C D S

Hexham, Northumberland, NE46 1RS Tel: 01434 603351 (Fax: 01434 609774)
South of Hexham. Nearest main road: A695 from Hexham to Newcastle.

5 Bedrooms. £25–£30 (less for 4 nights or more). All have own bath/shower/toilet. No smoking.
Dinner (by arrangement). £20 for 3 courses, wine and coffee, at 8pm or at times to suit guests. Vegetarian diets if ordered. No smoking.
2 Sitting-rooms. With open fire (in one), TV (in one), piano (in one). No smoking.
Large garden

Approached through woods by nearly half a mile of drive, Loughbrow House is a small mansion originally built in 1780. Many of the rooms have 18th-century proportions, such as the enormous drawing-room, where ancestral portraits and other paintings look down on a grand piano and some of the family antiques with which the house is mostly furnished. A smaller, cosier sitting-room is used when the house is not fully occupied.

Upstairs, the sizeable bedrooms include two single rooms and one with its own dressing-room (containing a child's bed, if required). Bathrooms, too, are spacious.

From the house, Patricia Clark runs a 400-acre agricultural and sporting estate. Her particular interest (she is also a keen shot and teaches bridge) is the large garden which, along with the farm, supplies almost all the produce for the table. A typical menu – available when enough people are dining – might be jellied borscht with salmon caviar, pheasant with chestnuts and seasonal vegetables, fruit pavlova, and a bottle of wine.

Though the house stands in seclusion high above Hexham, with splendid views almost to the Scottish border, the historic town is only a mile away.

V

Northumberland

MARKET CROSS GUEST-HOUSE

C D PT X

1 Church Street, Belford, Northumberland, NE70 7LS Tel: 01668 213013

South-east of Berwick-upon-Tweed. Nearest main road: A1 from Alnwick to Berwick.

3 Bedrooms. £20–£25 (less for 7 nights or more). Bargain breaks (for groups only). Available: own bath/shower/toilet; TV. No smoking.
Light suppers if ordered.
1 Sitting-room. No smoking.
Garden

When the Great North Road ran through Belford, this 200-year-old house was part of the Black Swan coaching inn next door. These days, with the village long since bypassed, you might on a fine morning breakfast in the stableyard once used by the London to Edinburgh stages, for this is now a patio looking on to a neat garden where John and Jill Hodge's Dalmatians romp. Otherwise, breakfast is served in a pine-furnished dining-room (where you may recognize, in caricature form on the wall, John in his former role as a Tyneside policeman). Upstairs, the newly refurbished bedrooms are decorated in bold colours and have good views of the hills, which just hide the sea a few miles away. With the Reivers' Way and Farne Islands nearby, this house appeals to walkers and birdwatchers (and to golfers like the Hodges).

Picturesque Belford is a quiet place: you can dine either at the Black Swan or more elaborately at the Blue Bell, just across what used to be the market place.

Reader's comment: Excellent accommodation and decoration.

Northumberland

ORCHARD HOUSE

C PT S

High Street, Rothbury, Northumberland, NE65 7TL Tel: 01669 620684

South-west of Alnwick. Nearest main road: A697 from Morpeth to Wooler.

6 Bedrooms. £23–£25. All have own bath/shower/toilet; TV. No smoking.
1 Sitting-room. With open fire. No smoking.
Small garden

E-mail: jpickard@orchardguesthouse.co.uk

Rothbury, a pleasant little market town with some interesting shops, stands in the very centre of Northumberland, and so many of the pleasures of that large and underestimated county are within an easy drive: the Roman wall to the south, Holy Island to the north, and in between countryside which can change from open moorland to woods and arable fields within a few miles, with picturesque villages and historic monuments for punctuation.

The Georgian house, which stands well aside from Rothbury's bustling main street, has been popular with readers for years. It is now run by Jean Pickard, who used to be a teacher. To commemorate the long-gone orchard, there is an engraved glass panel of an apple tree in the front door. Rooms are all light and neatly laid out. You can choose places for evening meals from the menus which Jean will send you when you book.

Reader's comments: In all respects excellent – food, courtesy, accommodation, cleanliness, and a charming hostess.

PHEASANT INN

C D M P T S

Stannersburn, Northumberland, NE48 1DD Tel/Fax: 01434 240382
North-west of Hexham. Nearest main road: A68 from Corbridge to Jedburgh.

8 Bedrooms. £25–£30. Bargain breaks. All have own shower/toilet; TV. No smoking.
Dinner. From £15 for 4 courses and coffee, at 7–9pm. Vegetarian or other special diets if ordered. Wine available. No smoking. **Light suppers.**
2 Lounge bars. With open fires.
Small garden

Close to Kielder Water, this is everything one wants a country inn to be – nearly four centuries old, stone-walled and low-beamed and in particularly lovely countryside. The Kershaws are determined to keep it unspoilt. The bedrooms, however, are modern, in a former hemel (farm implements store) and barn; many of them are on the ground floor.

The main bar (where very good snacks are served) is big and beamy, with a stone fireplace and some agricultural bygones, such as hay-knives and peat-spades; and a stuffed pheasant appropriately sits on the window-sill.

The dining-room is light and airy, with raspberry-coloured walls and pine furniture. Food is freshly prepared – one interesting starter is avocado with grapefruit and Stilton; trout comes with a sauce of yogurt and herbs.

Readers' comments: Delightful country inn. Mr Kershaw and his family could not have been more friendly and courteous, our room was spotlessly clean, the food truly delicious – we look forward to a return. A real pub, very good food, friendly and helpful staff.

V

SHIELDHALL

C(2) **D S**

Cambo, Northumberland, NE61 4AQ Tel/Fax: 01830 540387
West of Morpeth. Nearest main road: A696 from Newcastle to Otterburn.

6 Bedrooms. £23.50–£24.50 (less for 3 nights or more). All have own bath/shower/toilet; TV. No smoking.
Dinner (by arrangement). £18 for 4 courses and coffee, at 7pm. Vegetarian or other special diets if ordered. Wine available. No smoking. **Light suppers** if ordered.
3 Sitting-rooms. With open fire, TV. No smoking (in two). **Bar.**
Large garden
Closed in December and January.

Eighteenth-century stone buildings enclose a courtyard with lawn and flowerbeds, the former barns to left and right providing very well-equipped ground-floor bedrooms for visitors – each with its own entrance. Meals are taken in a beamed dining-room in the centre, furnished with antiques and an inglenook fireplace (Celia's typical dinner might comprise soup, coq au vin, vanilla fruit with home-made yogurt ice cream, and local cheeses – with produce from the garden and orchard); and to one side are sitting-rooms (one with library) for visitors.

Stephen Robinson-Gay is a professional cabinet-maker, happy to show visitors the workshops where he makes or restores furniture. Most of the work in all the rooms is his. For instance, beyond the arched doorway of the mahogany room is a colonial-style bed with very fine inlay, and in the oak room a Flemish-style four-poster with carved canopy. One workshop is just up the road at Capability Brown's birthplace, now excellently restored to house much else of interest.

Readers' comments: Super place. Fantastic holiday; everything you said and much more; lovely couple, food delicious.

Northumberland

THORNLEY HOUSE

D S X

Allendale, Northumberland, NE47 9NH Tel: 01434 683255
South-west of Hexham. Nearest main road: A69 from Newcastle towards Hexham.

3 Bedrooms. £21 (less for 7 nights or more). Bargain breaks. Available: own bath/shower/toilet.
Dinner. £13 for 3 courses and coffee, at about 7pm. Vegetarian or other special diets if ordered. No smoking.
2 Sitting-rooms. With TV, piano. No smoking.
Large garden

E-mail: e.finn@ukonline.co.uk

Allendale Town is a large village in a sheltered valley amid some of the most open scenery in England – deserted grouse moors and breezy sheep pastures which stretch for uninterrupted miles. On the outskirts of the village is this large and solid inter-war house in a well-tended garden with seating arranged in conversational groups. Woods and fields surround it.

Eileen Finn is a keen cook, and though guests are offered conventional fare (vichyssoise soup, breaded chicken, salad, and sticky prune cake, for example), she needs only a little encouragement to cook a dish from Mexico, where she lived for eight years, or from another of the many countries to which she has paid long visits. A fine Steinway grand piano attracts musicians, who sometimes play duets with Eileen. Rooms are spacious and light.

Readers' comments: Delightful venue. Nice house, excellent room. Superbly quiet and comfortable. Wonderful food. Outstanding. Most welcoming. Piano duets a real bonus. Very comfortable, excellent breakfast.

Northumberland

WEST CLOSE HOUSE

PT S X

Hextol Terrace, Hexham, Northumberland, NE46 2AD Tel: 01434 603307
Nearest main road: A69 from Newcastle to Carlisle.

4 Bedrooms. £21–£26 (less for 4 nights or more). Available: own shower/toilet. No smoking.
Light suppers only. Vegetarian or other special diets if ordered. No smoking.
2 Sitting-rooms. With TV. No smoking.
Small garden

Only 10 minutes' walk from the centre of characterful Hexham, West Close House is in a quiet, leafy cul-de-sac. Designed by an architect for himself about 75 years ago, it is a red-brick villa comfortably and decoratively furnished. The prize-winning gardens, enclosed by tall beech hedges, are beautifully tended, with seats and a revolving summer-house at the back. Patricia Graham-Tomlinson provides varied breakfasts; also simple snacks.

There are excellent Italian, Indian and Chinese restaurants among others in Hexham. The abbey here was founded in the 7th century. The crypt survived the depredations of the Danes, and you can see Roman inscriptions on some of the stones: it was built of material taken from Hadrian's Wall, some of the best sites on which are close.

V

Readers' comments: The best so far: a winner. Made to feel at home. Breakfast and accommodation excellent. Food is exceptional, the standard of accommodation is the finest we have found.

WESTLEA

C(2) M PT

29 Riverside Road, Alnmouth, Northumberland, NE66 2SD Tel: 01665 830730
South-east of Alnwick. Nearest main road: A1068 from Newcastle to Alnwick.

6 Bedrooms. £20–£28. Bargain breaks. Available: own bath/shower/toilet; TV; views of estuary. No smoking.
Dinner (by arrangement). From £12 for 4 courses and coffee, at 6.30–7pm. No smoking.
1 Sitting-room. With TV.
Small garden

This is a very comfortable modern guest-house facing the Aln estuary, immaculately kept by Janice Edwards. One attractive bedroom (wildflower fabrics and cane bedheads) opens on to the sunny front garden; others vary in size and style but all are well equipped. The upstairs sitting-room has a balcony from which to enjoy the river view.

Breakfasts are imaginative; and for dinner there may be such dishes as beef, salmon, Cheviot lamb (with Northumbrian baked suet-puddings) or game pie. For the way she runs Westlea, Janice has received many awards. As many visitors come repeatedly for long holidays, booking well ahead is essential.

Readers' comments: Nothing was too much trouble. Excellent food and an amazing choice for breakfast. Excellent value for money. Very impressed with warmth of welcome and unrivalled concern for guests. Overall excellence. Very comfortable. Dinner exceptional.

Prices are per person sharing a room at the beginning of the year.

Where wine is not available (meaning it is on sale or can be fetched for you), you are nearly always welcome to bring in your own drinks.

Many houses in this book are situated in or very near to Areas of Outstanding Natural Beauty and protected Heritage Coasts. For a selection of these houses, see p.xi.

THANK YOU . . . to those who send details of their own finds, for possible future inclusion in the book. Do not be disappointed if your candidate does not appear in the very next edition. Recommendations from unknown members of the public are never published without verification, and it takes time to get round each part of England and Wales in turn. Please, however, do not send details of houses already featured in many other guides, nor any that are more expensive than those in this book (see page xiv).

NOTTINGHAMSHIRE

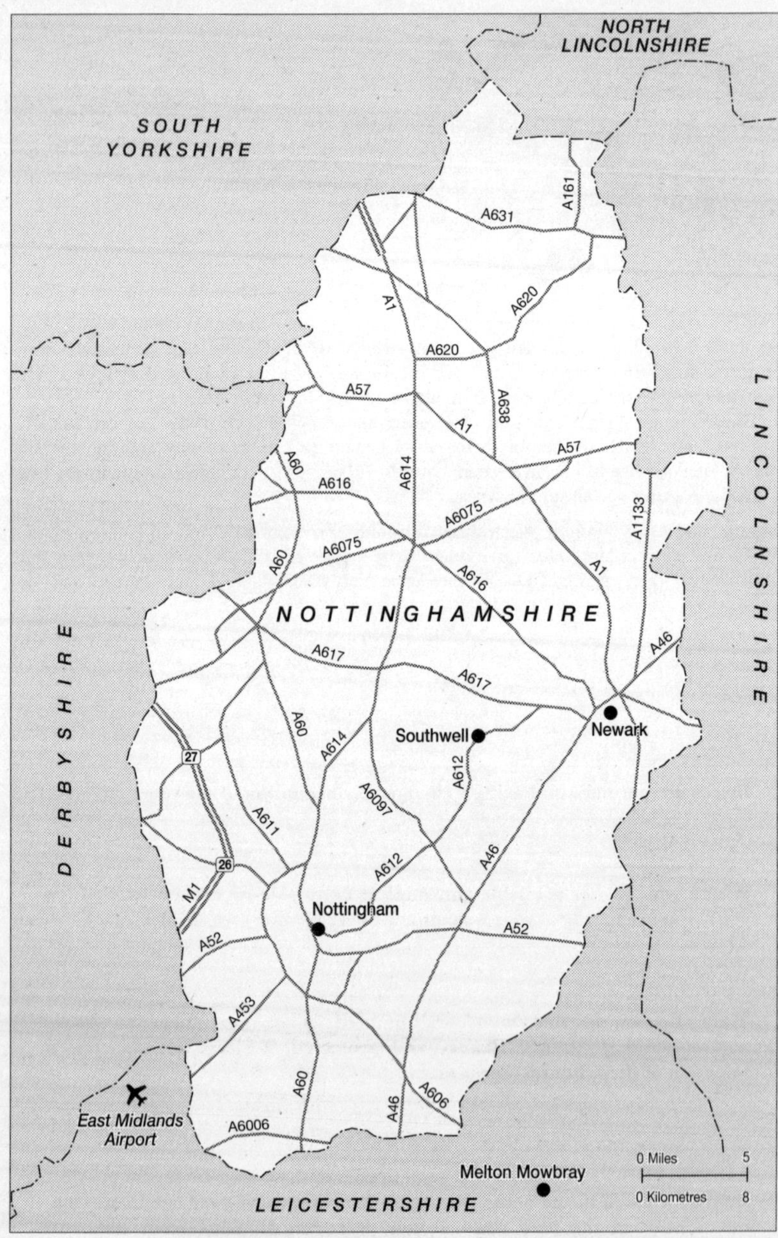

For explanation of code letters and V symbol, see inside front cover.

ARCHWAY HOUSE **C D S**

Kirklington, Nottinghamshire, NG22 8NX Tel: 01636 812070 (Fax: 01636 812200)
West of Newark. Nearest main road: A617 from Newark to Mansfield (and M1, junction 27).

3 Bedrooms. £23–£27 (less for 3 nights or more). Available: own bath/shower/toilet; TV. No smoking.
Dinner (by arrangement for 4 people or more only). £22 for 4 courses and coffee, at 7–9pm. Vegetarian or other special diets if ordered. Wine available. No smoking. **Light suppers** if ordered.
2 Sitting-rooms. With open fire, TV. No smoking (in one).
Large garden

E-mail: mcgarrigle@archway-house.co.uk

In the early 1900s, the owner of a coalmine built himself this spacious mansion, its big bay windows overlooking croquet or tennis lawns, with chestnut trees now grown to a great height. As the grounds are bounded by a haha, there is an uninterrupted view of the surrounding fields and parklands. Snowdrops and wood anemones abound early in the year.

Erica McGarrigle has furnished the rooms with antiques, Victorian paintings, big sofas, and mahogany and silver in the formal dining-room where an apricot carpet complements walls of dark green. Trained at the Tante Marie cookery school, Erica serves evening meals for groups, otherwise you dine at one of the many pubs and restaurants in the area. Another of her skills is furniture decoration, examples of which are to be seen around the house.

From the handsome, panelled hall, a staircase rises to well-proportioned bedrooms, one of which has an Edwardian-style, black-and-cream tiled bathroom. There's a snooker table, six-hole golf course and heated swimming-pool for guests' use.

Readers' comments: Warmly welcomed, excellent dinner, tastefully furnished. Excellent. Such civilization! **V**

HALL FARM HOUSE **C**

Gonalston, Nottinghamshire, NG14 7JA Tel: 01159 663112 (Fax: 01159 664844)
North-east of Nottingham. Nearest main road: A612 from Nottingham to Southwell.

3 Bedrooms. £25. One has own bath/shower/toilet; TV available.
Light suppers if ordered. Vegetarian or other special diets if ordered. Wine available.
2 Sitting-rooms. With open fires, TV. Piano.
Large garden

To the attractions of the house itself, which was built early in the 18th century, are added the varied pleasures of a pretty garden which include rosebeds, a large heated swimming-pool, tennis court, fish-pond and vegetable garden from which come fruit and other produce for the table. Stables have been converted to provide a games room (with table tennis).

Rosemary Smith's visitors eat either in the beamed and quarry-tiled dining-room or in the big kitchen. The sitting-rooms, also beamed and with oak floors, have antiques and, in one, mallard-patterned sofas around the brick fireplace. Bedrooms are attractive.

For guests wanting more than a light snack, there is a choice of five country pubs within two miles of the house, all serving good food.

Visitors come for a variety of reasons – to enjoy the area's Robin Hood attractions, browse through the many antique shops, follow riverside walks, or visit stately homes.

Readers' comments: Made to feel like family friends; very friendly and informal. Thoroughly enjoyed our stay. **V**

Nottinghamshire

HOLLY LODGE

CMPTX

Ricket Lane, Blidworth, Nottinghamshire, NG21 0NQ Tel: 01623 793853 (Fax: 01623 490977)

North of Nottingham. Nearest main road: A60 from Nottingham to Mansfield (and M1, junction 28).

4–5 Bedrooms. £25–£27 (less for 4 nights or more). Available: own bath/shower/toilet; TV. No smoking.
Light suppers if ordered.
1 Sitting-room. With open fire, TV. Piano. No smoking.
Large garden

What remains of great Sherwood Forest lies to the north of Nottingham, and here you will find Ann Shipside's Victorian hunting-lodge. It is near the estate of ancient Newstead Abbey which became Byron's home: it and its grounds are open to the public. Most of the visitors' immaculate bedrooms at the Lodge are in converted stables opening on to a grassy court with chairs. In the main house, a Laura Ashley suite with mahogany-fitted bathroom is particularly attractive. One can sit under the grapevine and fuchsias of the conservatory to enjoy a view of old roses and woodland, or by a log fire in the sitting-room. Dinners are available at many local restaurants and pubs.

The Lodge is surrounded by 15 acres of land where horses and Shetland ponies roam; there is also a tennis court and woodland walk. The World of Robin Hood (at Haughton) and the historic towns of Southwell, Newark and Nottingham are all within easy reach.

Readers' comments: The most congenial accommodation we have found. Everything was done with a smile. Rooms beautifully appointed.

Nottinghamshire

OLD FORGE

C DPTX

Burgage Lane, Southwell, Nottinghamshire, NG25 0ER Tel: 01636 812809 (Fax: 01636 816302)

North-east of Nottingham. Nearest main road: A612 from Nottingham to Southwell.

5 Bedrooms. £25. Available: own bath/shower/toilet; TV. No smoking.
Light suppers if ordered. Vegetarian or other special diets if ordered. Wine available. No smoking.
1 Sitting-room. No smoking.
Small garden

Flower-baskets hang on the pale pink house where once a blacksmith lived and worked. The forge itself is at the back and the great stone rim round which iron for wheels was hammered now lies idle by the lily-pool in the little patio-garden. This is overlooked by a small quarry-tiled conservatory, itself dominated by a giant 40-year-old Monastera.

Hilary Marston has filled the 200-year-old rooms with eye-catching period pieces such as a very old 'log cabin' quilt from Boston (now used as a wall-hanging), Staffordshire figures, a tapestry chair stitched by a great-aunt, and a Victorian brass bed.

Each bedroom has its own character and charm: one with a view of historic Southwell Minster, floodlit at night. The beamed breakfast-room is delightful. For full evening meals, there is a choice of eating-places within a few minutes' walk.

V

Readers' comments: Comfortably furnished, each room very individual. Warm welcome. Well-appointed rooms. Outstanding breakfast. First class. Excellent rooms. Superb breakfast, altogether a pleasant experience. Charming house and garden.

SULNEY FIELDS

C D

Colonel's Lane, Upper Broughton, Nottinghamshire, LE14 3BD
Tel: 01664 822204 (Fax: 01664 823976)
North-west of Melton Mowbray. Nearest main road: A606 from Melton Mowbray to Nottingham.

5 Bedrooms. £25–£30 (less for 3 nights or more). Available: own bath/shower/toilet; TV. No smoking.
1 Sitting-room. With open fire, TV.
Large garden
Closed in late December.

Panoramic views over the Vale of Belvoir stretch in front of this handsome 18th-century house, entered through a pretty 'gothick' porch filled with flowering plants. The large and airy sitting-room has a wall of tall windows making the most of this scene. Its coral walls are well matched by the armchairs and oriental carpets.

Hilary Dowson's bedrooms are equally handsome. A big pale blue one, with fine mahogany furniture and good paintings, has a shower-room and an adjoining room, which makes it ideal for families; the pink room has a bay window for enjoying those views. Outside is a sheltered, unheated swimming-pool. Hilary will occasionally do dinners for parties of six or more guests, but there are two good dining-pubs within a mile.

Melton Mowbray is famous for pies (visit Ye Olde Pork Pie Shoppe) and Stilton cheese, made in Colston Bassett village where you can buy it direct. Other villages (with interesting churches) worth a visit include Waltham-on-the-Wolds (carved monks) and Bottesford (monuments, and witchcraft associations). Nottingham itself is just a short drive away.

Some houses offer special discounts to readers using the current edition of this book. Always state you are an SOTBT reader when ringing to book or when using E-mail.

Complaints about matters which could not have been settled on the spot will be forwarded to proprietors. Please enclose a stamped addressed envelope if you want your complaint acknowledged.

Prices for single occupancy may be higher than those quoted here. Houses that charge singles no more, or only 10% more, than half the price of a double room (except possibly at peak periods) are indicated by the 'S' symbol.

To find the right accommodation in the right area at the right price, use an up-to-date edition of this book – revised every year. For an order form for the next edition (published in November), send a stamped addressed envelope, with 'SOTBT 2003 in the top left-hand corner, to Explore Britain, Alston, Cumbria, CA9 3SL.

OXFORDSHIRE

Book well ahead: many of these houses have few rooms. Do not expect dinner if you have not booked it or if you arrive late.

ASHEN COPSE

S

Oxfordshire

Coleshill, Oxfordshire, SN6 7PU Tel: 01367 240175 (Fax: 01367 241418)
North-east of Swindon. Nearest main road: A420 from Swindon to Oxford (and M4, junction 15).

3 Bedrooms. £23–£25 (less for 7 nights or more). One has own shower/toilet. No smoking.
1 Sitting-room. With open fire, TV. No smoking.
Large garden

E-mail: pat@hodd.demon.co.uk

A long drive leads past pheasant woods to this 300-year-old house built of stone and brick; and around lie the 600 acres of the Hoddinotts' farm, near Highworth.

There is a particularly good family room separate from the rest – very big and light, with its own shower-room. By the staircase to another room are row upon row of colourful rosettes won at pony shows by the Hoddinotts' daughter. From this bedroom you can look beyond the small swimming-pool (unheated) to the famous Uffington White Horse and the prehistoric Ridgeway. Inn food is available in the village.

This is good walking country. From Ashen Copse there is a footpath all the way to Great Coxwell Barn, built by monks in the 13th century. Another goes all round Badbury Clump (site of an Iron Age fort), which is prettiest at bluebell time and from which there are fine views. Also in the vicinity are attractive villages such as Lechlade, Buscot with a National Trust mansion, and Kelmscot (Tudor manor house where William Morris lived).

Readers' comments: Attractive house, pleasant welcome and attention. A tremendously positive experience.

V

BURLEIGH FARM

C S X

Oxfordshire

Bladon Road, Cassington, Oxfordshire, OX29 4EA Tel: 01865 881352
North-west of Oxford. Nearest main road: A40 from Oxford to Witney.

2 Bedrooms. £22.50–£25. Both have own bath/shower/toilet; TV. No smoking.
Light suppers if ordered.
Large garden

E-mail: gcook@farmline.com

In the 18th century, the farming scene was drastically changed by the Enclosure Acts. Hedges were planted to enclose fields, and farmhouses were built in remote spots among them, into which villagers moved as tenants of the lord. Burleigh was one such 'enclosure farm' on the great Blenheim estate. It is still owned by the Duke of Marlborough, and farmed these days by Jane and Michael Cook.

The stone house combines historic character (stone floors, log fires) with modern comfort. From some rooms there are distant glimpses of Oxford's spires and from others of Blenheim Palace, a romantic prospect when the setting sun glints on the far windows. Visitors are welcome to look round the farm and to follow footpaths through its fields to Bladon church, where Churchill is buried. Little Cassington is even more historic – Bronze and Iron Age relics have recently been found, and the church is Norman.

Readers' comments: Very efficient and well furnished. Warm welcome. Most friendly, welcoming, and extremely helpful and knowledgeable about local amenities.

COURT FARM

C PT X

Mawles Lane, Shipton-under-Wychwood, Oxfordshire, OX7 6DA
Tel: 01993 831515 (Fax: 01993 831813)
South of Chipping Norton. Nearest main road: A361 from Chipping Norton to Burford.

3 Bedrooms. £22.50–£25. Available: own bath/shower/toilet; TV. No smoking.
1 Sitting-room. With TV. No smoking.
Small garden

E-mail: belinda@courtfarmbb.fsnet.co.uk

Appleyards and Indian Runners inhabit the pond in front of this handsome 17th-century, Cotswold-stone farmhouse. A working farm no more, it was once part of neighbouring Shipton Court's manorial estate. Guests' accommodation is in an adjacent cottage which, until it was restored and renovated by Jonathan and Belinda Willson, was last occupied by Land Army girls in 1943.

In the whitewashed and beamed breakfast-room (a former wash-house), Belinda serves traditional English fare (eggs come from her own hens or ducks) on rustic-style Italian pottery. Overhead hangs one of Jonathan's ingenious chandelier creations; he also sought out such finds as the lead lights, stained glass and 18th-century window, which have been used to embellish interior walls and doors. Bedrooms – the best one in apricot and cream, with a wrought-iron bedhead and its own entrance – are cosy and comfortably furnished. Guests can relax in the little sitting-room or outside in a sheltered courtyard. The ancient Shaven Crown hotel in the village is good for evening meals.

V The Oxfordshire Way, for walkers and cyclists, passes by the village church; while southward lies the tourist honeypot of Burford.

Oxfordshire

THE CRAVEN

C M S X

Fernham Road, Uffington, Oxfordshire, SN7 7RD Tel: 01367 820449
South-west of Oxford. Nearest main road: A420 from Oxford to Swindon (and M4, junction 14).

6 Bedrooms. £20–£35 (less for 3 nights or more in winter and 7 nights year-round). Bargain breaks. Available: own bath/shower/toilet. No smoking.
Dinner (by arrangement). From £19.50 for 3 courses and coffee, at 7pm. Vegetarian or other special diets if ordered. Wine available. No smoking. **Light suppers** if ordered.
1 Sitting-room. With open fire, TV.
Large garden

E-mail: Carol@thecraven.co.uk

Three hundred years ago, this cream-walled and thatched house was a hostelry – later described in *Tom Brown's Schooldays*. One of the best bedrooms is on the ground floor – its four-poster hung with cabbage-rose chintz, its pillows in embroidered Victorian pillowslips; in the pretty bathroom is an antique weighing-machine. Upstairs, where passages and steps turn this way and that, are other rooms, equally attractive. The separate stable-room has a beautifully carved oak bed and an art nouveau stained-glass panel in the shower-room.

The beamed sitting-room, with a log fire in its inglenook, has among other antiques a particularly splendid grandfather clock made in Lincolnshire.

Carol Wadsworth serves dinners at a big pine table in her huge L-shaped kitchen or occasionally in the brick-paved courtyard among tubs of plants. A typical dinner: watercress soup; lamb with herb crust; summer pudding with cream. Sunday lunches too.

V *Readers' comments:* Charming place and proprietor. Friendly. Special and enjoyable. Nothing too much trouble, house most attractive, dinner delicious.

FORDS FARM

Ewelme, Oxfordshire, OX10 6HU Tel: 01491 839272
South-east of Oxford. Nearest main road: A4074 from Wallingford towards Oxford (and M40, junction 6).

2 Bedrooms. £24–£25. Available: own bath/shower/toilet; TV. No smoking.
1 Sitting-room. With TV. No smoking.
Small garden

Ewelme is Old English for 'spring source', and to this day a spring runs alongside the main street of this picturesque village. It has been associated with the Chaucer family since the 15th century when Alice Chaucer, granddaughter of the famous poet, founded a community school and church here, as well as some almshouses grouped round a courtyard. Very early examples of brick buildings, they survived the Reformation and are still in use today. Centuries later, the novelist Jerome K. Jerome lived in the village and is buried in the churchyard.

Marlene Edwards's family has farmed here since the early 1900s and it is where she spent much of her childhood. The attractive, part 15th-century farmhouse is approached via a lawned courtyard with, to one side, a tithe barn and on the other, a granary and old stables which at one time housed 28 working horses. Bedrooms are well appointed and comfortable, and the cosy, beamed dining-room has a large inglenook fireplace with pewter mugs hanging above.

There are two pubs a short distance away for evening meals. Stonor Park and Henley are near, as is the Ridgeway for lovely walks.

GORSELANDS HALL C D M PT X

Boddington Lane, North Leigh, Oxfordshire, OX29 6PU Tel: 01993 882292
(Fax: 01993 883629)
North-east of Witney. Nearest main road: A4095 from Woodstock to Witney.

Oxfordshire

6 Bedrooms. £22.50–£25 (less for 4 nights or more). Available: own bath/shower/toilet; TV. No smoking.
1 Sitting-room. With TV. No smoking.
Large garden

E-mail: b&b@gorselandshall.com

Within a short stroll of East End's Roman villa stands this comfortable, Cotswold-stone guest-house, which was originally part of the Blenheim estate. Built round three sides of a square, it has an attractive stone-slated roof, a feature once characteristic of the locality. Off the stone-flagged hall (where guests are likely to be greeted by Daisy, a bouncy golden Labrador) is the sunny, country-style breakfast-room, with polished wood floor, individual modern pine tables, a large dresser and original paintings by a family friend.

Since taking over, Nigel and Debbie Hamilton (both former teachers) have renovated the bedrooms to a high standard of modern comfort and convenience. Colour schemes are light and fresh, much use has been made of pine and all have fitted cupboards.

In the grounds, there is a grass tennis court, croquet lawn and badminton court, while indoors, the spacious sitting-room accommodates a snooker table. For dinner, the Hamiltons recommend the popular Woodman pub in North Leigh.

Gorselands is close to both Oxford and historic Woodstock, in addition to spectacular Blenheim Palace and Churchill's grave at Bladon.

V

Oxfordshire

THE GRANARY

C(2) M PT S

Main Street, Clanfield, Oxfordshire, OX18 2SH Tel: 01367 810266
South-west of Witney. Nearest main road: A4095 from Witney to Faringdon.

3 Bedrooms. £21–£25 **(less for 7 nights to readers of this book).** One has own bath/toilet. No smoking.
1 Sitting-room. With TV. No smoking.
Garden

A willow-fringed stream runs alongside the village road as it pursues its course to the Thames. On the other side are an 18th-century cottage, Victorian shop and old granary that have been turned into a guest-house. There is a beamed dining-room, and guests have their own neat sitting-room. The most spacious bedroom is on the ground floor (with its own bathroom); the others – pleasant and cottagey in style, with double-glazing – are above. Throughout, Rosina Payne's house is spotless, airy and decorated in light and pretty colours. (Good meals are available at the nearby Clanfield Tavern.)

This part of the Cotswolds is full of interest. The lanes lead one to such famous sights as Bourton-on-the-Water, Stow-on-the-Wold, Bibury watermill, Burford (and its wildlife park), Witney's farm museum or old Minster Lovell Hall. Just along the road is Radcot and the oldest bridge over the Thames, from which (in summer) narrow-boat trips set out for 18th-century Lechlade. And William Morris's Kelmscott Manor is close.

V *Readers' comments:* Warm and friendly. Accommodation excellent, breakfast delicious. We couldn't praise enough.

Oxfordshire

HOME FARM HOUSE

C(10) X

Middle Aston, Oxfordshire, OX25 3PX Tel: 01869 340666 (Fax: 01869 347789)
North of Oxford. Nearest main road: A4260 from Oxford to Banbury (and M40, junctions 9/10).

2 Bedrooms. £23–£25 (less for 4 nights or more). Both have own bath/shower/ toilet; TV. No smoking.
Light suppers if ordered.
Large garden

E-mail: cparsons@telinco.co.uk

The original sundial sits above the entrance door of this attractive, 17th-century stone farm-house, with its lovely views over the Cherwell Valley. Glen and Caroline Parsons have furnished their home in traditional country style. The oak-beamed dining-room, decorated in warm autumnal shades, has a large inglenook fireplace and an ancient stone-mullioned window. Bedrooms, in pastel colours, are spacious and comfortably furnished, one featuring an art deco bed. Both have views of the garden where Caroline's love of plants is much in evidence. The garden is open annually under the National Gardens Scheme.

Close by is Steeple Aston which, with its pretty, grey stone buildings, is a good example of an enclosed village. Also near is Rousham House, a fine Jacobean mansion built by Sir Robert Dormer in 1635 and still owned by the same family. The beautiful garden here, designed by 18th-century architect and landscape gardener William Kent, remains almost perfectly preserved.

For evening meals, the Parsons recommend the White Horse in Duns Tew or La Galleria restaurant in Woodstock, both a short drive away.

LENWADE

C D PT X

3 Western Road, Henley-on-Thames, Oxfordshire, RG9 1JL Tel/Fax: 01491 573468
Nearest main road: A4130 from Maidenhead to Wallingford (and M4, junctions 8/9).

3 Bedrooms. £25–£30. All have own shower/toilet; TV.
Light suppers if ordered. No smoking.
1 Sitting-room. With open fire, TV. No smoking.
Small garden

E-mail: lenwadeuk@compuserve.com

Tucked away in a quiet and leafy residential part of Henley, just outside the town centre, Lenwade is quite a find. A large, Victorian, semi-detached house swathed in wisteria and with a front garden brimming with plants, it is the home of Jacquie and John Williams (and their two cats).

The hallway is dominated by an extraordinary stained-glass window in Pre-Raphaelite style, depicting an unknown martyr; the mid-morning sun streams through it filling the hall with colour. Jacquie has taken the luminescent colours of the window as her inspiration for the decor elsewhere. In one bedroom, scarlet acanthus leaf curtains are offset by pale, two-toned wicker furniture. Another, overlooking the walled garden, has a blue colour scheme: striped quilts, gingham curtains and forget-me-not patterned tiles in the bathroom.

The Williams are expert at ensuring guests enjoy their stay: Jacquie was an air stewardess and John the cabin service director for a major airline. The house is well placed for Heathrow as well as Windsor, Eton and Oxford, or just a leisurely boat trip on the Thames. There are plenty of eating-places nearby.

V

THE MOUNT

C

Eastgate, Hornton, Oxfordshire, OX15 6BT Tel: 01295 670762 (Fax: 01295 670899)
North-west of Banbury. Nearest main road: A422 from Banbury to Stratford-upon-Avon (and M40, junction 11).

Oxfordshire

2 Bedrooms. £25. Both have own bath/toilet; TV. No smoking.
Dinner (by arrangement). £15–£20 for 2–3 courses and coffee, at times to suit guests. Vegetarian or other special diets if ordered. No smoking.
1 Sitting-room. With open fire. No smoking.
Walled garden

E-mail: LCrln@aol.com

It was a prosperous yeoman farmer who originally built this dignified house of locally quarried stone in 1680. Located in a quiet, unspoilt village – complete with thatched pub, maypole and 12th-century church – the exterior was commented upon by architectural historian Nikolaus Pevsner, but within, too, it retains many authentic period features.

One steps straight into the dining-hall where Caroline Larkin may serve such meals as cranberry and feta cheese salad, chicken breasts in an orange and sage marinade, and lemon meringue roulade. Afterwards, guests can retire to the elegant but informal sitting-room, with its impressive stone fireplace. (The cellar below is of interest, containing both a well and the lower half of a Roman coffin!)

Upstairs, the principal bedroom is particularly attractive: ivory walls with original panelling are complemented by Colefax & Fowler chintz curtains, and a burgundy-covered Victorian chesterfield stands on the old oak floorboards. The next-door bathroom, with window-seats and a cheval mirror, is equally appealing.

Caroline is happy to advise on gardens and great houses to visit in the vicinity. Edgehill (Civil War battlefield) is close by and Stratford itself just 20 minutes' drive away.

V

Oxfordshire

OLD FARMHOUSE

C(12) **PT**

Station Hill, Long Hanborough, Oxfordshire, OX29 8JZ Tel: 01993 882097 (Fax: 01993 880008)
North-east of Witney. Nearest main road: A4095 from Woodstock to Witney.

2 Bedrooms. £22–£24 (less for 3 nights or more). Bargain breaks. One has own shower/toilet; TV. No smoking.
Light suppers if ordered. Vegetarian or other special diets if ordered. No smoking.
1 Sitting-room. With open fire, TV. No smoking.
Garden

E-mail: old.farm@virgin.net

At 17th-century Old Farmhouse, Vanessa Maundrell serves meals (vegetables come from the garden) in a stone-flagged dining-room with a dresser full of blue Spode china. One sitting-room has her collection of some 40 pot-lids over the inglenook. Beams, rugged stone walls and deep-set windows with far views are complemented by flowery fabrics and family treasures. Breakfast, which includes home-made bread and preserves, is sometimes served in the new conservatory. Outside is a pretty cottage-garden with old iron pump among the foxgloves.

There is ample parking space here and guests are welcome to leave their cars while sightseeing in Oxford (only 10 minutes away by train). Oxford's colleges, churches and museums need no description, but there is always something new to be seen for those who stay several days. At the 'Oxford Story' you ride (literally) back through 800 years of history; Curioxity is a 'hands-on' science gallery. At Magdalen College is a version of Leonardo's 'Last Supper', even better – some say – than the one in Milan.

V *Readers' comments:* Made very welcome. Most comfortable room, excellent breakfast.

Oxfordshire

OLD RECTORY

C(8) **S**

Hinton Waldrist, Oxfordshire, SN7 8SA Tel: 01865 821228 (Fax: 01865 821193)
South-west of Oxford. Nearest main road: A420 from Oxford to Swindon.

3 Bedrooms. £20–£25 (less for 3 nights or more). Available: own bath/toilet; TV. No smoking.
Light suppers if ordered. No smoking.
1 Sitting-room. With TV, piano. No smoking.
Large garden

There are ancient cruck-beams in the kitchen of Sue and Martin Taylor's elegant home, for it was originally a mediaeval hall. The bedrooms and wood-panelled sitting-room were added in the 17th century, while the front of the house, which includes a dining-room with fine views over the Thames Valley, is Victorian Gothic in style.

In the spacious, flagstoned entrance hall, a wide staircase sweeps up to the first floor where there is a good-sized bedroom with red-and-cream striped walls, chintz curtains and matching headboards. On the second floor are two cosy, beamed attic rooms separated by a sitting-area and bathroom.

The house is surrounded by lovely gardens with old-fashioned roses, evergreen shrubs and a herbaceous border that is particularly colourful in early summer. There is a paddock and tennis court too. On warm days, tea may be served on the terrace.

For evening meals, the Taylors recommend the Blue Boar in nearby Longworth or the Lamb in Buckland (about two miles away). Hinton Waldrist is on the edge of the Cotswolds and Sue will advise guests on the many places of interest hereabouts.

V

PINKHILL COTTAGE C

45 Rack End, Standlake, Oxfordshire, OX29 7SA Tel: 01865 300544 (Mobile: 07776 365256)

South-east of Witney. Nearest main road: A415 from Witney to Abingdon.

1 Bedroom. £24 (less for 3 nights or more). Has own shower/toilet. No smoking.
1 Sitting-room. With TV. No smoking.
Garden

E-mail: pinkhill@madasafish.com

Standing near the edge of a tranquil Thames Valley village is this pretty, white-painted thatched cottage whose origins probably date back to the 17th century. Here, Jane Dodds provides secluded and tastefully decorated accommodation in an annexe, which has been converted from what was once a stable and hayloft extension. Guests have sole use of a neatly furnished sitting-room (with its own entrance) where Jane serves tea and home-made shortbread on arrival. This is also where breakfast is usually taken.

Behind a board-and-latch door, a private staircase leads up to the serene, oak-beamed bedroom, with sloping ceilings, fresh white walls and an immaculate en suite shower-room. Both here and elsewhere are watercolours painted by husband Christopher's grandmother.

From a bench seat in the back garden, guests can watch the River Windrush flowing by and enjoy the variety of birdlife which frequents this peaceful spot. For dinner, there are two village inns offering a good choice of food within a few minutes' walk.

Reader's comments: Breakfast wonderful, plentiful, wholesome. Idyllic getaway – very private. Can't recommend it highly enough. Fabulous.

POPLARS FARM C(12) X

Claydon Road, Cropredy, Oxfordshire, OX17 1JP Tel: 01295 750561

North of Banbury. Nearest main road: A423 from Banbury to Southam (and M40, junction 11).

rear view

2 Bedrooms. £25–£30 (less for 3 nights or more). Available: own bath/shower/toilet; TV. No smoking.
Light suppers if ordered. No smoking.
Large garden

E-mail: colkathpoplars@supanet.com.

Although Whitakers have farmed the land here since the 1940s, the farmhouse itself is a mere eight years old. Built of local Hornton stone, it is surrounded by open countryside and 250 acres of arable fields. Inside, the extensive use of polished wood lends character to this otherwise all-modern home. From the maple-floored hall, a handsome oak staircase rises to bedrooms which are light, airy and comfortable. One is huge, with cream walls and carpet, and smart fitted cupboards providing plenty of hanging space. The second bedroom has a lemon and rust colour scheme and an adjacent bathroom which features an air-bath.

In her big farmhouse kitchen, warmed by an Aga, Katharine Whitaker offers guests tea and home-made biscuits on arrival, or she will prepare light snacks for those arriving late. Breakfast includes organic cereals and yogurt; eggs, bacon and sausages come from a neighbouring farm.

A 20-minute walk along the nearby Oxford Canal brings one into the attractive village of Cropredy, where Katharine recommends the Red Lion for evening meals. Oxford, Stratford, Warwick and the Cotswolds are all within a half-hour's drive.

V

RECTORY FARM

Northmoor, Oxfordshire, OX8 1SX Tel: 01865 300207 (Fax: 01865 300559)
South-west of Oxford. Nearest main road: A415 from Witney to Abingdon.

2 Bedrooms. £25 (less for 3 nights or more). Both have own shower/toilet. No smoking.
1 Sitting-room. With woodstove, TV. No smoking.
Large garden
Closed from mid-December to end of January.

Until a generation ago, this ancient stone farmhouse (the ogee arches of its fireplaces have been dated to the 15th century) was owned by St John's College, Oxford.

The deep-set windows are stone-mullioned, with views of fields and a great slate-roofed dovecote that was built in the 18th century. The Floreys' 400 acres are used for sheep, cattle and crops. In the house are Mary Anne's beautiful arrangements of dried flowers.

Having a growing family to look after, she provides breakfasts only, but there are many restaurants nearby. The breakfast/sitting-room has chamfered beams overhead, red Turkey rugs on the floor, tapestry armchairs, and a sideboard laden with Victorian silver-plate.

The bedrooms are particularly spacious, light and attractively decorated, their shower-rooms immaculate (outsize bath-towels much appreciated!); and their windows have farm or garden views. On the farm are Thames-side walks (fishing too).

Readers' comments: Quite outstanding; very welcoming and kind. Delightful stay; beautiful and spacious room, charming welcome. Very comfortable and quiet, with warm, friendly hosts; we recommend it highly – one of the best. Breakfasts were excellent; beautiful garden.

YOU AND THE LAW

Once your booking has been confirmed - orally or in writing - a contract exists between you and the proprietor. He/she is legally bound to provide accommodation as booked; and you are legally bound to pay for this accommodation. If unable to take up the booking - even because of sickness - you still remain liable for a very substantial proportion of the charges (in addition to losing your deposit).

If you have to cancel, let the proprietor know as soon as possible; then he/she may be able to re-let the accommodation (in which case you would be liable to pay only a re-letting cost or forfeit your deposit). Phone if you are going to arrive late.

(A note to overseas readers. It may be an acceptable practice elsewhere to make bookings at several houses for the same date, choosing only later which one to patronize; but this way of doing things is not the British practice and you are legally liable to compensate any proprietors whom you let down in this way.)

Isles of SCILLY

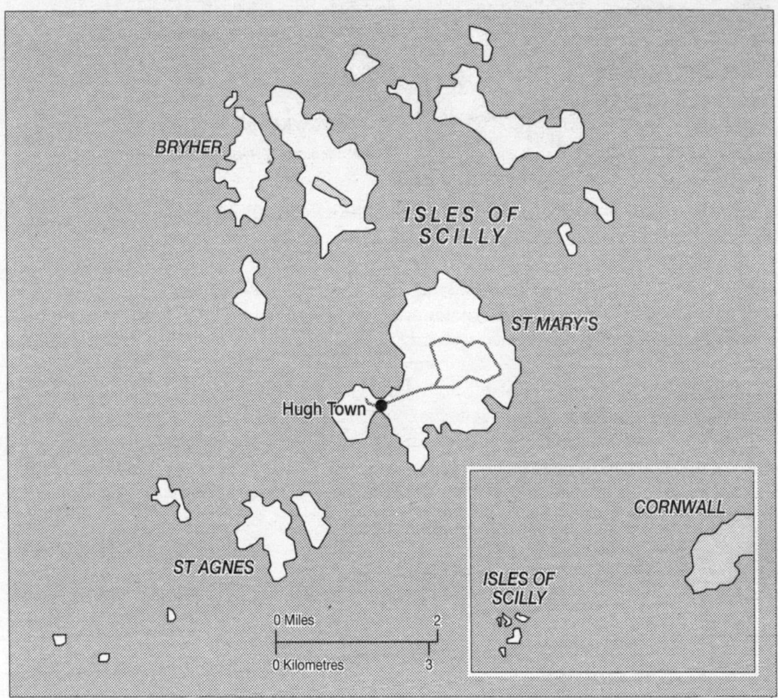

If you find places in England and Wales that you feel should be visited for possible inclusion in a future edition of SOTBT, please write and let us know. Send your descriptions (including full name of establishment, address and current b & b price per person) to Jan Bowmer, c/o Arrow Books, Random House, 20 Vauxhall Bridge Road, London, SW1V 2SA.

BANK COTTAGE

C(10) S

Bryher, Isles of Scilly, TR23 0PR Tel/Fax: 01720 422612

5 Bedrooms. £25–£30. Available: own shower/toilet; TV; views of sea; balcony. No smoking (some).
Dinner. £15 for 4 courses and coffee, at 7pm. Vegetarian or other special diets if ordered. Wine available. No smoking. **Light snacks** available.
1 Sitting-room
Garden
Closed from November to March.

E-mail: macmace@patrol.i-way.co.uk

Visitors here have a superb sandy beach (right outside) virtually all to themselves; beyond it is one of England's most beautiful seascapes, dotted with 22 islets.

Mac Mace works as a diver: sometimes diving for lobsters and crabs, sometimes for archaeological finds. He and his wife Tracy have a cottage built at least 300 years ago, but with later additions. The attractive rooms have low ceilings and thick walls to keep winter's gales at bay. Bedrooms are cheerful and bright. One en suite bedroom has its own balcony with sea view.

Many visitors are content just to sit all day in the colourful garden to enjoy the view of the bay; or they can use a small boat and go out fishing. Sunsets are outstanding.

Vegetables and loganberries are home-grown, rolls home-baked, eggs from the Maces' hens. A typical meal: fish pâté, a roast or casserole, and sherry trifle.

Visitors arriving by boat from St Mary's are met and their baggage taken up for them.

Readers' comments: Felt completely at home; happy and relaxed atmosphere. Comfortable room, excellent food. Simply delighted, a marvellous time. Nothing is too much trouble. Excellent food and accommodation, good hosts. Now a regular and much-loved destination.

THE BOATHOUSE

D S

Town Beach, Hugh Town, St Mary's, Isles of Scilly, TR21 0LN Tel: 01720 422688

5 Bedrooms. £23–£28. Most have views of sea.
1 Sitting-room
Closed from November to Easter.

With its feet in the sea (or the golden sands at low tide), this little house is down a quiet byway – yet only yards from the few shops and inns that constitute the town centre. Most of its neat pine-furnished bedrooms look over the sea and the stone jetty from which small boats regularly depart to other islands or on trips to see a lighthouse, seals or seabird colonies. The first-floor sitting-room (where complimentary tea or coffee can be had) opens on to a sun-trapping roof-terrace with seats and pots of plants. The breakfast-room has pretty tablecloths, white walls and cork floor. Hospitable Maureen Stuttaford and her sister Joan Collins are happy to make dinner reservations for guests at one of the local restaurants.

St Mary's, the principal island of Scilly, is only three miles long. Even its centre of action, Hugh Town, can hardly be called busy by mainland standards (though it does receive tides of day-visitors during high summer), and so it is easy to find any number of unfrequented coves or beaches close by.

Reader's comments: Immensely interesting hosts; friendliness and helpfulness itself; the best accommodation I have stayed at in the UK.

V

CARNWETHERS

C(11) **D M**

Green Lane, Pelistry Bay, St Mary's, Isles of Scilly, TR21 0NX
Tel/Fax: 01720 422415

rear view

9 Bedrooms. £45–£50 **including dinner** (less for 7 nights). All have own bath/shower/toilet; TV; views of sea (three). No smoking.
Dinner. 4 courses and coffee, at 6.30pm. Vegetarian or other special diets if ordered. Wine available. No smoking.
2 Sitting-rooms. With open fire, TV. **Bar.** No smoking.
Large garden
Closed from October to April.

Carnwethers is more than an ordinary guest-house (and a very good one, at that). Its owner is Roy Graham, well known as an underwater explorer, photographer and marine archaeologist. Even non-experts appreciate his library of books on maritime subjects and his immense knowledge of Scillonian history and ecology.

Every room is as neat as a new pin. There is a bar and lengthy wine list, a heated swimming-pool, sauna, games room and croquet lawn.

Meal times fit in with the times of Hugh Town activities, such as slide shows which are usually packed out, concerts, plays and the pubs. Local produce is much used by the chef. A typical meal: soup, roast turkey, and roly-poly pudding. Breakfast options include haddock and kippers. Bedrooms are agreeably decorated; some spacious ones open on to the very lovely garden. In the sitting-room, there are pictures of ships and seascapes. Diving, boating and fishing can be arranged.

Readers' comments: Happy, friendly atmosphere. Could not ask for more. Nothing is too much trouble. Complete satisfaction.

COASTGUARDS

D S

St Agnes, Isles of Scilly, TR22 0PL Tel: 01720 422373

3 Bedrooms. £33–£36 **including dinner.** Available: own bath/shower/toilet; views of sea. No smoking.
Dinner. 2 or 3 courses and coffee, at 7pm. Vegetarian or other special diets if ordered. No smoking.
1 Sitting-room. With open fire. No smoking.
Large garden
Closed from November to March.

A group of former coastguard cottages stands on a high point of St Agnes, a little island so unspoilt that there are no cars and no hotel. It is a paradise for those who want nothing more than sunshine early or late in the year, wildflowers, walks, birdwatching and peace.

Wendy Hick provides accommodation for guests in two adjacent cottages. She has furnished the rooms simply but attractively, with interesting objects around. The sitting-room has a William Morris suite and views out to the sea, polished board floors, and an open fire for chilly evenings. The food is all of a very good, homely style.

Visitors reach St Agnes via St Mary's, from which boats take them in 15 minutes to the little quay at St Agnes. (Wendy will supply all the times etc. for getting to Scilly.) Luggage is conveyed for them up the steep track that leads to the few cottages.

Readers' comments: Excellent in every respect. Good food, lovely scenery, such nice people. Warmly welcomed, well looked after, delicious food, excellent value; beautiful and peaceful place. Superb food and hospitality.

V

COVEAN COTTAGE

C(9) D S

St Agnes, Isles of Scilly, TR22 0PL Tel/Fax: 01720 422620

5 Bedrooms. £25–£32. Available: own bath/shower/toilet; TV; views of sea.
Dinner. £13.50 for 3 courses and coffee, at 7pm. Vegetarian or other special diets if ordered. Wine available. No smoking. **Light suppers** if ordered.
1 Sitting-room. With TV. **Bar.**
Small garden
Closed from November to January.

During the day the garden at Covean is abuzz with day-trippers as Peter and Heather Sewell, with their daughter Julie, have built a reputation for their teas and lunches. They were recently awarded the accolade of being one of the ten best places to eat in Cornwall and the Scillies.

But in the evening this most south-westerly of the isles, with its mere 65 inhabitants, regains its tranquillity. The rooms at the cottage are filled with flowers, and St Agnes carnations are much in evidence in the sea-facing conservatory where meals can be taken. Many of the paintings have been done by guests who have been inspired by the scenery to take up their brushes.

Most bedrooms have deep window-seats overlooking the sea. In one room there are blue-and-white frilled curtains, while another has a softly draped mini-canopy over a bed with crisp white sheets. For total privacy, there is also a garden cottage.

A typical dinner menu: cheese, cider and onion soup; duck in cherry sauce with sweet potatoes in a dressing; bread-and-butter pudding.

V

EVERGREEN COTTAGE

C D S

The Parade, Hugh Town, St Mary's, Isles of Scilly, TR21 0LP Tel: 01720 422711

5 Bedrooms. £25–£29.50. Bargain breaks. All have own shower/toilet. No smoking.
1 Sitting-room. With TV. No smoking.
Small garden

The glorious flowers in the small front garden of John and Anne Clare's 300-year-old cottage tell of a climate so mild that spring comes early, autumn stays late and winter hardly exists. Clustered around table and chairs are plants from Peru, the Canary Islands, South Africa and the Mediterranean.

The cottage, originally home to a seafaring captain, has been sympathetically restored to provide bedrooms with small casement windows and modern shower-rooms. The guests' sitting-room, with pink velvet chesterfield and cane furniture, has a huge map of the Scillies on one wall and a range of books covering the Clares' interests and those of their guests. Jostling for space is literature on walking, diving, bird life, flora and fauna – all of which draw visitors to the islands. Anne and John have also filled their cottage with another of their loves – Balinese wood-carvings.

The low-ceilinged breakfast-room is especially pleasant, and it is here that a local boatman calls daily to tell guests about various trips to other islands.

For evening meals, Hugh Town's pubs and restaurants are within a stone's throw of the cottage.

MORGELYN C(10)

McFarlands Down, St Mary's, Isles of Scilly, TR21 0NS Tel: 01720 422897

3 Bedrooms. £23–£24. Available: own bath/shower/ toilet; views of sea. No smoking.
1 Sitting-room. With stove, TV. No smoking.
Small garden
Closed from November to March.

E-mail: nick@scillyonline.co.uk

To Scillonians, Morgelyn is 'up country' which, on an island only six miles square, means it is not far from anywhere. A half-hour walk, with splendid views, takes you into Hugh Town, the small and unspoilt capital.

Everything about Morgelyn – Cornish for 'sea holly' – is restful, and Jane Lishman is a welcoming hostess. The guests' sitting-cum-breakfast-room is papered in the palest pink-and-cream stripes and one of the comfortable sofas has cream, green and pink checks, which blend well with the predominant colours of the room. The walls are hung with an eclectic mix of pictures.

Bedrooms have modern en suite shower-rooms and are immaculate.

Jane does not provide dinners, but there is a restaurant within a 15-minute stroll. Another walk enjoyed by guests is to Bant's Carn burial chamber and ancient village. The carn was the ancestral shrine of a small farming community, and it dates back to about 2000–1500BC, when the isles were all one large island.

Reader's comments: Very impressed with the welcome we received, the cooking and comfort. V

Private bathrooms are not necessarily en suite.

Months when houses are shown as closed are inclusive.

At houses where dinner is not served, a light supper can often be obtained (if ordered in advance), ranging from sandwiches to family 'pot luck'. (Packed lunches too.)

Addresses shown are to enable you to locate a house on a map. They are not necessarily complete postal addresses (though the essential post-code is included), and detailed directions for finding a house should be obtained from the owner.

SHROPSHIRE

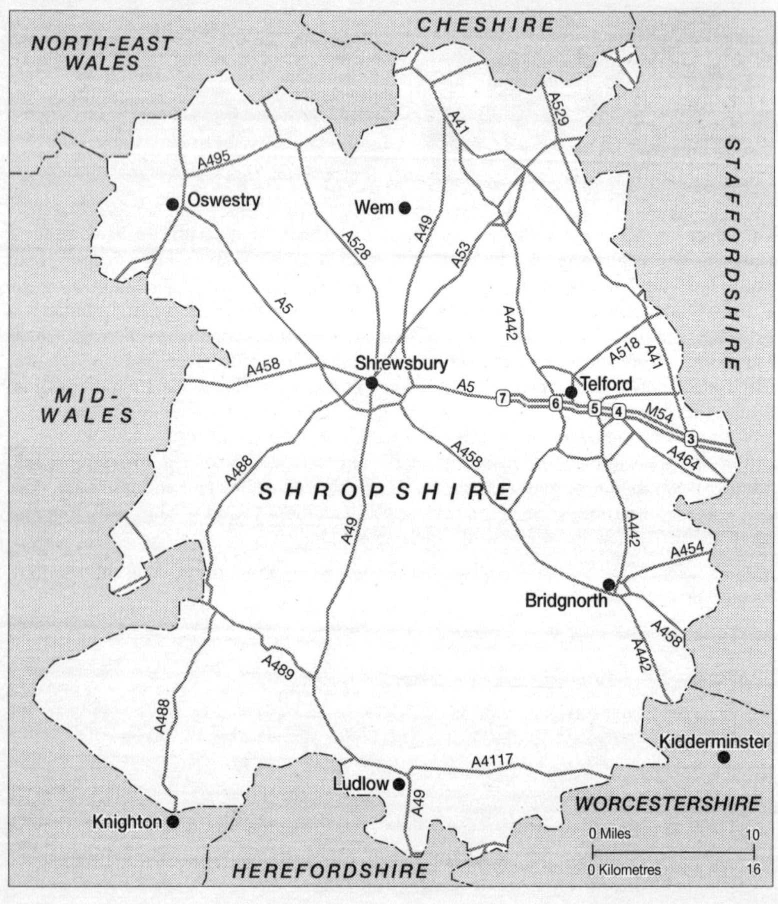

Facts (prices, etc.) at the top of entries are supplied by the proprietors themselves. While every effort is made to ensure that these are correct at the time of going to press, they may alter thereafter: please check when you book.

THE ALBYNES

Nordley, Shropshire, WV16 4SX Tel: 01746 762261
North of Bridgnorth. Nearest main road: A442 from Kidderminster to Telford.

3 Bedrooms. £22–£25 (less for 3 nights or more). Bargain breaks. Available: own bath/shower/toilet; TV. No smoking.
Dinner (by arrangement). £12.50 for 4 courses and coffee, at times to suit guests. Vegetarian or other special diets if ordered. No smoking. **Light suppers** if ordered.
1 Sitting-room. With stove, TV. No smoking.
Large garden

Older readers may have grown up with the nature books of Frances Pitt: this is the house where she lived and wrote them. It was orginally built in 1823 for the Burgher of Bridgnorth, who named it after his son Albinius. The dining-room was designed to accommodate fine carved panelling removed from a nearby Tudor house, and there is an elegant oak staircase that spirals its way up to the bedrooms. Several of these overlook the lake (or far hills), as does the sitting-room – furnished with antiques and gold brocade chairs. Twisting passages and steps, unusual curved doors and round-arched alcoves add to the character of the house.

Cynthia Woolley's husband farms the adjoining land – a mixture of arable fields and pasture. A typical dinner may comprise curried parsnip soup, grilled lamb chops with fresh herbs, and lemon-cream pudding.

Readers' comments: Wonderful cook; generous and friendly hostess. Wonderful hosts, lovely home.

V

BROWNHILL HOUSE

C PT S X

Ruyton XI Towns, Shropshire, SY4 1LR Tel: 01939 261121 (Fax: 01939 260626)
South-east of Oswestry. Nearest main road: A5 from Shrewsbury to Oswestry.

3 Bedrooms. £20–£22 (less for 2, 3 and 5 nights or more). All have own bath/shower/toilet.
Dinner (by arrangement). £10–£14 for 2–4 courses and coffee, at 6.30pm. Vegetarian or other special diets if ordered. Wine available. No smoking. **Light suppers** if ordered.
1 Sitting-room. With open fire, TV.
Large garden

E-mail: brownhill@eleventowns.demon.co.uk

It is the garden which brings most visitors here. Although when they moved in Roger and Yoland Brown had not the slightest interest in gardening, within a few years the potential of the large, steep site had converted them into enthusiasts and then experts. They have provided a variety of experiences for the visitor – here a grotto, there a Thai spirit house, 500 different shrubs, 20 kinds of fruit or nut, a vegetable garden with glasshouses.

As to the house itself, the bedrooms are comfortable and homely. Bathrooms are good. The beamed sitting-room has a huge stone fireplace. Meals are served in the large farmhouse-style kitchen, and may comprise such things as soup made from the garden's vegetables, stuffed pork with a crisp crumb coating, and a compote of garden fruit. Breakfasts are exceptional: bread is baked locally and jams are home-made by Yoland (who is an authority on the village, with its strange name).

Computer and e-mail facilities are available for guests' use.

Readers' comments: Most generous hosts, excellent hospitality. Very warm welcome and a really delicious meal. Wished we could have stayed longer.

Shropshire

BUCKNELL HOUSE

C(12) **D PT**

Bucknell, Shropshire, SY7 0AD Tel: 01547 530248
West of Ludlow. Nearest main road: A4113 from Ludlow to Knighton.

3 Bedrooms. £22 (less for 4 nights or more). All have own TV.
Light suppers sometimes. Vegetarian or other special diets if ordered.
1 Sitting-room. With open fire, TV, piano.
Large garden
Closed in December and January.

In the early 18th century, this huge and handsome house was a vicarage. The vicar would have approved of the equally handsome way in which locally born Brenda Davies has furnished it – the dining-room with Sheraton chairs and fine wallpaper; the sitting-room with big velvet armchairs, curtains of pale green silk; flowers everywhere. Bedrooms are just as good, with lovely country views. All are spacious; one has antique furniture, floral fabrics and wicker armchairs. Breakfasts here are substantial (the honey is home-produced, marmalade home-made).

The grounds (garden and watermeadows) are secluded, looking across the valley of the River Teme to Wales. There are rosebeds and croquet lawn, shooting and scenic walks. The surrounding woodlands and hills are full of wildlife. Mediaeval Ludlow, the historic Marches, the 'Black-and-White Village Trail' and Offa's Dyke are in the vicinity. At Craven Arms is the county's Secret Hills Centre. Guests dine in local village inns.

Readers' comments: Wonderfully comfortable bed, breakfast an ample repast, some of the most beautiful countryside in England. Outstanding amenities; marvellous people. Delightful couple; nothing was too much trouble. Looked after us splendidly.

Shropshire

FITZ MANOR

C D S

Fitz, Bomere Heath, Shropshire, SY4 3AS Tel/Fax: 01743 850295
North-west of Shrewsbury. Nearest main road: A5 from Shrewsbury to Llangollen.

3 Bedrooms. £23–£30 (less for 7 nights or more). No smoking.
Dinner (by arrangement). £15 for 4 courses and coffee, at times to suit guests. Vegetarian or other special diets if ordered. No smoking. **Light suppers** if ordered.
2 Sitting-rooms. With open fire, TV. No smoking in one.
Large garden

This outstanding manor house was built about 1450 in traditional Shropshire style – black timbers and white walls. It is at the heart of a large arable farm.

The interior is one of the most impressive in this book. A vast, blue dining-room with parquet floor and Persian carpet overlooks rosebeds, pergolas and yew hedges. It is furnished with antiques, paintings by John Piper and a collection of Crown Derby. In the oak-panelled sitting-room there are damask and pink velvet armchairs around the log fire.

Bedrooms differ in size. For instance, adjoining one huge room with armchairs is a white cottage-style bedroom – a useful combination for a family.

Dawn Baly's candlelit dinners may include home-made pâté, casseroled pheasant with home-grown vegetables, chocolate mousse, and cheeses.

In the grounds are a heated swimming-pool and croquet lawn.

V

Readers' comments: Lovely place – quite magical. Dinner was extremely well cooked, abundant and well presented. No attention to detail spared. Quite the most outstanding.

FOXLEIGH HOUSE

C(8) **D PT S**

Foxleigh Drive, Wem, Shropshire, SY4 5BP Tel/Fax: 01939 233528
North of Shrewsbury. Nearest main road: A49 from Shrewsbury to Whitchurch.

Shropshire

3 Bedrooms. £20–£23 (less for 4 nights or more). Bargain breaks. Available: own bath/toilet; TV. No smoking.
Dinner (by arrangement). £12 for 4 courses and coffee, at 7pm. No smoking. **Light suppers** if ordered.
1 Sitting-room. With open fire. No smoking.
Small garden
Closed from mid-December to January.

E-mail: foxleigh01@aol.com

Well tucked away in this little market town is handsome Foxleigh House, the most memorable feature of which is the fine sitting-room. Its cocoa walls, coffee ceiling and Chinese carpet are an excellent setting for antiques that include inlaid tables and a series of Hogarth prints. Bay windows open on to the croquet lawn and its towering Wellingtonia.

In the dining-room, Barbara Barnes serves such meals as avocado, roast lamb, trifle, and local cheeses. The bedrooms have art deco suites of figured maple, and the hall a gallery of ancestral portraits.

Wem still has many historic buildings, and Shrewsbury itself is near. So is 18th-century Hawkstone Park, now restored, with follies, underground grotto and glorious views.

Readers' comments: Can't praise too warmly. Made us feel so cared for. Particularly kind and helpful. Very, very comfortable and roomy; meals delicious. Very tastefully furnished; breakfast one of the best we have ever had. Excellent hospitality. Very good accommodation. V

MONAUGHTY POETH

C(12) **D PT S**

Llanfair-Waterdine, Shropshire, LD7 1TT Tel: 01547 528348
North-west of Knighton (Powys, Wales). Nearest main road: A488 from Knighton to Shrewsbury.

Shropshire

2 Bedrooms. £22 (less for 4 nights or more). Both have own TV.
1 Sitting-room. With open fire, TV, piano.
Small garden
Closed in December and January.

Here, where the border between Wales and Shropshire runs, two sisters grew up in the 1940s: Brenda (now of **Bucknell House**) and Jocelyn. Later they wrote a nostalgic history of their parish, tiny though it is, and Jocelyn has also written a book for young children about birds. In an Area of Outstanding Natural Beauty yet within easy reach of the historic towns of Ludlow and Hereford, Monaughty Poeth has an 800-year-old history, for it once belonged to the Cistercians of Abbey Cwmhir: Monaughty means 'monastery grange' and Poeth 'burnt' – the house burnt down and was rebuilt in the 19th century. This is where Jocelyn, married to farmer Jim Williams, lives and welcomes visitors.

The accommodation at Monaughty is in traditional farmhouse style, with comfort the keynote, and in every room are Jocelyn's pretty flower arrangements. Visitors dine at local village inns. For walkers, Offa's Dyke and Glyndwr's Way are close by.

Readers' comments: Treated like royalty! Enjoyed every comfort. Warmest of welcomes. Large, pretty bedroom and lovely view. Wonderful concern for her guests. Extremely friendly. Idyllic location. Charming and unassuming people. Lovely farmhouse.

Shropshire

OLD CIDER HOUSE

M PT S

1 Lion Lane, Cleobury Mortimer, Shropshire, DY14 8BT Tel: 01299 270304
West of Kidderminster. Nearest main road: A4117 from Cleobury Mortimer to Ludlow.

2 Bedrooms. £25 (less for 3 nights or more). Available: own bath/shower/toilet. No smoking.
1 Sitting-room. With woodstove, TV. No smoking.
Small garden

E-mail: lennox@old-cider-house.fnet.co.uk

Within sight of Cleobury Mortimer's crooked church-spire, down a narrow lane which was once the major route into this attractive market town, lies the Old Cider House – a welcome sight for weary drovers approaching journey's end with a serious thirst to quench. One steps straight into the low-ceilinged dining-room, where the oak beams have been dated to the 16th century and there is an unusual Orkney chair with oatstraw back. Through an alcove to one side lies the book-filled sitting-room (a wood-burning stove has been fitted in the stone wall between the rooms, providing comfort to both); on the other lies a bedroom with an excellent shower-room adjoining. Upstairs is another attractive bedroom, with a Lloyd Loom chair, pine furniture and bright fabrics; like the pretty tiled bathroom, it has a beamed ceiling.

Stroma Lennox does not serve dinner, since the various eating-places of Cleobury Mortimer are within a few minutes' walk. The town lies between the Wyre Forest and the Shropshire Hills; Wenlock Edge is not far away.

V

Shropshire

OLD VICARAGE

C D PT X

Leaton, Shropshire, SY4 3AP Tel/Fax: 01939 290989
North of Shrewsbury. Nearest main road: A5 from Shrewsbury to Oswestry.

3 Bedrooms. £20 (less for 7 nights or more). Available: own bath/shower/toilet; TV. No smoking.
Light suppers if ordered. Vegetarian or other special diets if ordered. No smoking.
1 Sitting-room. With open fire, TV.
Large garden

E-mail: m-j@oldvicleaton.freeserve.co.uk

Leaton's Old Vicarage was built in 1859 for an archdeacon: hence the many pointed or trefoil-arched windows, the arcading in the sitting-room, handsome floor-tiles and doors of ecclesiastical design. One very big bedroom has a bay window and another an oriel from which to enjoy views of the garden. One Victorian bathroom is particularly attractive. As well as breakfasts, with such unusual options as trout with mushrooms and tomatoes, Joan Mansell-Jones serves snack suppers; much is home-grown or home-made.

Almost islanded within a loop of the River Severn, Shrewsbury is a treasury of superb black-and-white buildings with several fine churches, gardens (Darwin, born here, is commemorated in a statue) and museums. It deserves repeated visits to explore twisting lanes (with such curious names as Dogpole, Shoplatch or Coffeehouse Passage), the castle, and the main square with flower-baskets hung around an open-pillared market hall.

Readers' comments: Beautiful house and garden, kind friendly welcome. We were really spoilt.

V

SEVERN TROW

M

Church Road, Jackfield, Ironbridge, Shropshire, TF8 7ND Tel: 01952 883551
South of Telford. Nearest main road: A442 from Telford to Bridgnorth (and M54, junctions 4/5).

3 Bedrooms. £23–£28. Available: own bath/shower/toilet; TV; views of river. No smoking.
1 Sitting-room. With open fire,TV. No smoking.
Small garden
Closed in November and December.

Through the Ironbridge gorge, scenic birthplace of the Industrial Revolution, sailing-barges called trows bore goods downriver to Bristol. The Severn Trow provided the men with beer, dormitory lodgings and brothel. Then it became a church hall.

The lounge (looking out over the garden towards the gorge) has a large 17th-century inglenook and a red and black quarry-tiled floor. In the dining-room, there is an outstanding mosaic floor.

Upstairs are excellent bedrooms with light colour schemes and interesting furnishings. One bedroom, with good bathroom and small kitchen area, is accessible from street level.

Very substantial breakfasts are provided by Pauline Hannigan but no evening meal. However, there are over two dozen eating-places within a mile radius.

Readers' comments: Most comfortable, wonderful welcome. Has to be seen to be believed. Superb breakfasts, extremely helpful. The best we have visited. Breakfast fruits a work of art! Friendly hostess. Enormous breakfast. Four-poster a delight. Nothing too much trouble.

UPPER HOUSE FARM

C D

Shropshire

Hopton Castle, Shropshire, SY7 0QF Tel: 01547 530319
West of Ludlow. Nearest main road: A49 from Ludlow to Craven Arms.

3 Bedrooms. £24–£25. All have own bath/shower/toilet; TV. No smoking.
Dinner (by arrangement). £14 for 4 courses and coffee, at 7pm. Vegetarian or other special diets if ordered. Wine available. No smoking.
1 Sitting-room. With open fire. No smoking.
Large garden
Closed in December.

A very beautiful garden surrounds this 18th-century house, and indoors everything is of an equally high standard: from the good carpets and the velvet armchairs grouped around the fireplace to the antiques and the excellent bathrooms. Beams and inglenooks complement the furnishings. You can enjoy a huge and sunny bedroom overlooking the picturesque ruins of Hopton Castle, and a stroll on the farm to look at cattle or Clun forest sheep. There's trout fishing to be had, free, in the river.

But above all it is Sue Williams's rich and imaginative cooking that brings visitors back. (Typically, vol-au-vent, pheasant casseroled in red wine, blueberry tart, and cheeses.)

The castle, which is on the farm's grounds, was built by the Normans; and in 1642 thirty Roundheads held it against 300 Royalists for three weeks.

Readers' comments: Cannot praise highly enough. Glorious countryside. Meals an absolute delight. Most charming and a wonderful cook. Lovely old house, splendid meals. Food with flair and imagination. Perfect in every way. Outstanding.

SOMERSET
(including Bath & North-East Somerset)

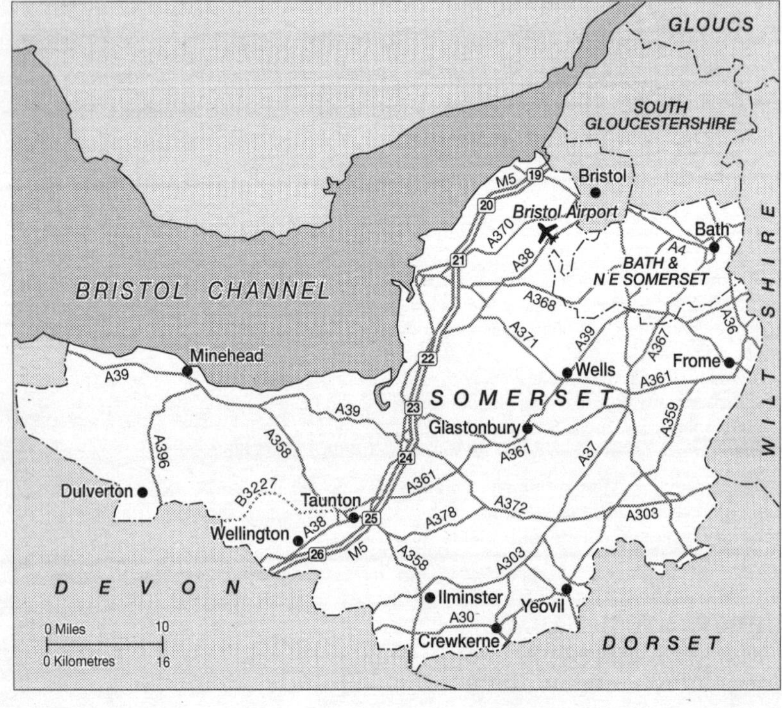

You stand a better chance of finding the right accommodation at the right price in the right area if you are using an up-to-date edition of this book, which is revised every year. Obtain an order form for the next edition (published in November) by sending a stamped addressed envelope, with 'SOTBT 2003' in the top left-hand corner, to Explore Britain, Alston, Cumbria, CA9 3SL.

ASTOR HOUSE

C PT X

14 Oldfield Road, Bath, Bath & North-East Somerset, BA2 3ND
Tel/Fax: 01225 429134
Nearest main road: A367 from Bath to Shepton Mallet.

6 Bedrooms. £22.50–£27.50 (less for 4 nights or more). All have own bath/shower/toilet; TV. No smoking.
1 Sitting-room. With TV. No smoking.
Garden

Among the bewildering variety of guest-houses in Bath, Astor House is quite a find: in a relatively quiet residential street, yet only minutes from buses and, to the more energetic, within walking distance of the abbey. The bow-fronted Victorian house is filled with knick-knacks and has been furnished with inspired purchases from Bath's many auction-rooms: cast-iron fireplaces in several bedrooms, a fine oak fire-surround in the cosy sitting-room. Three bedrooms are on the second floor, with sloping ceilings; one – No. 6 – has a splendid view down over the garden (complete with enormous walnut tree and nuts in season) and across the city to the heights of Lansdown beyond.

Before they took on Astor House as well in November 1999, Liz and Tony Peace ran a riverside pub in Bath, which they have built up into a popular restaurant serving meals seven nights a week. Guests wishing to dine there can cadge a lift in the evening with Tony; otherwise, Bath is very well endowed with eating-places to suit all pockets and tastes, and Liz will provide plates and cutlery for those who prefer a takeaway.

V

---

9 BATHWICK HILL

C(12) **PT S**

Bath, Bath & North-East Somerset, BA2 6EW Tel: 01225 460812
Nearest main road: A36 from Bath to Warminster.

Bath & North-East Somerset

2 Bedrooms. £25–£30. Both have own bath/shower/toilet. No smoking.
1 Sitting-room. With TV, piano. No smoking.
Walled garden

Gracious and elegant are the two words which spring to mind when entering this Bath-stone house, the home of Elspeth Bowman. Having spent most of her life abroad, Elspeth finally chose to settle in this late Georgian house, in one of the most attractive parts of Bath. National Trust fields spread out below and from some windows one can see the abbey, floodlit at night.

The guests' drawing-room and dining-room, like the rest of the house, are furnished with antiques and *objets d'art*. On warm mornings, breakfast can be taken in the conservatory. A curving staircase leads to bedrooms where chintz curtains in pinks, browns and sunny yellows match valances and padded headboards. A writing bureau is a feature of one bedroom; the other has a view of a flowering cherry tree.

Unusually for Bath, guests can leave their cars parked here. It is an easy, 15-minute stroll downhill to the city centre and a reliable bus service takes the strain out of the return journey. Just wandering among the Georgian perfection of Bath's streets and squares is a pleasure in itself.

Somerset

BEER FARM

C(12) **D S**

Bere Aller, Somerset, TA10 0QX Tel/Fax: 01458 250285
North-east of Taunton. Nearest main road: A372 from Langport to Bridgwater.

3 Bedrooms. £25–£32. Available: own bath/shower/toilet. No smoking.
Dinner (by arrangement). £17.50 for 3 courses and coffee, at times to suit guests. Vegetarian or other special diets if ordered. No smoking. **Light suppers** if ordered.
1 Sitting-room. With open fire, TV, piano. No smoking.
Large garden
Closed from mid-December to early January.

Lying below a ridge that is clothed with ancient hanging woods, Beer Farm is home to Susan and Philip Morlock. They came from Kent, where Philip was a fruit-grower and Susan an enthusiastic gardener and plant collector. Their present home, largely Georgian, is surrounded by gardens and an orchard.

Dinner is served in an elegant, low-ceilinged room where candlelight gleams on the china, crystal glasses and fresh flowers. Susan, a charming and relaxed hostess, who trained in catering management, might offer such dishes as salmon en croûte, raspberry and cinnamon pavlova, and cheese.

The colours throughout the house are pale and restful and the guests' drawing-room is filled with sofas, books and paintings (with a log fire for chilly evenings). The twin bedroom, with pink and white sprigged wallpaper, has a comfortable little sitting-area.

Beer Farm is well located for visiting local museums such as the Somerset Rural Life Museum at Glastonbury, where the social and domestic life of Victorian Somerset is recreated, and Taunton's Somerset County Museum. In addition, there are any number of interesting gardens, several belonging to the National Trust.

V

Bath & North-East Somerset

BRIDGE COTTAGE

D M PT

Ashley Road, Bathford, Bath & North-East Somerset, BA1 7TT
Tel: 01225 852399
East of Bath. Nearest main road: A4 from Chippenham to Bath (and M4, junction 18).

3 Bedrooms. £25–£32.50 (less for 2 nights or more). All have own bath/shower/toilet; TV. No smoking.
Light suppers if ordered. No smoking.
Small garden
Closed from November to March.

There are two bedrooms on the ground floor of beautifully converted Bridge Cottage; one has a particularly pretty bathroom, with flowery fitments, the other a luxurious blue-and-white shower-room. There is a little dining-room upstairs where guests take breakfast, and across the courtyard is another, equally attractive cottage, with its own patio garden. Tubs of begonias and petunias fill every corner, and there are 75 varieties of clematis.

As this edition went to press, we learned that Bridge Cottage had changed hands. The new owners are Daphne and Jack Mackay.

All the pleasures of Bath are within about 10 minutes by car (or bus), yet this little village perched on a hillside seems deep in the country. At nearby Bradford-on-Avon, steep roads converge at the mediaeval bridge with domed chapel-turned-lockup on it. It takes time to discover all Bradford's handsome houses, Saxon church, vast tithe barn and old inns. A few miles away are such lovely spots as Corsham, Lacock and the Chippenham–Calne area.

V

CALENDAR COTTAGE

C PT X

Somerset

Silver Street, Misterton, Somerset, TA18 8NB Tel: 01460 75680
South of Crewkerne. Nearest main road: A356 from Crewkerne to Dorchester.

3 Bedrooms. £22–£24. Bargain breaks. Available: own bath/shower/toilet; TV. No smoking.
1 Sitting-room. With open fire, piano. No smoking.
Small garden

Two 17th-century cottages have been turned into one pretty house, which retains many features of yesteryear – sloping ceilings, beams, wide casements and padded window-seats.

It formerly appeared in this guide as 'Yew Trees', but was renamed by its present owners, Derek and Judy Wood, as they felt it resembled the sort of picture-postcard cottage you would find on a calendar. The bedrooms are charming – each decorated with fabrics and colours chosen to suit the season after which it is named. Throughout are displays of Derek's lifetime collection of decorative plates. Downstairs, golds, russets and warm earth colours complement the old tiles in the entrance hall. The spacious breakfast/sitting-room has an open fire, as well as games and books for chilly evenings. Breakfast includes fresh and stewed fruit (often from the garden), marmalade made by Derek's father and local free-range eggs.

On arrival, guests are served tea in the secluded garden, with its lily-pond and towering copper beech. Judy, a keen gardener, enjoys sharing seeds and cuttings. For dinner, there are local restaurants and pubs, one of which is within a two-minute walk.

CASTLE FARM

C PT X

Somerset

Stoke-sub-Hamdon, Somerset, TA14 6QS Tel: 01935 822231 (Fax: 01935 822057)
West of Yeovil. Nearest main road: A303 from Andover towards Honiton.

3 Bedrooms. £20–£22.50 (less for 4 nights or more). All have own bath/shower/toilet; TV. No smoking.
Light suppers if ordered.
1 Sitting-area
Large garden

Part of the Duchy of Cornwall estate, Castle Farm is the home of Rob and Karen Hebditch and their young family. It is a handsome, 18th-century, Ham stone house commanding fine views of Ham Hill, an early Roman encampment (from beamed Bedroom 3), and St Michael's Hill at nearby Montacute (from the huge family room, with carved pine bedhead, full-size bunk beds, and the wide floorboards that betray its age). Room 2 is particularly attractive, with cream-painted walls enhanced by flowery borders and matching fabrics, interesting paintings, and a good bathroom. Karen serves hearty breakfasts in the warm farmhouse kitchen; for dinner, guests can choose between three very different eating-places in the village (including the highly praised, albeit expensive, Priory House restaurant).

This is a working mixed farm, with cattle, half-breed lambs, cereals and potatoes, surrounded by National Trust properties like Tintinhull House, the Treasurer's House at Martock, and magnificent Montacute House itself, an outpost of the National Portrait Gallery.

Reader's comments: Rob and Karen provided an efficient, quality service, and in a lovely setting; I highly recommend them.

CEDAR LODGE

C PT X

13 Lambridge, Bath, Bath & North-East Somerset, BA1 6BJ Tel: 01225 423468
On A4 from Bath to Chippenham.

3 Bedrooms. £23–£35 (less for 3 nights or more). Bargain breaks. Available: own bath/shower/toilet; TV. No smoking.
Dinner (by arrangement except in summer). £20 for 4 courses and coffee, at times to suit guests. Vegetarian or other special diets if ordered. No smoking. **Light suppers** if ordered.
1 Sitting-room. With open fire, TV. No smoking.
Garden

The 18th-century merchant who first owned this fine house celebrated peace when the American War of Independence ended by installing a window etched and painted with the American eagle bearing an olive branch. This is on a curved landing of the elegant staircase. At back and front are walled gardens, the latter with ample trees (as well as frog pools) to screen the verandahed house from the road into Bath: bus stop outside.

Derek and Hungarian-born Maria Beckett have furnished the house with antiques, an abundance of pictures and books, needlepoint cushions, and an alcove full of dolls and toys for visiting children. There is a tiny, stone-floored summer-house for reading and quiet contemplation. Maria, a cordon bleu cook, discusses guests' preferences beforehand, but dinner could comprise carrot-and-coriander soup, pheasant in red wine sauce, apple crumble, and local cheeses.

Upstairs are bedrooms with bay windows and handsomely panelled doors. One has a pine half-tester bed with lace drapery; another, a very wide four-poster and quilted spread.

Reader's comments: The home was warm with friendship, hosts more than gracious, very restful.

CREECHBARN

C D PT S

Vicarage Lane, Creech St Michael, Somerset, TA3 5PP Tel: 01823 443955
(Fax: 01823 443509)
East of Taunton. Nearest main road: A358 from Taunton to Ilminster (and M5, junction 25).

3 Bedrooms. £22–£31 (less for 3 nights or more). Available: own bath/shower/toilet. No smoking.
Dinner (by arrangement). £12.50 for 2 or 3 courses and coffee, at times to suit guests. Vegetarian or other special diets if ordered. **Light suppers** by arrangement.
1 Sitting-room. With TV, table tennis.
Large garden

E-mail: mick@somersite.co.uk

There has been a farm on this idyllic spot overlooking the Curry Moor since Domesday Book was compiled. In mediaeval times the property belonged to Muchelney Abbey until Henry VIII dissolved the monasteries; now, nearly five centuries later, the long-barn has been converted to the highest standards by Mick and Hope Humphreys. Books, Mick's photographs, and interesting souvenirs of his years in the Navy are everywhere; the attractive beamed bedrooms are comfortably furnished (one has a particularly pretty shower-room), and the huge studio/sitting-room is big enough for table tennis as well as more sedentary pursuits. In the dining-room, with its view over the Somerset Levels, Hope serves (if ordered in advance) such dinners as watercress soup, chicken breast with an almond crust, and a meringue pudding.

The cycle path along the Bridgwater & Taunton Canal is close; there are excellent walks on the doorstep; and an RSPB waterfowl sanctuary is nearby. Mick is involved, too, in the ongoing restoration of the 18th-century pleasure gardens on the Halswell estate, where the renovated Temple of Harmony bears comparison with the best of Stourhead.

CUTTHORNE

C D S

Luckwell Bridge, Wheddon Cross, Somerset, TA24 7EW Tel/Fax: 01643 831255
South-west of Minehead. Nearest main road: A396 from Exeter to Minehead.

3 Bedrooms. £25–£31. Bargain breaks. All have own bath/shower/toilet; TV. No smoking.
Dinner. £14 for 4 courses and coffee, at 7.30pm. Vegetarian or other special diets if ordered. No smoking.
Light suppers if ordered.
1 Sitting-room. With log stove, TV. No smoking.
Large garden

E-mail: durbin@cutthorne.co.uk

There has been a farm on this spot since the 1300s; the present house is 18th-century, with a slate-flagged porch and apricot walls, and here Ann Durbin produces candlelit dinners with much home produce (meat and game). Bedrooms in the house are excellently furnished, with exceptionally pretty embossed wallpapers and lovely Exmoor views; one has a carved and tapestry-hung four-poster, another an unusual carved French bed. In the sitting- and dining-rooms are antique rugs, log fires and brass-rubbings.

There is a courtyard where chickens roam, and a pond with exotic species of ducks and geese. Trout fishing and shooting available. (Two immaculate cottages have their own kitchens and dining facilities for either b & b or self-catering; guests can dine in the main house.)

In the heart of Exmoor, the house is also near the sands and sea.

Readers' comments: Excellent food, kind hosts, quiet setting. Attractive rooms, comprehensively equipped. The Durbins were most helpful. Good food, well presented.

V

DOLPHIN HOUSE

C(12) **PT**

8 Northend, Batheaston, Bath & North-East Somerset, BA1 7EH
Tel/Fax: 01225 858915 (Mobile: 07801 444521)
East of Bath. Nearest main road: A4 from Bath to Chippenham (and M4, junction 18).

rear view

2 Bedrooms. £25–£35 (with continental breakfast). Less for 3 nights or more. Both have own bath/shower/toilet; TV. No smoking.
Garden
Closed from late December to early January.

You may catch a glimpse through a window of two people beavering away in their workshop in this stately roadside house. It will be George and Jane Riley employing their talents as antique-restorers. It is not surprising, therefore, that their 200-year-old home is filled with choice and unusual pieces of furniture.

As there is no dining-room, Jane brings a substantial continental breakfast to the bedrooms, both of which are extremely spacious. The downstairs bedroom, with views of the terrace and sloping garden, has rug-strewn, polished floorboards and an early Victorian, gate-legged dining-table. Drawn close to the iron-grated fireplace, which is flanked by two large bronze candle-holders, is a comfortable sofa.

The *pièce de résistance* is, however, the upstairs bedroom, with a private sitting-room and further steps to a large bathroom. Jane has created a very French ambience in the sitting-room, which has toile wallpaper, cream brocade curtains and Persian rugs. Morning sun streams through the deep casements.

For dinner, there are pubs and restaurants within walking distance. The city of Bath is close at hand.

V

Somerset

DOUBLE-GATE FARM

C M

Godney, Somerset, BA5 1RX Tel: 01458 832217 (Fax: 01458 835612)
South-west of Wells. Nearest main road: A39 from Wells to Glastonbury.

8 Bedrooms. £22.50–£25. Available: own bath/shower/toilet; TV. No smoking.
3 Sitting-rooms. With stove (in one), TV, piano (in one). No smoking.
Small garden

E-mail: hilary@doublegate.demon.co.uk

History and legend mingle tantalizingly on the Somerset Levels, a fertile fen reclaimed over the centuries from the sea. One age-old belief identifies nearby Glastonbury as the fabled Isle of Avalon, the final resting-place of King Arthur.

Many visitors to Terry and Hilary Millard's mixed farm are following the trail of the Arthurian legends. Others are drawn by the birdlife supported by these unique wetlands, or by the fishing on the River Sheppey which runs at the foot of the garden.

Bedrooms are prettily decorated, spacious and well equipped, and some have fine views of the Mendip Hills. Three are in the main farmhouse, while the rest are in adjoining barn conversions, each with its own sitting-room. One ground-floor bedroom (and bathroom) has been fully adapted for wheelchair use. Disabled assistance dogs (only) are welcomed and children well catered for. A ground-floor laundry is also available.

Most guests finish their day in the games room, which houses a full-size snooker table, table tennis and darts board. They dine in the village pub next door or at other local inns.

V

Somerset

EAST LAMBROOK FARM

C(2) S

East Lambrook, Somerset, TA13 5HH Tel/Fax: 01460 240064
North-west of Yeovil. Nearest main road: A303 from Ilchester to Ilminster.

3 Bedrooms. £23–£24 (less for 4 nights or more). Available: own bath/shower/toilet. No smoking.
Light suppers if ordered. No smoking.
1 Sitting-room. With open fire, TV, piano. No smoking.
Large garden

The village of East Lambrook is famed for Margery Fish's listed garden which she created at the manor house, her home for 32 years. The garden has 5000 species and cultivars in tiny themed corners and is a favoured haunt of garden-lovers who stay with Nicola Eeles at East Lambrook Farm.

The date of 1685 on the western wall belies its age: when it was inspected by an architectural historian, he found mediaeval features. Nicola uses the flagged entrance hall, warmed by a wood-burning stove, as the breakfast-room. Here a large oak dresser holds her collection of Royal Copenhagen china. Throughout the house are reminders of the time Nicola spent in Zambia – such as a carved wall-panel of yoked African slaves and a series of pictures of Zambian sunbirds.

A piano in the guests' sitting-room is played occasionally by Nicola, a former piano teacher. Outside there is a tennis court.

One bedroom has a king-size double bed, and the others are given homely touches with favourite photographs, toys and books left behind by the Eeles' children.

V

EDGCOTT HOUSE

D PT S X

Porlock Road, Exford, Somerset, TA24 7QG Tel/Fax: 01643 831495
South-west of Minehead. Nearest main road: A396 from Exeter to Minehead.

Somerset

3 Bedrooms. £21–£24 (less for 3 nights or more). Bargain breaks. Available: own bath/shower/toilet; views of river.
Dinner. £15 for 4 courses and coffee, at 7.30pm. Vegetarian or other special diets if ordered. No smoking.
1 Sitting-room. With open fire, TV, piano.
Large garden

Trompe l'oeil murals, in 'Strawberry Hill gothick' style, cover the walls of the long dining/sitting-room. They were painted in the 1940s by George Oakes, who became a director of the distinguished interior decorating firm of Colefax & Fowler. The tall bay windows of this room open on to a tiled terrace from which there is a fine hill view beyond the old, rambling garden where yellow Welsh poppies grow in profusion. In the long entrance hall are Persian rugs and unusual clocks. Bedrooms are homely; throughout there is a mix of antique and merely old furniture, with more trompe l'oeil alcoves or doors.

Gillian Lamble's style of cooking is traditionally English and she serves such meals as mackerel pâté, roast lamb, lemon meringue pie, and cheeses.

Readers' comments: Mrs Lamble is kindness itself. A house of character. She went out of her way to be helpful. Food excellent. Will definitely return. A lovely house. A favourite. One of the best. Absolute find; food excellent.

V

GATCHELLS

C D X

Angersleigh, Somerset, TA3 7SY Tel: 01823 421580 (Mobile: 07808 164276)
South-west of Taunton. Nearest main road: A38 from Taunton to Wellington (and M5, junction 25).

Somerset

rear view

3 Bedrooms. £21–£27 (less for 5 nights or more). All have own bath/shower/toilet; TV. No smoking.
Dinner (by arrangement). £12–£13.50 for 2–3 courses and coffee, at times to suit guests. Vegetarian or other special diets if ordered. No smoking. **Light suppers** if ordered.
1 Sitting-room. With stove, TV, piano.
Large garden
Closed from end of October to early November.

E-mail: gatchells@somerweb.co.uk

Originally a mediaeval hall-house, built in 1425 on the site of a well by a local yeoman farmer, this stone, flint, thatch and cob cottage is surrounded on all sides by mature gardens and grounds (including orchards and a swimming-pool). Indoors, guests can relax in the olive-green, white and timbered sitting-room, which has a huge inglenook fireplace and pretty tapestry-covered footstools.

Off a landing dominated by a large photo montage of Queen Victoria and her extended family are attractive, thoughtfully decorated bedrooms – one with unusual furniture, another with patchwork quilts in autumnal colours. Bathrooms are equally good. In summer, Mandy Selhurst serves meals in the sunny conservatory looking out towards the Blackdown Hills; while in winter, guests eat in the big pine-furnished kitchen warmed by a blue Aga. A typical evening meal may be home-made watercress soup, a roast, and apple pie with clotted cream. All vegetables and soft fruits are home-grown. Undemanding walks are available directly from the grounds.

Gatchells is well placed for visiting the Quantocks, such grand country mansions as Barrington Court (National Trust) and glorious Hestercombe Gardens.

V

Somerset

HAWTHORNE HOUSE

C(12) **D X**

Bishopswood, Somerset, TA20 3RS Tel/Fax: 01460 234482
West of Ilminster. Nearest main road: A303 from Andover towards Honiton.

3 Bedrooms. £22.50 (less for 3 nights or more). All have own bath/shower/toilet. No smoking.
Dinner (by arrangement). £12.50 for 2 courses and coffee, at 6.30–7.30pm. Vegetarian or other special diets if ordered. No smoking.
1 Sitting-room. With open fire, TV. No smoking.
Large garden

The large window in the guests' sitting-room provides a clue to the building's history: until the 'new' shop was opened in 1924, Victorian Hawthorne House served as the village post office and stores, and when Sarah and Roger Newman-Coburn came here in 1986 they could still make out the marks left by the stock shelves on the interior walls. Today, however, the house has been attractively refurbished throughout: wallpapers and fabrics are exuberantly floral, bath- and shower-rooms immaculate, and the sitting-room is filled with comfortable chairs and sofas in which to browse through the wealth of local literature provided by the Newman-Coburns.

The conservatory/dining-room looks over the sloping, terraced garden, with wildlife pond at its foot, to the Blackdown Hills (an Area of Outstanding Natural Beauty) beyond. By arrangement, Roger – star pupil on his catering course – produces such dinners as pork braised in Somerset cider, and summer pudding or tarte tatin. Local spring water runs in the taps.

V

Readers' comments: Very good food, well presented; delightful surroundings, comfortable rooms; most helpful in every way.

Somerset

HIGHER LANGRIDGE FARM

C D S

Exbridge, Somerset, TA22 9RR Tel/Fax: 01398 323999
South of Dulverton. Nearest main road: A396 from Tiverton towards Dunster.

3 Bedrooms. £22–£25 (less for 3 nights or more). Available: own bath/shower/toilet. No smoking.
Dinner (by arrangement). From £13.75 for 3 courses and coffee, at 6.30–7pm. Vegetarian or other special diets if ordered. No smoking. **Light suppers** if ordered.
1 Sitting-room. With stove, TV, piano. No smoking.
Small garden

E-mail: info@langridgefarm.co.uk

Overlooking fields and rolling mid-Devon hills, this cream-painted 17th-century house is on a 400-acre beef-cattle and sheep farm which the Summers family have worked for six generations. From the long dining/sitting-room, with a wood-burner at one end and an inglenook fireplace at the other, guests may observe red deer while breakfasting on eggs from the farm's own hens, local sausages, English bacon, and, sometimes, Somerset yogurt and honey.

Spacious bedrooms, decorated in pale colours with flowery wallpaper borders, have traditional furnishings (there's a rocking chair in one) and good country views. All around is rural peace and quiet – broken only by the occasional sound of a cockerel crowing nearby. For dinner, Gill offers such meals as home-made vegetable soup, Exmoor roast lamb or fresh trout, and chocolate mousse.

V

Hereabouts, the Devon border weaves in and out and the landscape is dotted with attractive stone villages. At Molland, both the unspoilt church and inn are worth visiting; and at Hawkridge (another interesting church), a traditional craftsman makes walking sticks and candelabras from stags' antlers. Exmoor National Park is just a short drive away.

HIGHER ORCHARD

C PT S

Somerset

30 St George's Street, Dunster, Somerset, TA24 6RS Tel: 01643 821915
South-east of Minehead. Nearest main road: A39 from Bridgwater to Dunster.

3 Bedrooms. £20–£25 (less for 3 nights or more). Available: own bath/shower/toilet; TV; views of sea.
Light suppers if ordered.
1 Sitting-room. With open fire, piano. No smoking.
Small garden

Perched on a rise, with commanding views over the colourwashed cottages of mediaeval Dunster and out towards the sea, Higher Orchard is a tall Victorian house in Gothic style. It was built in 1864 for the daughter of a wealthy Norwich banker. One enters the house via a steep path, on either side of which Jan Lamacraft is creating a most attractive garden (there are seats where guests can relax and appreciate her green-fingered handiwork).

Rooms have restful colour schemes, original Victorian fireplaces, pine furnishings and fresh flowers. On two half-landings, stained-glass windows suffuse the house with a lovely light when the sun is shining.

For breakfast, Jan serves locally produced sausages and bacon, eggs from her own speckled hens and home-grown poached fruit. She can provide packed lunches for walkers and will ferry the car-less from Dunster station. In addition to many tea-rooms, there are at least eight restaurants for evening meals, all within walking distance.

Apart from Dunster itself (with National Trust castle, 15th-century church and octagonal yarn market), there is an excellent network of waymarked footpaths, the nearest being 50 yards from the house.

HIGHER WEST BARN

PT S X

Somerset

Witham Friary, Somerset, BA11 5HH Tel: 01749 850819 (Mobile: 07976 162207)
South of Frome. Nearest main road: A361 from Trowbridge to Shepton Mallet.

3 Bedrooms. £25–£30 (less for 4 nights or more). Available: own bath/shower/toilet; TV. No smoking.
Dinner (by arrangement). From £14.99 for 3 courses and coffee at times to suit guests. Vegetarian or other special diets if ordered. Wine available. No smoking.
Light suppers if ordered.
1 Sitting-room. With TV. No smoking.
Large garden

Parading peacocks and a clutch of ducks and hens roam round a stunning conversion of barns. They were once part of a friary farm, mentioned in Domesday Book, and have been developed by Anne Harrison and her husband, Haydon, a farmer.

Anne, who studied textile and fashion design, is an art teacher with a collector's eye for the stylish and exotic. In the elegant dining-room, lit by table lamps, she serves such evening meals as tomato and basil soup, fresh poached salmon, and tarte tatin. Dotted around are chairs with navy-blue French needlepoint cushions. There is also a French influence in one double bedroom. Here, above the brass and iron bedstead is a border of appliquéd velvet on silk, handstitched by French nuns, and even the curtains are in dark wine French velvet. Anne will turn this secluded upper floor, with sitting-room and bathroom, into a suite for special occasions.

The breakfast menu includes such options as scrambled eggs with smoked salmon. After meals, guests can relax in a large conservatory. Outside, trellises – covered in clematis, roses and jasmine – shelter a barbecue area which visitors are welcome to use.

Somerset

HIGHERCOMBE FARM

C(6) D

Dulverton, Somerset, TA22 9PT Tel/Fax: 01398 323616
North of Dulverton. Nearest main road: A396 from Bampton to Minehead.

3 Bedrooms. £22–£24 (less for 3 nights or more). Available: own bath/toilet; TV; balcony. No smoking.
Dinner (by arrangement). £15 for 3 courses and coffee, at 7pm. Vegetarian or other diets if ordered. No smoking. **Light suppers** if ordered.
1 Sitting-room. With stove, TV. Piano. No smoking.
Small garden
Closed from November to end of February.

E-mail: abigail@highercombe.demon.co.uk

On the very edge of Exmoor, up through a steep, wooded valley leading out of the 'hidden town' of Dulverton, you will find Highercombe set a quarter of a mile back from the road. It is a long, cream-washed modern house – with all its comfort and convenience – yet has the spacious rooms and low ceilings of a traditional farmhouse.

Bedrooms have pretty colour schemes (the best in cream and gold) and are named after fields on the 450-acre farm that Abigail Humphrey's partner Tom Flanagan runs. An artist friend made the delicate stencils on the walls.

The large sitting/dining-room has distant views, right to Dartmoor and the South Devon coast. At separate dark wood tables Abigail serves dinner (by lanternlight) which might comprise broccoli and Stilton soup, a casserole or roast, and one of several delicious puddings. Navy napery matches the carpet and chesterfield, and a big inglenook is surrounded by comfortable armchairs. You may be offered a complimentary farm tour by Land-Rover; and you can walk straight on to the moor where red deer roam freely.

V *Reader's comments:* Most comfortable stay; nothing too much trouble; very friendly.

Somerset

LARCOMBE FOOT

C(8) D S

Winsford, Somerset, TA24 7HS Tel/Fax: 01643 851306
North of Dulverton. Nearest main road: A396 from Dulverton to Dunster.

4 Bedrooms. £20 (less for 7 nights or more). Two have own bath/shower/toilet; views of river (from all).
Dinner (by arrangement). £12.50 for 4 courses and coffee, at 7.30pm. Vegetarian or other special diets if ordered. Wine available. **Light suppers** if ordered.
1 Sitting-room. With open fire, TV.
Large garden
Closed from December to March.

E-mail: larcombefoot@talk21.com

A single-room shepherd's hut built some 400 years ago has grown through the centuries into a long, creeper-clad, white house set in a marvellous position.

It is easy to find. First look for the dovecote, then glance upwards, and there, enjoying a vantage-point on the rooftop, are the birds. Valerie Vicary's visitors can enjoy similar views from both the warm and gracious dining-room and sitting-room. Here, there are open fires to relax by or sunlit window-seats where guests may look out for deer on the bracken-covered hill, which rises steeply above the River Exe.

Throughout the house is an interesting collection of pictures and porcelain, much of which was collected by Valerie during her postings as an army wife. Bedrooms are simply furnished. One, which is particularly attractive, has William Morris fabrics. Bathrooms are only shared if the bedrooms are occupied by parties travelling together.

Dinner is served round a large and highly polished table. The menu might include crab vol-au-vent, chicken and mushroom casserole, and a military pudding of ginger snaps, cream and sherry. Packed lunches are also available. V

MANOR FARM **C M P T S X**

Wayford, Somerset, TA18 8QL Tel/Fax: 01460 78865 (Mobile: 04676 20031)
South-west of Crewkerne. Nearest main road: A30 from Crewkerne to Chard.

3 Bedrooms. £22–£25. Available: own bath/shower/toilet; TV. No smoking.
1 Sitting-room. With open stove, TV, organ. No smoking.
Large garden

This imposing Victorian manor house commands views over the Axe Valley to the hills beyond. Ponds stocked with fish for anglers feed into the river below and here the elusive kingfisher can be sighted. For walkers, the Liberty Trail, once trodden by supporters of the Duke of Monmouth, passes through the bottom of Austin and Theresa Emery's garden. The Emerys, who used to run their own pub/restaurant, serve breakfast either in a spacious room which is filled with sunlight or outside on the terrace – both have sweeping rural views.

The bedrooms, sprigged and flowery, are wonderfully peaceful and guests can gaze down upon the Emerys' herd of Highland cattle.

Sightseers have a choice of gardens (such as those at Forde Abbey and Tintinhull), Cricket St Thomas wildlife park (used for the TV series 'To The Manor Born') or the natural attractions of the Dorset coast, much of it owned by the National Trust. There are lovely walks in the surrounding countryside, while towns such as Crewkerne, Lyme Regis and Honiton provide happy hunting-grounds for collectors of antiques or crafts.

Somerset

MARSH BRIDGE COTTAGE **C D X**

Dulverton, Somerset, TA22 9QG Tel: 01398 323197
West of Dulverton. Nearest main road: A396 from Tiverton towards Dunster.

3 Bedrooms. £17–£21 (less for 7 nights or more). All have own bath/shower/toilet; TV; views of river. No smoking.
Dinner (by arrangement). £13 for 4 courses and coffee, at 7pm. Vegetarian or other special diets if ordered. No smoking. **Light suppers** if ordered.
1 Sitting-room. With open fire, TV. Piano.
Small garden

Following the River Barle out of Dulverton and across a white stone and iron bridge, one comes to this small cottage on the edge of a woodland walkway to Tarr Steps (one of Exmoor's most popular beauty-spots). Built in the 1860s as a gamekeeper's cottage for the local big estate, it has gradually been attractively extended by Carole and Jon Nurcombe.

Bedrooms are fresh and prettily decorated, with very good bathrooms and lovely river views. In the compact dining-room, Carole serves such home-cooked meals as roasted red pepper and tomato soup, baked gammon, lemon meringue pie, and cheese to finish.

A sloping back garden is planted with mauve, mulberry and white heather, while the front lawn (where cream teas are served in summer) runs down to the river's edge. Fishing is available; riding and clay-pigeon shooting can be arranged. Visitors are welcome to leave their cars here while exploring the surrounding countryside – drying facilities and packed lunches for walkers are provided on request.

Readers' comments: Setting is idyllic; spotlessly clean and beautifully furnished; food is excellent; nothing too much trouble. Cannot praise highly enough; wonderful b & b, glorious countryside. A wonderful holiday, cannot wait to go back.

Somerset

MELON COTTAGE VINEYARD

C D S X

Charlton, Radstock, Somerset, BA3 5TN Tel: 01761 435090

South-west of Bath. Nearest main road: A367 from Radstock to Shepton Mallet.

2 Bedrooms. £17–£22. One has own shower/toilet.
Light suppers if ordered. No smoking.
Large garden

Nestling in the Somerset hills, midway between Wells and Bath, is Melon Cottage Vineyard from the 200 vines of which come about a thousand bottles of dry white wine each year (go in October to see the harvest, and in spring for the bottling). It is known that the Romans, too, had vineyards in the area. Virginia and Hugh Pountney's cottage has 39-inch stone walls, parts dating from mediaeval times. There are small stone-mullioned windows; one large bedroom is under the exposed rafters of the roof. Guests may relax in the garden (with ancient well) in fine weather. (The Somerset Wagon in Chilcompton serves excellent meals.)

Somerset is a county of great beauty, its landscape punctuated by impressive church towers from the resplendent Perpendicular period of mediaeval architecture, big stone barns and little stone villages. Geology is what accounts for its great variety, with buildings made up of stone that ranges from lilac to gold (for every quarry is different), and a landscape of hills and levels contrasting with one another. Nearby Downside Abbey is worth a visit for its tranquillity; and for the golfer, there are four good courses within a 10-mile radius.

Readers' comments: Very comfortable. Excellent hospitality. Made very welcome.

Bath & North-East Somerset

OLD BOATHOUSE

C PT

Bath Boating Station, Forester Road, Bath, Bath & North-East Somerset, BA2 6QE

Tel: 01225 466407

Nearest main road: A36 from Bath to Warminster.

4 Bedrooms. £24–£30 (less for 3 nights or more). Available: own bath/shower/toilet; TV; views of river; balcony. No smoking.
1 Sitting-room. With open fire, TV, piano. No smoking.
Large garden

The Old Boat House is a rare survival: an unspoilt Victorian boating-station with distinctive black-and-white verandah overlooking a quiet, willow-fringed reach of the River Avon, and with an open-topped launch available in season to take you (free) into the centre of Bath – unless you prefer to punt or row yourself. Four generations of Hardicks have built, repaired and hired out wooden skiffs and other craft here: you can still see these being clinker-built in the traditional way.

Bedrooms are simply furnished. Some face the rambling garden and trees; the best has windows on two sides and a verandah overlooking riverbank and geese (as does the sitting-room). A small cottage in the garden has two tiny bedrooms and its own spacious sitting-room. Separate from the house is a riverside restaurant, also with verandah.

Bath itself deserves at least a week-long stay and the surrounding countryside is full of interest. In the city centre there is much to see: the abbey, Roman temple and baths, the botanical gardens, the shopping arcades, several worthwhile museums and art galleries. On Saturdays there's a flea market with good bargains.

V

PARE MILL

CDS

Somerset

Hagley Bridge, Waterrow, Somerset, TA4 2AS Tel: 01984 623865
North-west of Wellington. Nearest main road: B3227 from Taunton to Bampton (and M5, junction 26).

3 Bedrooms. £18 (less for 7 nights or more). Bargain breaks. All have views of river. No smoking.
Light suppers if ordered. Vegetarian or other special diets if ordered. No smoking.
1 Sitting-room. With stove,TV. No smoking.
Garden

E-mail: r.sargent@bintemet.com

In a peaceful valley, down winding, high-hedged lanes flecked with primroses in spring, you eventually arrive at this secluded, trim white cottage on the banks of the River Tone (fishing available). Here, Hazel Sargent (a retired secondary school teacher) gives guests a warm welcome in her immaculate and tastefully furnished home – children, in particular, are happily catered for.

Breakfast, served in the attractive dining-room where there is a mix of old and modern pine, may include a herby omelette, kedgeree or home-made fishcakes. Bread is home-baked; honey comes from the Sargents' own bees. Upstairs, off a long corridor hung with original Posy Simmonds cartoons, are pretty bedrooms in creams and white which look out over the river and garden, where visitors can picnic in summer under the watchful eye of a flock of Jacob sheep.

Guests dine at the Rock Inn, Waterrow, or at the Globe, Appley (both a drive away). In the vicinity are some of the area's finest houses and gardens – Gaulden Manor, Hestercombe, Knightshayes Court (NT) and Cothay Manor, for example.

Readers' comments: Excellent hospitality; lovely old house. Idyllic setting.

PICKFORD HOUSE

CMPTSX

Somerset

Bath Road, Beckington, Somerset, BA11 6SJ Tel/Fax: 01373 830329
South of Bath. Nearest main road: A36 from Bath to Warminster.

4 Bedrooms. £17–£20 (less for 4 nights or more). Available: own bath/shower/toilet; TV; views of river; balcony. No smoking.
Dinner (by arrangement). £15 for 3 courses and coffee, from 7pm. Vegetarian or other special diets if ordered. Wine available. No smoking. **Light suppers** if ordered.
1 Sitting-room. With open fire, TV, piano. **Bar.**
Large garden

E-mail: AmPritchar@aol.com

Sometimes parties of friends take the whole of this hilltop house for a gourmet weekend together – for Angela Pritchard is a cordon bleu cook. On such weekends, the guests are invited to choose their menu for a candlelit dinner of six courses with appropriate wines. Traditional Sunday lunches too.

Even on everyday occasions Pickford House food is exceptional. Angela offers a three-course dinner that might include: mushrooms in Dijon sauce in a filo basket, lamb with leeks and ginger, and a sweet with mulberries from the garden.

The house is one of a pair that were built from honey-coloured Bath stone in 1804. The furnishings are comfortable, with three modern bedrooms in the old school house (one with kitchen adjoining).

Readers' comments: Excellent: accommodation and dinner beyond praise. Welcome relaxed, warm and personal. Great care to make us comfortable. First class. Excellent; remarkable value, especially the evening meal. B & b at its best. Sheer delight; meals superb.

V

Somerset

RIVERSIDE GRANGE

C(10)

Tanyard Lane, North Wootton, Somerset, BA4 4AE Tel: 01749 890761
South-east of Wells. Nearest main road: A39 from Wells to Glastonbury.

2 Bedrooms. £22–£22.50 (less for 7 nights or more). Available: own bath/shower/toilet; TV; views of river. No smoking.
Large garden
Closed from mid-December to early January.

A hidden haven awaits visitors at the end of Tanyard Lane. There, an old tannery dating from 1852, which supplied leather to Clarks for gloves, has been transformed into a spacious house with large windows and tranquil views. The home of Pat English and her husband Colin, a naval commander, it is filled with furniture, paintings and china bought in Hong Kong during a posting there. The Chinese rose colours and the Ming blue are carried through to carpets, curtains and the elaborate bedlinen. Framed in the window of the breakfast-room is an adjoining cider orchard, twice winner of an award for the best Somerset orchard. The only sound at night is the soft rippling of the stream which snakes below the walls of the house. Guests dine at the local pub, a two-minute walk.

Both Wells (with its 13th-century cathedral, bishop's palace and Europe's oldest mediaeval street) and Glastonbury are just a short drive away. Riverside Grange is also popular with shoppers looking for a bargain: Clarks Village, in nearby Street, has over 40 outlets selling clothes and other goods at factory prices.

V

Somerset

SELWORTHY FARM

C(12) **PT S**

Selworthy, Somerset, TA24 8TL Tel: 01643 862577
West of Minehead. Nearest main road: A39 from Minehead to Porlock.

2 Bedrooms. From £20. Available: own bath/shower/toilet; TV. No smoking.
1 Sitting-room. With log-burner, TV. No smoking.
Large garden
Closed from November to February.

The road into this small hamlet rises to the white-painted church at the top of the hill, and from here there are quite magnificent views across Porlock Vale and up the heather-covered slopes to Dunkery Beacon. Picturesque Selworthy is a noted beauty-spot, where the thatched cottages, built in 1828 for retired workers from the Holnicote estate, are now owned by the National Trust.

Also on National Trust land, at the edge of this hamlet, is the home of Graham and Hazel Leeves, who run a 200-acre sheep, cattle and horse farm. It is easy to see horses are their first love, as the attractive rooms of their farmhouse are filled with pictures, paintings and sculptures of the racehorses they breed to run in point-to-points.

Along with much use of pine, burnished copper and brass ornaments have been displayed against a restful colour scheme of predominantly cream, beige and soft greens. Similar colours are used in the comfortable bedrooms where Hazel, an attentive hostess, has provided electric blankets.

For dinner there is a restaurant close by, or Porlock (10 minutes' drive) has a wide choice of eating-places.

V

SHORES FARM HOUSE

C S

Frogs Street, Lopen, Somerset, TA13 5JR Tel: 01460 240587
(Mobile: 07788 186616)
West of Yeovil. Nearest main road: A303 from Andover towards Honiton.

Somerset

3 Bedrooms. £22–£23 (less for 3 nights or more). All have own bath/shower/toilet; TV. No smoking.
Dinner (by arrangement). From £10 for 2–3 courses and coffee, at 7–8pm. Vegetarian or other special diets if ordered. No smoking. **Light suppers** if ordered.
1 Sitting-room. With stove. No smoking.
Walled garden

E-mail: arouston@compuserve.com

In the middle of the conservation village of Lopen (where, it is said, a young rector of Limington was put in the stocks for disorderly conduct after imbibing too freely at the Lopen feast; he later rose to become a cardinal and Chancellor of England, Thomas Wolsey by name) stands this thatched former farmhouse. Built in the 17th century of local Ham stone, it is now the home of Sue and Alastair Rouston. Cosy bedrooms have beamed bathrooms and board-and-latch doors; three people travelling together might share a self-contained suite comprising twin room, shower-room and a very pretty white-painted single with honeysuckle borders. A fine stone-mullioned window admits light over the staircase; downstairs, blue leather sofa and chairs cluster round the inglenook in the sitting-room, and the dining-room boasts an unusual carved wooden panel above the handsome fireplace. Here Sue serves such dinners as home-made soup, steak-and-kidney pie, and lemon meringue.

The area is awash with famous gardens like East Lambrook (designed by Margery Fish) and the National Trust properties at Barrington Court and Tintinhull; fine houses too.

V

TOWN MILLS

C PT X

Dulverton, Somerset, TA22 9HB Tel: 01398 323124
Nearest main road: A396 from Tiverton towards Dunster.

Somerset

5 Bedrooms. £20–£27 (less for 7 nights or more). Available: own shower/toilet. TV.
Small garden

Bed-and-breakfast with a difference awaits one at this substantial Georgian-style house, tucked away behind Dulverton's high street. A mill and house have been recorded on this site since 1540 (Dulverton once boasted four mills) and the mill-leat still runs alongside the front courtyard. Inside, behind large sash windows are spacious bedsitting-rooms, each individually decorated, furnished and equipped to a very high standard. One pristine white and pale green room on the ground floor has its own separate lounge area; two upstairs have their own log fires.

A full English breakfast and a warmed loaf of bread are brought to your room by Jane Buckingham, who checks guests' preferences the night before. In each room there are comfortable armchairs or a sofa, TV, breakfast-table (with cereal packets), toaster and tea/coffee-making facilities. Complete privacy and peace are ensured.

For other meals, a good French/English restaurant, two tea-rooms serving cream teas and hearty pub food are all just minutes' walk away. Dulverton is an ideal base for exploring Exmoor and a whole range of country pursuits (walking, riding, fishing and shooting) are locally available.

V

Bath & North-East Somerset

WENTWORTH HOUSE

C(5) **M PT**

106 Bloomfield Road, Bath, Bath & North-East Somerset, BA2 2AP
Tel: 01225 339193 (Fax: 01225 310460)
Nearest main road: A367 from Bath to Shepton Mallet.

18 Bedrooms. £25–£50 **(but to readers who show the current edition of this book on arrival, 5% less for 2 nights, 10% less for 3 nights).** Bargain breaks. Available: own shower/toilet; TV.
Dinner. £10–£13 for 2–3 courses and coffee, at 6–7.30pm. Vegetarian or other special diets if ordered. Wine available. **Light suppers** if ordered.
Bar
Small garden

E-mail: stay@wentworthhouse.co.uk

The big, four-storey house was built for a coal merchant over a century ago. It is a fine building of creamy stone, furnished and equipped to very good standards by Theresa Boyle. The dining-room has a glass extension overlooking the swimming-pool (heated). Some of the nicest rooms are below this: they not only open on to the garden but in some cases are suites, each consisting of a small sun-room with armchairs and glass walls beyond the bedroom. Top-floor rooms have the finest views over the city; four first-floor bedrooms have four-posters.

The dinner menu (with choices) includes such dishes as scallop and crab roulade, chicken with apricots in mushroom, bacon and brandy sauce, and sticky-toffee pudding or assorted local ice creams. With breakfast cereals come bowls of various seeds and fresh fruit salad; home-made banana bread and flapjacks too. There is an ample carpark, and a bus stops just outside, saving you the steep walk up from the city after a day's sightseeing.

V *Readers' comments:* Very comfortable. Beautifully appointed. The room was lovely.

Somerset

WHITTLES FARM

C(12)

Beercrocombe, Somerset, TA3 6AH Tel/Fax: 01823 480301 (Mobile: 0780 3919337)
South-east of Taunton. Nearest main road: A358 from Ilminster to Taunton (and M5, junction 25).

3 Bedrooms. £25–£27 (less for 3 nights or more). All have own bath/shower/toilet; TV. No smoking.
Dinner (by arrangement). £15 for 4 courses and coffee, at 6.30pm. Wine available. No smoking.
2 Sitting-rooms. With open fire. No smoking in one. Bar.
Large garden
Closed from December to mid-February.

E-mail: dj.cm.mitchem@themail.co.uk

The excellence of the accommodation and Claire Mitchem's delightful personality make for an exceptional farmhouse holiday at Whittles Farm. At the end of a lane leading nowhere, part of the house dates back to the 16th century (hence the beams and inglenook of the sitting-room). Every bedroom is attractively decorated.

A typical dinner menu may include: boeuf bourguignonne accompanied by four vegetables and a salad; queen of puddings with clotted cream; fresh fruit.

There are excellent woodland walks, and drives along lanes which vary at every turn. Within easy reach are the National Trust's Barrington Court and the gardens at Hestercombe House; the coasts both north and south; and the county town of Taunton: the Vivary gardens here are well worth a visit, and also the castle (with exceptionally good museum).

Readers' comments: We liked it very much. Cannot speak too highly of the care and attention. Immaculate working farm, charming hostess, very comfortable room, delicious breakfast. This was a delight, rather like a luxurious hotel. Excellent meal.

V

WIGBOROUGH FARM

C S

Wigborough, Somerset, TA13 5LP Tel/Fax: 01460 240490
West of Yeovil. Nearest main road: A303 from Ilminster to Wincanton.

3 Bedrooms. £23–£25. Bargain breaks. Available: own bath/toilet. No smoking.
Light suppers if ordered. Vegetarian or other special diets if ordered. Wine available. No smoking.
1 Sitting-room. With open fire, TV, piano. No smoking.
Large garden
Closed from mid-December to March.

But for a fire in 1585, this mansion would doubtless have been one of England's oldest. Only one wing was rebuilt: even so, it remains among the most impressive of the houses in this book.

Outside are pinnacled gables, carved Tudor roses, handsome dripstones above mullioned windows – all in tawny Ham limestone. Inside are ogee arches, stone floors and iron-studded doors; there are still spit-racks above one of the huge fireplaces. One ground-floor room has a minstrels' gallery (now a bedroom) overlooking the great refectory table and its leather chairs.

Guests' bedrooms (varying in size and style) are on the second floor: the most outstanding has oak walls, its panels decoratively carved with arches and pilasters, and a four-poster bed.

From many windows are views of lawns with specimen trees, old stables and the walled vegetable garden. (Joan Vaux provides light suppers only.)

Readers' comments: As if out of a dream! Very loath to leave this most beautiful place and the relaxed generosity and the warmth of these charming people. A truly magnificent building in a most peaceful setting. Delicious food and excellent company.

WOOD ADVENT FARM

C(10) **S X**

Roadwater, Somerset, TA23 0RR Tel/Fax: 01984 640920
East of Minehead. Nearest main road: A39 from Bridgwater to Minehead.

5 Bedrooms. £22.50–£25.50 (less for 3 nights or more). Bargain breaks. Available: own bath/shower/toilet; TV. No smoking.
Dinner (by arrangement). £15 for 4 courses and coffee, at 7.30pm. Vegetarian or other special diets if ordered. Wine available. No smoking. **Light suppers** if ordered.
2 Sitting-rooms. With open fires, TV (in one), piano (in one). No smoking (in one).
Large garden
E-mail: info@woodadventfarm.co.uk

Everything about this imposing house and its surroundings speaks of solid continuity. The Brewer family have farmed the land since the 1700s and the farmhouse, the home of John and Diana Brewer, was built in the early 1800s. Rooms here are grand and beautifully furnished with family heirlooms. The drawing-room, where a deep pink carpet matches the pink flowers in the curtains, has been set aside for reading and writing. A second sitting-room is used by guests wanting to play board games or plan a day's outing.

Bedrooms are stunning. One in soft creams and greens has Queen Anne beds. Another, with mahogany beds, has its own little sitting-room-cum-dressing-room. All are supplied with bathrobes and carafes of Wood Advent mineral water, which is recommended by whisky drinkers!

The original farmhouse kitchen is now the dining-room (decorated in bold blues and yellows). Dinner might comprise fresh smoked mackerel pâté, tenderloin of Somerset pork in cream and cider, and hazelnut meringue roulade. Sunday lunch is also available.

In the grounds are a tennis court, heated swimming-pool and facilities for clay-pigeon shooting.

WOOD LANE HOUSE

C PT S

Butleigh, Somerset, BA6 8TG Tel: 01458 850354
South of Glastonbury. Nearest main road: A361 from Shepton Mallet to Glastonbury.

3 Bedrooms. £21–£25 (less for 7 nights or more). All have own shower/toilet; TV. No smoking.
Small garden
Closed from late December to early January.

This cosy, relaxed home has been converted from the former stables of a dower house, where Michael and Jane Gillam used to live. One cottage-style bedroom, nestling under the sloping eaves, has patchwork quilts and views of the orchard where sheep graze. A downstairs bedroom, in which the pinks, greens and cream of the curtains are offset by ecru covers, is furnished with small chairs, prettily upholstered by Jane. Pot-plants, books and pictures add further character to the bedrooms, while in the shower-rooms Jane has thoughtfully supplied such things as toothpaste, talcum powder and shower-gels.

The breakfast-room, where guests sit round a mahogany table, is also equipped with sofa and armchairs as it doubles as a sitting-room.

Outside, the walls of the house are festooned with jasmine and roses. Pathways wind beneath flower-covered arches, and seats are positioned in sun-trapping spots. Guests can dine at a pub which is a two-minute walk away.

Glastonbury's abbey stands on the site which is believed to be the birthplace of Christianity in England. Within easy reach are Cheddar Gorge and Wells Cathedral.

For a list of SOTBT houses that are in or close to the great National Parks of England and Wales, see p.ix.

Readers' comments quoted in the book are from letters sent directly to us: they are not supplied via the proprietors.

Major tourist attractions, such as Stratford-upon-Avon, Bath and Cambridge, can often be easily reached from houses in adjacent counties.

Some proprietors stipulate a minimum stay of two nights at weekends or peak seasons; or they will accept one-nighters only at short notice (that is, only if no lengthier booking has yet been made).

STAFFORDSHIRE

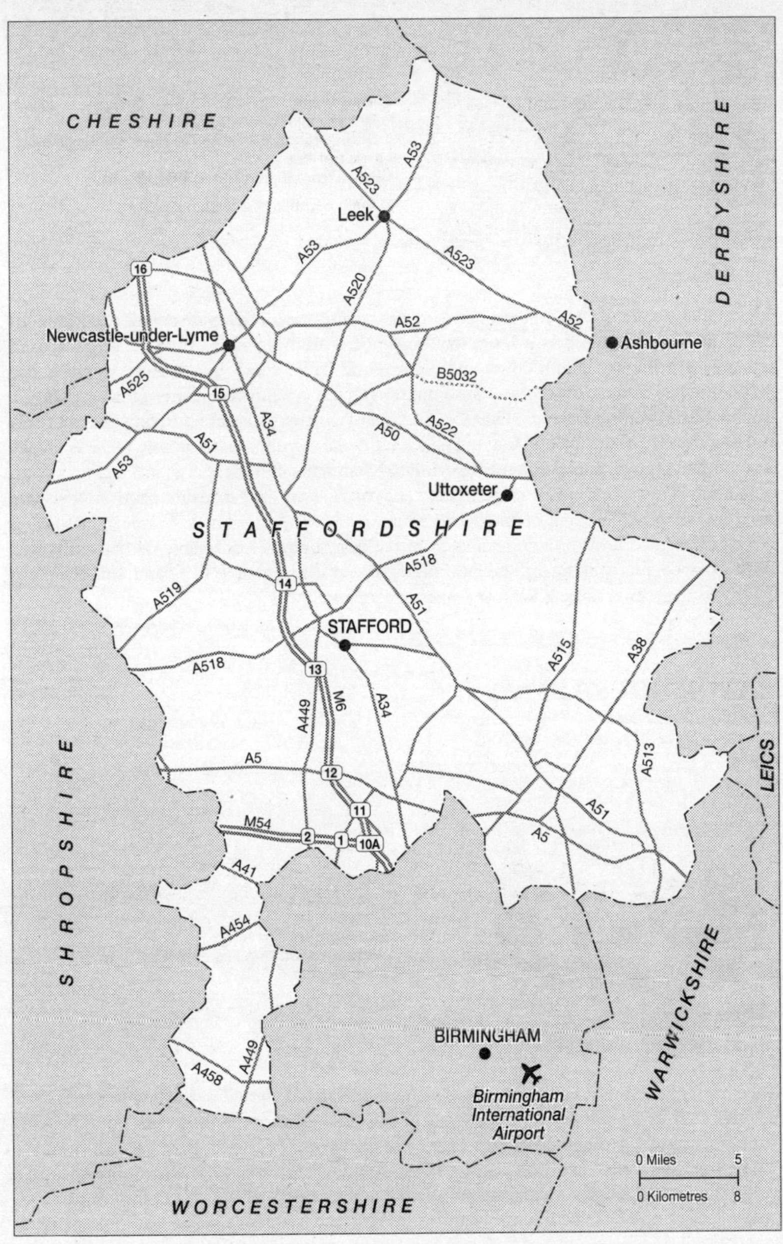

Prices are per person sharing a room at the beginning of the year.

Staffordshire

BEECHENHILL FARM

C

Ilam Moor Lane, Ilam, Staffordshire, DE6 2BD Tel/Fax: 01335 310274
North-west of Ashbourne. Nearest main road: A515 from Ashbourne to Buxton.

2 Bedrooms. £25–£30 (less for 2 nights or more). Both have own shower/toilet. No smoking.
1 Sitting-room. With open fire/stove, TV. No smoking.
Large garden
Closed from November to mid-March.

E-mail: beechenhill@btinternet.com

Perched on a south-facing hillside between the beauty-spots of Dovedale and the Manifold Valley, Beechenhill Farm is a long, low house built from limestone two centuries ago. It overlooks grazing sheep and cows, and picturesque Ilam village. Sue Prince, an artist, has decorated the rooms with style and imagination and there is much evidence of her handicraft around – from embroideries to stained glass. One of the two pleasant bedrooms is a light and spacious family room, with a draped bed. Traditional farmhouse breakfasts include home-made organic yogurt and Beechenhill porridge. No dinners, but there are local inns.

Author William Horwood stayed here; and you'll find the farm described as 'the best place in the world' by one of the moles in his *Duncton Quest*. There's a pretty garden, a specially designed farm trail and walks from the front door. This organic dairy-farm is also ideally placed for walking in the beautiful park of Ilam Hall (NT), and for exploring Dovedale – a scenic route known as Little Switzerland.

V

Staffordshire

MANOR HOUSE FARM

C S

Prestwood, Denstone, Staffordshire, ST14 5DD Tel: 01889 590415 and 01335 343669 (Fax: 01335 342198)
North of Uttoxeter. Nearest main road: B5032 from Cheadle to Ashbourne.

3 Bedrooms. £22–£26 (less for 3 nights or more). Bargain breaks. Available: own bath/shower/toilet; TV. No smoking.
Light suppers if ordered.
1 Sitting-room. With open fire, TV.
Large garden

E-mail: cm_ball@yahoo.co.uk

Once his family farmed here, but now Christopher Ball has turned to dealing in antiques; a fact reflected in the handsome furnishings of the 17th-century house. It was built of sandstone from nearby Hollington quarry.

High-backed settles flank the log fire in the sitting-room, which has stone-mullioned bay windows in its thick walls – with fine hill views. On the oak-panelled walls of the dining-room hang oil paintings. The bedrooms (with beams and exposed stone walls) have four-posters. The latest to be acquired by the Balls is a fine antique example with its original drapes.

The terraced garden is particularly attractive: weeping ash, pinnacled summer-house (it was once the cupola on a hospital roof), steps ascending between clipped yews, a tennis court and croquet lawn. You can barbecue your own meat if you wish.

Reader's comment: Excellent.

Staffordshire

OLD HALL

C D

Poolside, Madeley, Staffordshire, CW3 9DX Tel/Fax: 01782 750209
West of Newcastle-under-Lyme. On A525 from Newcastle-under-Lyme to Whitchurch (and near M6, junction 15).

3 Bedrooms. £25–£30. Bargain breaks. One has own shower/toilet; TV (in all). No smoking.
Dinner (by arrangement). £15 for 3 courses and coffee, at 7pm. Vegetarian or other special diets if ordered. No smoking. **Light suppers** if ordered.
1 Sitting-room. With woodstove, TV, piano. No smoking.
Large garden

Cheshire is famous for its black-and-white houses, and this – though just over the county boundary – is a good example, with its beams and gables. In the sitting-room there is a grand piano by the woodstove, and sometimes music-stands as well, for Mary Hugh is a professional viola player. Through oak-boarded doors is the dining-room, where guests are served with, for example, watercress soup or cheese soufflé, beef sirloin in mushroom and pepper sauce, and chocolate roulade – cooked by Ann O'Leary, a professional caterer.

Bedrooms have low beams, antiques and handsome brass door-fittings. The tiled bathroom with its huge bath is almost unchanged since the 1920s, when it was one of the first illustrated in *Ideal Home*.

Off the breakfast-room is a high-Victorian conservatory. In the two-acre garden, with pond and pergola, are croquet and tennis lawns.

Readers' comments: Very good. Wonderful house. Serene atmosphere. First-class food.

Staffordshire

PORCH FARMHOUSE

C(12) **D PT S**

Grindon, Staffordshire, ST13 7TP Tel/Fax: 01538 304545
South-east of Leek. Nearest main road: A523 from Leek towards Ashbourne.

3 Bedrooms. £25 (less for 7 nights). Bargain breaks. Available: own bath/shower/toilet; TV. No smoking.
Dinner (by arrangement). £15 for 3 courses and coffee, at 7pm. Vegetarian or other special diets if ordered. No smoking. **Light suppers** if ordered.
1 Sitting-room. No smoking.
Garden

Grindon lies 1000 feet high, above the Peak District's lovely Manifold Valley. Sally Hulme and her husband Ron came upon the village on a walking tour and moved to this large 500-year-old limestone cottage some 17 years ago.

The beamed cottage is comfortable and smartly furnished. Meals are taken in the dining-room hung with Victorian 'lace' plates, and a lovely old oak dresser displays a collection of glass and silver. A typical menu: cream of mushroom and garlic soup; salmon in spring onion and ginger sauce; and brandied chocolate and mint mousse. Traditional breakfasts are complemented by a good choice of fresh and dried fruits.

Bedrooms, all excellently equipped, are decorated with Liberty chintzes and oriental prints.

Despite the village's isolated position, it lies only three miles from a National Express bus stop (with phone box nearby), and the Hulmes are able to collect visitors from there.

Readers' comments: Very welcoming. Perfect meals; very comfortable. First-class accommodation, cooking excellent. Wonderful – can't speak too highly. Entertained most royally. Lovely home, friendly personality. Cannot fault it.

STANSHOPE HALL

C S

Stanshope, Staffordshire, DE6 2AD Tel: 01335 310278 (Fax: 01335 310470)
North-west of Ashbourne. Nearest main road: A515 from Ashbourne to Buxton.

3 Bedrooms. £25–£38 (less for 3 nights or more). Available: own bath/toilet; TV. No smoking.
Dinner (by arrangement). £20 for 3 courses and coffee, at 7.30pm. Vegetarian or other special diets if ordered. Wine available. No smoking. **Light suppers** if ordered (when dinner not available).
1 Sitting-room. With open fire, piano.
Large garden

E-mail: naomi@stanshope.demon.co.uk

Built in 1670 by Cromwell's quartermaster, Jackson, the Hall has seen many changes. It was greatly extended in the 1780s and when, at nearby Ilam, a great mansion burnt down in the 19th century, salvaged fireplaces were re-installed here. Later a theatrical designer made it his home, embellishing it with all sorts of trompe l'oeil effects. The murals with peacocks and trees in the sitting-room are in the manner of Rex Whistler, while in the entrance hall a stairway and arches of Hopton stone contrast with painted marbling.

Recently, local artists have repainted bedrooms with decorative murals (bathrooms too).

Not only the ambience but also the food provided by Naomi Chambers and Nick Lourie is out of the ordinary. A typical dinner menu: carrot-and-ginger soup, followed by lamb in red wine and honey, then either gooseberry ice cream or Bakewell tart.

V *Readers' comments:* A real home from home. Food excellent. Very relaxing and enjoyable break. Warm and comfortable with excellent views. Faultless; food exceptionally good. Charmed with the history and decor.

Houses which accept the discount vouchers on page ii are marked with a V symbol next to the relevant entries.

Many houses in this book are situated in or very near to Areas of Outstanding Natural Beauty and protected Heritage Coasts. For a selection of these houses, see p.xi.

COMPLAINTS: If anything was not of reasonable standard (e.g. chilly bedroom or badly cooked food) you are entitled to claim a reduction on your bill, but *only if* you had previously told the proprietor and given him or her a chance to put matters right. In a court case involving a restaurant meal, it was ruled that, because a customer had not made a specific complaint at the time, he had no right subsequently to withhold payment (he had cancelled his cheque). The moral is obvious: if dissatisfied, you are expected to say so at once and not later. Houses are regularly inspected; and complaints will be forwarded to proprietors for their comments. Write to: Jan Bowmer (SOTBT), c/o Arrow Books, 20 Vauxhall Bridge Road, London SW1V 2SA. Please enclose a stamped addressed envelope if you want her to acknowledge receipt of your complaint.

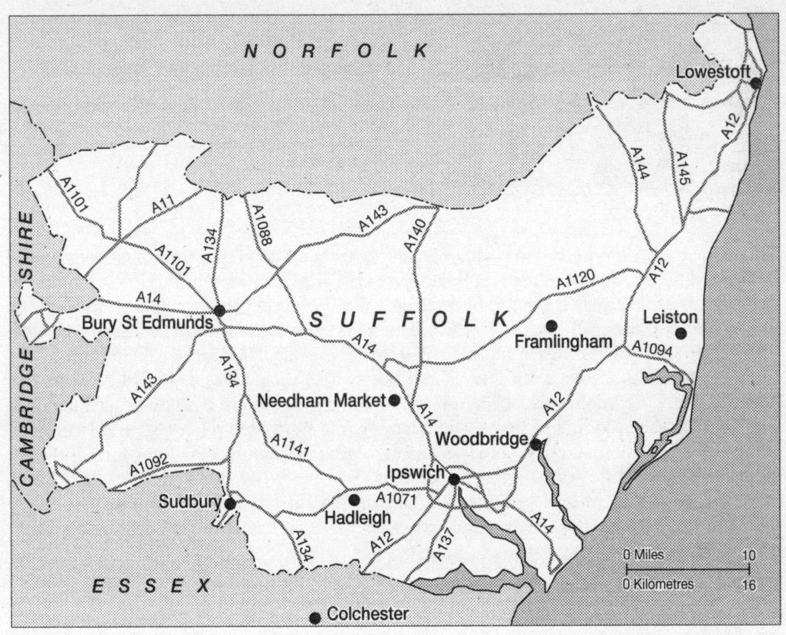

HELPING OXFAM

In the eastern part of Suffolk, 30 bed-and-breakfast houses are in a scheme under which one-third of whatever you pay is given to Oxfam. Between them over £200,000 has been raised. The scheme was originated by Rosemary Schlee, at whose own very lovely home – with equally lovely garden – visitors are also welcomed. Charges vary from £16–£20 per person (according to the facilities and location of each house); and all have been inspected. From Easter to October, on Friday and Saturday nights, expect to pay £2–£4 more per person. On departure, every visitor is given an official receipt for the one-third that goes to Oxfam. Phone Mrs Schlee: 01394 382740 for full details.

THE ALDERS

C D S X

Potters Street, Theberton, Suffolk, IP16 4RL Tel: 01728 831790
North of Leiston. Nearest main road: A12 from Woodbridge to Kessingland.

3 Bedrooms. £18–£19 (less for 2 nights or more). No smoking.
Light suppers if ordered. Vegetarian or other special diets if ordered. No smoking.
1 Sitting-room. With open fire, TV. No smoking.
Large garden

This old cottage, pink-washed in traditional Suffolk style, is a good base for exploring the nearby Heritage Coast, as well as the RSPB nature reserve at Minsmere, which is just a short walk away. The reserve arranges tutored birdwatching throughout the year, including introductory courses for the interested but uninformed. The more experienced watcher might opt for the 'Dawn Chorus and Breakfast' at sunrise in May or the evening 'Nightjar Watch' in June.

Janet Baxter is a keen animal lover and has two of each: cats, dogs and semi-retired horses. Guests' bedrooms are plainly furnished and the bathroom is shared, but there is a washbasin in each room. The homely and comfortable sitting-room (shared with Janet) has plenty of local information to browse through, after a hearty breakfast which includes home-made jams and eggs from Janet's chickens.

As an alternative to birdwatching or a walk in the surrounding woodlands, you might visit one of Suffolk's numerous small vineyards. The one at Bruisyard also has a large ornamental herb garden with plants and grapevines for sale.

Reader's comments: Comfortable rooms, complete peace and quiet.

BOUNDARY FARM

C X

Framlingham, Suffolk, IP13 9NU Tel: 01728 723401 (Fax: 01728 723877)
North of Woodbridge. Nearest main road: A1120 from Stowmarket to Yoxford.

3 Bedrooms. £20–£25 (less for 4 nights or more). Bargain breaks. Available: own bath/shower/toilet; TV. No smoking.
Light suppers if ordered.
1 Sitting-room. With TV. Piano. No smoking.
Large garden

Farmland still surrounds this 17th-century house, but Katherine and Gerry Cook do not work the land and the only animals about are of the domestic variety: a few chickens providing breakfast eggs, carp in the pond and Holly the Bernese mountain dog to woof a welcome.

Katherine used to be a florist and still makes attractive displays for the house. Examples of her other skills in crochet and watercolour-painting are also dotted around. There is a neat sitting/dining-room furnished in cottage style, where Katherine offers guests tea and cake on arrival. The best bedroom, decorated in shades of pink with a rose-sprig-patterned blue carpet, has a handsomely carved antique bedstead and an en suite bathroom in maroon and white.

For evening meals, guests go to the Queen's Head at Dennington. The village church here is worth visiting for its exceptionally rich and varied furnishings. Framlingham itself has an historic 12th-century castle from which Mary Tudor set out to claim the throne.

V

Readers' comments: Enjoyed the large English breakfast. Really impressed by the hospitality. The room was one of the best we have had; Mrs Cook made us very welcome.

EDGE HALL HOTEL

C D PT

Suffolk

2 High Street, Hadleigh, Suffolk, IP7 5AP Tel: 01473 822458 (Fax: 01473 827751)
West of Ipswich. Nearest main road: A1071 from Ipswich towards Sudbury.

8 Bedrooms. £25–£40 (less for 3 nights or more). Bargain breaks. All have own bath/shower/toilet; TV. No smoking (some).
Dinner. £21 for 3 courses and coffee, at 7pm. Vegetarian or other special diets if ordered. Wine available. No smoking. **Light suppers** if ordered.
1 Sitting-room. With open fire, piano.
Large garden

Hadleigh, once a rich wool town, went through bad times but is now prospering again. One of the High Street's many fine historic buildings to have been rejuvenated is a Tudor house with Georgian façade which is now this private hotel. The well-proportioned rooms have been furnished with style, and attractive wallpapers chosen for each one. In all the spacious bedrooms there are thick-pile carpets and good furniture. The sitting-room has glass doors opening on to the walled garden where an annexe has some bedrooms (for smokers).

Angela Rolfe, previously a teacher, does all the cooking and uses home-grown raspberries, strawberries, vegetables and other produce from the kitchen garden. She serves soup, roasts, organic vegetables and desserts such as raspberry pavlova, ginger meringues, rhubarb and ginger fool (ordering ahead is always necessary).

Readers' comments: Absolutely excellent. High standard. One of the very best. Made to feel at home; room superb and food likewise.

GAVELCROFT

C D M PT X

Suffolk

Holton, Suffolk, IP19 8LY Tel: 01986 873117
South-west of Lowestoft. Nearest main road: A144 from Bungay to Halesworth.

2 Bedrooms. £21–£23 (less for 7 nights or more). Bargain winter breaks. Available: own bath/shower/toilet; TV. No smoking.
Light suppers if ordered.
1 Sitting-room. With open fire/stove, TV. No smoking.
Large garden

Many refugees from 16th-century religious persecution on the Continent settled in Suffolk, often finding themselves employment in the local wool and silk-weaving trades. Gavelcroft was once home to such folk, its name deriving from the Dutch for 'gabled croft', and the Dutch gable-ends and dormers remain today. Now Sarah and Mike Hart live here. Sarah, a former speech therapist, looks after you, while Mike makes and restores double-basses in his workshop (which you may visit).

Accommodation here is cosy and private. One bedroom, decorated in celadon green and yellows, is on the ground floor and overlooks the apple orchard. The larger bedroom, in warm pinks and cream, with comfortable chairs, is in the eaves, converted from what was once an apple store. The low-beamed and stone-floored dining-room has antique and walnut furniture.

For dinners, there is a wide choice of eating-places in the vicinity.

It is only a few miles to picturesque Southwold or the wild Suffolk coast, or in fine weather you might take a peaceful riverside walk to the old market town of Halesworth.

Readers' comments: Homely and friendly atmosphere. The most perfect hosts.

Suffolk

MANORHOUSE

C(12)

The Green, Beyton, Suffolk, IP30 9AF Tel: 01359 270960
East of Bury St Edmunds. Nearest main road: A14 from Bury to Stowmarket.

4 Bedrooms. £24–£28 (less for 7 nights or more). Available: own bath/shower/toilet; TV. No smoking.
Dinner (by arrangement). £18 for 3 courses and coffee, at 7pm. Vegetarian or other special diets if ordered. No smoking. **Light suppers** if ordered.
1 Sitting-room. No smoking.
Large garden

E-mail: manorhouse@beyton.com

The beamed and panelled sitting/dining-room of this typical Suffolk long-house overlooks the village pond, and the geese resident there sometimes waddle past the window at breakfast time, as if pre-arranged by Kay and Mark Dewsbury, thus completing a picture of idyllic village life. Generous breakfasts here include home-made jams and eggs from the Dewsburys' own chickens. Dinner may comprise leek-and-potato soup, game casserole, and lemon mousse, all with fresh local ingredients. While dining you may admire Kay's collection of Staffordshire figures, and the rural landscapes painted by her mother.

The bedrooms in the house overlook the village green and pond, and are beautifully furnished. The yellow room, with a swagged voile hanging above the bed, has art deco-style lamps and pictures. Two more, in a barn conversion, are also well furnished, with a sofa in each; one has French windows and its own patio. Close by you might visit Blackthorp Barn with a summer music programme and a craft fair in November and December; or sample wine at Wyken Hall vineyard, with its good restaurant and attractive gardens.

Readers' comments: Delightful, tastefully restored and spotless. Breakfast excellent. Blissful bathroom. Excellent, spacious rooms.

Suffolk

MULBERRY HALL

C

Burstall, Suffolk, IP8 3DP Tel: 01473 652348 (Fax: 01473 652110)
West of Ipswich. Nearest main road: A1071 from Ipswich towards Sudbury.

2 Bedrooms. £21–£25 (less for 3 nights or more). Available: own bath/shower/toilet. No smoking.
Light suppers if ordered.
1 Sitting-room. With open fire, TV, piano. No smoking.
Large garden

E-mail: pennydebenham@hotmail.com

Cardinal Wolsey owned this house in 1523 and it is Henry VIII's colourful coat-of-arms which embellishes the inglenook fireplace in the big sitting-room – pink, beamed and with a grand piano. From this a winding stair leads up to well-equipped bedrooms. There is a small dining-room with raspberry walls and wheelback chairs around an oak table where Penny Debenham serves breakfast. In addition to the usual bacon and eggs, there are such options as devilled kidneys and kedgeree, as well as local apple juice, chilled melon and home-baked bread. Guests can dine locally.

Outside is an exceptional garden. Beyond a brick-paved terrace is a lawn with long lavender border, and a pergola leads past a rose garden to the tennis court.

V *Readers' comments:* Beautiful house; will visit again. A lot of loving care. Bedrooms light and airy, extremely comfortable; breakfast a highlight. Warm welcome, lovely house, superb breakfast. Very relaxed. Appreciated the style, welcome and comfort.

OLD VICARAGE

C D S X

Suffolk

Higham, Suffolk, CO7 6JY Tel: 01206 337248
North of Colchester. Nearest main road: A12 from Colchester to Ipswich.

3 Bedrooms. £25–£30 (less for 3 nights or more). Available: own bath/shower/toilet; TV; views of river.
Light suppers sometimes. Vegetarian or other special diets if ordered. No smoking.
1 Sitting-room. With open fire, TV. No smoking.
Large garden

Standing near a tranquil village, this elegant Tudor house (its walls colourwashed in warm apricot) is surrounded by superb views.

Meg Parker's taste is evident in every room: lovely colours, pretty wallpapers and chintzes, antiques, flowers and log fires all combine to create a background of great style. In the breakfast-room, bamboo chairs surround a huge circular table of mock marble; bedrooms are equally attractive, with individual touches everywhere. Outside is a pretty south-facing garden (with unheated swimming-pool).

Most visitors dine at the acclaimed Angel, in Stoke-by-Nayland.

Readers' comments: Perfect! Delightful weekend; privileged to be there. Most beautiful house. Very friendly. Thoroughly enjoyed it, superb. Food of highest standard, attention to detail outstanding. Splendid home and hospitality. Very interesting, friendly hostess. V

PIPPS FORD

C(5) **D M PT S**

Suffolk

Needham Market, Suffolk, IP6 8LJ Tel: 01449 760208 (Fax: 01449 760561)
North of Ipswich. Nearest main road: A14 from Ipswich to Bury St Edmunds.

6 Bedrooms. £20–£36 (less for 3 and 7 nights or more). Bargain breaks. Available: own bath/shower/toilet; views of river. No smoking.
Dinner. £19.50 for 3 courses and coffee, at 7.30pm. Vegetarian or other special diets if ordered. Wine available.
3 Sitting-rooms. With open fire, TV, piano.
Large garden
Closed from mid-December to mid-January.

E-mail: b&b@pippsford.co.uk

On a stretch of the River Gipping that has been designated an Area of Outstanding Natural Beauty stands a large Tudor farmhouse once owned by Hakluyt. Raewyn Hackett-Jones has made patchwork quilts or cushion-covers for every room and searched out attractive fabrics for curtains or upholstery. Many of the beds are collectors' pieces; even the bathrooms are attractive. Some bedrooms are in converted stables, with sitting-room.

This is a house of inglenook fireplaces, sloping floors, low beams and historic associations. Meals may be served in a flowery conservatory, a vine overhead.

Breakfasts are exceptional. From an enormous choice, you could select exotic juices; home-made sausages; cinnamon toast or waffles; kidneys, mackerel, fishcakes. Popular dinner dishes include: avocado and smoked salmon baked with cheese; breast of duck with port; home-made ice creams and traditional puddings.

Readers' comments: Delightful house, beautifully furnished; food and service outstanding; one of the best holidays ever. A fitting climax to our wonderful trip with your book. Charming and talented hostess. Very welcoming. Meals superb; so comfortable and pretty.

Suffolk

SHIP STORES

C M PT(limited) **X**

22 Callis Street, Clare, Suffolk, CO10 8PX Tel: 01787 277834 (Fax: 01787 277183)
North-west of Sudbury. Nearest main road: A1092 from Long Melford to Clare.

5 Bedrooms. £22–£25 (less for 3 nights or more). Bargain breaks. Available: own bath/shower/toilet; TV. No smoking.
Dinner (by arrangement). £8.50 for 2 courses and coffee, at 7–8pm. Vegetarian or other special diets if ordered. Wine available. **Light suppers** if ordered.
1 Sitting-room. With TV.

E-mail: shipclare@aol.com

Miles from the sea, this one-time inn was originally called the Sheep, not the Ship. Now it is a small shop run by Colin and Debra Bowles, with en suite bedrooms and an upstairs sitting-room for guests. It is a place of low beams, creaking floors, undulating roof and cream-plastered front: full of character. In the dining-room there is solid elm furniture locally made. There are two more en suite rooms in a flint-walled annexe. For dinner, Debra serves such meals as a roast, followed by apple pie. Bread and croissants are home-baked.

Clare is a place to explore on foot, to enjoy all the details of its ancient houses – plaster-work decoration, exuberant inn signs, the old priory. It is close to Cavendish, Sudbury and other attractive places in Suffolk such as Kentwell Hall and gardens, Long Melford (good for antique-hunting), Clare country park, the Colne Valley steam railway, Gainsborough's house, Hedingham Castle and Melford Hall.

V *Reader's comments:* A beautiful, charming and superbly run establishment.

Suffolk

SOUTH HILL HOUSE

C(8) **PT**

43 Southgate Street, Bury St Edmunds, Suffolk, IP33 2AZ Tel: 01284 755650 (Fax: 01284 752718)
Nearest main road: A134 from Sudbury to Bury St Edmunds (and A14).

3 Bedrooms. £23.50–£27 (less for 2 nights or more). Available: own bath/shower/toilet; TV. No smoking.
Small garden

E-mail: southill@cwcom.net

The simple Georgian exterior of South Hill House, described by Charles Dickens as 'a large, old, red-brick house, just outside the town', belies both its history and the generously sized, comfortable accommodation within. Reputedly taking it as the model for the school in *Pickwick Papers*, Dickens often read to the young ladies at Miss Amelia Hitchen's select establishment which occupied the building in the 1860s.

Sarah and Anthony Green (previously farmers), their family and dog Pernod now live here. All the bedrooms are spacious, with room to sit and relax. The largest room has a luxurious bathroom with mocha-coloured suite and sunken bath. Extraordinarily, in times of Catholic repression this room was an oratory, the bedroom being its meeting-room. Breakfast, in the stone-slabbed and oak-furnished dining-room, includes local sausages and smoked dry-cured bacon. There are plenty of restaurants a short walk away in the town, and much to see there too: lovely architecture, the beautiful Abbey Gardens, museums, an art gallery and the handsomely restored Theatre Royal.

Reader's comments: Absolutely sincere, heartwarming hospitality.

STAGE DOOR

CSX

1 & 2 Fen Cottages, Aldringham, Suffolk, IP16 4QR Tel: 01728 452961
South of Leiston. Nearest main road: A1094 from Friday Street to Aldeburgh.

2 Bedrooms. £20 (less for 3 nights or more). No smoking.
Light suppers if ordered.
Large garden

Informality and remoteness are the hallmarks of Stage Door. The Drakes' home borders North Warren nature reserve, and wildlife often spills over into the rambling garden. The cottages were designed by local architect, painter and poet Cecil Lay, whose eclectic style combines patterned brickwork, great buttressed chimneys and pargeting to pleasing effect.

Generous breakfasts are served in a farmhouse kitchen where holiday postcards jostle for space with good paintings, some of which are landscapes of Jean and Bryan's native New Zealand. Jean's speciality is a delicious omelette made with eggs from her chickens and parsley from the garden. Bread is freshly baked and the crystal clear water comes from the Drakes' own borehole. The simply furnished bedrooms have comfortable chairs (there is no sitting-room) and the bathroom is shared.

Jean and Bryan go out of their way to ensure you enjoy your stay. If persuaded, Bryan may talk to you about his operatic career – he sang in many premières of Benjamin Britten's operas. There is much to see and do hereabouts: summer theatre repertory at Aldeburgh, concerts at Snape, or a floating lunch aboard an ex-Navy supply vessel on the rivers Alde and Ore.

WESTERN HOUSE

CSX

High Street, Cavendish, Suffolk, CO10 8AR Tel: 01787 280550
North-west of Sudbury. On A1092 between Long Melford and Clare.

3 Bedrooms. £17 (less for 3 nights or more).
Large garden

Twice made redundant, Peter Marshall decided he would instead make a living from his best asset: his attractive 400-year-old house in the historic village of Cavendish.

He and his wife Jean (who teaches singing) are vegetarians, so at one end they started a wholefood shop, full of the smells of dried fruit and fresh herbs, and refurnished several bedrooms to take bed-and-breakfast guests. Options include all kinds of good things (such as their own muesli, eggs, mushrooms, tomatoes and home-made bread) but no bacon. They will recommend various restaurants in the village, at Long Melford or in Sudbury.

Each beamed bedroom, reached via zigzag corridors, is neat, pretty and spacious – well equipped with chairs, table, etc. One at the front (which looks on to the main road through the village) has a fresh cream and white colour scheme extending even to the sheets. One of the nicest features is the large and informal garden.

Readers' comments: Excellent, with very good breakfasts. Much enjoyed it; and the shop is excellent. Extremely comfortable; warm welcome. Absolutely excellent, high standard. Charming and interesting people. Extremely attractive.

V

SURREY

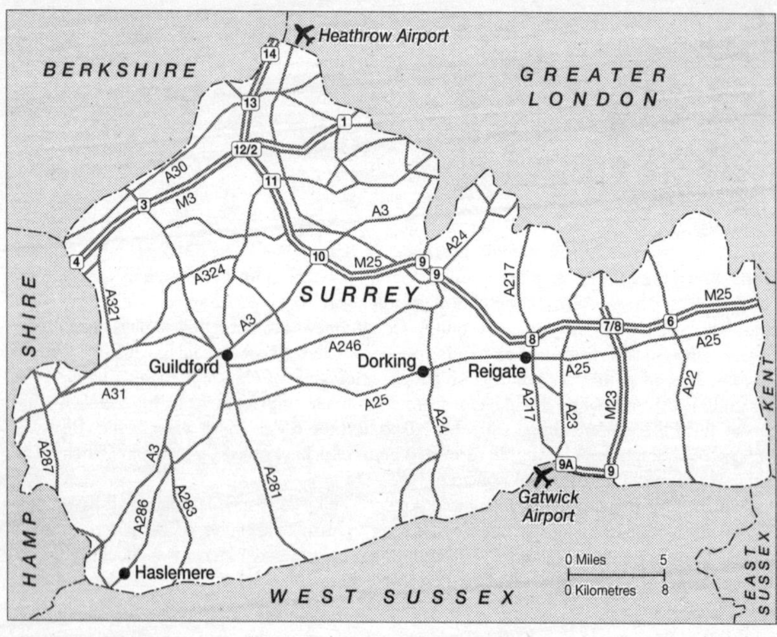

APPLYING FOR INCLUSION IN SOTBT Many proprietors ask for their houses to be included in this book, and – although few can be accepted – such applications are welcomed, particularly from areas not already well covered; *provided that* the b & b price is within the book's limits (see page xiv). Ideally, either dinner or light snacks should be available in the evening. There is no charge for an entry but, compiling the book being expensive, nearly all proprietors make a contribution at the end of each year (no bills are issued). Every house has to be visited first and it may be some time before this takes place. Brochures, prices, menus, etc. should be posted to: Jan Bowmer (SOTBT), c/o Arrow Books, 20 Vauxhall Bridge Road, London SW1V 2SA. No phone calls please.

BARN COTTAGE

C D S

Surrey

Church Road, Leigh, Surrey, RH2 8RF Tel: 01306 611347

South-west of Reigate. Nearest main road: A25 from Reigate to Dorking (and M25, junction 8).

2 Bedrooms. £25–£30. Bargain breaks. Both have TV. No smoking.
Dinner (by arrangement). £15 for 4 courses and coffee, at 7–9.30pm. Vegetarian or other special diets if ordered. Wine available. **Light suppers** if ordered.
1 Sitting-room. With open fire, TV, Piano.
Large garden
Closed at Easter.

The barn dates back to the 17th century and was converted in the 1930s. Original beams are much in evidence, as are mahogany antiques and pieces of Copenhagen china, the latter collected over the years by Pat Comer. Her tapestries cover chairs in the sitting- and dining-rooms; and she sells dolls which she knits.

Lattice-paned windows look out on to immaculate lawns, lovingly tended by the Comers. One can sit on the patio and enjoy the beautiful view of a garden and fish pond. There are swings and a sandpit to keep children amused, a swimming-pool and a hard tennis court.

Evening meals might include smoked salmon mousse, coronation chicken, chocolate-and-orange slice, and cheese.

The Comers will drive visitors to nearby Gatwick Airport or Redhill Station (regular trains into central London); and cars can be left here for a small daily charge.

Reader's comments: Charming and very comfortable house, could not have been made to feel more at home.

V

BEEVERS FARM

C

Surrey

Chinthurst Lane, Bramley, Surrey, GU5 0DR Tel/Fax: 01483 898764

South of Guildford. Nearest main road: A281 from Guildford to Horsham.

3 Bedrooms. £18–£25. One has own bath/shower/toilet; TV (in all). No smoking.
Light suppers if ordered. No smoking.
Large garden
Closed from December to January.

E-mail: beevers@onetel.net.uk

It is the genuine warmth and openness of Shelagh and Jim Cook's personalities that recommend a stay here. This plain, modern house just outside the village provides neat and simply furnished bedrooms decorated in pastel shades. The Cooks previously had plant nurseries on their surrounding land until these were destroyed in the 1987 hurricane. Now the land is deliberately left wild, and hazel and elder trees tangle with willows. The result is that you may see rabbits, pheasants or even deer. There was probably a vineyard here in ancient times; Jim dug up old vines and a Roman quern stone when the house was being built.

The Cooks keep their own chickens and bees, the resultant produce being served at breakfast, together with home-made preserves from the garden's fruit. There is no sitting-room, but in fine weather guests may sit in the plant-packed conservatory. There are plenty of restaurants in the village and Shelagh will do packed lunches for walkers – the 30-mile Downs Link joining the North and South Downs is nearby. A disused railway route, it is now popular with walkers and cyclists.

Reader's comments: Very comfortable, exceptional hospitality.

V

Surrey

BULMER FARM

C(12) **D M PT S X**

Holmbury St Mary, Surrey, RH5 6LG Tel: 01306 730210
South-west of Dorking. Nearest main road: A25 from Dorking to Guildford (and M25, junction 9).

8 Bedrooms. £23–£25. Available: own shower/toilet; TV. No smoking (some).
1 Sitting-room. With open fire, TV. No smoking.
Large garden

In the folds of Surrey's high North Downs a number of very picturesque villages lie hidden, and Holmbury is one. Near the centre stands Bulmer Farm, built about 1680. One steps straight into a large dining-room with gleaming furniture, and through this to an attractive sitting-room – a room of pink walls and old beams, logs crackling in the inglenook. It opens on to the large garden (with croquet).

Upstairs are pleasant, spacious bedrooms. Five additional and very comfortable rooms (with en suite showers) have been created in outbuildings for guests staying two nights or more. B & b only, but the area is full of inns offering good meals.

Outdoors, David Hill will show you the lake he created a few years ago, now a haven for herons, kingfishers, Canada geese and other wildfowl: it won a conservation award.

Readers' comments: Made so welcome, made to feel like one of the family. Picturesque, restful. Ultra quiet. Friendly, helpful owners. A great time. Very good accommodation and lovely area. Area wonderful, excellent place to stay to visit London.

V

Surrey

CHERRY TREES

C M PT S

Gomshall Lane, Shere, Surrey, GU5 9HE Tel: 01483 202288
East of Guildford. Nearest main road: A25 from Guildford to Dorking (and M25, junction 9).

4 Bedrooms. £25. Available: own bath/shower/toilet; TV. No smoking.
1 Sitting-room. With open fire. No smoking.
Large garden
Closed from mid-December to mid-January.

Picturesque Shere with old cottages around a stream is one of Surrey's beauty-spots. Here is Cherry Trees, a traditional 'twenties brick and tile-hung house in a garden of winding flowerbeds and colourful shrubs (with seats in leafy nooks from which to enjoy hill views). One of the bedrooms is on the ground floor, in former stables overlooking the pretty garden. There is also a swimming-pool for guests to use. Breakfast is served in a cream-walled room with oak dresser and leaded casements; for dinner, Olwen Warren recommends the White Horse inn and the 12th-century Kinghams restaurant, both a few yards away.

Dorking and Guildford (the latter with castle ruins, river trips and a good theatre) are each well worth a day's visit. Clandon Park and Polesden Lacey (stately homes) are close by, and so is Hatchlands (NT house with an interesting collection of musical instruments).

Reader's comment: Excellent location and perfect treatment.

Surrey

DEERFELL

C S

Blackdown Park, Fernden Lane, Haslemere, Surrey, GU27 3LA Tel: 01428 653409 (Fax: 01428 656106)

South of Haslemere. Nearest main road: A286 from Haslemere to Midhurst.

3 Bedrooms. £20–£23. Available: own bath/shower/toilet; TV. No smoking.
Dinner (by arrangement). £10 for 2 courses and coffee, at 7pm (not Sundays). Vegetarian or other special diets if ordered. No smoking. **Light suppers** if ordered.
1 Sitting-room. With open fire. No smoking.
Large garden
Closed from mid-December to mid-January.

Originally the coach house to a neighbouring mansion, Deerfell stands near the summit of Black Down, a Stone Age stronghold 8000 years ago, which rises to almost 1000 feet.

Its conversion from coach house to home was well done, retaining such features as stone-mullioned windows and latched board doors, but with such modern additions as a glass sun-room and a marble fireplace. Elizabeth Carmichael has decorated it with antiques, old rugs and colour schemes which are predominantly warm reds and cream. Bedrooms are comfortable and spacious. Navaho rugs adorn the staircase wall. Meals (which are usually served in the handsome dining-room with grandfather clock, piano and an ancestral portrait of William IV's physician) are well cooked, ample and unpretentious – for instance, moussaka and treacle tart or chocolate cheesecake.

London is only 45 minutes away by train from Haslemere.

Readers' comments: Very comfortable and pleasant stay. Lovely home. Felt relaxed and rested. Everything very much to our liking. Total peace and quiet. Warm and friendly. V

Surrey

HIGH EDSER

C D PT

Shere Road, Ewhurst, Surrey, GU6 7PQ Tel: 01483 278214 (Fax: 01483 278200)

South-east of Guildford. Nearest main road: A25 from Guildford to Dorking.

3 Bedrooms. £25–£30. No smoking.
Dinner (by arrangement). £8.50 for 2 courses or £10 for 3 courses and coffee, at 7pm. Vegetarian or other special diets if ordered. No smoking. **Light suppers** if ordered.
1 Sitting-room. With TV. No smoking.
Large garden

E-mail: franklinadams@highedser.demon.co.uk

Ewhurst means 'yew wood', and the great stump of an ancient yew stands like a monolith in the garden of this handsome 16th-century house where Carol and Patrick Franklin-Adams live. From the hall paved with York stone, where Carol has exposed some of the old wattle-and-daub construction, a winding staircase leads to smart bedrooms (with very low doorways). One bedroom has an oak floor, lovely yellow-and-blue tulip-patterned curtains and a pretty blue-and-white buttoned armchair, an example of Carol's upholstery skills. Another, with four-poster bed, is decorated in peach and terracotta, with a charming antique embroidery of a garden scene on one wall. From this room you look out over the garden, which is carpeted with daffodils in spring. There is croquet, a tennis court, and also a heated swimming-pool which guests may use by arrangement.

Meals are taken in the lattice-paned dining-room in front of an ancient, carved oak fire-surround. Evening meals may comprise simple soup and quiche or, more elaborately, Stilton and walnut pâté, pork with honey and chilli sauce, and lemon pudding. Afterwards, visitors can retire to the snug sitting-room to plan the next day's sightseeing.

Surrey

NURSCOMBE FARMHOUSE

C(10) **PT S**

Snowdenham Lane, Bramley, Surrey, GU5 0DB Tel: 01483 892242
South of Guildford. Nearest main road: A281 from Guildford to Horsham.

3 Bedrooms. £25–£30 (less for 4 nights or more). Available: own bath/toilet; views of lake. No smoking.
Dinner (by arrangement). £10 for 2 courses and coffee, at 7.30pm. Vegetarian or other special diets if ordered. No smoking.
1 Sitting-room. With open fire, TV. No smoking.
Large garden

There are few houses in this book that have both their own tennis courts and a private lake: Nurscombe Farmhouse, set in a quiet valley, is one. It is also exceptionally beautiful. A cream-walled, half-timbered house swathed in wisteria, it was built in the 15th century and added to in the 1600s. Bedrooms are prettily furnished, one with yellow-striped walls and views of the lake. The pale oak-panelled sitting-room is spacious and comfortable, some sofas grouped around the open fire and others at the far end of the room, which looks out on to the garden.

The high-ceilinged dining-room is the 17th-century addition made by a prosperous yeoman farmer. Here, among many family photos and paintings, Jane Fairbank serves breakfasts which include home-made jams and honey from her own bees. An evening meal might comprise fish pie or rabbit stew, followed by hot chocolate soufflé or bread-and-butter pudding. Close by is Elizabethan Loseley House (where the popular ice creams and yogurts are produced). Also worth a visit is Winkworth Arboretum, which has lovely autumnal colour or carpets of bluebells in spring.

Readers' comments: Wonderful view; luxury which could have cost four times as much in a hotel.

Surrey

SIXPENNY BUCKLE

C M PT

Gransden Close, Ewhurst, Surrey, GU6 7RL Tel: 01483 273988
South-east of Guildford. Nearest main road: A281 from Guildford to Horsham.

2 Bedrooms. £20–£25 (less for 4 nights or more). One has own shower; TV (in both). No smoking.
Light suppers if ordered. Vegetarian or other special diets if ordered. No smoking.
Garden

Although only some 25 years old, this bungalow has very much its own character, thanks to retired pharmacist Derek Mortimore and his wife Pat. Their immaculate garden is full of variegated shrubs, with a lovely sward of healthy lawn. At one end are a heated swimming-pool and changing-room which guests may use. The Mortimores even have their own vine from which Derek makes his wine – with varying degrees of success, he says. Bedrooms, smart and spotless, are decorated in pastel shades. The family room has comfortable seating (there is no sitting-room).

Breakfast is served in the cosy maroon-and-cream dining-room. Pat also provides afternoon tea on the lawn; for dinner, she recommends the Bull's Head pub nearby. With the Surrey hills all around, the house is a good base from which to try the many walks in the area. Close at hand are Wattlehurst Farm with friendly farm animals and the Hannah Pescha Sculpture Garden at Ockley, which has an exhibition of sculpture and ceramics in a dramatic watergarden setting. Gatwick Airport is 30 minutes away.

V

STURTWOOD FARM **C D**

Partridge Lane, Newdigate, Surrey, RH5 5EE Tel: 01306 631308 (Fax: 01306 631908)
South-east of Dorking. Nearest main road: A24 from Dorking to Horsham (and M23, junctions 9/9a).

rear view

3 Bedrooms. £22.50–£35. Available: own shower/ toilet; TV. No smoking.
Light suppers if ordered. Vegetarian or other special diets if ordered.
Large garden

Honeysuckle twining with climbing roses bedecks the whitewashed walls of this attractive farmhouse, the oldest parts of which date back to 1777. Only some 20 years later a local curate thought the land so poor that Newdigate was 'the last place in the world I should choose to farm in'. Nevertheless, Bridget and Roger Mackinnon farmed here successfully for 20 years, and now offer comfortable and homely accommodation. The best bedroom, with sofa to relax on (there is no sitting-room), has walnut headboards, antique furniture and an en suite shower-room.

The dining-room, where breakfast is served, looks out over a pond and has interesting antique furniture as well as old sporting prints on the walls. This house has the advantage of proximity to Gatwick Airport, yet is well away from flight-paths. You may leave your car here for a small charge.

For evening meals, Bridget recommends the Surrey Oaks or the Six Bells, both in Newdigate.

Reader's comment: Very comfortable indeed.

THE WALTONS **C D PT X**

5 Rose Hill, Dorking, Surrey, RH4 2EG Tel/Fax: 01306 883127
(Mobile: 07802 469953)
Nearest main road: A24 from Leatherhead to Horsham (and M25, junction 9).

4 Bedrooms. £25–£35 (less for 3 nights or more). Bargain breaks. All have TV. No smoking.
Dinner (by arrangement). £15.50 for 3 courses and coffee, at 6.30–8pm. Vegetarian or other special diets if ordered. Wine available. No smoking. **Light suppers** if ordered.
Small garden

E-mail: thewaltons@rosehill5.demon.co.uk

There's a hidden corner in Dorking: an oval green, high up, where horses graze (within minutes of the High Street). Around this conservation area pretty villas were built in 1830, one of which is now the home of Margaret Walton. She has chosen lovely fabrics and wallpapers while retaining such features as graceful cast-iron fireplaces and even rather splendid Victorian baths. The bedroom with the best view is on the first floor: beyond Dorking's mellow rooftops you can see Ranmore Common (NT) and Denbies' huge vineyard (open to visitors for tastings). In the handsome dining-room, Margaret provides candlelit dinners (such as smoked salmon, chicken fricassée, pavlova), Sunday lunches and snacks. Breakfast is sometimes served on the sunny terrace overlooking a secluded garden.

The surrounding area of woodland and hills is one of the finest beauty-spots near the capital, truly rural, and dotted with footpaths to follow, historic churches and villages with craft and antique shops. The Royal Horticultural Society's gardens at Wisley are near, too. V

SUSSEX
(East and West)

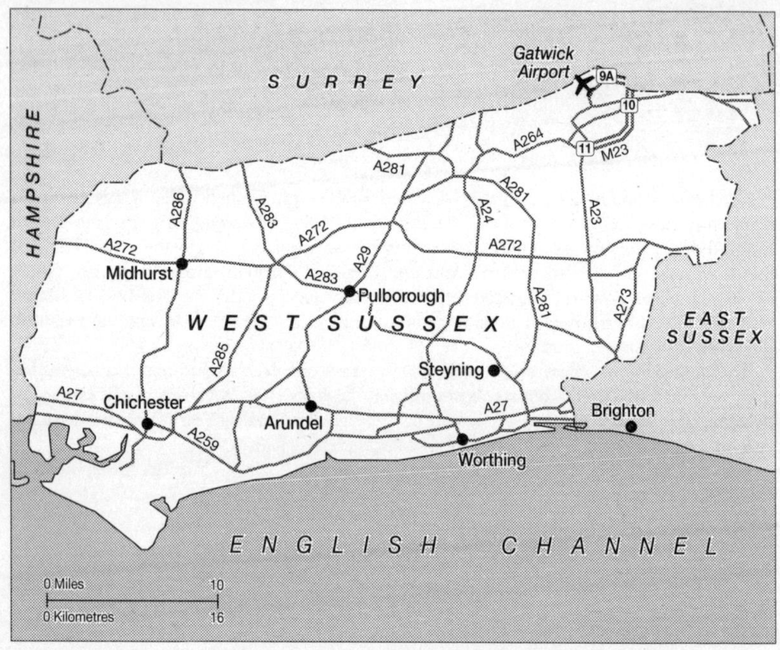

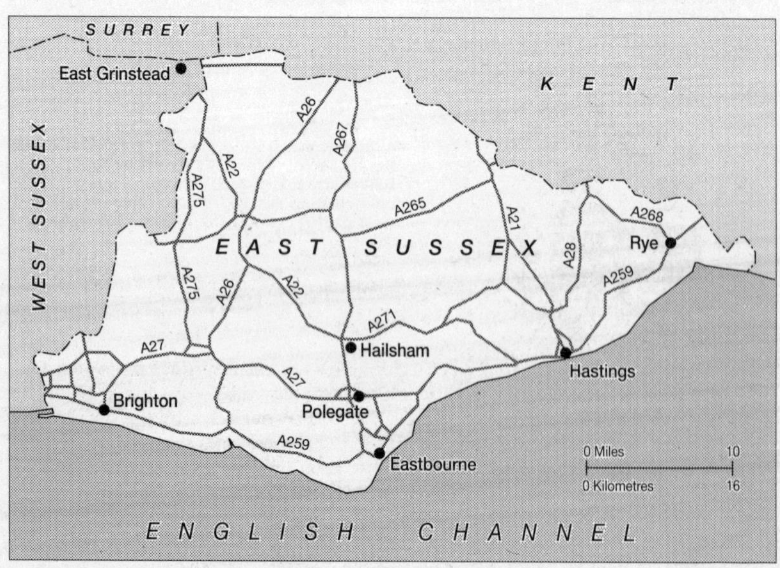

ASH FARM

C D PT S X

Filching, East Sussex, BN26 5QA Tel: 01323 487335 (Fax: 01323 484474)
South of Polegate. Nearest main road: A27 from Polegate to Lewes.

3 Bedrooms. £20–£25 (less for 3 nights or more). Bargain breaks. Available: own bath/shower/toilet; views of sea; balcony (one). No smoking.
Dinner. £10.50 for 2 courses and coffee, at 7.30pm. Vegetarian or other special diets if ordered. No smoking. **Light suppers** if ordered.
2 Sitting-rooms. With open fire (in one), TV. No smoking.
Large garden

Having run a busy London coffee-house for many years, Geoff and Pat Steer decided to exchange the rigours of the city for a somewhat less frenetic lifestyle. Ash Farm was 'naught but four damp walls and a roof' when bought, says Geoff, but the attraction of living here will be immediately apparent. This mid-Victorian whitewashed building clings to the side of a downland ridge, surrounded on all sides by verdant rolling hills. With direct access on to the South Downs Way, a popular pre-breakfast stroll to the top of a nearby hill is rewarded by splendid views across Weald and downland for some twenty miles.

Geoff's breakfasts, served in the conservatory, sometimes include home-made apple juice, and Pat's evening meals might comprise pork in cider, followed by blackberry-and-apple pie. The small bedrooms, simply furnished, have lovely views. One (once the hayloft) has a balcony with steps leading down to a pretty walled garden.

There is much to see in the area: Clergy House (NT), Firle House and the Filching Manor Automobile Collection (vintage cars exhibited in the grounds of a fine manor house, also home to the famous Bluebird world-record-beating boats).

V

ASHLANDS COTTAGE

C(12) PT X

Burwash, East Sussex, TN19 7HS Tel: 01435 882207
North-west of Hastings. Nearest main road: A265 from Hurst Green to Heathfield.

2 Bedrooms. £18–£22 (less for 2 nights or more). No smoking.
Light suppers if ordered.
1 Sitting-room. With TV.
Large garden

The garden of this pretty, lattice-paned cottage adjoins the estate of Batemans – a great 17th-century house that was Kipling's last home (it is now open to the public). Beyond its herbaceous beds and neat brick paths is a far view across the scenery that inspired 'Pook's Song' and you can glimpse Pook's Hill from the garden.

Trained as a singer, Nesta Harmer made her home here after many years spent in Bermuda; the pretty mahogany beds in one room came from there. Both rooms have wide views and a light, airy feel.

Beyond the garden is a wood in which Nesta has cleared a glade and planted woodland flowers. The inns and restaurants of Burwash are two minutes' walk away.

Readers' comments: Beautifully furnished, magnificent views. Home-from-home service, restful and delightfully furnished. Superb views, very comfortable. Very personal and gracious attention. View from our bedroom truly magnificent. Very generous and helpful.

V

East Sussex

BARONS GRANGE

C(12) **D PT**(limited) **S**

Readers Lane, Iden, East Sussex, TN31 7UU Tel: 01797 280478 (Fax: 01797 280186)

North of Rye. Nearest main road: A268 from Rye to Hawkhurst.

3 Bedrooms. £22.50–£27.50 (less for 3 nights or more). Bargain breaks. Available: own bath/shower/ toilet; TV. No smoking.
Light suppers if ordered.
2 Sitting-rooms. With open fire (in one). No smoking.
Large garden

A few miles from the Cinque Port of Rye, Barons Grange is a handsome Georgian house set in 600 acres of farmland. It was the family home of James Ramus and he now farms there (fruit, corn and sheep), while Joy offers bed-and-breakfast accommodation in some style. There is a light and airy sitting-room with chintz and velours sofas and chairs, antique furniture, family photos, and trophies from successes at three-day eventing. French windows lead to a sunny conservatory with grapevine trailing overhead, where guests may take breakfast, perhaps after an early-morning dip in the solar-heated pool. There is also a tennis court with equipment provided.

Bedrooms in pastel pinks are neat and well appointed. Guests can dine at the pub-restaurant in Iden, half a mile away.

Nearby Rye was the setting for E. F. Benson's *Mapp and Lucia* stories. Sometime mayor of the town, Benson lived in Lamb House (NT), the former home of Henry James. There is a weekly sheep and general market to visit as well as a heritage centre with an authentic town model.

V *Readers' comments:* Made us feel totally at home. Very comfortable. Nice relaxed atmosphere.

East Sussex

BATES GREEN

Arlington, East Sussex, BN26 6SH Tel/Fax: 01323 482039

North-west of Eastbourne. Nearest main road: A22 from Eastbourne to East Grinstead.

3 Bedrooms. £25–£35 (less for 4 nights or more). Bargain breaks. All have own bath/shower/toilet; TV. No smoking.
Light suppers (in winter only) if ordered.
1 Sitting-room. With log fire. No smoking.
Large garden

Goliath poppies mingling with tiny blue borage: that is the kind of unexpected juxtaposition of colour and scale which delights Carolyn McCutchan and makes her lovely garden so memorable. It is open to the public annually under the National Gardens Scheme, but visitors staying at the house can enjoy its colours all the year round. There are unusual plants everywhere, a tennis court, and a big bluebell wood which is a carpet of colour every May.

The house itself is tile-hung in traditional Sussex style. It began life in the 18th century as a gamekeeper's cottage on the Michelham Priory estate, but has since been much enlarged. The sitting-room is beamed and panelled, with flowery cretonne armchairs around the log fire. The dining-room has leaded casements opening on to the garden. From the brick-floored hall, stairs rise to the pretty bedrooms and bathrooms.

The Old Oak Inn at Arlington has good food. Arlington Reservoir, a nature reserve rich in birdlife, as well as Michelham Priory (and gardens) are worth visiting.

Readers' comments: Lovely house and garden, sumptuous bedrooms. Best we have been to. Beautiful house, wonderful hosts. A splendid b & b; most comfortable, welcoming and attractive.

BUNCTON MANOR FARM

C D PT X

Steyning Road, Wiston, West Sussex, BN44 3DD Tel: 01903 812736
(Fax: 01903 814838)
North-west of Steyning. On A283 from Steyning to Storrington.

2 Bedrooms. £20 (less for 3 nights or more in winter). Bargain breaks. Both have TV. No smoking.
Dinner (by arrangement, but not during harvest time). £14 for 2 courses and coffee, at 7–7.30pm. Vegetarian or other special diets if ordered. No smoking. **Light suppers** if ordered.
1 Sitting-room. With stove, TV.
Large garden

E-mail: bunctonmanor@email.com

There has been a manor house hereabouts since Saxon times, when the people of Buna settled on an enclosed farm or 'tun' in about AD500. The present moated brick building, at the foot of Chanctonbury Ring, is therefore relatively young, dating back only some five or six hundred years.

Nancy Rowland, brought up in Jamaica, came to England as a chef in her father's hotel. Now in the smart dining-room, which overlooks the moat and great yew tree (as do the bedrooms), she serves such meals as steak-and-kidney pudding, followed by pears poached in lemon and ginger. The packed lunches are particularly useful for walkers: the house is near the mid-point of the South Downs Way. Bedrooms (and the sitting-room shared with Nancy and Chris) are homely and comfortable.

There is much of interest locally: an isolated Norman chapel, once part of the manor, and, in pretty Steyning, St Andrew's with its grand nave, one of the best Norman churches in Britain. In Bramber is the fascinating St Mary's House (open in spring and summer), originally a monastic inn, and rich in historic and literary associations.

West Sussex

CONQUERORS

C M PT(limited) **X**

Cowbeech Hill, Herstmonceux, East Sussex, BN27 4PR Tel: 01323 832446
(Fax: 01323 831578)
North-east of Hailsham. Nearest main road: A271 from Hailsham to Battle.

3 Bedrooms. £20–£24 (less for 3 nights or more). Bargain breaks. Available: own bath/shower/toilet; views of sea. No smoking.
Dinner (by arrangement). £15 for 3 courses and coffee, at 7–8pm. Vegetarian or other special diets if ordered. No smoking. **Light suppers** if ordered.
1 Sitting-room. With open fire, TV. No smoking.
Large garden

E-mail: conquerors@ukgateway.net

Built in 1930 for a newspaper owner, this house has an Arts and Crafts feel to its architecture, complemented by Kate and Terry Short's choice of furnishings and ornaments. There are period pieces of furniture and lighting throughout, and the high-beamed sitting-room features a Charles Rennie Mackintosh fireplace. Beyond the galleried entrance hall, visitors eat in a triple-aspect sun lounge, with marvellous views over the terrace and garden towards Pevensey Bay. An evening meal might comprise casseroled pork in mustard sauce, followed by chocolate mousse with rum-soaked amaretti, and cheese.

Bedrooms, all on the ground floor, are decorated with flair and have 1920s and 1930s costume designs on display (linguist Kate worked for a theatrical costumier). One has an excellent shower-room with disabled facilities. Terry (a former financial consultant) encourages one to wander about the grounds – feather-footed bantams, peacocks, pheasants and ducks are in residence. Good local walks include the rural Cuckoo Trail, an 11-mile walk along the route of a disused railway track, with partial access for the disabled.

Reader's comments: Spectacular views, utterly peaceful, wonderfully welcoming hosts.

East Sussex

V

DOWNFIELDS

C(10) S

Level Mare Lane, Eastergate, West Sussex, PO20 6SB Tel: 01243 542012
West of Arundel. Nearest main road: A27 from Chichester to Arundel.

1 Bedroom. £20–£25 (less for 3 nights or more). Has own bath/toilet; TV. No smoking.
Garden

Having spent many years abroad, Margaret Cane and her late husband Peter eventually settled in this attractive late 1930s house. One enters through an archway into a light-filled hall. The stairway features a set of Chinese silk prints and watercolours which reflect Margaret's love of dogs (you will already have met Ollie, her friendly mongrel). Upstairs, on the spacious landing, a window-seat and comfortable chairs invite one to linger and view the gently rising garden which culminates in an apple orchard. Among a collection of photographs is one of the *Ark Royal*, on which Peter served.

The bedroom, in delicate pink, has smart French patchwork quilts, Sanderson floral fabrics and witty canine pictures by Cecil Aldin. Traffic noise from the nearby A27 is minimal.

In the breakfast-room, which is handsomely furnished with Victorian chairs and a circular rosewood table, Margaret's own tapestry pictures hang on the walls along with a large, gilded wooden panel depicting young girls picking oranges. An adjoining, bright sun lounge leads into the garden.

V Goodwood House, Denmans Garden and Fontwell racecourse are all close by, as is an ample choice of dining-pubs.

EASTON HOUSE

C S

Chidham Lane, Chidham, West Sussex, PO18 8TF Tel: 01243 572514
(Fax: 01243 573084)
West of Chichester. Nearest main road: A259 from Chichester towards Portsmouth.

3 Bedrooms. £21–£25. One has own bath/toilet. No smoking.
1 Sitting-room. With log stove, TV, piano. No smoking.
Small garden
E-mail: eastonhouse@chidham.fsnet.co.uk

Every corner of this Tudor house has been filled by Mary Hartley with unusual antiques and trifles. A modern white-and-red poppy wallpaper contrasts with old beams, oriental rugs with stone-flagged floor, scarlet folkweave curtains with antique furniture. All around is a fine collection of mirrors (Spanish, art deco, rococo) and pictures of cats. Mary is musical, and guests are welcome to play on the Bechstein or join in chamber music sessions. It's a free-and-easy atmosphere, a house full of character and cats. Bathrooms are pretty.

Although only breakfast is served, visitors are welcome to linger in the comfortable lime-green sitting-room with its log stove (where tea is served on arrival); or in the garden, under the shade of magnolia and walnut trees.

V *Readers' comments:* Peaceful house with great character. A marvellous place. Mrs Hartley anticipates her guests' every need. Excellent. Most comfortable, helpful and friendly.

HOLLY HOUSE

C D M P T S X

Beaconsfield Road, Chelwood Gate, East Sussex, RH17 7LF Tel: 01825 740484 (Fax: 01825 740172)

South of East Grinstead. Nearest main road: A275 from East Grinstead to Lewes.

East Sussex

5 Bedrooms. £23–£25 (less for 7 nights or more). Bargain breaks. Available: own shower/toilet; TV; balcony.

Dinner (by arrangement). £16 for 3 courses and coffee, at times to suit guests. Vegetarian or other special diets if ordered. No smoking. **Light suppers** if ordered.

1 Sitting-room

Large garden

E-mail: db@hollyhousebnb.demon.co.uk

In the hamlet of Chelwood Gate (once literally a gate into Ashdown Forest) is Holly House where former teacher Dee Birchell welcomes guests to rooms given character by her flair for spotting 'finds' such as iron balustrades salvaged from a great house and old furniture she re-upholstered herself. Some bedrooms are on the ground floor, each with its own good shower-room; one upstairs has a balcony over the garden with its azaleas and magnolias, fish-pond and small, heated swimming-pool. Garden produce goes into such meals as leek soup, chicken in sherry and mushrooms, and gingernut gâteau.

In the area there is plenty to enjoy (in addition, the south coast is soon reached): Ashdown Forest (miles of footpaths); the beauty-spot of Ditchling Beacon; the Bluebell Line steam train; Wakehurst Place (garden) and Standen (Arts and Crafts house) – both NT.

Readers' comments: Comfortable, pretty home; friendly service, well-equipped room. Keith and Dee's warmth make one feel like family.

V

HURSTON WARREN

C D S X

Golf Club Lane, Wiggonholt, West Sussex, RH20 2EN Tel: 01798 875831 (Fax: 01798 874989)

South-east of Pulborough. Nearest main road: A283 from Petworth to Shoreham.

West Sussex

3 Bedrooms. £18.50–£25 (less for 3 nights or more). Available: own bath/toilet. No smoking.

Large garden

E-mail: kglazier@btinternet.com

Approached down a winding private road, this imposing Lutyens-style house and its grounds is almost like a country estate. Built in 1930 by architect William Harkess, who lived there for 15 years (he also designed the adjoining golf club-house), the house retains many authentic 'thirties details. It is now the home of John and Kate Glazier (he, a hatter and sculptor; she, a former nurse). All around are examples of John's sculptural works, including a 17-acre woodland sculpture trail (workshops are held in summer).

Inside, doors have rounded arched panels and windows are leaded. A fine oak staircase leads to bedrooms with tiled fireplaces, individual period furnishings and unusual paintings. One bathroom has a cupboard door which drops down to form an ironing board.

Breakfast (with much organic produce) is served round a long refectory table with Spanish leather chairs. A collection of 19th-century English watercolours hangs on the walls here. For evening meals, there are good pubs in Pulborough.

Reader's comments: The house is beautiful, the antique furniture exceptional and the food delicious. The welcome from our hosts was unstinted.

V

West Sussex

LITTLE OREHAM FARM

S

off Horn Lane, Henfield, West Sussex, BN5 9SB Tel: 01273 492931
North-west of Brighton. Nearest main road: A281 from Horsham towards Shoreham.

3 Bedrooms. £22.50–£23.50 (less for 3 nights or more). Bargain breaks. Available: own bath/shower/toilet; TV. No smoking.
Dinner (by arrangement). £15 for 3 courses and coffee, at about 6.30pm. Vegetarian or other special diets if ordered. No smoking. **Light suppers** if ordered.
2 Sitting-rooms. With open fire, TV. No smoking.
Large garden

Inside this brick and timbered house, 300 years old, rooms have beams and oak-mullioned or lattice-paned windows. There is a great inglenook fireplace with iron fireback as old as the house itself (a collection of big copper vessels is housed on its slate hearth), and red tiles cover the dining-room floor.

One of the well-furnished bedrooms for visitors (pine furniture and sprigged fabrics) is in a converted outbuilding, but meals are taken in the house itself: typically, Josie Forbes provides (if these are ordered in advance) such dinners as lettuce soup, salmon with watercress sauce, and strawberry tartlets.

Readers' comments: Beautiful surroundings; most charming lady and a marvellous cook; made me so welcome I am planning to return. Very friendly and warm. Peaceful. My best ever stay, ambience of house remarkable.

V

East Sussex

OLD VICARAGE

C(8) PT

66 Church Square, Rye, East Sussex, TN31 7HF Tel: 01797 222119
(Fax: 01797 227466)
Nearest main road: A259 from Folkestone to Hastings.

5 Bedrooms. £25–£36 for a suite (less for 3 nights or more). **5% less to readers of this book staying 3 nights from April to October, excluding bank holidays.** Bargain breaks. Available: own bath/shower/toilet; TV; views of sea (from one). No smoking.
Light suppers if ordered. Vegetarian or other special diets. Wine available.
1 Sitting-room
Small garden

E-mail: OldVicarageRye@tesco.net

This pink-and-white, largely 18th-century house is virtually in the churchyard, a peaceful spot since it is traffic-free and the only sound is the melodious chime of the ancient church clock. One steps straight into a very pretty sitting-room, chintz sofas complemented by Laura Ashley fabrics. Curved windows, antiques and fresh flowers complete the scene.

The bedrooms are prettily decorated, mostly with old pine furniture and flowery fabrics. Two have elegant four-posters. Those at the front have views of the church; others, of Rye's mediaeval roofscape. Henry James wrote *The Spoils of Poynton* while living here in 1896.

Breakfasts include home-made and local produce. For dinner Julia Lampon-Masters recommends (after offering guests sherry) one of Rye's many restaurants or she will do snack suppers.

Readers' comments: Outstanding. Charm and helpfulness of the owners gave us a perfect weekend. Very beautifully furnished and comfortable rooms. Friendly hosts. Fantastic – best breakfast I've ever had. Beautiful garden room. Huge and delicious breakfast.

V

PENDRAGON LODGE **D X**

Watermill Lane, Pett, East Sussex, TN35 4HY Tel: 01424 814051
North-east of Hastings. Nearest main road: A259 from Hastings to Rye.

3 Bedrooms. £25–£28.50 (less for 3 nights or more). Bargain breaks. All have own bath/shower/toilet; TV. No smoking.
Light suppers only.
1 Sitting-room. With piano. No smoking.
Small garden

The quiet hamlet of Pett is a mixture of modern and older dwellings, and Pendragon Lodge, a solid Victorian house, once contained the village bakery. Dianna Epton has taken much care over the decor of the immaculate bedrooms, each with its own colour scheme. The blue room has an attractive old French bedstead and bathroom with a big free-standing tub, while the pale green room takes its tone from an antique needlepoint rug in subtle shades. Dianna enjoys searching out treasures in the numerous antique shops of nearby Rye. Breakfast (which includes home-made muesli and preserves) and light suppers only, but the Two Sawyers pub, five minutes' walk away, is convenient for evening meals.

There is a Forestry Commission wood to ramble through; Pett beach is close; and cliff-side paths lead you to Old Hastings town to the west, or pretty Winchelsea to the east. Planned by Edward I, it is a place of flint and brick buildings and ancient fortified gateways. Mediaeval cellars attest to the town's role as a once-important port for the Gascony wine trade. A little museum details the history of the Cinque Ports. V

PINDARS **C(10) PT**

Lyminster, West Sussex, BN17 7QF Tel: 01903 882628
South of Arundel. On A284 from Littlehampton towards Arundel.

3 Bedrooms. £19–£24 (less for 7 nights or more, November to March). Bargain breaks. Available: own bath/shower/toilet; TV. No smoking.
Dinner. £15 for 3 courses and coffee, at 7pm. Vegetarian or other special diets if ordered. No smoking. **Light suppers** if ordered.
1 Sitting-room. With TV. No smoking.
Large garden

The Newmans themselves designed this attractive house on the road between Littlehampton and historic Arundel, with its castle and cathedral.

Some of the light, bright bedrooms overlook the beautiful garden at the back, where stonework contrasts with beds that brim with flowers and shrubs (there is a swimming-pool too). Off the sitting-room – furnished with antiques – there is a conservatory. Garden produce goes into such meals as mushroom-and-spinach soup, chicken in a pimento sauce, and apple crumble with home-made ice cream: Jocelyne loves cooking. Breakfast may include kedgeree or fishcakes; preserves and scones are home-made.

Sunny rooms are furnished with Paisley sofas, Victorian miniatures and other characterful touches, and the Newmans have a variety of paintings collected when they ran an art gallery in Arundel.

Readers' comments: Warm welcome, delightful room. Artistically decorated, very comfortable, much care and attention to detail. Superior ambience, facilities and service. Immaculate. Delicious food. Beyond our expectations; hospitality and food excellent. V

West Sussex

RACEHORSE COTTAGE

C(5) D PT

18 Nepcote, Findon, West Sussex, BN14 0SD Tel: 01903 873783
North of Worthing. Nearest main road: A24 from Dorking to Worthing.

2 Bedrooms. £20–£25.
1 Sitting-room. With open fire, TV.
Small garden

The flint-walled hamlet of Nepcote is almost part of 18th-century Findon village, celebrated for its two racing stables (and very ancient church). This explains the name of the cottage, for which the previous owner chose a roadside position where he could watch strings of horses and their jockeys go by on their way to the surrounding South Downs for daily exercise. He built it in traditional Sussex style: upper storey weatherboarded, doors panelled.

It is a pleasant, unpretentious home with an L-shaped sitting/dining-room. Trim bedrooms have velvet bedheads and views of the Downs. Denis Lloyd grows his own produce, and for breakfast Jean offers stewed fruit as well as bread, muesli and jam which are all home-made. (Findon has three pubs and restaurants for evening meals.)

For walkers, the South Downs Way is close by, and the coastal resorts of Brighton, Worthing and Littlehampton are within easy driving distance.

Reader's comment: Everything necessary for comfort.

West Sussex

REDFORD COTTAGE

Redford, West Sussex, GU29 0QF Tel/Fax: 01428 741242
North-west of Midhurst. Nearest main road: A272 from Midhurst to Petersfield.

3 Bedrooms. £24–£28. Available: own bath/shower/toilet; TV. No smoking.
Light suppers if ordered. Vegetarian or other special diets if ordered.
2 Sitting-rooms. With open fire, TV, piano.
Large garden

In this secluded spot, which was without electricity until the 1970s, David Angela, a retired diplomat, and his wife Caroline have made a delightful home from what is basically a Tudor farm cottage with enlargements that make its rooms zigzag this way and that. The big L-shaped sitting/dining-room has a stone hearth with iron fireback dated 1626, a baby grand piano and, in one arm of the L, green velvet chairs around a circular table where breakfast is served. Numerous paintings and cretonne armchairs furnish the rest of the beamed room.

Glass doors lead to a patio of York stone where daffodils flower in spring and geraniums in summer.

There is a second, snug little sitting-room exclusively for visitors using the adjoining ground-floor bedroom. The bedroom itself is delightful – leaded windows on each side, tufted white spread, and its own shower-room. Two more bedrooms upstairs overlook plum and apple trees, with occasional glimpses of deer which stray in from the woods. A peaceful setting and yet only one and a quarter hours from London.

RIVER PARK FARM

C S

Lodsworth, West Sussex, GU28 9DS Tel: 01798 861362
East of Midhurst. Nearest main road: A272 from Petworth to Midhurst.

3 Bedrooms. £20. No smoking.
Light suppers if ordered (not Wednesdays, Thursdays and Fridays).
1 Sitting-room. With stove, TV. No smoking.
Large garden
Closed from November to Easter.

The farm (of 340 acres of corn, bullocks, sheep and poultry) is in a secluded position among woods where, if you are up early enough, you may encounter deer. There is a 4½-acre lake with plentiful carp and ducks, and in front a pretty garden. The house itself, built in 1600, is old and beamy with comfortable bedrooms along twisting passageways. In the dining-room Pat Moss has a strikingly colourful collection of green leaf plates and wooden ducks.

Pat does not do full-scale dinners (available elsewhere locally) but has a list of homely dishes like meat pie or macaroni cheese, and such puddings as banana chocolate sundae. Bread is home-baked and eggs free-range. Coarse fishing available. Many people come for the local walks and birdwatching.

Readers' comments: Enjoyed ourselves so much that we have twice visited for a week. Marvellous setting and house, kind hosts, good food. Outstanding. Warm, relaxed, friendly atmosphere, lovely farm. House charming, surroundings idyllic, rooms comfortable.

V

UPTON FARMHOUSE

C(3) **D PT X**

Upper Brighton Road, Sompting, West Sussex, BN14 9JU Tel: 01903 233706
East of Worthing. Nearest main road: A27 from Brighton to Worthing.

West Sussex

3 Bedrooms. £22.50–£25 (less for 3 nights or more). Bargain breaks. Available: own bath/shower/toilet; TV. No smoking.
Light suppers if ordered. Vegetarian or other special diets if ordered. Wine available.
1 Sitting-room. With open fire, TV. No smoking.
Large garden

Close to Worthing is the old village of Sompting, with a Rhenish-style Saxon church. Behind the handsome 18th-century façade of this house are parts built in the 15th century. The bedrooms – which have soft colours, deep, velvety carpets, private bathrooms, and views over farmland – are all spacious, immaculate and well equipped. Breakfast is served on lace tablecloths, with locally smoked kippers offered as an option. The massive sitting/dining-room is very comfortably furnished – its walls lined with prints of old sailing ships. Penny Hall is a particularly caring hostess.

The area round here is not only scenic but full of gardens, stately homes, Roman remains and castles to visit. Walkers enjoy wending their way up to Cissbury Ring, a prehistoric hill fort. South coast resorts within easy reach include not only sedate Worthing but also Brighton, celebrated for its oriental-style Pavilion and sophisticated pleasures. At Shoreham, nearby, there is a museum of D-Day aviation.

Reader's comments: Warm welcome, excellent food.

V

WARWICKSHIRE

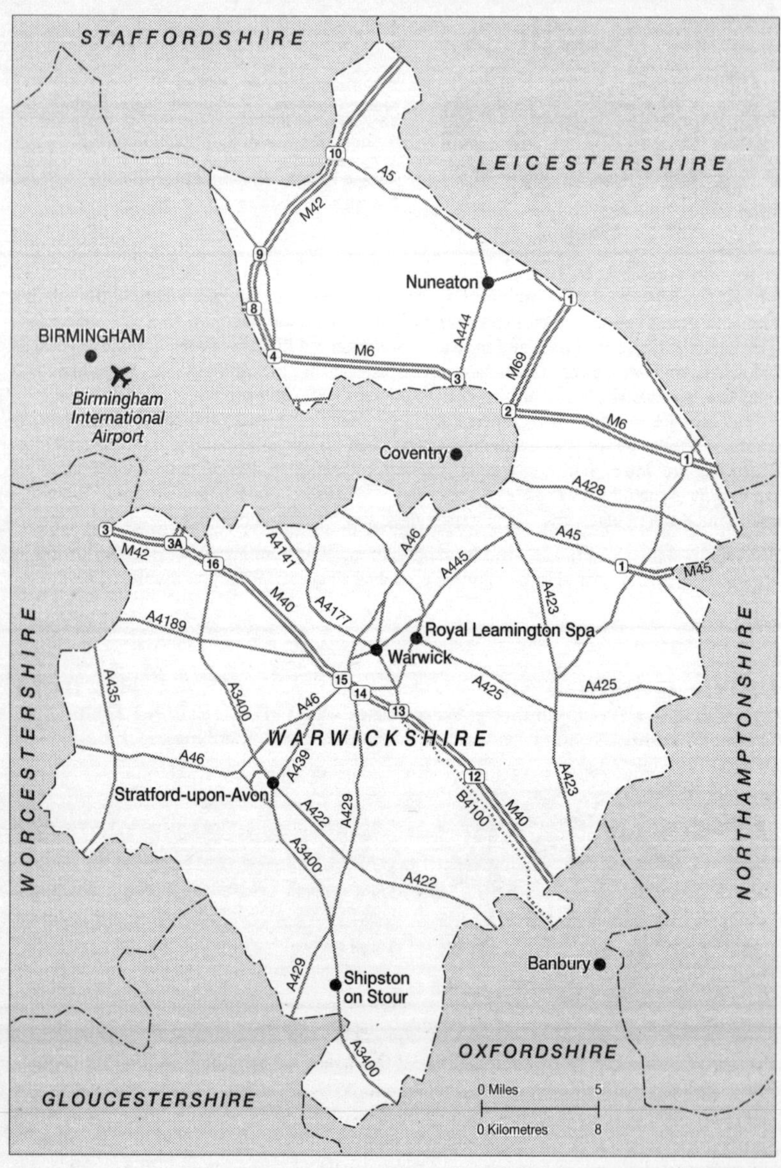

Major tourist attractions, such as Stratford-upon-Avon, Bath and Cambridge, can often be easily reached from houses in adjacent counties.

ASHBY HOUSE

C PT S

Long Compton, Warwickshire, CV36 5LB Tel/Fax: 01608 684286
South of Shipston on Stour. On A3400 from Shipston towards Chipping Norton.

2 Bedrooms. £20–£23 (less for 3 nights or more). Available: own bath/shower/toilet; TV. No smoking.
Dinner (by arrangement). £15 for 3 courses or £12 for 2 courses and coffee, at times to suit guests. Vegetarian or other special diets if ordered. No smoking. **Light suppers** if ordered.
1 Sitting-room. With open fire, TV. No smoking.
Small garden

E-mail: epfield@fieldashby.demon.co.uk

Long Compton lies between the woods of Weston Park and patchwork fields which rise to the ancient Rollright Stones on the Oxfordshire border. At the south end of the village, Victorian Ashby House is built of Cotswold stone and has been stylishly and comfortably furnished by Charlotte and Paul Field. Off the chequerboard-tiled hallway is a coffee-and-cream sitting-room, full of family pieces such as silver-framed photos and Charlotte's collection of china fowl on the marble mantelpiece.

In the royal-blue and gold dining-room, Charlotte, a professional caterer, serves such meals as guinea-fowl with creamed leeks, followed by strawberry meringue roulade. Bedrooms are smart and with plenty of reading matter. The garden has a collection of unusual trees including a Judas, a Tortuosa willow and a Maidenhair. The house is on the main road, but traffic is slow through the village and rooms double-glazed.

Readers' comments: Charming hosts, nothing too much trouble, wonderful food served in very comfortable surroundings. We were warmly welcomed. Charlotte's cooking is superb. Excellent accommodation and even better food.

V

BLACKWELL GRANGE

C(10) M S

Warwickshire

Blackwell, Warwickshire, CV36 4PF Tel: 01608 682357 (Fax: 01608 682856)
South of Stratford-upon-Avon. Nearest main road: A3400 from Stratford towards Oxford (and M40, junctions 11/12).

3 Bedrooms. £25–£30 **to readers of this book only** (less for 4 nights or more). Bargain breaks. All have own bath/shower/toilet. No smoking.
Dinner (by arrangement). £15 for 2 courses and coffee, at times to suit guests. Vegetarian or other special diets if ordered. No smoking. **Light suppers** if ordered.
1 Sitting-room. With open fire, TV. No smoking.
Large garden

E-mail: blackwell.grange@saqnet.co.uk

Stone-flagged floors and deep-set windows with chamfered mullions give this Elizabethan Cotswold house great character – but the Vernon-Millers had a tremendous task to give it modern comfort too. Liz has decorated the rooms with style – beribboned curtains in a pale pink bedroom, for instance; very nice bathrooms. An en suite, ground-floor bedroom, overlooking the garden, has been specifically designed for disabled guests.

An inglenook fireplace is the setting for a collection of country bygones such as ratchet cranes for hanging pots over the fire, and other kitchen tools. Dinner could consist of such dishes as roast lamb, followed by lemon meringue pie or home-made ice cream.

Outside is a thatched barn, and among the staddlestones (rick-stones) of the garden strut the Wyandotte bantams which provide breakfast eggs.

Readers' comments: Outstanding accommodation and warmth of hospitality. Most charming hostess. Kind and attentive. Garden delightful.

V

Warwickshire

CRANDON HOUSE

C(12)

Avon Dassett, Warwickshire, CV4 72AA Tel: 01295 770652 (Fax: 01295 770632)
South-east of Royal Leamington Spa. Nearest main road: A423 from Banbury to Coventry (and M40, junctions 11/12).

5 Bedrooms. £20–£25 (less for 7 nights or more). Bargain breaks. All have own bath/shower/toilet; TV. No smoking.
Light suppers if ordered.
2 Sitting-rooms. With log stove, TV.
Large garden

E-mail: crandonhouse@talk21.com

A 'hostess of the year' award was once won by Deborah Lea – the most unassuming of people – who with her brother runs this farmhouse on a smallholding where a few rare British white cattle, sheep and poultry roam free. One can sit in the sunny living-room to watch the geese and ducks enjoying life, with a view of hills beyond. There is a separate television room with log stove, and a terrace outside. Everything about the house, built in the 1950s, is solidly comfortable. The pink or blue bedrooms have nice pieces of furniture (a walnut suite, for instance, and a shellback brocade chair) and large windows.

There is a choice of pubs for evening meals within a mile. Breakfast options include porridge, kippers and smoked haddock. Packed lunches can also be provided.

V *Readers' comments:* We felt extremely welcome, no detail was overlooked. Splendid hosts, house immaculate. Pride of place goes to Crandon.

Warwickshire

DOCKERS BARN FARM

C(8) D

Oxhill Bridle Road, Pillerton Hersey, Warwickshire, CV35 0QB Tel: 01926 640475 (Fax: 01926 641747)
South-east of Stratford-upon-Avon. Nearest main road: A422 from Stratford to Banbury (and M40, junction 12).

3 Bedrooms. £21–£24 (less for 5 nights or more). Available: own bath/shower/toilet; TV. No smoking.
Garden

E-mail: jwhoward@onetel.net.uk

It would be hard to envisage a more tranquil and secluded spot, yet one so conveniently placed for visiting some of the country's best-known tourist honeypots: Stratford, Warwick and the Cotswolds are all easily accessible.

Down a mile-long country track, past fields of sheep and the Howards' Shetland ponies, you eventually come to this imaginatively converted, 18th-century threshing barn. In the adjoining former granary (with its own entrance), guests have a tastefully decorated suite, with a modern wrought-iron four-poster bed, small sitting-area and bathroom. The front door of the main house opens into a flagstoned dining-hall which looks out on to a semi-wild garden and pond. All around are fine old furnishings, family heirlooms and portraits of John's ancestors.

Tucked under the rafters are cosy and characterful bedrooms with exposed beams. Here and there, Carolyn has colourwashed rough-plastered walls and added such artistic touches as stencilled stars on one bedroom ceiling. Ten acres of this peaceful smallholding are devoted to wildlife conservation – deer, hares, kestrels, buzzards and even badgers may be V observed. Guests can dine well within a five-mile radius.

FORTH HOUSE

C D M P T X

44 High Street, Warwick, CV34 4AX Tel: 01926 401512 (Fax: 01926 490809)
(M40, junction 15, is near.)

2 Bedrooms. £25 **(one room for readers of this book only)**–£35. Less for 3 nights or more. Bargain breaks. Both have own bath/shower/toilet; TV. No smoking.
Light suppers if ordered.
2 Sitting-rooms. With open fire (in one), TV. No smoking.
Small garden

E-mail: info@forthhouseuk.co.uk

Past the antique and craft shops of the busy High Street is a terrace of trim Georgian houses; overhead looms Warwick Castle. Not exactly 'off the beaten track'. But behind no. 44 lies a secret place: a long garden stretching far back. Stone steps and paths flank the lawn; an ancient wisteria clambers high, and a fountain splashes. Here is found an entire garden-suite for visitors: virtually a flat with its own kitchen, and all on the ground floor. It is not only spacious but very pretty – blue-and-white stripes on the bathroom curtains, the bath's sides clad with pine. There's another bedroom at the back of the house, on the first floor. This has a pine table and rush chairs for meals (if you want to take these in privacy), and a sofa. Both the upstairs bedroom and ground-floor sitting-room have bay windows overlooking Elizabeth Draisey's lovely back garden.

Readers' comments: Best equipped room we've had; large and quiet. Highly recommended.

HILL HOUSE

C(13) **S**

off Mancetter Road, Caldecote, Warwickshire, CV10 0RS Tel: 024 76396685
North-west of Nuneaton. Nearest main road: A5 from Atherstone to Hinckley (also M69, junction 1; and M42, junction 10).

3 Bedrooms. £22.50–£25. Available: own bath/shower/toilet; TV; views of river; balcony. No smoking.
Dinner (by arrangement). £15 for 3 courses and coffee, at 7.30pm. Vegetarian diets if ordered. Wine available. No smoking. **Light suppers** if ordered.
1 Sitting-room. With open fire, TV. No smoking.
Large garden

A rough track leads to 18th-century Hill House – brimming with antiques and bric-a-brac collected by Jane Cox, from rococo mirrors to a naive portrait of the Queen. All contribute to the distinctive character of the house (where once Edward VII kept a mistress, it is said). Several bedrooms overlook arches where coaches used to be housed. There are a games room, canalside walks, panoramic views across the River Anker, and a goat to divert visitors. Dinner comprises such traditional dishes as vegetable soup, cottage pie, and lemon meringue tart (vegetarian dishes are a speciality).

Nuneaton has the George Eliot museum, and all around are places associated with her (Arbury Hall, in particular) and the scenes she so vividly described. This lesser-known part of Warwickshire has attractions waiting to be discovered. The National Exhibition Centre and Coventry Cathedral are near; and close by, in Leicestershire, is historic Bosworth where the celebrated battle in which Richard III was defeated is re-enacted from time to time.

LOWER ROWLEY C(8)

Wasperton, Warwickshire, CV35 8EB Tel/Fax: 01926 624937
South of Warwick. Nearest main road: A429 from Warwick to Moreton-in-Marsh (and M40, junction 15).

2–3 Bedrooms. £22.50–£24 (less for 3 nights or more). Available: own bath/shower/toilet; TV; views of river (from one). No smoking.
1 Sitting-room. No smoking.
Small garden

E-mail: CliffordVeasey@lower-rowley.freeserve.co.uk

At the edge of a village, where traces of an Iron Age settlement and Roman and Saxon burial mounds have been found, is this 1960s house where Carol and Cliff Veasey welcome bed-and-breakfast guests.

Although bedrooms are not large, they have been very comfortably and considerately equipped. From the blue-and-white room – which has a handsome walnut wardrobe, blue wicker armchairs and a compact shower unit – there are superb views over the River Avon. The twin room, equally immaculate, has pale yellow and green 'Country Diary' fabrics and its own neat, tiled bathroom.

The Veaseys (she a former nurse, he an engineer) are a friendly couple and their pride in their home, with its attractive mix of antique and modern furnishings, is evident. Breakfast is served on an old oak gate-legged table in the sunny conservatory, which overlooks the flowery garden. Here, guests can relax or wander on down to the peaceful banks of the Avon.

V Warwick Castle, Charlecote Park (NT), Stratford and the Royal Showground at Stoneleigh are all within easy reach. There is ample choice of nearby pubs at which to dine.

LOXLEY FARMHOUSE C D

Stratford Road, Loxley, Warwickshire, CV35 9JN Tel/Fax: 01789 840265
South-east of Stratford-upon-Avon. Nearest main road: A422 from Stratford to Banbury (and M40, junction 15).

2–3 Bedrooms. £25–£32 (less for 7 nights or more). Two have own bath/shower/toilet; TV.
Large garden

Loxley is a hilltop village with a diminutive church. Just downhill from here Loxley Farm is tucked away: a rare cruck-house of half-timbering and thatch, parts dating back to the 13th century. Charles I stayed here during the battle of Edgehill.

Inside, everything is in keeping with the style of the ancient house: low ceilings with pewter pots hanging from the beams, flagged floors, small-paned windows, oak doors. In the dining-room, where Anne Horton serves breakfast, leather chairs surround a large oak table.

Two suites with sitting-rooms are in a separate, half-timbered, thatched, 17th-century barn conversion. In the main house a double room is sometimes available for guests.

Readers' comments: Idyllic surroundings. Much care and attention. Most welcoming and comfortable. Not a jarring note. The most delightful of all. Have enjoyed Mrs Horton's hospitality over the past ten years. Pleasant place and very pleasant people.

MINE HILL HOUSE **C D X**

Lower Brailes, Warwickshire, OX15 5BJ Tel: 01608 685594
South-east of Shipston on Stour. Nearest main road: A3400 from Stratford towards Chipping Norton (and M40, junction 11).

2 Bedrooms. £25–£35. Available: own bath/toilet; TV. No smoking.
Dinner (by arrangement). £20 for 3 courses and coffee, at 7.30–9pm. Vegetarian or other special diets if ordered. **Light suppers** if ordered.
2 Sitting-rooms. With open fire/stove, TV. No smoking in one.
Large garden

Standing alone at the top of a hill on the Cotswold borders, Mine Hill House has wonderful views across the patchwork fields of five counties. An 18th-century farmhouse surrounded by old outbuildings, the decor within is stylish and smart. The best bedroom, in blue with oakleaf-patterned walls, has its own bathroom in matching colours. The other room is a pretty pink-and-white twin, with thick beams and wicker and bamboo bedside tables.

Hester Sale is a cordon bleu cook and might offer you warm goat's cheese salad with lardons as a starter, followed by chicken breasts stuffed with roast peppers in a red pepper and basil sauce, then frozen chocolate mousse with caramel oranges and mint. While dining you can look at the Sales' collection of modern art. Many of the paintings throughout the house are by Hester's mother, an internationally exhibited artist. One snug sitting-room has a coal fire; another grander one, decorated in vibrant colours, has more paintings.

This is an area rich in Civil War history, and a short walk away are the ominously named Traitor's Ford and Gallows Hill. Stratford, Banbury and Oxford are within easy reach.

NORTHLEIGH HOUSE **C D M**(limited)

Five Ways Road, Hatton, Warwickshire, CV35 7HZ Tel: 01926 484203 (Fax: 01926 484006)
North-west of Warwick. Nearest main road: A4177 from Warwick towards Solihull (also M40, junction 15; and M42, junction 5).

7 Bedrooms. £25–£30 (less for 3 nights over the weekend). Available: own bath/shower/toilet; TV; balcony (one). No smoking.
1 Sitting-room. With woodstove. No smoking.
Garden
Closed in December and January.

Sylvia Fenwick – a vivacious personality – has had an immensely varied career and at Northleigh House she has turned her creative energy to decorating every room with great elegance and style. Each bedroom has an individual theme and many verge on the luxurious. A large, ground-floor blue room has its own sofa and kitchenette; the Victoria room, in gentle shades of mushroom and muted rose-pink, has a collection of 19th-century plates and lithographs; while in the vibrant Italian room, a verdigris wrought-iron bedhead has a complementary chandelier and lampstands. All are very thoughtfully equipped with fridges concealed within capacious cupboards, and grab rails and magnifying make-up mirrors in the equally smart bathrooms.

Breakfast is served on mahogany tables overlooking the pretty, shrub-filled garden. For evening meals, Sylvia gives guests a map (and sample menus) of local eateries, three of which are gourmet-standard pub-restaurants.

Readers' comments: First class! Immaculate. A very warm and hospitable lady. Her scrambled eggs are heavenly! We loved this place. Well equipped and luxurious. Warm welcome, comfortable stay. Sylvia is a real character.

PARK FARM

C(12) **S X**

Spring Road, Barnacle, Warwickshire, CV7 9LG Tel: 024 76612628
North of Coventry. Nearest main roads: M69 and M6 (junction 2).

2 Bedrooms. £22. Both have TV. No smoking.
Dinner (by arrangement). £16 for 3 courses and coffee. Vegetarian or other special diets if ordered.
Light suppers if ordered.
1 Sitting-room.
Large garden

The Roundheads burnt down the original house: several great Civil War battles took place in this region. This one was built about 1670. Outside it stand fine yews and within are such handsome features as the balustered staircase. All around is the 200-acre farm.

The house is immaculate, furnished with antiques and decorated in restful colours. In the pale cream sitting-room is an attractive suite upholstered in vanilla damask. The big dining-room has windows at each end, and here Linda Grindal serves such meals as home-made pâté, chicken and broccoli casserole with dauphinoise potatoes, and blackcurrant shortcake. Upstairs are pleasant bedrooms – fine walnut beds in the yellow one, a prettily draped one in the pink room; and a very good bathroom.

V *Readers' comments:* Wonderful dinner, wicked breakfasts. The Grindals are delightful. Accommodation first class. Pretty home, gracious host. Made to feel most welcome. Wonderful – fantastic home cooking and the most generous of hospitality.

PEAR TREE COTTAGE

C(3) **PT**

Church Road, Wilmcote, Warwickshire, CV37 9UX Tel: 01789 205889
(Fax: 01789 262862)
North-west of Stratford-upon-Avon. Nearest main road: A3400 from Stratford to Birmingham (and M40, junction 15).

7 Bedrooms. £24–£30 (less for 7 nights or more). All have own bath/shower/toilet; TV. No smoking.
2 Sitting-rooms. With TV. No smoking.
Large garden

E-mail: mander@peartree.co.uk

Mary Arden, Shakespeare's mother, grew up in the big red brick house near this half-timbered cottage, which is of much the same date. One steps into a hall with stone-flagged floor (of blue lias, once quarried at Wilmcote), oak settle, other antiques and bunches of dried flowers.

In the beamed dining-room, country Hepplewhite chairs and colourful Staffordshire pottery figures show well against rugged stone walls. There's a little television room and a pretty reading-room opening on to the gardens. Bedrooms (reached by steps and turns all the way) have very pleasant colour schemes. Some are in a new extension.

Outside are two gardens, a stream, stone paths and seats under old apple-trees. Although Margaret Mander does not serve evening meals, there are kitchens in which guests can prepare their own snack suppers, and two inns serving good food in the village.

V *Readers' comments:* Ideal in all respects. Have always received most kind and courteous attention and a wonderful breakfast. Very friendly. Excellent. Exceptional.

POND COTTAGE

C(13) S

The Green, Warmington, Warwickshire, OX17 1BU Tel: 01295 690682
South-east of Stratford-upon-Avon. Nearest main road: B4100 from Banbury to Warwick (and M40, junctions 11/12).

2 Bedrooms. £22 (less for 4 nights or more). Available: own bath/shower/toilet.
Light suppers if ordered.
1 Sitting-room. With open fire, TV.
Small garden
Closed in December and January.

The village of Warmington, near the M40, is so tucked away that few tourists find it. Around a sloping green with duck-pond are ranged rows of cottages built from local stone, and Pond Cottage is one of these. Vi Viljoen has furnished its rooms with great elegance – gleaming antique furniture and silver contrast with the rugged stones of the sitting-room walls. One pretty bedroom is all blue – from the silk bedspread to the birds-and-flowers wallpaper.

The cottage is well placed for visiting not only Warwick Castle and Stratford but such stately homes as Upton House (wonderful collection of paintings) and Blenheim Palace. The National Herb Centre is very close by, and the Heritage Motor Centre (with over 300 historic British cars) is just six miles away.

Readers' comments: Delicious food, extremely good value. Like staying with a friend, every need anticipated.

V

SHREWLEY POOLS FARM

C PT

Haseley, Warwickshire, CV35 7HB Tel: 01926 484315
North-west of Warwick. Nearest main road: A4177 from Warwick towards Solihull (also M40, junction 15; and M42, junction 5).

2 Bedrooms. £22.50–£27.50 (less for 3 nights or more). Both have own bath/toilet; TV; views of lake (from one). No smoking.
Dinner (by arrangement). £15 for 3 courses and coffee, at times to suit guests. Vegetarian or other special diets if ordered. No smoking. **Light suppers** if ordered.
1 Sitting-room. With woodburner, TV. No smoking.
Large garden

E-mail: cathydodd@hotmail.com

Families are warmly welcomed at this mellow old farmhouse which is surrounded by a particularly attractive garden, where bantam chickens roam free. Also in the grounds are sheep, geese, turkeys, and Saddleback pigs which may be spotted by the large lake as you approach the house.

Built in 1640, the brick and timbered farmhouse, with a listed barn, stands at the heart of a traditional mixed working farm. Inside, there are beams, low doorways, sloping corridors and an original quarry-tiled hall with an inglenook fireplace. Chintz sofas and armchairs are drawn round the hearth in the peaceful sitting-room. Up a steep wooden staircase is an airy family room (spacious enough for four), which has cream and rosy floral fabrics and is equipped with such extras as an iron, shoe-cleaning kit and even a spare dressing-gown. Cathy Dodd can provide high chairs and cots as well as toys, games and puzzles to keep young ones amused.

Breakfast eggs, sausages and bacon are all home-produced. The Aga-cooked dinner might comprise poached salmon or the farm's own gammon, lemon meringue pie or jam roly-poly, and English cheeses.

V

Warwickshire

SUGARSWELL FARM

C(12) X

Shenington, Warwickshire, OX15 6HW Tel: 01295 680512 (Fax: 01295 688149)
South of Stratford-upon-Avon. Nearest main road: A422 from Stratford to Banbury.

3 Bedrooms. £21–£25. All have own bath/toilet; TV. No smoking.
Dinner (by arrangement). £22.50 for 3 courses and coffee, at 6.30pm. Vegetarian or other special diets if ordered. No smoking. **Light suppers** if ordered.
1 Sitting-room. With open fire, TV. No smoking.
Large garden

Rosemary Nunnely is a cook of cordon bleu calibre – her greatest delight is preparing meals. Visitors who stay with her are likely to get something very different from ordinary 'farmhouse fare': for instance, seafood gratin, followed by fillet steak in a sauce of port, cream and garlic, with crème brûlée to finish.

The house is modern but made from old stones taken from a demolished cottage. It has big picture-windows, and a striking staircase with 18th-century portraits. Sofas are grouped round a huge stone fireplace in the sage-green sitting-room. Guests sit on Chippendale chairs to dine; and one side of the dining-room has a glass wall filled with Rosemary's collection of Crown Derby. Upstairs are elegant bedrooms – one with a sofa from which to enjoy woodland views, and a very large bathroom decorated in bright mulberry.

Readers' comments: Time capsule of the good life! Charming hostess, delightful accommodation. Superb welcome, superb cooking. An outstanding cook. First class. We have been back nine times. A truly beautiful house and excellent food. Wonderful holiday.

Warwickshire

WHITE HOUSE

C X

Burton Dassett, Warwickshire, CV47 2AB Tel/Fax: 01295 770143
South-east of Royal Leamington Spa. Nearest main road: B4100 from Warwick to Banbury (and M40, junction 12).

3 Bedrooms. £22.50. All have own shower/toilet; TV. No smoking.
Light suppers if ordered.
1 Sitting-room. With open fire, TV, piano. No smoking.
Garden

E-mail: lisa@whitehouse10.freeserve.co.uk

Nestling on a hillside within undulating Burton Dassett Country Park, this white-painted house has wide, open views which, on a clear day, extend over 40 miles towards the Malverns in Worcestershire. The accommodation here is homely and modest, but musical Lisa Foxwell has created a most welcoming atmosphere, much enlivened by the presence of her West Highland terriers.

Upstairs, past a landing-alcove housing one of Lisa's pianos and her impressive collection of music certificates, are neat, simply furnished bedrooms, decorated predominantly in shades of pink and white. Two have the benefit of those superb country views.

Beige-checked sofas and armchairs, with crochet throws, are drawn round the fireplace in the comfortable sitting-room. There is a baby grand in one corner and over the mantelpiece hangs a huge photograph of the two terriers. Although sandwich suppers are available, most people dine at nearby pubs.

In addition to scenic walks straight from the front door, this is a good base for sightseeing: Banbury, Leamington Spa, Warwick, Stratford and the Cotswolds are all within 30 minutes' drive. Motoring-enthusiasts head for Gaydon Heritage Motor Centre, serious walkers for the Fosse Way.

V

WILLOW CORNER

C(12)

Armscote, Warwickshire, CV37 8DE Tel: 01608 682391 (Mobile: 07803 710149)
South of Stratford-upon-Avon. Nearest main road: A3400 from Stratford to Shipston on Stour.

3 Bedrooms. £25 (**one room for readers of this book only**) –£29. All have own shower/toilet; TV. No smoking.
1 Sitting-room. No smoking.
Small garden

E-mail: willowcorner@compuserve.com

Warwickshire

As one enters this archetypal English cottage – thatched roof, Cotswold-stone walls, leaded windows – the sound of wind chimes tinkling in the breeze provides a hint of what lies within. For Trish and Alan Holmes have added a distinct Eastern flavour to their 300-year-old, beamed and timbered home. From the intricately carved Rajashtani sideboard in the flagstoned hall to the framed fragments of sari beading and the splendid Oriental carpets, everywhere you look there are interesting artefacts acquired by the Holmeses during their many years overseas (Alan was in the diplomatic service).

Bedrooms here are exceptionally attractive – stylishly and individually decorated, with colour-coordinated Indian fabrics and soft furnishings. Shower-rooms, too, are particularly good.

To one side of the main lounge, dominated by a huge inglenook fireplace, is the formal dining-area where Trish serves breakfast round a table elegantly laid with silverware and blue-and-white china.

Guests can relax in a private sitting-room or outside in the pretty cottage-garden. The Fox & Goose, serving sophisticated food, is a minute's stroll away.

Reader's comments: Very warm welcome, bedrooms delightful; highly recommended; would certainly stay again. **V**

WOODSIDE

C D M S

Langley Road, Claverdon, Warwickshire, CV35 8PJ Tel: 01926 842446
(Fax: 01926 843697)
West of Warwick. Nearest main road: A4189 from Warwick to Henley-in-Arden (and M40, junction 15).

Warwickshire

5 Bedrooms. £23–£28 (less for 7 nights or more). Bargain breaks. One has own shower/toilet; TV (in all). No smoking.
Light suppers if ordered.
1 Sitting-room. With open fire, TV. No smoking.
Large garden

Woodside, built in 1917 as a shooting-lodge, has its own wildlife reserve. Hillside woods, untouched since mediaeval times, have rare old trees and traces of ancient farming techniques. Furnished with antiques, the house has two bedrooms on the ground floor, while upstairs there are three more, including a sunny family room complete with rocking chair. Doreen Bromilow does not provide full dinners, but there are plenty of eating-places in the vicinity.

Rural quiet surrounds the house – and yet it is only a few miles from Birmingham's National Exhibition Centre and international airport, Stratford-upon-Avon, Warwick and Coventry. Readers of Edith Holden's *Country Diary of an Edwardian Lady* will be familiar with a number of place-names around here such as Knowle, with half-timbered houses; and Packwood House (NT) which has a lovely garden and fine furniture inside.

Reader's comments: Very comfortable, food very well prepared.

Isle of WIGHT

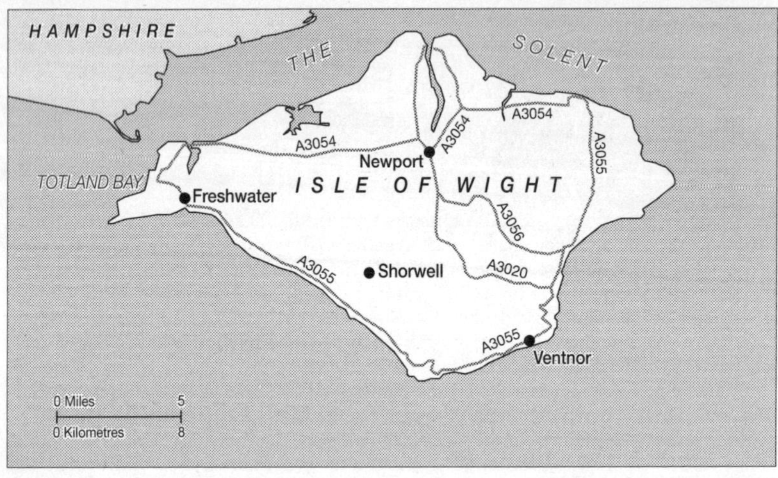

YOU AND THE LAW

Once your booking has been confirmed - orally or in writing - a contract exists between you and the proprietor. He/she is legally bound to provide accommodation as booked; and you are legally bound to pay for this accommodation. If unable to take up the booking - even because of sickness - you still remain liable for a very substantial proportion of the charges (in addition to losing your deposit).

If you have to cancel, let the proprietor know as soon as possible; then he/she may be able to re-let the accommodation (in which case you would be liable to pay only a re-letting cost or forfeit your deposit). Phone if you are going to arrive late.

(A note to overseas readers. It may be an acceptable practice elsewhere to make bookings at several houses for the same date, choosing only later which one to patronize; but this way of doing things is not the British practice and you are legally liable to compensate any proprietors whom you let down in this way.)

NORTH COURT

C PT

Shorwell, Isle of Wight, PO30 3JG Tel: 01983 740415
South-west of Newport. Nearest main road: A3055 from Totland to Ventnor.

3 Bedrooms. £23–£25 (less for 3 nights or more). All have own bath/toilet; TV. No smoking.
Light suppers if ordered.
1 Sitting-room. With open fire, piano. No smoking.
Large garden

Swinburne and his girl cousin used to play the organ that stands in the hall of this 17th-century manor house – a big, stone-flagged room with logs piled high around the stove.

The house is now the home of John and Christine Harrison, portraits of whose ancestors hang on the walls of the large dining-room with mahogany tables and marble fireplace. The great staircase was reputedly designed by Grinling Gibbons, and nearly every room has handsome detailing from that period – arched or scallop-framed doorways, egg-and-dart mouldings, shuttered windows in thick stone walls. All bedrooms are large, with armchairs.

Impressive though the house is, the really outstanding feature is the large and undulating garden with many plants of botanical interest. You can wander through woodlands or down terraces to a stream with water-plants, try to tell the time from a sundial in the knot garden, look down into the ancient bath-house, wander through arches of wisteria or lilac, play croquet . . . As only snacks are served, dinner for most people always involves a stroll through this lovely garden (opened to the public occasionally) to reach the nearby Crown Inn.

Reader's comments: A lovely place! Delightful couple and very helpful.

STRANG HALL

C PT S

Uplands, Totland Bay, Isle of Wight, PO39 0DZ Tel/Fax: 01983 753189
West of Freshwater. Nearest main road: A3054 from Yarmouth to Freshwater.

Isle of Wight

3 Bedrooms. £22.50–£25 (less for 7 nights or more). Available: own bath/shower/toilet; TV; views of sea. No smoking.
Dinner. £17.50 for 2 courses and coffee, at times to suit guests. Vegetarian or other special diets if ordered.
Light suppers if ordered.
1 Sitting-room. With open fire. No smoking.
Large garden

Totland Bay, one of west Wight's loveliest and least crowded beaches, can be reached on foot from the bottom of Strang Hall's garden. This Arts and Crafts-style house lies in the hills above the bay and is an ideal base from which to explore the island – by car, bus or the well-marked and extensive system of footpaths which crisscross it.

The house is decorated in bold period colours and is full of interesting pictures, china, tapestries and curios collected over the years by Vera McMullen and Robin Vetcher. In the sunshine-yellow dining-room overlooking the bay, Vera serves copious cooked breakfasts which also include unusual home-made preserves and home-pressed apple juice; an evening meal might be pheasant followed by banana strudel. She will prepare picnics for guests, sometimes including such treats as a fresh sponge cake. Bedrooms are all individual and have the original fitted oak furniture made locally by a ship's carpenter. If you are lucky, you may glimpse the badgers in the garden, and certainly children will enjoy feeding the donkeys there.

Reader's comments: Wonderful hosts, so welcoming to our children.

V

UNDER ROCK

PT

Shore Road, Bonchurch, Isle of Wight, PO38 1RF Tel: 01983 855274
East of Ventnor. Nearest main road: A3055 from Ventnor to Shanklin.

3 Bedrooms. £22–£26 (less for 4 nights or more). Available: own bath/shower/toilet; TV. No smoking.
Dinner. £13 for 3 courses and coffee, at 6.30pm. Vegetarian diets if ordered. No smoking. **Light suppers** if ordered.
1 Sitting-room. With open fire, piano. No smoking.
Large garden

The little village of Bonchurch with its subtropical climate and pretty duck-pond has associations with many Victorian literary figures, among them Elizabeth Sewell, Thackeray, Carlyle, Swinburne (buried at the 'new' church) and Dickens, who wrote much of *David Copperfield* here. He declared Bonchurch 'smashing' and the view from the top of St Boniface Down, beneath which Under Rock stands, as 'only to be equalled on the Genoese shore of the Mediterranean'.

The house itself, of unusual design, with wings coming off a central roundel, was home to Edmund Peel, poet nephew of Sir Robert. James Pritchett and Rod Woodward now offer accommodation in a peaceful atmosphere. Bedrooms have nice old furniture and original paintings, and there are many antique lamps, including a Moorish brass lantern which lights the hallway. James's cooking has unusual touches such as savoury scones at breakfast. A typical dinner: toast with Brie and redcurrant jelly, cottage pie, and apple crumble.

V Bonchurch is well placed for visits to the Heritage coasts as well as the many man-made attractions on offer. The island is perhaps best visited in spring, when tourists are few.

For explanation of code letters and V symbol, see inside front cover.

When writing to the managing editor, if you want an acknowledgment please enclose a stamped addressed envelope.

Prices are per person sharing a room at the beginning of the year. However, for the best rooms in the house or later in the year, you may well be asked for more.

Addresses shown are to enable you to locate a house on a map. They are not necessarily complete postal addresses (though the essential post-code is included), and detailed directions for finding a house should be obtained from the owner.

WILTSHIRE

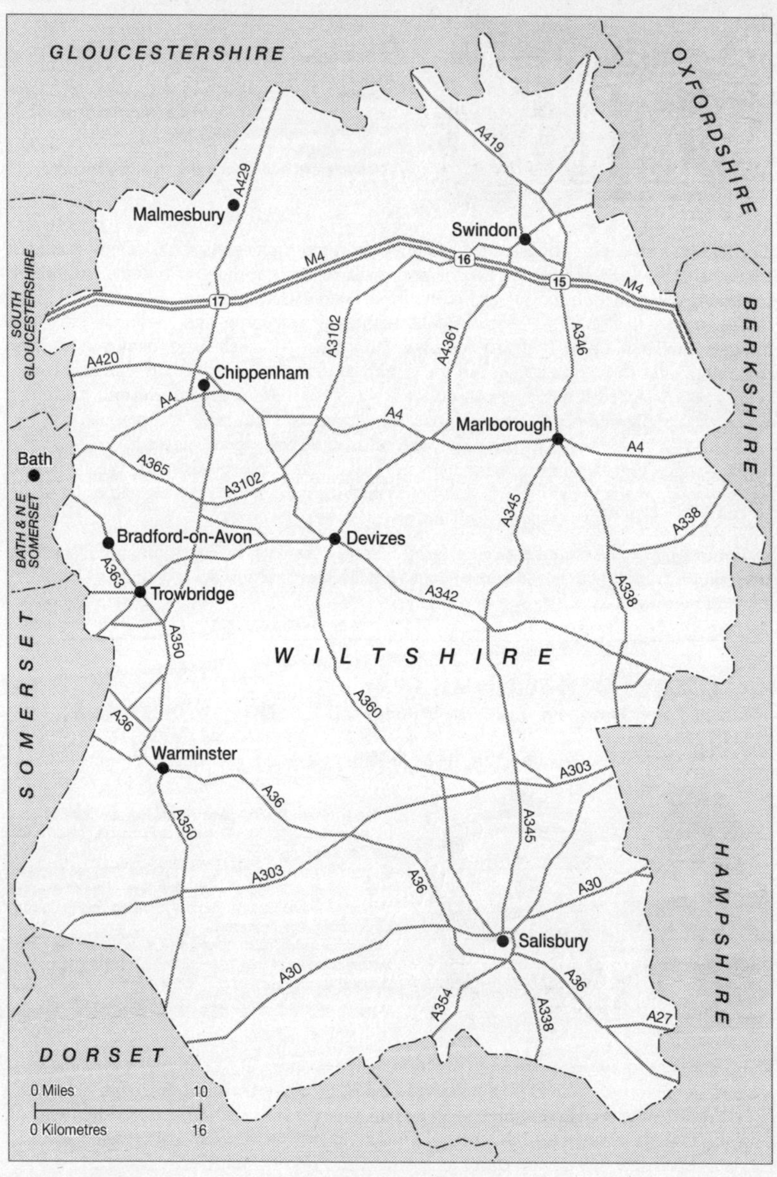

Some houses offer special discounts to readers using the current edition of this book. Always state you are an SOTBT reader when ringing to book or when using E-mail.

Wiltshire

AVONSIDE

C(10) PT S

Winsley Hill, Limpley Stoke, Wiltshire, BA2 7JJ Tel/Fax: 01225 722547

South-east of Bath. Nearest main road: A36 from Bath to Warminster.

2 Bedrooms. £23 (less for 4 nights or more). Views of river. No smoking.
Dinner (by arrangement). £15 for 3 courses with aperitif and coffee, at 7.30pm. **Light suppers** if ordered.
1 Sitting-room. With open fire.
Large garden
Closed from mid-December to mid-January.

A typical English country house, built of honey-coloured Bath stone, the Challens' secluded home stands on the banks of the River Avon: walks along it or the nearby canal and fishing are among the attractions of this very scenic area. Bath itself is close by.

Ursula has furnished the sitting-room with tangerine armchairs, oriental rugs and antiques that show up well against walls painted peach, on which hang many paintings by Peter who, after serving as a major in the Gurkhas, turned to a completely different career as an artist. Attached is a heated conservatory where orchids are grown. Beyond, there is a serene view of the well-kept lawn and landscaped grounds, with tennis and croquet.

Other rooms are equally pleasing, with attractive wallpapers and leafy views. The Challens offer visitors pre-dinner drinks (no extra charge). Typical of the kind of meal Ursula serves: avocado pâté; chicken in honey-and-mustard sauce with vegetables from the garden; a brûlée of brown sugar, cream and yogurt over raspberries.

Readers' comments: Wonderful people, very friendly. Elegant; lovely meals. The Challens make one feel like their house-guests. Excellent accommodation and food. Very comfortable and relaxing – good meals, too.

Wiltshire

BRADFORD OLD WINDMILL

PT

4 Masons Lane, Bradford-on-Avon, Wiltshire, BA15 1QN Tel: 01225 866842 (Fax: 01225 866648)

East of Bath. Nearest main road: A363 from Bath to Trowbridge (and M4, junction 17).

3 Bedrooms. £24.50 **(one room for readers of this book only)**–£49.50. All have own bath/shower/toilet; TV. No smoking.
Dinner (by arrangement). £20 for 3 vegetarian courses and coffee, at 8pm (on Monday, Thursday and Saturday only). Special diets if ordered. No smoking.
Light suppers if ordered.
1 Sitting-room. With open fire, TV. No smoking.
Small garden
Closed in January and February.

E-mail: sobt@distinctlydifferent.co.uk

The original windmill here ceased to function in 1817, and today its stump is simply a very unusual stone house, perched on a hillside within picturesque Bradford-on-Avon.

It is now in the imaginative care of Peter and Priscilla Roberts, a much-travelled couple (engineer and teacher) who have brought back finds from the Far East, New Zealand, Tahiti and Australia which now decorate the rooms.

Every room has its own character and shape: some are circular. In the sitting-room, William Morris sofas and furniture of stripped pine face a log fire. One bedroom has a circular bed with a spread patterned with wildflowers and butterflies. In another, there is a water-bed covered with a patchwork bedspread.

Breakfasts are imaginative and suppers range from wholesome 'soup trays' to an occasional Thai meal. All evening meals must be booked in advance.

V *Readers' comments:* Everything you could want. Very friendly, I thoroughly enjoyed my visit.

BULLOCKS HORN COTTAGE

C(12)

Charlton, Wiltshire, SN16 9DZ Tel: 01666 577600 (Fax: 01666 577905)

North-east of Malmesbury. Nearest main road: A429 from Cirencester to Chippenham (and M4, junction 17).

2 Bedrooms. £25–£30 (less for 3 nights or more). Both have own bath/shower/toilet. No smoking.
Dinner (by arrangement). £14–£20 for 2–3 courses and coffee, from 7–9pm. Vegetarian or other special diets if ordered. **Light suppers** if ordered.
1 Sitting-room. With open fire, TV.
Garden

E-mail: Legge@bullockshorn.clara.co.uk

For three centuries, cattle on their way from Malmesbury to Highworth Market would stop and water at the dew-pond in the peaceful hamlet of Bullocks Horn. The 150-year-old cottage here, surrounded by nearly an acre of garden with open farmland beyond, has been much extended by its present owners, Liz and Colin Legge. One enters the house via the light and airy conservatory filled with plants. Meals are taken here, or sometimes in the garden when the weather is fine. The Legges usually dine with their guests.

The sitting-room, with its plum-coloured walls and cream curtains, has a lovely Regency writing desk and an 18th-century square piano. French windows lead on to a pretty cottage garden and on summer days meals such as gazpacho, tarragon chicken with salad or vegetables from the Legges' kitchen garden, and summer pudding with home-made ginger ice cream are served in the rose-clad arbour. Bedrooms are comfortable, with buttermilk walls, chintz fabrics and cotton sheets. Family portraits line the staircase.

The gardens at Hodges Barn as well as Bath, Bristol and Cheltenham are within easy reach.

Readers' comments: Most kind; I very much enjoyed their delightful cottage. A lovely place, peaceful; beautiful garden; made to feel like a family guest.

Wiltshire

CHURCH HOUSE

C(12) **X**

Grittleton, Wiltshire, SN14 6AP Tel: 01249 782562 (Fax: 01249 782546)

North-west of Chippenham. Nearest main road: M4 (junctions 17/18).

4 Bedrooms. £24.50–£29.50 (less for 4 nights or more). Bargain breaks. Available: own bath/shower/toilet; TV.
Dinner (by arrangement). £15.50 for 4 courses, wine and coffee, at 8pm. Vegetarian or other special diets if ordered. No smoking. **Light suppers** if ordered.
1 Sitting-room. With log fire. Piano.
Large garden

Church House began life in 1740 as a huge rectory. Around it are lawns with immense copper beeches (floodlit at night), an orchard, a covered swimming-pool, a croquet lawn, and a walled vegetable and fruit garden. Anna Moore produces imaginative meals if these are ordered in advance. A typical menu: peaches or pears stuffed with Stilton; flamed pheasant; tarte tatin; British cheeses, fruit, and wine (included in the price).

The house has handsome and finely proportioned rooms. Guest-rooms are furnished with antiques; some have their bathroom facilities behind screens.

Anna and her family treat all visitors as house-guests and she often escorts overseas visitors on sightseeing tours.

Readers' comments: Anna Moore is an excellent cook. Bedrooms spacious and most comfortable. Peaceful. Lovely beds, charming house. Happy memories.

V

Wiltshire

THE COTTAGE

C

Westbrook, Bromham, Wiltshire, SN15 2EE Tel: 01380 850255
North-west of Devizes. Nearest main road: A3102 from Calne to Melksham (and M4, junction 17).

3 Bedrooms. £25. All have own shower/toilet; TV.
Large garden

E-mail: RJSteed@cottage16.freeserve.co.uk

Converted stables, weatherboarded and pantiled, provide the accommodation in The Cottage. The quiet hamlet nearby was once the home of Thomas Moore, the Irish poet.

Inside, the roof beams are still visible. The bedrooms (on the ground floor) have been furnished in keeping with the style of the building. Through the windows one can sometimes see deer and rabbits, with a distant landscape created by Capability Brown. At breakfast there will be local produce, home-made muesli and compote of fruit. Gloria Steed holds menus for a variety of excellent nearby eating-places and will make reservations for guests.

There is an immense amount to see and do in the neighbourhood. Close by are such lovely spots as Corsham (with splendid Elizabethan mansion and the unusual Bath Stone Quarry Museum), Lacock (13th-century abbey, 18th-century houses and museum of photographic history) and Bowood House, with the gardens and parklands that were laid out by Capability Brown.

V *Readers' comments:* Full of charm and character. We couldn't have asked for more.

Wiltshire

EASTCOTT MANOR

C D S

Eastcott, Wiltshire, SN10 4PL Tel: 01380 813313
South of Devizes. Nearest main road: A360 from Devizes to Salisbury.

4 Bedrooms. £23–£27 (less for 3 nights or more; and **15% reduction to readers of this book for 3 nights, December to February**). Available: own bath/shower/toilet; TV. No smoking.
Dinner (by arrangement). £20 for 4 courses, wine and coffee, at 7.30pm. Special diets if ordered. No smoking.
Light suppers if ordered.
1 Sitting-room. With open fire, TV. No smoking.
Large garden

As early as 1150 there was a house on this spot. The present building has parts dating back to the 16th century, but every century since has added its contribution. Furnishings vary. Most are fine antiques – the refectory table in the dining-room (its walls hung with ancestral portraits) is 400 years old, for instance; and one alcove houses Crown Derby and other porcelain. Up the oak staircase with barley-sugar balusters are attractive bedrooms; the largest has blue-and-white panelled walls with big sash windows at each end and rural views. There is also a conservatory.

In outbuildings or paddocks are always some of the Firths' horses: they have trained many well-known 'trials' horses. Janet's other great interest is cookery, for which she has a number of diplomas. A typical meal, served on a generous help-yourself basis: fish soufflé, lamb provençale, caramelized fruit, and cheeses (vegetables and fruit are home-produced).

V *Readers' comments:* Lovely house. Friendly and helpful. Delicious food. Very much enjoyed. Kind and welcoming. Delicious supper.

ENFORD HOUSE

C D PT S

Enford, Wiltshire, SN9 6DJ Tel: 01980 670414
South-east of Devizes. Nearest main road: A345 from Marlborough to Salisbury.

3 Bedrooms. £17.50. Bargain breaks. No smoking.
Light suppers if ordered.
1 Sitting-room. With open fire, TV.
Garden

The 18th-century house (once a rectory) and its garden are enclosed by thatch-topped walls – a feature one finds in those parts of Wiltshire where, stone being non-existent, a mix of earth and dung with horsehair or else chalk blocks were used to build walls (which then needed protection from rain). The house has pointed 'gothick' windows on one side, doors to the garden on another. Antiques furnish the panelled sitting-room, which has a crackling fire on chilly nights. Bedrooms are simple, fresh and conventionally furnished.

Although Sarah Campbell no longer serves full evening meals, excellent food is available at the village pub. The Campbells are very knowledgeable about the area – not just its historic sights (Stonehenge is only a few miles away) but also its wildlife – and can tell guests where to go for the finest views and the best walks.

Readers' comments: Everything quite delightful. A charming hostess and excellent food. Very comfortable. Pleasant and relaxed time. **V**

Wiltshire

FARTHINGS

PT S X

9 Swaynes Close, Salisbury, Wiltshire, SP1 3AE Tel/Fax: 01722 330749

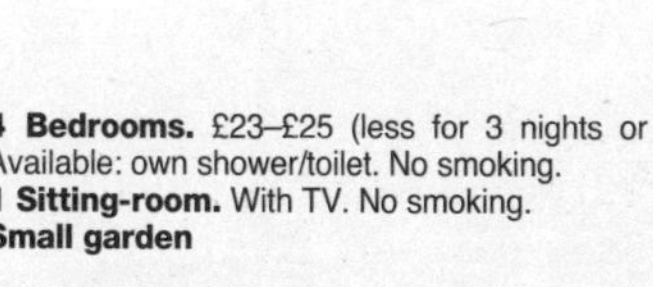
4 Bedrooms. £23–£25 (less for 3 nights or more). Available: own shower/toilet. No smoking.
1 Sitting-room. With TV. No smoking.
Small garden

Farthings is very central (there's a view of the cathedral spire over rooftops) yet very quiet. It has a garden with brimming flowerbeds, for gardening is one of retired teacher Gill Rodwell's many hobbies. All rooms are neat, tidy and pleasantly furnished. At breakfast, the choices include croissants and much else.

Salisbury is also known as New Sarum (new in 1220!) because the first town was elsewhere, on the hill now known as Old Sarum which began as an Iron Age fort. When it was decided to rebuild on a better site, the new cathedral, with the tallest spire in England, was surrounded by grass and big walls to keep the township that followed at a respectful distance. Within the precincts of the cathedral is Mompesson House, a beautiful Queen Anne building with a fine collection of paintings, china, glassware and period furnishings.

Readers' comments: Excellent value for money. Gleamingly clean. Delighted. A treasure. Accommodation and breakfast first rate. Lovely house. Charming and kind owner. Comfortable and spacious; furnished and equipped to a high standard. Garden a delight.

Wiltshire

FERN COTTAGE

C(12) X

74 Monkton Farleigh, Wiltshire, BA15 2QJ Tel: 01225 859412 (Fax: 01225 859018)
South-east of Bath. Nearest main road: A363 from Bath to Bradford-on-Avon.

rear view

3 Bedrooms. £25 **to readers of this book only in January** –£30 (less for 3 nights or more). All have own bath/shower/toilet; TV. No smoking.
Light suppers sometimes. No smoking.
Small garden

In one of the many pretty villages scattered over the lovely countryside around Bradford-on-Avon nestles Fern Cottage, home of Jenny and Christopher Valentine and now a haven for those who wish to visit the Bath area without staying in the city itself. Jenny does not serve dinner, but the nearby 17th-century coaching inn is excellent, and neither Bath nor Bradford-on-Avon is more than five miles away. Breakfast is served in the dining-room, where there is a black-leaded range in the old fireplace and the colours of the pretty floral curtains are picked up by the Chinese rug. Portraits of Christopher's great-great-grandparents hang on the walls.

Bedrooms are immaculate, with board-and-latch doors and brass bedheads, and across the secluded guests' garden, with lily-pond and magnolias, is a separate suite. Best of all is the conservatory, where guests have lingered for hours in the comfortable, white-painted chairs under the passion flowers, reading, playing games or just dreaming the time away.

V *Reader's comments:* Delightful, very warm welcome, very comfortable, excellent breakfast.

Wiltshire

HEATHERLY COTTAGE

Ladbrook Lane, Gastard, Wiltshire, SN13 9PE Tel: 01249 701402
(Fax: 01249 701412)
South-west of Chippenham. Nearest main road: A4 from Bath to Chippenham (and M4, junction 17).

3 Bedrooms. £23–£25. Bargain breaks. Available: own bath/shower/toilet; TV. No smoking.
Light suppers if ordered. No smoking.
Large garden

You will indeed find heather growing in the garden of this much extended 17th-century cottage, lovingly tended by Jenny and Peter Daniel. There are fruit trees, too, whose produce provides home-made preserves for breakfast, and there are chickens providing fresh eggs.

Guests stay in the original part of the house, built of Bath stone. The beamed bedroom on the ground floor is spacious, with private corridor leading to a large white bathroom. The upstairs bedrooms, in pastel shades, with flowery duvets and matching curtains, have fine views towards Corsham, Lacock and the Westbury White Horse. In the entrance hall is a hand-carved sideboard known as a credence table. These were used in the past when testing food for poison before serving it.

As there is no sitting-room, guests are welcome to relax in the dining-room or in the garden in summer. For dinner, you could try the George in Lacock or the White Horse in Biddestone, both about two miles away. There is much to see and do in the area and, for golf enthusiasts, there is a one-hole golf course in the garden!

V

HERB COTTAGE

C S

Wiltshire

99 Bradford Leigh, Wiltshire, BA15 2RW Tel: 01225 865554
East of Bath. Nearest main road: A363 from Bath to Bradford-on-Avon.

2 Bedrooms. £25 (less for 2 nights or more). Available: own bath/shower/toilet; TV. No smoking.
Light suppers only. Vegetarian or other special diets if ordered. No smoking.
1 Sitting-room. With stove, TV, piano. No smoking.
Garden

Down a path bordered on one side by Suzanne Wise's organic fruit and herb bed and on the other by her daughter's dramatic wood totem symbols is a 200-year-old converted farmhouse filled with more good things: individually designed wooden furniture and glass sculptures (many for sale); rococo mirrors on bedroom walls; and books everywhere. One of the simply furnished bedrooms is on the ground floor, with its own spacious shower-room and a lovely view northwards over countryside. Upstairs is another bedroom, with an attractive chest of drawers and carpeted bathroom, and a small room adjoining for accompanying child or relative.

Most guests dine at the Plough Inn at the end of the lane, but nearby Bradford-on-Avon has several pubs with good food, and Bath with its almost infinite variety of restaurants is only five miles away. Suzanne's interest in holistic health is reflected in her breakfasts: there is always a compote of home-grown fruit on the table, along with nuts, raisins, yogurt and good bread, and any dietary requirement can be catered for with notice.

V

LITTLE LANGFORD FARMHOUSE

C(12)

Wiltshire

Little Langford, Wiltshire, SP3 4NR Tel: 01722 790205 (Fax: 01722 790086)
North-west of Salisbury. Nearest main road: A36 from Wilton to Warminster.

3 Bedrooms. £25–£27 (less for 3 nights or more). Available: own bath/shower/toilet; TV. No smoking.
Light suppers if ordered. Vegetarian or other special diets if ordered. No smoking.
1 Sitting-room. With open fire, piano. No smoking.
Large garden
Closed from mid-December to mid-January.

E-mail: bandb@littlelangford.co.uk

This is a farmhouse on the grand scale – with crenellations, lancet windows and a turreted entrance hall, it is a fine example of Victorian 'gothick' architecture. Topsy Helyer continues the Victorian theme in her decor, using damask curtains and good period furniture. One bedroom has a finely carved Arts and Crafts suite, another blue striped walls and brass bed. Two have their original window-shutters, stripped down to a warm golden pine. Guests can use the billiard room or relax on the secluded terrace.

The house is situated in the rolling downs of the Wylye Valley and on fine days you can see as far as one of the Wiltshire white horses, some 45 miles distant. Guests are welcome to observe working life on this dairy and arable farm or follow the downland walks the Helyers have mapped out. In this Area of Special Scientific Interest there are numerous butterfly and wildflower species to spot. Such attractions as Wilton House, Salisbury and Longleat are short drives away, or one can visit nearby Heale Gardens, where there are many gardens in formal settings as well as watergardens and a Japanese tea-house.

V

Wiltshire

LONGWATER

C(5) **D M**

Lower Road, Erlestoke, Wiltshire, SN10 5UE Tel/Fax: 01380 830095
South-west of Devizes. Nearest main road: A360 from Devizes towards Amesbury.

3 Bedrooms. £22–£28 (less for 3 nights or more). Available: own bath/shower/toilet; TV; views of lakes.
2 Sitting-rooms. With open fire/stove, TV. No smoking in one.
Large garden

Longwater is a modern, long-house-style bungalow at the centre of an organic farm with various hens, ducks and geese in residence (as well as Pam Hampton's three cats). There are also 40 acres of woodland for walks, and licensed fishing in season in the larger of the two lakes on the land (from which the house takes its name). Bedrooms, decorated in pastel shades and chintzes, are either on the ground floor of the main house or in a separate family annexe. All the rooms have good wheelchair access; fridges and microwaves, too.

Guests may sit in the large conservatory or the more cosy but spacious sitting-room, both with panoramic countryside views. Pam Hampton is a keen collector, be it of blue and white china, of gleaming copper pans and jugs, or even of telephone boxes – an old red one sits outside the house. No evening meals, but the village pub is just 250 yards away, or you can dine at one of the many hostelries in the surrounding villages.

This is an ideal base from which to explore Wiltshire. Visit nearby Devizes in particular, which has fine churches and architecture, the Wiltshire Museum of Archaeology, and a famous system of 29 canal locks.

Wiltshire

ROSEGARTH

West Grafton, Wiltshire, SN8 3BY Tel: 01672 810288
South-east of Marlborough. Nearest main road: A338 from Hungerford to North Tidworth.

2 Bedrooms. £20–£22 (less for 7 nights or more). Both have own bath/toilet. No smoking.
1 Sitting-room. With TV. No smoking.
Large garden

Rosegarth is a picturebook, 16th-century, thatched cottage in a hamlet a few miles south of Marlborough and ancient Savernake Forest. Guest accommodation is self-contained at one end of the house. Bedrooms (reached via a steep narrow staircase) are simply furnished, with whitewashed walls and candlewick bedspreads. The comfortable sitting-room has a pink and pistachio colour scheme, and a pretty display of colourful Bohemian glassware set in one window.

Anne and Rick Ruddock-Brown take much care over their guests' wellbeing, with thoughtful touches such as posies of fresh flowers in each bedroom, and, although evening meals are not offered, they have menus from good restaurants within a five-minute drive. You may amble about the garden, where squirrels leap amongst the tall larch and spruce and where pheasants spend the winter. So far, Rick has spotted 43 species of bird.

Nearby Marlborough is a handsome and historic town, with one of the widest high streets in the country. Its famous public school, Marlborough College, is well worth a visit when open to the public, and there are adult summer schools covering a broad range of subjects.

Readers' comments: Lovely garden. Have stayed on four occasions.

SPIERS PIECE FARM

C D S

Wiltshire

Steeple Ashton, Wiltshire, BA14 6HG Tel: 01380 870266
East of Trowbridge. Nearest main road: A350 from Melksham to Westbury.

3 Bedrooms. £18–£19 (less for 7 nights or more). One has TV. No smoking.
Light suppers if ordered. Vegetarian or other special diets if ordered. No smoking.
1 Sitting-room. With open fire, TV. No smoking.
Large garden

In the 15th and 16th centuries, Steeple Ashton was one of the many Wiltshire villages to profit from the local wool trade. Today it is a picturesque and peaceful spot, with a fine parish church, old manor house, market cross and domed lock-up for miscreants.

Spiers Piece Farm, on the edge of the village, is a neat early Victorian house, the home of Jill and Pat Awdry – distant relatives of the Rev. W. Awdry, creator of Thomas the Tank Engine. Bedrooms are prettily furnished in yellows, pinks and creams. Downstairs, the dining-room has a fine set of Robert Thompson 'House of Mouse' pale oak furniture and equine portraits on the walls. Here Jill serves enormous, traditional farmhouse breakfasts, with such alternatives as fruit and yogurt always available too. Afternoon tea with home-made cake is sometimes served, and in the evening most guests eat at the Lamb-on-the-Strand in nearby Semington or at the village pub.

Reader's comments: First-class food and accommodation; helpful and welcoming; we felt at home from the outset.

V

STAG COTTAGE

C D P T S X

Wiltshire

Fantley Lane, Zeals, Wiltshire, BA12 6NX Tel/Fax: 01747 840458
South-west of Warminster. Nearest main road: A303 from Wincanton to Amesbury.

3 Bedrooms. £18–£20 (less for 5 nights or more). Available: own bath/shower/toilet; TV. No smoking.
Light suppers if ordered. No smoking.
1 Sitting-room. With wood-burner, TV. No smoking.
Small garden

In the 17th century, Stag Cottage, with its thatched roof and antlers above the front door, was the middle one of three farm labourers' cottages. Today, the thatch and the antlers remain, but the cottages now form one dwelling, with bed-and-breakfast accommodation.

Marie and Peter Boxall will serve hot snacks all year round in the beamed dining-room, with its collection of cream jugs and old thatching-needles above the inglenook fireplace. For dinner, they recommend the White Lion, a five-minute walk away, or the Smithy in nearby Charlton Musgrove.

Bedrooms are small and cosy (windows are double-glazed), with quilted headboards and matching curtains made by Marie. Framed examples of her talent for embroidery hang in one room while in another is a piece of artwork which the couple acquired while living in Rio de Janeiro. The whitewashed walls of the landing are filled with family photos, including some of children whom the Boxalls have fostered in the past.

Children are very welcome here and special china is provided for them as well as a supply of colouring books and pencils. Baby-changing facilities and packed lunches are also available.

V

WELAM HOUSE C

Bratton Road, West Ashton, Wiltshire, BA14 6AZ Tel: 01225 755908
East of Trowbridge. Nearest main road: A350 from Westbury to Chippenham.

3 Bedrooms. £18–£19 (less for 3 nights or more). Available: own bath/shower/toilet. No smoking.
Light suppers if ordered. Vegetarian or other special diets if ordered. No smoking.
1 Sitting-room. With open fire, TV. No smoking.
Large garden
Closed from December to March.

This former vicarage was built from Bath stone in 1840 in the 'gothick' style so fashionable then – hence the pointed windows, arched fireplaces and stained glass in the hall (with the crest of Lord Long, a great local landowner at the time). There is exceptionally decorative plasterwork, particularly in the turquoise sitting-room, which has an egg-and-dart design in the ceiling coving and a bay with intricate rope mouldings. Outside is a lawn with lily-pool, bowling green and putting; alternatively, there is the shady canopy of a weeping cherry under which to recline in the Cronans' deckchairs on a sunny day.

Nearby Trowbridge is a town of handsome stone buildings that were built by rich cloth-merchants descended from Flemish weavers who fled here during times of religious persecution. Another weavers' town is Westbury, which is overlooked by the huge white horse cut into the chalky downs in the 18th century. The vast green undulations of Salisbury Plain have changed little over the centuries; its grandeur is as imposing as ever.

Readers' comments: Very comfortable. Excellent value. Lovely, peaceful house.

For a list of SOTBT houses that are in or close to the great National Parks of England and Wales, see p.ix.

Where wine is not available (meaning it is on sale or can be fetched for you), you are nearly always welcome to bring in your own drinks.

At houses where dinner is not served, a light supper can often be obtained (if ordered in advance), ranging from sandwiches to family 'pot luck'. (Packed lunches too.)

Prices for single occupancy may be higher than those quoted here. Houses that charge singles no more, or only 10% more, than half the price of a double room (except possibly at peak periods) are indicated by the 'S' symbol.

WORCESTERSHIRE

You stand a better chance of finding the right accommodation at the right price in the right area if you are using an up-to-date edition of this book, which is revised every year. Obtain an order form for the next edition (published in November) by sending a stamped addressed envelope, with 'SOTBT 2003' in the top left-hand corner, to Explore Britain, Alston, Cumbria, CA9 3SL.

CLAY FARM

C

Clows Top, Worcestershire, DY14 9NN Tel: 01299 832421
West of Kidderminster. Nearest main road: A456 from Kidderminster to Tenbury Wells.

3 Bedrooms. £20–£25. All have own shower/toilet. No smoking.
Light suppers if ordered. Vegetarian or other special diets if ordered.
1 Sitting-room. With open fire, TV.
Large garden

Although the bedrooms at Clay Farm are perfectly comfortable, with delicately patterned fabrics, cream-and-gold furniture, and pretty china doorhandles, there is no denying that their most striking features are outside, not in: the views from this 1970s house are truly spectacular. Wyre Forest lies to north and east, the Shropshire Hills to the north-west; closer to the house itself are its own extensive pasture land and woods. There are three lakes where Mick Grinnall will teach you the rudiments of fly-fishing, and coarse fishing and clay-pigeon shooting instruction are available as well.

Breakfast is plentiful, with local free-range eggs; Ella recommends for dinner the Colliers Arms a couple of miles away, or the Sun & Slipper at Mamble. Afterwards, you can sink deep into the dusky pink 'buffalo-skin' sofa and chairs in front of a log fire in the sitting-room, or in summer (when the house disappears under a multitude of pot-plants and hanging-baskets) relax in the adjoining sun-lounge to watch the sun go down over the trout lake.

There is a station on the Severn Valley steam railway at nearby Bewdley – irresistible to some.

Readers' comments: Breakfast was wonderful; lovely views; an absolute bargain.

Worcestershire

COWLEIGH PARK FARMHOUSE

C(7) **D PT**

Cowleigh Road, Great Malvern, Worcestershire, WR13 5HJ
Tel/Fax: 01684 566750
Nearest main road: A449 from Worcester to Ross-on-Wye (and the junction of the M5 with the M50).

3 Bedrooms. £25–£27 (less for 5 nights or more). Available: own bath/shower/toilet; TV. No smoking.
Dinner. £14 for 3 courses and coffee, at 7pm (Monday–Friday only). Vegetarian or other special diets if ordered. Wine available. No smoking. **Light suppers** if ordered.
1 Sitting-room. With open fire, piano. No smoking.
Large garden

The half-timbered house is 350 years old, and some of its beams are even older. On driving up to the door, there is a tranquil scene – snowy alyssum spreading over old stone walls, an ancient cider-press on the brick terrace. (The Worcestershire Way starts here.)

Beyond the slate-flagged hall, Sue Stringer has furnished the low-beamed rooms attractively – comfortable antique chairs are placed round a large inglenook in the main sitting-room. In the dining-room there is a yew refectory table with 18th-century rush-seated chairs. Bedrooms have deep-pile carpets, stripped pine, board-and-latch doors, and soft colours. One has a particularly pretty view, of lily-pool and rock garden.

A typical meal: Stilton-and-apple soup, goulash, and blackcurrant gâteau.

The house has its own piped Malvern water.

Readers' comments: Warm, hospitable and friendly. Wished we could have stayed longer. Very relaxing and comfortable home. Pretty rooms. Charming home. Made very welcome. Food excellent and plentiful. Really nice welcome. Delicious breakfasts. Super house.

GREENLANDS

C D S X

Uphampton, Worcestershire, WR9 0JP Tel: 01905 620873 (Mobile: 07775 742626)
North of Worcester. Nearest main road: A449 from Worcester to Kidderminster.

4 Bedrooms. £18–£25. Available: own bath/shower/toilet. No smoking.
Light suppers if ordered. Vegetarian or other special diets if ordered. No smoking.
1 Sitting-room. With open fire, TV.
Garden

E-mail: xlandgreenlands@onetel.net.uk

The oldest part of black-and-white Greenlands dates back to around 1580: beams from this period are abundant, including one massive tree-trunk (still with some bark attached) stretching overhead for the length of the sitting-room. It is a house of steps and low ceilings, angles and dark crannies, in which the modern decorative touches supplied by Chris Crossland, a skilled upholsterer, sit very easily beside old oak chests and corner cupboards, and cosy open fires. Thanks to sloping ceilings and low-set windows, the bedrooms upstairs are particularly attractive; the ground-floor room (in the modern part of the house) has a spacious en suite shower-room and colourwashed woodwork.

The house was probably originally a land-worker's or fruit-picker's cottage. Although the cider orchards which used to flourish hereabouts are largely gone now, the Fruiterer's Arms down the road still brews its own beer: a plus for CAMRA enthusiasts.

By arrangement, Chris will occasionally provide light suppers, but there are excellent pubs and a more upmarket restaurant in the attractive market town of Ombersley nearby. **V**

MOUNT PLEASANT FARM

C(5)

Childswickham, Worcestershire, WR12 7HZ Tel/Fax: 01386 853424
South of Evesham. Nearest main road: A46 from Evesham towards Tewkesbury.

3 Bedrooms. £23–£25 (less for 3 nights or more). Available: own bath/shower/toilet; TV.
1 Sitting-room. With open fire, piano.
Large garden

On a quiet road between Evesham and the Cotswold jewel of Broadway (bypassed now, but definitely worth a detour if you are in the area) lies this early Victorian farmhouse, filled with a pleasing mix of antique and simply comfortable furniture: old wooden bedsteads and Laura Ashley fabrics in the bedrooms; cream-painted walls and floral upholstery in the sitting-room; wide stripped-pine doors throughout, and an attractive slate fireplace with pine surround in the dining-room. The best bedrooms have magnificent views over the surrounding farmland and countryside, as far as Broadway Tower – 18th-century folly cum landmark – cresting a rise to the south-east.

Helen Perry is renowned for her breakfast, but for evening meals (when she is busy with chores on the farm) recommends the village pub in Childswickham, a mile or so down the road; it has real ales too.

Right on the northern edge of the Cotswolds, Mount Pleasant is a good base from which to visit such deservedly popular towns as Chipping Campden and Moreton-in-Marsh; further west, the attractions of the Malvern Hills beckon.

Readers' comments: Made very welcome indeed; very comfortable; breakfast was excellent. **V**

Worcestershire

OLD PARSONAGE FARMHOUSE D

Hanley Castle, Worcestershire, WR8 0BU Tel: 01684 310124
South-east of Great Malvern. Nearest main road: A38 from Worcester to Tewkesbury (also M5, junctions 7/8; and M50, junction 1).

rear view

3 Bedrooms. £21.50–£27.50 (less for 3 nights mid-week **to readers of this book only**). All have own bath/toilet. No smoking.
Dinner. £16.90 for 4 courses and coffee, at 7.30pm. Vegetarian or other special diets if ordered. Wine available. No smoking.
2 Sitting-rooms. With open fire, TV. No smoking in one.
Large garden

E-mail: OPWines@aol.com

It is not just the surrounding views of the Malvern Hills or the handsome 18th-century house of mellow brick which makes this worth seeking out: Ann Addison has a flair for both cookery and interior decoration, while Tony is a wine expert.

You enter the house via a vaulted entrance hall, then through double doors into the sandalwood sitting-room. On the right is the pale sea-green drawing-room with its arched Georgian windows and marble Adam fireplace. The sunflower-yellow dining-room has the original brick hearth and bread oven. Upstairs are elegant bedrooms.

A typical meal: mushrooms and herbs in puff pastry; chicken breasts with prawns in cream and brandy; bramble mousse; cheeses.

Readers' comments: High standard of imaginative food. Superb standards and unrivalled personal service. Very friendly. Most welcoming and comfortable. Skills in every department quite exceptional. Lovely home, lovely couple, lovely food. Hope to return.

V

Worcestershire

ST ELISABETH'S COTTAGE D S X

Woodman Lane, Clent, Worcestershire, DY9 9PX Tel: 01562 883883
East of Kidderminster. Nearest main road: A456 from Kidderminster to Birmingham (and M5, junctions 3/4).

3 Bedrooms. £24–£27 (less for 3 nights or more). Bargain breaks. Available: own bath/shower/toilet; TV. No smoking.
Dinner (by arrangement). £12 for 3 courses and coffee, at variable times. Wine available. No smoking.
Light suppers if ordered.
1 Sitting-room. With open fire, TV. No smoking.
Large garden

The 18th-century cottage has been much extended over the years and is now quite a large house, surrounded by a particularly beautiful garden. There is a willow-fringed pool which attracts herons and other wildlife, shrubs, a big sloping lawn and swimming-pool.

Sheila Blankstone has furnished her home elegantly with, for instance, pink chintz and a fine inlaid walnut table and cabinet in one of the bedrooms. Huge picture-windows make the most of garden views. In addition to the large sitting-room there is a small 'snug'. Some visitors will appreciate having their own entrance to their bedroom, and the choice of continental breakfast in their room or a cooked breakfast in the dining-room. Sheila will sometimes do dinners, such as melon, roast lamb, cheese and fruit – or visitors may use her kitchen. Vegetables are grown in the garden. Central Birmingham is only 20 minutes away, and the Black Country Museum in Dudley is worth a visit.

Readers' comments: Bedroom was the largest and most elegant we have ever stayed in. Made most welcome.

V

THE STEPS

C D X

6 High Street, Feckenham, Worcestershire, B96 6HS Tel: 01527 892678
South-west of Redditch. Nearest main road: A441 from Birmingham towards Evesham.

3 Bedrooms. £20–£22 (less for 3 nights or more). One has own shower/toilet. No smoking.
Dinner (by arrangement). £10 for 2 courses or £12 for 3 courses and coffee, at 7.30–8.30pm, or times to suit guests. Vegetarian or other special diets if ordered. No smoking. **Light suppers** if ordered.
1 Sitting-room. With open fire, TV.
Small garden

The buildings of Feckenham are an architectural student's delight: handsome Queen Anne houses jostle half-timbered Tudor frontages, while the 800-year-old lodge on the village green is said to have been used by King John when he hunted the royal forests with which this area was once covered. The Steps is one of the youngsters, a double-fronted Georgian house which Jenny Thomas has decorated to a very high standard: a pale green paper with watered-silk effect in the quiet back bedroom, Laura Ashley and candy-stripes in the others. The pastel sitting-room stretches the length of the house and its French windows open out to the garden where the Thomases' ducks and cats wander at will.

In the wood-floored dining-area, Jenny will provide such evening meals as soup, fish pie with fresh vegetables, and a traditional pudding or fruit salad; the village has two pubs with good food as well. Feckenham is within easy reach of Stratford, Warwick, Worcester and the Cotswolds; and the National Exhibition Centre (Birmingham) is only 30 minutes away. Birdwatchers appreciate the natural wetland which lies a couple of miles from the village.

TARN

D PT

Long Bank, Bewdley, Worcestershire, DY12 2QT Tel: 01299 402243
West of Kidderminster. Off A456 from Kidderminster to Tenbury Wells.

rear view

4 Bedrooms. £20. No smoking.
1 Sitting-room. With TV, piano. No smoking.
Large garden
Closed in December and January.

Until 1923, two adjacent workers' cottages stood on this site close to the Georgian town of Bewdley; then they were knocked into one, and some 50 years later Topsy Beves and her family completed the transformation into the gracious red-brick house Tarn is today. It takes quite a leap of the imagination to realize that a century ago two families of six children each grew up in an area the size of the present kitchen.

Having approached the house down a long winding drive, one enters through the slate-floored hall, off which lies a magnificent split-level library, complete with a Pleyel grand and a square piano. Cork-tiled floors are spread with fine old rugs; Liberty fabrics cover comfortable chairs from which to look out at Topsy's magnificent garden. Glass doors from the dining-room (with very pretty chandelier) open on to a terrace with fig tree and rambling vine – a summer breakfast here is a memorable event. Upstairs are four bedrooms (two are singles) furnished in a light, practical style; and a number of bath- and shower-rooms.

TYTCHNEY GABLES

C D S X

Boreley, Ombersley, Worcestershire, WR9 0HZ Tel: 01905 620185
North of Worcester. Nearest main road: A449 from Worcester to Kidderminster.

2 Bedrooms. £18–£20 (less for 3 nights or more). One has own toilet. No smoking.
Light suppers if ordered. Vegetarian or other special diets if ordered. No smoking.
1 Sitting-room. With open fire, TV, piano. No smoking.
Garden

One of the black-and-white houses which characterize this part of England, Tytchney Gables started life as a 16th-century hall-house, with what are now the dining-area and the kitchen open to the rafters. The dividing wall still shows its original beams and panelling; in the sitting-room, a portion of the wattle-and-daub construction is exposed beneath a protective glass screen. Deep inglenooks, board-and-latch doors and sloping floorboards abound. Not a house for the unsteady: the shared toilet is on the second floor and steeply angled; the family shower-room one flight down.

Margaret Peters – a professional mezzo-soprano who likes nothing better than making music with her guests, be they concert pianists or just enthusiasts – grew up in the farmhouse you can see from the dining-room window; the views from the bedroom windows are even more spectacular, to the Malvern Hills in one direction, Abberley Hill in another. This is good walking country with many popular rambles taking in the River Severn.

A wide choice of eating-places within a four-mile radius caters for all tastes and pockets.

Reader's comments: A real gem; nothing was too much trouble.

Months when houses are shown as closed are inclusive.

Book well ahead: many of these houses have few rooms. Do not expect dinner if you have not booked it or if you arrive late.

Some proprietors stipulate a minimum stay of two nights at weekends or peak seasons; or they will accept one-nighters only at short notice (that is, only if no lengthier booking has yet been made).

Facts (prices, etc.) at the top of entries are supplied by the proprietors themselves. While every effort is made to ensure that these are correct at the time of going to press, they may alter thereafter: please check when you book.

YORKSHIRE

(including East Riding of Yorkshire, North Yorkshire and West Yorkshire)

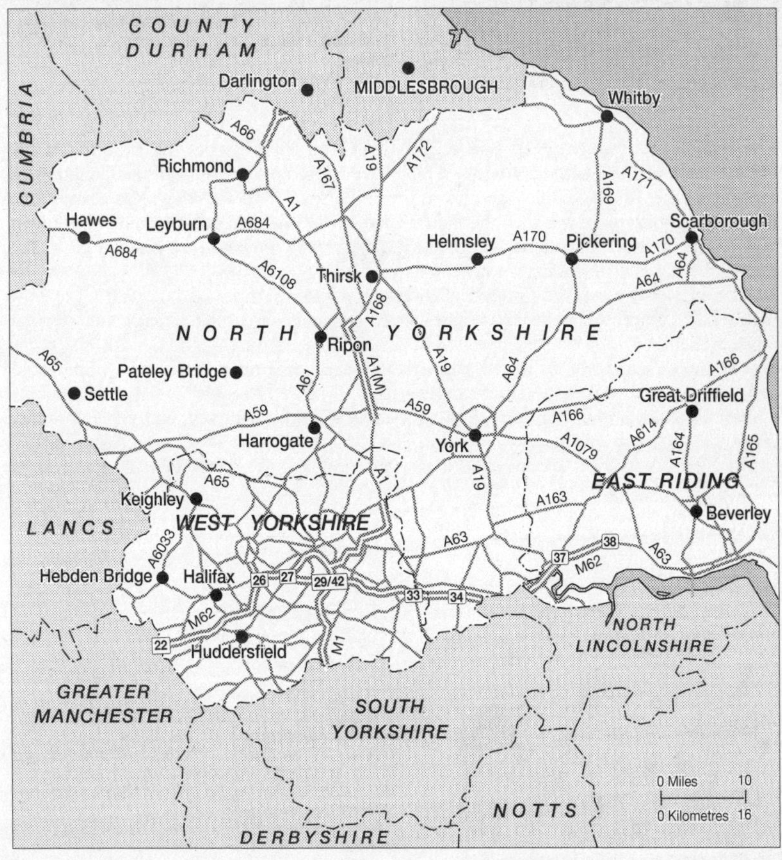

If you find places in England and Wales that you feel should be visited for possible inclusion in a future edition of SOTBT, please write and let us know. Send your descriptions (including full name of establishment, address and current b & b price per person) to Jan Bowmer, c/o Arrow Books, Random House, 20 Vauxhall Bridge Road, London, SW1V 2SA.

North Yorkshire

AINDERBY MYERS FARM

CSX

Bedale, North Yorkshire, DL8 1PF Tel: 01609 748668 or 748424
South-east of Richmond. Nearest main road: A1 from Boroughbridge to Scotch Corner.

4 Bedrooms. £20–£23. Available: own bath/shower/toilet; TV. No smoking.
Dinner (by arrangement). £10 for 3 courses and coffee, at 7pm. Vegetarian or other special diets if ordered. No smoking. **Light suppers** if ordered.
2 Sitting-rooms. With open fire, TV, piano. No smoking.
Large garden

The homely style which greets one at this farmhouse almost belies the antiquity of the place: mentioned in Domesday Book, it may have housed one of William the Conqueror's sons for a time. In the Middle Ages, it was the property of Jervaulx Abbey, and what is now the guests' sitting-room was then the monks' chapel – its Norman doorway remains, though now on the interior. A keystone over the arch through which the house is entered shows the date of the last major building works: 1664.

The interior is a rambling warren of rooms, and Valerie Anderson permutates the bedrooms and bathrooms according to guests' requirements (a second sitting-room may be made available).

The large farm includes mixed arable land, sheep, free-range hens on a commercial scale, and geese. It is run by Valerie's three sons.

When dinner is available, it might be vegetable soup, roast turkey, and apple crumble. Otherwise, guests go to the Greyhound in Hackforth or another of the pub restaurants in which North Yorkshire abounds. Well worth a visit are the lovely lakeside grounds of Thorpe Perrow arboretum.

V

North Yorkshire

BANK VILLA

C(5) PT

Masham, North Yorkshire, HG4 4DB Tel/Fax: 01765 689605
North-west of Ripon. Nearest main road: A6108 from Ripon to Leyburn.

6 Bedrooms. £20–£27.50 (less for 4 nights or more). Available: own bath/shower/toilet; views of river.
Dinner (by arrangement). £18 for 4 courses and coffee, at 7.30pm. Vegetarian or other special diets if ordered. Wine available. No smoking. **Light suppers** if ordered.
2 Sitting-rooms. With TV (in one). No smoking.
Garden

Bank Villa is a late Georgian stone house standing behind its front garden on the edge of Masham. Lucy Thomson has furnished and decorated it with enthusiasm and is constantly enhancing the interiors. There are large and luxurious bedrooms on the first floor and simpler but characterful rooms under the attic rafters, some giving (in winter at least) a glimpse of the River Ure at the foot of the hill. Two sitting-rooms provide guests with the choice of TV or conversation. The smaller (television-free) 'parlour' leads to a conservatory, beyond which is a terraced garden.

Lucy, who used to be a hotel-trade executive, is a keen cook, and in the colourful dining-room she might serve you with a starter such as scallops and bacon, followed by soup, rack of lamb with red wine and redcurrant sauce, and chocolate-and-orange bread-and-butter pudding.

Masham is a town of character with some individual shops and a big market square which fills with sheep for the September fair. You can tour the well-known independent brewery up the lane at the side of Bank Villa.

V

THE BARN

CMS

Caldbergh-in-Coverdale, Middleham, North Yorkshire, DL8 4RW
Tel: 01969 640674
South of Leyburn. Nearest main road: A6108 from Masham to Leyburn.

3 Bedrooms. £19 (less for 3 nights or more). One has own bath/toilet. No smoking.
1 Sitting-room. With stove, TV. No smoking.
Large garden

In an isolated hamlet – little more than a couple of farms and a phone box – this conversion was designed by an architect to take maximum advantage of the particularly fine countryside which surrounds it. The beamed bedrooms all have good views, and there is a conservatory at the end of the Turners' sitting-room from which to contemplate the large garden and the landscape of hills, trees and dry-stone walls. At the far end, the garden is semi-wild and runs down to a ghyll. From the front door many walks are possible to suit all levels of fitness.

Inside, the large and pleasantly uncluttered sitting-room, with plain colours for the walls and carpet, has a glowing stove within a terracotta-painted recess. One bedroom is meant for two children (or it can serve as a second small sitting-room).

Although Marjorie Turner does not provide evening meals, in nearby Middleham – a large and picturesque village – there is a choice of places where guests can dine well. Here also is one of the area's ruined castles, this one famous for its close associations with Richard III (and the mediaeval Middleham Jewel), and an arts workshop run by a sculptor, with a bookshop attached.

BRAMWOOD

PT

19 Hallgarth, Pickering, North Yorkshire, YO18 7AW Tel: 01751 474066
Off A170 from Thirsk to Scarborough.

rear view

8 Bedrooms. £20–£25 (less for 5 nights or more). Bargain breaks. All have own shower/toilet; TV. No smoking.
Dinner (by arrangement). £15 for 3 courses and coffee, at 6.30pm. Vegetarian or other special diets if ordered. No smoking. **Light suppers** if ordered.
1 Sitting-room. With open fire. No smoking.
Small garden

The best approach to this 18th-century guest-house is from the back, through an old archway built for coaches – racks for the horses' tack and an old forge still survive, but beyond what was once the stable yard there is now a pretty and secluded garden, with clematis scrambling up old walls and an apple-tree. The breakfast-room overlooks it.

Bramwood is now run by the Hacketts – Steve, who was connected with the construction industry, and Georgina, who was in the floristry business. They have improved the bedrooms, including Laura Ashley wallpapers, and Steve has taken to cooking with enthusiasm. He produces such meals as carrot-and-coriander soup, chicken Italian, and a choice of sweets. High teas are sometimes served as an alternative to dinner during the summer. In the dining-room is old oak furniture, which the Hacketts have collected, and an open fire.

Pickering is at one end of the North York Moors Railway (a good way of seeing this National Park) and also has the Beck Isle Museum of Rural Life and a castle.

Reader's comments: Very capable hosts; we were very well looked after; breakfasts were generous; would certainly stay again.

V

BROOM HOUSE

C M P T

Egton Bridge, North Yorkshire, YO21 1XD Tel: 01947 895279 (Fax: 01947 895657)
South-west of Whitby. Nearest main road: A171 from Middlesbrough to Whitby.

6 Bedrooms. £21.50–£24 (less for 5 nights or more). Bargain breaks. All have own bath/shower/toilet; TV. No smoking.
Dinner (by arrangement). £12.95 for 3 courses and coffee, at 6.30–7.30pm. Vegetarian or other special diets if ordered. No smoking.
1 Sitting-room. With open fire. No smoking.
Garden

E-mail: welcome@broomhouseegtonbridge.freeserve.co.uk

The wooded Esk Valley runs through the heather-covered North York Moors National Park. On the outskirts of one of the villages it shelters is this 19th-century farmhouse, which has been well restored by David and Maria White. Maria is very skilled at colourwashing and has done each room in a different colour, some with a stencilled frieze. She has found unusual iron bedsteads and has made much use of handsome sisal floor-covering.

One bedroom has a French window leading on to the well-tended garden, while at the top of the house are characterful rooms with beams and sloping ceilings. The dining-room, with painted wooden furniture, contains a big cast-iron range where a log fire sometimes burns. Here Maria, who is a qualified chef, offers a choice of dishes which might include Stilton pâté, salmon fillet with lime dressing, and gooseberry meringue.

The Esk Valley Railway runs past the house and provides a good way of enjoying the scenery. Whitby and the coast are not far; and a few miles away is Goathland, the moorland village made famous by the television series 'Heartbeat'.

V

CLAXTON HALL COTTAGE

C P T S X

Claxton, North Yorkshire, YO60 7RE Tel/Fax: 01904 468697
North-east of York. Nearest main road: A64 from York to Malton.

side view

3 Bedrooms. £22.50–£27.50 (less for 3 nights or more). Bargain breaks. All have own bath/shower/toilet; TV. No smoking.
Dinner (by arrangement). £12.50 for 3 courses and coffee, at times to suit guests. Vegetarian or other special diets if ordered. No smoking. **Light suppers** if ordered.
1 Sitting-room. With stove. No smoking.
Large garden

E-mail: claxcott@aol.com

Built in the early 19th century and more recently extended, this used to be the servants' quarters for Claxton Hall (now gone). On the ground floor, spaces flow into one another, so that the sitting-room at the foot of the staircase runs into the beamed dining-room, with the entrance hall adjoining. The recent modernization has been carried out by Martin and Carol Brough, much of it by Carol herself, as she is an accomplished woodworker.

Upstairs, the bedrooms (the best with a canopied bed) look over trees and fields with, in one direction, the road to York beyond – visible, but not audible; the city is only 10 minutes away. So is Castle Howard, the Vanbrugh masterpiece made even more famous by the television adaptation of *Brideshead Revisited*. Further on is Malton, a pleasant market town where the museum has a rich archaeological collection.

The Broughs, being local people, are well informed about sights other than the famous ones. When dinner is required, it might consist of leek-and-potato soup, roast chicken (with Yorkshire puddings, of course), and a fruit pie. Otherwise, many inns in the area have excellent restaurants.

V

CRIB FARM C(7) **S**

Long Causeway, Luddenden Foot, West Yorkshire, HX2 6JJ Tel: 01422 883285
West of Halifax. Nearest main road: A58 from Rochdale to Halifax (and M62, junction24).

4 Bedrooms. £18–£20. Bargain breaks. Available: own bath/shower/toilet; TV. No smoking.
Dinner (by arrangement). £8.50 for 3 courses and coffee, at 6.30pm. Vegetarian or other special diets if ordered. Wine available. No smoking. **Light suppers.**
1 Sitting-room. With open fire, piano.
Small garden
Closed in November and December.

A necessary break to change horses on the long cross-Pennine journey from Lancashire to Yorkshire brought this 17th-century moorland house into being, for originally it was a coaching inn. Centuries later it became – and still is – a dairy-farm, though its role as a haven for travellers continues too. The Hitchen family have been here since 1815 and a framed auction notice on the wall proves it.

The spacious old house has a warm and hospitable atmosphere, with rooms decorated in light and cheerful colours. Pauline's dinners (when available) might comprise home-made asparagus soup, home-reared turkey with garden vegetables, and a choice of puddings, or cheeses. Butter is home-made.

Readers' comments: A welcoming family. Very comfortable and easy. A very happy week. Warmth of hospitality matched only by splendid breakfasts.

CROFTS C(12) **S X**

Carlton Husthwaite, North Yorkshire, YO7 2BJ Tel/Fax: 01845 501325
South-east of Thirsk. Nearest main road: A19 from Thirsk to York.

rear view

2 Bedrooms. £22 (less for 2 nights or more). Available: own bath/toilet. No smoking.
Light suppers if ordered.
1 Sitting-room. With open fire, TV. No smoking.
Garden

Two cottages, built of the warm-coloured bricks and tiles typical of this part of Yorkshire, have been made into one house, now the home of the Corbetts, Diane and Dan (cricket umpire and ex-banker). Behind is the garden, and beyond lies the paddock where the family pony grazes and the hens lay the free-range eggs you can have for breakfast. Three ebullient dogs greet you on arrival, and there is a cat too.

Much of the furniture was made in Kilburn, at the original one of the cabinet-makers' workshops which now proliferate in the surrounding villages: you can identify it by a carved mouse on every piece. The two bedrooms, twin or double, are furnished in dark oak or pine respectively. They are not let separately (except to a party of three or more) so that guests have the exclusive use of the bathroom.

For evening meals, there is a good pub just across the road or plenty of others in villages a drive away.

Reader's comments: Felt right at home, beautiful house, very cosy, breakfasts with a wide variety of choices; owners how friendly! A really excellent experience all round.

V

York

THE DAIRY

C M PT

3 Scarcroft Road, York, YO23 1ND Tel: 01904 639367
Nearest main road: A64 from Leeds to York.

5 Bedrooms. £25–£27.50. Available: own bath/shower/toilet; TV. No smoking.
Courtyard garden

In York, just outside the city walls, close to historic Clifford's Tower and the interesting Castle Museum, is The Dairy, which was just that until some years ago: a milk churn now planted with flowers stands in the creeper-hung yard at the back. Rooms are cottagey in style, with original Victorian joinery, plasterwork and fireplaces, furnished with colourful fabrics and stripped pine. One of the best, off the yard, is the room where Yorkshire curd was made; another has the use of a big Victorian bath. The breakfasts, which Phil Hunt and Chris Andrade provide, consist almost entirely of organic wholefood and can be vegetarian. For dinner, there is an award-winning restaurant next door, or a big choice within walking distance.

York hardly needs description, with its carefully conserved streets, its city walls, the Minster and the railway museum. Tourist attractions abound, from the parish churches with their notable stained glass, to Jorvik, the elaborate re-creation of the Viking settlement which was the first such attraction to use modern technology to reproduce the past.

V

North Yorkshire

EDEN HOUSE

PT S

120 Eastgate, Pickering, North Yorkshire, YO18 7DW Tel: 01751 472289
(Fax: 01751 476066)
On A170 from Thirsk to Scarborough.

3 Bedrooms. £21–£23 (less for 7 nights or more). Bargain breaks. All have own bath/shower/toilet; TV. No smoking.
Dinner (by arrangement). £14.50 for 3 courses and coffee, at 7pm. Vegetarian or other special diets if ordered. Wine available. No smoking.
1 Sitting-room. With open fire.
Garden

E-mail: edenhouse@breathemail.net

With years of experience as hoteliers behind them, Adrian and Gaby Smith are food and wine enthusiasts who bake their own bread, make their own sausages and preserves, and grow their own vegetables. Visitors are offered in the morning a choice for dinner, which might include shellfish Mornay; lamb fillet with rosemary and Cumberland sauce; and caramelized custards.

The house is a pair of 250-year-old cottages in a terrace in the small town of Pickering. Though it is on the main road, noise from traffic has never proved a problem. Rooms overlook the long garden, where the Smiths have made a pond; there is also private carparking.

The bedrooms are bright and neat, and very thoughtfully equipped, even down to shoe-polishing kits and dressing-gowns. Downstairs, the dining-room and cosy little sitting-room are furnished with country antiques and cretonne-covered chairs.

Readers' comments: Everything immaculate and cosy, delicious evening meal, wish we could have spent longer.

V

FOREST FARMHOUSE

C D PT S

Mount Road, Marsden, West Yorkshire, HD7 6NN Tel/Fax: 01484 842687
South-west of Huddersfield. Nearest main road: A62 from Oldham to Huddersfield.

West Yorkshire

3 Bedrooms. £18–£20.
Dinner (by arrangement). £7 for 3 courses and coffee, at 7pm. Vegetarian or other special diets if ordered.
Light suppers if ordered.
1 Sitting-room. With stove, TV, organ.
Small garden

Standing at 1000 feet, Forest Farmhouse is surrounded by a golf course (which visitors can often use) and moorland, much of it owned by the National Trust, at the top of the Peak District National Park. There was never a forest: the word is used in its sense of a hunting-ground and, at least according to the deeds of the house, the royal family still has the right to use it. This is a typical farmhouse of its kind, built of dark gritstone at least 200 years ago, with mullioned windows and stone-slated roof. Inside, the beamed wooden ceilings are low and the guests' sitting-room has a big stone fireplace. Bedrooms, some with exposed masonry, have pine fittings.

Genial Ted and May Fussey run the place with walkers in mind (the open moors and the nearness of the Pennine Way attract them here). May provides, for example, home-made soup or grilled grapefruit, pork steak in breadcrumbs with fresh vegetables, and chocolate pudding with white sauce. All bread is home-made.

Climbing, angling and hang-gliding are some of the pastimes available nearby.

V

GRASSFIELDS

C D PT X

Wath Road, Pateley Bridge, North Yorkshire, HG3 5HL Tel: 01423 711412
(Fax: 01423 712844)
North of Harrogate. Nearest main road: A59 from Harrogate to Skipton.

North Yorkshire

9 Bedrooms. £25 **(to readers of this book only)** –£29.50. Less for 3 nights or more. Bargain breaks. All have own bath/shower/toilet; TV.
Dinner. £18.50 for 3 courses and coffee, from 7pm. Vegetarian or other special diets if ordered. Wine available. No smoking. **Light suppers** if ordered.
1 Sitting-room. With open fire. **Bar.**
Large garden

E-mail: grassfields@nidderdale.co.uk

This country house hotel is set back from the road, in its own gardens: it is a handsome Georgian building with a new conservatory, surrounded by lawns and trees. Most rooms are spacious and comfortably furnished, one with a four-poster bed. Barbara Garforth studies her visitors' interests and provides helpful information on local areas of note, including many local walks.

Meals are prepared from local vegetables and produce whenever possible, including free-range eggs and Nidderdale lamb. A typical dinner menu: game terrine, roast rack of lamb, and fresh fruit crème brûlée – all in generous quantities. Alternatively, a more flexible bistro menu is available in the conservatory, where breakfast is also served. There is a wide selection of wines.

Pateley Bridge is an interesting small town (in an Area of Outstanding Natural Beauty). In Nidderdale, there are crags, glens and How Stean gorge.

Readers' comments: Most helpful. Very fine food. Good food and plenty of it. Thoroughly enjoyed our stay. Wonderful. Very friendly atmosphere. Very comfortable, delightful atmosphere, splendid location. Lovely, peaceful location, kind hostess.

V

York

THE HEATHERS

C(10) **PT**

54 Shipton Road, Clifton-Without, York, YO3 6RQ Tel/Fax: 01904 640989
On A19 from Thirsk to York.

8 Bedrooms. £18–£35. Available: own bath/shower/toilet; TV. No smoking.
1 Sitting-room. No smoking.
Garden
Closed in January.

E-mail: thghyork@globalnet.co.uk

As well as being very pleasantly furnished, The Heathers has a number of advantages in a city not short of guest-houses: it is easy to find and has its own carparking when you have done so. Whilst it is not 'off the beaten track', the road it is on takes you, by means of a bus ride or brisk walk, straight to the pedestrianized historic city centre, with the Minster just inside the city walls.

The inter-war house offers a range of bedrooms: the best has a large bay window and overlooks the long garden. Those at the front give a view of pasture and sports fields on the other side of the road, any noise from which is minimized by the shrubbery in the front garden beyond the parking spaces.

The breakfast/sitting-room has balloon-back chairs round circular tables, and capacious settees. All the rooms have been decorated by Graham and Heather Fisher in light, bright colours, with imaginative use of draperies.

For dinner, central York offers plenty of choice, but there are good places to eat near at hand in Clifton.

North Yorkshire

HIGH WINSLEY COTTAGE

Burnt Yates, North Yorkshire, HG3 3EP Tel: 01423 770662
North-west of Harrogate. Nearest main road: A61 from Harrogate to Ripon.

4 Bedrooms. £22–£24 (less for 3 nights or more). All have own bath/shower/toilet. No smoking.
Dinner (from September to end of April). £14 for 3 courses and coffee, at 7pm. Vegetarian or other special diets if ordered. Wine available. No smoking. **Light suppers** if ordered (all year).
2 Sitting-rooms. With open fire, TV (in one). No smoking.
Large garden
Closed in December and January.

Off the road leading to Brimham Rocks is a one-time farm cottage now much extended, which has been modernized with care by Clive and Gill King. From the parquet-floored dining-room one steps down to a sitting-room where soft sofas face a log fire and sliding glass doors open on to a terrace with views to the far hills. Outside are the Kings' Wensleydale sheep – a rare breed with long curly wool.

Colour schemes have been well chosen. A blue-and-white bedroom has a matching bathroom; Laura Ashley briar-roses predominate in another, furnished with antiques; a large room has windows on two sides and comfortable armchairs from which to enjoy the views.

Gill puts as much care into making the simplest dishes as into a dinner such as lemons with a stuffing of smoked fish, pork in spiced orange sauce, and apple jalousie. Her own or local produce is used; bread is home-baked. (Two village pubs also serve meals).

Readers' comments: Very beautiful and cosy. Charming host and hostess. The best cooking we ever had in the UK. A haven of peace, delightfully furnished rooms. A lovely stay, food good. Nothing but praise. First-rate b & b. Accommodation and food excellent.

HOLME HOUSE
C D S X

Piercebridge, North Yorkshire, DL2 3SY Tel/Fax: 01325 374280
West of Darlington. Nearest main road: A67 from Darlington to Barnard Castle (and A1 to Scotch Corner).

2 Bedrooms. £24–£25 (less for 3 nights or more). Both have own bath/shower/toilet. No smoking.
Light suppers only. Vegetarian or other special diets if ordered.
1 Sitting-room. With open fire, TV, piano.
Large garden

Piercebridge is a carefully conserved village and Holme House is just outside it, over the North Yorkshire border by a matter of yards. Down a tarmac farm road, it is a spacious Georgian house furnished with antiques and with many sporting prints and watercolours around. Guests breakfast at a long, stripped-pine farmhouse table. Anne Graham's family are animal-lovers, and there is a variety of livestock at the adjoining farm, which is managed by her husband. The two bedrooms have splendid views of open countryside. For dinner, visitors have a choice of good food at nearby village pubs.

Piercebridge was settled by the Romans, who have left many remains in the vicinity: by the village are a fort and a bridge – or was it a lock? The controversy about what is left is the subject of a book. Apart from Darlington, famous in railway history, the nearest town is Barnard Castle, with a picturesque market place and the remarkable collections in the château-style Bowes Museum, founded by an ancestor of the Queen Mother.

Readers' comments: Wonderful welcome, warm and hospitable. Idyllic.

V

North Yorkshire

KELLEYTHORPE FARM
C D PT S

Great Driffield, East Riding of Yorkshire, YO25 9DW Tel: 01377 252297
On A614 from Market Weighton to Great Driffield.

2 Bedrooms. £19–£22 (less for 2 nights or more). Available: own bath/shower/toilet; views of lake.
Dinner (by arrangement). £12 for 3 courses and coffee, at 7pm. Vegetarian or other special diets if ordered. No smoking. **Light suppers** if ordered.
1 Sitting-room. With open fire, TV.
Large garden

This big 18th-century farmhouse, partly rebuilt after wartime bombing, has been in the Hopper family since the early 1800s. It takes its name from 'kell', the Anglo-Saxon word for spring, many of which rise in the small lake just at the back of the house. The bay window of the large sitting/dining-room overlooks the lake (as does one bedroom), and there is a terrace with chairs from which guests can watch the ducks and – with luck – kingfishers. This is the source of the River Hull, which gives the downstream city its name. There are lakeside and woodland walks on the 200-acre farm.

In spite of the size of the house, with its wide staircase hung with oil paintings, this is not a formal place, and family antiques – old furniture, pewter and silver – are scattered around almost casually.

Dinner here might consist of smoked trout or asparagus; pork fillet en croûte; and a fruit pudding. The farm's excellent beef and pork are on sale.

V

East Riding of Yorkshire

North Yorkshire

KNOX MILL HOUSE

C(12) PT

Knox Mill Lane, Harrogate, North Yorkshire, HG3 2AE Tel/Fax: 01423 560650

North-west of Harrogate. Nearest main road: A61 from Harrogate to Ripon.

3 Bedrooms. £22.50. Available: own bath/shower/toilet; views of river. No smoking.
Light suppers if ordered.
1 Sitting-room. With open fire, TV. No smoking.
Small garden

In a quiet, tree-lined lane just outside Harrogate, this 18th-century house was the home of the owner of the adjoining corn mill. Bedrooms overlook the stream into which the mill-race used to run, and from two the remains of the waterwheel can be glimpsed. Beyond is open countryside. The downstairs rooms, built into the riverbank, have curious arched, cellar-like recesses; in one is the breakfast-table, with a book-lined alcove to one side. One can sit under a beamed ceiling, by a stone fireplace, or else by the stream and hope to spot the resident kingfisher.

Peter (sometime golf professional) and Marion Thomson do not serve dinners because there is such a big choice of restaurants and tea-rooms in Harrogate, just up the main road. Here one can sample the foul-smelling but supposedly beneficial spa water, go to the theatre, or visit the famous gardens of Harlow Carr.

V *Readers' comments:* Stayed longer than we had booked; situation nothing short of idyllic. Friendly atmosphere and character.

North Yorkshire

LABURNUM HOUSE

C(5) PT

31 Topcliffe Road, Thirsk, North Yorkshire, YO7 1RX Tel: 01845 524120

Nearest main road: A168 from Thirsk towards Ripon.

3 Bedrooms. £21–£22.50 (less for 3 nights or more). All have own bath/shower/toilet; TV. No smoking.
1 Sitting-room. With open fire. No smoking.
Small garden
Closed from December to February.

Liz Ogleby's hospitality was much appreciated by readers who stayed at her old home in Thirsk. She has now moved to a newly built house on the outskirts of the town, and has taken with her many of her antiques: grandfather and skeleton clocks and fine side-tables in the sitting-room, for example – though the sumptuous armchairs are new! In the breakfast-room there is a substantial oak table with Windsor chairs round it and, against the walls, a French walnut sideboard and a display of old guns. Bedrooms are all large, especially the family room, with settee; on the walls are such pictures as old prints of Thirsk market 150 years ago or historic photoprints of Whitby. Views are of playing-fields.

Although the house is on a fairly busy road, it is spacious enough for traffic – beyond the big tree which gives it its name – to be hardly noticeable.

For dinner, you can go to one of the villages in the vicinity or into Thirsk.

V *Readers' comments:* Hospitality as great as ever, breakfast superb. Rooms equally comfortable, welcome as warm. Breakfasts continue to be notable for quantity and quality. Quite lovely. Completely delighted; a memorable and comfortable stay.

LASKILL FARM

C D M P T S X

Bilsdale, near Helmsley, North Yorkshire, YO62 5NB Tel/Fax: 01439 798268

North-west of Helmsley. Nearest main road: A170 from Thirsk to Helmsley.

rear view

6 Bedrooms. £25–£30. Bargain breaks. Available: own bath/shower/toilet; TV; views of lake, river.
Dinner. £13.50 for 3 courses and coffee, at 7pm (on 2 nights a week only). Vegetarian or other special diets if ordered. Wine available. **Light suppers** if ordered.
1 Sitting-room. With open fire.
Large garden

E-mail: suesmith@laskillfarm.fsnet.co.uk

This stone farmhouse lies in a hilly, wooded area of great scenic splendour ('Herriot country'), and close to famous Rievaulx Abbey. Its courtyard is made pretty with stone troughs, flowers and rocks; and around lie 600 acres with cattle and sheep.

In the sitting/dining-room is oak furniture hand-carved by local craftsmen. Here Sue Smith serves home-made soup or pâté before a main course which is likely to comprise meat and vegetables from the farm, followed by (for instance) lemon meringue pie or an interesting selection of cheeses.

Two bedrooms are in a beamy outbuilding and open on to the lawn. Two others, more recently converted, are in another farm building. These rooms have their own bathrooms.

Readers' comments: Food quite superb. Wonderful place, surrounding countryside cannot be bettered. Fed royally; cosy and warm in accommodation superior to any hotel. Friendly hostess providing excellent food. One of the best. A delight; good value for money. **V**

LAUREL MANOR FARM

C D P T S X

Brafferton-Helperby, North Yorkshire, YO61 2NZ Tel: 01423 360436 (Fax: 01423 360437)

East of Ripon. Nearest main road: A1 from Wetherby to Catterick.

3 Bedrooms. £25–£30 (less for 3 nights or more). Available: own bath/shower/toilet; TV; views of river.
Dinner (by arrangement). £25 for 4 courses and coffee, at 7.30–8.30pm. Vegetarian or other special diets if ordered. Wine available. **Light suppers** if ordered.
1 Sitting-room. With open fire.
Large garden

E-mail: laurelmf@globalnet.co.uk

The Keys have been Yorkshire landowners for 300 years (though not at this farm), so this house is rich with family portraits and antiques. Less venerable are the models and pictures of Spitfires and other aircraft, explained by Sam Key's many years in the RAF.

Standing on a knoll, this tall, 18th-century house has fine views – of the village church from two bedrooms and from the terrace. It is surrounded by the Keys' 28 acres – a hobby farm but enough land to provide lamb for the table and to support some rare breeds. There is also enough for a tennis court and a croquet lawn. There is angling, too.

Ann, who specialized in cookery at her finishing school, and Sam, who also cooks sometimes, join visitors at the oak dining-table for such candlelit meals as prawns in garlic butter; roast lamb from the farm with home-grown vegetables; summer pudding; and then cheese.

Families like the self-contained suite of two bedrooms (with bathroom).

Readers' comments: Rooms are delightful; pleasant, attentive but relaxed hosts.

THE MOHAIR FARM

C D S X

York Road, Barmby Moor, East Riding of Yorkshire, YO42 4HU
Tel: 01759 380308 (Fax: 01759 388119)
East of York. On A1079 from York to Market Weighton.

2 Bedrooms. £16.50. Bargain breaks. Both have own bath/toilet; TV.
Large garden

This would be a good choice for anyone who wants to see the city of York but prefers to stay in the country. And they will stay on an intrinsically interesting farm as a bonus. For this is the only farm in the country where the main enterprise is angora goats, whose long silky hair provides mohair. Lesley Scott formed her flock about 15 years ago, and visitors can buy knitting yarn made from their hair.

The farmhouse is decorated with some imagination, though there is no sitting-room. The family room, however, is spacious, with armchairs and a writing table. Ask to hear the story of Peter's great-grandfather's will, which hangs on the breakfast-room wall. The farm, which is well away from the road, is on the site of a Roman settlement with a pottery.

Massage, Bowen therapy and Indian head massage (by Lesley) are available by appointment for evenings and weekends, and guided walks (by Peter) are on offer. Those who do not want to travel the 10 miles into York to dine have a fair choice in Pocklington, the nearest town.

V *Readers' comments:* Exactly as described; delightful. Breakfasts excellent; nothing too much trouble.

East Riding of Yorkshire

NUMBER ONE

C D P T S X

1 Woodlands, Beverley, East Riding of Yorkshire, HU17 8BT
Tel/Fax: 01482 862752
Nearest main road: A1079 from York to Beverley (and M62, junction 38).

3 Bedrooms. £20–£23 (less for 5 nights or more). Bargain breaks. One has own bath/shower/toilet. No smoking.
Dinner (by arrangement). £12 for 4 courses and coffee, at 7pm. Vegetarian or other special diets if ordered. No smoking. **Light suppers** if ordered.
1 Sitting-room. With open fire, TV. No smoking.
Small garden

Like York but on a smaller scale, Beverley consists of a minster rising from a warren of small streets within what was once a moated town – 'made for walking in' (John Betjeman). Number One is in a dignified and relatively quiet late-Victorian terrace.

The Kings have furnished the house with some brio, using wallpapers and bright colours to good effect. There is an abundance of house-plants, books and pictures, and some quirky decorative touches: a pair of antlers hung with assorted hats, for example. There is a grandfather clock on the landing, which leads to well-windowed bedrooms.

V Sarah King provides for dinner a choice of several courses which might include grilled courgettes with walnuts and goat's cheese, a meat or fish main course, and a choice of out-of-the-ordinary puddings. Over coffee, which comes with chocolates, the Kings like to talk to their guests in front of the sitting-room fire.

OLDSTEAD GRANGE

C(10)

Oldstead, North Yorkshire, YO61 4BJ Tel: 01347 868634
East of Thirsk. Nearest main road: A170 from Thirsk to Helmsley.

3 Bedrooms. £25–£36 (less for 2 nights or more). All have own bath/shower/toilet; TV. No smoking.
Light suppers if ordered.
1 Sitting-room. With open fire, TV. No smoking.
Garden

E-mail: anne@yorkshireuk.com

Several generations of the Banks family have farmed here since the property was confiscated from the monks of Byland Abbey, the ruins of which are nearby. The house was built in the 17th century, but there are reminders of its earlier history, such as the collection of querns (hand-mills) turned up by the plough. Mostly arable, the farm's rolling acres include some permanent grasslands and woods, which shelter much wildlife. You may see it on one of the walks suggested in the informative folder in your bedroom.

The individually decorated bedrooms overlook the garden or farm buildings. They have been particularly well kitted out by Anne Banks, even to home-made biscuits and chocolates on the teatray. There are some unusual options for breakfast, served at an oak table which, like much of the furniture, is a product of one of the many North Yorkshire craft workshops.

If you want more than a light supper, you could be driven to one of the excellent pub-restaurants which abound in the vicinity, and then back to relax by the sitting-room fireplace, built of cobbles ploughed up on the farm.

V

ORCHARD HOUSE

S

Marton, North Yorkshire, YO62 6RD Tel: 01751 432904
West of Pickering. Nearest main road: A170 from Kirkby Moorside to Pickering.

North Yorkshire

3 Bedrooms. £23–£25 (less for 3 nights or more). Bargain breaks. All have own bath/toilet. No smoking.
Dinner (by arrangement for 4 people or more only). £12.50 for 2 courses and coffee, at 7pm. Vegetarian or other special diets if ordered. Wine available. No smoking.
1 Sitting-room. With open stove, TV. No smoking.
Large garden

Orchard House is one of the stone houses that face each other across the wide village street. It was built in 1784 as a farmhouse, and in the next century part was briefly a shop. Immediately inside the front door is the dining-room, with open fireplace. Walls are painted terracotta, except for one which consists of an expanse of stripped panelling. Paul Richardson is a wine connoisseur and a keen cook, producing, on occasion, such two-course meals as stuffed pork fillet followed by spiced pears.

There is a large, light sitting-room with walls of pale yellow, carpeted like the rest of the ground floor with handsome woven sisal, and with well-filled bookshelves. Throughout the house, the interior design is particularly pleasant, which is not surprising since Alison Richardson is an architect. The long garden goes down to the River Seven, where fishing is possible. Sometimes breakfast (exceptional) is served in the garden room.

Readers' comments: Standard of accommodation very high; too good to be hidden from a wider audience. Quite exceptional; decorated with taste and style; excellent and enthusiastic hosts; cooking to a high standard. Very happy with the accommodation and friendly atmosphere.

V

North Yorkshire

PARK END

C(8) **D M S X**

Kearton, North Yorkshire, DL11 6PL Tel: 01748 886287
West of Richmond. Nearest main road: A6108 from Leyburn to Richmond.

3 Bedrooms. £20. All have own bath/toilet. No smoking.
Dinner (by arrangement). £10 for 3 courses and coffee, at times to suit guests. Vegetarian or other special diets if ordered. No smoking. **Light suppers** if ordered.
1 Sitting-room. With stove, TV. No smoking.
Small garden

High above beautiful Swaledale, this remote house went with a lead-miner's smallholding. The Mansfields have extended what became Jennie's family's holiday cottage by restoring the adjoining barns and, at the behest of the National Park authority, they maintained the external appearance so two of the guest bedrooms have the barns' original openings as windows. The largest bedroom, on the ground floor, used to be a stable and its bathroom a pigsty. In the sitting-room there is a large collection of books on this interesting part of the country; Roger and Jennie are themselves well informed about the geology and topography of Swaledale, since they were both teachers involved in outdoor education.

This is great walking country – the Coast-to-Coast route is not far – and so Jennie is used to catering for hearty appetites with, usually, soup, followed by (for example) chicken casserole and then chocolate mousse. More sedentary people can simply make the most of the view of Swaledale from the flagged terrace.

V *Reader's comments:* Most attractive and comfortable; wonderful hosts – could not have been more attentive to our needs; excellent breakfasts and evening meals.

North Yorkshire

POND COTTAGE

C PT S

Brandsby Road, Stillington, North Yorkshire, YO61 1NY Tel: 01347 810796
North of York. Nearest main road: A19 from York to Thirsk.

2 Bedrooms. £20–£22 (less for 3 nights or more). Bargain breaks. Both have own toilet. No smoking.
Light suppers if ordered. Vegetarian or other special diets if ordered. No smoking.
1 Sitting-room. With TV. No smoking.
Small garden
Closed from December to February.

In a barn adjoining this tiny primrose-yellow cottage is a treasure-trove of domestic bygones. For the Thurstans are antique dealers, specializing in 'kitchenalia' and pine furniture. The 18th-century house itself is furnished with antiques, and its shelves and nooks are filled with curios. There are collections of coronation mugs and Staffordshire dogs in the low-beamed sitting-room, where high-backed wing chairs are grouped around an inglenook fireplace. This is a house of twists and turns, unexpected steps and low windows. Its pleasant bedrooms overlook a terrace with stone troughs of flowers, a croquet lawn and a natural pond.

Dianne serves only breakfast and light suppers because the area is very well supplied with eating-places. Stillington is almost equidistant from the city of York, the coast, the North York Moors and the Dales – each offering totally different holiday experiences needing many days to explore.

V *Readers' comments:* A brilliant discovery. Fantastic treatment. Accommodation and catering excellent. Wonderful. Outstanding. Delightful and caring hostess. Nothing too much trouble. Friendly and welcoming family, very comfortable, good value.

PONDEN HOUSE

C D P T S

Stanbury, West Yorkshire, BD22 0HR Tel: 01535 644154
South-west of Keighley. Nearest main road: A6033 from Hebden Bridge to Keighley.

West Yorkshire

3 Bedrooms. £22–£23. Available: own shower/toilet.
Dinner (by arrangement). £13 for 3 courses and coffee, at 7pm. Vegetarian or other special diets if ordered. Wine available. **Light suppers** if ordered.
1 Sitting-room. With stove, piano.
Small garden and wooded grounds

On the site of an old farmhouse and barn Brenda Taylor has created a house which combines the best of old and new, where works of modern art and craft blend with reclaimed stone and wood, imaginatively used. By the table in the sitting/dining-room hangs a big photo-collage by David Hockney of Ponden Hall across the lane. (Supposedly the Thrushcross Grange of *Wuthering Heights*, it was owned by Brenda when it was in this book – it is now a private house.) On the other side of the room, a woodstove stands under a big Gothic arch of stone, with settees around it. In all the rooms are good pictures and wall-hangings, and the colour schemes in the bedrooms – ivory and flame, soft blues and purple – are striking.

Brenda is a creative and generous caterer, and dinner might consist of a robust vegetable soup, chicken breasts with Puy lentils and an assortment of vegetables and salad, and a chocolate roulade. Breakfast eggs and bacon are particularly good.

Three miles away are the Brontës' Haworth and the Worth Valley Steam Railway; Top Withens, the original of Wuthering Heights, is a walk away. **V**

PROSPECT END

C M P T X

8 Prospect Terrace, Savile Road, Hebden Bridge, West Yorkshire, HX7 6NA
Tel/Fax: 01422 843586
West of Halifax. Nearest main road: A646 from Halifax to Burnley (and M62, junctions 21/24).

West Yorkshire

2 Bedrooms. £20 (less for 3 nights or more). Bargain breaks. Both have own shower/toilet; TV. No smoking.
Light suppers if ordered.
1 Sitting-room. With TV. No smoking.
Small garden

Terraced houses used to be built one on top of another to fit the steep slopes of Hebden Bridge. A pair of these have been united to form Prospect End, where the guest-rooms are approached through the garden, while the kitchen/breakfast-room above them is at street level and the sitting-room windows look on to treetops. The two en suite bedrooms, in pale pink, are neat and well equipped. Ann Anthon will provide light suppers, but most guests go to the many restaurants in the town, which has become something of a cultural centre for the south Pennines and has some interesting shops. The local beauty-spot is Hardcastle Crags (NT), with riverside walks; and Haworth, home of the Brontës, is close.

In the nearby city of Halifax, the Piece Hall is an enormous Italianate building of the 18th century, where the handloom weavers of the area came to sell their pieces of cloth. As well as a museum devoted to that cottage industry, there are dozens of shops and galleries, and exhibitions and performances are held there. Also in Halifax is Eureka!, a purpose-built museum for children (aged 3 to 12) with lots of hands-on features. **V**

North Yorkshire

SEVENFORD HOUSE C

Thorgill, Rosedale Abbey, North Yorkshire, YO18 8SE Tel: 01751 417283 (Fax: 01751 417505)

North-west of Pickering. Nearest main road: A170 from Thirsk to Scarborough.

3 Bedrooms. £22.50. Available: own bath/shower/toilet; TV. No smoking.
Light suppers only. Vegetarian or other special diets if ordered. No smoking.
1 Sitting-room. With open fire, piano.
Large garden

Rosedale Abbey now exists only in the name it gave this quiet village. It was something of an iron-mining Klondike in the late Victorian era, when Sevenford House was built on its outskirts, and there was glass-making here in the 16th century. Glass-blowing has recently been revived with distinction by two craft-workers in the village; there is also a pottery where you can have a lesson.

The house, with its spacious rooms, has been decorated and furnished in keeping with its period by Linda and Ian Sugars; on the walls are a lot of photoprints of local Victorian characters by Frank Meadows Sutcliffe of Whitby.

Visitors have a choice of two good restaurants in the village. On the airy grouse-moors which surround it, a National Park, are England's best-preserved stretch of Roman road, prehistoric standing stones and mediaeval crosses.

V *Readers' comments:* Beautiful old house; very warm welcome; made most comfortable.

North Yorkshire

SHALLOWDALE HOUSE C(12) PT

West End, Ampleforth, North Yorkshire, YO62 4DY Tel: 01439 788325 (Fax: 01439 788885)

South-west of Helmsley. Nearest main road: A170 from Thirsk to Pickering.

3 Bedrooms. £25 **to readers of this book only** –£40 (less for 3 nights or more). All have own bath/shower/toilet; TV; balcony (one). No smoking.
Dinner (by arrangement). £22.50 for 4 courses and coffee, at 7.30pm. Vegetarian or other special diets if ordered. Wine available. No smoking.
2 Sitting-rooms. With open fire. No smoking.
Large garden

E-mail: stay@shallowdalehouse.demon.co.uk

Anton van der Horst and Phillip Gill had no intention of buying a modern house but they could not resist this 1960s one, sited on a rise just outside Ampleforth and excellently planned to give every room a good view of the surrounding countryside. Readers who stayed at Phillip and Anton's previous house in Masham will know that they have furnished and decorated this one with unusual judgement and originality: the furniture ranges from an ornate old Friesian clock in the sitting-room to classic 1960s chairs in the bedrooms, where specially made quilts match the printed curtains. One bedroom is almost a private suite; also upstairs is a small and tranquil second sitting-room. Good pictures abound.

You can walk up the solitary valley after which the house is named or even through woods to the top of Sutton Bank.

The practice of outstanding cooking continues, a typical meal being smoked haddock with spinach and chives; braised lamb with flageolets; bread-and-butter pudding made with panettone; and cheese.

Readers' comments: Food as good as the priciest restaurants. Energetic, cheerful and efficient. Excellent food and pleasant proprietors.

SPROXTON HALL

S

Sproxton, North Yorkshire, YO62 5EQ Tel: 01439 770225 (Fax: 01439 771373)
South of Helmsley. Nearest main road: A170 from Thirsk to Helmsley.

3 Bedrooms. £24–£28 (less for 3 nights or more). Bargain breaks. Available: own bath/shower/toilet; TV. No smoking.
Light suppers if ordered.
1 Sitting-room. With open fire. No smoking.
Large garden
Closed in late December and January.

E-mail: info@sproxtonhall.demon.co.uk

Under a high-beamed ceiling, deep chintz-covered armchairs and a settee face a stone wall with an open fireplace in the large sitting-room, with plentiful antiques around. The bedrooms in this 17th-century house are just as prettily furnished, with flowery fabrics and sprigged wallpaper, and the double rooms have brass half-tester beds with crisp draperies. (The bathrooms too are pretty – Margaret Wainwright is understandably house-proud!) Views are of a trim garden beyond which are the fields of this large mixed farm; or of a farmyard, with hills in the background.

Margaret does not serve full dinners, for the area has excellent pub restaurants. It is also rich in 'sights' – castles, mansions, gardens, and the famous ruined abbeys of the Cistercian monks. One imposing castle is at nearby Helmsley, a picturesque market town with superior shops and galleries. Many of the villages in the area are very attractive, with their carefully conserved houses of honey-coloured stone and red pantiled roofs.

Reader's comments: Excellent value, a beautiful house, genuine Yorkshire hospitality.

V

WHASHTON SPRINGS FARM

C(5) S

Whashton, North Yorkshire, DL11 7JS Tel: 01748 822884 (Fax: 01748 826285)
North-west of Richmond. Nearest main road: A1 from Catterick to Scotch Corner.

8 Bedrooms. £24–£25 (less for 7 nights or more). Bargain breaks. All have own bath/shower/toilet; TV. No smoking in some.
1 Sitting-room. With open fire. No smoking. **Bar.**
Small garden
Closed from mid-December to end of January.

Far more handsome than the average farmhouse, 18th-century Whashton Springs has great bow windows and other detailing typical of this fine period in English architecture. Around it is a large, mixed farm run by two generations of Turnbulls. It is high among wooded hills, with superb views of the Dales and of a stream with mediaeval bridge below.

Fairlie Turnbull has decorated each bedroom differently. One, for instance, has flowery fabrics, broderie anglaise on the bedlinen, pretty Victorian antiques and a bow window; another, a four-poster with William Morris drapery and buttoned velvet chairs. Others in a converted stable-block are more modern in style (velvet bedheads, flowery duvets and pine furniture); most of these overlook a courtyard where tubs and stone troughs brim with pansies and petunias; one has a garden view.

Readers' comments: Very comfortable. Made very welcome. High praise. Lovely surroundings and easy access to many places. Charming proprietors, accommodation excellent. Exceptional value for comfort, amenities, atmosphere and personal welcome.

WHITFIELD

C D PT S

Helm, Askrigg, North Yorkshire, DL8 3JF Tel/Fax: 01969 650565
West of Leyburn. Nearest main road: A684 from Hawes to Leyburn.

2 Bedrooms. £23 (less for 2 nights or more). Both have own bath/shower/toilet; TV. No smoking.
1 Sitting-room. With open fire. No smoking.
Small garden

E-mail: empsall@askrigg.yorks.net

Once a house, then a barn, and now a house again, Whitfield was built in the 17th century. Named after the ridge of fells behind it, the house stands at nearly 1000 feet above sea level. All the rooms face south, with excellent views across upper Wensleydale to Addlebrough, the hill on top of which a prehistoric settlement is being excavated.

Visitors breakfast, under a pine-beamed ceiling, at a big mahogany table. By it is a grandfather clock made in Askrigg, where there were once no fewer than 18 clock-makers. Now the village, which is where episodes of 'All Creatures Great and Small' were filmed, has several good restaurants. One could walk there by one of the footpaths which pass just by the house.

Ex-teacher Kate Empsall has furnished the house conventionally and comfortably, with armchairs round the open fireplace beyond the dining-table. She has also added some individualistic touches, such as collections of antique cycle lamps and glass bottles. Lush flowers surround the house, by which a herd of dairy cows passes twice daily in summer, to the interest of many guests.

V

WIDDALE FOOT

C S

Hawes, North Yorkshire, DL8 3LX Tel/Fax: 01969 667383
South-west of Hawes. Nearest main road: A684 from Hawes to Sedbergh.

3 Bedrooms. £19–£22. Available: own bath/shower/toilet; views of river. No smoking.
1 Sitting-room. With open fire, TV. No smoking.
Large garden
Closed from November to March.

Every visitor comments on the ornate glazed cabinet which stands by the mahogany table in the breakfast-room here, a fantastically carved piece of distinctly oriental appearance but unknown origin. It is an exotic thing to find in a 19th-century Yorkshire farmhouse, which has been greatly improved by Margaret and Roy Hill. Reached by its own road, the house has a little river rushing past it, which you can contemplate from the sitting-room windows, the bedrooms, or the pleasant garden just outside. Beyond graze the Hills' Hebridean sheep, a rare breed, who occupy the surrounding 13 acres of land.

This is notable walking country – you can start from the house on a green footpath. The area is equally known for the historic Settle–Carlisle railway: the road to the house continues on to the famous Ribblehead viaduct (and thence to Ingleton, with waterfalls and caves). In the other direction, Hawes is only three miles away. This is where to have dinner (a good choice of places), but it should be visited during the daytime as well for the folk museum and the interesting ropeworks, and to buy antiques, old books or Wensleydale cheese.

V

WILLERBY WOLD FARM

C(5)

Staxton, North Yorkshire, YO12 4TF Tel: 01944 710747 (Fax: 01944 710281)
South of Scarborough. Nearest main road: A64 from Malton to Scarborough.

2 Bedrooms. £20–£22.50 (less for 3 nights or more). Both have own bath/shower/toilet; TV; views of sea (one). No smoking.
Dinner (by arrangement). £12.50 for 3 courses and coffee, at times to suit guests. Vegetarian or special diets if ordered. Restricted smoking. **Light suppers** if ordered.
Large garden

E-mail: willerbywold@amserve.net

Though it is in fact Victorian – built in 1865 – this large farmhouse has retained a degree of Georgian elegance, with well-proportioned rooms within a simple exterior. Built of the mellow red brick characteristic of this part of Yorkshire, it is at the heart of an 800-acre mixed farm in a tranquil agricultural area.

One bedroom is very large, with a settee. The smaller room, equally graceful, has a view of the flourishing rose garden. (A sitting-room is made available only when both rooms are occupied.) There is also a tennis court.

Virginia Sutton does not usually offer a full evening meal – there are good pubs at which to dine within a mile or two – but when she does, it could comprise pork chops ardennaise, sponge pudding, and cheese. This will be served in the blue-papered dining-room at a long mahogany table which, like much of the rest of the furniture, is a family antique.

Nearby Scarborough has all the attractions of a traditional seaside resort, plus the theatre where Alan Ayckbourn's plays are always premiered. Filey and Flamborough Head are a drive away.

WILLOW TREE COTTAGE

C(5) D

North Yorkshire

Boltby, North Yorkshire, YO7 2DY Tel: 01845 537406 (Fax: 01845 537073)
North-east of Thirsk. Nearest main road: A170 from Thirsk to Scarborough.

1 Bedroom. £22.50. Has own bath/shower/toilet; TV; balcony. No smoking.
Dinner (by arrangement). £12 for 3 courses and coffee, at times to suit guests. Vegetarian or other special diets if ordered. No smoking. **Light suppers** if ordered.
Garden

E-mail: townsend.sce@virgin.net

A sinuous lane winds through woods and fields to this one-time keeper's cottage on the edge of a neat village of warm sandstone houses. With the Townsends' hens, geese and a few sheep outside, the house is perched on the edge of a hillside which gives a long vista of the Vale of York. In an extension added a few decades ago to this 19th-century house is particularly spacious and comfortable accommodation. Not only is the pastel-decorated bedroom large – large enough for there to be an extra-big double bed, armchairs and a table, and for another bed to be easily added if required – but there is a well-equipped kitchenette off it for guests to prepare simple meals if they wish.

Diana Townsend serves breakfast in the room, and dinner too when it is available (this might consist of avocado, roast beef, and ice cream). Otherwise, the inn in the next village is recommended – the drive is worth it for the view halfway there.

Readers' comments: Accommodation luxurious, wonderful view of the lovely surroundings; very friendly and helpful. Lovely b & b; pleasant and helpful; highly recommended.

V

North Yorkshire

WOOD VIEW

CDX

The Green, Austwick, North Yorkshire, LA2 8BB Tel: 01524 251268
North-west of Settle. Nearest main road: A65 from Settle to Kirkby Lonsdale.

6 Bedrooms. £22–£32 (less for 2 nights or more). Bargain breaks. Available: own bath/shower/toilet; TV. No smoking.
Dinner (by arrangement). £12–£15 for 2–3 courses and coffee, at 6–7.30pm. Vegetarian or other special diets if ordered. Wine available. No smoking. **Light suppers** if ordered.
1 Sitting-room. With open fire. **Bar.**
Large garden

The symmetrical front and small windows belie the size of this early 18th-century one-time farmhouse, for it is a capacious place. The biggest and best-equipped rooms are the attics, which are crossed by great wooden beams. Jenny Suri has furnished them and the other bedrooms with matching modern suites. Downstairs there is a large sitting-room with a bar off it; both have stone fireplaces. In the dining-room Jenny serves straightforward meals, with a choice at each course: one might pick crab cocktail, chicken in white wine sauce, and bread-and-butter pudding.

Austwick is a village of stone houses and it stands in an area rich with spectacular geology. Hill-walking enthusiasts will know the Three Peaks (Ingleborough, Pen-y-Ghent and Whernside), but there is much to be seen by the less energetic: notably waterfalls, enormous caves, and the effects of glaciation many ages ago. The limestone 'pavements' in the imposing fells a few miles away are famous.

V

Houses which accept the discount vouchers on page ii are marked with a V symbol next to the relevant entries.

Many houses in this book are situated in or very near to Areas of Outstanding Natural Beauty and protected Heritage Coasts. For a selection of these houses, see p.xi.

Complaints about matters which could not have been settled on the spot will be forwarded to proprietors. Please enclose a stamped addressed envelope if you want your complaint acknowledged.

THANK YOU . . . to those who send details of their own finds, for possible future inclusion in the book. Do not be disappointed if your candidate does not appear in the very next edition. Recommendations from unknown members of the public are never published without verification, and it takes time to get round each part of England and Wales in turn. Please, however, do not send details of houses already featured in many other guides, nor any that are more expensive than those in this book (see page xiv).

REGIONAL DIRECTORY OF HOUSES AND HOTELS IN

WALES

Prices are per person sharing a double room, at the beginning of the year. You may be quoted more later or for single occupancy.

Prices and other facts quoted at the head of each entry are as supplied by the proprietors.

Sitting-room at Upper Trewalkin Farm, Powys (see page 332)

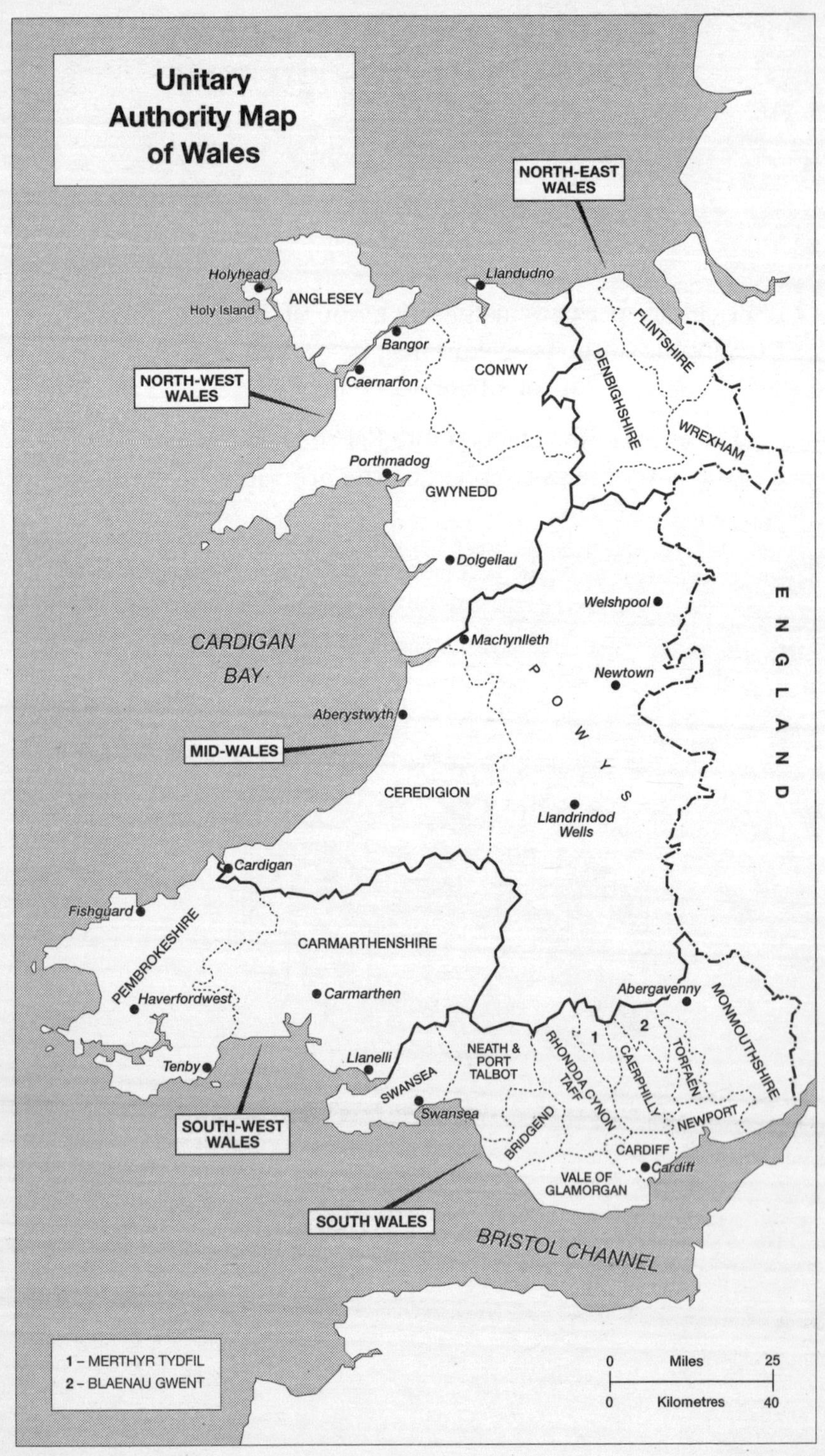

Unitary Authority Map of Wales
NORTH-EAST WALES
Holyhead
Holy Island
ANGLESEY
Llandudno
Bangor
Caernarfon
NORTH-WEST WALES
CONWY
FLINTSHIRE
DENBIGHSHIRE
WREXHAM
Porthmadog
GWYNEDD
Dolgellau
Welshpool
ENGLAND
CARDIGAN BAY
Machynlleth
Newtown
POWYS
Aberystwyth
MID-WALES
CEREDIGION
Llandrindod Wells
Cardigan
Fishguard
PEMBROKESHIRE
CARMARTHENSHIRE
Haverfordwest
Carmarthen
Abergavenny
MONMOUTHSHIRE
1
2
NEATH & PORT TALBOT
RHONDDA CYNON TAFF
CAERPHILLY
TORFAEN
Llanelli
Tenby
SWANSEA
Swansea
BRIDGEND
NEWPORT
CARDIFF
Cardiff
VALE OF GLAMORGAN
SOUTH-WEST WALES
SOUTH WALES
BRISTOL CHANNEL
1 – MERTHYR TYDFIL
2 – BLAENAU GWENT
0 Miles 25
0 Kilometres 40

NORTH-WEST WALES
(including Anglesey, Conwy and Gwynedd)

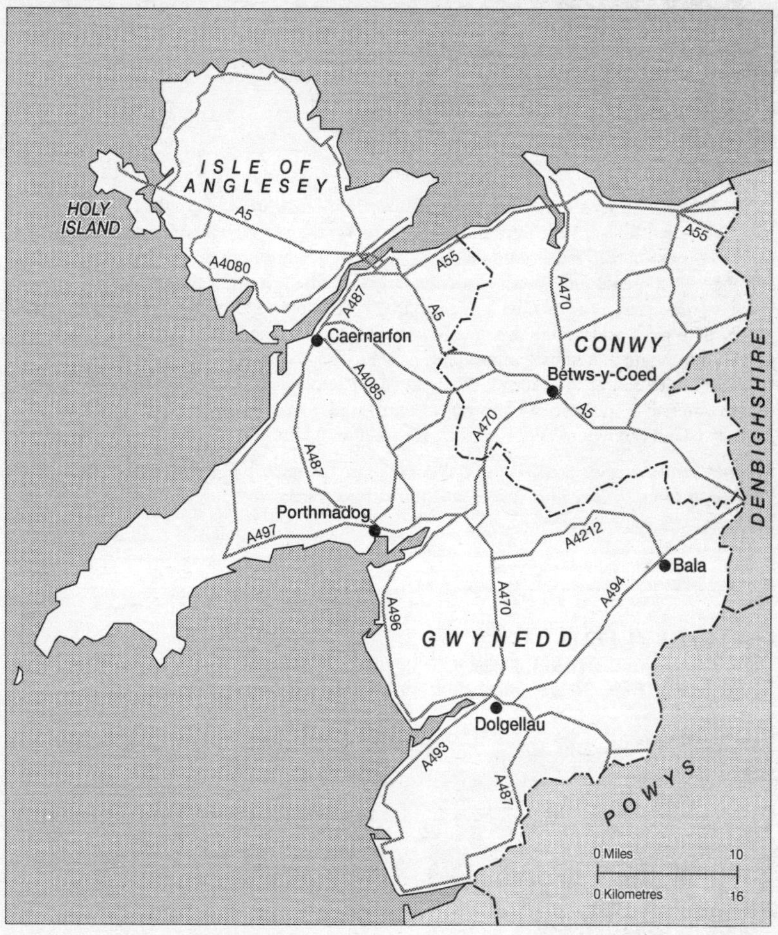

Addresses shown are to enable you to locate a house on a map. They are not necessarily complete postal addresses (though the essential post-code is included), and detailed directions for finding a house should be obtained from the owner.

BRONANT

C D P T S X

Bontnewydd, Gwynedd, LL54 7YF Tel: 01286 830451
South of Caernarfon. Nearest main road: A487 from Caernarfon to Porthmadog.

3 Bedrooms. £18–£19 (less for 3 nights or more). Bargain breaks. Views of sea. No smoking.
2 Sitting-rooms. With TV, organ. No smoking.
Small garden

At the top of the Lleyn Peninsula (looking over the Menai Strait to Anglesey) is this handsome Victorian house, kept in immaculate order by Megan Williams and her nieces, who run a tea-room here. Their traditional Welsh teas are really authentic: the gingerbread, *bara brith* (speckled bread) and Welsh cakes regularly take first prizes at county shows.

Most rooms are spacious, with Welsh tapestry bedspreads in rich colours and views of sheep, pine trees and mountains. Some windows have stained glass depicting apples and pears, appropriate to a house where good, natural food excels.

Right at the end of the Lleyn is Mynydd Mawr, a National Trust headland with coastal views comparable to those of Cornwall's Land's End. Over two miles of choppy waters lies Bardsey Island (known to pilgrims as the isle of 20,000 saints).

V

Readers' comments: Spacious, comfortable bedroom. A great place with spectacular views. Very good value. Marvellous cakes. Beautiful and comfortable house; Megan Williams and her nieces charming.

CWM HWYLFOD

C S

Cefn-ddwysarn, Gwynedd, LL23 7LN Tel/Fax: 01678 530310
North-east of Bala. Nearest main road: A494 from Bala towards Corwen.

3 Bedrooms. £20 (less for 7 nights or more). With TV. No smoking.
1 Sitting-room. With open fire, TV. No smoking.
Large garden

'Meeting of drovers' roads' is a rough translation of the name Cwm Hwylfod: a remote inn-turned-farm in the hills at Cefn-ddwysarn, still retaining its 400-year-old character. The Bests (civil engineer and teacher) bought it on impulse when holidaying in this spectacular area above the Dee Valley, falling in love with its odd-shaped walls, beams, deep-set windows, log fires, and screen wall of old timbers which once separated people from cows and hayloft. They keep 300 sheep as well as other livestock: children love the streams, sheepdogs, collecting eggs and exploring footpaths.

Bedrooms are simple. For evening meals, Joan recommends the Plas yn Dre restaurant in Bala (a 10-minute drive) where the food is good, the ambience child-friendly and the owner very welcoming.

V

Readers' comments: Received most warmly. Children in seventh heaven! Will certainly return.

LLWYNDÛ FARMHOUSE

C D PT X

Llanaber, Barmouth, Gwynedd, LL42 1RR Tel: 01341 280144 (Fax: 01341 281236)
West of Dolgellau. Nearest main road: A496 from Barmouth to Harlech.

7 Bedrooms. £25–£35. Bargain breaks. Available: own bath/shower/toilet; TV; views of sea. No smoking.
Dinner (by arrangement). £16.45 for 3 courses and coffee, at 7.30pm. Vegetarian or other special diets if ordered. Wine available. No smoking. **Light suppers** if ordered.
1 Sitting-room. With open fire, TV. No smoking.
Large garden

E-mail: Intouch@llwyndu-farmhouse.co.uk

In 1597, this handsomely built house was already of considerable consequence in the neighbourhood. The walls are immensely thick, and the living-room huge; one ceiling-beam is over two feet thick, and great blocks of granite form the fireplace. New discoveries continue to come to light – for instance, a 16th-century oak-mullioned window.

Most bedrooms have views (and sounds) of the sea, and two have four-poster beds – also excellent bathrooms. One room has a dressing-room, another its own stone stair to the garden; some are in a converted granary. Everywhere are attractive furnishings, and great pieces of driftwood from the beaches stand here and there like sculpture.

Peter and Paula Thompson are very keen cooks, preparing such meals as parsnip-and-apple soup, lamb in a mushroom and cinnamon sauce, rhubarb-and-banana pie.

Readers' comments: House has tremendous character. Lovely food, great value. Delightful situation, friendly welcome. Food superb. Excellent hostess and cook. Stunning views.

MELIN MELOCH

C(5) D S

Llanfor, Bala, Gwynedd, LL23 7DP Tel: 01678 520101 (Mobile: 0370 978790)
East of Bala. Nearest main road: A494 from Corwen to Bala.

4 Bedrooms. £20–£24.50 (less for 4 nights or more). Bargain breaks. Available: own bath/shower/toilet; TV. No smoking.
2 Sitting-rooms. With open fire, TV. No smoking.
Large garden
Closed in January.

This 13th-century watermill is a galleried house with pretty bedrooms. Through an arch by the big stone fireplace in the beamed sitting-room is a great table flanked by pews, where Beryl Fullard serves breakfast. For evening meals, the Fullards will drive guests to and from a good restaurant in Bala.

The miller's cottage has a ground-floor bedroom and spacious family suite; other rooms are in a granary. Everywhere are paintings and antique Welsh oak furniture. Richard has landscaped the large gardens, making the most of the stream, the waterfall and the ponds, and has annually received an award for his work.

The River Meloch feeds the mill-race (*melin* means mill), which drives a Pelton wheel, a Victorian form of waterwheel which Richard has restored.

Readers' comments: Spectacular. Location excellent. Lovely house. Perfection. The house is a beauty. Absolutely wonderful time. Never-to-be-forgotten, unique house. Garden is the heart and soul of this place. Perfect hosts.

PLAS GOWER

C S X

Llangower, Gwynedd, LL23 7BY Tel/Fax: 01678 520431
South-west of Bala. Nearest main road: A494 from Dolgellau to Bala.

2 Bedrooms. £22–£24 (less for 4 nights or more). Bargain breaks. Both have own bath/shower/toilet; TV; views of lake. No smoking.
Dinner (by arrangement). £8.50 for 3 courses and coffee, at times to suit guests. Vegetarian diets if ordered. No smoking. **Light suppers** if ordered.
1 Sitting-room. With open fire, TV. No smoking.
Large garden

Above the less-frequented side of Lake Bala is this 18th-century house, which has very fine views across lily-pond and lake to the mountains of Snowdonia. One enters past a cascade of begonias in the verandah to rooms furnished handsomely, with Victorian watercolours of Wales and such interesting features as an old spinet converted into a desk. There is a particularly elegant bathroom. A previous owner was the Welsh poet Euros Bowen who lived here until 1973, but the site has been inhabited since 1312 and Olwen Foreman has a sampler which lists all owners from then until now. She enjoys telling visitors about lesser-known routes to follow and cooking for them traditional meals such as leek soup, Welsh lamb, and blackberry-and-apple crumble. Her sister, too, takes b & b guests – at **Plas Penucha** in Flintshire.

Bala is Wales's largest lake, surrounded by wild hills offering scenic walks and drives among peaks nearly 3000 feet high. The loftiest road in Wales runs from Bala to Dinas Mawddwy, a very pretty village: footpaths lead to waterfalls.

V

ROYAL OAK FARMHOUSE

C(5) PT S

Betws-y-Coed, Conwy, LL24 0AH Tel: 01690 710427
Nearest main road: A5 from Betws-y-Coed to Llangollen.

2–3 Bedrooms. £20–£22 (less for 7 nights or more). Available: own bath/shower/toilet; views of river. No smoking.
1 Sitting-room. With open fire, TV. No smoking.
Large garden

Royal Oak Farmhouse is a small, partly 13th-century watermill. Although so central, the mill is hidden in a little valley with a deep salmon pool close by. The lattice-paned windows, great stone fireplace, carved oak settle and very pretty bedrooms give this guest-house great character. Two bedrooms, with private bathroom, are let as a family suite.

Elsie Houghton serves only breakfast, but there are good eating-places in Betws.

Four wooded valleys meet at this village, with a high plateau looming above it. Walkers use it as a centre to explore in every direction, the serious ones making for Snowdon but most for the riverside paths, the Gwydyr Forest, any of several lakes or waterfalls, or the Fairy Glen, one of the area's finest beauty-spots.

Also in the vicinity are such sights as Dolwyddelan Castle, Ffestiniog power station (guided tours) and the cavernous slate mine at Llechwedd (you are conveyed by train through Victorian scenes underground).

TY GWYN HOTEL

C D M P T S X

Betws-y-Coed, Conwy, LL24 0SG Tel/Fax: 01690 710383 or 710787
On A5 from Betws-y-Coed to Llangollen.

13 Bedrooms. £17–£45 (less for 5 nights or more). Bargain breaks. Available: own bath/shower/toilet; TV; views of river; balcony (one).
Dinner. A la carte, from 7–9pm. Vegetarian or other special diets if ordered. Wine available. **Light suppers** if ordered.
1 Sitting-room. With TV. **Bar** with open fire.

A former coaching inn, Ty Gwyn ('white house'), although on a road, has quiet bedrooms at the back. The Ratcliffes have a flair for interior decoration, and every bedroom – small or large – is beautiful, many with en suite bathrooms (prices vary accordingly). The most impressive is an attic suite with four-poster and sitting-room; the most convenient for anyone with mobility problems, a pretty ground-floor room.There is an ancient, beamed bar (fire glowing in the old black range) and a very comfortable sitting-room.

Cooking is done by chef Martin, the Ratcliffes' son, whose specialities include exotic dishes like pigeon with oyster mushrooms in Madeira, or Thai-style king prawns. These meals are served in a picturesque dining-room: antique furniture, crochet, crystal and silver on the tables. Even the bar snacks are interesting. Young children may stay free.

Readers' comments: Lovely setting, wonderful room. Good food. Very good, and a really beautiful attic suite. The highlight of the tour; have put real thought into vegetarian menu.

TY MAWR FARM

C D X

Llanddeiniolen, Gwynedd, LL55 3AD Tel/Fax: 01248 670147
North-east of Caernarfon. Nearest main road: A487 from Caernarfon to Bangor.

rear view

3 Bedrooms. £22–£25 (less for 3 nights or more). Bargain breaks. All have own bath/shower/toilet; TV.
Dinner (by arrangement). £12.50 for 3 courses and coffee, at 6–7pm. Vegetarian or other special diets if ordered. **Light suppers** if ordered.
2 Sitting-rooms. With open fire/stove, TV.
Large garden

Eighteenth-century Ty Mawr is on a 150-acre farm where once-rare 'badger-faced' sheep are bred, now often bought as pets. Superb views of Snowdonia are one of the attractions of staying here; another is young Jane Pierce's cooking of such meals as prawns in puff pastry, lamb with baked leeks and other vegetables, and trifle. In two beamy sitting-rooms and elsewhere are a mixture of antiques and family possessions, pretty fabrics and colours, flowery armchairs grouped around a log stove.

One is in the heart of Snowdonia here, with Caernarfon in one direction and Bangor in the other. The rugged grandeur of the mountain passes is in complete contrast to the tranquil countryside around the farm, with wildflowers and birds in abundance. The island of Anglesey is soon reached; some of its sandy beaches sheltered and others open to Atlantic breakers, ideal for surfing. There are preserved railways – steam at Ffestiniog, rack-and-pinion up to Snowdon's summit; and, of course, some sensational castles – Caernarfon in particular, but also Beaumaris, Penrhyn and Conwy.

V

Y WERN

C(5) X

Llanfrothen, Gwynedd, LL48 6LX Tel/Fax: 01766 770556

North-east of Porthmadog. Nearest main road: A4085 from Penrhyndeudraeth to Caernarfon.

5 Bedrooms. £19–£23 (less for 2 nights or more). Available: own bath/shower/toilet. No smoking.
Dinner (by arrangement). £13.50 for 3 courses and coffee, at 7pm. Vegetarian or other special diets if ordered. No smoking.
1 Sitting-room. With stove, TV, piano. No smoking.
Large garden

Alder trees gave their name to Y Wern when it was built as a farm in the 16th century. Now the home of Tony Bayley, it is a beamy house with homely furniture, deep-set windows, slate floors and stone inglenooks; the best hill views are to be had from the cottagey second-floor bedroom under the rafters. A plaque over the front door is dedicated to the 18th-century *eisteddfod* bard Richard Jones. The dinner menu varies according to seasonal produce, but a meal might consist of barbecued peppers, chicken or salmon, and sticky-toffee pudding. It is sometimes served on the terrace but usually in the old kitchen.

The house is well placed for touring the beautiful Lleyn Peninsula and visiting such other sights as Portmeirion and Harlech Castle (splendid views of Snowdonia from the battlements). You can walk from the house up on to the mountains behind, or to Plas Brondanw gardens (where there are also great views) by footpath.

V *Readers' comments:* Memorable meals. Very peaceful and friendly. Shall certainly return.

SOME WELSH PLACE NAMES

Aber	River mouth	**Hafod**	Summer dwelling
Afon	River	**Hen**	Old
Bach/Fach	Little	**Hendre**	Winter dwelling
Bryn/Fryn	Hill	**Llan**	Parish
Cae/Gae	Field	**Llwyn**	Copse
Caer/Gaer	Fort	**Llyn**	Lake
Coed	Woods	**Mawr**	Big
Cwm/Gwm	Valley	**Mynydd**	Mountain
Dol	Bend	**Nant**	Valley
Dref/Tref	Town	**Pentre**	Village
Du	Black	**Plas**	Mansion
Dy/Ty	House	**Rhaeadr**	Waterfall
Eglwys	Church	**Rhos**	Moor
Gwyn/Wyn	White	**Ynys**	Island

NORTH-EAST WALES
(including Denbighshire, Flintshire and Wrexham)

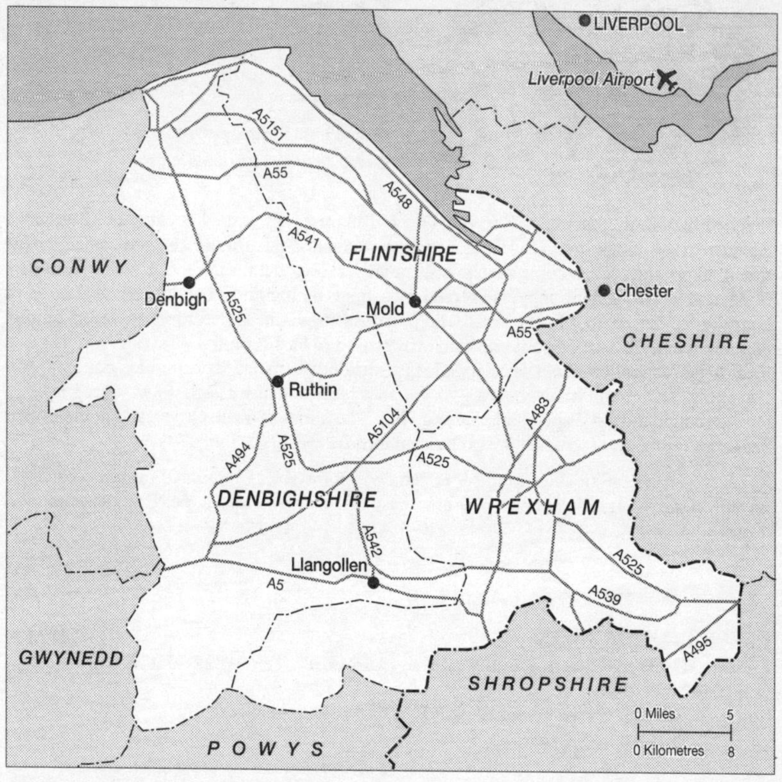

Prices for single occupancy may be higher than those quoted here. Houses that charge singles no more, or only 10% more, than half the price of a double room (except possibly at peak periods) are indicated by the 'S' symbol.

DEE FARMHOUSE

C D S

Rhewl, Llangollen, Denbighshire, LL20 7YT Tel: 01978 861598
North-west of Llangollen. Nearest main road: A5 from Llangollen to Corwen.

2 Bedrooms. £22–£25 (less for 3 nights or more). Bargain breaks. Available: own bath/shower/toilet; views of river. No smoking.
Light suppers if ordered. Vegetarian diets if ordered. No smoking.
2 Sitting-rooms. With open fire (in one). No smoking.
Small garden
Closed from November to March.

E-mail: harman@activelives.co.uk

Perched high in the hamlet of Rhewl is Dee Farmhouse – so named because the River Dee lies just below its garden. Once this was a slate-miners' inn (hence the slate floor downstairs). From the garden come artichokes, spinach, herbs, etc. for the soups which form part of Mary Harman's light suppers (served in a huge dining-kitchen), as well as roses and lavender for her rooms. In the small and pretty sitting-room are antiques; cases of butterflies are in a beamy sitting-room upstairs which used to be a hayloft.

Nearby Llangollen is not only a walking centre but home of the international *eisteddfod* every July. National Trust properties in the area include Chirk Castle (best visited in May for the rhododendron display) and Erddig Hall. The abbey of Valle Crucis and horse-drawn boat trips on the historic canal are other local attractions.

V

Readers' comments: Fine old furniture, extremely comfortable. Concerned for one's comfort. Lovely view. Wonderful cook; pleasant, easy friendliness; house perfect; peaceful and restful.

North-East Wales

EYARTH STATION

C D M X

Llanfair-Dyffryn-Clwyd, Denbighshire, LL15 2EE Tel: 01824 703643
(Fax: 01824 707464)
South of Ruthin. Nearest main road: A525 from Ruthin to Wrexham.

6 Bedrooms. £23 **to readers of this book only** –£25 (less for 3 nights or more). Bargain breaks. Available: own bath/shower/toilet. No smoking.
Dinner. £11 for 2 courses and coffee, at 7pm. Vegetarian or other special diets if ordered. Wine available. No smoking. **Light suppers** if ordered.
2 Sitting-rooms. With log stove, TV. No smoking.
Bar.
Large garden
Closed in January and February.

E-mail: eyarthstation@amserve.net

Ruthin is an attractive little town with half-timbered houses and a crafts centre. Just south of here, a disused railway station is now an unusual – and unusually excellent – guest-house. It has been imaginatively converted and furnished by Jen Spencer. Outside, all is white paint and flowers. Ground-floor bedrooms have such touches as canopied bedheads; some (more simply furnished) are in what were the porters' rooms. Excellent bathrooms (even a bidet). What was once the waiting-room is now a very large sitting-room (one of two) with a balcony just above the fields: big sofas, log stove and thick carpet make this particularly comfortable. The conservatory/dining-room – once the platform – overlooks a small, well-heated swimming-pool which gets the afternoon sun. Jen offers meals with such dishes as chicken breasts in white wine sauce with salad and garlic bread, followed by apple pie.

V

Readers' comments: Excellent accommodation, and welcoming. Delightful lounge and grounds. Meals superb. One of the best places. Exceptional food, wonderful hosts.

FRON HAUL

C D S X

Bodfari, Denbighshire, LL16 4DY Tel/Fax: 01745 710301
North-east of Denbigh. Nearest main road: A541 from Denbigh to Mold.

3 Bedrooms. £23–£25 (less for 7 nights or more). Bargain breaks. Available: own bath/shower/toilet; TV; balcony. No smoking.
Dinner (by arrangement). From £10.50 for 4 courses and coffee, at 8pm. Vegetarian or other special diets if ordered. No smoking. **Light suppers** if ordered.
1 Sitting-room. With open fire, TV, organ. No smoking.
Large garden

Fron Haul ('breast of the sun') guest-house is perched high on the edge of the lovely Vale of Clwyd. Originally the home of a Victorian surgeon, it has balconies from which to enjoy the wonderful view – or you can relax in the sitting-room, conservatory or tea gardens. Bedrooms are comfortable and homely. The house is much used by long-distance walkers – it is on the Offa's Dyke path.

Gwladys Edwards provides an à la carte choice for dinner, with such dishes as salmon, steak or lamb from Fron Haul's farm. (Lunches too. Bread and cakes are home-made.)

Northward is St Asaph, with Britain's smallest cathedral; and at Dyserth, there is a spectacular waterfall and a stately home (Bodelwyddan Castle) with fine gardens – it is an outstation of London's National Portrait Gallery.

Readers' comments: Excellent food (super sweet trolley!). Made very welcome and nothing too much trouble. Stayed on numerous occasions. Unfailingly helpful. Comfort and food memorable.

V

THE MOUNT

C(12) **D PT**

Higher Kinnerton, Flintshire, CH4 9BQ Tel/Fax: 01244 660275
South-west of Chester (England). Nearest main road: A55 from Chester to Conwy (and M56, junction 16).

3 Bedrooms. £25–£30 (less for 2 nights or more). Available: own bath/shower/toilet; TV. No smoking.
Dinner (by arrangement). £20 for 4 courses and coffee, from 7.30pm. No smoking.
1 Sitting-room. With open fire, TV, piano. No smoking.
Large garden

Because of Rachel Major's enthusiasm for gardening, among the attractions of staying here are the fine grounds (sometimes open under the National Gardens Scheme) with herbaceous beds, flowering shrubs and cedar and other trees as mature as the early Victorian house itself. The garden also supplies fresh produce for the table.

Rooms are spacious, with (for instance) yellow panelling in the dining-room and a prettily carved fireplace as the focal point in a very long, coral-walled sitting-room. Guests often relax among the plumbago in the conservatory or (more energetically) on the croquet lawn or tennis court, with views of the Peckforton Hills in Cheshire beyond.

For dinner, Rachel (a cordon bleu cook) might serve soup, baked trout with home-grown vegetables, strawberry ice cream, and cheese. Her other accomplishment is canvaswork, of which there are many examples around the house.

The historic city of Chester with its manifold attractions is easily reached from here.

North-East Wales

PLAS PENUCHA

C S X

Caerwys, Flintshire, CH7 5BH Tel: 01352 720210
North-west of Mold. Nearest main road: A55 from Chester to Conwy.

4 Bedrooms. £22.50–£25 (less for 4 nights or more). Bargain breaks. Available: own shower/toilet. No smoking.
Dinner (by arrangement). £11.50 for 4 courses and coffee, at 7pm. Vegetarian or other special diets if ordered. No smoking. **Light suppers** if ordered.
2 Sitting-rooms. With open fire/stove, TV, piano. No smoking in one.
Large garden

Nêst Price is a harpist and violinist who used also to run the North Wales Music Festival; and this is her ancestral home. Spanish gold financed the original building (sited on top of a spring), home of one of Elizabeth I's buccaneers, but it has been much added to and altered by successive generations.

In the main room, there is a genial greeting, *Aelwyd a Gymhell*, carved on the oak beam across the fireplace: it means 'A welcoming hearth beckons'. Very appropriate in this hospitable house! There is another sitting-room (with built-in log stove), the blue in its oriental rugs on the polished wood-block floor matched by the blue damask sofas; books line one wall and Elizabethan panelling another. Bedrooms are attractive and comfortable; and Nêst is an excellent cook of such meals as soup; rack of Welsh lamb; syllabub; Welsh cheeses. Outside is a large garden, with a view towards the Clwydian Hills.

V *Reader's comments:* First-class atmosphere, facilities, food and comfort.

Prices are per person sharing a room at the beginning of the year.

For explanation of code letters and V symbol, see inside front cover.

Some houses offer special discounts to readers using the current edition of this book. Always state you are an SOTBT reader when ringing to book or when using E-mail.

At houses where dinner is not served, a light supper can often be obtained (if ordered in advance), ranging from sandwiches to family 'pot luck'. (Packed lunches too.)

MID-WALES
(including Ceredigion and Powys)

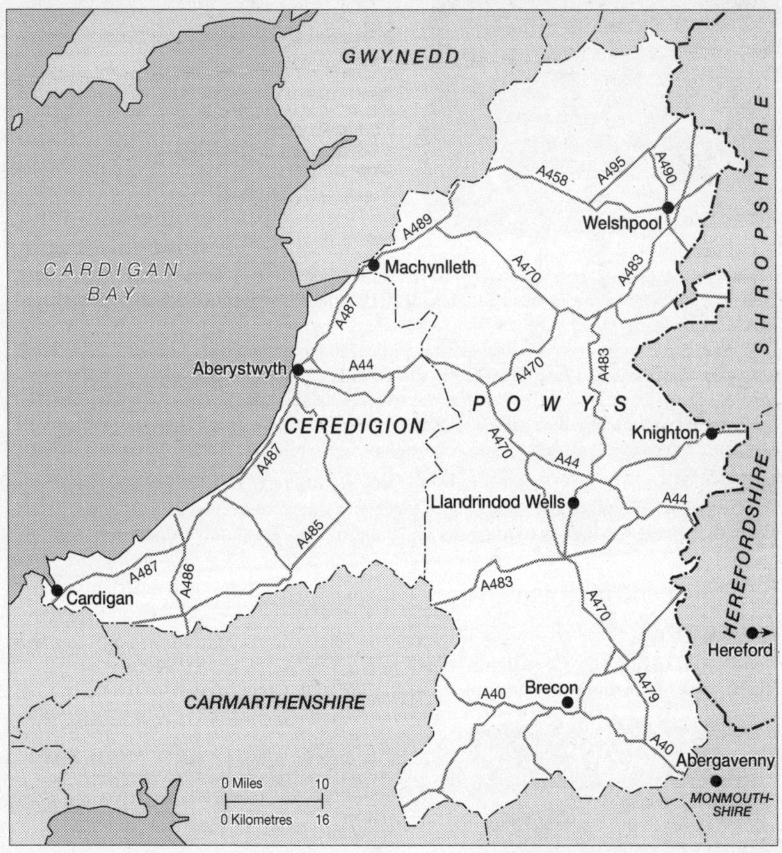

You stand a better chance of finding the right accommodation at the right price in the right area if you are using an up-to-date edition of this book, which is revised every year. Obtain an order form for the next edition (published in November) by sending a stamped addressed envelope, with 'SOTBT 2003' in the top left-hand corner, to Explore Britain, Alston, Cumbria, CA9 3SL.

BRON HEULOG

C PT S X

Waterfall Road, Llanrhaeadr-ym-Mochnant, Powys, SY10 0JX
Tel: 01691 780521
North of Welshpool. Nearest main road: A483 from Welshpool to Oswestry.

3 Bedrooms. £23–£26 (less for 2 nights or more). Bargain breaks. All have own shower/toilet; TV. No smoking.
Dinner (by arrangement). £15 for 3 courses and coffee, at 7pm. Vegetarian or other special diets if ordered. No smoking.
1 Sitting-room. With open fire. No smoking.
Large garden

E-mail: kraines@enta.net

There is a very lovely drive through hills, moors and woods from Bala to the Tanat Valley. Here, on the way to the country's highest waterfall, is this handsome stone house of 1861 which, as its name (*bron*) suggests, is on a hillside.

Karon and Ken Raines have decorated the house to an immaculate standard. Period furniture, pine shutters and a fine Chinese carpet complement Ken's collection of militaria in the rosy sitting-room; original prints line the elegant curving staircase. Bedrooms are named after the flowers suggested by their colour schemes; one has a four-poster. The shower-rooms are excellent. A typical meal: Stilton soup, French lamb casserole, and flambé bananas.

Readers' comments: Food delicious, hosts friendly yet discreet. House beautiful, wonderful view, standard of decor the highest, meals excellent value. Superb food; lovely hosts, generous with their time. Pleasant room, quiet and comfortable. Absolutely delightful.

Mid-Wales

BRONIWAN

D S

Rhydlewis, Llandysul, Ceredigion, SA44 5PF Tel/Fax: 01239 851261
North-east of Cardigan. Nearest main road: A487 from Cardigan to Aberaeron.

3 Bedrooms. £23–£25 (less for 7 nights or more). Available: own bath/shower/toilet. No smoking.
Dinner. £14.50 for 3 courses and coffee, at 7.30pm. Vegetarian or other special diets if ordered. No smoking. **Light suppers** if ordered.
1 Sitting-room. With log stove, TV. No smoking.
Large garden

E-mail: Broniwan@compuserve.com

Within easy reach of National Trust beaches, on a rocky hillside stands this ivy-clad, grey stone house, built in 1867, with much use of pitch-pine.

Carole and Allen Jacobs combine organic farming with teaching English as a foreign language. They have a small herd of Aberdeen Angus beef-cattle, hens and a large vegetable garden. The rooms are very attractive with, for instance, striped wallpaper, Welsh tapestry bedspreads, watercolours, books and old Staffordshire pottery figures.

A typical dinner: watercress soufflé, home-raised beef (with garden vegetables), pears in white wine.

Broniwan is well placed for a holiday full of varied interest. In one direction is the long sandy coastline around great Cardigan Bay, dotted with such pleasant little fishing villages as Aberaeron and Llangranog and with seals and dolphins to be seen; inland are hill walks among gorse and heather where butterflies and buzzards fly. There are old market towns along the bank of the River Teifi and coracle-fishing, and the Welsh Wildlife Centre at Cilgerran. The gardens at Aberglasney are a 45-minute drive away.

BRYNARTH

C(10) **D M S**

Lledrod, Ceredigion, SY23 4HX Tel/Fax: 01974 261367

South-east of Aberystwyth. Nearest main road: A485 from Tregaron to Aberystwyth.

Mid-Wales

7 Bedrooms. £22–£24 (less for 3 nights or more). Most have own bath/shower/toilet. No smoking.
Dinner (by arrangement). £14 for 3 courses and coffee, at 7pm. Vegetarian or other special diets if ordered. Wine available. No smoking. **Light suppers** if ordered.
2 Sitting-rooms. With stove (in one), TV (in one). No smoking. **Bar.**
Large garden
Closed from November to February.

E-mail: brynarth.guesthouse@virgin.net

A very pretty group of white stone buildings, over three centuries old, encloses a big courtyard with lily-pool, flowering shrubs and benches of stone and timber; around are seven acres of grounds. Sally and Chris Prickett – Chris a former colonel in the Australian army, most recently defence attaché to the UN – love the contrast with their previous home on Manhattan where, from their high-rise apartment at roughly the same altitude as Brynarth, they looked down on an area containing several million souls; now their view encompasses a few dozen sheep!

The bedrooms, in the converted barn, are delightful: white-painted stone walls, beams, good wooden furniture and excellent bathrooms create an old-world atmosphere combined with a degree of comfort which is bang up to the minute. In the slate-flagged farmhouse, with inglenook and comfortable sofas, Sally serves such imaginative dinners as spiced apple soup or a brazil nut roast as a starter, followed by wild salmon in a mustard and white wine sauce, and then home-made hazelnut ice cream. In another converted outbuilding is a games room with darts, pool and table tennis.

V

BURNT HOUSE

C(12) **D S**

Trelydan, Powys, SY21 9HU Tel: 01938 552827

North of Welshpool. Nearest main road: A490 from Welshpool to Guilsfield.

Mid-Wales

2 Bedrooms. £20–£22 (less for 3 nights or more). Bargain breaks. One has own bath/toilet.
Dinner. £12.50 for 3 courses and coffee, at 7pm. Vegetarian or other special diets if ordered. **Light suppers** if ordered.
1 Sitting-room. With open fire/stove, TV.
Large garden
Closed from December to February.

Not far from the Georgian market town of Welshpool is mediaeval Burnt House. Above a big, open-plan sitting/dining-room with ample sofas are two attractive bedrooms. One – in the oldest part of the house – has exposed timbers and pretty walnut beds. The other has a view of the Berwyn Mountains; its bathroom is outstanding – textured tiles around the built-in bath. Summer visitors see the garden at its best: Tricia Wykes won the 'Wales in Bloom' award for hotels, pubs and guest-houses throughout North Wales in 1994, 1996 and 1997. Tricia used to cook cakes professionally and so, after perhaps home-made pâté and pork fillet in a sauce of cream and sherry, one may be offered a gâteau or a tempting meringue confection.

Trelydan is very near to the English border, Offa's Dyke and the Shropshire towns of Oswestry and Shrewsbury. In the opposite direction lie lakes Vyrnwy and Bala.

Readers' comments: Hospitality and cuisine excellent. Truly marvellous. Enjoyed every minute. Excellent value for money. Delightful place, peaceful and so comfortable. Cottage warm, welcome equally so; dinners delicious. In a class of its own, wonderful food.

V

CWMLLECHWEDD FAWR

C S

Llanbister, Powys, LD1 6UH Tel/Fax: 01597 840267
North of Llandrindod Wells. Nearest main road: A483 from Llandrindod Wells to Newtown.

2 Bedrooms. £20. Bargain breaks. Both have own bath/shower/toilet; TV (on request). No smoking.
Dinner (by arrangement). £10 for 3 courses and coffee, at 8pm. Vegetarian or other special diets if ordered. No smoking. **Light suppers** if ordered.
1 Sitting-room. With open fire, piano. No smoking.
Large garden
Closed in March and April.

Negotiating a twisting track, you turn a corner and suddenly Cwmllechwedd Fawr comes into view in the distance, a 180-year-old farmhouse perched alone on the hillside in a rugged valley. This organic farm is the peaceful and stylish home of John Underwood, a former antiquarian bookseller, and John Rath, a distinguished opera singer. Also in residence are numerous cats, two dogs, chickens and geese. Truly remote, so walking shoes and wellies are useful in bad weather.

Now completely refurbished, bedrooms, both with lovely country views, have teak floors with kilim rugs and interesting prints on the walls. Afternoon tea is offered on the terrace in warm weather, where later you may be served such dinners as cold cucumber and yogurt soup, home-grown lamb, and delicious home-made ice cream to finish. In colder weather, dinners indoors are candlelit, in a dining-room with a great Welsh dragon painted above the hearth. The adjoining sitting-room, shared with the hosts, has comfortable sofas, contemporary paintings and plenty of local information to help plan your days out.

Mid-Wales

DYSSERTH HALL

C(8) S

by Powis Castle, Welshpool, Powys, SY21 8RQ Tel/Fax: 01938 552153
South of Welshpool. Nearest main road: A483 from Welshpool to Newtown.

4 Bedrooms. £22.50–£25 (less for 3 nights or more). Some have own bath/shower/toilet. No smoking.
Dinner (by arrangement). £15 for 3 courses and coffee, at 7.30–8pm. Vegetarian or other special diets if ordered. Wine available. No smoking. **Light suppers** if ordered.
1 Sitting-room. With open fire, TV, piano. No smoking.
Large garden
Closed from December to February.

A crag of red rock and a moat provided strong defences for 13th-century Powis Castle, from which the princes of Powis ruled much of Wales. The management of their descendants' estates was in the hands of Paul Marriott until he retired. His 18th-century manor house is close to the castle (now National Trust).

Paul and Maureen's elegant home is furnished with fine antiques, well-chosen wallpapers and fabrics – delicate clematis paper in one bedroom, blue brocade on the walls of the dining-room, for instance. There are good paintings everywhere. From a paved terrace with rosebeds one can enjoy the view across the Severn Valley to Long Mountain. (Tennis court in the grounds.)

Dinner may be a candlelit meal of avocado and prawns, Welsh lamb, meringues or, possibly, local cheeses. Vegetables come from the Victorian kitchen garden.

V *Readers' comments:* Warm and welcoming, dinner very good. Wonderful comfort.

THE FFALDAU

C(12) **PT**

Llandegley, Powys, LD1 5UD Tel/Fax: 01597 851421
East of Llandrindod Wells. On A44 from Kington to Rhayader.

3 Bedrooms. £24–£28 (less for 7 nights or more). Available: own bath/shower/toilet. No smoking.
Dinner. £16 for 3 or 4 courses and coffee, at 7pm in winter and 7.30pm in summer, or at times to suit guests (not Thursdays and Sundays). Vegetarian or other special diets if ordered. Wine available. No smoking.
Light suppers if ordered.
3 Sitting-rooms. With stove, TV. No smoking. **Bar.**
Large garden

E-mail: langstaff@ffaldau.co.uk

Mid-Wales

Roses climb up stone walls, rustic seats overlook beds of heather, and a variety of wild birds does not always confine its attention to the bird tables outside, but has been known to venture indoors to assist Michael Langstaff at his computer. The resident hoya plant, too, ignores conventional boundaries and flamboyantly embraces the bathroom adjoining one of the attractive bedrooms.

Ffaldau ('sheepfold') began life around 1500 as a long-house. Old features like the polished slate-flagged floors and beamed ceilings have been retained and restored, and upstairs one can see the cruck construction of the house. Mullioned windows are set into the stone walls, and a log stove stands on an old inglenook hearth. When Michael and Carol came here in 1999 their aim was to offer tranquillity and 'time for people', and indeed the combination of unobtrusive care, good food (Carol was recently runner-up for the title of Mid-Wales Cook of the Year) and the glorious surrounding countryside tempts their visitors to return repeatedly.

Dinner might comprise a home-made soup or mousse, salmon-stuffed chicken parcels, and a seasonal fruit pudding or chocolate concoction.

V

GLYNDWR

C

Pen-y-Bont-Fawr, Powys, SY10 0NT Tel: 01691 860430
North-west of Welshpool. Nearest main road: A483 from Oswestry to Welshpool.

3 Bedrooms. £20–£25. All have own bath/shower/toilet; TV. No smoking.
Dinner (by arrangement). £12 for 3 courses and coffee, at 7pm. Vegetarian or other special diets if ordered. No smoking.
1 Sitting-room. With open fire. No smoking.
Small garden

Mid-Wales

In the beautiful and little-known Tanat Valley, Henry and Gillian Cooper live at 17th-century Glyndwr, once the village inn. Behind is a pretty riverside garden with views of the Berwyn Mountains. From the front door one steps down straight into the welcoming living/dining-area, whose huge open fireplace is supported by a massive oak beam. Up the twisting staircase the cottagey bedrooms have good bath- and shower-rooms, and there is off-street parking at the side of the house – a boon in this small village with its narrow, winding streets. Dinner might comprise spiced grapefruit or mushroom toast, followed by lamb-and-potato pie or salmon parcels, and summer fruit compote or rich bread-and-butter pudding.

Lake Vyrnwy, nearby, is not only picturesque but surrounded by 5000 acres of woods. At the foot of grouse moors one finds Pistyll Rhaeadr, the country's highest waterfall. Small villages, inns and agricultural shows add to the interest of this very scenic area. Motoring is a traffic-free pleasure, alternating between roads that feel as if on top of the world and lanes that plunge deep into valleys.

Mid-Wales

RHYDLEWIS HOUSE

C S

Rhydlewis, Llandysul, Ceredigion, SA44 5PE Tel/Fax: 01239 851748
East of Cardigan. Nearest main road: A487 from Cardigan to Aberaeron.

3 Bedrooms. £22–£24 (less for 7 nights or more). Bargain breaks. Available: own bath/shower/toilet; TV. No smoking.
Dinner (by arrangement). £15 for 4 courses and coffee, at 7pm. Vegetarian or other special diets if ordered. No smoking. **Light suppers** if ordered.
1 Sitting-room. With stove, TV. No smoking.
Large garden

It was the vast inglenook fireplace at the heart of what had become a delapidated shell that first caught Judith Russill's imagination and inspired her to bring Rhydlewis House back to life. For many years the building housed a general supply store selling – along with more everyday items – bowler hats that were made on the premises.

The care and attention to detail which some readers may remember Judith for at her previous home (Wye Barn in Tintern) are again evident here at every turn. In the long sitting-room, rough textured green-and-cream crewelwork curtains perfectly complement the blue-green hues of the stone walls. Because she once worked for the celebrated furniture-designer John Makepeace, Judith has a number of very lovely and unusual studio pieces. Bedrooms are equally smart and attractive.

Welsh food is the highlight of Judith's menus. Following a platter of locally smoked trout and salmon, you may be offered a succulent rack of lamb, then plum fool and a board of Welsh cheeses. In addition to Judith's own pretty garden, there are other grander ones nearby.

V *Reader's comments:* Beautiful house; we were fed like lords.

Mid-Wales

TALBONTDRAIN

C D PT(limited) **S**

Uwychygarreg, Powys, SY20 8RR Tel: 01654 702192
South of Machynlleth. Nearest main road: A489 from Machynlleth towards Newtown.

4 Bedrooms. £20–£22.50 (less for 7 nights or more). Bargain breaks. Some have own bath/shower/toilet. No smoking.
Dinner (by arrangement). £11 for 2 courses and coffee, at 7.30pm. Vegetarian or other special diets if ordered. No smoking. **Light suppers** if ordered.
1 Sitting-room. With open fire, pianola. No smoking.
Large garden

E-mail: talbontdrain@btclick.com

Hilary Matthews used to live in London before restoring this remote, slate-floored house, high in the hills, furnishing it very simply but with attractive colours and textures. No car is needed here: Hilary will book a taxi at Machynlleth station to drive you up her long, twisting lane; and she provides particularly well for children. She serves such two-course meals as lamb and pepper casserole, followed by home-made damson ice cream. Her breakfasts feature Welsh specialities: for example, 'Glamorgan sausage', a type of cheese croquette. Some guests enjoy her excellent pianola as an after-dinner treat.

Talbontdrain (its name means 'thorn tree at the end of the bridge') is in a varied area of woodland, waterfalls, moors and sheep pastures; utterly peaceful. Around the house are goats, wagtails and chickens; inside are warmth and comfort. The centre for Alternative Technology and Y Tabernacl (a modern arts centre with concerts, exhibitions and an August music festival) are popular local attractions.

V *Readers' comments:* Friendly; good food and company; extremely comfortable. Beautifully situated. Very friendly and interesting. Enriching atmosphere, beautiful environment.

TREWALTER

C(4) D

Llangorse, Powys, LD3 0PS Tel/Fax: 01874 658442
East of Brecon. Nearest main road: A40 from Abergavenny to Brecon.

3 Bedrooms. £22–£26.50 (less for 2 nights or more). All have own bath/shower/toilet. No smoking.
1 Sitting-room. With open fire, TV.
Large garden

E-mail: Bradleys@trewalter.freeserve.co.uk

It is the views which put the finishing touches to Victorian Trewalter's elegant bedrooms; large armchairs are placed in window embrasures to make the most of a panorama which stretches from the Black Mountains to the Brecon Beacons. The rooms themselves are decorated in restful pastel shades – except one, north-facing, which Ann Bradley has fitted out in rich and dramatic damson. Downstairs, breakfast is served in a dining-room whose dresser houses a charming collection of willow-pattern and other blue-and-white china. For evening meals, guests can stroll to the local pub or drive to one of the many good eating-places in the area.

This is superb walking country, even if you do not want to tackle the mountain paths. Forest trails are well way-marked; and there are guided walks, too. In addition, there are plenty of castles to visit and nearby Brecon has a Norman cathedral. Steam trains, craft workshops, waterfalls and the Big Pit Museum of Mining at Blaenavon are other attractions of the area.

Reader's comments: Charming and helpful hostess; bedrooms very comfortable and attractive.

V

Mid-Wales

TY CROESO HOTEL

C D S X

The Dardy, Crickhowell, Powys, NP8 1PU Tel/Fax: 01873 810573
North-west of Abergavenny. Nearest main road: A40 from Abergavenny to Brecon.

8 Bedrooms. £24–£35 (less for 2 nights or more on half-board basis only). Bargain breaks. All have own bath/shower/toilet; TV; views of river.
Dinner. £16.95 for 3 courses and coffee, from 7–9pm. Also à la carte. Vegetarian or other special diets if ordered. Wine available. **Light suppers** if ordered.
1 Sitting-room. With open fire, piano. **Bar.**
Large garden

E-mail: tycroeso@ty-croeso-hotel.freeserve.co.uk

The name means 'house of welcome', a far cry from its early Victorian origins as a workhouse. It was used as such up to the Second World War. Now it is run very professionally by Mandy and Ian Moore and their daughter Karen as a small hotel of character.

Bedrooms vary in size. The majority have magnificent panoramic views, for the hotel is perched on a hillside in the Brecon Beacons, above the River Usk. Rooms are individually furnished. Bath- and shower-rooms are very good, and single rooms as attractive as doubles. One huge and particularly elegant bedroom has a four-poster and a sitting-area.

The restaurant has a Welsh dresser against a rugged stone wall and fresh flower arrangements on the tables. A typical meal: avocado and grapefruit with coriander dressing; chicken breast in plum and brandy sauce; syllabub of honey and ginger (several choices at each course). A 'Taste of Wales' dinner is also available.

Readers' comments: Fresh home cooking. Cuisine almost as good as French. Ideal hosts; service, food and accommodation could not be better. Excellent menus and wine lists. Good value; imaginative food; first-class venue for a short break.

V

Mid-Wales

TYNLLYNE FARM C(10)

Llanigon, Powys, HR3 5QF Tel: 01497 847342
West of Hereford (England). Nearest main road: A438 from Hereford towards Brecon.

2 Bedrooms. £24–£26. Available: own bath/shower/toilet; views of river. No smoking.
Light suppers if ordered.
1 Sitting-room. With open fire, TV, piano. No smoking.
Large garden
Closed from mid-September to Easter.

Just within the Welsh border is this working dairy-farm with a big H-shaped house built in the year of the Spanish Armada: Tynllyne – 'house by the lake'. Low beams, three-foot-thick stone (or oak plank) walls and the turned balusters of the wide oak staircase all date from that period. One bedroom has a high brass bed with a particularly fine, beamed bathroom. Outside is a terrace (with barbecue), an immaculate lawn, and a stream-and-woodland nature trail. For breakfast, Lynda Price offers home-made preserves and dishes cooked with local ingredients.

Three historic towns are equidistant from the farm: Brecon (ancient cathedral, antique and craft shops, museums and castle ruins), Hereford (mediaeval city with a very fine cathedral, home to the famous *Mappa Mundi*) and the former spa of Builth Wells in the lovely Wye Valley. Even nearer is 'book city', Hay-on-Wye, where there is a choice of places for evening meals. But for many the wide open spaces of the Black Mountains are an even greater attraction.

Mid-Wales

UPPER TREWALKIN FARM C(5) S

near Talgarth, Powys, LD3 0HA Tel/Fax: 01874 711349
East of Brecon. Nearest main road: A479 from Talgarth towards Crickhowell.

3 Bedrooms. £23 (less for 2 nights or more). All have own bath/toilet. No smoking.
Dinner (by arrangement). £13.50 for 4 courses and coffee, at 7pm (not Tuesdays and Sundays). No smoking. **Light suppers** if ordered.
2 Sitting-rooms. With log-burner and TV (in one). No smoking.
Small garden
Closed from mid-November to mid-April.

The reputation of hospitable Meudwen Stephens has spread far and wide: she is often invited to do overseas tours promoting Wales and its food. So one thing of which you can be sure is a good dinner – such as courgette and tomato soup, lamb chops cooked in white wine and mushrooms (accompanied by garden vegetables), bread-and-butter pudding or lemon syllabub.

But there is more to Upper Trewalkin than this. In the 16th century it was a long-house (animals at one end, family at the other), built on a site previously owned by a Norman knight. It was updated in the 18th century, although many original features were retained.

From many rooms there are superb views of the Black Mountains. Some walls are of exposed stone, some attractively papered. At every turn are paintings by local artists.

The farm is in the Brecon Beacons National Park, an area of great interest to birdwatchers and walkers alike. Llangorse Lake is near and here, at the quieter end, grebes nest.

Readers' comments: Excellent home cooking, delightful hostess, comfortable accommodation. A gem.

SOUTH-WEST WALES
(including Carmarthenshire and Pembrokeshire)

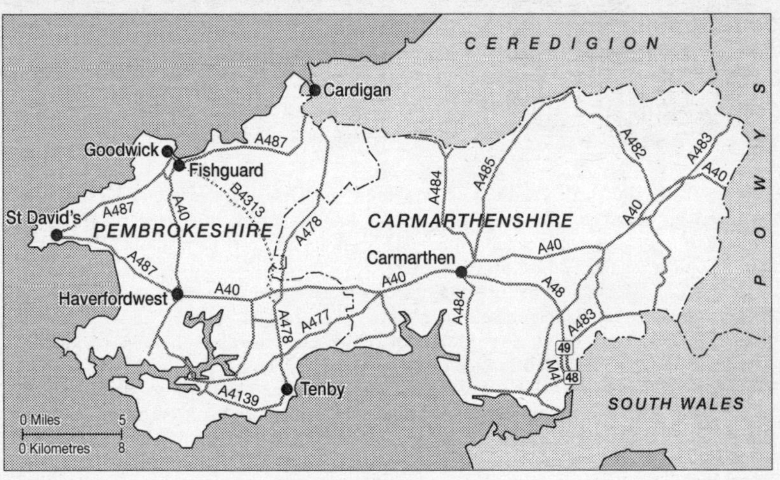

COMPLAINTS: If anything was not of reasonable standard (e.g. chilly bedroom or badly cooked food) you are entitled to claim a reduction on your bill, but *only if* you had previously told the proprietor and given him or her a chance to put matters right. In a court case involving a restaurant meal, it was ruled that, because a customer had not made a specific complaint at the time, he had no right subsequently to withhold payment (he had cancelled his cheque). The moral is obvious: if dissatisfied, you are expected to say so at once and not later. Houses are regularly inspected; and complaints will be forwarded to proprietors for their comments. Write to: Jan Bowmer (SOTBT), c/o Arrow Books, 20 Vauxhall Bridge Road, London SW1V 2SA. Please enclose a stamped addressed envelope if you want her to acknowledge receipt of your complaint.

South-West Wales

ALLENBROOK

M(limited) **PT**(limited) **S**

Dale, Pembrokeshire, SA62 3RN Tel: 01646 636254 (Fax: 01646 636954)
South-west of Haverfordwest. Nearest main road: A40 from Carmarthen to Haverfordwest.

4 Bedrooms. £25 (less for 7 nights or more). Available: own bath/shower/toilet; TV; views of sea. No smoking.
Light suppers if ordered
2 Sitting-rooms. With open fires, piano (in one). No smoking.
Large garden

E-mail: allenbrook@talk21.com

Landing with 2000 men in 1485, it was from the Dale peninsula that Henry Tudor launched his successful campaign to gain the English throne and establish the Tudor dynasty. It is an area rich in wildlife, particularly on the offshore islands, while Dale itself is now a popular boating and windsurfing centre.

Allenbrook looks across the bay and has very much the air of a gracious, small country house. Bedrooms (including one on the ground floor) are light, spacious and elegantly furnished. In addition to the smaller sitting-room downstairs, there is a morning-room on the first floor which is decorated in pale blues and greens. Throughout the house, alongside numerous hunting prints – John Webber is a keen horseman – you will see many examples of Elizabeth Webber's accomplished paintings. She sometimes takes her inspiration from the peacocks that wander about the garden, through the bluebell wood and down to the brook which gives the house its name. For evening meals, the Griffin Inn in the village is a short stroll away.

V *Reader's comments:* Bedrooms exceptional, beautiful garden, the owners especially warm and friendly.

South-West Wales

COACH HOUSE COTTAGE

C D PT S

The Square, Goodwick, Pembrokeshire, SA64 0DH Tel/Fax: 01348 873660
North-west of Fishguard. Nearest main road: A40 from Goodwick to Haverfordwest.

1 Bedroom. £16. Has own TV; views of sea. No smoking.
Dinner (by arrangement). £8.50 for 2 courses and coffee, at times to suit guests. Vegetarian or other special diets if ordered. No smoking. **Light suppers** if ordered.
1 Sitting-room. With stove, TV. Piano. No smoking.
Small garden
Closed in December.

E-mail: Lizmaxwell@aol.com

Tucked away behind Goodwick's small square is Elizabeth Maxwell-Jones's home, where there is a multitude of pictures, books and interesting objects.

One reaches it up 20 steps beside a rushing mountain brook and enters through a stable-type door, straight into the dining-kitchen. From the pretty little bedroom, with its pine-panelled walls and sloping ceiling, are hill views and a glimpse of the sea; the long-distance Pembrokeshire Coastal Path runs close by.

Elizabeth is an accomplished cook who serves, for example, excellent chicken Marengo and summer pudding – all made with organic ingredients. Guests are offered tea and home-made Welsh cakes on arrival.

The cottage is conveniently situated very close to Fishguard Harbour (ferries to Ireland). The footpath up the side of the cottage leads to the old Pilgrim's Way from Cardigan to St David's, which takes in many ancient religious sites.

Reader's comment: Extraordinarily kind and considerate.

CWMTWRCH

C D M

Nantgaredig, Carmarthenshire, SA32 7NY Tel: 01267 290238 (Fax: 01267 290808)
North-east of Carmarthen. Nearest main road: A40 from Carmarthen to Llandeilo (and M4, junction 49).

6 Bedrooms. £25–£40. Available: own bath/shower/toilet; TV.
Dinner. £22.50 for 4 courses and coffee, from 7.30pm. Vegetarian or other special diets if ordered. Wine available. No smoking. **Light suppers** if ordered.
2 Sitting-rooms. With stove, TV. No smoking in one.
Bar.
Large garden

E-mail: jen4seasons@aol.com

The name of this farmhouse-turned-hotel means 'valley of the wild boar'. Nothing so wild now disturbs the peace of this civilized spot where Jenny Willmott and her husband, Bill, have transformed a group of old farm buildings with great sensitivity. The restaurant has stone walls painted white, slate floor and boarded roof above. At one side, the kitchen is open to view; on the other is a conservatory overlooking the courtyard. The food is exceptional, with such dishes as hot red onion and feta cheese tart, fresh salmon or boned Barbary duck, and a flan of grapes among the choices. Bread is baked daily. All rooms have interesting and lovely objects, paintings and pottery (for sale). Bedrooms (full of character) are in the house or in former stables. One ground-floor room has its own sitting-room. There is a heated indoor swimming-pool. The National Botanic Gardens are a 10-minute drive away.

Readers' comments: Marvellous. Food excellent. Helpfulness and friendliness had to be seen to be believed. First class. Good food, friendly hosts, comfort and quiet. Delicious dinner. Professionally run; cosy and tastefully decorated. One of the very best. V

DOLAU

C PT(limited)

Felingwm Isaf, Nantgaredig, Carmarthenshire, SA32 7PB Tel: 01267 290464
East of Carmarthen. Nearest main road: A40 from Carmarthen to Llandeilo (and M4, junction 49).

3 Bedrooms. £21–£25 (less for 3 nights or more). Available: own bath/shower/toilet; TV; views of river. No smoking.
Dinner (by arrangement). £12.50 for 3 courses and coffee, at times to suit guests. Vegetarian or other special diets if ordered. No smoking. **Light suppers** if ordered.
1 Sitting-room. With stove, TV. No smoking.
Large garden

E-mail: brightdolau@aol.com

Old buildings and a rushing stream provide clues to this whitewashed, 19th-century cottage's former life. *Felingwm* means 'valley of mills' and Dolau was one of the hundreds of small woollen mills that were once integral to Welsh rural-industrial life.

Carol and Bill Bright's modernized home has comfortable and spotless bedrooms in pinks and blues. There is a small reading-room off the larger conservatory, in addition to the cosy sitting-room. For dinner, Carol may offer you a Greek salad, then baked sea-trout (sewin), and a summer-fruit tart for pudding. In the grounds are pleasant waterside walks and a picnic-area.

Garden-lovers will want to visit the recently opened National Botanic Gardens and the rediscovered gardens at Aberglasney, both a very short drive away. This is a good area to spot red kites and there is a viewing hide at Llynllech Owain. At Bronwydd is a working steam railway and pottery producing fine tableware. Llanstephan, whose dramatically sited castle was a favourite with Romantic painters, is a particularly charming, quiet coastal village.

Reader's comments: A magic combination of idyllic countryside, friendly hospitality and delicious food. V

DOLAU ISAF FARM C S

Mynachlog-ddu, Clunderwen, Pembrokeshire, SA66 7SB Tel/Fax: 01994 419327

South of Cardigan. Nearest main road: A478 from Cardigan to Tenby.

3 Bedrooms. £20–£25 (less for 7 nights or more). Bargain breaks. Available: own bath/shower/toilet. No smoking.

Dinner (by arrangement). £12.50–£15.50 for 2–3 courses and coffee, at 7pm. Coeliac vegetarian or other special diets if ordered. No smoking. **Light suppers** if ordered.

1 Sitting-room. With log-burner, TV. No smoking.

E-mail: vivlockton@tinyworld.co.uk

Vivienne and Douglas Lockton's isolated livestock farm lies at the heart of 'bluestone country', an area rich in prehistoric remains. The dolerite stone, which glistens blue when wet, was hewn from the Preseli Hills to build such monuments and stone circles as those at Pentre Ifan and Gors Fawr nearby, as well as Stonehenge.

Set amidst rolling hills – *dolau isaf* means 'lower meadows' – this thick-walled and white-washed farmhouse offers comfortable, homely accommodation, where the atmosphere is friendly and informal. Bedrooms, decorated in pinks and yellows, have thoughtful touches such as posies of fresh flowers. Vivienne cooks good meals, with the emphasis on local produce. Dinner might comprise chicken breast in cream, mushroom and garlic sauce, followed by blackberry and apple crumble. Packed lunches are available, too.

The Locktons keep angora goats; and mohair yarn, knitwear and rugs are for sale. On the outskirts of the village is a monument to the Welsh poet Waldo Williams, who lived here and whose poetry derived much inspiration from the area. Narberth is good for hunting out antiques, while the ruins of Cilgerran Castle and St Dogmaels Abbey are just short drives away.

V

South-West Wales

EAST HOOK FARMHOUSE C D X

Portfield Gate, Pembrokeshire, SA62 3LN Tel: 01437 762211 (Fax: 01437 779060)

West of Haverfordwest. Nearest main road: A487 from Haverfordwest towards St David's.

3 Bedrooms. £22.50–£30 (less for 3 nights or more). All have own bath/shower/toilet; TV. No smoking.

Dinner (by arrangement). £15 for 3 courses and coffee, at 7pm. Vegetarian or other special diets if ordered. No smoking. **Light suppers** if ordered.

1 Sitting-room. With stove, TV. No smoking.

Garden

E-mail: jen.easthook@virginnet.co.uk

Although there are records of a dwelling here dating back to the mediaeval period, the present house has a 17th-century interior behind a Georgian porticoed façade. It is the home of Jen and Howard Patrick and their two young sons, and the centre of a 180-acre sheep farm. The comfortable and spotless bedrooms, decorated in pastel pinks, have attractive old pieces of furniture and good bathrooms. In the sitting-room, there is a crackling stove for chilly evenings.

Evening meals, prepared using local produce, are well presented and plentiful. Salmon mousse might be followed by a traditional roast, with sherry trifle to finish.

The Pembrokeshire Coast Path is easily reached from here. For guests who prefer more leisurely exercise, there is golf at Haverfordwest. This is an area rich in castle ruins, with those at Wiston, Roch, Llawhaden and Haverfordwest open to visitors. Picton Castle, home to the same family for eight generations, has 40 acres of woodland gardens to explore and a significant collection of artworks by Graham Sutherland.

Reader's comments: A quiet rural setting where I was very warmly welcomed; nothing too much trouble.

V

FFERM-Y-FELIN **CSX**

Llanpumsaint, Carmarthenshire, SA33 6DA Tel: 01267 253498 (Fax: 01267 253579)
North of Carmarthen. Nearest main road: A485 from Carmarthen to Lampeter.

2 Bedrooms. £24–£25 (less for 3 nights or more). Bargain breaks. All have own bath/shower/toilet; TV; views of lake (from one). No smoking.
Dinner (by arrangement). £14 for 4 courses and coffee, at 7–8.30pm. Vegetarian or other special diets if ordered. No smoking. **Light suppers** if ordered.
1 Sitting-room. With open fire, TV, piano. No smoking.
Large garden

E-mail: anne@ryderowen.freeserve.co.uk

Fferm-y-Felin, or 'mill farm', is the 18th-century home of Anne Ryder-Owen: a place of particular interest to birdwatchers. You can be told where to spot pied flycatchers, buzzards and even the rare red kite. Beyond the dining-room is a sitting-room so large that it has a fireplace at each end; pink, buttoned velvet sofas and a walnut piano contrast with rugged stone walls. Anne serves snacks or such meals as corn-on-the-cob, wild trout, and apple crumble; breakfast options include laverbread and cockles.

This would be a good place for a family holiday: the farmhouse stands in 15 acres of countryside, with a large lake and interesting waterfowl as well as other livestock. Self-catering accommodation too, with meals provided in the main house if wanted. Aberglasney Gardens and the National Botanic Gardens are half an hour away by car.

Readers' comments: Wonderfully looked after. Food excellent and plentiful. Kind, considerate, welcoming. Truly spectacular holiday; one of the best meals I have ever had. A most delightful and welcoming lady.

V

LLANDDINOG HOUSE C(7) **PT**(limited) **S**

Llandeloy, Pembrokeshire, SA62 6NA Tel/Fax: 01348 831467
East of St David's. Nearest main road: A487 from Haverfordwest to St David's.

South-West Wales

3 Bedrooms. £25–£28 (less for 7 nights or more). Available: own bath/shower/toilet; TV. No smoking.
1 Sitting-room. With TV. No smoking.
Large garden

E-mail: llanddinoghouse@solvawales.freeserve.co.uk

Tucked away inland, a couple of miles from the coast, Gloria Jones' and Ken Droy's attractive modern home is part faced in stone cut from the local quarry at Solva. Indoor plants and muted colours have been used to create a relaxing atmosphere, which complements the quiet surrounding countryside. Neat and well-equipped bedrooms look north to the lighthouse at Strumble Head and west to St David's Head. In an attempt to encourage wildlife, a seven-acre paddock at the front of the house has been planted with 6000 trees.

The sitting-room is shared with Gloria and Ken, who are a welcoming and friendly couple (she was once a dancer, while he has a keen interest in cycling and flying). There is plenty of information on local walks. One particular ramble leads you to standing stones at Tremaenhir and then down into the fishing village of Solva (well supplied with eateries for evening meals). From the cliffs on either side of the village are remarkable views across St Brides Bay in one direction and to Ramsey Island – home to seals, sea birds and red deer – in the other.

V

South-West Wales

MANOR HOUSE HOTEL

C D P T S

Main Street, Fishguard, Pembrokeshire, SA65 9HG Tel/Fax: 01348 873260
Nearest main road: A40 from Haverfordwest to Fishguard.

6 Bedrooms. £25–£32 (less for 3 nights or more). All have own bath/shower/toilet; TV; views of sea. No smoking.
Dinner. From £18 for 3 courses and coffee, at 7–8pm. Vegetarian or other special diets if ordered. Wine available. No smoking. **Light suppers** if ordered.
1 Sitting-room. Bar.
Small garden

In the main street of Fishguard (but with quiet rooms overlooking the sea at the back) is Manor House Hotel, built in the 18th century. Most rooms are spacious and stylishly furnished. One has an art deco theme; while another has Edwardian furniture. In a room on the ground floor, antiques are for sale. Austrian-born Beatrix Davies has given the small hotel a reputation for its food. There is always a wide à la carte choice that includes such dishes as smoked fish pancake in a lightly curried sauce; rack of local lamb; chocolate, raisin and rum slice. Ralph Davies keeps an interesting and varied wine list. From the garden (where you can take breakfast) there are fine views across the sea to Dinas Head.

Fishguard, a picturesque port, is on a coastline so spectacular that it has been designated a National Park: windswept and dramatic cliffs alternate with sunny, sheltered coves.

Readers' comments: Very hospitable hosts; comfortable, spacious room; good dinner with creative cuisine.

South-West Wales

OLD COURT HOUSE

C(5) **D M**(limited) **PT S**

Trefin, Pembrokeshire, SA62 5AX Tel: 01348 837095
North-east of St David's. Nearest main road: A487 from St David's to Fishguard.

3 Bedrooms. £23.50 (less for 3 nights or more). Bargain breaks. All have own bath/shower/toilet; TV. No smoking.
Dinner (by arrangement). £14.50 for 3 courses and coffee, at 7.30pm. No smoking. **Light suppers** if ordered.
1 Sitting-room. With open fire. No smoking.
Small garden

E-mail: oldcourthouse@netscapeonline.co.uk

Trefin lies halfway between St David's (Britain's smallest cathedral city) and the port of Fishguard, on an elevated part of the coastline which affords scenery of exceptional grandeur. Once the ecclesiastical court of a local bishop, Lynne and Steve Brodie's 200-year-old cottage is a place of twisting corridors and low ceilings. The snug sitting-room, well supplied with books and CDs, has an orthopaedic 'back chair', and in the brightly decorated dining-room are examples of local pottery and artwork. There is a particularly attractive, self-contained bedroom in a ground-floor annexe, with modern Swedish furnishings and rough-plastered cream walls.

V

Lynne's cooking is very much a draw here: she is cordon vert trained and runs vegetarian cookery courses for those wishing to expand their culinary horizons. As you might expect, menus (vegetarian *only*) are interesting and varied. Breakfast could comprise baked grapefruit, followed by grilled tomatoes with wholegrain mustard and chives, home-made smoked Cenarth cheese sausages and scrambled free-range eggs. Such a hearty meal might well precede a trek along the coastal path, only five minutes' walk from the house.

OLD VICARAGE

Moylegrove, Pembrokeshire, SA43 3BN Tel: 01239 881231 (Fax: 0870 136 2382)
West of Cardigan. Nearest main road: A487 from Cardigan to Fishguard.

3 Bedrooms. £23–£30 (less for 7 nights or more). All have own shower/toilet; views of sea. No smoking.
Dinner (by arrangement). £16 for 3 courses, at 7pm. Vegetarian or other special diets if ordered. Wine available. No smoking.
1 Sitting-room. With open fire, TV. No smoking.
Large garden
Closed from December to February.

E-mail: stay@old-vic.co.uk

An air of quality and comfort pervades every room in this substantial Edwardian house, set on a sweeping lawn with glimpses of Cardigan Bay not far away. The unusual slate and turf wall of the garden is traditional to the area. High up in the countryside, the house has superb views, for it is on the edge of the Pembrokeshire Coast National Park.

Fine rugs cover the floors, particularly in the dining-room, where Patricia and David Phillips serve such meals as home-made soup, baked salmon with Parmesan and parsley, chocolate pecan pie or farmhouse cheeses.

The large bedrooms have restful colour schemes, flowery duvets and good bathrooms.

Within a mile, the long Pembrokeshire Coastal Path passes on its way, following the dramatic cliffs, beaches and steep valleys that make this coast so outstanding.

Readers' comments: Excellent; food ample and imaginative. A wonderful week in a splendid location; rooms and food of a very high standard. Accommodation of the highest standard; excellent hosts. Perfect blend of friendliness and discretion.

SOAR HILL

C D PT S X

Cilgwyn Road, Newport, Pembrokeshire, SA42 0QG Tel: 01239 820506
East of Fishguard. Nearest main road: A487 from Fishguard to Cardigan.

South-West Wales

3 Bedrooms. £18–£22 (less for 3 nights or more). Available: own bath/shower/toilet; TV; views of sea. No smoking.
Light suppers if ordered. No smoking.
1 Sitting-room. With stove, TV. No smoking.
Large garden

E-mail: soarhill@hotmail.com

The Pembrokeshire hills are where Jean Dunham's roots lie, for she was born and brought up at Soar Hill, which was then her parents' working farm. After teaching home economics and spending much of her life abroad, she recently returned to the family home, very quickly imprinting her own style and personality upon it. The smart and airy, cream-and-terracotta sitting-room, converted from an old cow shed, has damask-dressed windows on all sides and lovely views of the surrounding Nevern Valley. Bedrooms have clean lines, with quality furnishings and bedlinen, and well-designed bathrooms. There is an additional walk-in shower downstairs for guests' use.

Breakfasts include traditional Welsh dishes, as well as such continental options as fruit compote and pastries. Jean is a keen walker and her knowledge of the area is invaluable to guests. One walk she suggests takes in the prehistoric Pentre Ifan burial chamber, Castell Henllys hill fort and the ancient woodlands at Ty Canol. For evening meals there is a well thought-of eatery at Gellifawr, a short drive away.

WYCHWOOD HOUSE

C D PT X

Penally, Pembrokeshire, SA70 7PE Tel/Fax: 01843 844387
South of Tenby. Nearest main road: A4139 from Tenby to Pembroke.

3 Bedrooms. £25–£30 (less for 7 nights or more). Bargain breaks. Available: own bath/shower/toilet; TV; views of sea; balcony. No smoking.
Dinner (by arrangement). £17.50 for 3 courses and coffee, at 7.30pm. Vegetarian or other special diets if ordered. No smoking. **Light suppers** if ordered.
1 Sitting-room. With open fire, TV. No smoking.
Garden

The quiet village of Penally, overlooking monastic Caldey Island, is a perfect spot from which to explore Pembrokeshire's historic coastline, and this 1930s house provides accommodation of great comfort and style. One attractive bedroom, in cool blue and white, has a bathroom with original art deco fitments; another, with sea views, has a four-poster bed and pretty chintz curtains. Downstairs, off the hallway with its gleaming parquet floor, is a large and comfortable sitting-room with coloured oriel windows.

Lee Ravenscroft is a keen and inventive cook, often offering meals with an Asian slant: his wife Mherly comes from the Philippines. After salmon, prawn and horseradish-cream parcels, you might have a green pork curry with coconut and limes, then banana and sultana crêpes. High tea is also available.

There is much to keep one occupied hereabouts – two golf courses almost on the doorstep, a quiet beach, and a coastal walk to Tenby (with mediaeval town wall, Tudor Merchant's House and a fine art gallery). Laugharne (Dylan Thomas associations) is a short drive away,
V while closer by are several interesting churches, including 6th-century St Govan's Chapel.

YOU AND THE LAW

Once your booking has been confirmed – orally or in writing – a contract exists between you and the proprietor. He/she is legally bound to provide accommodation as booked; and you are legally bound to pay for this accommodation. If unable to take up the booking – even because of sickness – you still remain liable for a very substantial proportion of the charges (in addition to losing your deposit).

If you have to cancel, let the proprietor know as soon as possible; then he/she may be able to re-let the accommodation (in which case you would be liable to pay only a re-letting cost or forfeit your deposit). Phone if you are going to arrive late.

(A note to overseas readers. It may be an acceptable practice elsewhere to make bookings at several houses for the same date, choosing only later which one to patronize; but this way of doing things is not the British practice and you are legally liable to compensate any proprietors whom you let down in this way.)

SOUTH WALES
(including Monmouthshire, Newport, Swansea and Vale of Glamorgan)

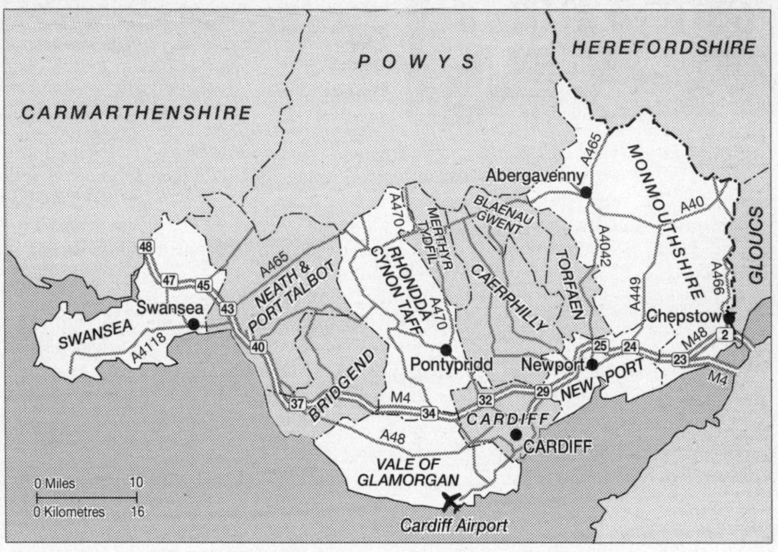

Facts (prices, etc.) at the top of entries are supplied by the proprietors themselves. While every effort is made to ensure that these are correct at the time of going to press, they may alter thereafter: please check when you book.

South Wales

CROSSWAYS HOUSE

C D PT

Cowbridge, Vale of Glamorgan, CF71 7LJ Tel: 01446 773171 (Fax: 01446 771707)
West of Cardiff. Nearest main road: A48 from Bridgend to Cardiff (and M4, junctions 33/35).

3 Bedrooms. £25–£35 (less for 7 nights or more). Bargain breaks. Available: own bath/shower/toilet; TV. No smoking.
Dinner (by arrangement). £15 for 3 courses and coffee, at 7–8pm. Vegetarian or other special diets if ordered. No smoking. **Light suppers** if ordered.
1 Sitting-room. With open fire, TV, piano. No smoking.
Large garden

E-mail: enquiries@crosswayshouse.co.uk

Crossways House has had a number of incarnations. Seventeenth-century in origin, it was renovated in 1921 in late Victorian 'gothick' style – turrets, elaborate carved woodwork and plastering. The owner then was a local shipping magnate who at the age of 55 took a teenage bride. She, alas, promptly ran off with an Indian prince. The house served as a hospital during the Second World War and is now divided into separate dwellings, in one of which Mandy and John Davies offer accommodation.

The bright bedrooms are attractively furnished: one, looking out over six acres of woodland, has a jade, marble-effect wallpaper and frog-patterned tiles in the bathroom. The sitting-room is shared with the Davieses and their teenage children. There is a wide choice of Welsh specialities at breakfast, including such vegetarian options as laverbread cakes and Glamorgan sausages (made with leeks and Caerphilly cheese). Mandy is happy to discuss evening meal preferences with guests.

Cowbridge is ideally placed for visiting historic Cardiff or further afield in Glamorgan.

V

Readers' comments: An excellent welcome and breakfast. We should have no hesitation in returning.

South Wales

FAIRFIELD COTTAGE

C(5) **D PT S**

Knelston, Gower Peninsula, Swansea, SA3 1AR Tel: 01792 391013
West of Swansea. On A4118 from Swansea to Port Eynon (M4, junction 47, is near).

3 Bedrooms. £18–£19.50 (less for 2 nights or more). TV (in one). No smoking.
Dinner. £13.50 for 4 courses and coffee, at 7pm. No smoking. **Light suppers** if ordered.
1 Sitting-room. With open fire, TV. No smoking.
Garden

The Gower peninsula is so scenic that there are few more attractive places. Knelston is roughly equidistant from north, west and south coasts.

Caryl Ashton's 18th-century home is a little white cottage made colourful by window-boxes, tubs and hanging-baskets of flowers. One steps straight into the sitting/dining-room from which a staircase rises between the joists to small but pretty, cottagey bedrooms. There is a very good bathroom.

One can take a complimentary aperitif by the inglenook fire or in the garden (it has a summer-house) before enjoying such a meal as gratin of haddock, roast Welsh lamb, home-made lemon meringue pie, and a selection of cheeses. Fruit and vegetables come from local farms, and yogurt, Welsh cakes and scones are home-made.

V

Readers' comments: Treated with particular care and love. Superb cook, wonderful hosts. All meals delicious; a most memorable experience. Friendly, helpful and very thoughtful. The best. House beautifully kept; extraordinarily kind. Really friendly, and what a cook.

LAWNS FARM

C S

Grosmont, Monmouthshire, NP7 8ES Tel: 01981 240298 (Fax: 01981 241275)

North-east of Abergavenny. Nearest main road: A465 from Abergavenny to Hereford.

3 Bedrooms. £20–£25 (less for 3 nights or more). Available: own bath/shower/toilet; TV; views of river. No smoking.
Light suppers if ordered. No smoking.
1 Sitting-room. With stove, piano. No smoking.
Large garden

E-mail: edna@ferneyhough8.freeserve.co.uk

Standing at the summit of rolling terraced meadows which rise from the banks of the River Monnow, this rather splendid 17th-century manor house offers considerable comfort and breathtaking vistas. Ferneyhoughs have been here for over 100 years, and Edna and John have put much effort into creating a stylish and friendly atmosphere.

Bedrooms are attractive (two are large). The double one, in duck-egg blue, has a fine old four-poster bedstead polished to a lustrous sheen, and views towards Grieg Hill and Grosmont Castle. Swagged chintz curtains in the sitting-room complement emerald-green sofas drawn around the fire. Breakfast – seated in the bay window of the dining-room, looking out over unspoilt countryside – is the perfect way to start your day, followed by a stroll in the imaginatively planned gardens. Restaurant bookings and taxis can be arranged; and for a special meal, try the renowned Walnut Tree at Llanddewi Skerrid.

Reader's comments: Friendly, helpful and welcoming; breakfasts superb; nothing was too much trouble. **V**

OLD RECTORY

C(10) **D PT S X**

Reynoldston, Gower Peninsula, Swansea, SA3 1AD Tel: 01792 390129
(Fax: 01792 390764)

West of Swansea. Nearest main road: A4118 from Swansea to Port Eynon (and M4, junction 47).

3 Bedrooms. £20 (less for 3 nights or more). One has own shower. No smoking.
Dinner (by arrangement). £12 for 3 courses and coffee, at times to suit guests. Vegetarian or other special diets if ordered. No smoking. **Light suppers** if ordered.
1 Sitting-room. With open fire, TV, piano. No smoking.
Large garden

E-mail: valerie.evans@reynoldston.com

A short distance from Knelston, Reynoldston is a rather straggling village merging into the bracken-covered hills of Cefn Bryn ('ridge of hills'), a stretch of moorland where ponies roam free and yellow waterlilies brighten the pools. It is an area dotted with castle ruins, prehistoric burial chambers and other traces of a far-distant history. The Old Rectory is a handsome, grey, slate-roofed house, part 17th- and part 18th-century in origin, which Valerie Evans has made into an elegant home, with guest bedrooms decorated in relaxing pastel shades.

The spacious and airy sitting-room has lovely old furniture and chintz-covered sofas and chairs grouped round the fireplace. French windows open on to the terrace where you may have breakfast in summer. Evening meals may start with lettuce soup, then tarragon-and-orange chicken, and gooseberry-and-elderflower soufflé to finish. The secluded garden is dominated by a magnificent Western Red Cedar, reminding one rather of an enormous and misshapen upturned umbrella-frame. The newly opened National Botanic Gardens of Wales are just under an hour's drive away.

Readers' comments: Tastefully and comfortably furnished. Nothing was too much trouble. **V**

South Wales

TYN-Y-WERN CDPTSX

Ynysybwl, Rhondda Cynon Taff, CF37 3LY Tel/Fax: 01443 790551
North of Pontypridd. Nearest main road: A470 from Pontypridd to Merthyr Tydfil (and M4, junction 32).

3 Bedrooms. £21–£25. Bargain breaks. Available: own bath/shower/toilet; TV. No smoking.
Dinner (by arrangement). £10–£13.50 for 2–3 courses and coffee, at times to suit guests. Vegetarian or other special diets if ordered. No smoking. **Light suppers** if ordered.
1 Sitting-room. With open fire.
Garden

The valleys of South Wales are gradually regaining the rural aspect they once had before coal-mining scarred the landscape. Little remains of the Lady Windsor colliery for which this solid Victorian house was the mine manager's residence – it is now almost surrounded by open countryside. Hermione Bruton has decorated her home in bold colours, mixing modern artwork with antiques to pleasing effect. In the blue dining-room, where Staffordshire figures and crystal decanters sit on an old oak Welsh dresser, she serves such evening meals as mushroom soup, chicken in apricot sauce, and apple flan for dessert. She is a member of the Soil Association, and much produce comes from her organic kitchen garden.

These valleys are very much walking country: the Taff Trail, for both walkers and cyclists, passes close to the village. In addition to Cardiff, nearby sightseeing attractions include St Fagans Welsh Folk Museum, Castell Coch and the Rhondda Heritage Park. A steam railway from Merthyr Tydfil takes you through beautiful scenery into the Brecon Beacons.

Readers' comments: Good food and hospitable ways. A very relaxing atmosphere, with a wonderful view across the valley.

South Wales

UPPER SEDBURY HOUSE CDPTSX

Sedbury Lane, Sedbury, Monmouthshire, NP16 7HN Tel: 01291 627173
East of Chepstow. Nearest main road: A48 from Chepstow towards Gloucester (and M48, junction 2).

6 Bedrooms. £19.50–£22.50 (less for 3 nights or more). Bargain breaks. Available: own bath/shower/toilet; TV.
Dinner. £10.50 for 3 courses and coffee, at 7pm. Vegetarian or other special diets if ordered. **Light suppers** if ordered.
1 Sitting-room. With open fire, TV.
Large garden

Sedbury, not marked on all maps, is tucked between Chepstow and the Severn estuary – quite close to the Severn Bridge. In rural Sedbury Lane stands an old farm, Upper Sedbury House, with cottagey bedrooms; and also an attic flat, usually let for self-catering but Christine Potts is happy to do meals for those guests too. (A typical dinner, using garden produce: pears in tarragon mayonnaise, casserole of beef, fruit crumble.) There is a swimming-pool, unheated; badminton, etc.; and the Offa's Dyke footpath runs near the house.

In the immediate vicinity are Tintern Abbey's particularly beautiful ruins and the scenic splendour of both the Wye and the Usk valleys. Chepstow has an impressive Norman castle overlooking the harbour.

Also within easy driving distance are the Forest of Dean and historic Monmouth. Henry V was born in the castle, and Nelson stayed here – hence the naval temple on Kymin Hill, commanding far views. Then there is Raglan, with spectacular castle remains nearby.

V

THE WENALLT

C D S

Gilwern, Monmouthshire, NP7 0HP Tel/Fax: 01873 830694
West of Abergavenny. Nearest main road: A465 from Abergavenny to Merthyr Tydfil.

8 Bedrooms. £19.50–£24 (less for 7 nights or more). Bargain breaks. Available: own bath/shower/toilet. No smoking.
Dinner (by arrangement). £13 for 4 courses and coffee, at 7.30pm. Vegetarian or other special diets if ordered. Wine available. No smoking. **Light suppers** if ordered.
1 Sitting-room. With open fire. No smoking. **Bar** with TV.
Large garden

The name, 'wooded hill', was given to this remote stone house when it was first built as a long-house: though most of it dates from about 1600, some parts are a good deal older. What is now a bar once housed cattle, and the bedroom above, hay to feed them; the sitting-room was a dairy. And from many windows in this hilltop guest-house you can see for miles. Farmer Brian Harris and his wife Yvonne made many improvements when they came here and in the new dining-room installed a stone fireplace from Tredegar House; Brian also converted a stone cow-byre to make more bedrooms.

There are scores of cups won at horse shows (Brian is now a judge at these), and other touches that give the house individuality – from a stuffed pheasant on a hearth to the beribboned fabrics in one of the bedrooms.

Meals are well above average – for example: stuffed courgette flowers (in season), a sorbet, turkey in walnut sauce, and the lightest of apple strudels.

Readers' comments: Friendly and helpful. Food excellent. Our spacious room was furnished with lovely antiques. Enjoyed so much that I extended my stay. Food and service excellent. **V**

WEST USK LIGHTHOUSE

Lighthouse Road, St Brides Wentlooge, Newport, NP10 8SF Tel: 01633 810126 or 815860 (Fax: 01633 815582)
South-west of Newport. Nearest main road: A48 from Cardiff to Newport (and M4, junction 28).

4 Bedrooms. £25–£40. Available: own bath/shower/toilet; TV; views of sea/river. No smoking.
Dinner (by arrangement). £15 for 3 courses and coffee, at 7pm. Vegetarian diets if ordered. No smoking. **Light suppers** if ordered.
1 Sitting-room. With open fire. No smoking.
Large garden

E-mail: lighthouse1@tesco.net

The ex-lighthouse is not tall as most lighthouses are, and considerably bigger in circumference. In 1821, it was on an island where the Severn and Usk run into the sea (since then land has been reclaimed). On one side the loudest sound is of the sea when the tide comes racing in, on the other only the occasional mooing cow can be heard. The walls are over two feet thick, with wedge-shaped rooms. From the slate-paved hall a spiral stair rises to the bedrooms, attractively decorated. The sitting-room has cane furniture (and sometimes a meditation pyramid). There is a lamp-room with seats from which to watch ships go by and the spectacular sunsets.

The house is run in an informal way by Frank Sheahan, with relaxation classes and aromatherapy sessions available – even a flotation tank. For meals, a short conventional menu.

Readers' comments: Charmingly and artistically furnished and very unusual; peaceful. An inspired conversion. Friendly and open-minded host. Location excellent. **V**

EXPLANATION OF CODE LETTERS

(These appear, where applicable, with each entry.)

C Suitable for families with children. Sometimes a minimum age is stipulated, in which case this is indicated by a numeral; thus **C**(5) means children over 5 years old are accepted. In most cases, houses that accept children offer reduced rates and special meals. They may provide cots and high chairs; or games and sports for older children. Please enquire when booking. And do not expect young children to be lodged free, as babies are. Families which pick establishments with plenty of games, swimming-pool, animals, etc., or that are near free museums, parks and walks, can save a lot on keeping youngsters entertained. (Readers wanting total quiet may wish to avoid houses coded **C**.)

D Dogs permitted. A charge is rarely made, but it is often a stipulation that you must ask before bringing one; the dog may have to sleep in your car, or be banned from certain rooms.

M Suitable for those with mobility problems. Needs vary: whenever we have used the code letter **M**, this indicates that not only is there a ground-floor bedroom and bathroom, but these, and doorways, have sufficient width for a wheelchair, and steps are few. For precise details, ask when booking.

PT Accessible by public transport. It is not essential to have a car in order to get off the beaten track because public transport is mostly available, albeit on a somewhat infrequent basis in many deep rural areas. Houses indicated by the code **PT** have a railway station or coach stop within a reasonable distance, from which you can walk or take a taxi (quite a number of hosts will even pick you up, free, in their own car). The symbol **PT** further indicates that there are also some buses for sightseeing, but these may be few. Ask when booking.

S Indicates those houses which charge single people no more, or only 10% more, than half the price of a double room (except, possibly, at peak periods).

X Visitors are accepted at Christmas, though Christmas meals are not necessarily provided. Some hotels and farms offer special Christmas holidays; but, unless otherwise indicated (by the code letter **X** at top of entry), those in this book will then be closed. Even if a house is not shown as being open at Christmas, it may open immediately thereafter – please enquire.

V Houses which accept the discount vouchers on page ii of this book.

INDEX OF TOWNS IN ENGLAND WHICH HAVE SOTBT HOUSES NEARBY

INDEX OF TOWNS IN WALES WHICH HAVE SOTBT HOUSES NEARBY

READER PARTICIPATION

1 It would be very helpful if you will let me know your opinion of places from this book at which you have stayed. Please post this to: Jan Bowmer (SOTBT), c/o Arrow Books, 20 Vauxhall Bridge Road, London SW1V 2SA. **If you wish for an acknowledgment please enclose a stamped addressed envelope.**

Names of establishments	**Your comments (with date of stay)**

2 If you find other places in England and Wales you think should be visited, for possible inclusion in a future edition, please will you send me your description (including price and address), with brochure. **No expensive places, please.**

Your name and address (capitals) ______________________________

____

Date ________________ Occupation (optional) ____________________

____

READER PARTICIPATION

1 It would be very helpful if you will let me know your opinion of places from this book at which you have stayed. Please post this to: Jan Bowmer (SOTBT), c/o Arrow Books, 20 Vauxhall Bridge Road, London SW1V 2SA. **If you wish for an acknowledgment please enclose a stamped addressed envelope.**

Names of establishments	**Your comments (with date of stay)**

2 If you find other places in England and Wales you think should be visited, for possible inclusion in a future edition, please will you send me your description (including price and address), with brochure. **No expensive places, please.**

Your name and address (capitals) ______________________________

____

Date ______________ Occupation (optional) ______________________

____